*Columbia University Studies
in Jewish History, Culture,
and Institutions*

EDITED UNDER THE AUSPICES OF THE
CENTER FOR ISRAEL AND JEWISH STUDIES
COLUMBIA UNIVERSITY

NUMBER ONE
From Spanish Court to Italian Ghetto

Las
EXCELENCIAS
DE LOS HEBREOS.

Por el Doctor
YSHAC CARDOSO.

EL QUE ME ESPARSIO ME RECOGERA.

Impreſſo en AMSTERDAM en caſa de
DAVID DE CASTRO TARTAS.
El Año de 1679.

Title page of Isaac Cardoso's *Las Excelencias de los Hebreos* (Amsterdam, 1679)

From Spanish Court to Italian Ghetto

ISAAC CARDOSO:
A Study in Seventeenth-Century Marranism and Jewish Apologetics, by
YOSEF HAYIM YERUSHALMI

NEW YORK & LONDON
Columbia University Press
1971

Yosef Hayim Yerushalmi is Professor of Hebrew
and Jewish History at Harvard University.

This study, prepared under the Graduate Faculties of Columbia
University, was selected by a committee of those faculties to receive
one of the Clarke F. Ansley awards given annually by Columbia
University Press.

Copyright © 1971 Columbia University Press
Library of Congress Catalog Card Number: 76-109544
ISBN 0-231-03286-2
Printed in the United States of America

For Ophra

זכרתי לך
חסד נעוריך
אהבת כלולתיך
לכתך אחרי במדבר
בארץ לא זרועה

Contents

Contents

Illustrations

Recent years have witnessed a reawakening of interest, both scholarly and popular, in the history of the Spanish Inquisition and of some of its main victims, the Marranos. On the one hand, from among the Spanish historians and theologians there have emerged a number of gifted apologists for that institution, which had fallen into great disrepute during the nineteenth century. Some of them felt that the price Spain had paid for the hard regime of its Holy Office had not been too high. Led by German-trained Bernardino Llorca, these scholars insisted that because, with the Inquisition's aid, the country had maintained its historic continuity from its medieval orderliness and consistently Catholic *Weltanschauung*, it had been spared much of the confusion and intermittent inner upheavals which characterized the evolution of the Western democracies. Some of their disciples in other Spanish-speaking countries as far away as Argentina now began speaking in Torquemadean terms of the "redemptive" quality of violence.

At the same time another school of Spanish historians, led by Américo Castro, penetrated more deeply into the roots of Spanish culture and attributed much of its uniqueness and richness to its assimilation of many ingredients of Iberia's glorious Jewish and Moorish heritage. Still another group of more dispassionate students of Spain's extraordinary past, under the guidance of Francisco Cantera Burgos and José María Millás Vallicrosa, began sifting the enormous mass of archival and literary records preserved in Spain.

Foreword

For more than a quarter century, their Instituto Arias Montano at the Universities of Madrid and Barcelona has published a number of excellent books and a fine specialized quarterly, *Sefarad*, which have helped illumine many vital factors of Spanish Jewish history, literature, and thought.

On their part, Jewish historians, who in the nineteenth century with a few noteworthy exceptions had been predominantly Germano-centric in their approach and even later extended their horizons in the main only to the East European segment of the Jewish people, have begun evincing greater interest in the Sephardic world. Yitzhak Baer and his disciples paved the way for a keen reappraisal of the achievements and failures of the great medieval Jewish communities on the Iberian Peninsula and their offshoots in many lands. Other scholars have begun to analyze more searchingly the roots of the West European and American Jewish communities which to a very large extent owed their modern foundations to the Marrano dispersion. After all, today more than half of world Jewry lives in the Western Hemisphere alone. Simultaneously, there has been a growing scholarly involvement in the historic fate of the North African and Middle Eastern Jewries, intensified by the growing concentration of Jews in Mandatory Palestine and, still more, in the new State of Israel. Here, too, one half of Israel's population has been recruited from the eastern communities with their high ratio of descendants of the erstwhile exiles from Spain and Portugal.

Moreover, as other great diasporas—for example, those of the French Huguenots, the English Puritans, the Polish patriots of the early nineteenth century, or the twentieth-century Jewish refugees from Hitler's Europe—the Marrano dispersion in the early modern period in its sheer struggle for survival had to perform great pioneering services for its own people and for civilization at large. Yet the story of both the respective pioneering groups and the individual path-finders in the economic as well as in the cultural sphere has only begun to be elucidated by recent authors.

Professor Yerushalmi's excellent biography of Isaac Cardoso is an important landmark in this field. In his dramatic presentation he shows the transition of this talented physician and thinker from a life among the privileged minority of intellectuals in royal Madrid to a more obscure and precarious existence as a secret Judaizer and later as a professing Jew in Venice and Verona. From being a friend of the confirmed anti-Jewish dramatist, Felix Lope de Vega, whose death he mourned in a moving oration, Cardoso gradually developed into one of the most brilliant apologists for modern Judaism and a wide-ranging philosopher building bridges between his Jewish heritage and Western culture. He accomplished all that while retaining his rational frame of mind, in contrast to his brother Abraham who became a leading Hebrew mystic and a follower of the pseudo-Messiah, Sabbatai Zevi.

In his own modest and calm, yet searching and deeply felt, reappraisal of Jewish life in the dispersion, Isaac became one of the outstanding pioneers in the Jewish entry into Western culture which ultimately, in a way unforeseen by him, paved the way for Jewish Emancipation. Described in an equally restrained and persuasive manner, on the basis of extensive research in many widely scattered sources, published and unpublished, Yerushalmi's biography of this distinguished pioneer is, indeed, an illuminating *exemplar vitae humanae* and a fascinating contribution to learning.

Salo W. Baron

Preface

The "Marranos" are today once more in the forefront of historical research, and this after more than a century of scholarship has already yielded a veritable library on the subject. In the last decade or so, intensified archival work in the Peninsula has brought to light materials of prime importance, and has revealed how far we have yet to go before even the documentary basis for future study may be regarded as satisfactory. There has been a renewed emphasis on the history of the Marranos in the sixteenth and seventeenth centuries. Important studies have been undertaken on their economic role, in both Spain and Portugal, as well as abroad. The social and idealogical impact of *conversos* and their descendants on the cultural history of Spain is the subject of searching and often dramatic investigations. The influence of Marrano emigrants on certain religious and intellectual trends in the Jewish world has begun to be studied in depth. These and other ramifications of the problem are surveyed in the opening chapter of the present study and need not detain us here. It is the particular nature of the study itself which requires some preliminary explanation.

Despite all the advances which have been made, Marrano research has not yet overcome some basic dichotomies which could not but affect its results.

In part this has been due to the very nature of the subject. The Marranos have, after all, both a "Peninsular" and a "Jewish" history, and it is not surprising that the two aspects have often been treated as separate entities. The cleavage is perhaps most evident in the case of those Marranos who, over a span of several centuries, fled from Spain and Portugal, and emerged elsewhere as professing Jews. These had, in a sense, two lives, one prior to their departure, and another subsequent to it. Inevitably, it is the former which has generally attracted the historian of Spain, and the latter which has engaged the Jewish scholar. By and large each has brought to bear on the subject his own distinct methodology, frame of reference, and technical equipment. Most archival research on the post-Expulsion period has been the work of Peninsular scholars, while it is the Jewish historian who has had access to the Hebrew sources, and hence to the inner life of the Sephardic diaspora. Another serious division which has often characterized the study of the Marranos is between their literary history and their social history, with the heaviest concentration on the first. Even then, the writings of former Marranos have usually been treated and discussed with little reference to the lives of the authors.

It should hardly require special pleading, I think, to insist that all these elements are merely different facets of the same phenomenon, and that ultimately one cannot be understood without the other. Inquisitorial documents must be integrated with rabbinic sources, Iberian with Hebrew literature, Peninsular social history with Jewish communal history, if genuine perspective is to be attained.

This study is an exploratory attempt to combine such various approaches, and to see what can be learned by applying them to one man: the seventeenth-century Marrano physician, philosopher, and apologist, Isaac Cardoso.

While the method and aim are deliberate, the specific choice of subject was somewhat fortuitous, the result of a sudden personal interest. I first knew of Isaac Cardoso only as a name which I encountered often in the course of my reading, and as the brother of the Sabbatian mystic Abraham Cardoso, to whom so much attention has been devoted by Professor Gershom Scholem and his disciples. Some years ago I saw a reproduction of the frontispiece of Isaac's *Las excelencias de los hebreos* in the catalogue of an Oxford bookseller, but, as with most of the other tempting items of Spanish and Portuguese Judaica which were offered for sale, I found the price rather prohibitive. Only weeks later, by a stroke of luck, a somewhat inaccessible corner of a bookshop in New York yielded a copy which I was able to ransom from the dust for a mere pittance. As I finally began to read the text itself, I was captivated by what appeared to me a major classic of Jewish apologetics. Turning back to the scholarly literature I found that the book had been frequently mentioned, but never even adequately described—praised, but not analyzed. Kayserling and others gave some bare biographical facts about Cardoso's life in the Peninsula, quite insufficient to illumine the work itself, but enough to intrigue me all the more. The author of the *Excelencias*, I learned, had apparently moved in the highest society in Madrid, had written a number of medical and scientific works in Spanish and Latin, had even published a funeral oration on Lope de Vega. I became extremely curious to find out more about the two lives of Cardoso, that of the Spanish physician and that of the passionate Jewish apologist, and to seek out, if possible, some of the strands that united the two in the same person. This study is the result.

Lacunae, of course, remain, and no one can be more aware of them than I. It would perhaps have been the better part of prudence to choose to study a Marrano with some prior indication as to what documentary sources might be available for him. Instead, I first chose the man, and resolved to learn what I could. My quest for Cardoso led me to retrace his own journeys, and I have thus searched through the proverbial haystack in the archives and libraries of Portugal, Spain, and Italy. He has often proved to be an elusive quarry. Two potentially major sources on which I at first based high hopes proved to be nonexistent. The most abundant font of information for the Peninsular life of a Marrano is usually to be found in his inquisitorial dossier. Cardoso, however, was never tried by the Inquisition, and in this respect we can hardly allow our thirst for documents to begrudge him his good fortune. More frustrating is the disappearance of the registers of the Sephardic community of Verona, when the city was occupied by the Nazis during the Second World War, for me a small symbol of the larger human tragedy.

Nevertheless, my search has brought its compensations as well, some of them quite unexpected, both in the materials I have been able to examine, and in the various methodological approaches which those materials compelled me to adopt as I went along. It is for others to judge whether I have adequately coped with the questions that have arisen. I hope, at least, that the right questions have been asked, and that their implications are not confined to Cardoso alone.

A number of technical observations may be of use to the reader. For reasons which will be explained in the first chapter, I have used the term "Marrano" to denote only those men and women whose Judaizing propensities are either established or highly probable. Otherwise I have employed the religiously neutral term "New Christian" which here merely indicates that the person is of known Jewish descent, but implies no ideological evaluation. I have, however, frequently referred to Iberian "antisemitism" and "antisemites," well aware that such nineteenth-century terms are essentially anachronistic, and perhaps especially so in the Peninsula, where, in the period we are discussing, there were formally no Jews. To have done otherwise would have been to make a fetish of semantics. "Anti-Converso" or "anti-New Christian" is not really satisfactory, being too restrictive, while "anti-Conversoism" or "anti-New Christianism" is too clumsy to tolerate. If the term "antisemitism" is anachronistic, it is so in the very same way that the New Christian was called "Jew" by his Iberian adversaries, and in that sense alone it is even appropriate.

In quoting from primary sources, especially Latin, Spanish, and Portuguese, I have generally transcribed the texts as they appear in the original, with no attempt to modernize the orthography or introduce all the necessary accents. I have departed from this practice in cases of obvious misprints, and in instances where a word, as given, may prove ambiguous or unclear to the reader. Citations from the Bible in English have been given according to the Jewish Publication Society translation, except in a few instances where I felt the use of the citation required that the translation be altered.

While adhering to a biographical framework, this study is not, strictly speaking, a biography. It is rather, as the subtitle indicates, a study of seventeenth-century Marranism and Jewish apologetics

—as reflected in the life of one man. This will explain, for example, why I have gone into considerable detail in discussing such matters as the case of the *Cristo de la Paciencia*, or the antisemitic tract of Juan de Quiñones. Both illumine important aspects of the *milieu* which Cardoso knew. If the book lays any particular claim to novelty, it is precisely in its attempt at a comprehensive study of an individual Marrano, taking account of both his life in the Peninsula and his later Jewish career, his experience and his thought, seen as an organic whole. Should it persuade others of the need for similar investigations. I shall consider my labors amply rewarded.

My first book also provides a first opportunity to indicate my indebtedness to those who have so great a share in it.

It is more than ordinary bonds of filial obligation which move me to begin by expressing my profound gratitude for the high privilege of being the son of Hava and Yehuda Yerushalmi. I cannot write publicly of the measure of their love and self-sacrifice, but I must record something of what they gave me besides. In our home in New York my mother brought me the rich Jewish traditions of Pinsk, and my father, the Hebrew humanism of Odessa. Together they led me into an enchanted palace of Jewish learning, folklore, and song from which I shall always draw sustenance. East European Ashkenazim both, they had no inkling that I would someday devote myself to Sephardic studies. Yet it was they who gave me my very first awareness of "Marranos" when I was ten years old, in a children's biography of Don Isaac Abravanel, written in Yiddish. My mother, alas, did not live to see this book appear. She passed away five months ago, on the eve of Passover, when I had already begun the final revisions. May the book prove a source of some consolation to my father.

I have been equally fortunate in the teachers I have had. To my revered master Professor Salo Wittmayer Baron, foremost of Jewish historians in our time, I owe more than I can say. He was my guide and mentor throughout my years of graduate study at Columbia University, and both my master's thesis and the present work were written under his direction. In the finest tradition of Jewish teaching he has been more than a teacher. From the day

I first stepped into his office he has taken the closest interest in my progress at every turn, and his solicitude and efforts for my personal welfare have never ceased. The Foreword he has graciously added to my book is thus only the latest link in the long succession of his favors to me. My fondest hope is that I shall prove worthy to be numbered among his disciples.

Three other teachers must be singled out among the many from whom I have profited. My historical studies with Professor Zvi Ankori at the Jewish Theological Seminary of America and later at Columbia were decisive experiences. The erudition and enthusiasm which he communicated had much to do with my own decision to become an historian, and the friendship into which our relationship soon ripened enabled me to learn as much from him in private conversation as in class. Professor Shalom Spiegel of the Seminary remains indelibly in my mind, not only for his unforgettable lectures on Hebrew poetry in medieval Spain, but as a truly Renaissance figure to whom nothing in Jewish or universal culture is alien. The "sea of the Talmud" was charted for me at the Seminary by Professor Saul Lieberman. His unrivaled ability to make an ancient text come to life remains an inspiration.

My work on this book was greatly facilitated by Sr. Pierre Audubert of Madrid. Together with his charming wife Betty and their young son José, he opened to me his home and made it my own. When I was back in New York, and as I needed more materials, he undertook to procure the microfilms and photostats for me. I extend my warm thanks also to Sra. Mina Ryten of Lisbon for making my stay in Portugal such a pleasant one; to Mr. Rod W. Horton, Cultural Attaché at the United States Embassy, and Prof. Kurt Jacobsohn of the University of Lisbon; to D. Luís Silveira, Inspector General of Portuguese Archives and Libraries, whose letter opened all doors to me; and to Sr. Alfonso Cassuto for a memorable evening spent in his home, when he showed me his magnificent library of rare Sephardica. In Madrid D. Ramón Paz, the distinguished director of the Manuscript Division of the Biblioteca Nacional, offered not only help, but friendship. Professor Cecil Roth, formerly of Oxford, was kind enough to send me some useful notes on the Venetian archives, and I received important information on the Verona *pinkasim* from Professor Shlomo Simonson of Tel-Aviv University. Professors Haim Beinart of Jerusalem and I. S. Révah of Paris sent me some very encouraging letters. Their prompt replies to the queries of a stranger were for me an affecting reminder of the bonds that can link the international scholarly community.

Both my graduate work and my research trips abroad were facilitated at various times by financial assistance from individuals and institutions. I wish to thank Mrs. Joy Ungerleider and Mr. Richard Scheuer of Larchmont, N. Y., for their early faith in me; the Society for Religion in Higher Education for awarding me a Kent Fellowship; and the National Foundation for Jewish Culture, for its very generous travel grant.

I am deeply beholden to Dr. Milton Rosenbaum and Dr. Maurice S. Nadelman for their encouragement and support.

My debt to my alma mater, Columbia University, is great on many counts. I am grateful to the University for naming me to a President's Fellowship, and for affording me my first opportunity to teach while still a doctoral student; to the Ansley Awards Committee for having chosen my dissertation to receive the 1966 Ansley Award, thus making possible the publication of this book; to Columbia University Press, and especially to Messrs. Henry Wiggins and Harry W. Segessman for their patience and genuine understanding in undertaking the arduous task of publication. In addition to Professor Baron, Professors Isaac Barzilay, Gerson D. Cohen, and Gonzalo Sobejano turned my doctoral "defense" into a creative scholarly conversation. Their helpful comments have been incorporated in this book.

I owe my invitation to join the Harvard University faculty two years ago largely to the initiative of Isadore Twersky, Littauer Professor of Hebrew Literature and Philosophy, and chairman of the Department of Near Eastern Languages and Literatures. Our close professional association and personal friendship in a stimulating intellectual environment continue to be for me a major source of gratification, while his keen interest in my work has been a welcome spur in bringing this book to its final completion.

Two generous friends in the university community gave me more help than I had the right to expect. Anne Whitman, who had already placed her rich classical erudition at my disposal in translating some of the Latin texts, also read the final draft with incomparable devotion and vigilance. Raimundo Lida, Professor of Romance Languages and Literatures at Harvard, readily agreed to my last-minute request that he merely review the Spanish citations. Instead, in the midst of his own very busy schedule, he went on to read the entire book. As though this were not enough, he then spent hours with me at his home in a discussion which made me wish I had known him when I first embarked on this study.

It remains my pleasant duty to thank those individuals, archives, and libraries, who have furnished the materials for my work: The Keeper of Oriental Books, Bodleian Library, Oxford; Dr.ª Carlota Gil Pereira of the Biblioteca Nacional and Dr.ª Maria Francisca de Oliveira Andrade of the Arquivo Nacional da Torre do Tombo, Lisbon; the Archivo Histórico Provincial y Universitario, Valladolid; the Archivo Universitario, Salamanca; the Archivo Histórico Nacional and Biblioteca Nacional, Madrid; the Bibliotheca Marciana and Archivio di Stato, Venice; the Biblioteca Comunale and Archivio di Stato, Verona; Nello Pavoncello, formerly Chief Rabbi of Verona; the Jewish National and University Library, Jerusalem; the staffs of the libraries of Columbia University, Jewish Theological Seminary of America, New York Public Library, New York Academy of Medicine, and Hispanic Society of America, and of the Widener and Houghton Libraries, Harvard University.

Miss Sybil Wyner of Elizabeth, New Jersey, typed the manuscript in record time. A grant from the Clark Fund at Harvard made the additional revisions possible. Miss Elisabeth Shoemaker, my editor at Columbia University Press, has enhanced the whole with her good taste and vast technical experience. All have my heartfelt thanks.

Finally, in dedicating this book to my wife, I merely formalize what already belongs to her.

Yosef Hayim Yerushalmi

Cambridge, Massachusetts
Elul, 5728/September, 1968

AHN	Archivo Histórico Nacional (Madrid)
AHP	Arquivo Histórico Português (or: Portuguez)
AUS	Archivo Universitario, Salamanca
Antt	Josephus, *Antiquities*
AUV	Archivo (Provincial y) Universitario, Valladolid
B.A.E.	Biblioteca de Autores Españoles
BEPJ	Biblioteca Española-Portugueza-Judaica
BNM	Biblioteca Nacional (Madrid)
HSA	Hispanic Society of America (New York)
HUCA	*Hebrew Union College Annual*
JE	*The Jewish Encyclopedia*
JQR	*Jewish Quarterly Review*
MGWJ	*Monatsschrift für Geschichte und Wissenschaft des Judentums*
(N.S.)	New Series
(O.S.)	Old Series
PL	*Patrologiæ Cursus Completus*, series Latina, ed. by J. P. Migne
REJ	*Revue des études juives*
Responsa	(for any collection of *She'elot u-teshubot* which bears no other title)
Semanario erudito	Semanario erudito, que comprehende varias obras inéditas, críticas, morales, instructivas, políticas, históricas, satíricas y jocosas de nuestros mejores autores antiguos y modernos
ṢNṢ	*Sefer Ṣiṣat Nobel Ṣebi*
TB	Babylonian Talmud
TP	Palestinian Talmud
ZGJD	*Zeitschrift für die Geschichte der Juden in Deutschland*

MARRANOS IN THE SEVENTEENTH CENTURY

> And what will it profit our lord and king
> to pour holy water on the Jews, calling
> them by our names, 'Pedro,' or 'Pablo,'
> while they keep their faith like Akiba or
> Tarfon? . . . Know, Sire, that Judaism is
> one of the incurable diseases.
> —Solomon ibn Verga, *Shebet Yehudah*

THERE ARE even today areas in the Iberian Peninsula where, more than four and one half centuries after the Expulsion from Spain and conversion in Portugal, the name "Jew" elicits only an uncertain response from the local inhabitants. Returning from a trip through the Spanish or Portuguese provinces, a Jewish traveler can still regale his friends by describing how, upon identifying himself as a Jew, the villagers could associate the term only with the Jews of the Bible. It is to be presumed that with the continuing expansion of tourism and the further settlement of Jews in the Peninsula such experiences will soon be a thing of the past. Until quite recently, however, the anecdote was a common one. For the masses in Spain and Portugal the name *judío* (or *judeu*) had become, at best, an exotic and archaic evocation; it no longer corresponded to a reality.

But this was not always so. The Jew did not disappear suddenly from the mind of the Spanish people in 1492, nor did Judaism lose all significance in Portugal after the mass baptism of 1497. In the sixteenth and seventeenth centuries, and even later, Peninsular presses still sent forth books and tracts directed *contra los judíos de nuestros tiempos* (against the Jews of our times [!]). Alleged Judaizers continued to be penanced or relaxed for burning by the inquisitorial tribunals, and the populace flocked to the public spectacle of the *auto-da-fé*. Long after the last synagogues had been dedicated to the Virgin, Spanish and Portuguese pulpits rang with denunciations of the Jewish perfidy. The "Jew" was still an object of satire on the stage and in the doggerel of urchins in the streets. Rumors of Jewish plots to subvert Spain could yet pass swiftly through the *barrios* of Madrid. A Spaniard or Portuguese who aspired to honors or offices had very much to worry, in presenting his genealogy for inspection, lest a Jew be found clinging to a remote branch of the family tree. The *sambenitos* which had been worn by those reconciled by the Inquisition hung afterwards through decades and generations in the churches where their grandchildren prayed. Broadsides posted in public places still displayed a list of characteristic Jewish ceremonies, and called upon the faithful to denounce those whom they knew to be following the execrable rites of the Law of Moses.

To a Spaniard or Portuguese of the seventeenth century the phrase "Jews of our times" was neither an abstraction nor a euphemism. It might well apply to some of his own neighbors, even though they bore authentic Iberian Christian names, and he saw them regularly at Mass in the cathedral, and the walls of their homes were adorned with the conventional pious pictures. There was no guarantee that this seemingly unimpeachable orthodoxy was not a mere façade, and that among themselves these people did not practice occult Jewish rites. For they were, after all, *cristianos nuevos* (Port., *cristãos novos*), "New Christians," descendants of those many Jews who had been baptized in the fourteenth and fifteenth centuries. In the seventeenth century these New Christians still constituted a distinct and important class within Iberian society, and in the popular mind the line between "New Christian" and "Jew" was often blurred. The one seemed merely a metamorphosis of the other. Had not the Inquisition consistently revealed how many of the seed of the original Conversos were still Jews at heart? One might perhaps be somewhat wary of hurling the epithet *marrano* or *judío* at a person, for this was considered to be so grave an insult as to be prohibited by law. But it did not really matter which term one chose to use. In the consciousness of seventeenth-century Spain and Portugal the "Jew" was not merely an historical reminiscence; he was, in effect, a contemporary. How are we to understand this phenomenon?

THE "PORTUGUESE" IN SPAIN

The long campaign to obliterate Spanish Judaism which began with the pogroms of 1391 appeared, by the latter half of the sixteenth century, to be finally crowned with success. Isolated after the expulsion in 1492 of all professing Jews, the Conversos in the ensuing decades ultimately lost the strength, and perhaps the will, to maintain their Jewish ties in the midst of a ruthless program of persecution and repression. The available evidence, admittedly incomplete, indicates that by this time crypto-Judaism had been atomized by the hammer blows of the Inquisition, and that Spanish Marranism had lost its former élan, except perhaps in certain small and remote localities.[1] Those Conversos who did not flee to other lands, and who had not perished at the stake, appeared, to the degree that they were accepted, largely merged into the general population, and attempting to live as faithful Catholics. From the mid-sixteenth

---

[1] On the waning of Spanish Marranism in the 16th century see Henry Charles Lea, *A History of the Inquisition of Spain* (New York, 1907), III, 234 f. Cf. Cecil Roth, *A History of the Marranos* (Philadelphia, 1947), pp. 85 f.; Julio Caro Baroja, *Los judíos en la España moderna y contemporánea* (Madrid, 1961—), I, 452 f., 460.

An interesting example of the survival of crypto-Judaism in a relatively isolated community is that of Badajoz in Estremadura, near the Portuguese border. The list of *sambenitos* of that town has been published and analyzed by Antonio Rodríguez-Moñino in his "Les Judaisants à Badajoz de 1493 à 1599," *Revue des études juives*, CXV (1956), 73–86. More such instances could undoubtedly be found were it not for the fact that the surviving records of the Spanish Inquisition are quite incomplete. See the remarks of I. S. Révah, "Les marranes," *REJ*, CVIII (1950–60), 35 f. n. 1, noting also the need for a comprehensive study of the Spanish Inquisition up to 1580.

century onward, the Spanish Inquisition turned increasingly from the prosecution of Judaizers to that of Protestant and other heresies. Those nonconformist impulses which still retained some vitality among the offspring of the Conversos seem to have found an outlet in mystical or Erasmian currents within Spanish Catholicism itself.[2] While the presence of this leaven is of considerable interest for the intellectual history of Spain, the fact remains that in the course of the sixteenth century the Spanish Conversos disappear, progressively, from the ken of Jewish history.

If Spain in the seventeenth century was obsessed once again with a Judaizing heresy, that was due to the massive influx, beginning after 1580, of the Portuguese New Christians.

Both the genesis and the development of the Converso problem in Portugal differed significantly from that of Spain. Lusitanian Jewry had not suffered the slow debilitative process of erosion which their Hispanic brethren had endured from 1391 to 1492. Their inner strength had not been sapped by periodic massacre, waves of conversionist panic, and a culminating expulsion of those who had remained constant. When, in 1497, the death knell sounded for open

---

[2] The New Christian share in the propagation of 16th-century Erasmian and allied tendencies has been fully demonstrated by Marcel Bataillon in his study of *Érasme et l'Espagne* (Paris, 1937). Cf. also Eugenio Asensio, "El erasmismo y las corrientes espirituales afines," *Revista de filología española*, XXXVI (1952), especially pp. 56–69.

In recent decades Spanish scholars have evinced an ever growing interest in the Converso provenance of various major figures in the spiritual and intellectual history of their country. Thus, it has been ascertained by Abdón M. Salazar that the father of Luis Vives was burned at the stake in 1526, and that before the age of ten the philosopher himself attended clandestine Jewish services. (Cited by Américo Castro, *The Structure of Spanish History* (Princeton, 1954), p. 577, n. 42). Similarly, the grandfather of Santa Teresa of Ávila was reconciled for Judaizing by the Inquisition of Toledo in 1485. See Narciso Alonso Cortés, "Pleitos de los Cepedas," *Boletín de la Real Academia Española*, XXV (1946), 85–110; cf. H. Serís, "Nueva geneologia de Santa Teresa," *Nueva revista de filología hispánica*, X (1956), 364–84. The real or alleged Converso ancestry of other Spanish luminaries is examined by Antonio Domínguez Ortiz, *La clase social de los conversos en Castilla en la edad moderna* (Madrid, 1955), pp. 155–89, by Castro (*Structure*, pp. 569, 575) and by Caro Baroja (*Judíos*, vol. II, pt. iii, chs. 9–10), all with ample bibliographies.

4

Jewish life in Portugal, it came in the form of a sudden and total conversion by force of all Portuguese Jewry. The mass baptism decreed by King Manoel engulfed both the native Portuguese Jews and those Jewish exiles from Spain who, some five years earlier, had refused to pay the price of conversion and had sought refuge across the frontier.[3]

Crypto-Judaism among the New Christians of Portugal was to prove hardy enough to survive for centuries. In attempting to explain this remarkable endurance scholars have usually stressed two factors. In contrast to Spain it is argued that conversion in Portugal, being entirely and literally forced, overcame thousands of faithful Jews and not only the religiously weak, while at the same time it included some of the most tenacious elements from Spain itself. Moreover, after 1497 some four decades were to elapse before the introduction of the Portuguese Inquisition. This respite allowed the Conversos ample time to accommodate themselves to conditions and to create viable forms of crypto-Jewish life.[4] However, while these factors certainly played a part in the formation of Portuguese Marranism, they are insufficient to explain the phenomenon as a whole. After all, in Spain, at least in 1391, it was not only the weakest elements who were converted. And, while the Portuguese Conversos faced no Inquisition between 1497 and 1536, the same was true of the Spanish Conversos from 1391 to 1478. Moreover, the latter, during all this time, had before their eyes the example of a living Judaism professed in the homes, schools, and synagogues of the *aljamas*. In Portugal, conversion and the extinction of open Jewish life occurred simultaneously.

But perhaps it is precisely here that the key should be sought. What was of decisive import in Portugal was the fact that there the *community itself* was converted, *in toto*, whereas in Spain the

---

[3] Portuguese Jewry in the 15th century is surveyed by Meyer Kayserling, *Geschichte der Juden in Portugal* (Leipzig, 1867), chs. 4–7, and J. Mendes dos Remédios, *Os Judeus em Portugal*, I (Coimbra, 1895), chs. 4–5. A study of Portuguese Jewish history prior to 1497, based on extensive archival research comparable to that which has been lavished on the Jews of medieval Spain, is still a major desideratum.

[4] See Roth, *Marranos*, pp. 61 f.; cf. Révah, "Les marranes," p. 36.

community had remained throughout, even though eroded and diminished in number, outside the pale of conversion. Schematically, we might outline the progression in both countries as follows:

In Spain: a) Before 1391 The Jewish community.

  b) 1391–1492 Conversos *plus* the Jewish community.

  c) After 1492 Conversos *minus* the expelled Jewish community.

In Portugal: a) Before 1497 The Jewish community.

  b) After 1497 A converted Jewish community, minus individual exiles.

In effect, Portugal skipped the intermediate phase through which Spain had passed: the existence, side by side, of Conversos and a normative Jewish community. Consequently, the intervals between conversion and the establishment of the Inquisition (1391–1478 in Spain, 1497–1536 in Portugal) are, although superficially parallel, not at all analogous in the two countries. We must try to envision at least some of the implications of this fundamental datum. It means first that in Portugal, unlike Spain, there was no period of tension between Conversos and professing Jews, for after 1497 all who had been Jews were suddenly converts. Portuguese Jewry thus evaded the corrosive intracommunal and intrafamilial ruptures which conversion had brought to Spanish Jewry, and which had plagued the latter through much of the fifteenth century. Moreover, in Spain, where conversion had engulfed only a part of Jewry, the energies of those who had remained professing Jews were still channeled into the normative community and its institutions up to the very time of the Expulsion. In Portugal all Jewish energies were immediately absorbed in 1497 into the converted community. Individual social ties remained intact. Though formal instruments of social control abruptly lost their force, age-old communal bonds could not be unraveled overnight. Surely in the wake of the great catastrophe the unwillingly baptized rabbis and scholars did not suddenly cease to teach and guide, albeit surreptitiously, nor did the men who had been prominent in the community immediately lose their influence. Undoubtedly there were Jews who had previously lacked only the initiative or the courage to convert voluntarily as individuals, and who now welcomed the forced mass baptism as an opportunity to live as Christians with a clear conscience. But for the many who remained constant at heart, the possibility of a viable crypto-Jewish life must have been vastly enhanced by the fact that the social base so essential to such a life had been transmuted, but not really obliterated.

Apart from its social consequences, the simultaneous conversion in Portugal of the entire Jewry of the country must have had an even deeper impact on the self-image of the Conversos themselves. We have already noted that the presence in fifteenth-century Spain of an ongoing Jewish community provided the Conversos with an example of living Judaism. Of this the Portuguese convert was deprived. But, by the same token, there was no normative community in Portugal to serve him daily as a visible reminder that he was now outside its fold, or to place his Jewish identity in doubt. Here conversion was, in a real sense, normative for the corporate Jewish group. This was now "Jewry"; there was no other. It is that very corporate character of conversion in Portugal which invested the Portuguese converts with the cohesion and solidarity of having shared one destiny from the very outset. A Spanish New Christian in later times might well speculate whether his forbears had accepted baptism under duress during a pogrom in 1391, or perhaps out of conviction at the time of the Disputation of Tortosa, or in order to remain in Spain at the time of the Expulsion. The Portuguese New Christian was not prey to such ambiguities. He knew, or he could assume, the collective origins of his entire group, indeed of all the New Christians in the land. His fathers had not entered Christianity as individuals; they had been swept up in the common fate of all Jewry. Thus, to a degree not paralleled by the Spanish New Christians, those of Portugal possessed a genuinely historical group character of which, as we shall see, Portuguese society was itself instinctively aware. In terms of sheer number, it may well be that more Jews had been converted in Spain than in Portugal. But the essential difference between conversion in the two countries was not quantitative, but qualitative. Despite the collapse of its traditional structure and institutions, a converted Portuguese Jewry

7

retained, at least initially, much of the vital force and solidarity of the community itself.

Possessed of this strength, the Portuguese Conversos could take full advantage of the years prior to the establishment of the Inquisition. It is in the period from 1497 to 1536 that the New Christians penetrated into the highest echelons of Portuguese commerce and finance. But it is also during this time that various modes of crypto-Jewish life became firmly entrenched among thousands of them. The group vitality which we have stressed was amply manifested time and again in the elaborate negotiations of the New Christians to prevent the introduction of the Inquisition. Throughout the transactions with king, Pope, and Curia, involving the most arduous diplomatic activity abroad and the raising of huge sums of money at home, the Conversos moved collectively through their spokesmen and representatives. They acted, in fact, as a group in whom the earlier communal traditions of Portuguese Jewry still manifested a considerable measure of their original vigor. It was not for lack of common effort or leadership that the endeavor ended in failure. In 1536 John III obtained papal consent for the establishment of the Inquisition in his domains. The first formal *auto-da-fé* was held in Lisbon in 1540. By 1547, after some temporary setbacks, the Portuguese Inquisition was in full and unimpeded operation. It was often to exceed in ferocity its Spanish prototype and counterpart.[5]

Through an unexpected development in the Peninsula, however, the destinies of the New Christians in the two kingdoms were fated to converge and to attain a new dimension. In 1580 Portugal was annexed to Spain in a personal union under Philip II. The Portuguese New Christians, who had by now endured more than forty years of intense inquisitorial harassment, placed great hopes in the union, though these were not immediately realized. When the Portuguese Cortes met to swear its allegiance to Philip, the estates insisted that no Conversos be admitted to any office. At the same time the latter petitioned the king for the total abolition of legal

---

[5] The period 1497–1536 is treated in great detail in Alexandre Herculano's classic, *Da origem e estabelecimento da Inquisição em Portugal* (3 vols., Lisbon, 1854–59).

distinctions between New and Old Christians, and asked also that the Crown intervene to obtain for them a General Pardon from the Holy See. Philip denied both these requests. When he came to Lisbon to be crowned, he personally attended an *auto-da-fé* held on April 1, 1582. All the legal disabilities remained in force.[6]

Nevertheless, the union ushered in a new era. As, periodically, freedom of movement was obtained, there began an ever-increasing emigration of New Christians from Portugal into Spain.[7] This influx, which eventually reached massive proportions, was doubly motivated. Compared to the radical decline of the Portuguese economy, Spain, wealthier and politically dominant, seemed now a land full of opportunities. Again, relative to the fury of inquisitorial persecution in Portugal, Spain must have appeared, in the eyes of many, almost a refuge. Though Portugal had been annexed, the Portuguese Inquisition was not merged with that of Castile, but remained autonomous. Only the nomination of the Inquisitor General belonged to the Spanish Crown. Between 1581 and 1600 the three Portuguese tribunals held no less than fifty *autos-da-fé*. Most significantly, however, the Spanish Inquisition did not punish crimes against the faith which were committed in Portugal. At least as late as 1630, a decade before Portugal regained its independence, there was still no formal provision for extradition, and Castilian tribunals did not usually honor such requests from the Portuguese inquisitors.[8]

Thus the lure of new economic horizons and the desire to find some measure of relief from religious persecution combined, after 1580, to alter radically the geographical distribution of the Peninsular New Christians. Around 1599 the Spanish Dominican Fray Augustín Salucio, pleading for the elimination of legal discriminations between New and Old Christians, could still muster the

---

[6] J. Lúcio d'Azevedo, *História dos Christãos-Novos portugueses* (Lisbon, 1921), pp. 149 f.

[7] On emigration after 1580 and its effects, see Lea, *Inquisition*, III, 266 f.; Roth, *Marranos*, pp. 85 f.; Domínguez Ortiz, *Clase social*, p. 82.

[8] Lea, *Inquisition*, III, 265 f., 278.

argument that Judaizers hardly exist in the Spain of his time.[9] By 1640 the royal chronicler José Pellicer y Tovar cries out in frustration that "one of the calamities which must be considered with the greatest attention and grief is to see Spain filled on all sides with Jews, enemies of our Holy Catholic Faith!"[10] His voice is only one among many. A Spain which, in the late sixteenth century, had thought itself largely freed of Jewish concerns, now found itself in the seventeenth century obsessed once more with the age-old problem. The pendulum, after completing its arc, had swung back to its point of origin. The incursion into Spain of Portuguese New Christians was of such dimensions and impact that, to the Spaniards of the seventeenth century, "Portuguese" was virtually synonymous with "Jew." So close was the identification that in 1646 the Jesuit Sebastián Gonzáles could describe several Portuguese, who had been arrested by the Inquisition in Madrid, as having been imprisoned simply *for what they are*.[11] The Portuguese people themselves complained that often, when traveling abroad, they were automatically stigmatized as Judaizers, simply because of their land of origin.[12]

---

[9] "Pues quién no vé en quán diferente estado se halla ahora el reyno, y quánta seguridad hay en general de la gente que tiene alguna raza?" in Augustín Salucio, *Discurso acerca de la justicia y buen gobierno de España en los estatutos de limpieza de sangre*, printed in *Semanario erudito*, XV (Madrid, 1788), 165.

[10] "De verdad, una de las desdichas que se deben reparar con mas atención y lástima, es ver a España tan llena por todos lados de Judíos, enemigos de nuestra Santa fe Católica," in José Pellicer y Tovar, *Avisos históricos, que comprehenden las noticias y sucesos particulares, ocurridos en nuestra monarquía desde al año de 1639*, in *Semanario erudito*, XXXI (Madrid, 1790), 165.

According to the calculations of Albert Girard there were, around the year 1640, some 2,000 Portuguese merchants in Seville alone, and most of them were New Christians. See his *Le commerce français à Séville et Cadix au temps des Hapsbourg* (Paris, 1932), pp. 39 f.

[11] "Tres días ha prendieron también por la Inquisición á siete ú ocho portugueses *por lo que suelen*" (*Cartas de algunos PP. de la Compañía de Jesus sobre los sucessos de la monarquía entre los años de 1634 y 1648*, in *Memorial Histórico Español*, XVIII [Madrid, 1864], 420; letter of October 23, 1646).

[12] "Portuguezes e judeus já são synônimos," writes the great 17th-century Portuguese Jesuit, Padre António Vieira. See his *Obras inéditas* (Lisbon, 1856), III, 93. For other similar citations see Edward Glaser, "Referencias antisemitas

The "Portuguese" in Spain

One of the effects of the entry of the Portuguese New Christians was the recrudescence of the activity of the Spanish Inquisition which, as we have noted, had shown a diminishing interest in Judaizers in the decades prior to 1580. Already in 1595 ninety-eight Judaizers appeared at an *auto* in Seville.[13] Beginning in 1625 the majority of those charged with Judaizing by the Inquisition of Córdoba were "Portuguese" living in Andalucía.[14] Throughout the seventeenth century no Spanish *auto de fe* will lack them. Most of the accused will be of Portuguese origin and will bear Portuguese names. To some degree, the advent of the "Portuguese" also revived crypto-Jewish tendencies among the Spanish New Christians. In any case, as far as may be learned from the partially preserved records of the Spanish Inquisition, the problem of Judaizing heresies did not recede again until the middle of the eighteenth century.[15]

"Marranism" in Spain during this second phase thus exhibited a remarkable tenacity. Nevertheless, it should be clear that, although all New Christians may have been generically suspected of Judaizing, they were by no means all of them Judaizers. The "Mar-

---

en la literatura peninsular de la Edad de Oro," *Nueva revista de filología hispánica*, VIII (1954), 41, n. 5.

The Spaniards themselves often suffered from being called "Marranos" by foreigners. There is abundant material on this in Arturo Farinelli's *Marrano: storia di un vituperio* (Geneva, 1925), especially pp. 67–71. Nevertheless, there was a difference. In the case of the Portuguese the identification as Jews was already so complete that no other epithet was required. "Portuguese" alone sufficed.

[13] Domínguez Ortiz, *Clase social*, p. 83.

[14] See *Colección de los autos generales y particulares de fé, celebrados por el Tribunal de la Inquisición de Córdoba. Anotados y dados a luz en 1836 por el Lic. Gaspar Matute y Luquin* (Madrid, 1912).

[15] As late as 1720 a secret "synagogue" of some twenty families, whose members had held services since 1707, was uncovered in Madrid. In 1714 they had elected a rabbi, whose name was sent to the Jewish community of Leghorn for confirmation. Probably as a result of this scandalous revelation, there began a new wave of inquisitorial activity in which, between 1721 and 1727, at least 820 cases of Judaizing were tried in Spain. See Lea, *Inquisition*, III, 30 f. Compare now, in greater detail, Caro Baroja, *Judíos*, III, 46–79 ("Los judaizantes de Madrid en los primeros años del reinado de Felipe V"), and 80–118 ("La gran represión final").

ranos" were a *part* of the New Christian group, but were not coextensive with it. Only if we bear this distinction in mind can we hope to arrive at an appreciation of Marranism itself, especially as it was manifested in the seventeenth century.

THE "MEN OF THE NATION"

Let us first examine the larger entity.

Against the background of Peninsular life in the seventeenth century the New Christians confront us, before all else, as a social class which had been compelled, through the generations, to bear the curse and stigma of its Jewish origins. While individual families of Converso descendants in this period could be absorbed successfully into the Old Christian society, the majority remained a separate, unintegrated group. The basic pattern had already crystallized in the fifteenth century with the formulation in Spain of the first statutes of so-called *limpieza de sangre* (purity of blood), barring those of Jewish or Moorish ancestry from various offices, titles, and honors. These discriminatory provisions, which can be traced formally to the famous *Sentencia-Estatuto* of Toledo (1449), were themselves the expression of a deeply ingrained resentment of the Conversos. Alien to traditional Christian teaching, essentially subversive of the tremendous missionary effort previously exerted against Spanish Jewry by church and state, the statutes of *limpieza* incarnated the paradoxes posed by the very success of that effort.[16]

---

[16] The most comprehensive study of the statutes, their development, and the debates they engendered is available in Albert A. Sicroff's important monograph *Les controverses des statuts de pureté de sang en Espagne du XVᵉ au XVIIᵉ siècle* (Paris, 1960). Much of Domínguez Ortiz, *Clase social*, is devoted to the same subject. Cf. also Caro Baroja, *Judíos*, II, 267–323. Américo Castro's contention (*Structure*, pp. 525 ff.) that Spanish ideas on *limpieza de sangre* were a heritage derived from the Jews of Spain is, I believe, effectively refuted by Sicroff (p. 88, n. 98). For another criticism see Caro Baroja, II, 297. Sicroff also rejects the suggestion of Domínguez Ortiz that the antecedents are to be sought in the statutes of certain military brotherhoods of the 13th and 14th centuries, for these were patently

The "Men of the Nation"

Until masses of its Jews had been brought to the baptismal font, Spain, along with the rest of medieval Europe, had viewed the Jewish problem in one dimension: as a problem of religious conversion. It was precisely when conversion had been achieved on an unprecedented scale that there had ensued a realization of the basic inadequacy of the conversionist solution. For in the eyes of the rest of the population nothing beneficial had been accomplished thereby. Names had been altered, religious allegiances had shifted, but, even discounting the question of religious sincerity, today's Christian was still recognizable as yesterday's Jew. What was even worse, his conversion had only made him more dangerous as a competitor, and, because he could now present a Christian façade, his influence appeared all the more insidious. A comparable reaction followed in Portugal in the wake of the forced baptism of 1497.[17] In both countries the professing Jew had at least been a clearly defined entity. He had lived in his own quarter. He could be hedged about with restrictive laws and be made to pay special taxes. An individual convert could always be welcomed. But, when thousands of Jews had been baptized within the space of a few decades, it seemed to many as though the Jews had been transported bodily, though under another guise, into the very midst of the Christian social fabric. Here was a new and ambiguous breed that fitted into no familiar category, somehow neither Jew nor Christian. Baptism, whether forced or voluntary, appeared to have served primarily to

---

motivated by political and social, rather than religious and racial, considerations.

An analogue may be found, however, in the discriminatory provisions against Jewish converts in the Visigothic codes. Curiously, none of the aforementioned scholars has seen fit to discuss the Visigothic legislation in this context. Castro's general insistence on the break in continuity between Visigothic and later Christian Spain does not affect the importance of Visigothic legal precedents. Unfortunately, beyond the treatment of the Jews in Visigothic law, we know almost nothing of Jewish life in Spain during that period. For a succinct analysis of all available information on Visigothic Jewry, see Salo W. Baron, *A Social and Religious History of the Jews* (2d ed.; New York, 1957), III, 33–46.

[17] Hostility to the Portuguese New Christians reached its initial climax in April, 1506, when violent anti-Converso riots erupted in Lisbon. See Mendes dos Remédios, *Judeus em Portugal*, I, 308–20; D'Azevedo, *Christãos-Novos*, pp. 59 f.

invalidate all the former legal disabilities. The Jewish chronicler Solomon ibn Verga, himself an exile from Spain, undoubtedly reflects the mood of many Spanish Christians in his day when, in a fictitious dialogue, he records the advice allegedly given by a courtier to a king of Spain:

There is nothing to be gained by their conversion. They will rather become overweening against the true Christians, without fear, once they are held to appear as Christians. And the laws of the kingdom which used to be given while they were Jews will no longer be issued.[18]

The statutes of *limpieza* must be understood in this context. They originated as an attempt, ultimately successful, to find new juridical means to impose legal restrictions against the Converso, now that the old laws which had been formulated against professing Jews no longer applied. Thus they mark the ironic retaliation of Iberian society against the intrusion of the Jew through a conversion toward which that same society had labored so assiduously.

The older Jewry laws had been predicated on a distinction in religion. The Jew belonged to a different community of faith which was tolerated within the Christian state, but for which a special body of legislation was necessary and justifiable. If new barriers were to be erected they could no longer be based on a divergence of faith which, theoretically at least, no longer existed. Though it might conceivably be embellished with theological rationales, the only foundation remaining for special legislation against the Converso and his descendants was necessarily an *ethnic* one. Not faith but *blood* was to be the decisive factor. In subsequent centuries apologists for the statutes would try to justify them by general allegations concerning the heretical proclivities of the descendants of the Jews. But significantly, *anyone* of known Jewish ancestry, regardless of his personal piety, belonged automatically to the class of those subject to the statutes. *Limpieza de sangre* came to overshadow *limpieza de fe*.

Despite the alarm over the Converso threat Spain did not easily

---

[18] Solomon ibn Verga, *Shebet Yehudah*, ed. A. Shoḥat (Jerusalem, 1957), no. 64, p. 129.

accept the statutes of *limpieza* in the initial phases. For a religion which had come into the world proclaiming its indifference to the distinction between Jew and Greek, the theological objections were obvious. In addition, some authorities sensed immediately the potential dangers of such laws for a land in which Christian, Jewish, and Moorish blood had mingled for centuries. When the *Sentencia-Estatuto*, excluding persons of Jewish extraction from municipal offices in Toledo, was passed in 1449 at the instigation of the *alcalde mayor* Pedro Sarmiento, the subsequent outcry caused it to fall into abeyance. It was opposed by the king, by the Pope, and by prominent clergy and statesmen. But although the controversy over *limpieza de sangre* was to continue for centuries in both Spain and Portugal, the progress of the statutes was inexorable. The century following 1449 saw a gradual multiplication of the statutes, adopted sporadically by various corporate bodies in Spanish society.[19]

The most serious impetus came in 1547, when a new statute, instituted by the archbishop Juan Martínez Silíceo, was promulgated in the Cathedral Chapter of Toledo. Again, as before, there was considerable vocal opposition. But this statute was destined to stand and, indeed, to serve as the classic model. In 1555 it was ratified by Pope Paul VI and a year later it was upheld by Philip II, thus setting the seal of royal and papal approval on a practice that was already firmly established.[20] It is noteworthy that this development took place just at the time when the last discernible vestiges of crypto-Judaism were disappearing and the Spanish New Christians seem to have been on the threshold of complete assimilation. Yet from this point on *limpieza de sangre* rapidly became an official requirement for entry into almost any important honor or office in Spain. As the network of statutes multiplied, it was hard to find a significant area of Spanish public life which did not require of the candidate *pruebas de limpieza*, certifying him to be free of the stain of Jewish or Moorish blood. From Spain the statutes passed to

---

[19] On the *Sentencia-Estatuto* and the reactions to it see Sicroff, *Controverses*, pp. 32–62. The proliferation of statutes of *limpieza* up to 1547 is traced *ibid.*, pp. 88–94. Cf. Domínguez Ortiz, *Clase social*, pp. 26–50.

[20] Sicroff, *Controverses*, ch. III, pp. 95–139.

15

Portugal. When the Portuguese New Christians began to flow into Spain after 1580, they found the statutes rampant everywhere. By the seventeenth century the corporations in Spain with requirements of *limpieza* included: the military orders (Santiago, Calatrava, Alcántara, and others); judicial tribunals, among them the Inquisition itself; cathedrals and Chapters; various religious orders; the *colegios mayores* at the universities; certain provinces and towns; public and municipal offices; brotherhoods and confraternities.

The statutes, and the mentality they represented, perpetuated the distinction between New and Old Christians for centuries. They thus helped to maintain a class consciousness even among those descendants of the original Conversos whose Jewish awareness had atrophied. The fact is that few of them were able to forget their origins completely, even if they may have wished to do so. The statutes were as forceful a reminder of their Jewish extraction as the insults to which they were often subjected in daily life. For the term "New Christian" was both a social stigma and a legal category. The two pressures reinforced one another sufficiently to mark the entire group as a class apart.

But there was also another factor which contributed significantly to the self-awareness of this class. If legal disabilities and social barriers provided the negative impulses, the economic sphere provided a positive catalyst.

It is no accident that in sixteenth- and seventeenth-century Portugal one of the recurring synonyms for *cristãos novos* is *homens de negócios*—"Men of Affairs." The phrase is a terminological witness to the fact that in the Portuguese mind the New Christians were, above all, the men of business and commerce.[21] This appraisal was not unjustified, for in these centuries the New Christians were ubiquitous in every area of Portuguese commerce and high finance.

---

[21] A striking parallel is to be found in Southern Italy several centuries earlier. There, subsequent to the mass conversion of Jews in 1290–93, official usage tended to designate the descendants of the converts not merely as *neofiti* but, synonymously, as *mercanti*. See Vito Vitale, "Un particolare ignorato di storia pugliese: neofiti e mercanti," in *Studi di storia napoletana in onore di Michelangelo Schipa* (Naples, 1926), pp. 233–46.

At times, indeed, they seemed in a position of almost total control.[22] Much of overseas trade was in their hands. They virtually monopolized the traffic in sugar, slaves, spices, and other colonial commodities.[23] Their commercial links extended to the mercantile colonies of New Christian *émigrés* scattered throughout the world, as well as to the Jewish centers of Europe and the Near East. Often these also proved to be family ties. Various members of the same families could be found living in Portugal as New Christians, in France as "Portuguese," and in Holland, Italy, or the Ottoman Empire as Jews. Far from being an obstacle, the dispersion and diverse religious affiliations of the various relatives often gave them all a decided advantage over their commercial rivals in the international arena.[24]

Within Portugal itself the New Christians of the sixteenth and seventeenth centuries may be regarded as approximating a bour-

---

[22] "Porque esse poco o mucho dinero que tiene el Reyno, ellos [i.e., the New Christians] lo manejan . . ." writes Duarte Gómez Solis in 1622 in his *Discurso sobre los comercios de las dos Indias,* ed. Moses Bensabat Amzalak (Lisbon, 1943), p. 20. Speaking of the Portuguese empire, he continues: "Y de todo esto es el nerbio el comercio, *que solo se sustenta entre los mercaderes de la casta Hebrea,* que con sus industrias lo ilustraron, y sin ellos quedavan todos los comercios perdidos, y acabados, porque la nobleza de los cristianos viejos no se precia de mercaderes, ni quando lo sea no tiene la industria de los de la casta Hebrea." (*Ibid.,* pp. 120 f. My italics.)

[23] Antonio Domínguez Ortiz, *Política y hacienda de Felipe IV* (Madrid, 1960), p. 127.

[24] An instructive example of the worldwide dispersion of one family with an extreme diversity of religious commitments will be found in I. S. Révah's genealogical reconstruction of "Une famille de 'Nouveau-Chrétiens': les Bocarro Francês," *REJ,* CXVI (1957), 73–87. The complex networks of many New Christian mercantile enterprises may now be examined in Hermann Kellenbenz's massive study of *Sephardim an der Unteren Elbe: Ihre wirtschaftliche und politische Bedeutung vom Ende des 16. bis zum Beginn des 18. Jahrhunderts* (Wiesbaden, 1958). Focusing mainly on the Sephardic communities of Hamburg, Glückstadt, Altona, and some lesser satellites, Kellenbenz has been able to trace their lines of commercial contact with the Iberian Peninsula and around the world. Particularly rich in genealogical information, the book should serve as a model for much needed economic histories of other Sephardic centers in Holland, France, and Italy.

geoisie. They were, classically, the urban middle class.[25] After the union of 1580 they came to occupy a similar position in Spain. In both countries the New Christians were particularly suited to fill the vacuum between a peasantry which could not rise and an aristocracy whose disdain for all forms of commercial activity was proverbial. From this vantage point, we should also understand an aspect which has perhaps not been sufficiently stressed—that in the sixteenth and seventeenth centuries the New Christians performed an economic function and occupied a socioeconomic position somewhat analogous to that of their Jewish forebears in the Middle Ages. The *homem de negócios*, whether a modest tradesman, tax farmer, or court financier, was descended by more than blood alone from the Jew of the *aljama*.[26]

Bonds of economic interest and endeavor must have enhanced significantly the sense of group cohesion among the New Christians of the Peninsula. Though representatives of all occupations were to be found among them, and a considerable number were simple artisans and petty merchants, they were on the whole a prosperous class. Some, indeed, amassed huge fortunes. Although their wealth was a perpetual subject for attack and propaganda by their enemies,

[25] On the generally urban and bourgeois character of the New Christians see Domínguez Ortiz, *Clase social*, pp. 143–45; Frederic Mauro, "La bourgeoisie portugaise au XVIIᵉ siècle," *XVIIᵉ siècle* (Bulletin of the Société d'Étude du XVIIᵉ Siècle), no. 40 (1958), pp. 235–57; A. J. Saraiva, *História da cultura em Portugal*, III, 30. Saraiva's thesis that the Portuguese New Christians were *exclusively* a socioeconomic entity, with no real religious or ethnic significance of their own, is analyzed and rejected by Révah, "Les marranes," pp. 47–52.

[26] One is tempted to speculate further that this continuity of economic function may contribute to an understanding of the different fates suffered by the Jews of Spain and Portugal in the climactic last decade of the 15th century. In the final analysis Ferdinand and Isabella may have found it *possible* to expel all professing Jews from Spain precisely because the large Converso group would still remain to fulfill the traditional Jewish economic roles. By the same token, Manoel's reluctance to expel the Jews from Portugal becomes more comprehensible in view of the absence of a Converso class in his realm. His final decision to enforce mass baptism resolved the dilemma, for, while destroying open Jewish life in his realm, it enabled him to retain his Jews. Certainly it was only because they were indispensable to the economy that the New Christians of the 17th century did not share the fate of the *Moriscos*, expelled by Philip III in 1609.

18

the New Christians were very much aware that their economic usefulness and power constituted their greatest safeguard. Privileges and pardons affording them some respite from the Inquisition, or granting them permission to emigrate, had to be bought from the Crown, and money was essential to any negotation. As in their general position within the economy, so in their particular relation to the royal treasury, the position of the New Christians as a class was not without parallel to that of their medieval Jewish forebears.[27]

But in the final analysis the essence of the group is not to be grasped through the role it played, nor can it be defined merely within a sociological framework. The economic, social, and even religious configurations of the Conversos, are but the variables which derive from a fundamental substructure, whose character is conveyed with particular force in the use of another term throughout the Portuguese documents of the sixteenth and seventeenth centuries. The equation *cristãos novos = homens de negócios* yields simply: *homens da nação*—"the Men of the Nation."[28] No qualifying adjective

---

[27] The granting of such privileges to the New Christians in the 16th century, their periodic revocations and renewals, and the fiscal manoeuvres which attended the transactions, are described by Herculano, *Origem, passim.;* cf. J. Mendes dos Remédios, "Os Judeus e os perdões gerais, de D. Manoel ao Cardeal-Rei," *Biblos*, I (1925), 631–55, reprinted as ch. 2 of his *Judeus em Portugal*, II (Lisbon, 1928), 43–67. In the 17th century, during the reigns of Philip III and Philip IV, the avarice of the Crown in exploiting the Pardons became even more obvious. See *infra*, ch. II.

[28] Variants: *gente da nação, os da nação Hebrea* (or merely *os da nação*), etc. For the interesting conflate *os da nação dos christãos novos*, see the edict of 1579 issued by Dom Henrique in Mendes dos Remédios, *Judeus em Portugal*, II, 60.
A preference among the Conversos themselves to be called *homens da nação* is alleged by one of their most virulent adversaries in the 17th century, the Portuguese Vicente da Costa Mattos. (He claims that they avoid the use of *cristãos novos* because they abhor any form of the name "Christian".) See his *Breve discurso contra a heretica perfidia do iudaismo* (Lisbon, 1623), pp. 148 f. Though the reason adduced by him is suspect, he may have been correct about the practice itself. In an anti-inquisitorial tract of the 17th century, often erroneously attributed to Padre Vieira, we are told of a conversation between several New Christians after a peasant had offered to sell them some hares and one of them had refused to buy. His friend wanted to know the reason, and said to him: "*Todos somos de uma nação;* bem podeis dizer porque não quisestes aquellas lebres."

was necessary. Everyone understood what was meant. If the term *cristãos novos* had a theological ring to it, and *homens de negócios* emerged directly from the economic realm, the phrase *homens da nação* had an exclusively ethnic impact. The "Nation" is the Jewish nation, understood in Portugal as including anyone of Jewish origin. No more eloquent testimony is needed to demonstrate for us that the primary category with which we are dealing is an ethnic one, though it is conditioned by socioeconomic factors.[29] Here, then, is the profounder meaning of that conversion of the total community in Portugal, whose significance in another context we have already remarked. As the medieval Jewish community represented a "national" unit of a nation in exile, so the converted community is not a mere agglomeration of individuals. It continues in the eyes of the Portuguese to possess a national characteristic, which indeed it bequeaths to subsequent generations.[30]

(*Noticias reconditas do modo de proceder da Inquisição com os seus presos*, in António Vieira, *Obras escolhidas*, ed. António Sérgio and Hernâni Cidade, IV [Lisbon, 1951], 211. My italics.)

[29] While there was considerable intermarriage at various times, the ethnic continuity of the New Christians was generally reinforced by endogamous tendencies, especially among those who Judaized. See the evidence in Révah, "Les marranes," pp. 49–50, and Caro Baroja, *Judíos*, I, 395–403. The subject is also treated in rabbinic responsa of the 17th century. Thus Yom Tob Zaḥalon asserted that, if a Converso family in the Peninsula was found to intermarry with Old Christians, it was ostracized by the others. See his *Responsa* (Venice, 1694), no. 148. A similar opinion was held by Joseph ibn Leb (d. 1579), *Responsa* (Amsterdam, 1762), I, no. 15, adding that, though reluctant to marry Christians, many Conversos had Christian paramours. Joseph Trani, *Responsa* (Venice, 1645), Eben ha-'ezer no. 18, agreed that the Conversos were largely endogamous, but insisted it was simply out of fear that an Old Christian spouse would betray their secrets.

[30] That there is some fundamental reality of the Jewish nation which may survive religious conversion was already grasped intuitively by Isaac Abravanel, though he discussed the implications only in a messianic context. See, *inter alia*, his *Mashmi'a yeshu'ah* (Offenbach, 1767), fols. 24v, 52v–54r, and Commentary on Isaiah 43:2–7. In effect, according to Abravanel, religious conversion cannot bring about the ethnic assimilation of the Jews, and the Conversos are by no means removed from the collective destiny of the Jewish people. That destiny continues to be shared by all who are of Jewish *origin*, i.e., "the Ingathering shall

It should be stressed that this survival of the ethnic "national" group provided the very ground on which Marranism might flourish, and that without it the phenomenon of Marrano religion would have been ephemeral at best. In other words, it was the continuing existence in the Peninsula of a *metamorphosed Jewish "nation"* which was basic to the very possibility of a *metamorphosed "Judaism,"* in whatever form that might assume.

MARRANISM:
SOME METHODOLOGICAL PROBLEMS

That a secret Judaism indeed existed among the New Christians, and that many of the "Men of the Nation" were really crypto-Jews, has generally been accepted as axiomatic in Marrano historiography. It is only in recent years that some voices have been raised to deny radically the very notion of the Jewish character of the Marranos. Marranism, it is claimed, died out very rapidly among the Conversos, actually in the first generation. The Spanish Inquisition was only the instrument employed in an attempt to destroy the Converso class, and it fabricated the charge of crypto-Judaism in fifteenth-century Spain merely in order to proceed against the Conversos. At most, inquisitorial persecution may have stimulated a short-lived revival of Jewish awareness. On the whole, however, what we call "Marranism" was a fiction deliberately created and retained as a weapon by the enemies of the New Christians.[31]

Though I firmly disagree with these propositions, the present

---

be for the Children of Israel who are called Jacob, *and also for the Marranos who are of their seed* (Comm. ad Isa. 43:7). (My italics.) Cf. the remarks of Yitzhak Baer, *Galut* (New York, 1947), p. 64, and B. Netanyahu, *Don Isaac Abravanel: Statesman and Philosopher* (Philadelphia, 1953), pp. 203 f.

[31] So Ellis Rivkin, "The Utilization of Non-Jewish Sources for the Reconstruction of Jewish History," *JQR* (N.S.), XLVIII (1957–58), especially pp. 191–203. "The documents of the Inquisition cannot be used as evidence for the religious life of the Conversos, but as a source only *for what the Inquisition wanted the people to believe about the Conversos*" (*ibid.*, p. 191). (My italics.) See the critique of Rivkin's

study would derive scant benefit from a detailed polemic on the reality of Marranism in the fifteenth century.[32] Even if it were demonstrated conclusively that the Spanish Marranos had effectively shed their Jewish identity prior to the establishment of the Inquisition, this would by no means rule out the existence of a clandestine Judaism in subsequent periods. Conversely, I assume that no array of evidence for a genuine Marranism in the seventeenth century will necessarily persuade the proponents of the thesis as to its existence in the fifteenth. For the fact is that any crypto-Jewish phenomenon after 1478 is automatically attributed by them to the stimulus of the Inquisition itself.[33] Nonetheless, the thesis does have implications for the later periods as well. Despite the obvious differences between the fifteenth- and seventeenth-century situations, such methodological problems as the comparative reliability of rabbinic responsa and inquisitorial documents are common to both.[34] Above all, the question of defining so essentially vague a

---

construction by Révah, "Les marranes," pp. 45–47. The most serious and thorough attempt to sustain such a thesis is B. Netanyahu's exhaustive study of *The Marranos of Spain from the Late XIVth to the Early XVIth Century According to Contemporary Hebrew Sources* (New York, 1966). A companion volume on non-Hebrew sources is in preparation.

[32] The reader is referred to the review of Netanyahu's book by Gerson D. Cohen in *Jewish Social Studies*, XXIX (1967), 178–84, with whose strictures my own generally coincide.

[33] E. g., Netanyahu, *Marranos of Spain*, p. 3: "It was not a powerful Marrano movement that provoked the establishment of the Inquisition, but it was the Inquisition that caused the temporary resurgence of the Spanish Marrano movement." Cf. *infra*, n. 62.

[34] Netanyahu recognizes that the forced conversion of Portuguese Jewry in 1497 introduced a new configuration to the Marrano problem. However, since he makes no real distinction between Spanish and Portuguese Marranism, he argues that this new "cycle" of Marranism ended "a century later with the same evaluation of the Portuguese Marranos that we found expressed regarding their Spanish predecessors when the former were about to complete *their* cycle" (*Marranos of Spain*, pp. 74 f.). As proof he cites the denial of the Jewishness of the Marranos by R. Jacob de Boton and by R. Isaac Gershon. With the exception of R. Joseph ibn Leb, he neglects to mention other equally prominent 17th-century rabbis who regarded the Marranos as Jews (see, e.g., *infra*, nn. 37, 39, 42). In any case, the problem of evaluating the responsa, be they pro or contra, remains.

term as the "Jewishness" of the Marranos merits our close attention, if only because it forces us to consider the nature of Marrano religion, and the peculiar circumstances of Marrano life.

Let us recognize at the outset that few phenomena can be more elusive of historical scrutiny than a secret religion whose subterranean life has been documented largely by its antagonists. In the case of Marranism we are, of course, largely dependent on the inquisitorial dossiers preserved in the Spanish and Portuguese archives. Here are recorded myriad interrogations and confessions of New Christians which are replete with the most minute details concerning their Jewish beliefs and practices. On the other hand, there exist also a considerable number of responsa written by rabbis of the sixteenth and seventeenth centuries, which impugn the Jewish character of the Marranos, or regard them as total Christians. How are these conflicting testimonies to be properly evaluated and reconciled?

The basic credibility of the inquisitorial documents is the more easily established, and to do so it is not necessary to enter into the controversy on the original aims of the Spanish Inquisition itself. We can easily concede that its purposes were not exclusively religious but were mixed with certain political and pragmatic considerations. Still, one fact is germane: the archival records of the Inquisition were kept in the very strictest secrecy for the use of inquisitors alone, and remained so until the abolition of the Holy Office in the nineteenth century. To regard these documents as a means of spreading the fiction of crypto-Judaism for propaganda purposes presents a strange dilemma. It would mean that, in recording the details of Judaizing practices into the dossiers of the accused, the inquisitors were purposely transcribing a tissue of lies for the perusal of other inquisitors who were engaged in the same conspiracy. But this is manifestly absurd. Certainly we must approach these documents critically, bearing in mind the possibility of false denunciations, motives of confiscation, confessions extracted under torture, and similar factors. This is merely an invitation to the exercise of scholarly caution. It cannot possibly justify an a priori rejection of masses of inquisitorial documents spanning some three centuries and ranging from Spain and Portugal to Goa in the east and Chile in the west. Of distortions there may be many, but the recording of Judaizing confessions was not an intramural game.[35] To view the inquisitors as involved in what amounts to a universal conspiracy of fabrication is to ignore the mentality of men of a bygone day, and to flatter them with Machiavellian intentions and capabilities somewhat beyond their reach. Indeed, in one seventeenth-century case which I shall analyze in detail in chapter III, that of the so-called *Cristo de la Paciencia*, there seems to be little doubt that the victims were innocent of the specific charge on which they were convicted. However, that conclusion is to be derived not from a generic dismissal of the reliability of inquisitorial documents but, quite to the contrary, by examining the internal evidence contained in the comprehensive dossiers so meticulously assembled in the case. As we shall see, the inquisitorial notaries did not level the recorded testimonies of witnesses to conform to one another, nor did they omit or disguise the doubts which even some of the inquisitors themselves entertained as to the guilt of the accused. Even in this case, where justice was perverted, the documents were not.

The problem of the rabbinic Responsa is more complex.[36] One can certainly present an array of rabbis, from Spanish exiles of the fifteenth century to Turkish authorities of the seventeenth, who expressed their dismay at the Marranos of Spain and Portugal and denied that they were to be any longer considered as Jews. One can also point to a significant number who thought otherwise.[37] But

---

[35] For a similar approach to the reliability of Jewish information recorded in the 13th and 14th centuries by the Papal Inquisition, see my study, "The Inquisition and the Jews of France in the Time of Bernard Gui," *Rutgers Hebraic Studies*, I (1965), especially pp. 34–60 (on the Jewish information in Gui's *Practica Inquisitionis*).

[36] The standard surveys of the Responsa literature bearing on the Marranos are H. J. Zimmels' *Die Marranen in der Rabbinischen Literatur* (Berlin, 1932), and Simha Assaf, "The Marranos of Spain and Portugal in the Responsa Literature" (Hebrew), *Me'assef* (of the Palestine Historical and Ethnographical Society), V, 19–61; reprinted in his *Be-'oholey Ya'akob* (Jerusalem, 1943), pp. 145–80.

[37] See, e.g., Samuel b. Abraham Aboab (1610–94), *Debar Shemuel* (Responsa; Venice, 1702), no. 45, fol. 18 f. Asked whether the descendants of the original Conversos are apostates, Aboab replied that this was true only of those who had

before one marshals a wealth of citations from rabbinic literature on either side, one should really consider that these sources have only a limited bearing on the Marrano situation in the Peninsula.

When the rabbis of the Sephardic diaspora dealt with the question of the "Jewishness" of the Marranos in their Responsa, their frame of reference was quite clear. They were almost invariably preoccupied with the very real problem of the *legal* status of the Marrano *as it affected their own communities*. They were forced to deal with the concrete problems which arose whenever Marrano emigrants arrived in a Jewish center and difficult cases had to be settled concerning marriage and divorce, levirate ties, inheritance, and a host of other legal complications. In assessing, whether positively or negatively, the Jewish status of the Conversos who were still in Spain or Portugal, each rabbi must have had in mind the practical consequences of his broad definition for the specific cases which came before him. The rabbinic evaluations of the Jewishness of the Conversos were therefore derived from a consideration of the problems of the emigrants interacting with the diaspora communities, rather than an objective appraisal of Marrano life within the Peninsula. This, in turn, often presented the rabbis with a frustrating alternative. For what might seem to be leniency and tolerance with regard to the theoretical status of the Conversos who remained in Spain and Portugal might necessarily mean an unmitigated harshness toward those who fled and returned openly to the Jewish fold.

To give but one common example: It frequently occurred that a Converso woman whose husband had died, and whose brother-in-law remained in the Peninsula, would arrive in an Italian or

---

a personal knowledge of Judaism and knew that "idolatry" is forbidden. But their children, who never knew the light of the Torah, are no different from Jewish children who live captive among non-Jews or among Karaites, whom Maimonides treats leniently. Cf. Yom Tob Zaḥalon, *Responsa*, no. 148, emphasizing the constancy of the Marrano women of Portugal, "from whom Torah and Judaism shall yet go forth!" (On this Responsum see *infra*, n. 39.) By far the harshest voice in the 17th century is that of Jacob de Boton (d. 1687), who claims that the Spanish Conversos are worse than Christians, and are to be treated more severely than ordinary apostates. See his *'Edut be-Ya'akob* (Salonika, 1720), no. 72, fol. 222.

Marranos in the Seventeenth Century

Turkish Jewish community and desire to remarry. Should the rabbinic authorities put forth the view that the Conversos of Spain and Portugal were still considered as Jews, the results for this woman could be disastrous, for then she would still be subject to levirate marriage with the brother of her deceased husband. If he should refuse to leave the Peninsula and perform the ceremony of release (*haliṣah*), she might remain an *'agunah* for the rest of her life, unable ever to marry according to Jewish law.[38]

Can one really doubt that such practical and humane considerations, rather than sober historical appraisals, were prominent in the minds of those rabbis who ruled the Marranos to be Christians? These negative Responsa are of great value for the study of the impact of Marrano emigration in the Jewish world from the fifteenth to the eighteenth centuries; they are most often irrelevant to an understanding of the realities of Marranism within the confines of the Peninsula itself. If Responsa be used at all, greater weight in the discussion may well be given to those of the rabbis who, *despite* the legal hazards involved, persisted in regarding the Peninsular Conversos as Jews. It is hard to conceive that rabbis such as Yom Tob Zaḥalon in the seventeenth century insisted on the Jewish status of the Conversos out of asperity toward those who fled and returned to open Jewish life.[39] If these rabbis were willing to risk a harsh

---

[38] Such cases in the 17th century are widely recorded. Partial references in Zimmels, *Marranen*, p. 14, n. 7.

The problem of the force of levirate ties was, of course, contingent on the more basic question of the validity of Converso marriages performed in the Peninsula. The answer to either of these problems would necessarily require taking a stand on the general issue of defining the theoretical status of the Peninsular Conversos in Jewish law.

[39] One of the most comprehensive discussions in the 17th century of the Jewish status of the Marranos is to be found in Yom Tob Zaḥalon's *Responsa*, no. 148, fols. 123r–125r. Written sometime between 1604 and 1615, it contains summaries of the literature on the subject until that time, and, what is more important, reflects the divergent opinions of contemporary rabbinic authorities.

The question brought before Zaḥalon had already been treated by several rabbis, and its tone reveals the opinion which had already been formed by those who asked it: "There were two brothers among the Marranos of Portugal who already these past 120 years are born outside the Faith, and [Jewish] rites of

decision in the individual case in order to sustain the general principle, it at least suggests that they considered the Jewishness of the Iberian Marranos to be a reality which could not, in all conscience, be ignored.

But the relevance of the Responsa to Peninsular realities is also suspect on the theoretical plane. Even a casual reading reveals immediately that the rabbis who regarded the Conversos adversely were judging them by traditional canons of Jewish behavior and observance. From the Responsa one can generally abstract three major considerations which moved many rabbis to deny the entire Converso group a place in the House of Israel. They are: a) the progressive decline of Jewish observance; b) the violation of Jewish law not only in public, but also "in private, where there is no fear";

---

marriage have been forgotten by them, for they do not marry [Jewishly] at all, and they serve idols, and violate the Sabbath in public. And one of the brothers came from there with his wife and married her in our presence according to the laws of Moses and of Israel, and died childless. And the unfortunate young woman wrote to her levir [i.e., the brother-in-law] to come here [Venice?] since the door is open to come without fear, for the Marranos have paid a large sum of money to the king for permission to emigrate where they please. And the brother replied that he does not desire to come. . . ." Is such a woman subject to her levir (and hence to a *haliṣah* which cannot be obtained)?

Isaac Gershon, to whom the case was first presented, cited all the authorities who held that the Marranos are no longer Jews and ruled that, since the original marriage was invalid, the woman had no levirate ties. Two colleagues, Moses Galante and Abraham Gabriel, attached their approbations to this decision.

Zaḥalon, however, rejected all their arguments, and concluded that the Marranos in the Peninsula are Jews "even unto a thousand generations," that their marriages are valid, and that their levirate ties must be sustained. There is no suspicion that they intermarry with Christian women, for such instances are extremely rare.

Sometime before Zaḥalon's decision was received, the woman remarried. The question now arose as to whether the couple should be forced to separate. In reply, Zaḥalon wrote another Responsum (no. 201, fol. 157r) in which he accepted this marriage as a fact and ruled that, while efforts should continue to bring the levir from Portugal to perform *haliṣah*, the woman might remain with her husband. Thus, in the final analysis, even Zaḥalon felt obliged to ignore his theoretical position out of concern for the plight of the woman. For further details on both responsa, cf. Zimmels' *Marranen*, pp. 152 ff.

27

c) failure to emigrate from the Peninsula at those times when the means and opportunity were present.

The artificiality of these criteria is readily apparent. They are based on fixed categories from which the human and psychological dimensions are entirely absent. Undoubtedly, within the framework of that which the Jewish *halakha* expects of a professing Jew, the Conversos and their descendants were very poor Jews indeed. But is observance of precepts a realistic standard by which to judge them? Surely, if they were renegades from the point of view of a contemporary rabbi, this still does not mean that they could not also have been heretics in the eyes of an Inquisitor. "Public" and "private" also hardly provide an illuminating distinction in an atmosphere of universal fear where even children intentionally or unwittingly betrayed their own parents to the Holy Office. As for the pragmatic test of emigration and flight, we can apply it only *in retrospect* to those who actually took the step. For those who remained behind this test is inadequate. It glosses over the complexity of human motivations, and displays little tolerance for human frailties.

We have but to apply the rabbinic standards to Marrano figures in the seventeenth century of whose Jewish aspirations there is no doubt. Thus, it is relatively easy to perceive the "Jewishness" of those who had already emigrated, simply by considering their subsequent Jewish careers. But how would the rabbinic criteria avail us in assessing the life of the very same persons *prior* to their emigration? Had Uriel da Costa been apprehended before reaching Amsterdam, could these standards enable us to make any positive statement about his Jewish character? We should find no external manifestation of Jewish behavior in the young man who was treasurer of a church in Oporto and who, as he himself later wrote, was "educated in the Catholic Faith and observed all its precepts."[40]

---

[40] "Institutus fui, quemadmodum mos est illius regni, in religione Christiana Pontifica; et cum jam essem adolescens ac valde timerem damnationem aeternam, cupiebam exacte omnia observare." (Uriel da Costa, *Exemplar Humanae Vitae*, printed as an appendix to Philip van Limborch, *De Veritate Religionis Christianae* [Gouda, 1687], p. 346.)

But at the same time we should also have no inkling of the stirrings and yearnings in his troubled soul, which finally led him to reject Christianity and flee to Holland. By the same token, Isaac Cardoso emerges in the ghetto of Verona as a major Jewish figure. But as Dr. Fernando Cardoso in Madrid he would hardly be considered a Jew, if tested by the norms of some of the Responsa.[41]

What are we to say then, of the thousands of New Christians who did not take the decisive step of emigrating from the Peninsula? How many other Da Costas or Cardosos were there who did not have the courage to leave? Surely this does not of itself prove anything as to their secret beliefs and hopes. There were numerous factors behind this reluctance to depart which, though perhaps inadequate in the view of many rabbis, were still real enough. The universal hesitation of human beings to uproot themselves and brave the unknown is too obvious to require comment. The deep attachment of the Spanish and Portuguese New Christians to the lands of their birth should also come as no surprise when we ponder the tenacity and nostalgia with which Sephardic Jewry itself perpetuated its Iberian heritage through the centuries and throughout the world.

But there were also mundane problems which must be taken into serious account. The real dangers to be faced in attempting to flee the Peninsula are underscored both by those who took the step and by some of the rabbis themselves.[42] So pervasive was the fear of

---

[41] Abravanel certainly understood that no outward signs of Jewish observance were to be expected from the Marranos, but rather the fulfillment of "with all thy heart and with all thy soul" (Deut. 6:2). See *Mashmi'a yeshu'ah*, p. 54r:

ובקשתם משם — ר״ל, מתוך אותה העבודה שתעשו מפני האונס תבקשו את ה' אבל לא יהיה זה במעשה המצוות, מפני הפחד, כי אם בכל לבבך ובכל נפשך.

[42] Da Costa, *Exemplar*, p. 347, speaking of his flight from Portugal: "Itaque navem adscendimus, *non sine magno periculo*, (non licet illis qui ab Hebraeis originem ducunt a regno discedere sine speciali Regis facultate)...." (My italics.)

In a Responsum written in 1655, Jacob Sasportas speaks of "those [Marranos] whose entire effort is to come [to a Jewish community], and who have risked their lives and endangered themselves ... and the 'Uncircumcised' detected them and caught them like thieves in the act, and decreed death upon them ... and they gave up their lives for the sanctification of His Name." See his collected Responsa, *'Ohel Ya'akob* (Amsterdam, 1737), no. 3.

inquisitorial reprisal that, even at those times when royal permission to emigrate was granted, we hear that some did not take advantage of the opportunity lest it prove a deliberate trap to expose them as Judaizers.[43] Considerations of livelihood and family were even more important. There were New Christians who desired to leave, but who persuaded themselves that it would be best first to amass a sum of money, so they would later have the means with which to begin a new life in another land. We hear even of some who, through their commercial contacts, managed periodically to transfer funds to Italy or Holland in preparation for their eventual departure.[44] We may regard their caution as misguided and their prudence as lacking idealism, but such behavior is essentially no different from that manifested by Jews in other times and places. Certainly the family problem provided the most emotional and heartbreaking alternatives, especially when the impulse to flee was not shared by all. Sometimes the spouse was of Old Christian stock, and the problem all the more acute. In a Responsum of the seventeenth century we read of a Converso whom "they requested to come three times, and he could flee without fear, but he does not desire to come, saying, 'I love my wife and children who are Christian.' "[45]

---

[43] Assaf, *Be-'oholey Ya'akob*, p. 165.

[44] The physician Felipe de Nájera, reconciled for Judaizing by the Inquisition of Toledo in 1610, affirmed that the goal of many Portuguese New Christians was to make a fortune of eight or ten thousand ducats in Spain, and then to flee to a Jewish community abroad. See Caro Baroja, *Judíos*, I, 458. His trial is discussed *ibid.*, II, 197–206. On Marranos transferring funds to Italy see the Responsa of Rafael Meldola (d. 1748), *Mayim rabbim* (Amsterdam, 1737), II, no. 30.

Of unusual interest is the case of Manuel Cortizos de Villasante, perhaps the most powerful and influential of the "Portuguese" at the court of Philip IV, and a *Caballero* of the Order of Calatrava, who died in 1651. In the inquisitorial proceedings which were then begun, it was discovered that he had been a Judaizer well known to the Amsterdam community, and had even deposited there a fund of 600,000 *escudos* to be held for him in trust. For his career see Caro Baroja, *Judíos*, II, 103–22.

[45]

» וקראוהו לבא זה שלש פעמים ויכול למלט נפשו בלי פחד, ואינו רוצה לבא, באומרו —
אהבתי את אשתי ואת בני שבגויות… «

(Yom Tob Zaḥalon, *Responsa*, no. 148). On the case, see *supra*, n. 39.

In the absence of any other information about such a man we are simply not in a position to judge him categorically as totally bereft of Jewish consciousness. Nor can we pronounce this verdict over the many who, even though married within the New Christian group, were faced with a similarly painful choice.

If we are to perceive the meaning of Marranism in the seventeenth century, we must not approach the problem with preconceived notions as to what constitutes "Jewishness" nor, least of all, with legalistic definitions. Rather than superimpose external criteria which derive from traditional Jewish life and behavior, thereby ignoring the genuine peculiarities of the Converso position, we should try to confine ourselves to an inductive method.

PERSISTENCE OF MARRANISM

That Marranism was not a figment of the inquisitorial imagination, but a living current of crypto-Judaism, first becomes evident when we contemplate what the Marranos contributed to the Jewish world of the seventeenth century. Any student of the period must encounter at every step a galaxy of illustrious Jewish personalities who were either themselves born as New Christians in the Peninsula, or who had New Christian parents. To give a full and detailed account of a long and impressive list would be an idle venture. Suffice it to say that the catalogue would include eminent rabbis, physicians, polemicists, communal leaders, men of letters, grammarians and scholars, mystics and messianic enthusiasts. But even then it would include only the famous, those who left a marked imprint on Jewish life. Around them were the anonymous, the thousands who came from the Peninsula to various Jewish centers, whose biographies have not been preserved. Traces of their migration may be found in the Responsa literature itself. To be sure, some fled for fear of their lives or because of harassment by the Inquisition. But others came of their own volition, out of an active desire to live as Jews. Had they sought only safety, they could have found it as well outside the ghetto or the Jewish street. Certainly at the time of their arrival their Jewish knowledge was often minimal and distorted. Yet the yearning which impelled them to seek the God of Israel in Amsterdam, Venice, or Constantinople, remains difficult to understand unless there existed a continuing crypto-Jewish tradition in the Peninsula itself. If, between one hundred and two hundred years after the extinction of the last vestiges of organized Jewish life in Spain and Portugal, this force was still strong enough to graft these withered branches back onto the trunk of the Jewish people, it must have been considerable.[46]

This and more. If the emigration of New Christians was motivated solely by fear or convenience, we should expect that, once across the border, the emigrants would have been content to live in the various Christian lands as Catholics. Clearly, there were many individuals who chose this path. Beyond the Peninsula there were no statutes of *limpieza* to vex them.[47]

---

[46] In this connection we should also consider the dramatic discovery in the twentieth century of Marrano communities in northern Portugal. However atrophied or distorted their Jewish beliefs and practices, the very existence of these pathetic remnants of Portuguese Jewry is a monument to the power of the original impulses, which did not completely die out despite the ravages of more than four centuries. On these communities see Samuel Schwarz, *Os Cristãos-Novos em Portugal no século XX* (Lisbon, 1925); Nahum Slouschz, *Ha-anusim be-Portugal* (Tel-Aviv, 1932); J. Leite de Vasconcellos, *Etnografia portuguesa*, ed. M. Viegas Guerrero, IV (Lisbon, 1958), ch. 4: "Cristãos-Novos do nosso tempo em Trás-os-Montes e na Beira" (pp. 162–255).

[47] There is ample material in rabbinic and general sources of the 17th century on Converso emigrants who continued to live as Catholics. This was so even in cities where there existed open Jewish communities. For example, Joseph ibn Leb (*Responsa*, no. 19) refers to such persons not only in "Flanders," but in Venice itself:

אין סומכין על העדויות של האנוסים בהיותם בגיות בפלאנדיש או בויניציה•

Jacob Sasportas tells of a Marrano who fled with his three sons to Amsterdam. Both he and the two youngest returned to Judaism. The oldest son, however, remained a Christian even then. See Sasportas, *'Ohel Ya'akob*, no. 59:

ראובן מאנוסי הזמן העיר ה' את רוחו ובא הוא ושלשה בניו לעיר אמשטרדם יע״ה להתיהד ולקבל עליהם עול מלכות שמים• וכן עשה הוא ושני בניו הקטנים, כי הגדול לעומת כשבא כן הלך משוך בערלתו וחזר לסורו...•

The reluctance of some New Christians to embrace Judaism even after emigration was often the subject of intense propaganda activity by Sephardic Jews, of whom many were themselves former Marranos. See, e.g., the letters of Elijah

It is therefore all the more impressive to see how groups of New Christians, throughout the sixteenth and seventeenth centuries and in all parts of the world, strove successfully to establish *Jewish communities*, often through great hardships and perseverance. The pattern is almost everywhere the same. At the end of the sixteenth century the small group of New Christians who arrived in Amsterdam took immediate steps to found a real Jewish community which was rapidly to become one of the glories of the Jewish world. Again, in Hamburg, or in Leghorn, Jewish communities were established. In the south of France, in Bordeaux, Bayonne, and other localities, the New Christian immigrants entered into a protracted struggle to erect their synagogues, over the vehement opposition of the Church. In Brazil the New Christians of Pernambuco took immediate advantage of the Dutch conquest to emerge as professing Jews. After the Portuguese reconquest the exiles who came to the West Indies and to New Amsterdam again established Jewish communities. The examples can be multiplied. The phenomenon as a whole must seem strange indeed unless we recognize that, however we define them, there existed intense Jewish motivations among thousands of New Christians in the seventeenth century.[48]

Montalto to Dr. Pedro Rodríguez in St. Jean de Luz (Cecil Roth, "Quatre lettres d'Elie de Montalto: contribution à l'histoire des marranes," *REJ*, LXXXVII (1929), 137–65), and the similar efforts of Immanuel Aboab among the New Christians in Southern France and Antwerp (Roth, "Immanuel Aboab's Proselytization of the Marranos," *JQR* (N.S.), XXIII (1923–33), 121–62. There is only a partial truth in Padre Vieira's sweeping assertion that, once abroad, even the sincere Catholics among the New Christians invariably succomb to Judaism: "porque, saindo de Portugal muitos que eram verdadeiros cristãos . . . vendem e perdem a Fé . . . porque é certo que uns resistem seis meses, outros um ano e dois, e quase todos andam primeiro vacilando entre uma e outra crença, até que finalmente se rendem e se circuncidam con grande triunfo do Demónio e da perfidia, e afronta do baptismo e Fé católica de Cristo " (*Obras escolhidas*, ed. António Sérgio and Hernâni Cidade, IV (Lisbon, 1951), 30 f.).

[48] On the Marrano beginnings of the various communities see the following For Amsterdam: J. S. da Silva Rosa, *Geschiedenis der Portugeesche Joden te Amsterdam* (Amsterdam, 1925) and, for later and more specialized studies, the "Literatuurlijst" in Hk. Brugmans and A. Frank, eds., *Geschiedenis der Joden in Nederland*, Pt. I (Amsterdam, 1940). For Hamburg: A. Cassuto, "Neue Funde zur ältesten

Marranos in the Seventeenth Century

The New Christian panorama, however, was as large and variegated as life itself. Within the Peninsula the situation differed
according to time and place. The Spanish Conversos of the fifteenth
century, recently baptized, and in contact with open Jewish communities, can hardly be equated with those of a century or two
after the Expulsion. The Portuguese New Christians in the early
sixteenth century, prior to the introduction of the Inquisition, faced
a different array of forces than did their contemporaries in Spain.
At any time, the life of the New Christians in the large cities was
different from that in the more remote rural areas where they
formed smaller but more compact clusters.

One can also broadly distinguish several different types among
the descendants of the original Conversos with reference to the
degree of their assimilation. Many New Christians in the seventeenth
century were convinced Catholics and sought nothing more than
to fuse quietly into the general population. Others, though equally
sincere in their Catholic convictions, were subjected to inquisitorial
pressures and fled abroad, where they continued by choice to live
as Christians. Some were simply opportunists, indifferent to religious
or ideological issues, whose actions were determined exclusively by
practical self-interest. Of this category some even left to join Jewish
communities and later, having failed to make their fortunes, returned
to Spain or Portugal to be reconciled to the Church. Both among
the convinced Catholics, at home and abroad, and among the
cynics there were always those who did not hesitate to serve as
informants for the Inquisition.[49]

Geschichte der portugiesischen Juden in Hamburg," *Zeitschrift für die Geschichte der
Juden in Deutschland*, III (1931), 58 ff.; Cecil Roth, "Neue Kunde von der
Marranen-Gemeinde in Hamburg," *ibid.*, II (1930), 228 ff.: further literature in
the rich bibliography to Kellenbenz, *Sephardim an der Unteren Elbe*. For Leghorn:
Cecil Roth, "Notes sur les marranes de Livourne," *REJ*, XCI (1931), 1–27. For
Bordeaux: Théophile Malvezin, *Histoire des juifs de Bordeaux* (Bordeaux, 1875).
For Bayonne: Henry Leon, *Histoire des juifs de Bayonne* (Paris, 1893). For Brazil:
Arnold Wiznitzer, *The Jews of Colonial Brazil* (New York, 1960).

[49] A striking instance of a New Christian who returned to the Peninsula, after
living abroad as a Jew, and who delivered important information to the Inquisition, may be found in Cecil Roth's, "The Strange Case of Hector Mendes Bravo,"

Finally, many New Christians were "Marranos." But here again we are not dealing with a uniform or static image. The Marrano is himself a complex variable. What has been termed the "religion of the Marranos" displays only a few fundamental traits which can be isolated.[50] One may speak at best of common *conditioning* factors —primarily, the need for secrecy, the general absence of Jewish books or actual models of normal Jewish life, and the pervasive influence of generations of Christian education and environment. As for expression, one can point to an inner deprecation of Christianity as idolatrous and a consequent rejection of its salvational claims; the atrophy or disappearance of traditional Jewish observances; a fairly obvious syncretism, natural under the circumstances; a reliance on the Old Testament as the most readily available textbook of Judaism; a tendency toward messianism. Beyond this point it becomes increasingly difficult to generalize, and one finds that even the characteristics already mentioned must be modified to take account of many individual cases which do not fit such patterns. My study of Cardoso, for example, ultimately forced me to open afresh the question of how much postbiblical Jewish information was available to certain Marranos in the Peninsula, in a way that I did not at all anticipate when I began. But here, precisely, lies the value of studying the individual Marrano.

For Marranism, though arising out of a common matrix, and apparently subject to a given set of limitations, expressed itself in many ways. We can all too readily concede that by the seventeenth century most Marranos were completely cut off from an organic Jewish tradition. But we are thereby ignoring those who were exposed to some Jewish life and teaching during business trips

---

Hebrew Union College Annual, XVIII (1934–44), 221–45. In 1617 Mendes Bravo presented to the Inquisition of Lisbon a denunciation of Portuguese living as Jews in Venice, Hamburg, and Amsterdam, with a detailed list of names. Cf. the important denunciations given in 1635 to the Inquisition of Toledo by Capt. Estevan Ares da Fonseca in Caro Baroja, *Judíos*, III, App. xxix, pp. 332–36.

[50] Information on religious practices and beliefs may be found scattered through almost any study of the Marranos. Cecil Roth's "The Religion of the Marranos" (*JQR*, N.S., XII (1931), 1–35) remains the only monograph devoted entirely to the subject, but synthesizes data from a span of more than three centuries.

abroad.[51] The Marrano prayers which have come down to us show that, while there was a heavy reliance on the Psalms, other prayers seem to have been created by Marranos themselves, and there were also some prayers which mirrored various texts of the traditional Jewish liturgy.[52] In the midst of the decay of Jewish observances, some rituals showed a surprising resiliency, at times long after their

---

[51] The possibilities inherent in such excursions are vividly illustrated by the testimony of Diego Nuñez Silva before the Inquisition of Toledo in 1661. Nuñez Silva farmed the royal rents in Ávila, but had traveled on occasion to Bayonne in France. There he had been present at various Jewish ceremonies and services, notably those in the house of Diego Rodríguez Cardoso, a leader of the Marrano community. In his testimony (published in part by Caro Baroja, *Judíos*, III, App. xxxvi, pp. 350-52) he was able to recall almost verbatim many passages from the liturgy, especially from the 'Amida. Cf. the case of Gonzalo Báez de Paiba who, after being released in 1657 from an inquisitional prison, determined to go to Rome. On the way he stopped in Bayonne, where his sister, in an effort to bring him to Judaism, had him read the Ferrara Bible and various other Jewish works in Spanish. On him see *ibid.*, I, 470–74.

Undoubtedly there were a significant number of other Spanish and Portuguese Conversos who were exposed to similar experiences when visiting cities which contained Jewish communities. That there was considerable mobility back and forth across the French border can be amply documented. Cf., in this connection, Z. Szajkowski, "Trade Relations of Marranos in France with the Iberian Peninsula in the 16th and 17th Centuries," *JQR* (N.S.). L (1959–60), 69–78.

[52] In his deposition of 1624 to the Inquisition of Goa, António Bocarro Francês stated that the Psalms and the "Song of the Three Children" ("trium puerorum," from the apocryphal Additions to Daniel, placed in the Vulgate after ch. 3) are popular prayers among the Portuguese Marranos. See Pedro A. d'Azevedo, "O Bocarro Francês e os Judeus de Cochim e Hamburgo," *Arquivo histórico português*, VIII (1910), 189. From the same testimony we have an example of an original Marrano prayer, to be recited in Church while the Host was raised ("Solo altissimo domino Deo Israel debetur omnis honor et gloria, quia ipse est Deus super omnes Deos . . ." etc. (*Ibid.*, p. 187.) Cf. also the moving prayers of Brites Henriques, a twenty-one-year-old girl, recorded in 1674 by the Inquisition of Lisbon. (Schwarz, *Os christãos novos*, pp. 95–105.) The following prayer to be said upon rising in he morning, recorded in 1590 by the Inquisition of Toledo in the case of one Juan López de Armenia, may contain an echo of the traditional *Modeh 'Ani:* "Alabado sea el Señor que me a amanecido bivo y sano y seguro y en paz de la tiniebla de la noche; me de su luz y vida y gracia para que le sirva. Amen." (Cited by Caro Baroja, *Judíos*, I, 423.)

original meaning had been forgotten.[53] The rite of circumcision represented the utmost danger, as it was potentially an indelible death warrant for its bearer. We may therefore confidently assume that most Marranos refrained from the practice. And yet—both inquisitorial and Jewish sources insist that even in the seventeenth century there were still cases of circumcision in the Peninsula.[54]

---

[53] An especially intriguing example is that of "sweeping the house the wrong way" (*varrer a casa as avessas*), i.e., sweeping the dirt from the entrance toward the inside of the room, rather than out through the door. In his valuable analysis of the Portuguese sermons preached at *autos-da-fé* ("Invitation to Intolerance," *HUCA*, XXVII [1956], 353 f.), Edward Glaser has noted that this is the Judaizing rite most frequently discussed and ridiculed by the inquisitors. Glaser found no explanation for the practice in the sermons and could only cite, with some misgiving, the assertion of Francisco Manoel de Mello that "the Jews sweep toward the inside of the house so that they shall not . . . throw out their possessions."

However, the real origin of the rite is clearly stated in a contemporary Jewish source. Referring to the inquisitorial allegation, Moses Hagiz (1671-1750) explains that long ago it was a custom of the Spanish Jews not to sweep through the doorway *out of reverence for the "mezuzah" on the doorpost*. See his *Mishnat ḥakhamim* (Wandsbeck, 1713), p. 53r:

מנהג קדום היה בספרד שהיו נזהרים מלכבד הבית מלפנים ולחוץ, אלא מן הפתח היו מתחילין לכבד את הבית ומוליכין האשפה לפנים, לכבוד המזוזה. ומטעם זה עד עכשו בפורטוגל כומרי החקירה אחת מהאשמות שמטילין על האנוסים כדי לחייבם הוא זה, שאומרים להם שיש עדות שהם מכבדים את הבית מן הפתח ולפנים.

If the Marranos really observed this custom long after there were no *mezuzot* to be seen on their doorposts, and if they were at all aware of its original intent, its retention seems particularly poignant.

[54] The grave risks incurred through circumcision in the Peninsula are self-evident. Certainly every suspected Judaizer brought before the Inquisition was physically examined as a matter of routine. In three cases before the Inquisition of Toledo, during a span of some eighteen years, we find the name of the same examiner, which suggests that this may have been part of his permanent function. Thus in 1652 the surgeon Pablo Collaço (or Collazos) examined the aged Manuel Cardoso for circumcision, with negative results (Caro, *Judíos*, I, 469). In 1656 he examined Juan López de Castro, accused of spitting at an image of the Virgin (*ibid.*, I, 463). Again, in 1670, he examined Fernando Gil de Espinosa, and found him circumcised (*ibid.*, I, 476, n. 54).

According to the denunciation delivered on May 15, 1635, by Capt. Estevan Ares de Fonseca (*supra*, n. 49) certain rich "Jews" in Madrid had contracted with a "master of circumcision" in Amsterdam named Isaac Farque to come to the capital and perform the operation on their sons. Farque came under the assumed

Marranos in the Seventeenth Century

Some Marranos kept their Jewish feelings locked in their hearts. Others appear to have met together for regular liturgical services.[55] There were Marranos who managed successfully to rationalize their religious position by evolving what might be termed a theology of secrecy.[56] On the other hand, others were prey to an overwhelming

---

name of Antonio de Aguiar and allegedly received much money for his services. For further information along these lines see Roth, *Marranos*, p. 390, n. 1. That some Marranos circumcised while still "in the land of their foes" was asserted in 1604 by Joseph Trani (*Responsa*, 'Eben ha-'ezer, no. 18) although they transgressed many other commandments because they read the Bible without its oral interpretation. Cf. Assaf, *Be-'oholey Ya'akob*, p. 147, n. 13; Zimmels, *Marranen*, p. 79, n. 1; Solomon Amarillo (d. 1722), *Kerem Shelomo* (Salonika, 1719), no. 27, on an eight-day-old child circumcised in the Peninsula despite the great danger. One must, however, also entertain the possibility that, due to the risks involved, some circumcisers may not have performed an actual circumcision, but may have merely drawn a drop of blood (*hatafat dam berit*). For allegations concerning such a practice in receiving adult proselytes in 14th-century France, see my study of Bernard Gui, pp. 58–60.

[55] Such was the group discovered in Coimbra in the early 17th century, in a case which achieved wide notoriety. In 1619 Antonio Homem, famous as a preacher and professor of canon law at the university, was imprisoned by the Inquisition and accused of being the high priest of a crypto-Jewish congregation formed since the Pardon of 1605. The alleged practices of the group show an extreme degree of syncretism, and included a confraternity patterned after the Catholic cult of the saints, to revere the martyred Judaizer Fray Diogo da Assumpção. Homem was garroted and burned in 1624. The case has been studied extensively. See especially António José Texeira, *António Homem e a Inquisição* (Coimbra, 1895), and António Baião, *Episódios dramáticos da Inquisicão portuguesa*, I (Porto, 1919), 109–29.

[56] This rationalization assumed various forms. According to Diego de Simancas (Pseud.: Didaco Velásquez), *Defensio statuti Toletani* (Antwerp, 1575), fol. 70 f., the Conversos explained their not having chosen martyrdom by citing Deut. 5: 30 ("so that ye may live"), which is indeed a *locus classicus*. More elaborate was the typological use of the Book of Esther which transformed the Jewish queen, hiding her true faith in order to save her people, into the archetypal Marrano. See Roth, "Religion of the Marranos," pp. 26 f.

Similar use was made of the Apocrypha. Samuel Aboab (*Debar Shemuel*, no. 45) states that the Marranos hold Christianity to be forbidden only as *belief*, but that when one believes in one's heart that this idolatry is nothing, there is no divine punishment for the external observation of its rituals. The proof text for this notion was the "Letter of Baruch ben Neriah" (i. e., the so-called *Epistle of Jeremy* in the Apocrypha, especially vv. 5–6). This interpretation is discussed at length

sense of guilt which accompanied them even long after they had returned to Judaism elsewhere in the world.[57]

The "religion of the Marranos" thus ran the entire gamut, from the most attenuated awareness of Jewish roots, to a readiness to endure martyrdom for the "Law of Moses."[58] Perhaps the most felicitous term for the phenomenon as a whole has been proposed by I. S. Révah. He has called Marrano religion "a *potential* Judaism, which entry into a Jewish community transformed most often into a real Judaism."[59] This characterization is certainly valid. Its only deficiency lies in beginning at the point when the Marrano is already "Judaizing" in one form or another. I believe that, with a slight shift of emphasis, we should go back farther. Paraphrasing Professor Révah's statement, it is perhaps even more fundamental to recognize that, even before he began to Judaize, every New Christian was a

---

and vigorously combated by Immanuel Aboab in his *Nomologia* (Amsterdam, 1629), Pt. II, ch. 18, pp. 213–17. That, given conditions in Spain, dissimulation of religion was a necessity, is categorically maintained by another prominent Jewish figure who had undergone the Marrano experience, Isaac (Balthasar) Orobio de Castro. See Limborch, *De veritate religionis christianae*, p. 178.

[57] On penances sought by former Marranos see the references in Assaf, *Be'oholey Ya'akob*, pp. 179 f. Cf. the example of the former Marrano Isaac b. Nahmias, who habitually signed his name as *ba'al teshubah* (The Penitent), *REJ*, LXXXVII, 216.

The penitential personality is particularly manifest in the wealthy Abraham Israel Pereyra (d. 1699), at one time president of the Portuguese Jewish community in Amsterdam, who was born Thomas Rodríguez Pereyra in Madrid. See the moving invocation in his *La certeza del camino . . . dedicada al Señor Dios de Israel, en lugar de sacrificio sobre su Ara, por expiación de peccados del autor* (Amsterdam, 1666), and especially pp. 141 ff. ("De la miserable vida de los que viven en idolatria").

[58] Admittedly most Judaizers convicted by the Inquisition chose, if possible, to be reconciled and penanced. Yet the 17th century produced its real martyrs as well. See the section entitled "Testigos de la unidad de Dios" in Isaac Cardoso's *Las excelencias de los hebreos* (pp. 316 ff.), and my discussion *infra*, ch. VIII.

[59] "En réalité . . . le 'Judaisme' des marranes était essentiellement un Judaisme *potentiel* que l'entrée dans une communauté juive transformait le plus souvent en Judaisme réel." ("Les marranes," p. 55). Révah has found this idea already adumbrated in the 16th century by the Portuguese writer João de Barros. See his edition of the latter's *Ropica Pnefma*, I (Lisbon, 1952), 123.

potential Marrano, whom any of a variety of circumstances could transform into an active Marrano.

An examination of the lives of seventeenth-century Marranos reveals how different the stimuli could be. Even New Christians who were, from childhood, the products of a thoroughly Catholic education, and who regarded themselves as Catholics, could be suddenly awakened to reclaim their Jewish birthright. The Inquisition itself certainly had a ramified effect in this regard. Many who might have been content to live undisturbed as Christians were moved to despise the Christian faith after they had experienced inquisitorial persecution. In his poetic paraphrase of the Psalms, written in the safe haven of Amsterdam, David Abenatar Melo (d. *ca.* 1646) declared that the Inquisition and its prisons were "the school where he was taught the knowledge of God."[60] The grim drama of the *autos-da-fé*, though a festive occasion for most of the crowd, could well lead the more sensitive to reject a religion in whose name such horrors might be unleashed. There were also many who, finding their way into the mainstream of Spanish society blocked by the statutes of *limpieza* or by other forms of discrimination, proceeded out of this negative collision to a positive examination and acceptance of their ancestral roots. Others rejected the Christian faith on intellectual and ideological grounds. Once this occurred, it was natural for these New Christians at least to entertain the possibility of the Jewish faith as a viable alternative.

Finally, there were those who possessed an active family tradition of crypto-Judaism. The poet João (Moseh) Pinto Delgado speaks movingly of his parents in Portugal, who "planted in my soul the trees of the Most Holy Law, whose fruits were late in coming."[61]

---

[60] "La Inquisición habia sido para él escuela a donde se le habia enseñado el conocimiento de Dios." See José Amador de los Ríos, *Estudios históricos, políticos y literarios sobre los Judíos en España* (Madrid, 1848), pp. 521 ff.; Meyer Kayserling, *Sephardim: Romanische Poesien der Juden in Spanien* (Leipzig, 1859), pp. 169 ff.

[61] "Por aver ya mis progenitores plantado en mi alma los árboles de la Santissima Ley, de que tardaron los frutos." (I. S. Révah, "Autobiographie d'un Marrane: édition partielle d'un manuscrit de João [Moseh] Pinto Delgado," *REJ*, CXIX [1961], 93).

We shall see that there is reason to suppose some such family tradition in the upbringing of Isaac Cardoso as well.

In sum, the Marrano potential existed in any New Christian of the seventeenth century, so long as he was even barely aware that he was of Jewish extraction. Given such an awareness, no matter whence it derived nor how minimal it was, the potential could be activated at any time by either positive or negative forces, often by a combination of both. To be sure, hatred of the Converso played an important part. But it is futile to speculate as to how much Marranism owed to external pressures or to inner impulses. It surely varied with the individual. To state blandly that the Inquisition or the statutes of *limpieza* preserved Marranism in the Peninsula is merely to offer a new twist to the old theory that hatred alone has preserved the Jewish people.[62] Already the ancient Talmudic parable

---

[62] That discrimination against the New Christians preserved crypto-Judaism in the Peninsula was already a favorite dogma of those who, from the 16th to the 18th century, argued for the abolition of the statutes of *limpieza* (see *infra*, ch. III). The same notion was advanced on other grounds by Spinoza in a well-known passage of the "Theological-Political Treatise." There it was used as an illustration of his general principle: "quod autem Nationem odium eos (i.e., the Jews) admodum conservet. . . ." Ignoring, whether willfully or by inadvertence, the statutes of *limpieza* in Spain, Spinoza wrote: "Cum Rex Hispaniae olim Judaeos coegit Regni Religionem admittere, vel in exilium ire, perplurimi Judaei pontificorum Religionem admiserunt; sed quia iis qui religionem admiserunt, omnia Hispanorum naturalium privilegia concessa sunt, iique omnibus honoribus digni existimati sunt, statim ita se Hispanis immiscuerunt ut pauco post tempore nullae eorum reliquiae manserint, neque ulla memoria. At plane contra iis contigit quos Rex Lusitanorum religionem sui imperii admittere coegit, qui semper, quamvis ad religionem conversi, ab omnibus separati vixerunt, nimirum quia eos omnibus honoribus indignos declaravit." (*Tractatus Theologico-Politicus*, in *Opera*, ed. Carl Gebhardt, III (Heidelberg, 1926), ch. 3, pp. 56 f.).

Yet it is precisely the presence of intense social discrimination and inquisitorial terror in *both* countries which raises the question as to why the fate of Marranism was different in each. One cannot have it both ways. If the statutes or the Inquisition preserved Marranism, then Marranism should not have declined in Spain. Conversely, if Marranism was destroyed by the Spanish Inquisition of the 15th and 16th centuries, why could not the Portuguese Inquisition accomplish the same in the 16th and 17th? Since the external pressures were similar, one must assume an *internal* difference in the very genesis and character of the two New Christian groups.

had compared the Jews to the olive which only when beaten and crushed yields its oil. While such adages may serve a homiletic purpose, they do not really illumine a specific historical situation which, when it confronts us with the concrete individual, seems both to sustain and confute the rule.

THE EMIGRANTS

The vicissitudes of those Marranos who emigrated to other lands were quite as variegated as their experience in the Peninsula itself, and had ramified effects on the Jewish communities which attempted to integrate them.

For the general history of the seventeenth century, the extreme importance of exiles has long been appreciated. "In every country in Europe," writes Sir George Clark, "were men driven from home by the persecution of their religious beliefs . . . with their own ideas striking against those they found in their foreign homes like steel on flint." Within Jewry, the great era of exiles and wanderers had commenced even earlier with the cataclysm of the Spanish expulsion, and was augmented during the next two hundred years by an ongoing exodus of Spanish and Portuguese Marranos. While some of these became the vanguard of Jewish resettlement in Western Europe or the pioneers of Jewish colonization in the New World, thousands of others were absorbed by the established communities of the now far-flung Sephardic diaspora.

In the fifteenth and early sixteenth centuries the arrival of the Spanish exiles and their interaction with local Jewries had often been fraught with difficulties. Wherever they came, the Sephardic Jews constituted a new and dynamic element which generated considerable friction and generally gained a rapid ascendancy. But, after all, those exiles had been professing Jews who arrived and mingled with other Jews from whom they differed only in custom and culture. A much more volatile potential was represented by the Marranos who came in their wake to return to Judaism during the sixteenth and seventeenth centuries, bringing with them ideas and attitudes which derived, not merely from a different Jewish environment, but from a life lived in a totally gentile world. It was through these emigrants that Marranism became a critical factor in Jewish history.

For Jewry, no less than for Christendom, the seventeenth century was an era of profound ideological ferment, in which the effects of forces unleashed during the previous century became ever more manifest. The great trauma of the Spanish expulsion had been spiritual as well as physical, and had affected not only the Sephardic Jews but the entire people. At the very core it had raised the perennial problem of Jewish exile and suffering to a new level of urgency. Jews in the sixteenth century had groped for a new understanding of the ancient enigmas, and had responded with novel departures in historiography, mysticism, and messianism.[63] In the seventeenth century the messianic passion stimulated earlier by the spread of Lurianic Kabbalah would finally erupt in the worldwide explosion of the Sabbatian movement, with its concomitant antinomian elements. In the social and economic spheres wealthy merchants with international horizons and allegiances already chafed at the provincial limitations of a corporate Jewish community which retained its medieval structure and character. Nor was Jewry immune to the raging intellectual conflicts of the age. Within the communities of Holland, France, and Italy were individuals and small groups of Jews who had been deeply affected by the rationalist and skeptical currents of the times, though they did not often risk excommunication by avowing their ideas in public. At the same time even those who remained firmly within the bounds of tradition and community often revealed a decidedly modern intellectual and cultural orientation. The secular culture of many Dutch and Italian Jews anticipated the Berlin Haskalah of the eighteenth century and was, in some respects, more naturally acquired, mature, and broadly based.[64]

---

[63] For some of these developments see Baer, *Galut*, pp. 69 ff.; Abraham Neuman, "The Shebet Yehudah and Sixteenth Century Historiography," in *Louis Ginzberg Jubilee Volume*, English Section (New York, 1954): Gershom Scholem, *Major Trends in Jewish Mysticism* (3d ed.: New York, 1954), pp. 245 ff.

[64] In a stimulating discussion of what he has termed "Italian and Dutch Haskalah," Salo Baron has stressed that "all the fundamentals of the Haskalah . . .

Marranos in the Seventeenth Century

In all the welter of competing ideas the Marrano emigrants played an unusually vital role. Against the backdrop of an age which produced a number of significantly "modern" developments in Jewry, they stand out as perhaps the first modern Jews. By virtue of the years each had spent in the Peninsula, these former Marranos constituted the first considerable group of European Jews to have had their most extensive and direct personal experiences completely outside the organic Jewish community and the spiritual universe of normative Jewish tradition. Moreover, as nominal Christians in Spain and Portugal they had enjoyed full access to the mainsprings of Western theological, philosophic, and scientific learning. In a time when Jews were barred from most European universities, or allowed only sporadic attendance at some, many former Marranos were alumni of Coimbra, Salamanca, Alcalá, or even Toulouse and Paris. Their emotional, religious, and educational experiences as Marranos were hardly calculated to prepare them for life in a Jewish society which, despite the cracks and breaches in its spiritual ramparts, still preserved largely intact the integrity of its traditions. In the return of Marranos to open Jewish life these antitheses were bound to produce interesting, and sometimes violent, repercussions.

The problematics inherent in the reaction of Marrano emigrants to Jewish life were clearly perceived by Orobio de Castro, and stated by him with the force of one who had himself stepped forth from Marranism into Judaism:[65]

---

had become more and more marked in Italy and Holland long before Mendelsohn." See his *Social and Religious History of the Jews*, II (1st ed.: New York, 1937), 205–12, 139 f., n. 13).

[65] The passage appears in the prologue to his *Epístola invectiva contra Prado*, written at the end of 1663 or early in 1664.

Dr. Juan de Prado, the object of Orobio's polemic, was a physician and former Marrano who had fled from Spain and had become a Deist while in Antwerp. He arrived in Amsterdam around 1655 and soon succeeded in gathering about him a small group of young men from the Yeshiva to whom he expounded his ideas. Twice, in 1656 and in 1657, Prado was censured by the *Mahamad*, the second time being placed under the Ban. Unwilling, for personal reasons, to sever his ties with the community, he formally recanted his views, though continuing to hold them in private. Thanks to the researches of Carl Gebhardt and I. S. Révah we

Those who withdraw from Idolatry[66] to the Provinces[67] where liberty is granted to Judaism are of two kinds:

Some who, upon reaching the desired haven and receiving the seal (of circumcision), direct all their will to love the Divine Law and try to learn, within the grasp of their understanding, that which is necessary in order to observe scrupulously the sacred precepts, laws, and ceremonies, which they and their forefathers had forgotten in Captivity. They humbly listen to those who, raised in Judaism and having learned the Law, are able to explain it. As soon as they can, they make themselves proficient, each one according to his state and capability, in the laudable modes, traditions, and customs, which Israel observes throughout the world, so as to order their lives in the service of God and avoid the errors which were formerly caused by ignorance. They come, ill with ignorance, but, since they are not accompanied by the horrible sickness of pride, they recuperate easily, tasting the holy and healing medicine which the compassion of their brothers offers to them. For, when they arrive, all of the latter, from the greatest rabbi to the most minor layman, try to teach them so that they shall not err in the observance of the Divine Law.

Others come to Judaism who, while in Idolatry, had studied various profane sciences such as logic, physics, metaphysics, and medicine. These

---

now know that he exerted a marked influence on Spinoza in the critical period preceding and following the latter's excommunication. It was Gebhardt who recognized the importance of the *Epístola invectiva* and of Prado himself for an understanding of the heterodox circles in the Jewish community of 17th-century Amsterdam, and for the impact of this milieu on the young Spinoza. In 1922 he published excerpts from the *Epístola* in his *Die Schriften des Uriel da Costa* (= Bibliotheca Spinozana, vol. II), pp. 242 f. He cited it again in his special study of "Juan de Prado," *Chronicon Spinozanum*, III (1923), pp. 271 f. The entire relationship has now been reexamined and amplified with new documentary and literary materials by Révah in his *Spinoza et le Dr. Juan de Prado* (Paris, 1959). In my translation I follow Révah's Spanish text (*ibid.*, pp. 89 f.).

For a strikingly similar passage in a letter of Abraham Cardoso, see *infra*, ch. VII.

[66] In Marrano apologetics and polemics, "Idolatry" commonly denotes Catholicism.

[67] Probably the United Provinces of the Netherlands are specifically meant here. In any event, Orobio's remarks would hold true for any Jewish community to which Marranos made their way.

arrive no less ignorant of the Law of God than the first, but they are full of vanity, pride, and haughtiness, convinced that they are learned in all matters, and that they know everything; and even though they are ignorant of that which is most essential, they believe they know it all. They enter under the felicitous yoke of Judaism and begin to listen to those who know that of which they are ignorant, [but] their vanity and pride do not permit them to receive instruction so that they may emerge from their ignorance. It seems to them that their reputation as learned men will diminish if they allow themselves to be taught by those who are truly learned in the Holy Law. They make a show of great science in order to contradict what they do not understand, even though it be all true, all holy, all divine. It seems to them that, by making sophistic arguments without foundation, they are reputing themselves to be ingenious and wise. And the worst of it is that they also spread this opinion among some who, because of either their youth or bad nature, presume themselves clever, and who, even though they don't understand a thing of that which the foolish philosopher says against the Law of God, act nonetheless as if they understood him, in order not to admit that they do not understand him, and thus still to be regarded as understanding. These succeed in making such a philosopher even more prideful. His pride grows, and so does his impiety, so that without much effort the ignorant philosopher, as well as those who hold him in affection, falls into the abyss of apostasy and heresy.

So much for the basic cleavage. In reality, however, the responses of Marrano emigrants betrayed a number of additional subtleties. Orobio himself goes on to enumerate three subdivisions among the heretics. The worst are labeled "atheists," and defined as those "who dare deny Sacred Scripture, although they exculpate themselves by admitting a First Cause." Then there are Jews who "believe in God, give their assent to the Sacred Text, but hold in abomination the explanation which God Himself, in His supreme providence, has given to the Law." Finally, those who believe in both the written and the Oral Law, but who reject the "hedges" of ordinances which the rabbis erected around the Law.[68] To these categories we must add at least one other, that of the Marranos who found their deepest

---

[68] The text in Révah, *Spinoza*, pp. 126 f.

spiritual affinity with Jewish mysticism, most notably the heretical mysticism of the Sabbatian movement.[69]

Orobio's observations were made in the heat of a polemic in which there was no room for empathy with those he attacked, nor any attempt to evaluate their underlying motivations. It is at this point that he fails us. For the collision of many Marrano emigrants with traditional Judaism was clearly due to more than mere pride or perverse obstinacy. If we recall their Peninsular background, we must recognize that the problem of adjusting to their new lives within the Jewish community was truly enormous. The Marrano who arrived as an adult had not only to undergo circumcision, but also to acquire rapidly a large fund of Jewish skills and knowledge without which even minimal participation in the life of the community would be impossible. The habits, ideas, and attitudes which other Jews had inherited naturally, and in which they had been educated during their formative years, had now to be compressed and assimilated by mature men in a very short time.

To help meet this critical need there arose in the sixteenth and seventeenth centuries an extensive literature whose central aim was to make the storehouse of Jewish knowledge available in the Spanish and Portuguese languages.[70] It was the first large corpus of Jewish

---

[69] On the Marrano element in Sabbatian ideology, especially after the conversion of the messiah, see *infra*, ch. VII.

[70] Since the pioneering efforts in the mid-19th century of Amador de los Ríos (*Estudios históricos, políticos y literarios sobre los judíos en España*) and Kayserling (*Sephardim*), both antiquated in many respects, there has been no attempt at a comprehensive study of Hispano-Portuguese Jewish literature. Much spadework still needs to be done even in bibliography. An exhaustive and scientifically ordered bibliography of printed books and pamphlets with complete collations would be a boon to scholarship. There is an even more serious need for a catalogue of the manuscripts scattered in libraries and collections around the world.

At the moment Kayserling's *Biblioteca Española–Portugueza–Judaica* (Strasbourg, 1890) remains the standard guide. It is to be supplemented by J. S. da Silva Rosa, *Die spanischen und portugiesischen gedruckten Judaica in der Bibliothek des Jüdischen Portugiesischen Seminars Ets Haim in Amsterdam: Eine Ergänzung zu Kayserling's Biblioteca*, etc. (Amsterdam, 1933). See also the additions to Kayserling by Antonio Elías de Molíns in *Revista crítica de historia y literatura*, VI (1901), 210–18. The serious student must still have recourse to some of the great older Spanish and Portuguese bibliographies, which often contain more ample information.

thought to be rendered by Jews into a modern European tongue, and covered a wide range of material. Included were translations of the Bible, of classical rabbinic literature, and of the major philosophic works of the Middle Ages. From Jewish law and liturgy there were translations of the prayerbook, treatises on the 613 commandments, halakhic manuals, and abridgments of the *Shulḥan 'Arukh*. In general we may regard the ends to which this literature was addressed and the method it applied as the reverse of those which were later to characterize the Berlin Haskalah. For if the disciples of Mendelsohn employed Hebrew as a means to spread secular enlightenment among the Jews of Germany, here the secular Spanish and Portuguese vernaculars were being used to spread Jewish enlightenment among the returning Marranos.

The Hispano-Portuguese literature of the sixteenth and seventeenth centuries was not confined to translations and summaries of classics. Original works were produced in history and theology. Belles-lettres were represented by poetry and drama on Jewish themes. But by far the most important creation was in the area of polemics and apologetics. Here the needs of the day and the special qualities of Marrano experience combined to produce a contribution of unusual force and relevance. The polemics were aimed simultaneously in several directions. While actually intended to refute the claims of Christianity and often addressed to Christian adversaries, they could serve at the same time as an arsenal from which to convince wavering Marranos of the need to embrace Judaism fully and openly. If the writer was himself a former Marrano, his critique of Christianity was in essence also a personal testimonial, a justification of his own choice of Judaism. The defense of Judaism was also conducted on two planes, for while it was important to vindicate the Faith in the eyes of the outside world, it was sometimes even more imperative to defend the Oral Law from the attacks to which it was subjected within Jewry itself. In any case, the issues which were hammered out in Spanish and Portuguese were not the subjects of an academic exercise, but the burning problems of thinking and feeling men. If the Marranos had so large a share in this apologetic and polemical activity, that is because they were themselves the bridge which had brought the age-old confrontation between Jewry and Christendom to a new pitch of intensity and intimacy. The Jew who had been born in Lisbon and now lived in the Amsterdam Jodenbreestraat, or he who had spent his childhood in Madrid and now worshiped in the Scuola Spagnuola in the Venetian Ghetto, spanned both worlds. Certainly there had been Jewish apologists and polemicists in the past who displayed wide erudition in Christian sources (though not quite comparable to that of seventeenth-century Marranos who had studied theology under Spanish Jesuits). But the novelty of Marrano apologetics and polemics goes far beyond the relative degree of its Christian learning. The knowledge which these writers had of Christianity was derived not merely from books, but from their own personal experience of Christian life, ritual, and liturgy. They are thus the first body of Jewish writers *contra Christianos* to have known Christianity from *within*, and it is this which endows their tracts with special interest.

In Marrano apologetics and polemics we have a mirror to the turbulence of the age and the difficulties of the Marrano adjustment to Jewish life. Orobio de Castro was dismayed that the encounter engendered heretical reactions among the emigrants. We must look at the matter differently. That these Marranos often found it impossible to make the transition to a Judaism alien in so many respects to their experience and expectations is in no way remarkable. The real marvel is that some Marranos were able, despite their background, to embrace a complete Jewish orthodoxy, to immerse themselves thoroughly in Jewish tradition, and to become intellectual and communal leaders in seventeenth-century Jewry. Our astonishment should be elicited not by the discontented, the disillusioned, the "heretics," but rather by those who managed "to direct all their will to love the Divine Law."

Isaac Cardoso is a prime case in point, and in choosing him as the object of my study I need hardly emphasize that he is representative of only one segment in the broad spectrum of seventeenth-century Marranism. Nevertheless, the stage on which his life unfolds will prove to be wide indeed. His is an odyssey which will lead us through two seemingly irreconcilable civilizations: those of Iberian Catholicism and Italian Judaism. We shall have to pause along the way to enter some of the bypaths of Peninsular science, medicine, and philosophy, of courtly and literary circles in the Spanish capital, of Jewish messianism, of ghetto life in the city of Romeo and Juliet. We shall encounter Spanish grandees and men of letters, rabbis and antisemites, and Marranos whose lives followed different courses than his. Throughout, we shall try to keep attuned to the changing nuances in Cardoso's personal evolution, and yet bear in mind that he who ultimately wrote one of the most eloquent and passionate of Jewish apologia is the same man who in his youth had commemorated, in elegant Castilian verse, the death of a bull in the arena. Insofar as we are able, we must try to uncover the factors of continuity which made the transition possible. It is an intricate way from the one to the other. Let us begin the journey.

BEGINNINGS OF A CAREER

> Como se dá caso de um advogado, um
> homem de negócio de trato grosso . . .
> um médico, um fidalgo nos livros de El-
> Rei, como são muitos cristãos novos, haja
> de pôr seu filho ao oficio de sapateiro ou
> outro semelhante?
> —Padre António Vieira, *Papel a favor dos
> cristãos-novos*

EVEN the bare outlines of Isaac Cardoso's life have hitherto been blurred. Though it was generally agreed that he was born in Portugal, the exact date and place have been disputed. Kayserling wrote that he was born in Celorico da Beira in 1615, a view which was subsequently adopted by most modern scholars.[1] On the other hand, Amador de los Ríos and the medical historian Anastasio Chinchilla asserted that he was born in Lisbon.[2] In his classic bibliography of Spanish medicine, Hernández Morejón also designated Lisbon as Cardoso's native city, but placed his birth at the beginning of the seventeenth century.

---

[1] See Kayserling, *BEPJ*, p. 33, and his article on Cardoso in *JE*, III, 574. Cf. Augusto d'Esaguy, *Apontamentos da historia da medicina* (Lisbon, 1931), p. 22; Harry Friedenwald, *The Jews and Medicine* (Baltimore, 1944), II, 716.

[2] Amador, *Estudios*, p. 565; Anastasio Chinchilla, *Anales históricos de la medicina en general, y biográfico-bibliográficos de la española en particular: Historia de la medicina española*, I (Valencia, 1841), 84. Lisbon was also proposed by E. H. Lindo, *The History of the Jews of Spain and Portugal* (London, 1848), p. 367.

Curiously, both he and Chinchilla assumed that Cardoso, who later emerged openly as a Jew in Italy, had originally converted from Judaism to Christianity.[3] Neither recognized the incongruity of such a "conversion" in seventeenth-century Spain or Portugal where there were no professing Jews to begin with. Menéndez y Pelayo cited both Lisbon and Celorico as possible birthplaces, without specifying a date.[4] To compound the confusion, it was occasionally suggested that some of the books published in Madrid by Fernando Cardoso, as he was then known, may have been the work of another physician, Fernando Rodrigues Cardoso.[5]

We can most easily pick our way through the tangle of conflicting opinions by tracing them back to their ultimate roots in the references to Cardoso by the early bibliographers. That Cardoso was born in Celorico da Beira was already stated in his own lifetime by Nicolás Antonio, who recorded this information in 1672, but gave

---

[3] Chinchilla, *Anales históricos;* Antonio Hernández Morejón, *Historia bibliográfica de la medicina española,* I (Madrid, 1842), 110.

[4] *Historia de los heterodoxos,* II, 595.

[5] Such reservations were expressed by August Hirsch, *Biographisches Lexicon der Hervorragenden Aerzte aller Zeiten und Voelker* (Vienna and Leipzig, 1884–88). Cf. Harry Friedenwald, *Jewish Luminaries in Medical History* (Baltimore, 1946), p. 52.

However, there can be no doubt that our Cardoso composed the works attributed to him and published in Madrid in the 1630s. The other, Fernando Rodrigues Cardoso, died in 1608. Barbosa (*Biblioteca lusitana,* II, 52) lists only two printed works of his, neither of which was published in Spain. The confusion arises only from his mention of two works in manuscript, a Discurso del Vesuvio, and a Vida de Lope de Vega, both of them subjects treated by our Cardoso as well. Kayserling remarked that it is difficult to conceive such a double coincidence (see *Sephardim,* p. 344, n. 238) and suggested that the MSS. which Barbosa cited were probably those of Fernando Cardoso himself. This is surely the case, and it is therefore unfortunate that Barbosa gave no indication as to the location of the manuscripts. But in the end there is no need even to speculate. The works of the 1630s can all be linked to one another by internal evidence. Moreover, their subjects and ideas appear in Cardoso's major philosophic treatise, published years later when he was living in Italy as a professing Jew, and one work may have been incorporated therein *in toto*. The possibility remains that Fernando Cardoso and Fernando Rodrigues Cardoso were somehow related.

no date for his birth.[6] Antonio's notice, the first to appear, was
followed directly by that of Bartolocci, writing in 1683, who relied
on it completely. (The notion that Cardoso had first passed from
Judaism to Christianity, and subsequently reverted, obviously arose
much later from a hasty misreading of Bartolocci's statement that
he was *descended* from those Jews who had formerly adopted the
Christian faith and then denied it.)[7] In the eighteenth century
neither Basnage, Wolf, nor Barbosa Machado deviated from what
had been written previously about Cardoso's origins.[8] The first to
propose Lisbon as his birthplace was Rodríguez de Castro, but he
was writing almost a century after Cardoso's death, and offered no
facts to sustain his contention.[9] Nor, in common with those who
had preceded him, did he propose a date. In fact, no specific date
was suggested until late in the nineteenth century. Kayserling's
statement that Cardoso was born in 1615 appears, on closer examination, to have been taken from Graetz.[10] While the latter mentioned Cardoso only peripherally, it is rather strange that Kayserling
did not find this date incompatible with the fact that by 1632
Cardoso was already something of a celebrity in Madrid and had
commenced to publish his scientific works.

The key to a sound documentation of Cardoso's origins was

---

[6] Nicolás Antonio, *Biblioteca hispana nova* (Rome, 1672), I, 283: "Ferdinandus
Cardosus, Lusitanus de Celorico Beirae oppido. . . ."

[7] Giulio Bartolocci, *Bibliotheca magna rabbinica*, III (Rome, 1683), no. 1008,
p. 921: "R. Isaac Cardosus Lusitanus, progenie Iudaeus *ex ijs qui olim fidem Christi
susceperant, postea abnegarunt*. Nascitur Celorici de Fruta Pagi Provinciae Beyrae.
In S. Baptismi unda vocatur Ferdinandus. . . ." (My italics.) As a matter of fact,
any ambiguity is dispelled by Bartolocci's Hebrew superscription to the entry:

ר׳ יצחק קארדוסו מפורטוגאל, רופא ופילוסוף שהיה משיחי ואחר כך נעשה יהודי.

[8] J. Basnage, *Histoire des Juifs depuis Jésus Christ jusqu'à présent* (The Hague, 1716),
IX, Pt. 2, pp. 737 f.; Johann Christoph Wolf, *Bibliotheca Hebraea*, III (Hamburg
and Leipzig, 1727), 612 f.; Diogo Barbosa Machado, *Bibliotheca lusitana*, II (Lisbon,
1747), 20.

[9] Joseph Rodríguez de Castro, *Biblioteca española*, I (Madrid, 1781), 582.

[10] Graetz, *Geschichte*, X, 232. Before the appearance of Graetz's history, Kayserling merely stated that Cardoso was born at the beginning of the seventeenth
century. See his *Sephardim*, p. 189, and *Geschichte der Juden in Portugal*, p. 302.

already available more than sixty years ago, but no one made use of it. In 1903 Richard Gottheil published a number of documents from Spanish inquisitorial archives. One of these was a list of "Portuguese" in Madrid who had testified at various trials in defense of others accused of Judaizing in 1634.[11] Among the persons so mentioned was a Dr. Fernando Cardoso, described as a "native of Trancoso, physician in the Calle de las Infantas," who had testified in the trial of one Bartolomé Febos.[12] By coincidence, in 1903 there also appeared the catalogue of the documents of the Inquisition of Toledo preserved in the Spanish national archives, which listed the trial of Febos in the section of *Judaizantes,* with precise indications for the dossier.[13] All the necessary materials were therefore available for further investigation. Unfortunately Gottheil published his list without comment, and it was ignored by other scholars. So the matter rested until recently.

Although unaware of Gottheil's monograph, Julio Caro Baroja came across the same list and realized its significance.[14] Turning to the actual testimony in the trial of Febos, he found that Cardoso described himself then (1634) as being thirty years old.[15] Thus, while

---

[11] *Memoria de algunos portugueses que viven en Madrid que han dicho sus dichos en defensas de reos portugueses presos en el S.^{to} off.^{o} con nombres de vecindad y naturaleza dellos año de 1634.* See Richard J. H. Gottheil, "The Jews and the Spanish Inquisition (1622–1721)," *JQR* (O.S.), XV (1903), 229–32.

[12] "El doctor Fernando Cardoso natural del Trancoso medico en la calle de las Infantas" (*Ibid.,* p. 231).

[13] *Archivo Histórico Nacional: Catálogo de las causas contra la fe seguidas ante el Tribunal del Santo Oficio de la Inquisición de Toledo* (Madrid, 1903), p. 180: "*Febos (Bartolomé),* negociante, portugués, vecino de Madrid. Se le aplico el tormento. Resultado de la causa: Condenado. Años: 1632–1636. Legajo 146, número 238." (Under a new system of classification the signature at present is Leg. 146, num. 4.)

[14] The *Memoria (supra,* n. 11) printed by Gottheil appears as Appendix xxvii ("Lista de 'Sospechosos': 1634") in Caro Baroja's *Judíos en la España moderna,* III, 326–29. It should be noted also that Appendix xxx, *ibid.,* pp. 336–44 ("Una lista de Judaizantes portugueses con conexiones con Francia, hecha en tiempos de Felipe IV") is identical with the list published by Gottheil, "Jews and the Spanish Inquisition," pp. 224–29.

[15] Cardoso's deposition is printed in Caro Baroja, *Judíos,* III, App. xxviii ("Los doctores Fernando Cardoso y Miguel de Silveira declaran a favor de un procesado

the notation in the list gave the place of his birth, the testimony itself easily enables us to fix the date as well. Cardoso was born in Trancoso in 1603/4. The date 1615, unacceptable for logical reasons, and the suggestion of Lisbon, may be confidently dismissed. On the other hand, the tradition initiated by Nicolás Antonio that Cardoso was born in the Portuguese province of Beira, is vindicated in essence. Both Trancoso and Celorico are situated there, and their proximity may easily have led to a confusion of the two.

BEIRA ALTA

The town of Trancoso, in the district of Piñel (Pinhel), is situated three leagues from Celorico in a spacious and gay countryside whose verdure continually preserves its freshness. It is surrounded by walls, with a beautiful castle, five gates, 300 residents and nobility, divided into six parishes. [It contains] a convent of Franciscan Friars, another of nuns of the same Order, a Casa de Misericordia, and a good hospital. It holds a preeminent vote in the Cortes, has its Fair on Saint Bartholomew's Day the twenty-fourth of August, market on Thursdays each week, for its arms a castle and an eagle on a shield, and is abundant in grain, wine, greens, game, fowl and cattle. . . ."[16]

The description is by Rodrigo Méndez Silva, himself a native of Celorico who became royal historiographer to the king of Spain and whose life was to be intimately affected by Cardoso. He

---

por el Santo Oficio"), pp. 330–32. On Febos cf. Caro's remarks in his inaugural address at the Real Academia de la Historia entitled *La sociedad criptojudía en la corte de Felipe IV* (Madrid, 1963), pp. 45 f. His special study of the case was to appear in the second volume of the *Homenaje a Don Ramón Carande y Thovar*. On Cardoso's participation in the trial cf. *infra*, ch. IV.

[16] Rodrigo Méndez Silva, *Población general de España* (Madrid, 1645), fol. 191r. For its size, Trancoso was an important town in the Portuguese Middle Ages. The affluence of some of its residents in Cardoso's time is evident in some beautiful 17th-century houses which have survived. On its general history see the elaborate article in the *Enciclopedia Luso-Brasileira* (*s.v.* Trancoso) which does not, however, deal with any Jewish aspects.

undoubtedly saw Trancoso in his youth, and his lines conjure up a pleasant image of a small but prosperous town in Beira Alta, the northern portion of the province. Viseu, the chief city of Beira Alta, is situated some 45 kilometers to the west. Within a radius of 25 kilometers are the town of Pinhel directly to the east, and the city of Guarda to the south. Celorico is but "three leagues" (about 15 kilometers) away, also to the south. Eastward from Trancoso it is only about 30 kilometers to the Spanish border.

Here, as we know now, in 1603/4, Fernando Cardoso was born of a New Christian family. Though this is the name by which he was to be known in Spain, it is likely that at his baptism it was given to him in its Portuguese form: Fernão (Fernam), The surname, Cardoso, is extremely common in Portugal to this day. To my knowledge, it is not to be encountered among medieval Portuguese Jewry. Presumably it was one of the Christian surnames adopted by converted Jews after the mass baptisms of 1497.[17]

There had been an established Jewish community in Trancoso

---

[17] In this connection it may be of interest to note that a definite link exists between the name Cardoso and certain branches of the famous Aboab family. The latter had been one of the most distinguished Jewish families in medieval Spain, and some of its members arrived in Portugal in 1492, only to be caught in the mass baptisms of 1497. At least four different Portuguese names were apparently adopted by various Aboabs after their conversion: Dias, Fonseca, Faleiro, and Cardoso. (See Roth's remarks in *JQR*, XXIII (1932–33), 124, n. 8.) Conversely, after fleeing from the Peninsula and settling in Jewish communities, the name Aboab would be reassumed, or sometimes coupled with the Portuguese name by which such former Marranos continued to be known to the municipal authorities. We have, for example, a list of members of the Hamburg Jewish community delivered in 1644 to the Inquisition of Lisbon, in which, for once, both the Portuguese and the Jewish surnames are recorded. There we find a Gonçalo Cardoso, alias Abraham Aboab, and a João Gomez Cardoso, alias Uzua (*sic*) Aboab. (The list was published by Pedro A. d'Azevedo in the *Arquivo histórico português*, VIII (1910), and reprinted by Roth in *ZGJD*, II (1930), 234.) Similarly, Eliau Aboab Cardoso is reputed to have organized the first synagogue in Hamburg (see *BEPJ*, p. 2), while another of the same name was to be found in Brazil (Wiznitzer, *Colonial Brazil*, p. 137). On an Abraham Aboab Cardoso in Verona, see *infra*, ch. V. Of course we have no proof that Fernando Cardoso's parents were related to any of these particular Cardoso families of the Marrano diaspora, but the possibility cannot be ruled out.

in the Middle Ages, of which almost nothing is known. Its existence is attested by the fact that in 1395 the Jews of Trancoso are recorded as having to pay a new *serviço* to the king.[18] After 1497 it is certain that a considerable number of Jewish converts continued to reside in the town. But this New Christian community was to suffer a sudden and brutal disruption in the sixteenth century. In 1543, at a time when the violence of the Portuguese Inquisition began to be felt, numerous denunciations were being gathered in the districts of Viseu and Aveiro, which also implicated the communities in the eastern part of Beira province. Shortly afterwards an inquisitorial commissioner appeared in Trancoso and forbade all New Christians to leave the town, adding that anyone who disobeyed would automatically be branded a heretic. This order, together with the calls for denunciations which began to be issued by the local clergy, apparently produced a mass hysteria among the New Christians. Most of them abruptly fled and left everything behind, even, we are told, their children. Thirty-five adults who remained in the town were arrested. As the news spread through the countryside some five hundred armed peasants from the surrounding area rushed into Trancoso to pillage the homes of the fugitives. Many children were seen wandering in the neighborhood, clamoring for their parents. The New Christians who had been imprisoned were transferred to Evora and cast into the dungeons of the Inquisition.[19]

Thus, in the mid-sixteenth century, New Christian activity in Trancoso had come to a complete halt. The community into which Cardoso was born must have been reconstituted in the decades after 1550. Though some of the former inhabitants may have returned when conditions became more favorable, the new community must have also included many New Christians who were not indigenous

---

[18] A. Braamcamp Freire, "Tombo da comarca da Beira," *Arquivo histórico português*, X (1916), 215.

[19] Herculano, *Da origem*, III, 142 f. We may note at this point that Trancoso was also the birthplace of Bandarra, the cobbler–prophet, who initiated a Portuguese messianic movement in the previous decade (1530–40). Though himself apparently an Old Christian, his movement had very wide currency among the New Christians of the area. For details, see *infra*, ch. VII.

to the place. We cannot know for certain to which group the Cardoso family belonged. Following the establishment of the Inquisition there was a progressive migration of thousands of Portuguese New Christian families from the large cities to small hamlets in rural areas. While the pattern is still not entirely clear, the north appears to have been particularly attractive to them, especially the north-eastern provinces of Beira and Trás-os-Montes, and the towns which lay not far from the Spanish frontier. Even within Beira itself there was a perceptible movement northward. It has been noted that in the sixteenth century the New Christian concentration within the province was mostly in Beira Baixa.[20] By the seventeenth century Beira Alta became one of the centers of New Christian settlement.

Moreover, the small towns of Beira sent forth a considerable number of important personalities in seventeenth-century Marranism. Even if we focus our attention on Celorico and Trancoso alone, we are confronted with several intriguing examples. From Celorico came the aforementioned Rodrigo Méndez Silva, who was to end his days in an Italian ghetto, as well as the physician and poet Miguel de Silveyra (Port.: da Silveira), author of the epic *El Macabeo*.[21] Among the most prominent New Christians born in Trancoso and later prosecuted for Judaizing was Juan Nuñez Saravia, one of the most affluent and powerful of the *assentadores* in Madrid during the reigns of Philip III and Philip IV.[22] We may

---

[20] See, e.g., Maximiano Lemos, *Amato Lusitano: a sua vida e a sua obra* (Porto, 1907), pp. 2 f.

[21] On Rodrigo Méndez Silva see *infra*, chs. IV and V; on Miguel de Silveyra, ch. IV. For a discussion of the New Christians in Celorico see Manoel Ramos de Oliveira, *Celorico da Beira e o seu concelho através da historia e da tradição* (Celorico, 1939). As might be expected, the author considers Cardoso a native of the place (p. 168).

[22] Born *ca.* 1580, Juan Nuñez Saravia passed most of his life at the court in Madrid, where his wealth and influence were very great. In 1607 his father had gone to live in Bordeaux, presumably in order to Judaize. Already in 1612 Juan Nuñez was denounced to the Inquisition, but he managed to elude punishment. A new investigation was begun in 1630, and numerous depositions against him were collected in the next few years. The charges included the practice of Jewish rites, aiding Portuguese fugitives from the Inquisition, conspiring in the assassination of a New Christian woman who was about to turn informer, sup-

further consider, parenthetically, that in the list of "Portuguese" defense witnesses in the inquisitorial trials of 1634 to which allusion has already been made, several are recorded as having been born in Trancoso.[23] Also a native of Trancoso was the scholar Tomás de Pinedo (1614–79), a figure of considerable interest for us.[24] His father, as he informs us, was of the Pinheiro family, and his mother a Fonseca. At an early age he came to Madrid, where he received a superior education in Jesuit schools, and counted Nicolás Antonio among his friends. At some point, however, he fell prey to the grudges of enemies who denounced him to the Inquisition. Fortunately he was able to elude arrest and flee to Holland where he settled as a professing Jew and took the name Isaac. In 1678 he published his *magnum opus* in Amsterdam, a voluminous commentary to the work of the sixth-century geographer Stephen of Byzantium

---

porting Jews who came to Madrid from abroad, distributing funds to synagogues in Holland, etc. Throughout the proceedings, and even under torture, he denied everything. On October 13, 1637, he appeared with his brother at an *auto* held in Toledo, where he abjured *de vehementi*, and was sentenced to pay a fine of 20,000 ducats. This comparatively light sentence was undoubtedly due to the intervention of powerful friends. The case has been studied independently by Antonio Domínguez Ortiz, "El proceso inquisitorial de Juan Nuñez Saravia, banquero de Felipe IV," *Hispania*, No. 61 (1955) pp. 559–81, and Caro Baroja, *Judíos*, II, 60–67.

[23] See the documents in Gottheil, "Jews and the Spanish Inquistión," pp. 229 ff. (= Caro, *Judíos*, III, 326 ff.). The witnesses, and the trials in which they testified, are listed as follows: In defense of Enrique Nuñez Saravia (the brother of Juan Nuñez Saravia), "Balthasar enrriquez natural del Trancoso hermano de Jorge enrriquez en la calle de Alcala de 52 a.ˢ," and 'Fran.ᶜᵒ de Amezqueta natural del Trancoso posa en la calle de S. migel como sale a la de alcala de 56 anos." In defense of Simon López Méndez, "Antonio suarez natural del Trancoso anda en comissiones. Viue en la calle del soldado casas de Catug.º de 70 a.ˢ." Furthermore, in the list of Judaizers, mostly Portuguese in southern France, which the inquisitors culled in 1637–38 from the case of Manuel Rodríguez (Gottheil, pp. 224 ff.; Caro, *Judíos*, III, 337 ff.), we find a Gaspar Trancoso in Biarritz, and a Trancoso López in Bordeaux, the latter described as "grande doctor." For the very interesting case of the physician Felipe de Nájera, also a native of Trancoso, already alluded to in passing (*supra*, ch. I, n. 44), see Caro, II, 197–206, and *infra*, ch. VII.

[24] Kayserling had already drawn attention to him in his "Thomas de Pinedo, eine Biographie," *MGWJ*, VII (1858), 191–202.

on the cities of the world.[25] The huge tome, containing the Greek epitome, a Latin translation, and detailed glosses to every rubric, also in Latin, reveals Pinedo as a master of classical erudition who possessed also a good working knowledge of Hebrew. Though Pinedo wrote no specifically Jewish work, the Amsterdam Jewish poet Daniel Levi (Miguel) de Barrios, also a former Marrano, speaks of him as a faithful Jew, and there can be no doubt that he died within the fold of the Jewish community.[26]

---

[25] The full title reads: *ΣΤΕΦΑΝΟΣ ΠΕΡΙ ΠΟΛΕΩΝ. Stephanus de Urbibus quem primus Thomas de Pinedo Lusitanus Lati jure donabat & Observationibus Scrutinio Variarum Linguarum, ac praecipue Hebraicae, Phoeniciae, Graecae et Latinae detectis illustrabat . . .* (Amsterdam, 1678). The title page also contains an engraving of bees gathering pollen from flowers, above which appears the Hebrew motto: הטובים מכל בחרתי.

The information that Pinedo was born in Trancoso is found in the epitaph which he composed for himself and placed at the end of his "Admonitio ad Lectorem": Advortite mortales/ hic jacet/ Thomas de Pinedo Lusitanus/ qui primum orientem solem vidit/ in Lusitanie oppido Trancozo/ ortus/ ex nobili illius regni familia/ paterna Pinhera/ materna Fonseca/ Madriti penes patruum educatus/ literis apud Jesuitas operam dedit/ domo profugus/ nullius criminis at invidiae reus/ has oras appulit/ antequam abiret ad plures/ in sui memoriam/ hoc cenotaphium per Stephanum sibi excitavit/ id volebat vos scire/ Valete." For his bitter attacks on the Spanish Inquisition see fols. 106, 319, 364.

[26] Pinedo was lauded in his lifetime by De Barrios, *Coro de las Musas* (Brussels, 1672), p. 224. In his *Triumpho del govierno popular en la Casa de Jacob* (n.p., n.d.; *ca.* 1684?), p. 18, the latter refers to "mi amigo Thomas de Pinedo" and speaks explicitly of "el zelo que lo atropella por la ley mosaica."

On the other hand, the 17-century German scholar Johann Wülfer wrote that he heard Pinedo himself give great praise to Jesus. (See his *Theriaca Judaica* [Nuremberg, 1681], p. 44.) Kayserling dismissed this allegation completely, pointing out that the only two references to Jesus in Pinedo's book (the correct indications are: fol. 163, n. 3, *s.v.* Betlema, and fol. 198, n. 51, *s.v.* Galilaei) mention Jesus simply as one of the famous men of those places. Yet Wülfer's assertion is perhaps not entirely without foundation. Although, after his entry into the Jewish community, Pinedo certainly did not concede the divinity of Jesus, it is quite possible that he was prepared to grant him, as a spiritual figure, an honored place in human history. We have a clue in Pinedo's treatment of Christianity itself, to which he was willing to attribute an important role in the religious advancement of civilization. Thus, after describing the monstrous superstitions of Egypt, he states (fol. 37, n. 50, *s.v.* Aegyptus): "Non satis etiam aestimari

Even these few indications may serve to give us some insight into the nature of the New Christian communities of Celorico, Trancoso, and their environs. Though the area was somewhat remote, the towns small, and the general economy agrarian, we are patently dealing here with neither an ignorant peasantry nor a debased proletariat, but with a fairly affluent and cultured group. It is a society which has both the desire and the means to give some of its sons the best education then available in the Peninsula. Others are channeled into commerce and high finance. The group is dynamic, mobile, ambitious. When the horizons of Beira prove too confining, these New Christians find a broader field of activity in other places. Some make brilliant careers in the Spanish capital and, presumably, in other large cities. We may surmise, moreover, that it was a tightly knit society, probably small in number, and united by an intricate web of family ties. Among those persons mentioned earlier, Pinedo, born in Trancoso, and Silveyra, born in Celorico, were related.[27] It must have been a common phenomenon. When

---

potest, quantum Christianae religioni debeatur, quae tot religionum monstra sustulit." But, significantly, Pinedo conceded this role to the Christian religion only in its youth. Most revealing in this respect is his biting comment on a history of Germany whose author claimed that the primitive Germans knew the Catholic mystery of the Trinity, and a Spanish work which attempted to prove that the patriarch Jacob, as well as Muhammad, adored the Cross: "Quae quando uterque illorum scripserunt, pace eorum dixerim, vel dormitabant, vel delirabant. Quasi hujusmodi deliramenta religioni Christianae vires adderent, quae sua adolescentia adeo fuit robusta, ut omnia religionum monstra sustulerit. At illa Cluverii, ac D. Joannis de la Portilla magis movent risum, quam stomachum . . ." (fol. 59, n. 80, *s.v.* Alamani).

Wülfer certainly knew Pinedo as a Jew, and described him as such. Similarly Johann Albert Fabricius, *Bibliotheca Graeca*, III (Hamburg, 1708), 53: "A. 1678 Amstelodami fol. lucem adspexit Stephani Epitome illustrata animadversionibus copiosis et Latina versione Judaei Lusitani Thomae de Pinedo. . . ." Also germane with regard to his Jewish sympathies is Pinedo's summary refutation of ancient antisemitic charges (fol. 331, n. 94, *s.v.* Judaea).

[27] Pinedo, *Stephanus de urbibus*, fol. 532, n. 72, *s.v.* Paros: "Eam etiam honoravit Michael da Silveyra, *cognatus noster*, qui pariter cum Epicis Hispaniae Poetis in bicipiti Parnasso decertavit (hac honorifica mentione ei parentare volumus) sic enim de Paro canit in suo Maccabeo. . . ."

Beginnings of a Career

Rodrigo Méndez Silva, writing of Celorico, tells us that it contains three hundred inhabitants (i.e., heads of families), "the greater part of them *noble families*," the list reads at times like a catalogue of some of the most famous New Christian families of the seventeenth century.[28] Since many of the original Conversos of Spain and Portugal had adopted the names of noble houses this is hardly surprising, though it makes the problem of establishing genealogical relations all the more difficult. The Cardosos, whom Méndez Silva includes in his survey, were indeed to be found in Celorico. The name occurs frequently in archival documents of the town, and some, to least, may have been related to the Cardosos of Trancoso.[29]

---

[28] Méndez Silva, *Población general de España*, fol. 189r (on Celorico): "Habitanla trecientos vezinos, la mayor parte nobles familias, Aragones, Cabrales, Cardosos, Almeydas, Ossorios, Coellos, Abreos, Tabares, Rosas, Fonsecas, Sarabias, Cuñas, Carballos, Pimenteles, Meyreles, Herreras, Arauxos, Belosos, Salvados, Macedos, Sousas, Gamas, Pinas, Paez, Diaz, Mendez, Andradas, Siqueiras, Açevedos, Escobares, Silvas, Gomez, Figueredos, Costas, Amarales, Vaez, Fernandez, Pachechos, Lopez, Silveyras, Valles, Antunez, y Feijos."

It is well known that both in Spain and in Portugal many of the original Conversos tended to adopt the names of the nobility. This is one of the New Christian practices which so galled the Spanish antisemite Francisco de Torrejoncillo. See his *Centinela contra judíos* (Pamplona, 1691), p. 194, where he says of them: "Muchos vemos que se honran con dezir, que son Guzmanes, Mendozas, Zuñigas, y Toledos; y como por otra parte no dizen sus acciones con el nombre, ellas descubren la ficcion de su nobleza." He then proceeds to compare them to the chameleon.

[29] The baptismal registers of Celorico da Beira from the end of the 16th century are preserved in Lisbon in the parish archives (*Arquivo dos Registros Paroquiais*) of the Arquivo da Torre do Tombo. Of the three parishes of Celorico I have examined the following registers which are extant. (In each instance B. = baptisms, C. = marriages, O. = deaths.)

Santa Maria. Liv. 1: B. 1590–1623; C. 1590–1622; O. 1575–1622. (One volume is missing. The next begins in 1650.)

São Martinho. Liv. 1: B. 1560–1620; C. 1558–1620; O. 1561–1620. Liv. 2: B. 1620–1698; C. 1620–1699; O. 1621–1698.

São Pedro. Liv. 1: B. 1606–1660; C. 1606–1658; O. 1606–1659.

In the baptismal register of Santa Maria alone, the following Cardosos appear between 1593 and 1606.

fol. 12r: Bernardo Cardoso, godfather (1593); fol. 18v: Antonio Cardoso, godfather (1596); fol. 24v: Bernardo Cardoso, godfather (at the baptism of João,

When actual family ties did not exist between the New Christians of the two towns, there must have been other links of business or friendship. Certainly, given the special nature of the New Christian group, many must at least have been known to one another. Thus we learn that Tomás de Pinedo knew Rodrigo Méndez Silva. (It is to be hoped, however, that Pinedo held the latter's character in

---

son of Antonio and Caterina Saraiva, 1599); fol. 25v: Isabel Cardosa and Duarte Rois, parents of the child Branca. Domingas Cardosa, godmother, (1599); Isabel, daughter of Manoel Cardoso Coelho and Felippa d'Almada (1599); fol. 26r: Mathias, son of Antonio da Fonseca de Pina and Illena Cardosa (1600); fol. 27v: Isabel Cardosa, godmother (1601); fol. 29r: Francisca Cardosa, daughter of Bernardo Cardoso, and Antonio Saraiva, godparents at the baptism of Simão, son of Antonio Fernandez and Maria Nuñez (1601); fol. 29v: Domingas Cardosa, godmother (1602); fol. 30r: Beatris, daughter of Duarte Roiz and Isabel Cardosa. João Roiz and Domingas Cardosa, godparents (1602); Francisca Cardosa, godmother of Manoel, son of Antonio Saraiva (1602); Bernardo Cardoso Cabral, and Helena Cardosa, wife of Antonio da Fonseca, godparents (1602); fol. 30v: Domingas Cardosa, godmother (1603); Elias, son of Manoel Cardoso d'Almeida (Isabel Saraiva, godmother) (1603); fol. 31r: Maria, daughter of Luis Cardoso and Maria Fernandez (1603); fol. 31v: Isabel Cardosa, godmother (1603); Felipe, son of Antonio Gomez Alvarez and Domingas Cardosa (1603?); fol. 33r: (*illegible*), son of Duarte Roiz and Isabel Cardosa (1604); Antonio Cardoso do Toural, godfather (1604); Paulina, daughter of Antonio da Fonseca de Pina and Illena Cardosa (1604); fol. 33v: Antonio Cardoso, godfather of Francisco, son of Antonio Saraiva (1604); Leonor, daughter of Antonio Gomes Alvares and Domingas Cardosa (1606).

We cannot be certain, of course, that these and other Cardosos of Celorico were related to those of Trancoso, or that they were even necessarily New Christians. However, given the proximity of the two towns, and the close association revealed in the register between Cardosos, Saraivas, Nuñez, etc., the latter is at least a strong possibility. It must also be pointed out that combinations of the name Cardoso with some of those which appear as relatives or godparents in the baptismal lists of Celorico can be found throughout the Marrano diaspora of the seventeenth century. For example, the family Ruiz Cardoso appears in the early Jewish communities of Amsterdam and Hamburg, Fernández Cardoso in the latter city, and Cardoso de Fonseca among persons tried for Judaizing by the Inquisition. Nor is New Christian provenance ruled out by the appearance in the register (fols. 35v, 36v, 40v, 43r) of a priest, "o padre Manoel Cardoso," described in one place as a subdeacon, brother of Maria Cardosa, who served as godfather several times between 1606 and 1611. (On the popularity of the priesthood as a career for New Christians see Roth, *Marranos*, pp. 79 ff.)

higher esteem than he did his knowledge of Latin, Greek, and Hebrew).[30]

Nowhere in his writing does Cardoso speak of his early childhood, and we are therefore left to speculate that in most respects it was probably similar to that of thousands of other sons of New Christian families. The boy must have gone with his parents to church, learned the catechism, and received his first instruction from the priest, just like any young Catholic. All this is to be expected. The real question is not one of standardized outward behavior, but of the inner life of the Cardoso household. After all, there were Marranos in the seventeenth century who judaized in their maturity, but whose parents and families were devout Catholics, and there were others whose judaizing tendencies first derived from within their family circle. To which type can we assign the family of Fernando Cardoso?

We possess one small but precious clue in an autobiographical passage written many decades later by Fernando's younger brother Miguel, in which he states flatly: *And when I was six years old, my parents told me that I am a Jew.*[31] To be sure, these words were written in retrospect, long after Miguel had left Spain and had emerged as a professing Jew. But that is no reason to reject his testimony outright. Many other Marranos in the Peninsula were informed by their parents of their Jewish lineage and faith in the same abrupt manner. The only point which elicits some surprise is the early age which he mentions. Generally, Marranos seem to have waited until their children had passed the age of thirteen before initiating them into their secret heritage.[32] Indeed, Orobio de Castro notes that the greatest danger to Marranos comes from the children, and that therefore the parents divulge such information to them only at the

---

[30] Pinedo, *Stephanus de urbibus*, fol. 507 n. 15, *s.v.* Odysseis: "Rodericum Méndez Silva in libro, cui titulum fecit *Población general de España*, virum in Hispaniae rebus doctum, sed qui Latinas, Graecas, Hebraeas literas numquam salutaverat."

[31] The passage occurs in MS. Adler no. 1653, 10 (beginning אני המכונה), most of which was published by Carlo Bernheimer, "Some New Contributions to Abraham Cardoso's Biography," *JQR* (N.S.), XVIII (1927–28), 112:

ובהיותי בן ו' שנים הודיעוני אבותי שאני יהודי.

[32] Roth, *Marranos*, pp. 179 f.

age of twenty.[33] Yet, although the possibility remains that Miguel may have been exaggerating on this score, we cannot deny that the Cardosos may have been an exception. In any event the question of age is of secondary importance. The real relevance of Miguel's statement is that it enables us to assume that the same information was revealed to Fernando years before, when he was himself a child. It would imply, at least, that the parents were in some sense active Marranos, and that their "Marranism," whatever its form and content, was a family tradition transmitted from one generation to the next. Of his early education at home Miguel found it significant to relate only that at the age of twelve he read the Bible *in Latin* for himself, and that later his father was able to resolve his perplexity concerning the Tetragrammaton and its relation to the nameless First Cause of the philosophers. Such problems are admittedly not the usual concern of twelve-year-olds. But even were we to accept the statement at face value, we have no evidence from Miguel of a teaching in the home which was nurtured, however remotely, from postbiblical Judaism. Naturally we must bear in mind that this supposition, derived *ex silentio*, is hardly conclusive. It is to be regretted that Miguel did not see fit to discuss some of the Marrano customs and rituals which may have been practiced in the Cardoso household, for it was here, rather than on the level of ideas, that Jewish traditions often manifested their greatest tenacity. In sum, we can learn from Miguel only that the family felt themselves in some sense to be Jews, that religious questions were discussed, and that the home was obviously a cultured one. It must suffice us to know that the seed of Jewish consciousness may well have been planted in Fernando Cardoso by his parents, though we must be careful not to exaggerate its importance. Such a seed was poor enough and could easily have remained barren.

---

[33] See Nahum Sokolow, *Barukh Spinoza u-zemano* (Paris, 1929), pp. 167 f. Cf. Zimmels, *Marranen*, pp. 77 f., 143 f.

INTO CASTILE

At some point in Cardoso's youth the family left Portugal and settled in Spain. The move definitely took place before 1623 when, as we shall see, he was at the University of Valladolid. Since by that time he had already received baccalaureate degrees in arts and medicine, almost certainly from a Spanish university, we may place the *terminus ad quem* for his arrival in Spain around 1615. However, it may yet be possible to narrow the date even further. Indeed, though it cannot be proved with absolute certainty, there are strong grounds to suppose that Fernando Cardoso reached Spain as a very young child. Some weight may be given the fact that in his writings Cardoso's culture reveals itself as almost exclusively Hispanic, and is expressed in an idiom devoid of Portuguese echoes. It is almost superfluous to add, in this regard, that his books and poems were all written in Latin or Spanish, never in Portuguese. Admittedly, these are insufficient criteria, since there were other authors in Spain who had spent their entire youth in Portugal and yet wrote purely in Castilian. In Cardoso's case, however, such factors may assume some additional significance when they are viewed in conjunction with the unfolding of events in Portugal itself.

It was early in the reign of Philip III (1598–1621) that the hopes of the Portuguese New Christians for an amelioration of their condition began to be fulfilled. Unlike his father, the new monarch and his ministers were amenable to financial persuasion. In fact, the period in which Cardoso was born was marked by some notable transactions and concessions. Already in 1601, three years before his birth, the New Christians of Portugal were granted permission to emigrate, with a promise never again to renew the prohibition. The privilege was bought, of course, with a huge sum of money, a pattern which would be repeated time and again. Always eager for funds, Philip and his minister Lerma were temporarily satisfied, and when a delegation of Portuguese prelates journeyed to Spain the following year to complain, they were rebuffed.[34] Nor was this

---

[34] On the granting of the permit and the mission of the clergy, see D'Azevedo,

all. Upon the promise of further sums the Crown had interceded with the Holy See. On August 23, 1604, Clement VIII issued a Brief of Indulgence to the New Christians for crimes then pending before the Inquisition. The pardon was published in the three Portuguese inquisitorial centers on January 16, 1605, and as a result several hundred prisoners were released. Reaction followed swiftly. In Portugal riots broke out in Lisbon and Coimbra, while in Spain too there were manifestations of strong popular disapproval.[35] Nevertheless, the royal permit to emigrate and the papal pardon had the effect which might have been anticipated. New Christian emigration from Portugal to Spain, noticeable since the union of 1580, though still somewhat surreptitious, now swelled to such proportions as to cause grave alarm.[36] For the next several years the migration continued unabated. But this phase of the Portuguese influx into Spain was to draw to a close. Philip, after all, was not in the least concerned about the personal problem of the New Christians, and was becoming very much worried about the money they had promised but which was being paid too slowly for his liking. In 1607, impatient with the progress that had been made, he ordered that the descendants of Jews now residing in Spain must contribute to the payment for the pardon. In 1610, probably because the promised sum had still not been paid, the permission to leave Portugal was revoked.[37]

Christãos novos, pp. 155 ff.; Lea, *Inquisition*, III, 267; Mendes dos Remédios, *Judeus em Portugal*, II, 70 ff.

[35] The Brief ("Postulat a nobis") is published in the *Corpo Diplomático Portuguêz*, XII (Lisbon, 1902), pp. 121–29. On the Portuguese riots see D'Azevedo, *Christãos novos*, p. 162. In Seville an *auto* had been scheduled for Nov. 7, when a messenger arrived from Valladolid with a sudden order for its suspension. There was great disappointment among the populace. However, after the intervention of the Inquisitor General, the *auto* was finally celebrated (Domínguez, *Clase social*, p. 86).

[36] In 1605, for example, the province of Guipúzcoa, traditionally hostile to New Christian incursions, accused the immigrants of illegal commerce, exporting precious metals, and usurping the profits and business of the local inhabitants. See Domínguez, *Política y hacienda*, p. 128.

[37] On the decree of 1607 see Domínguez, *Clase social*, p. 87; for the withdrawal of the permit, *idem*, *Política y hacienda*, p. 128.

We shall therefore consider it most likely that the Cardosos took advantage of the new opportunities prior to that date, and crossed the frontier into Castile between 1604 and 1610. This would mean that Fernando left Portugal before the age of six.

Patently, the parents did not choose to flee abroad to a Jewish center though they could have done so. We know, in fact, that the development of the pardons in this period was followed with intense interest abroad by the Sephardic Jewish communities. It was fully expected that the Portuguese Marranos would seize the opportunity to come to the lands where Judaism was openly recognized.[38] That the Cardoso family did not elect to leave the Peninsula merely indicates that, even if they were aware of their Marrano heritage, it was not sufficient to overcome whatever practical and private motivations restrained them from taking such a decisive step. I have attempted to demonstrate earlier that Marranism and a reluctance to abandon the Peninsula are by no means incompatible attitudes.

Whether immediately or subsequently, it is certain that in Spain the family settled in the Castilian town of Medina del Rioseco, for

---

[38] Both the expectation abroad and the subsequent disappointment are well reflected in a question addressed to Joseph b. Moses Trani, in which we read (*Responsa* [Venice, 1645], no. 18, fol. 20r):

שאלה על אנוס שמת ולו אח במקום האנוסים שנאנסו זה קך (?) שנה והוא בן ס' שנה ומתאחר לבא עם שהמלך יר''ה נתן פטור בעד ז' שנים שכל הרוצה לפנות יפנה, ועם שמתו לו אביו ואמו ואשתו, והוא אמיד, ועודנו שם...

(The period of "120 years" since the beginnings of Marranism is undoubtedly an error. Zimmels [*Marranen*, p. 154] is correct in assuming that the pardon mentioned here is that of 1604.) For another reference to it see Yom Tob Zaḥalon, *Responsa*, no. 148 (*supra*, ch. I, n. 39). In general among the Sephardic communities there was a tendency to look askance at those who, it was presumed, had the means or chance to flee, but remained nonetheless. In the case of Diego Gómez de Salazar, which we shall consider later, a witness who had been in Amsterdam asserted that when the Jews heard of his imprisonment (1659), some stated that God had permitted it, because, although he had held to the law of Moses while poor, when he became rich he did not come to Holland in order to observe the Law freely (Caro, *Judíos*, I, 421).

On the other hand, the violently antisemitic Padre Francisco de Torrejoncillo alleged, with obvious exaggeration, that after the pardon of 1604 some 2,000 New Christian families left for Holland (*Centinela contra Judíos*, p. 150).

it was there, in 1627, that Miguel Cardoso was born.[39] The fact that the two brothers were thus separated in age by some twenty-three years is certainly noteworthy, and may prove of some value to us when we consider their personal relations later in life. It should not impel us, however, to postulate that the two were necessarily born of different mothers.[40] At a time when marriages were contracted at a comparatively early age, brides of fifteen or sixteen being very common, there is nothing intrinsically improbable in such a gap. When she gave birth to Miguel, Fernando's mother may not yet have attained the age of forty. Of other siblings we know definitely of a girl but, other than the fact that she was blind many years later, we possess almost no information about her.[41]

Unless the Cardosos had some relatives or special acquaintances

---

[39] The place of birth is given by Miguel himself in the aforementioned biographical sketch published by Bernheimer (*JQR*, XVIII, 112). The baptismal register (Libro de B. no. 8, años 1624–44) in the Parroquia de Santa Maria of Medina de Rioseco was examined by Padre Gabriel Pellitero Fernández, but he was unable to find a Miguel Cardoso. Nevertheless there can be no doubt that Miguel really meant Rioseco, since he also translated the name into Hebrew as "Dry River." Thus:

אני המכונה פעם מב״א ר״ת מיכאל בן אברהם ופעם אמ״ק אברהם מיכאל קארדושו מן האנוסים אשר בספרד· נולדתי בעיר ריאושיקו ר״ל נהר יבש...

The phrase "of the Marranos who are in Spain" led Bernheimer to doubt that the family originated in Portugal. But Miguel is simply referring here to the actual situation of the family, which was indeed in Spain when he was born.

The date, 1627, is furnished by an epistle written by Miguel in 1669. There he states that in 1649 he was twenty-two years old. See Gershom Scholem, "A letter of Abraham Michael Cardoso to the Rabbis of Smyrna" (Hebrew), *Zion*, XIX (1954), 15.

[40] Caro Baroja's speculation (*Sociedad criptojudía*, p. 106, n. 17) that Fernando and Miguel were perhaps not brothers at all may be dismissed completely. The Jewish sources, inaccessible to him, offer conclusive proof. See *infra*, ch. VII.

[41] She apparently followed Miguel (Abraham) to the Near East in later years, and may have lived in his house. In a letter enumerating the signs and wonders which have occurred in his household, Miguel relates that she was able miraculously to regain her sight during the night on which his son Ephraim was born, and again on the day of his circumcision. See Isaac Raphael Molho and Abraham Amarillo, "Autobiographical Letters of [Abraham] Cardoso" (Hebrew), *Sefunot*, III/IV (Jerusalem, 1959–60), 230 f.

in Rioseco, their reasons for choosing this particular place of residence remain a puzzle. Located in the province of Valladolid, but pertaining to the archdiocese of Palencia, Medina del Rioseco is situated between the two cities, almost two hundred kilometers north of Madrid. There is evidence that some Jews lived in the town during the fifteenth century, though apparently not in sufficient number to constitute a separate *aljama*.[42] If Rioseco had any special meaning for New Christians in the seventeenth century, it has hitherto not come to light. Yet it was there, if our previous suppositions have been correct, that Fernando Cardoso may well have passed the remainder of his childhood. It would not be very long before he would dedicate his first book to the titular duke of Rioseco. But that was after he had already entered a wider and more vibrant world than Trancoso or Rioseco could ever offer.

THE UNIVERSITY YEARS

"Why is a swordmaker automatically considered *limpio*, while a physician is invariably held to be a Jew?"

Such is the plaintive question posed early in the reign of Philip IV by the authors of a petition for reforms in the investigation of *limpieza de sangre*.[43] Though the popular opinion was certainly an exaggeration, it could not have arisen but for the fact that many New Christians were unusually prominent in the medical profession. Despite recurring antisemitic attacks, New Christian physicians were widely employed in the Peninsula, and their presence was strongly and specifically felt. When, at the beginning of the seventeenth

---

[42] In a list of tax apportionments drawn up in 1474 for Don Enrique IV we find the Jews of Medina del Rioseco, along with those of some other towns, subsumed in conjunction with the *aljama* of Aguilar de Campoo (J. Amador de los Ríos, *Historia social, política y religiosa de los judíos de España* [reprint; Madrid, 1960], III, Appendix III, p. 998). On two Jews from Rioseco who refused in 1490 to pay a tax, see Fritz Baer, *Die Juden im Christlichen Spanien*, II: *Kastillien/ Inquisitionsakten* (Berlin, 1936), no. 388, p. 428.

[43] Cited by Sicroff, *Controverses*, p. 211.

century, there took place a considerable emigration of such physicians from Portugal, the movement was sufficiently marked to attract the serious attention of the authorities. A census taken in 1614 revealed that many New Christian doctors had passed over into Spain, others had left the Peninsula entirely, and some had even migrated beyond Europe.[44] The investigations of Friedenwald and others have amply revealed how many Spanish and Portuguese physicians, some of them with international reputations, emerged from the New Christian group.[45] It need hardly be reiterated by now that not all of them were Marranos. Yet the frequent appearance of physicians prosecuted for Judaizing by the Inquisition is more than mere accident.[46] Definite evidence of Marranism is afforded by the considerable number of important physicians who were active in the Peninsula and later professed Judaism elsewhere.[47]

The popularity of the medical profession among New Christians in Spain and Portugal was due to a variety of factors, among which the long and venerable tradition of Jewish medicine which lay behind them should not be ignored. In a number of New Christian families we find successive generations of physicians, the vocation passing directly from father to son. It would be most interesting to know if this was true of the Cardosos as well, since both Fernando and later Miguel chose the same field. But we must be careful to recognize that the phenomenon in general is not to be viewed as

---

[44] Pedro A. d'Azevedo, "Médicos cristãos novos que se ausentaram de Portugal no principio do século XVII," *Arquivos de historia da medicina portuguesa* (N. S.), V (1914), 153–72.

[45] See, e.g., the convenient catalogue of "Spanish and Portuguese Physicians after the Expulsion at the End of the Fifteenth Century" in Friedenwald, *Jews and Medicine*, II, 704–71.

[46] Some information will be found in the volume entitled *Médicos perseguidos por la Inquisición Española* (Madrid, 1855), and in almost all the important studies of peninsular medicine. A list of 239 physicians was culled by Alexander Marx from records of the Portuguese Inquisition now in the library of the Jewish Theological Seminary of America. Cf. Friedenwald, *Jewish Luminaries in Medical History* (Baltimore, 1946), p. 162.

[47] Friedenwald, *Jews and Medicine, passim.*

merely atavistic. Jewish participation in medicine has always been, at least in part, a product of social forces. A dynamic and articulate minority, so often blocked from other spheres of activity, channeled its energies into those forms of business and commerce which were open to it, while some of its intellectual elite was drawn to a higher profession which was not only attractive but accessible as well. This was as true of the New Christians in the sixteenth and seventeenth centuries as it had been of the Jews in the Middle Ages. What they inherited was not a set of mental characteristics but a somewhat analogous social situation to which they responded in kind. A maxim cited by Lope de Vega had it that the way to glory in Spain was via "ciencia y mar y Casa Real." For an intelligent and ambitious New Christian youth who might not be interested in trade and finance, and who found himself cut off by the statutes of *limpieza* from honors and dignities to which others could aspire, the first of the three paths could easily appear the most promising. With talent, diligence, and some luck, it might even lead to the "Royal House" itself.

It has often been asserted, though with no documentation, that Cardoso was an alumnus of the University of Salamanca and acquired his medical training there.[48] For the moment, however, we have conclusive proof only that he taught at the University of Valladolid, and it is practically certain that there he was also awarded his doctorate in medicine. To attempt a reconstruction of the progress of Cardoso's university years, it is necessary to begin with the evidence available for his connection with the latter institution.

Cardoso himself referred explicitly to his university career on but two occasions, and mentioned only his teaching. The more ample information is contained in the dedication of his first important work, in which he states that he had known Valladolid from the age of twenty-one, when he held the chair of philosophy at its

---

[48] So, e.g., d'Esaguy, *Apontamentos*, p. 23; Friedenwald, *Jews in Medicine*, II, 716. Menéndez y Pelayo, *Heterodoxos*, IV, 296, stated that he received his doctorate there.

university, and that when he was twenty-three years old he was a *pretendiente* at its major chairs of medicine.[49]

The archives of the University of Valladolid have preserved the records of Cardoso's first teaching appointment. They show that he was granted the *Cátedra de Filosofía* in May of 1624.[50]

Cardoso's own remarks and the university documents thus support one another, and both incidentally corroborate the date we have fixed for his birth. If he was born in 1603/4, then indeed, as he stated, he was approximately twenty-one when he became a *catedrático*. But the same documents yield further information. At the time he was granted the chair, Cardoso is described as a *Licenciado*, an intermediate grade between the baccalaureate and the doctorate which required a separate examination. We shall see, however, that already in 1625 he is referred to as "Dr. Cardoso," and that he must therefore have been awarded the doctorate at Valladolid sometime during that year.[51]

It remains for us to inquire whether he had studied at Valladolid from the very outset. Here an important clue is provided by Cardoso's application for his first teaching post, in which he describes himself as "Fernan Cardoso, Bachelor of Arts *incorporated* in this university."[52] The term clearly implies that Cardoso completed his baccalaureate at another institution, since an act of incorporation was required at Valladolid of all those who had received prior degrees elsewhere. According to the statutes, courses were recognized as valid for incorporation only if they were pursued at certain

---

[49] "i aviéndome conocido de veinte i un años Valladolid Catedrático de Filosofía en su Universidad, i de veinte i tres pretendiente a sus mayores Cátedras de Medicina . . ." (*Discurso sobre el Monte Vesuvio* [Madrid, 1632], fol. 1r-v of the preliminary material). That Cardoso taught at Valladolid was already stated by Antonio, *Bibl. hisp. nova*, "Pincianus olim medicae artis professor. . . ."

[50] AUV., Leg. 238 (3-7), fol. 12v. Cf. *infra*, n. 75.
All the pages in this and subsequent folders are unnumbered. For the sake of convenience I have assigned a pagination which follows the order in which they are found, even though the entries were not always made in the proper chronological sequence. The handwriting, I might add, is generally abominable.

[51] See *infra*, n. 81.

[52] AUV., Leg. 238 (3-7), fol. 5r. For the text of the application see *infra*, n. 63.

of the other Spanish universities, depending on the subject. Courses in theology and arts were accepted from Alcalá, Granada, and Seville; those in civil or canon law, as well as medicine, from Alcalá or the Spanish College in Bologna. Courses in all subjects and all degrees were accepted if they had been taken at the University of Salamanca.[53]

The only reference which Cardoso himself ever made to a stay in Salamanca is found in a casual remark which appears in a book he published many decades later:

At Salamanca we knew Zamora, an outstanding professor of medicine and mathematics, totally unfortunate in treating the sick, intent more on constellations and aspects of the stars than on opportunities for remedies, just as we have known many others remarkable for the same vanity and the same misfortune.[54]

As in any of his infrequent autobiographical remarks, this one is characteristically laconic. It does seem most probable that he is referring, not to a mere visit to the city of Salamanca, but to a period of study at its university. The depiction of the professor further indicates that he studied medicine there. If we join to this our knowledge of his incorporation at Valladolid after receiving earlier degrees at another school, we may safely assume, I think, that the latter was indeed the University of Salamanca.[55]

---

[53] On the general necessity for incorporation see statute no. 84 in Mariano Alcocer Martínez, *Anales universitarios: Historia de la Universidad de Valladolid*, I (*Libro de Bezerro* and *Estatutos;* Valladolid, 1918), lxxxvii. For the universities from which the various courses were recognized, cf. *ibid.*, no. 150, p. cxxv, and no. 173, p. cxxxiii.

[54] *Philosophia libera* (Venice, 1673), p. 177.

[55] My examination of the archives of the University of Salamanca has brought to light a Fernando Cardoso who, in 1621, received the baccalaureate in medicine. He appears annually in the student registers of the Faculty of Medicine during the years 1616–21. (Each volume is entitled Matrículas de todos los estudiantes en todas facultades desta Universidad de Salamanca, the relevant section beginning: "Estudiantes y Bachilleres que digeron ser en la facultad de medicina.") The precise references are: AUS., Leg. 321 (Matrículas ... 1616–17), fol. 144r; Leg. 322 (1617–18), fol. 141r; Leg. 323 (1618–19), fol. 142r; Leg. 324 (1619–20), fol. 140r; Leg. 325 (1620–21) fol. 141v. He successfully passed his examination

That Cardoso commenced his university studies at a relatively early age may be ascertained by simple computation. In 1625, at the age of about twenty-one, he possessed his doctorate in medicine. This was obviously preceded by a baccalaureate and *licenciatura* in the same subject which, in turn, required a preliminary degree of Bachelor of Arts. Even if all his studies had been continuous and without interruption, we must assume a total period of at least eight or nine years' study prior to the doctorate. Cardoso could not have been more than thirteen years old when he began, and may well have been even younger.

Examining more closely this important formative period in Cardoso's life one is immediately impressed by his precocity. An adolescent when he entered the university, he had barely passed his adolescence when he began to teach. It may be taken for granted that he did not unduly dissipate his time in the frivolities and escapades so notorious among the students depicted in the Spanish literature of the day. The encyclopedic erudition he displayed in later years must have been largely acquired at this time in long hours spent over his books. That learning which would eventually ornament his published works, with their innumerable citations of authorities famous and obscure, is of a content, and reflects a mentality, which will reveal themselves to us only if we consider the curriculum and training he absorbed during his student years.

The instruction offered by the Spanish universities in this period

---

on Friday, May 26, 1621, as may be seen in the Libros de actas de Bachilleramientos (Leg. 745, fol. 128 and Leg. 747, fol. 246).

Though it would not be difficult to reconcile this date with the information that our Cardoso was in Valladolid by 1623, several factors militate against identifying the two Cardosos as one and the same: a) The Cardoso in the Salamancan archives is listed throughout as a native of the Portuguese city of Viseu ("Fernan Cardoso, nal. de Viseo"); b) Already in Nov., 1616, when he began his medical studies, he is recorded as possessing his B.A. This means that he must have entered the university in the fall of 1612, at which time our Cardoso was only eight or nine years old. To be sure, neither of these points in isolation would present an insurmountable obstacle. Cardoso may have had some reason not to disclose his true place of birth. He may also have been an even greater prodigy than we think. But taken together, and in the absence of further evidence, these difficulties are sufficiently serious to render such an identification suspect.

was thoroughly traditional. Outwardly, to be sure, the schools were still flourishing, with rich endowments and many students. Of the three major universities Salamanca still retained primacy, boasting its seventy chairs, and continuing to attract an international student body to its halls. Alcalá could yet bask in the reflected glory of its heyday in the previous century. Valladolid was still an important center of study, and its alumni were to be found in high places throughout the realm. But the ferment of the sixteenth century was gone, and the Spanish universities had become, by now, cautious and conservative. A decadence was already manifest which, by the eighteenth century, would be total. In this respect, however, Spain was not unique. The other European universities of the time were hardly more daring or creative. Throughout Europe the universities of the seventeenth century saw their task not in innovation, but rather in the transmission of an approved body of past knowledge. There may be some merit to the common charge that in Spain the spirit of inquiry and experimentation suffered from a stifling atmosphere of absolutism and religious conformity. But for the sake of perspective it should be borne in mind that beyond the Peninsula conditions were often no more promising. If Galileo's recantation of 1632 was due to another Inquisition, that of Rome, let us remember that professors at Paris were later to be forbidden by the Parlement to express Cartesian views, and that the Sorbonne consistently condemned and refused to license almost all the important scientific works of the age. Those pioneers of the seventeenth century who laid the foundations of modern science, mathematics, and philosophy were often university graduates. But their most important work was generally done outside the university's confines. Finally, we should also consider that when Cardoso was a student in Spain the profound intellectual revolutions of the century were only on the horizon, and had not yet come into full view.[56]

---

[56] On the development of the Spanish universities in our period see C. M.ª Ajo G. y Sainz de Zuñiga, *Historia de las universidades hispánicas* (Ávila, 1958), especially vols. II and III. For student life, based largely on Salamanca, Gustave Reynier's *La vie universitaire dans l'ancienne Espagne* (Paris-Toulouse, 1902) offers a vivid portrait. I know of no single work which gives a richer insight into the remarkable

The University Years

The curriculum which Cardoso followed at the university did not differ radically from that which he might have pursued had he lived a hundred years before, nor from that which was studied by his contemporaries in Paris or Bologna. A typical course in a Spanish Faculty of Arts, considered a corridor towards admission to the higher professional faculties, normally lasted four years. It comprised, besides rhetoric, the following major subjects: The first year was devoted to "Súmulas," based on the *Súmulas logicales* of the thirteenth-century Petrus Hispanus; the second, to further studies in logic from Porphyry's Introduction to the *Categories* of Aristotle, and from the *Topics;* the third, to "natural philosophy," which included Aristotle's *Physics, Meteorologica,* and *De Anima;* the fourth year was given over to the *Metaphysics.*[57] Of course, all these were taught with commentaries and supercommentaries, some of them quite recent. But it was an essentially scholastic education, the ladder climbing from logic to metaphysics, just as it had in the Middle Ages.

Equally bound to the past was the study of medicine. For an insight into its content we have only to glance at the medical chairs at the University of Valladolid, of which there were five in Cardoso's time. In addition to a *Cátedra de Vísperas de Medicina,* one of *Método,* and another of *Zirujía,* it included a *Cátedra de Prima de Medicina de Avicena* and a *Cátedra de Prima de Hipócrates.*[58] The latter chair had been founded as recently as 1618 by the court physician Dr. Miguel Polanco, and was endowed by Philip III. The instruction of the chair in surgery, established in 1594, drew its texts almost exclusively from Galen.[59] At Valladolid, as elsewhere, the book still took precedence over clinical observation. Significantly, in 1630 the

---

mixture of old and new in 17th-century knowledge than vols. VI and VIII of Lynn Thorndike's monumental *History of Magic and Experimental Science* (New York, 1958).

[57] Reynier, *Vie universitaire,* p. 167.

[58] The chairs in medicine are described in Alcocer, *Universidad de Valladolid,* I, 70–77, 101. The Cátedra de Prima de Medicina de Avicena was not abolished until 1771, when another chair, "conforming more to Hippocrates," was substituted (*ibid.,* p. 253).

[59] *Ibid.,* p. 75. For material taught in the other medical courses, see pp. cxvii f.

Beginnings of a Career

students found it necessary to petition for the teaching of anatomy (presumably by dissection) in the *Cátedra de Método*.[60] Yet it would be unfortunate were we to lose sight of the fact that what appears quaint and archaic to us from the vantage point of our age did not seem so to Cardoso and the men of his time. This was medicine in the early seventeenth century. Even William Harvey (1578–1657) spoke with absolute reverence of "the divine Galen." Besides its proximity to the family home in Rioseco, the University of Valladolid must have attracted Cardoso by virtue of the substantial medical reputation it had acquired during the sixteenth century, when its faculty included such a major figure as Dr. Luis de Mercado,[61] physician to Philip II and later to Philip III. Of Cardoso's own teachers in medicine at Valladolid he singles out Dr. Antonio Ponce de Santa Cruz, himself a disciple of Mercado, and one of the most renowned physicians of his time.[62]

The steps by which one mounted the academic pyramid at the Spanish universities were, on the whole, minutely regulated and rigidly defined. Having taken his baccalaureate in arts, and most

---

[60] *Ibid.*, p. 73. An anatomical theater was apparently not established until 1771 (p. 253). At Salamanca the theater which had been opened in 1568 was closed eight years later.

[61] Mercado, a native of Valladolid, died some time before 1611 at the age of seventy-six. That he was a New Christian may be gathered from his inclusion in the list of famous Peninsular physicians of Jewish extraction compiled by Benedict de Castro in his apologetic work *Flagellum Calumniantium* (Amsterdam, 1631). There is no evidence that he judaized. For his works see Friedenwald, *Jews and Medicine*, I, 327–31. On other eminent physicians associated with the university, see Narciso Alonso Cortés, *Miscelánea Vallesolitana*, 3d ser. (Valladolid, 1921), pp. 133–46.

[62] Cardoso, *De febri syncopali* (Madrid, 1639), p. 35v. He held the *Cátedra de Prima de Avicena* from 1618 until his death and was, in addition, a court physician to Philip III and Philip IV. See Alcocer, *Universidad de Valladolid*, VII (*Biobibliografías de médicos notables;* Valladolid, 1931), 106–10. He was the author of the following medical treatises: *Tratado de las causas y curación de las fiebres* (Valladolid, 1600); *Dignotio et cura affectuum melancholicorum* (Madrid, 1622); *Exactissimae disputationes de pulsibus quibus Galeni et Avicennae doctrina philosophica perpenditur* (Madrid, 1622); *In Avicennae Primam Primi* (Madrid, 1622); *Praelectiones Vallisoletanae in librum magni Hipp. Coi de morbo sacro* (Madrid, 1631).

78

probably in medicine as well. Cardoso had also passed his examination for the *licenciatura* by the end of 1623. Though he must have been preparing for the doctorate as well, he felt himself ready for his first teaching post. The documents show that on December 9, 1623, notices were posted in Valladolid which proclaimed that three chairs in the Faculty of Arts had recently been vacated: in Logic, Súmulas, and Philosophy. Cardoso applied for the latter two, promising that, whichever one he should receive, he would then relinquish all claims to the other.[63] A similar application for the same chairs was submitted by another physician, the Licenciado Joseph Gonzáles.[64] The chair in Logic was sought solely by Dr. Juan Carrillo de Salcedo, a member of the powerful *Colegio Mayor de Santa Cruz* at Valladolid.[65] It may be that this alone discouraged others from opposing him. Cardoso and Gonzáles, however, would have to compete against one another.

Such competitions were usually conducted according to established procedures. Until that very year it had been the tradition at Valladolid, as at Salamanca and Alcalá, that it was not the professors who chose their colleague, but rather the students who chose their teacher. For each vacant chair an *oposición*, consisting of model lectures and debate on the part of the aspirants, was held publicly before the matriculated students of the respective faculty, after which they voted for the candidate of their choice. However, some months before Cardoso announced his own candidacy, an important change had taken place. Alarmed at frequent reports of irregularities and abuses in the election of *catedráticos*, Philip IV

---

[63] The notices on the vacant chairs are in AUV Leg. 238 (3–7), fols. 1r–3v. Cardoso's application, written in his own hand (*ibid.*, fol. 5r), reads as follows:

"Fernan Cardoso bachiller artista encorporado en esta universidad digo q. a mi noticia es venido q. V.md. tiene vacas tres cathedras de artes Sumulas, Logica, y Philosophia, yo me oppongo a las cathedras de Sumulas y Philosophia, y estoi presto de hazer los actos en declaracion q. llevando qualquiera de las dos cathedras me aparto del derecho de la otra. Supplico a V.md. me aya por oppuesto y me lo mande dar por testim.º pido iusticia.

(Signed) Fernan Cardoso"

[64] *Ibid.*, fol. 6r.

[65] Carrillo's application, *ibid.*, fol. 6r.

issued a decree on May 26, 1623, which entirely deprived the students of their vote, and placed the final award of university chairs in the hands of the Royal and Supreme Council in Madrid.[66] The actual procedure involved in this new means of selection was not spelled out in the decree, but it may be ascertained from a request for information sent to Valladolid by the council and preserved among our documents. It becomes clear that, although the students no longer voted, the *oposiciones* themselves were still held in much the same manner as before. Only now, in order to help the Council make its decision, it was the doctors, counselors, and *catedráticos* of the university who were to vote. Without being opened and counted, the sealed ballots were to be sent to Madrid along with other information on the qualifications of the candidates.[67]

Thus, despite the shift in final authority, the venerable institution of the *oposición* remained in all its details. The documents yield a fairly vivid picture of the proceedings.

On Sunday, December 17, 1623, Cardoso and Gonzáles were told to present themselves the next morning to choose a text for the *oposición*. Being "more recent" at the university than his adversary, Cardoso would be the first to lecture.[68] Accordingly, on Monday at 8:00 A.M. the two candidates came to the house of the rector. There, as was the custom, one of Aristotle's treatises (apparently the *Metaphysics*) was opened three times at random by a young boy,

---

[66] On this development see Alcocer, *Universidad de Valladolid*, I, 94, and Ajo, *Hist. de las universidades*, II, 48, III, 602 f., no. DXLVI.

In 1632 the king ordered a reversion to the old system, with the exception of chairs in theology and medicine. Provision of the latter remained in the hands of the council.

[67] AUV, Leg. 238 (3–7), fol. 10r-v.

[68] *Ibid.*, fol. 6v: "En valladolid a diez y siete dias del mes de diziembre de mil y seis y vte y tres el sr. Rtor mando se notifique a los lldos. Joseph gs. y fernan cardoso venir mañana lunes a tomar puntos para leer de opossn. como son obligados primero el mas nuebo y ansi lo mando. (Signed) Antonio arias."

Cf. fol. 7v: "son ambos medicos examinados y sin duda de bllrs. y el gs. de licenciado. es mas antigo gs."

On the rules and procedure for *oposiciones* at Valladolid, see Alcocer, *Universidad de Valladolid*, I, xcvii, cii f.

and Cardoso was asked to indicate his preference. Of the three passages which were shown to him, he chose the one "on Substance."[69]

Cardoso must have spent the rest of the day in intensive preparation. The next morning (Tuesday, the 19th) he delivered his lecture in the hall of Canon Law, and Gonzáles "argued" the points he had made.[70] Then it was the latter's turn to choose one of three passages taken from the same work and selected, as before, by chance. He chose the passage "on the Qualities"[71] and lectured on it the following day, while this time Cardoso delivered the critique.[72] Of course both lectures and arguments were given in Latin.

After this the *opositores* were given a day's respite. On Friday, December 22d, they were summoned again to choose their texts for the final stage of the competition. On this occasion the book to be opened was Aristotle's *Physics*. Cardoso selected the section "on the Infinite" (Bk. III, ch. 4), and that afternoon Gonzáles chose

---

[69] AUV, Leg. 238 (3–7), fol. 5v: "Lunes a los ocho de la mañana diez y ocho dias del mes de diz.ᵉ del dhᵒ año los dhᵒˢ opositores fernan cardoso y joseph gs. se allaron en casa del Rtor y al dhᵒ fernan cardoso como mas nuebo se le dio tres puntos para aver de leer en oposⁿ en un libro llamado aristoteles [*sic!*] y se abrio en tres puntos y de los que salieron escoxio el capitulo de sustancia que enpieza sustancia autem." No further details are given. The text was apparently read in Latin translation. That a young boy should open the books was specified in the university statutes, obviously to ensure the random quality of the choices.

[70] *Ibid.:* "Doy fee que en martes diez y nuebe del dhᵒ mes el dhᵒ fernan cardoso leio en opsn. en el general de canones de nuebe a diez de la mañana de los puntos que hubo excoxido presᵗᵉ [?] el dhᵒ joseph gs. que le arguyo como es costumbre. (Signed) Antonio arias."

[71] *Ibid.* fols. 6v-7r: "Martes diez y nuebe dias del mes de diziembre del año de mil y seis y vᵗᵉ y tres a los ocho de la mañana el dhᵒ joseph gs. opositor ... tomo puntos en el mismo libro llamado aristoteles que se abrio tres veces y de los que ... salieron escoxio para leer de oposicion el siguiente dia de quali & qualitate que enpieza qualitatem bero. ..."

[72] *Ibid.* fol. 7r: "Doy fee que oy miercoles veinte del dhᵒ mes y año de ocho a nuebe de la mañana el dhᵒ joseph gs. leio en oposn. en el general de canones de los puntos que excoxio presᵗᵉ [?] el dhᵒ fernan cardoso que le arguyo como es costumbre. Antonio arias."

to discuss the Continuum (Bk. VI, ch. 1).[73] They gave their lectures on Saturday, Cardoso speaking from 9:00 to 11:00 A.M., and González from 3:00 to 5:00 P.M.[74] Each lecture must have been followed again by criticism and debate. As far as their own effort was concerned, the candidates had now completed the somewhat grueling process which was expected of them. They had only to await the final decision which, since it was to come from Madrid, took some time. On March 23, 1624, the Royal Council sent its request for information to Alonso Niño, the rector of the university, and it was not until May that it rendered its verdict. The Council took the most simple course open to it under the circumstances, especially as it had no personal knowledge of either candidate. Since each had applied for both chairs, it decided to divide them between the two. González was granted the chair in Súmulas, and Cardoso that of Philosophy. Formal title was given to Cardoso by the *claustro* of the university on May 7th, and he was thus invested, for the first time, with the special hat of a *catedrático*.[75]

---

[73] *Ibid.:* "En valladolid viernes v^{te} y dos de diziembre de mil y seis y veinte y tres as. tomo segunda vez puntos en un libro llamado los phisicos de aristoteles fernan cardoso opositor y se abrio el dh^o libro tres veces y de los que salieron escoxio para leer de oposn. del capitulo 4° cum autem cientia naturalis.

"En el mismo dia a las dos de la tarde tomo puntos en el mismo libro el l^{do} joseph gs. oppositor y se abrio tres veces y de los que salieron escoxio para leer de oposn. en el libro sexto el capitulo primero si autem . . . continuum sunt."

[74] *Ibid.*, fol. 7v: "Leio de oposicion el l^{do} fernan cardoso sabado veinte y tres de diziembre de nuebe a once de los puntos que escoxio."

[75] *Ibid.*, fol. 12v: "En el pleito que ante nos el Rector y consiliarios de la Un^d real desta ciudad de V^d apendido y pende sobre la provision de la catedra trienia da artes en filosofia a que an leido opositores los licenciados joseph gs. y fernan cardoso. . . . Fallamos que la dicha cathedra de artes en philosophia asi vaca en esta Un^d es devida y perteneciente al licenciado fernan cardoso por la haber hecho de ella m^d su mag^d y señores de su supremo y real consejo y como a tal se la devemos de adjudicar y adjudicamos y de ella le hacemos titulo y colacion y canonica institucion por imposicion de un bonete que sobre su cabeca ponemos para que la tenga goce i usa por tiempo y espacio de tres a^s que corren y se quentan desde el pronunciam^{to} desta nuestra ssentencia en adelante . . ." (The date May 7, 1624, is given in the report of the *claustro*, fol. 12r).

The award of the chair in Súmulas to Joseph González is stated in similar terms (fol. 11r). Since he was the only candidate, Juan Carrillo de Salcedo was granted

The chair which he had earned was a temporary one awarded, as usual, for three years. But Cardoso was not to take advantage of his prerogative for the full span of time. It is possible that he began to teach immediately, in May, but our documentary information commences only in October, at the start of the new academic year. It was the custom at Valladolid for the *bedel* of the university to check on the number of lectures which the professors failed to deliver each month, and to record these, along with the fines incurred, in the Libro de cuentas de catedráticos. This register reveals that Cardoso taught from October, 1624, but that in each of the subsequent months he was absent from a significant number of lectures. It records further that in January, 1625, his chair became vacant, and that on May 17 it was given to the Licenciado Juan Gómez del Pinar.[76]

Lacking any information as to Cardoso's activities at this time, it is virtually impossible to determine what actually happened. Presumably he was relieved of the chair because his absences had been excessive. The university statutes specified that this penalty was to be imposed, in addition to the monetary fines, on any *catedrático* who absented himself from fifteen consecutive lectures without the express permission of the rector, which was given only in case of illness.[77] On the other hand, we hear at one point that

---

the chair of Logic earlier, on February 7th (fols. 8r, 9r). The notice given by Alcocer, (*Universidad de Valladolid*, III, *Expedientes de provisiones de catedras* [Valladolid, 1921], p. 273) that Cardoso was given the chair in Logic is therefore incorrect. He does not mention Cardoso among the *catedráticos* in philosophy where, as the documents show, he belongs; nor does he cite Joseph Gonzáles among the *catedráticos* in Súmulas.

[76] AUV, Lib. 291, Libro de cuentas de catedráticos 1616–1629, fol. 256v: "Cat^a de curso de Artes tienela el Sr. Licen^do Cardoso leese a las oras que las demas de artes y vale lomismo."

Cardoso missed 9 lectures in October, 20 in November, and 17 in December. In January the *bedel*, Pedro Vélez, noted: "Ubo v^te y un dias lectivos y por la dicha auss^a no se leyeron y se baco esta cat^a por estar en un sal^o [?] el d^ho licen^do cardoso en 15 deste mes, son del arca 21." The entry for May reads: "Ubo diez y siete dias lectivos llevo esta cathedra y se la dio poss^on al licen^do Juan gomez del pinar savado diez y siete deste mes de mayo . . . ."

[77] Alcocer, *Universidad de Valladolid*, I, xxviii, cxviii.

the chair became vacant because of Cardoso's "resignation," which may imply that his departure was voluntary.[78] At any rate, absences were a frequent phenomenon at Valladolid, and the register shows that almost every other chair was mulcted to a greater or lesser extent.[79] Perhaps because faculty absences were so rampant, no particular stigma seems to have attached to them. How else are we to explain the fact that this incident proved no serious obstacle to Cardoso's further advancement? For indeed at this very time Cardoso was invested with another position. The dossier which contains the documents of Juan Gómez del Pinar informs us that he received his chair when Cardoso ascended to that of Prima de Filosofía.[80]

Sometime in 1625 Cardoso also received his doctorate in medicine.[81] He must certainly have aimed for it all along, but in any event the statutes demanded that anyone who held a chair must

---

[78] AUV, Leg. 238 (3–8), fol. 3r (Application of Pedro de Ayngo): "digo que a mi noticia es venido como en esta Universidad esta vaca una cathedra de las trienias de artes *por dexacion* del D.ᵒʳ Cardosso su vlo. posedor. . . ."

[79] This may be seen in the annual summary of fines (Oct. 1624–Aug. 1625 recorded by the bedel (AUV, Lib. 291, fol. 257r-v). Cardoso's chair was mulcted for a total of 16,360 maravedis, but this included the months between January and May, when the chair was empty. Fines for other chairs ranged from 903 to 12,534 maravedis. They may have been deducted from salary payments.

[80] AUV, Leg. 238 (3–8): "Provision de la catedra de Súmulas vacante por ascenso del Lic. Fernando Cardoso a Prima de Filosofia, en el Lic. Juan Gomez del Pinar a 4 enero—17 mayo 1625."

There seems to be some confusion in the documents as to precisely which chair it was that Cardoso vacated. Here it appears to have been that of Súmulas. But the documents cited earlier from Leg. 238 (3–7) leave absolutely no doubt that Cardoso had received the chair of Philosophy, while the chair of Súmulas had gone to Joseph Gonzáles. The summary of fines (*supra*, n. 79) refers to three separate chairs, each called by the generic name "Cathedra de curso de Artes," one of them held by Juan Carrillo de Salcedo, the second by Joseph Gonzáles, and the third by Cardoso. From Leg. 238 (3–7), it is clear that these are, respectively, the chairs of logic, súmulas, and philosophy, in the Faculty of Arts. If the attribution to Cardoso of the chair in Súmulas is not an error, the reasons for it elude me.

[81] He is already referred to as "Dr. Cardoso" by Pedro de Ayngo in his application for Cardoso's chair, January 16, 1625 (*supra*, n. 78).

acquire the doctorate within two years. Once he had the title it was not long before Cardoso turned his eyes to the medical faculty. Though he may have begun to practice medicine in the city, apparently he was still intent on a university career. From his own remarks we have already noted that at the age of twenty-three (1626/7) he was a *pretendiente* for the *Cátedra de Prima de Medicina*,[82] a position somewhat analogous to that of the *Privatdozent* at central European universities in modern times. Unfortunately, the documents of this phase in Cardoso's association with the university seem to have been lost. We can well imagine that just as he had earlier to lecture on Aristotle in the contest for his first chair in philosophy, so now he had to do the same with a text selected from Hippocrates, Galen, or Avicenna.

The effect of some ten years of university study and teaching on Cardoso's development can hardly be overestimated. Here was an intellectual world in which the ancients were the arbiters of truth, in which the mind was nourished by classical and medieval thought, Latin was the language of study and instruction, and wits were sharpened in dialectical duels over the most abstruse of subtleties. All this was to leave on Cardoso an indelible imprint whose traces are strong throughout the works he wrote decades later. Even as he asserted his independence, even after he had undergone a profound ideological reorientation, something of the Spanish academician was to remain in him to the end of his days. If the environment in which the mind first reaches maturity is always hard to leave behind, this is doubly difficult when it has also provided the first taste of glory. And yet, despite his academic success, as a New Christian Cardoso could not have been oblivious of other, less pleasant aspects of life at Valladolid, even if they did not yet affect him personally.

It is no small matter to realize that Cardoso almost certainly witnessed his first *auto de fe* at Valladolid. Such an *auto* was held

---

[82] *Discurso sobre el monte Vesuvio* (see *supra*, n. 49); he speaks of it again in his *De febre syncopali* (fol. 2r of the preliminary material): "Despues de aver sido . . . Catedratico de Filosofia en Valladolid, y hecho a la Catedra de Prima de Medicina de las mayores demostraciones que se han visto en aquella Universidad. . . ."

in the city on October 4, 1623, a month before he submitted his application for the *Cátedra de Filosofía*.[83] Along with the municipal and ecclesiastical dignitaries and corporations, the university marched in the procession.[84] Most of the victims were accused of crimes ranging from Protestant heresy to bigamy, and were given a variety of penances. Of the two unfortunates who were burned at the stake, one was "a witch of Rioseco, a Jewess, who died in her Law."[85] The woman, in other words, had incurred the death penalty by her refusal to abjure, and even then had remained steadfast to the end.

But there were also other less dramatic, though more constant, reminders at Valladolid to make a New Christian sensitive to his situation. The *colegios mayores* affiliated with the major Spanish universities had been intended by their founders to serve an elite of poor but promising young men by providing them with support so that they might have an austere and tranquil milieu in which to pursue their studies. However, thanks in part to the immense funds which were lavished upon them, the colleges had changed their character completely by the seventeenth century. Far from being a means of equalizing opportunity they became a haven for sons of important families, closed and aristocratic corporations which, through powerful connections, favored their alumni with a sure avenue to the most desirable positions. While the universities themselves were generally more lax with regard to purity of blood, the *colegios mayores* almost from the outset required the very strictest proofs of *limpieza* not only from the candidates who wished to enter, but even from all those who worked there. The Colegio de San

---

[83] A contemporary *romance* on this auto has been published with a brief introduction by Narciso Alonso Cortés in his *Miscelánea Vallisoletana*, 5th series (Valladolid, 1930), pp. 5–21. A detailed description is to be found in BNM, MS 2354 (Relación del auto de la fé que se celebro en la ciudad de Vall^{ld} dia de San fra.^{co} 4 de octubre deste año de 1623).

[84] "Luego vino acompañando / que ha sido la vez primera / la ilustre Universidad donde florecen las ciencias / Los señores regidores / que la ciudad representan / tras las escuelas vinieron . . ." (N. Alonso Cortés, *Miscelanea Vallisoletana*, p. 16).

[85] "Las de los quemados heran de un beneficiado de balbeni . . . por apostata; la otra hera de una bruja de Rioseco, judía, que murió en su ley" (*Cartas de Andrés de Almansa y Mendoza*, cited *ibid.*, p. 6).

Bartolomé at Salamanca demanded it even of the cook and the water carrier.[86]

In Valladolid the Colegio de Santa Cruz possessed statutes of *limpieza* dated April 24, 1488, which had been established by the founder and the first students.[87] There could of course be no question of Cardoso belonging to this college, for the genealogical investigations conducted by the *colegios mayores* were known to be the most rigorous in all Spain. Perhaps he would not have wanted to enter in any case. But the very knowledge that, because of his ancestry, it was impossible was thereby already part of his consciousness. We shall never know what remarks about New Christians or "Jews" he may have heard in his contacts with fellow students or teachers. His daily life at the university may have been quiet enough, and we are not to imagine necessarily that he was preoccupied with such problems. But surely he must have been aware at various times of the intense hostility to New Christians which existed around him. Though not himself a member of Santa Cruz, it is hardly imaginable that he did not know of a practice which amply reflects the virulent racialism of the *colegiales,* and is reported by Torrejoncillo in the following words:

In the renowned Colegio de Santa Cruz of Valladolid, from which have emerged so many important and illustrious men that to refer to them all would consume much time and paper . . . there is an immemorial custom worthy to be pondered and publicized, to wit: that every year on Good Friday all the collegians gather in their refectory where, during the meal, the Passion of the Lord is read devoutly in Latin; and, after completing the meal, all those who have served and administered the meal leave the room or refectory, while the collegians remain alone behind closed doors. They place themselves in two rows in the said room or refectory, and the rector says the following words in a loud voice: *Quid vobis videtur de illis perfidis Iudaeis, qui hodie Christum Dominum nostrum*

---

[86] On the concern for *limpieza* at the Colegios Mayores see Domínguez Ortiz, *Clase social,* pp. 57–59; Sicroff, *Controverses,* pp. 89 ff., 222; Caro Baroja, *Judíos,* II, 271–73; María Anunciación Febrero Lorenzo, *La pedagogía de los colegios mayores a través de su legislación en el Siglo de Oro* (Madrid, 1960), pp. 63–68.

[87] Sicroff, *Controverses,* p. 90.

crucifixerunt? What shall we say, or what judgment can be made of those perfidious Jews who today crucified our Lord Jesus Christ? And, beginning soon with the oldest, each is obliged to say and refer to some family of tainted lineage, the place where it is found, and that all should beware of it. And thus, all the collegians having spoken that which they know, and having made a mockery of the Jews, they terminate the gathering, and leave the refectory.[88]

Beyond possible exposure to actively hostile elements in the environment, Cardoso naturally lived his life in conformity with that which was expected at a most Christian university, with its cycle of holy days and religious celebrations, especially those which the institution held in particular veneration. Along with all the other members of the university community, whose attendance was mandatory on such occasions, he walked in solemn procession each December on the *Fiesta de San Nicolás* from the Plaza de Santa María to the church in the city which bore the saint's name, for Vespers, High Mass, and the customary sermon. In the same month the *Fiesta del Angélico Doctor Santo Tomás* was celebrated in the convent of San Pablo, and the *Fiesta de San Juan Evangelista* in the university chapel. Similar solemnities were observed throughout the other months of the school year[89]. Each time he received an academic degree Cardoso had not only to take the oath upon the Gospels and the Cross but also, because of a recent development, to swear that he believed in the Immaculate Conception.[90]

That he read very extensively in the entire range of Christian thought from the Church Fathers to his own day becomes evident,

---

[88] Francisco de Torrejoncillo, *Centinela contra judíos*, fol. 67f. Cf. fol. 190.

[89] On religious celebrations at the University of Valladolid see Alcocer, *Universidad de Valladolid*, I, 165–77, xxxix f. (For complete list, see pp. cxix f.)

[90] Philip III took it upon himself to promote the cause of the Immaculate Conception in 1617. Between July and October he sent circular letters to Valladolid and other universities, asking them to manifest their sentiments on this matter to the Pope, "para que la aclamación de todos obligue a Su Santidad a caminar en este negocio." In 1618 the oath was imposed upon graduates of almost all the Spanish universities. See Ajo, *Universidades*, II, 47. The text of the oath at Valladolid is given *ibid.*, n. 117, and Alcocer, I, 175, n. 2. For the text of Philip's letter see Ajo, III, 571; Alcocer, I, 173.

as we shall see, upon perusal of his published works. Even though he was never formally enrolled in a theological faculty, he may have audited lectures in theology without matriculating.

Finally, it is interesting to consider that Cardoso could even have had the opportunity, if he so wished and thought it prudent, to study some Hebrew at Valladolid. The chair in Hebrew was first established in 1564, and seems to have been in fairly continuous use, although in 1584 and 1594 there was some problem in paying the professor. On May 21, 1610, the chair was consigned to a Don Pedro de Castro, *Hebreo*, at an annual salary of 20,000 maravedis. Some interesting data on this person are given in a royal order issued on October 30, 1612. Philip III wrote to the university that Pedro de Castro, "Hebreo de nazion," had reported the following: he was the son of a rabbi of Fez, and had formerly been very wealthy. But he had left everything behind in order to come to Spain together with two of his servants and accept the Catholic Faith. Having all been baptized, the servants received from the king a *merced* of 16 escudos per month, but he himself had not yet been granted anything. Since he is expert in the Hebrew language and holds the chair in that subject at the university, he requests the same, so that he may more easily continue with his work. Philip asked the university to assist De Castro each year "with what is just," but before acceding to his request he desired more information. The university replied that the chair was extremely useful, especially for Sacred Letters, and that Pedro de Castro was a most qualified person. They had assigned to him a salary of 12,000 maravedis for lack of more ample funds, and asked the king that the *merced* which he would grant should be subject to fines like all regular professorial salaries.[91] We are not informed as to how many years after this De Castro continued to occupy the chair. But it is nonetheless piquant to entertain the possibility that, among his varied experiences at the University of Valladolid, Cardoso may even have come into contact with a baptized Morrocan Jew.

[91] Alcocer, I, 82 f.; Ajo, III, 555, no DIII.

TO THE CAPITAL

Sometime between 1627 and 1630 Cardoso left Valladolid and went to Madrid.[92] It may well be that he had reached an impasse at the university and therefore saw in the capital a wider field for his ambitions. To be a *pretendiente* in the Faculty of Medicine may have been temporarily gratifying for a young man. But the salary was small, and the position often proved a frustrating trap in which, for years, one had "nothing more than hope."[93] The medical chairs with tenure, the so-called *cátedras de propriedad* were held at this time by men of greater seniority. Despite the fact that Cardoso reports, with no pretense of modesty, that he delivered some of the finest lectures in medicine ever heard at the university,[94] the prize of a tenured professorship apparently eluded him.

Though a causal connection need not necessarily be sought, it should be remarked also that Cardoso's arrival in Madrid coincided with an important external development. At this very time the movement of Portuguese New Christians to Madrid reached its greatest height, the result of a complex of political and economic factors. Increasingly enmeshed in the intricate convolutions of the Thirty Years War, drifting toward a major encounter with France, Spain had already overextended its commitments and was fighting on several scattered fronts. The drain on the resources of the treasury was enormous. In January, 1627, the country suffered the shock of a severe monetary crisis. Even before this there had been thoughts of replacing the Genoese bankers, who played such an important role in court finance, by the Portuguese. The plan seems to have emanated from the prime minister, Olivares, who virtually ruled

---

[92] The date 1630 as a *terminus ad quem* for Cardoso's arrival in Madrid is derived from his testimony at the inquisitorial trial of Bartolomé Febos (March, 1634), in which he stated that he had known the latter for the past four years. (AHN, Inq. de Toledo, Leg. 146, num. 238, 4, fol. 174r; Caro, *Judíos*, III, 330.)

[93] Reynier, *La vie universitaire*, p. 22.   [94] *De febre syncopali*. (See *supra*, n. 82

the land in Philip's name. Already in 1626 a group of wealthy Portuguese in Lisbon, New Christians with but one exception, had offered to provide 400,000 escudos for the war in Flanders in return for certain concessions in Madrid.[95] Thus begun, the negotiations led to the issuance on June 26, 1627, of a temporary Indulgence from the Inquisition to the New Christians of Portugal, together with a permit to emigrate.[96] Further transactions, often conducted over the active protests of the Portuguese clergy, produced additional benefits. With the intention of excluding foreigners from the commercial orbit of the Americas, in 1628 Philip qualified the *hombres de negocios* of Portugal to deal freely by land and sea, and to change their domicile.[97] On November 17, 1629, a royal decree again granted them liberty of movement and permission to dispose of their goods at will.[98] Though the intricacies of these and later negotiations

---

[95] Domínguez, *Política y hacienda*, pp. 129 f.; Caro, *Sociedad*, p. 41. Among the concessions requested was a permit to bring to Lisbon and to work 200,000 ducats of silver, as well as to engage in other transactions of a purely financial nature.

[96] Domínguez, pp. 129 f. The Indulgence was granted for three months. The exit permit specified that if they went to lands where Catholicism was forbidden, they could not return without royal license.

[97] Caro, *Judíos*, II, 56, regards this measure as of "exceptional importance in the history of the New Christians." It should be noted that as a result of this decree, though many settled in Spain, some went to the Low Countries and the German port cities.

[98] Girard, *Le commerce français à Séville*, p. 29; Domínguez, *Política y hacienda*. While the negotiations were still in progress, on May 23, 1629, the Portuguese bishops and theologians met at Tomar to protest. The discussions were characterized by antisemitic propaganda of the most vulgar kind. See J. Lúcio d'Azevedo, *Christãos-Novos*, pp. 194 ff. Apparently opposition in Portugal to any amelioration of the status of the New Christians was sufficiently fierce to subvert, at times, the decrees which came from Madrid. For the continuing complaints of the Portuguese New Christians, see the documents published by Elkan Adler in his "Les marranes d'Espagne et de Portugal sous Philippe IV," *REJ*, XLVIII-LI, which, despite the title, concerns only those of Portugal. The documents consist of petitions to the *Junta* formed in 1629 to consider the requests of the Portuguese conversos, and its own deliberations. Most of the members were generally in favor of concessions. The documents break off on January 1, 1632. On March 25th Philip sent a letter in which he stated that the amnesty to the Portuguese New Christians cannot be negated after 240,000 ducats have been accepted from them. He also defended

remain obscure at some points, the general outlines are sufficiently clear. Given the new opportunities, there took place after 1627 an exodus of New Christians from Portugal to Spain which was of truly unprecedented proportions. In particular, Madrid, because it was the seat of the court, and Seville, the center of overseas trade, were veritable lodestones, attracting perhaps the bulk of the emigrants. In 1633 Thomas de Cardona could report soberly from Lisbon that "commerce has ended in this city, and all the businessmen of substance have moved to this court (Madrid) and to Seville."[99] Even earlier, of course, Madrid had contained a significant New Christian population, and by 1622 the Portuguese antisemite Vicente da Costa Mattos was prepared to call it a "great refuge of Judaism."[100] Be that as it may, the real heyday of New Christian influence in Madrid, both by sheer number and by the power some New Christians wielded, may be placed in the decades of the thirties and forties, the very years when Cardoso made his home there. It was an auspicious time.

the sincerity of their conversion. Domínguez (*Clase social*, p. 114) does not think that even this letter finally resolved the controversy, since there is no corresponding legislative text.

[99] Domínguez, *Política y hacienda*, p. 132. Francisco Manoel de Mello tells of a parish in Lisbon from which more than 2,000 inhabitants, all wealthy, have departed for Madrid and Seville (*ibid.*, p. 138, n. 7). Nevertheless, Domínguez is justified in cautioning that only a tiny minority of the emigrants possessed great fortunes, and that the multitude were much less opulent, contenting themselves with farming the royal rents or with various forms of commerce (p. 131).

[100] Costa Mattos, *Discurso*, fol. 135r: "Madrid (grãde valhacouto do Iudaismo . . . sem culpa das justiças que não tem tanto conhecimento deste . . .)." In the margin: "Iudeos em Madrid estão como em seu sentro."

MADRID: DEBUTS AND COLLISIONS

Tu bolcán portentoso verifica
Teatro funeral de los mortales.
—Cardoso, *Soneto al Vesuvio*

MADRID, at the time of Cardoso's arrival, was a fascination and a paradox. Often somber in its architecture,
swollen with a constantly growing population, many
of its streets unpaved and filthy, it could yet astonish
any newcomer with a seemingly endless succession of brilliant spectacle and pageantry. For Madrid was "la Corte"—"The Court"
—and in that word lay both its designation and its justification.
Devoid of resources, of industry, even of the mellow venerability
which long memories had conferred upon Toledo or Valladolid,
Madrid could ignore those pedestrian qualifications which logic
ordinarily demands of capital cities. Here only one supreme fact
was important: the presence of the monarch made the city possible,
as a queen bee makes the hive. "Sólo Madrid es corte"—"Only
Madrid is the Court"—was the proud boast of the Madrileños. And
this was true, not only because the city had been restored to its
primacy since 1606, but also because it was indeed a striking contrast
to the rest of the country. At the end of the first decade of the
reign of Philip IV Madrid was the capital of a Spain sinking steadily
into ruin; but in the city itself one could easily have the illusion
that this was rather a capital worthy of the virile empire of a
Philip II. Here was channeled whatever was left of the wealth of
Spain and its colonies. Hither were drawn the idle, the ambitious,

93

Madrid: Debuts and Collisions

the seekers of pleasure or privilege, courtiers and courtesans, and a stream of curious foreigners eager to spend their time and their money in what was still, perhaps, the liveliest and most colorful court in Europe. As one historian has written, Madrid was then "like the last phosphorescent spot in a decaying body, and attracted by its brilliancy, when all the rest of Spain was dark."[1]

It must be noted, however, that in one respect the glitter was not merely external. If, around the year 1630, Spain was approaching the end of its political and economic prime, it was still basking in the golden age of its culture; and if Madrid was indeed the capital of a decaying empire, she was nonetheless still queen of a splendid domain in the arts. Amid the debauchery, the conspicuous waste and shallow exhibitionism which characterized so much of the social life of the city, there was also a genuine love of culture and a lavish patronage and enjoyment of the arts in all their forms.

For the sake of perspective it will help us to recall that the Madrid to which Cardoso came numbered among its residents Pedro Calderón, Francisco de Quevedo, Juan Ruiz de Alarcón, and Lope de Vega, the latter now an old man but still active. Around such luminaries were a host of lesser satellites, poets and dramatists who, if they did not quite possess the genius of the giants, were certainly endowed with important talents. The theaters of Madrid were exciting and packed to capacity, and the literary academies provided a congenial meeting ground for the creators and the connoisseurs. Among the nobility and the merely wealthy there raged a passion for the collection of paintings and other art treasures which brought

---

[1] Martin Hume, *The Court of Philip IV: Spain in Decadence* (London, 1907; new ed., New York, n. d.), p. 193.

For Madrid at this time, see Ramón de Mesonero Romanos, *El antiguo Madrid* (2 vols.; Madrid, 1881), and the illustrations in Federico Carlos Sainz de Robles, *Historia y estampas de la villa de Madrid*, Vol. I (Madrid-Barcelona, 1933). Abundant data on many aspects of daily life, society, and customs, will be found in the various volumes of José Deleito y Piñuela's series on *La España de Felipe IV*, e.g., *El Rey se divierte* (Madrid, 1935); *Sólo Madrid es corte* (1942); *Tambien se divierte el pueblo* (1944). See also Hugo Albert Rennert, *The Spanish Stage in the Time of Lope de Vega* (New York, 1909).

to Madrid the work of the finest Italian and Flemish masters. And at the court itself Diego Velásquez had already begun to record the entire human panorama which surrounded him, from the monarch to the dwarfs, in those inspired canvases which would someday confer on the court of Philip IV an unearned immortality.

A ROMAN ENTERTAINMENT

Cardoso must have come to Madrid bearing excellent recommendations and letters of introduction to important personages, for we find within a very short time he had gained access to the most fashionable courtly and artistic circles in the city. Though he earned his living from his medical practice, he had the broad intellectual interests of many physicians of his day, in an age when men of medicine were also serious amateurs of the arts and figures of some standing in society. By 1632, as we shall see, he was enjoying the patronage of the most august of the Spanish grandees, Don Juan Alonso Enríquez de Cabrera, the Admiral of Castile. Indeed, Cardoso may very well have had the latter's sponsorship from the very outset, since the Admiral was also the Duke of Medina de Rioseco, and the family may have been known to him from that town.[2]

At any rate, Cardoso's first printed work, a sonnet written in 1631, already places him in the company of some of the most prominent figures of the capital, and the circumstance for which it was written reveals some interesting facets of the milieu in which he now found himself.

We have observed that the court of Philip IV was known for the extravagance of its spectacles. Upon the slightest pretext, fabulous entertainments and theatricals were held in which Their Majesties eagerly participated. At other times the court was addicted to more strenuous amusements: equestrian displays, boar hunts in the

---

[2] Some such prior relationship may perhaps be inferred from the end of Cardoso's dedication to the Admiral of his book on Vesuvius, in which he speaks of his "obligation" to him. See *infra*, n. 10.

Madrid: Debuts and Collisions

Pardo, and, of course, the bullfights which accompanied almost every noteworthy event, and some not so worthy, and which were the delight of the populace. In one such fight held the year before, on June 19, 1630, no less than twenty bulls (and three men) had been killed in celebration of the peace treaty with England. Now, however, Olivares had a new diversion to offer his sovereign. Perhaps bullfights, by their very frequency, were already too commonplace for the jaded senses of the court. In anticipation of the second birthday of Prince Balthasar Carlos, heir to the Spanish throne, the prime minister decided upon something truly original: "to renew that exercise which was so applauded by the Roman Forum, and to regale their Catholic Majesties . . . by arranging for them a *fiesta* according to the ancient custom of Rome. . . ." The event, scheduled for October 13, 1631, would normally have taken place in the Plaza Mayor. However, a few months earlier, in July, half of that great square had been destroyed in a terrible fire which lasted three days. No sooner had the conflagration been extinguished—indeed, the ashes were still smoldering—than another bullfight had been held in the presence of the king and his court. During this *corrida* a house in the square caught fire again, and in the frantic rush of the panic-stricken crowd many were trampled and killed. By October the rebuilding of the Plaza Mayor had not yet been completed, and so Olivares' *fiesta* in Roman style was held on the thirteenth of that month in the Plaza del Parque.

The spectacle was certainly planned to display a ferocity which might rival that of the arenas in the ancient world. Its purpose was to see what would be the outcome of a general and spontaneous battle of diverse animals, and as usual everything had been prepared with elaborate care. Into the makeshift arena were sent a tiger, a bear, a bull, a horse, and a greyhound, as well as "other less important animals which might enhance the laughter and entertainment." The event had been well publicized. A huge crowd looked on as the beasts attacked one another, and the success, we are informed, was "beyond expectation." To the surprise and delight of all it was the bull which triumphed. After killing some of the other creatures "he traversed the circus as if he were the lord of it . . . and caused the rest to flee." So great was the terror now inspired by the bull that when certain men, covered with an ingenious wooden armor, entered the arena to goad the remaining animals, they still refused to fight.

And then came the unanticipated climax. "His Majesty saw the valor of that beast [the bull]. . . . He asked for an arquebus . . . took it gracefully, and, vigorously adjusting his cape, he took aim with such dexterity, and placed the shot so effectively, that he killed the bull."

In a court noted for the exuberance of its adulation, such a prodigious feat could not be passed over in silence. That single royal shot called forth no less than 90 laudatory poems by 89 poets, nobles, and courtiers. Within two or three weeks they were all published, together with a preface describing the event, by the royal chronicler Don Joseph Pellicer de Tovar, in a book which bore the resounding title: Amphitheater of Philip the Great, Catholic King of the Spanish Realms, Sovereign Monarch of the Indies, East and West, always August, Pious, Felicitous, and Supreme, Containing the Eulogies Which Have Celebrated the Fate He Has Dealt the Bull, in the Agonal Celebration of the Thirteenth of October, [etc.][3]

Cardoso too was represented in the volume.[4] His poem, which followed one by the playwright Francisco de Rojas Zorrilla, was a sonnet. Though possessing a certain ingenuity, it reflects the extravagant conceits of the time. The king is envisioned in quasi-divine terms. He is the "Spanish Numa" (a reference to Numa Pompilius, the legendary second king of Rome), and the "Christian Mars." He sends forth rays of light. The bull is depicted as gratefully

---

[3] *Anfiteatro de Felipe el Grande, Rey Catolico de las Españas, monarca soberano de las Indias de Oriente y Occidente, siempre Augusto, Pio, Feliz, i Maximo, contiene los elogios que han celebrado la suerte que hizo en el Toro, en la Fiesta Agonal de treze de otubre, deste año de M.DC.XXXI. Dedicale a su magestad Don Ioseph Pellicer de Tovar señor de la casa de Pellicer. Cronista de sus Reynos de Castilla i Leon con la proteccion del Excelentissimo Señor Don Gaspar de Guzman Conde, Duque, i Gran Canciller, con privilegio. En Madrid, por Iuan Gonçalez.* My descriptive quotations have been taken from fols. 3–11. At the end of the book there is an *aprobación* dated Nov. 3, 1631. A complete list of the poets is given by Bartolomé José Gallardo, *Ensayo de una biblioteca española de libros raros y curiosos* (Madrid, 1863–89), III, col. 1119.

[4] Pellicer, *Anfiteatro*, fol. 43v.

accepting its wound at the hands of the monarch, and dies happily, for in such a death it has earned a more triumphant life. Heaven, which has thus favored the king's right hand, announces thereby that lightning bolts from this shot shall become the "fulminating fire" of the world. Thus, the poet implies, this feat presages victories in Philip's wars as well.

We have, of course, no inkling from all this as to Cardoso's real mood when he watched the bloody doings in the arena.[5] Certainly he did not take Philip's shot as seriously as his sonnet would seem to indicate. Flattery of the king and the writing of occasional poems were fixed conventions of the time, useful for anyone who desired advancement and a place in society. Cardoso surely did not mind having his name associated with some of the others who appeared in the same volume, which included: Lope de Vega, Quevedo (two poems), Alarcón, Calderón, Cardoso's compatriot Miguel de Silveyra, the diplomat and political writer Diego de Saavedra Fajardo, Lope's disciple Juan Pérez de Montalván, the dramatist Antonio Mira de Amescua, the historian and playwright Antonio de Solís. If it was not beneath the dignity of such personalities to applaud the royal prowess in verse, we cannot expect that Cardoso, twenty-seven years old and ambitious, should have quibbled at what was, after all, an opportunity.

VESUVIUS

But a reputation is not built on a sonnet. A more serious occasion was soon to come which would impel Cardoso to publish, for the first time, a book of his own.

On Tuesday, December 16, 1631, there began one of the most violent eruptions of Mt. Vesuvius in recorded history. The volcanic activity did not subside until February, and even then there were periodic eruptions and earthquakes of diminishing intensity. During

---

[5] Cardoso's remarks much later in life about such contests will be examined *infra*, ch. VIII.

the worst of the cataclysm several thousand people lost their lives, and some 40 towns and villages in the vicinity were devastated.[6] The eruption, and the terrifying upheavals which had accompanied it, made an enormous impression throughout Europe. Between 1631 and 1634 more than 140 separate accounts of the eruption appeared. Most of these were eyewitness reports written in Italian, but there were others in French, German, Dutch, Latin, and even one in Polish.[7] Since Naples was, of course, a Spanish domain, it was only natural that the tragic event should arouse much interest in Spain itself. Madrid must have hummed with talk about the catastrophe, and in 1632 two treatises devoted to Vesuvius were published there. One of them was written by Cardoso.[8]

This work, entitled *Discurso sobre el Monte Vesuvio*, was completed by him sometime before June, 1632, and was dedicated, as was noted earlier, to the Admiral of Castile.[9] There is both a graceful

---

[6] The most thorough modern study of this eruption is that of M. H. Le Hon, "Eruption du Vésuve de 1631," *Bulletins de l'Académie Royale des Sciences, des Lettres et des Beaux Arts de Belgique* (2d series), XX (1865), 483–538.

[7] I have analyzed the following lists: a) Henry James Johnston-Lavis, *Bibliography of the Geology and Eruptive Phenomena of the More Important Volcanoes of Southern Italy* (2d ed; London, 1918), which yields 132 items on the eruption of 1631; b) Luigi Riccio, "Nuovi documenti sull'incendio Vesuviano dell'anno 1631," *Archivio storico per le province Napoletane*, XIV (1889), 489–555 (bibliography, pp. 539-55). Of a total of 232 items listed by Riccio, 142 were published between 1631 and 1634 and constitute separate works.

[8] Johnston-Lavis records 10 Spanish works of which 8 appeared in Naples. Riccio gives 8 in Spanish, 7 of them printed in Naples. Only the former lists Cardoso's *Discurso*.

Reports of the disaster reached Madrid in several languages. In a volume entitled *Sucesos del año 1631* in the Biblioteca Nacional, Madrid, (MS 2363), I found the following bound together with other materials: Descripcion de la montaña de Soma y del incendio que empezo en ella a 16 de Deze 1631 (fols. 234–38; in manuscript); Giulio Cesare Braccini, *Relazione dell'incendio fattosi nel Vesuvio alli 16 di decembre 1631* (Naples, 1631); *Metheorologicus discursus circa portentissimum et monstruosum partum Vesuvii (vulgo monte de Somma)* . . . (n.p., n.d.), by "Doctoris Vincenti Molis, regis familiae medici."

[9] *Discurso/ sobre el monte/ Vesuvio, insigne por sus/ ruinas, famoso por la muer/ te de Plinio/ del prodigioso incendio/ del año passado de 1631 i de sus causas natu/rales, i el origen verdadero de los terremotos, vientos, i tempestades./ Al Excelentissimo señor/ Almirante*

99

DISCVRSO SOBRE EL MONTE VESVVIO, INSIGNE POR SVS RVINAS, FAMOSO POR LA MVERTE DE PLINIO,

DEL PRODIGIOSO INCENDIO del año passado de 1631. i de sus causas naturales, i el origen verdadero de los terremotos, vientos, i tempestades.

AL EXCELENTISSIMO SEÑOR ALMIRANTE DE CASTILLA.

Por el Doctor Fernando Cardoso.

Con licencia. *EN MADRID.*

POR FRANCISCO MARTINEZ. Año M.DC.XXXII.

deference and a secure pride in the dedicatory preface, in which Cardoso does not hesitate to underscore the precocity of his achievements at the University of Valladolid, and offers to his patron "in a little work, great goodwill."[10]

Cardoso's scientific theories concerning volcanic phenomena need not, in themselves, detain us at this point. For the moment it is more important to remark that the theme which he treated was one which, of necessity, he could not have observed at first hand. That he chose to write about it is characteristic not only of Cardoso, but of the age in which he worked, and was a result of the education he had received. Direct observation was not yet of the essence; rather, erudition in the scientific authorities of the past, and evaluation and criticism of various opinions. The discourse necessarily moves on the theoretical rather than the experimental plane.

Once we accept these assumptions, we find that the work is written concisely, lucidly, and with a great deal of charm. In a time when the science of vulcanology had not yet been born, there is at least

---

de Castilla.| Por el Doctor Fernando Cardoso.| Con licencia. En Madrid.| Por Francisco Martinez.| Año M.DC.XXXII. 33 fols (numbered recto, 2–17) + Censura (June 21, 1632) and Licencia (June 23, 1632). The reader is asked to note that in this, as well as in all future first references to Cardoso's printed works, the diagonal slashes indicate the spacing of the lines as they appear on the title page.

[10] The full text of the dedication reads: "Los incendios del Vesuvio (Excelentissimo Señor) que con violencia suma destruyeron lo mas ameno de Campania, han sido ruina memorable a los siglos passados, i funesta tragedia a la posteridad. Sus secretos oculta la ignorancia, i atiende la admiracion, i tantos prodigios incitan justamente al conocimiento de sus causas, pues desvelado el gran Plinio en su noticia le costo la curiosidad la vida. Al temeroso Volcā que abrio el año passado de 1631 acompañaron varios temblores, vientos, pluvias, nieve, arco, i otras impressiones del aire, que debe cōtemplar el Filosofo, como lo hizo felizmente Calistenes discipulo de Aristoteles, i tambien Maestro de Alexandro, sobre el terremoto de Acaya: i aviendome conocido de veinte i un años Valledolid Catedratico de Filosofia en su Universidad, i de veinte i tres pretendiente à sus mayores Catedras de Medicina, me parecio digna empresa discurrir en esta materia tan propria, i ofrecer à V. Excelencia en obra pequeña voluntad grande, siendo en mi obligacion lo que en otros cuidado. Divierta à V. Excelencia este breve Discurso, entre tanto que ofrezco assumptos mayores. Dios guarde à V. Excelencia muchos años.—El Dᵒʳ Fernando Cardoso."

Title page of Cardoso's treatise on the eruption of Mount Vesuvius (Madrid, 1632)

Biblioteca Nacional, Madrid

an earnest effort to discover the natural causes of volcanic phenomena. The book is divided into seven short chapters, dealing with the following subjects: 1. A physical description of Vesuvius, its vegetation prior to the eruption, and its surroundings. 2. A survey of past eruptions, of which Cardoso counts eight before 1631. Rejecting the notion that the first eruption was the famous one in which Pliny the Elder perished, he places it in the time of Abraham, "in the year 1857 of the Creation." 3. A description of the eruption of 1631, obviously derived from some of the written reports which had come from Naples to Madrid. 4. The cause of volcanoes. 5. Causes of earthquakes. 6. Causes of winds. 7. Causes of the accompanying noises, and of the rainbow.

Among a number of interesting features of the work, several deserve particular mention.

Cardoso's attitude to his learned authorities is, on the whole, reverential. Most of his citations are from ancient Greek and Roman writers, with a few references to the Church Fathers. Of the moderns he singles out for particular approval Lorenzo Ramírez de Prado's commentary on Martial, and, perhaps significantly, Stephen de Castro's work on meteors.[11] Other than that, with but one exception, he does not cite his own contemporaries by name. Yet he betrays a definite desire to take an independent and critical stand toward the ancients themselves. "Freely did Aristotle philosophize, and freely do his disciples philosophize!"[12] Cardoso takes Aristotle to task on a number of points, but one can detect a feeling of trepidation when he does so. We hear almost a sigh of relief when he states: "Having argued with the common master, Aristotle, the battle with our contemporaries will be less difficult. . . ."[13] There is, on the other hand, a decided attraction to "the divine Plato," the *Timaeus* being quoted more frequently than any other work.[14] But always there is a marked reluctance to depart from Aristotle

---

[11] *Discurso*, fols. 3r, 15r. In the latter he has in mind Estêvão Rodrigues de Castro (1559–1627), *De meteoris microcosmi libri quator*, published in Florence in 1621. De Castro, born a New Christian in Lisbon, was later professor of medicine at the University of Pisa. See, on him, Friedenwald, *Jews in Medicine*, II, 453–55.

[12] *Discurso*, fol. 15v.   [13] *Ibid.*, fol. 12v.   [14] *Ibid.*, fols. 9r, 10r, 13v, 16r.

decisively. The imprint of the Valladolid curriculum is evident throughout.

The same hesitation is to be remarked in two other areas: astrology, and the relation between natural and supernatural causes.

Cardoso notes that the astrologers (along with Macrobius, Seneca, Pythagoras, Democritus, and Avicenna) believe that by a certain conjunction of heavenly bodies there can take place "naturally" a universal deluge, conflagration, or earthquake. Cardoso will have none of this, and he goes to some lengths to refute it. He observes that the astrologers "lightly attribute more power to the sky than that which its Creator infused into it at the beginning. . . ." They further presume to know that of which prophets themselves are ignorant. "Astrology always usurps more license than its originators granted to it and, if left unreprimanded, it precipitates itself into the greatest absurdities."[15] In another section Cardoso attacks the astrological explanation of the origin of winds, and states emphatically that "in this case it is not necessary to have recourse to the stars," since a more natural and simple explanation is at hand.[16] In essence, however, Cardoso's verdict on astrology remains qualified. "The constellations do not have power over all the earth, only upon part of it."[17] It becomes clear that the abuse, not the use, of astrological explanations is the reason for his irritation.

For if Cardoso objects to the astrologers' postulate of a potential universal destruction, it is not merely because logic negates their arguments, and certainly not because such a phenomenon is itself impossible. Indeed, such destruction could take place, but then it would be due neither to the constellations nor to a terrestrial causality. "It is an established matter in true philosophy that, just as there can be no universal fire or flood of water produced by natural causes, in the same fashion there can be no general earthquake, *unless it be miraculous*."[18] Though the bulk of Cardoso's treatise constitutes a search for natural explanations, the reality of divine intervention in the natural order is accepted as a matter of course.

---

[15] *Ibid.*, fol. 10v. For his criticism of astrology in later years, see *infra*, ch. VI.
[16] *Ibid.*, fol. 15v.　　[17] *Ibid.*, fol. 10v.　　[18] *Ibid.*, fol. 13v. (Italics mine.)

Madrid: Debuts and Collisions

God has often used destruction through upheavals in nature as a means to instill awe in man, to humble human pride, or to punish sin. Scriptural examples are given, from Sodom to the death of Aaron's sons. "Desiring to plant terror in the hearts of Israel, God presented Himself majestically amid thunder and lightning so that they might revere as terrifier Him whom they deprecated as lover."[19] The eruptions of Vesuvius itself are regarded by many authors as heralding various calamities. "And notwithstanding that this effect is natural, and proceeds from natural causes, rare prodigies of nature always carry with them great secrets, which Divine Wisdom has reserved unto itself. . . ."[20]

It remains for us to note one other element in the *Discurso* which gives some insight into Cardoso's theological and philosophical views at this time. At several points in the work Cardoso digresses to focus upon Pliny the Elder as a special target of attack. The latter's presence in a treatise on Vesuvius is, of course, quite natural, since he perished in an eruption. But Cardoso uses the opportunity to assail that unfortunate Roman with biting irony. What so arouses his ire is Pliny's well-known rejection of the afterlife, and especially his denial of the immortality of the human soul.[21] After briefly relating the story of Pliny's death, he writes: "He who in life was an impugner of immortality saw himself in death a witness to his own dung; eternalized by his evil [is] he who in his ignorance imagined himself perishable. . . ."[22] Shortly afterward Cardoso inserts a poetic "Epitaph" for Pliny which, he says, he had composed on another occasion.[23] Referring to Pliny's curiosity at the volcano, it concludes: "More attentive to his pen than to his doom/ he contemplated the secrets of nature/ and in so much absorption forgot

---

[19] *Ibid.*, fol. 11r.   [20] *Ibid.*

[21] Cardoso was evidently referring to such attacks of Pliny against the afterlife as that in which he argues that, had there been infernal regions, zealous miners would already have reached them with their tunnels (*Historia naturalis*, II.63.158). or his passionate declaration (*ibid.*, VII.55.190), "Unhappy one, what folly is thine that thou renewest life! Where will creatures ever find rest if souls in heaven, if shades in the infernal regions still have feeling?"

[22] *Discurso*, fol. 5r-v.   [23] *Ibid.*, fol. 5v.

the risk./ Once dead, from another world he saw his error/ for though he denied the immortal souls/ his death devised eternal life for him."

Thus, in his first book Cardoso had already touched upon a variety of themes which would prove of abiding concern to him: questions of natural science, the authority of Aristotle, the limits of astrology, the problem of causality, and, most interesting in a young man of twenty-eight, the immortality of the soul. We have every reason to suppose that the *Discurso* pleased not only the patron but also the learned public to which it was addressed. It must have marked for Cardoso a significant step forward. As his star began to rise, Madrid seems indeed to have begun to fulfill all the high expectations which he must have carried with him from Valladolid.

But merely to trace the upward curve of Cardoso's career in the capital would display to us only one facet of his experience. To the young physician and author life may have appeared suffused with the springtime of hope. To the New Christian, however, all was by no means joy and light. On the contrary, the same Madrid offered to his view an uglier and indeed tragic aspect. No sooner had Cardoso completed his study of Vesuvius than there occurred, perilously close to him, an eruption of a very different kind, with serious implications for his own existence.

TERROR IN THE CALLE DE LAS INFANTAS

On June 20, 1632, a day before Cardoso's *Discurso* received the censor's approval for publication, Madrid began to stir with intensive preparations for one of the greatest *autos de fe* ever to be held in the city.[24]

On that day, in accordance with established procedure, public notices were posted which announced that the *auto* would be held two weeks later. The standard of the Inquisition was carried through

---

[24] The details which follow are all taken from the anonymous *Relación del auto de la fé que se celebró en Madrid Domingo a quatro de Julio de MDCXXXII*, n.p. (Madrid?), 1632(?). For other contemporary reports see *infra*, n. 61.

the streets, and a proclamation was read to the populace. In the following days the Plaza Mayor resounded with the noise of hammers and saws as workmen constructed the necessary platforms and scaffolding. Care was taken to place the seats for the king and queen in those balconies which would afford them both shade and unobstructed vision. Others were busy preparing apartments in the houses around the square to provide Their Majesties and the royal entourage with opportunities for eating and refreshment. Meanwhile the prisoners were secretly transferred in one night from Toledo, where they had been held until now, to the new prisons of the Inquisition in Madrid. The work in the Plaza Mayor was completed with a final touch when awnings were stretched over the balconies and platforms reserved for royalty and nobility, "for the sun at that time was great, and vast the concourse of people which would be present on this occasion."[25]

On Saturday, July 3d, at 5:00 P.M., the Procession of the Green Cross emerged from the Colegio de Doña Maria de Arago. It was preceded by the standard of the Holy Office, displaying the arms of the Inquisition ("Misericordia et Justitia") on one side, and the arms of the king on the other, carried aloft by Cardoso's patron Don Alonso Enríquez de Cabrera, who was a familiar of the Inquisition. Next came the banners of the *Cruz Blanca* and the *Cruz Verde*. The procession wound its way to the royal palace and thence to the Plaza Mayor, where the *Cruz Verde* was placed at a specially constructed altar, and a guard stationed around it for the night.

Before dawn on July 4, the day of the *auto*, masses began to be celebrated at the altar, with a large crowd of people already in attendance. The various platforms began to be decorated with damasks of various colors, and when dawn broke another mass was sung by the Dominicans. The Spanish and German guard corps arrived to maintain order, and the Company of Archers to protect the king. By now the great square was almost filled. The councils of Castile, Aragón, Italy, Portugal, Flanders, and the Indies were seated. At 7:00 A.M. Their Majesties and the Infante Don Carlos left the palace in a coach, together with Olivares and other grandees,

---

[25] *Relación*, fol. 18 f.

their wives, and attendants. Entering the Plaza Mayor through the houses of the Count of Barajas, they too took their places. Meanwhile the procession of the accused had left the prisons of the Inquisition. As they made their way toward the square, along the route "there was such a number of people gathered for the occasion at the windows, doors, roofs, and scaffolds, that the imagination could not encompass it. . . ."[26]

The prisoners were finally marched into the Plaza Mayor, followed by the officials and dignitaries of the Holy Office and of the city of Madrid. The very last to enter was Cardinal Antonio Zapata, Inquisitor-General of the kingdoms of Spain. Ascending to the royal balcony he administered to Philip the oath that he would continue to defend the Faith and give all possible support to the Holy Office. With this ceremony the *auto*, which was to last until evening, was officially begun. A sermon was preached by Fray Antonio de Sotomayor, at this time confessor to the king, but himself soon to become the Grand Inquisitor. After the judges were sworn in, the sentences began to be read. As they stepped forward in turn, each of the prisoners held a yellow candle and wore the peaked paper hat (the *coroza*) on his head. Those who were to be relaxed for burning held a green cross in their hands. In all, 40 prisoners appeared in person. Twenty-four received penances for crimes other than Judaizing,[27] while nine were penanced for it. But of the seven who were sentenced to be burned at the stake, the proportion was reversed. Six of them were condemned Judaizers, and only one was not: a Genoese friar who had been convicted of heresy and sacrilege.[28] Finally, four Judaizers (two of them already dead, and the others having fled the country) were sentenced to be burned in effigy.

---

[26] *Ibid.*, fol. 32.

[27] Twelve for magic, witchcraft, pacts with demons, etc.; five for blasphemy; four for bigamy; two imposters, including one who had pretended to be an inquisitorial official.

[28] Fray Domingo Ramairón, arrested seven years earlier. "Sus errores fueron grandes, y en particular en los tocante al Santissimo Sacramento, no creyendo en las palabres de la consagración" (*Relación*, fol. 70).

Madrid: Debuts and Collisions

The core around which this great *auto* had been assembled was the ramified case of a group of Judaizers convicted of ritually beating an image of the Savior. Since the scandal had rocked Madrid, the figure had come to be known as *El Cristo de la Paciencia* —"The Patient Christ."

The broad facts of which the Madrid public was aware can be briefly stated. About a year and a half earlier, sometime before September, 1630,[29] a group of Portuguese New Christians residing in Madrid, both men and women, were arrested by order of the Inquisition and imprisoned in the dungeons of Toledo. It was alleged that they were all Judaizers, and that each week they would gather in the house of one Miguel Rodríguez and flagellate an image of Christ Crucified. Miraculously, the figure bled and wept on several occasions, asking his tormentors why they were mistreating him, but they callously ignored his pleas. In the months following their arrest most of the conspirators confessed their crimes and implicated others. All stood now in the Plaza Mayor, before an immense multitude, to hear the punishment for their heinous affront to God.

The penances meted out to those allowed to be reconciled to the Church were as follows:[30]

Sentenced to abjure *de vehementi*, to wear the *sambenito*, and to life imprisonment without any possibility of appeal, were: Luis de Acosta, native of Villaflor, forty-five years old; Francisco de Andrada, native of Alcobaz, twenty-eight years old; Guiomar de Vega, native of Viseu; Violante Núñez Méndez, "Portuguese," twenty-eight years old; Beatriz Enríquez, daughter of Miguel Rodríguez, sixteen years old. In addition, the twelve-year-old Catalina Méndez, born in Lisbon, was sentenced to wear the *sambenito* and to six months' imprisonment, after which she was to be placed in the house of some family who would instruct her in the Catholic Faith. On Simón Luis, a native of Gradis, thirty-nine years old, were imposed

---

[29] The date is revealed by the archival documents described *infra*, n. 36.

[30] *Relación*, fols. 57–64. In the list which follows the author has omitted one name, that of Victoria Méndez. Her dossier is extant in the inquisitorial archives (see *infra*, n. 36).

---

the *sambenito*, two hundred lashes, six years in the galleys, and then imprisonment for life. Elena Núñez, born in the same town, was to be similarly imprisoned after receiving one hundred lashes. And another twelve-year-old girl, Ana Rodríguez, the sister of Beatriz Enríquez, was to wear the *sambenito* and be imprisoned for one year.

Those for whose salvation the Inquisition had given up all hope and consequently "relaxed" to the state for execution were:

Beatriz Núñez, of whom we are told that "four friars of the orders of St. Francis and the Capuchins helped to support her, for being of the age of seventy years, her forces were few";[31] Fernan Báez, native of Torre de Moncorvo, sixty-six years old; Isabel Núñez Álvarez, wife of Miguel Rodríguez, native of Viseu, forty-five years old, of whom we are informed that "she showed signs of great repentance";[32] Leonor Rodríguez, wife of Fernan Báez, fifty-five years old; Miguel Rodríguez, the alleged leader of the group, native of Ferreirin, seventy years old; and Jorge Quaresma, native of Fermosilla, thirty-five years old.[33]

These six, together with the condemned Italian friar, were immediately turned over to the secular authorities. Riding on "humble beasts" they were led out through the Calle de los Boteros, flanked by soldiers on horseback to guard them from the angry crowd. The *auto* itself continued with the abjurations *de levi* of the bigamists, sorcerers, and imposters, and *de vehementi* of the remaining Judaizers. The hours dragged on. Those to be reconciled were submitted to the routine questioning of Cardinal Zapata: "Dost thou believe that God is One in essence and Three in person. . .?" "Yes, I believe. . . ." The Exorcism was intoned ("Immunde Spiritus . . ."). The Royal Choir chanted the psalm "Miserere mei Dominus." In a crescendo of prayer, including that for the turning of men from heretical error and depraved apostasy, "that is, from the Jewish

---

[31] *Ibid.*, fol. 65 f.   [32] *Ibid.*, fol. 66 f.

[33] Quaresma is the only one among those relaxed who does not seem to have been involved in the *Cristo de la Paciencia*, though he was condemned for Judaizing. He is described as *letrado*, and we are told: "assistieronle quatro Frailes Franciscos, y en su conversion passaron muchos lances, queriendo defender su opinion" (*Relación*, fol. 68).

superstition, the Mohammedan sect, and the Lutheran hersey," the *auto* came to an end at 6:00 P.M. The Plaza Mayor was emptied, the penanced were returned to their cells, and the Dominicans took the *Cruz Verde* to the Monastery of St. Thomas.

Later in the evening the condemned were brought to the *brasero*, the place of execution which had been rebuilt for the occasion outside the Puerta de Alcalá. The seven men and women were tied to stakes and exhorted by monks to confess. However,

although close to the fire, the hardness of their hearts was such that even at this point some of them did not wish to confess their crime. May God have mercy on their souls.

The confusion and crowd on this day were great throughout, and in the field they were even greater, the fire was huge, completing a punishment so well deserved precisely at 11:00 P.M. when the element disintegrated them into ashes, so that no memory even shall remain of such evil people. . . .[34]

But for some the memory did remain. Cardoso, for one, would remember the event to the very end of his days. We can easily imagine that any Portuguese New Christian living in Madrid at the time must have been terrified, wondering if the *auto* did not presage a general persecution. Moreover, the house of Miguel Rodríguez, as well as those of some of the other accused, stood in the Calle de las Infantas. We have already pointed out that this was the street in which Cardoso was living in 1634, and it is reasonable to assume that he had resided there earlier as well. Though he did not necessarily have personal contact with any of the group, for as we shall see they belonged to a vastly inferior social level, and although he himself was certainly never implicated in the matter, like other New Christians in the city he must have followed it with the keenest interest. We do not know if he was among the huge crowd in the Plaza Mayor on the day of the *auto*, or if he witnessed the burning. But the depth of his feeling is indicated above all by one salient fact. All of Cardoso's later works are characterized by a reticence to reveal autobiographical details

---

[34] *Ibid.*, fols. 94 f. The floggings were administered the next day.

which amounts to almost total silence. This is especially true of the two last great works which he composed when he was living as a Jew in Italy, and in which he rarely alludes to his prior life in Spain. We may be sure that on those few occasions when Cardoso does tell some personal anecdote, or when he refers to events of which he had personal knowledge, it points to an experience which was so intense that he cannot contain himself, but must speak of it. One such passage, inserted into a book he published fully forty-seven years later, constitutes Cardoso's own account of the events we have just described:

But so that one may see of how much the implacable hatred against a humble nation is capable, and how uncertain are the proofs which are derived from personal confession through tortures, let us conclude these unhappy events with that which occurred in Madrid in the year one thousand six hundred and thirty-two.

There came from Portugal to the Court some Portuguese Jews with their wives and little children. These were sent to school and, while conversing with the other children, the latter gave them dainties and delicacies and began to ask them if they were Jews, and whether at home their parents mistreated or whipped a Christ. At first they denied it. But, persuaded by the sweets which the others gave them, and by the teacher, who had little affection for this nation, and possessed more feigned than perfect piety, without realizing what they were saying they came to admit that which was imputed to them. And although these were minors of five or six years of age, when testimonies are null and void, for those influenced and prompted statements they arrested the parents who were ill in bed with tertiary fever brought on by the summer heat and the hardships of the journey, and submitted them to torture, old, poor, and infirm, exhorting them to confess and thereby be dealt with mercifully. Unable to endure the pain, they confessed that of which they were accused. Six or seven persons were burned, the sentences first being read to them in a public *auto*, at which it was declared that they flagellated a Christ, that they afterward burned it, and that between the lashes which they gave it, it said to them: "Why do you mistreat me?"

However, the physician who used to treat them, and the surgeon who bled them, saw clearly that in their house they had no figure or image whatsoever, of wood, metal, or paper.

The house was duly destroyed, and on its site was put as a memorial an infamous marker in the Calle de las Infantas, which referred to the

Madrid: Debuts and Collisions

episode of a Christ having been whipped and burned. But afterwards, since it seemed unbecoming, they took it away, and established on the site a Convent of Capuchin Friars. Such is the power of false testimonies and rigorous tortures that there are many who crave a single death, rather than to suffer interminable pains.[35]

The original dossiers of eight of the accused in the case of the *Cristo de la Paciencia* have been preserved in the inquisitorial archives.[36] Although Cardoso's account cannot be proved in every detail, there is enough information among these voluminous documents to sustain it and give it a large measure of credibility.

In reality we possess the documents of seven prisoners, since one dossier is that of a fugitive, Beatriz Rodríguez, who escaped before she could be apprehended.

We find, to begin with, that two of these seven persons, Fernan Báez and Victoria Méndez, were indeed tortured severely. Báez had voluntarily admitted to his interrogators that he practiced Jewish rites such as keeping the Sabbath, abstaining from pork, observing the Fast of Esther, etc. But even after his torture he denied the main charge of flagellating the Christ, and he continued to do so to the very end.[37] Victoria Méndez, a young woman of twenty-nine

---

[35] *Las excelencias de los Hebreos* (Amsterdam, 1679), pp. 405–6.

[36] *Archivo Histórico Nacional (Madrid): Inquisición de Toledo,* Leg. 140, no. 4: "Cristo de la Paciencia." (See also *Catálogo de la Inq. de Tol.,* pp. 171–72). The dossiers are found in the following order:

(1) Beatriz Enríquez (numbered recto, 1–105).
(2) Fernan Báez (numbered recto, 1–136).
(3) Victoria Méndez (numbered recto, 1–130).
(4) Violante Méndez (numbered recto, 1–137).
(5) Isabel Núñez Álvarez (no pagination; 157 fols.).
(6) Elena Núñez (no pagination; 105 fols.).
(7) Beatriz Rodríguez (no pagination; 61 fols.).
(8) Miguel Rodríguez (numbered recto, 1–163).

Caro Baroja has already noted that "la tesis de Cardoso tiene muchos visos de verosimilitud" (*Judíos,* II, 450). I am preparing a study of the entire case based on all the inquisitorial documents.

[37] AHN, *Inq. de Toledo,* Leg. 140, no. 4 (Dossier of Fernan Báez). His torture: fols. 97r–99v; his continued denial of the flagellation: fols. 120r–v; the sentence: fols. 123v–125r.

and mother of five children, denied at first that she was even a Judaizer, but then she acknowledged that she had observed the "Law of Moses" in Portugal.[38] Put to the torture, she still declared that she had no further information to offer. Her replies to her tormentors provide one of the most moving documents in the entire case.[39] She was extremely ill afterwards, and was visited in her cell by the Inquisitor Don Christóbal de Ybarra y Mendoza, but still she said that she had nothing to add. Even when the testimonies against her were read for the fifth time, she denied whipping the image. Only after a prolonged period of physical and mental agony, and when the inquisitorial counsel, Dr. Miguel Sánchez, advised her to confess or face dire consequences, did she finally agree to do so.[40]

Violante Méndez and Isabel Núñez Álvarez confessed only in the torture chamber, just before the torment was to begin.[41] The latter's husband, Miguel Rodríguez, confessed at his second hearing that he had Judaized since the age of fourteen, but denied the flagellation. Eight months later he admitted that as well. However, he still rejected certain details—the number of flagellations, passing the image through the fire, whipping it also in another house, that the image had spoken, etc. He was brought to the torture chamber on March 6, 1632, but he was not tortured. The physician in attendance advised that it would certainly kill him, and the inquisitors obviously wanted him alive for the impending *auto*.[42]

The statement by Cardoso that the group was poor, and the

---

[38] AHN, *Inq. de Toledo*, Leg. 140, no. 4, (Dossier of Victoria Méndez), fols. 62r ff.

[39] Her torture is recorded in the most vivid detail, *ibid.*, fols. 94v-99v.

[40] Her illness: *ibid.*, fol. 99v; continued denial of the charge: fol. 102r; Dr. Sánchez' advice, and her confession: fols. 110r ff.

[41] AHN, *Inq. de Toledo*, Leg. 140, no. 4, dossiers of Violante Méndez and Isabel Núñez Álvarez.

[42] AHN, *Inq. de Toledo*, Leg. 140 no. 4 (Dossier of Miguel Rodríguez). His initial confession to Judaizing: fols. 71r ff.; denial of the flagellation: fol. 81v. He confessed to this charge as well on August 13, 1631. His denial of details: fols. 111r ff.; the scene in the torture chamber: fols. 123r ff.

It is to be noted that Ferreirin, Rodríguez' birthplace, is near Trancoso.

general impression that these people were on a low social plane, can also be substantiated. The documents show that almost all of them were illiterate.[43] As for occupations, Miguel Rodríguez was, characteristically, a peddler.

But at the very heart of Cardoso's account is the story of how the entire affair began when the children babbled in school about their parents. True, we do not find this particular detail in the documents. But then, the dossiers themselves commence, in each instance, with the accused already in prison. The circumstances which led to the initial arrests are, except for the statement of the charge itself, glossed over in silence. Nevertheless, the documents do prove emphatically that some children certainly had a major rôle in bringing about the tragic fate of their own parents, and of the other adults as well.

Two such children were the young son and daughter of Miguel Rodríguez and Isabel Núñez Álvarez. The following facts are a summary of the information contained in the relevant documents.

On September 14, 1630, a certain Augustín de Vergara came before the Inquisitor Don Juan Dionisio Portocarrero in Madrid, to submit a voluntary deposition.[44] He related that during that very morning a Negro woman had appeared at his house, leading by the hand a little Portuguese boy whom he guessed to be about ten years old, and asked him if he had any use for the child, who was abandoned because his parents were imprisoned by the Inquisition. When De Vergara asked the boy why his parents had been arrested, the latter said it was because they had whipped a Christ in their apartment. Among other details, he said that they would also pass the image through a fire and then whip it again. These things were done in the presence of a large group of Portuguese men and women, some of whose names he recalled.[45] De Vergara thought the matter

---

[43] E.g., Dossier of Fernan Báez, fol. 46r: "Dixo que no sabe leer ni escribir ni a estudiado ninguna facultad, solo sabe acer una mala firma, que aun el no la sabe leer, y que no tiene libros prohibidos."

[44] Dossier of Miguel Rodríguez, fols. 25r-26r.

[45] He named Carlos López, Diego Feros, and Julian Díaz, none of whom appeared in the *auto* of 1632.

worthy of investigation, and had therefore brought the child to the Holy Office. .

The Inquisitor now personally interrogated the boy,[46] who seemed to him also to be aged nine or ten. Because he was so young, no oath was administered to him.

The boy said his name was Andrés Núñez, and that he was a son of Miguel Rodríguez "who sells Portuguese thread in the streets," and of Isabel Núñez, and that they lived in the Calle de las Infantas. (On another occasion the father himself told the inquisitors that Andrés was seven years old).[47] He was aware that his parents and siblings had been arrested about a week before, and were imprisoned in Toledo. He himself had remained in a neighbor's house, but had slept the night before in a field, lying in a wagon and covered with a sack. He also volunteered the information that near the family home there had lived a certain Doña Juana who had a little boy called Manuelillo. That woman had been killed.

Asked once more to state the reason for his parents' arrest, he answered that he had heard it was because they did not eat pork, but in reality it was because they tied a Christ with a rope and whipped him with thorns. Then his father had taken the figure by the feet, while his mother held its head, and they passed it through a fire. During these acts they did not allow him to enter the kitchen, but he was able to observe them from outside through an opening. He added that his parents did not go to mass. In the days after

----

[46] Dossier of Miguel Rodríguez, fols. 26r-28r.

[47] The children of Miguel Rodríguez and Isabel Nuñez Álvarez were enumerated by him at his first interrogation (fol. 68r) as follows:

1. Simón Rodríguez, 22 years old, "que no tiene off., q. esta casado con una moça de ferreir. y no la save el nombre. (On fol. 79r we learn that he lived in Madrid.)

2. Andrés, "de hedad de siete años."

3. Leonor Núñez, 20 years old, married to Manuel Núñez. She had been imprisoned by the Inquisition of Coimbra. (Documents from her case were sent by the Portuguese inquisitors to Toledo, and are placed in the dossier of her mother, Isabel Núñez Álvarez).

4. Beatriz Enríquez, 15 or 16 years old.

5. Ana (Rodríguez), 12 or 13 years old.

their arrest he had been in the house of Carlos López, one of those who was present at the flagellations. As for the woman who had been killed, she was a relative. López had warned him not to visit her house or speak of her to anyone.

"Andresillo," as he was sometimes called, was now placed temporarily in the house of Pedro de Salazar, an inquisitorial functionary. There he encountered Manuelillo, who had been detained for examination regarding the murder of his mother, Doña Juana de Silva. In the course of the conversation it was stated that Andresillo's brothers and sisters had avoided arrest by fleeing with the aid of an uncle.[48] An official report on the death of Juana de Silva brought the news that apparently she had been assassinated because she informed to the Inquisition.[49]

On September 8 Portocarrero took Andresillo to his parents' home in the Calle de las Infantas.[50] The plan and arrangement of the various apartments was noted, and the inquisitor satisfied himself that the boy could have peered into the kitchen while standing in the garden of the patio. Nearby was a rosebush which, according to the boy, had furnished the thorns for the flagellations. On September 10 Portocarrero informed the Inquisition of Toledo of his visit to the house, and forwarded Andresillo's testimony. The Toledan inquisitors were requested to search the confiscated property of Miguel Rodríguez and his wife, to see if there were an image of Christ hidden in some chest. No such object was ever found. On September 13 one Joseph de Cervantes, a weaver, presented himself before the inquisitorial commissioner in Madrid, Dr. Juan de la Peña. It seems that the Negro woman had first

---

[48] This information proved later to be incorrect. Of Andresillo's siblings only his brother Simón Rodríguez escaped arrest. His sister Beatriz Enríquez was arrested in August of 1631, and his other sister Ana Rodríguez at about the same time. Only Beatriz Rodríguez who, despite her name, was the daughter of Fernan Báez, succeeded in fleeing, along with Catalina de Acosta. As we have seen, they were later burned in effigy at the *auto*.

[49] Dossier of Miguel Rodríguez, fol. 29r.

[50] *Ibid.*, fols. 29v-30v. (There is a plan of the house and its garden patio on fol. 31.)

brought Andresillo to him before she had gone to Augustín de Vergara. In general he duplicated De Vergara's information, as did his wife, Juana de Moya.[51]

A most important development took place on September 17, when Andresillo was again brought to his parents' home, but this time in the company of Don Pedro Pacheco, a member of the Council of the Inquisition.[52] Now, under much closer questioning, he elaborated more details and became enmeshed in a host of contradictions and implausibilities. When asked to describe the size, color, and material of the image which had been whipped, he could only point to Pacheco and say that the Christ was as large as he, was dressed in black like him, and that he didn't know if it was made of wood or something else. "And soon the said Sr. Don Pedro Pacheco saw and examined the place where the said Andrés had declared they suspended the Christ . . . and there was not enough room there to hold a Christ of the size he had described." Pacheco also began to find other flaws in his testimony, and Andresillo became flustered. The questioning ceased, and the boy was returned to his cell.

In the following months there seems to have been much hesitation as to whether Andresillo's testimony was of any value and could be used. A note written in Toledo as late as May 23, 1631, remarks that, aside from being a child, he is also "of little capacity, and even variable in his depositions."[53]

By June 28, 1631, these qualms had been overcome. Since, in the normal procedure of the Inquisition, the accused was never confronted personally with the witness and was not even told his name, the problem was not serious. Andresillo was brought before the inquisitors in Madrid for the formal ratification of his testimonies.[54] He was told they would be used against his parents, and he confirmed them. Before the signatures of the adults present were affixed, he added spontaneously that the thorns used in whipping the Christ had been brought from Portugal, or so he had been advised to say, but that he had really seen them gathered near the house. Suddenly he produced a further refinement. His parents, he

---

[51] *Ibid.*, fols. 34r-35v.   [52] *Ibid.*, fols. 36r-39r.   [53] *Ibid.*, fol. 43r.
[54] *Ibid.*, fols. 45r-46v.

Madrid: Debuts and Collisions

said, would first attach pins to the thorns. During the flagellation the Christ spoke and asked why they were whipping him, and they replied that, although it sorrowed and vexed him, they had to do so, "and that is the truth of which he knows."

Some months later, on September 5, 1631, Andresillo's sister, Ana Rodríguez, was brought from Madrid and placed in the inquisitorial prison of Toledo. The girl was twelve years old. The dossier of her own trial is not extant, but summaries of her testimony were placed in the dossier of her father.[55] It is clear that at the beginning she knew nothing of the charge of whipping an image. On September 17 she admitted, "to unburden her conscience," that some years ago she had been initiated into the "Law of Moses" by the widow Beatriz Núñez. Then, on September 24, presumably after she became acquainted with the central charge, she asked for a hearing and confessed that her parents had whipped a Christ three or four times. She also implicated her sister Beatriz Enríquez, as well as Fernan Báez and his wife Leonor Rodríguez. But she denied that she had herself participated in the flagellation, as had been alleged in one of the testimonies against her. Once, when the image was whipped in her sister's bedroom, the Christ did speak. On May 15 she admitted her father had twice ordered her and her sister to hold the Christ while he and the others beat it. Since she was only an ignorant and obedient child, she had complied. She was now deeply sorry, and pleaded for mercy. We must understand that the surviving documents only summarize her admissions, but say nothing of the questions and promptings to which she was subjected in between. Obviously the terrified girl was by now more than willing to make any confession required of her. We have already noted that her sentence at the *auto* was comparatively light.

A full study of the case of *El Cristo de la Paciencia* would reveal an extremely tangled web of testimonies,[56] since most of the accused

---

[55] *Ibid.*, fols. 51r-52v.

[56] Among other charges, it was alleged that some members of the group had flagellated an image not only in Madrid, but also in Gradis, Portugal (Dossier of Victoria Méndez, fols. 110r ff.). However, there is no mention of this charge in the Portuguese inquisitorial documents concerning Leonor Nuñez (*supra*, n. 47).

118

were already imprisoned in August and September of 1630. We have focused only on the children, since they are the objects of our immediate concern.

For central to a proper understanding of the case is the fact that it unfolded in two consecutive but distinct stages, and we must distinguish between them. The group was first arrested on ordinary charges of Judaizing and, had no other factor intervened, the prosecution would have proceeded along normal lines. Not until the advent of Andresillo was the motif of the scourged Christ introduced, soon to completely overshadow all other aspects. On a purely theoretical plane one would be hard put to make a definitive judgement about this accusation one way or the other. Bizarre though it might appear, there is nothing intrinsically impossible in the notion that a group of mostly illiterate Marranos of the lowest classes might, out of crude superstition, express their hatred of Christianity through such a ritual. The inquisitorial documents make it clear, however, that this stage of the case revolved entirely around the testimony of Andresillo, and we find indeed that his denunciations were used in interrogating every one of the other prisoners.[57] This, despite his self-contradictions and blatant inventions; despite the fact that details of his statements are inconsistent with others given by his sister; despite his tender age and the recognition, even by the inquisitors, that his intelligence was low. The testimony of a child is not to be discredited merely because of age, for even children do tell the truth. But when the child is an Andresillo, and when his allegations are presented and developed in the manner we have traced, we must reject them.

In the light of all we have seen, it would thus be difficult to deny the basic credibility of Cardoso's account. Miguel Rodríguez, his wife, and the others may well have Judaized. Cardoso himself does not take issue with this. But the sensational charge of flagellating the Christ was surely false. Some of the inquisitors obviously believed

---

[57] Andresillo's depositions appear in their original form prefixed to the dossier of Miguel Rodríguez. In a summarized form they are found in all the other dossiers, e.g.: Beatriz Enríquez, fol. 8r; Fernan Báez, fol. 27r-v; Victoria Méndez, fol. 36r.

Madrid: Debuts and Collisions

it; others were not really deceived. In November, 1630, for example, the Council of the Inquisition in Madrid was not at all persuaded that Andresillo's testimony had much substance.[58] As one studies the case in depth, one receives the mounting impression that the *auto* of 1632 was above all a great show of strength on the part of the Inquisition, alarmed at the recent New Christian influx from Portugal. The theme of the flagellated Christ, probably originating in the unbridled fancies of children, was seized upon as a perfect means to arouse the passions of Madrid, and transform an otherwise ordinary case of Judaizing into a shocking *cause célèbre*.

In this the inquisitors succeeded. The emotional repercussions were explosive. Two days after the *auto* the house in the Calle de las Infantas was torn down, "and even the crowd, which had no tools, tore out stones and blocks from the foundations with their bare hands."[59] On its site was later erected the Capuchin Convento de la Paciencia to which Cardoso alluded.[60] *Fiestas* in honor of Christ Crucified, some of them lasting eight consecutive days, were held late into September throughout the capital. Several printed *relaciones* appeared, giving every detail of the *auto*. Poems and books on the scandal were published even years later. And in the immediate wave of outraged feeling which enveloped Madrid, Lope de Vega applied the greatest pen in Spain to a poem of one hundred and one stanzas: "Sentiments at the Offenses Done unto Our Good Christ by the Hebrew Nation"[61] of whose verses these examples will suffice:

---

[58] This may be gathered from the following note sent to Toledo by Portocarrero on Nov. 26, 1630:

"Un muchacho llamado Andres hijo de Miguel Rodriguez y de Isabel Nuñez q. estan presos en este santo officio a hecho contra sus Padres las declaraciones q. remito a Vs. *y aun q. al conss. no le an parecido de mucha sustancia* parece se deven juntar con el proceso de sus Padres de donde resultara el credito que se les deve dar . . ." (Dossier of Miguel Rodríguez, fol. 1r. my italics).

[59] *Relación*, fol. 100.

[60] It was torn down in 1837. For a picture of the edifice see Mesonero Romanos, *El antiguo Madrid*, II, 104, and Caro Baroja, *Judíos*, II, 329.

[61] *Sentimientos a los agravios de Cristo nuestro bien por la nación Hebrea*. It was first published in Part II of Lope's *La vega del Parnasso* (Madrid, 1637), but undoubtedly

Terror in the Calle de las Infantas

What wearies you, infidel? What fatigues you?
If He is a shadow, then whom do you punish?
If He is a block of wood, whom do you whip?
If He is a man, and dead, whom do you propose to kill?
—Unless you believe it is God whom you affront?!

. . .

Obdurate nation, whom Hadrian exiled,
And who, for our ruin, coming to Spain,
So oppresses and injures today
The Christian Empire

. . .

---

circulated earlier in manuscript. I have used the text in the *Colección de las obras sueltas . . . de D. Frey Lope de Vega Carpio*, X (Madrid, 1777), 16–35.

Among other Spanish works inspired by the case of the *Cristo de la Paciencia* are the following: Juan Gómez de Mora, *Auto de la Fé celebrado en Madrid este año de MDCXXXII, al Rey Don Philippe IIII N.S.* (Madrid, 1632); a manuscript report of the *auto* by Diego de Soto y Aguilar, in B.N. Madrid, MS 6751 (Auttos generales y partticulares, zelebrados por el Santto Ofizio en distinttas Ynquisiziones de estos Reynos de España, desde los Años de 1555 Astta el año de 1721), fols. 53r-62v (see Caro, *Judíos*, II. 421, nn. 155–56; 422, n. 157); Juan Antonio de Peña, *Discurso en exaltacion de los improperios que padecio la imagen de Cristo a manos de la perfidia Iudaica. Con Relacion de la magnífica Octava, Sermones, Letras y Procession que a estos Catolicos intentos hizo en el Real Convento de las Descalças la Serenissima y Religiosissima Infanta Sor Margarita de la Cruz* (Madrid, 1632); Juan de Ayala Fajardo, *Oracion panegirica Christo desagraviado de los Oprobrios que unos Hebreos le hizieron en su Sacrosanta Imagen . . . Aviase de Recitar al Rey nuestro Señor en el Convento de la Santissima Trinidad donde se hizo esta Fiesta, estorvolo el estar enfermo su Magestad* (Madrid, 1639); Fray Matheo de Anguiano, *La nueva Jerusalén, en que la perfidia hebraica reitero con nuevos ultrages la passion de Christo, salvador del mundo, en su sacrosanta imagen del Crucifixo de la Paciencia en Madrid; y augustos y perennes desagravios de nuestros Catholicos Monarcas, D. Phelipe IV el Grande, y D. Isabel de Borbon y de sus successores en su real Convento de la Paciencia de Christo de Menores Capuchinos* (Madrid, 1709).

The *auto* of 1632 also made a profound impression on the Sephardic diaspora. Manasseh ben Israel, *Esperança de Israel* (Amsterdam, 1650). p. 109, regarded the death of Philip's brother, the Infante Don Carlos, in the same month, as divine retribution for that event.

121

Madrid: Debuts and Collisions

Like Cain, who, because he killed his brother,
Wandered and fled, abhorred,
And lived for his infamy,
So with empty thought
Wanders the Hebrew, perfidious murderer,
Who took the life of the innocent Abel.

. . .

Since the Talmud exceeds one hundred precepts,
How has its observance not wearied you?

. . .

This sweet crucified Lord
Whom you insultingly whipped in His image . . .
Is the same you still expect.

. . .

You neither understand nor interpret
Divine Scripture,
Deceived by barbarous rabbis,
With so many fabulous madnesses.

. . .

O ingrate! O madman! O blind one!
That even blood does not move you!

We shall consider Cardoso's own relations with Lope de Vega in the next chapter. But we have not yet done with the *Cristo de la Paciencia*. A treatise written, like Lope's poem, in the climate of hatred which the case left in its wake, opens to our view still another dimension of the highest significance. It casts a new light, not only on Cardoso's reaction to the *auto* of 1632, but on the essential ambivalence of his life in Madrid.

THE ALCALDE DON JUAN DE QUIÑONES

If, as we presume, Cardoso's sparse later references to events he knew in Spain are generally to be taken as a reflection of profound impressions, the passage we are about to cite is doubly important.

The Alcalde Don Juan de Quiñones

The account of the *auto*, though personal, still refrained from giving any details about his own activities at the time it occurred. The following lines, written in the same work, constitute something even more precious—a rare autobiographical anecdote:

But we must not omit a charming episode which occurred in Madrid about thirty [*sic*] years ago, more or less. There was an *alcalde* of the Court named Don Juan de Quiñones, a curiously learned man of variable erudition and a huge library, who wrote several treatises and specialized books on such topics as the gypsies, the Bell of Velilla, and Vesuvius. And, among others, he compiled one concerning the material which we are discussing, proving that Jews have a tail, and that like women they are subject to menstrual periods, and blood, as punishment for the grave sin which they committed.

Within a very short time he developed hemorrhoids in certain parts, so great and huge, and accompanied by blood and pain, that they actually seemed tail-like. In the company of a surgeon I then said to him: "Your honor must also be liable in the sin of that death [i.e., of Christ], for we see in you the same affliction, and just as you have written that the Jews have a tail and blood, you too have the same."

And so, the conversation continuing in jest, he began to laugh and said that he did not agree with this, for he has been well proved to be an *hidalgo* of La Mancha, and the discussion moved on. But he remained with the defect which he imputed to the Jews.[62]

It is now possible to reconstruct the background of this passage, itself so uncharacteristic of Cardoso's usual lofty and solemn style.

Though posterity has hardly remembered him, Dr. Juan de Quiñones de Benavente was a well-known figure in the Madrid of Cardoso's time.[63] Born in Chinchón, he had a career which consisted of a slow but steady climb through the Spanish bureaucracy. Since 1614, when Philip III had appointed him *alcalde mayor* in the Escorial, he had served in various capacities. He had been an *alcalde*

---

[62] *Las excelencias de los Hebreos*, pp. 345–46, in the chapter entitled "Cola y sangre."

[63] This is the name as it appears in Nicolás Antonio, *Bib. Hisp. Nova*, II, 764. In addition to an ample, though incomplete, list of Quiñones' publications, Antonio, like Cardoso, also makes special mention of his library.

of the court in Madrid since 1625, a position which charged him with the maintenance of law and order, the pursuit of criminals, and a host of other functions in the king's service.[64] His duties often brought him into collaboration with the Inquisition, which depended on the secular authorities for much of its police work, and for the actual sentencing and execution of those whom it "relaxed." On several occasions Quiñones had apprehended Judaizers and handed them over to the inquisitors.[65] Nor was his zeal confined to them. Once he succeeded in capturing a "great Calvinist heretic" who attempted to bring Protestant books into Spain.[66] At an *auto* held in Madrid in January, 1624, a Catalan Franciscan, Benito Ferrer, received his sentence from Quiñones.[67] In 1631, near Sepúlveda, gypsies had allegedly intercepted and robbed a mail shipment from Flanders. Quiñones went to the area and succeeded in capturing thirty-four of the group. Five men were hanged and quartered.

---

[64] The date, as well as other autobiographical information, is provided by Quiñones himself on fol. 22 of a work which summarizes his services to the Crown: *Memorial de los servicios que hizo al Rey Don Felipe III nuestro Señor, que santa gloria aya, y que ha hecho a V. magestad, que Dios guarde; El Doctor Don Iuan de Quiñones Alcalde de Casa y Corte mas antiguo, en diferentes jornadas, causas graves que ha averiguado contra delinquentes, y castigos que se les dieron. y de otras ocupaciones que ha tenido, tocantes al bien publico* (n.p., n.d; [Madrid, 1643?]). The date of publication may be ascertained from fol. 27: "Aora este año de 643. . . ."

Quiñones died sometime before March 15, 1646. See *Archivo Histórico Nacional, Consejo de Castilla, Sala de Castilla, Sala de Alcaldes de Casa y Corte: Catálogo por materias* (Madrid, 1925). p. 756: "Valcarcel Velasquez (Francisco de), Título de Alcalde de Casa y Corte . . . en lugar de Juan de Quiñones, defunto. 15 Marzo 1646."

[65] "En la Corte, siendo Iuez Ordinario, prendi unos Iudios retajados . . . y les entregue a don Andres Pacheco, Inquisidor General de la Suprema, que entonces era" (*Memorial*, fol. 31).

[66] *Memorial*, fols. 28–30.

[67] Ferrer, expelled from two convents, became a "Lutheran and a Calvinist" and was alleged to be the son of a Jewess. One day, in a fit of madness, he destroyed a host in church during the mass. Relaxed by the Inquisition he was sentenced by Quiñones and another judge to the inevitable execution by burning. At the *auto* itself, held on January 21, 1624, Lope de Vega led the procession of inquisitorial familiars and commissioners. See on this Hugo A. Rennert and Américo Castro, *Vida de Lope de Vega* (Madrid, 1919). pp. 298 f, and Caro, *Judíos*, I, 176.

Others were flogged and sent to the galleys. The women and children were banished from the country.[68] Upon his return to Madrid Quiñones wrote a work directed to the king in which he urged that all gypsies be expelled from Spain.[69]

For, as we have already learned from Cardoso, Don Juan de Quiñones was also an author. He never wrote a sustained work, but rather treated any subject which struck his fancy, usually those which were occasioned by some immediate experience of his own. A treatise on locusts, published in 1620, was prompted by a plague in Castile which he had helped to eradicate in 1618.[70] Among his other works we find a study of some recently discovered Roman coins, which also appeared in 1620;[71] a discourse on the Bell of Velilla, which had allegedly rung again, by itself, in 1625;[72] an attack on a Frenchman who doubted that Francis I had been imprisoned in Madrid after the Battle of Pavia;[73] a treatise on the carbuncle and its virtues, after it was reported in 1634 that one had been found in Santander.[74]

We already have something of a composite picture of the man. He is a conscientious servant of the state, a bibliophile, an antiquary,

---

[68] *Memorial,* fols. 58–60.

[69] *Al Rey nuestro Señor el Doctor Don Iuan de Quiñones Alcalde de su Casa y Corte Discurso contra los Gitanos* (Madrid, 1631). He wanted them only expelled, but not killed: "No es mi intento, Señor, se les quite la vida . . ." (*Ibid.,* fol. 23r).

[70] *Tratado de las langostas* (Madrid, 1620). For the circumstances see *Memorial,* fol. 37.

[71] *Explicaciones de unas monedas de oro de Emperadores Romanos que se hallaron en el Puerto de Guadarrama* (Madrid, 1620). See *Memorial,* fols. 36 f.

[72] *Discurso de la campana de Velilla* (Madrid, 1625). See *Memorial,* fol. 38. On the popular belief in the miraculous ringing of the bells of Velilla, see José Deleito y Piñuela, *La vida religiosa española bajo el cuarto Felipe* (Madrid, 1952), pp. 196–202.

[73] *Suceso de la batalla memorable de Pavia* (Madrid, 1634). According to Nicolás Antonio he also translated from the French a *Tratado de la contrariedad de España y Francia,* and published it in 1635 under the anagram "Dr. Senonqui." This was probably the work which brought forth his own reply.

[74] *Tratado del Carbunco, donde se tratan sus virtudes, y de las otras piedras que estavan en el Racional del Sumo Sacerdote* (Madrid, 1634). See *Memorial,* fol. 38.

a dilettante of the arts. Lope de Vega devoted to him a stanza of his *Laurel de Apolo*.[75] He is an honored member of the community, a zealous patriot, a man convinced of the justness of his actions and the reward merited by his many services. His prejudices are very much those of the Spain of his time. That his country is superior to all others, that convicted heretics should be burned, are for him axioms which he would never think of questioning. "No greater offering or sacrifice [to God] can be made," he writes, "than to punish the iniquitous and perverse man."[76] Though Quiñones was not himself an inquisitor, we can ask for no better insight into the rationalizing mechanism of the inquisitorial mentality than this statement:

My purpose is not to glorify myself through the punishments which I have carried out, nor to delight myself by them . . . but only to give glory to God because crimes have been punished. For judges are called most saintly when evildoers are castigated. . . . And all that goes well is to be attributed neither to our talent nor our power, but to God alone, with much thanks to Your Majesty, because in your time, being so great a lover of justice and reverer of those who guard it, the deserved punishments have been meted out to the wicked and the delinquent.[77]

With these observations in mind, we may now approach the work which occasioned Cardoso's biting anecdote.

Quiñones did indeed compose a treatise which attempted to prove that Jewish males menstruate. Though never printed, the manuscript must have circulated widely at the time it was written.[78] The

---

[75] Lope de Vega, *Obras sueltas*, I, 21. He also mentions Quiñones in a letter to the Duque de Sessa dated Madrid, June 18–21, 1628 (*Cartas completas* [Buenos Aires, 1948]), no. 507, pp. 168 f.

[76] *Memorial*, fol. 40.   [77] *Ibid.*, fol. 43.

[78] Nicolás Antonio records it simply as: "Memorial a la Inquisición sobre un Judío que tenia menstruo. In 4." Gallardo (*Ensayo*, IV, col. 12) quoted Quiñones' own reference to this work in the Memorial (fol. 38). Caro Baroja, who was struck by Cardoso's anecdote, states: "He tenido algún interés en seguir la pista al libro sobre los judíos de don Juan de Quiñones. No lo he hallado" (*Judíos*, II, 446, n. 87).

It was my good fortune to stumble upon a copy of Quiñones' manuscript while

The Alcalde Don Juan de Quiñones

treatise, in the copy we have found, bears no formal title. It opens with a dedication to Fray Antonio de Sotomayor, confessor to the king and Inquisitor-General of Spain, and immediately relates the event which prompted its composition:

When, with majestic pomp, great solemnity, and the gravest authority, there was celebrated in this Court the *Auto de la Fe* on the fourth day of July, 1632, among other defendants who appeared in it was Francisco de Andrada[79] of whom it was said that he suffered every month the flux of blood which nature has given to women, and which is called menstruation. Some people doubted if this was certain, either because it seemed to them a rare thing, seldom seen, or because of not having read and pursued it. And so to satisfy them, and in order that they may know what has been written about this, it seemed to me proper to discuss it briefly and to state what I have found in this material. . . .[80]

The work may thus be considered another striking epilogue to the affair of the *Cristo de la Paciencia*. In a Spain preoccupied with purity of blood, accustomed to blood in the bull ring, and to the so-called *disciplinantes de sangre*, who in processions on Good Friday would whip themselves until their robes were stained with blood, there was perhaps sufficient psychological preparation for any phenomenon in which blood was involved. Then too, belief in miracles abounded, and knew no practical limits. If the flagellated image in the Calle de las Infantas could bleed and weep, why was it not equally plausible that Jewish males should bleed in punishment for the death of Him whom such images represent? Here is Quiñones:

In this perfidious mob of the Jews, that rebellious nation, incredulous tyranny, infamous cruelty, ferocious molestation, perjurous, obstinately proud, pertinacious, debased, without honor anywhere, but always seeking

examining certain inquisitorial materials at the Biblioteca Nacional in Lisbon. Only later did I realize that this MS had already been noted, but not discussed, by D'Azevedo (*Cristãos-Novos*, p. 218).
Quiñones' work is contained in B.N. Lisbon MS 868 (*Colecção Moreira*, II), fols. 73r-89r.
[79] He was one of the nine Judaizers penanced at the *auto* (*Relación*, fol. 57). His case is no longer extant in the inquisitorial archives.
[80] B.N. Lisbon, MS 868, fol. 73r-v.

it, deprived of kingdom and priesthood, exiled, a vagrant captive placed in perpetual servitude and abhorred by all . . . among other maledictions both corporal and spiritual, within and upon its body, for having so persecuted the true Messiah Christ our Redeemer as to put Him on a cross, there is one which is: that every month many of them show a flux of blood in the posterior parts as a perpetual sign of ignominy and opprobrium. . . .

The allegation itself was not new. It appears repeatedly in the Middle Ages,[81] and in various antisemitic Spanish and Portuguese books of the sixteenth and seventeenth centuries.[82] Its symbolic and psychological implications are exceedingly complex. Easily perceived is the fact that here the Jews are not merely punished for their crime by exile and the loss of kingdom and priesthood, as in traditional Christian theology. If Jewish males menstruate they are, in effect, no longer men but women, and the crime of deicide has been punished by castration. We shall, however, leave it to those more competent in psychoanalysis to investigate such matters, and confine ourselves to a literal summary of Quiñones' work, which has the distinction of being the only one in which this allegation is not a peripheral aside, but the central theme.

Except for the initial outburst quoted above, Quiñones' method betrays two fundamental characteristics. One is to adopt a calm and erudite tone, garnishing the arguments with whole paragraphs consisting solely of learned names, and thus exhuding an air of scientific and scholarly reliability; the other, to assume a seemingly dispassionate attitude, offering several alternative explanations for each point, as though leaving it to the reader to make up his own mind. A virulently antisemitic explanation of a phenomenon will be followed by the qualifying phrase "Others say. . . ." It is a technique used effectively in antisemitic literature at least since Tacitus. Beyond that, the work is quite confused, full of arbitrary

---

[81] Joshua Trachtenberg, *The Devil and the Jews* (New Haven, 1943; reprint, New York, 1961), pp. 51, 148.

[82] So, e.g., Costa Mattos, *Breve discurso contra a heretica perfidia do iudaismo*, fol. 131r-v; Torrejoncillo, *Centinela contra judíos*, fol. 174.

digressions into other antisemitic charges, as well as matters which are totally irrelevant to the Jews.

Desiring to prove conclusively that Jewish men really menstruate, Quiñones is at first hard put to find a basis for it in Scripture. He refers lamely to the curse in Deuteronomy that God will send upon the Jews the "sore" of Egypt, and states immediately that he is aware, of course, that many interpret this as meaning one of the Egyptian plagues, namely, boils.[83] Without pausing to explain why the verse should therefore be interpreted in any other manner, he goes on to cite "that which David said in a Psalm, that He smote His enemies in the posterior parts, giving them eternal shame,"[84] and adds: "I am not unaware that this verse has in mind the Philistines, when God struck them in the posterior parts, as is related in Scripture in the Book of Kings, because they took the Ark to Azoto, which some say is derived from *azote* [i.e., "whip"] . . . for which there came upon them such a great infirmity in so filthy a part of the body."[85] But it does not really matter, since "some cite the words in both places (i.e., Deuteronomy and Psalms) and apply them to that which must afflict the Jews for having persecuted and killed Christ our Lord."

Having exhausted the Old Testament, Quiñones turns to the New. Many authors say that when Pilate declared himself innocent of Christ's blood, those Jews who clamored that His blood be upon them and their children, together with their descendants, remained

---

[83] Quiñones was obviously thinking of Deut. 28: 27, but gives a typically lax paraphrase. The Vulgate has: "Percutiat te Dominus ulcere Aegypti, *et partem corporis, per quam stercora egeruntur, scabie quoque et prurigine:* ita ut curari nequeas."

[84] The reference is to Ps. 77: 66 in the Vulgate (= 78: 66 in the Hebrew): "Et percussit inimicos suos in posteriora opprobrium sempiternum dedit illis." Quiñones has taken *in posteriora* to mean "en las partes posteriores."

[85] The affliction of the Philistines with hemorrhoids after their capture of the ark is narrated in I Reg. (= I Sam.) 5–6. "Azoto" is of course the Phillistine city of Ashdod which the Vulgate translates as *Azotus*. In general, one cannot help wondering how much Quiñones' concern with these dubious "proofs" stemmed from a morbid fixation on his own malady.

with "the plague, stain, and perpetual sign of being affected each month by a menstrual flux."[86]

But now he offers an alternative, "natural" explanation. Some say that the Jews are simply exposed to the malady which the physicians call hemorrhoids, and that this in turn is caused by their food, which they ordinarily eat without salt. "Gordonio" states three reasons for the Jewish illness: they are ordinarily an indolent people, and thus possess a superfluity of melancholic humors; they are always full of fear and fatigue, and this multiplies their melancholic blood; and finally, it is also a divine punishment.[87] Other cases of male menstruation, not necessarily Jewish, are now reported. The authority of San Vincente Ferrer is adduced to show that the descendants of those who killed Christ are born with the right hand stuck to the head and covered with blood.[88] Others have stated that Jews menstruate on Good Friday, and that is why they are so pale, yellow, and discolored.

The Jews, however, have sought a potent cure in the ritual murder of Christian children, whose blood they drink in the vain hope that it will heal them.[89] They do not realize that it is only that blood which is offered daily in the mass which can cure them of the curse inherited from their fathers. Quiñones next presents a series of examples of ritual murder, full of vivid anecdote and the most lurid

---

[86] B.N. Lisbon, MS 868, fol. 74v. According to Quiñones, many cite St. Augustine as their authority for this interpretation, but he has not succeeded in finding the passage in the latter's writings.

[87] "Gordonio" is probably a reference to Bernardus de Gordonio, *Lilio de medicina* (anonymous Sp. translation of his *Lilium medicinae*) (Seville, 1495).

[88] So also Costa Mattos, *Discurso*, fol. 131v: "que os filhos dos Iudeos desta casta, quãdo nascem trazem a mão direita chea de sangue, e pegada na cabeça." Quiñones and others had available to them a recently published Spanish translation of this work, by Fr. Diego Gavilan Vela: *Discurso contra los Judíos, traducido de lengua portuguesa en Castellano* (Salamanca, 1631).

[89] B.N. Lisbon, MS 868, fol. 76r, citing Alonso de Espina's *Fortalitium fidei*, as well as "Thomas Cantipratano." The latter is Thomas of Cantimpré (13th cent.), whose *Bonum universale de apibus* (II, col. 29, no. 23) contains perhaps the first literary reference to the accusation of ritual murder against the Jews. An edition of this work appeared in Douai in 1627.

detail. Then, carried away in his attempt to demonstrate the Jewish lust for Christian blood, he offers his reader nothing less than a version of the Shylock legend. Here the setting is Turkey. A Jew lent money to a Christian to be returned on a certain date, but specified, in lieu of usury, "two ounces of flesh." Portia does not appear, but Suleiman, the Turkish sultan, saves the day in the familiar manner.[90]

With this, the discussion of male menstruation is temporarily halted. Having done with one infirmity, Quiñones goes on to elaborate on another: the Jewish odor.[91] For this, too, the Jews vainly drink Christian blood. Conversion to Christianity, however, can cure any of the Jewish diseases. Examples are given of miraculous cures after baptism, even among pagans. Of course, the Jewish odor has also been explained on natural grounds (the Jews eat strong-smelling foods like garlic and onions, etc.) but Quiñones insists that it, too, is a punishment from God, who wished this rebellious people to carry eternal signs of their guilt. There are many other physical signs. For example, the descendants of those Jews who spat at Christ cannot spit forward, and so the spittle runs down their beards and chests; and the progeny of those who blasphemed at the Cross cannot lift their heads to see the sky and stars.[92] Yes,

---

[90] B.N. Lisbon, MS 868, fols. 77v-78r, citing Martin del Río and "Adamo Kellerio." See Del Río's *Disquisitionum magicarum libri sex* (Lyon, 1604), II, 116. I have been unable to identify Adam Keller.

[91] B.N. Lisbon, MS 868, fols. 78r-79r.

[92] B.N. Lisbon, MS 868, fol. 8or-v. Cf. Costa Mattos, *Discurso*, fol. 135r. Torrejoncillo (*Centinela*, pp. 174, 178–82) cites a work by Antonio Caraffa, described as a converted Jew, which gives minute details of the curses placed on the descendants of each of the twelve tribes of Israel. E.g., Judah: 30 men of the tribe die each year as a result of betrayal; Reuben: all green vegetation around them withers in three days, and wherever they are buried, nothing grows; Gad: each March 25th, from morning to evening, they develop 15 thorns on the body which drip blood; Asher: their right hands are shorter than their left by a palm; Naftali: their children are born with four teeth, like pigs; Manasseh: at each new moon they feel pain throughout the body and bleed all day; Simeon: wounds develop on their hands and feet each March 25th; Levi: they cannot spit on the ground, only into the air, whence the spittle flies back in their faces. Caraffa allegedly saw all this among his Jewish contemporaries in Turkey. A work by

there are some sincere Catholics among the New Christians, but they are few, and not descended from the aforementioned Jews of old. Jews have notoriously large noses.[93] Some think they also have tails. Quiñones does not insist upon it, since he has found no other author who says so. But, on the other hand, there have been references to men with tails in Java and in Chile.

He now begins a lengthy excursus on physical signs in general as signifying divine punishment. In particular, Quiñones has elaborate information on the statue of salt into which God transformed Lot's wife when she looked back at Sodom.[94] Quiñones is, in fact, so obsessed with this statue that soon he cannot resist discussing its miraculous character. Pilgrims, for example, would break off pieces of salt from it, and yet the cavities would immediately be refilled. And, among its other marvelous capacities, the statue menstruated each month.

The murderers of St. Thomas Becket first cut off the tail from his horse, and so, after the murder, God caused all their descendants to be born with tails. "And if God has done such a thing for His servants, one should not be surprized that He has permitted the Jews to be born with the aforementioned stigma and mark of a flux of blood."[95]

There are also humanly imposed signs, analogous to the divine.

Antonio Caraffa entitled *Los* [sic] *doce maledíciones* [sic] *de los Judíos* is mentioned by Kayserling (*BEPJ*, p. 115) as existing in MS, but with no further indications. In the Lee M. Friedman Collection now in the Houghton Library of Harvard University I found an Italian pamphlet consisting of only a frontispiece and two pages, which lists the 12 curses of the tribes without further comment. The title page reads: *Dodici maleditioni quali ereditorno gli Hebrei per la morte da loro procurata e data al nostro Signore Giesù Christo sotto l'Imperio di Tiberio Cesare* (Perugia, 1617).

To place all 12 tribes in 1st-century Judea is, of course, a gross anachronism. I suspect that we have here an interesting, though absurd, polemical reaction to the claim, voiced by some Spanish and other Jews, that their ancestors were exiled from Judea long before the Crucifixion, and so could not have participated in it.

[93] B.N. Lisbon, MS 868, fol. 81r.   [94] B.N. Lisbon, MS 868, fols. 81r-82v.
[95] *Ibid.*, fol. 83r.

Such are the Jewish Badge, ordained by some kings of Castile, and the *sambenito* worn by those who are penanced by the Inquisition.

Strange physical signs are also found among other peoples, as are miraculous cures. In France some who claim descent from St. Hubert affirm that they can cure rabies. In Spain there are others who say they are of the family of St. Paul, that they have the mark of a serpent on their bodies, and are immune to snake bites. But, Quiñones adds indignantly, these and others "certainly deserve to take a cure in the galleys, because ordinarily they are lost, vagrant people, and what they do or say is either feigned or full of diabolical superstition, and therefore far from the Christian religion. . .!"[96] (This does not inhibit an elaborate discussion of the curative powers possessed by certain Catholic kings of France and Spain.)

After another dissertation on the nature of signs (the mark of Cain; the costumes of soldier, cleric, king, priest, and magistrate; the stigmata; the lopped-off ears of the thief and the pierced ear of the slave), Quiñones finally arrives at a practical conclusion: in examining suspects, the Inquisition should pay close attention to occult signs on the body. There should certainly be an examination for circumcision. The author himself was able to arrest three men in Madrid and deliver them to the Inquisition because they were circumcised.[97] Abstention from pork is another important sign. But the Inquisition must also be on the watch for something else as well:

If any are found who have this flux of blood they should be handed over to the Inquisition, since they cannot have ceased to be Jews or apostates. For if they have it they are not baptized, since with baptism it disappears; and if they are baptized and it happens to them each month, they are apostates . . . and thus, being always a manifestation of their sin and guilt . . . it seems to me . . . that an inquisition can be instituted against them, to verify which Law they observe, and which ceremonies they practice.[98]

With a final peroration to the Inquisitor-General, the work draws to a close.

---

[96] *Ibid.*, fol. 84v.   [97] *Ibid.*, fol. 88r.   [98] *Ibid.*, fol. 88v.

THE MASK

It has been necessary to dwell in some detail on Quiñones' treatise in order to gain some insight into the reality of Spanish antisemitism, as well as to appreciate the concrete quality of the work which must have so revolted Cardoso at the time. Only a reading of this manuscript could explain why he so vividly remembered the *alcalde* when writing his own culminating work decades later in Italy and, indeed, devoted a special section to the refutation of this particular libel against the Jews. The anecdote of the visit to Quiñones' sickbed is, despite its comic aspects, permeated with Cardoso's loathing for this man. Whether or not Cardoso really said what he claimed to have said to him is quite irrelevant. If he did not say those words to Quiñones, they are the words he wanted to say. If he did, then in essence he had to hide his revulsion in a jest. That aspect is of paramount importance.

For one thing has remained unstated until now. In 1632, at about the same time that Cardoso published his *Discurso sobre el Monte Vesuvio*, there appeared in Madrid another work on the same subject, entitled *El Monte Vesuvio*, dedicated to Philip IV.[99] Its author was Dr. Juan de Quiñones. A comparison of the two books would reveal many differences in content and detail, but the same universe of discourse. In Quiñones' book the treatise proper is followed by an appendix of poems devoted to Vesuvius, written expressly for this purpose by twenty-two different persons. Among them, in the company of Lope de Vega, Quevedo, Montalván, Silveyra, Vélez

---

[99] *El Monte Vesuvio, aora la montaña de Soma. Dedicado a Don Felipe el Grande nuestro Señor, Rey Catolico de las Españas, Monarca Soberano de las Indias Orientales, y Occidentales. Por el Doctor Don Iuan de Quiñones, Alcalde de su Casa y Corte* [Arms of Philip IV] *Con Licencia. En Madrid. Por Iuan Gonçalez. Año 1632.* 2 unnumbered fols. of preface + 56 numbered fols. of the treatise + 15 fols. of poems.

It is possible that, shortly before, Cardoso had already published his own *Discurso*, for Quiñones states in the preface: "Bien sé que aunque se han hecho otras relaciones y doctas, se podía agradezer este discurso."

Title page of Juan de Quiñones' treatise on Mount Vesuvius (Madrid, 1632)

Library of the Hispanic Society of America, New York

EL MONTE
VESVVIO,
AORA LA MONTAÑA
DE SOMA.

EDICADO A DON FELIPE
VARTO el Grande nuestro Señor, Rey Catolico de las Españas, Monarca Soberano
de las Indias Orientales, y
Occidentales.

OR EL DOCTOR DON IVAN DE
Quiñones, Alcalde de su Casa y Corte.

CON LICENCIA

En Madrid. Por Iuan Gonçalez. Año 1632.

de Guevara, Pellicer, and members of the military orders and of the Inquisition, is a sonnet by Cardoso.[100]

Only now do we begin to appreciate the situation in its totality. To contribute a poem to another's book in seventeenth-century Spain, whether it be offered or solicited, constituted, by convention at least, an act of friendship or a mark of esteem. We have thus arrived at the heart of the paradox. The future author of one of the most monumental apologia for Judaism contributes a sonnet to enhance a work by the author of a treatise on the menstruation of Jewish males. Both write scientific works on Vesuvius, and both could and probably did speak to each other often on matters of common interest. They move in the same social circles. If the anecdote is an indication, Cardoso may well have treated Quiñones' hemorrhoids as a physician. Outwardly all is politeness and gracious conviviality. And all the while the real thoughts and attitudes, the contempt he must have felt are concealed beneath a smile and locked in the recesses of the heart. We need no better illustration of what it meant to live as a New Christian in Madrid.

---

[100] The pages on which the poems appear are unnumbered. Cardoso's sonnet is placed between one by Don Luis Remirez de Arellano and another by Miguel de Silveyra.

Chapter iv

MADRID: FAME AND FLIGHT

> Los que quieren vivir con la libertad de
> las gentes entre delicias y regalos abun-
> dantes de bienes temporales, no pueden
> observar la Ley del Señor. . . .
> —Cardoso, *Las excelencias de los Hebreos*

D ESPITE the tragic events of 1632, Cardoso was to remain
in Madrid for fully fifteen years more, and to enjoy a
brilliant career. Notwithstanding the waves of hostility
against the New Christians which would rise and ebb
periodically, he must have felt that he had nothing to fear. This
is all the more striking when we consider that on at least one
occasion, less than two years after the great *auto*, he himself became
involved in a case then pending before the Holy Office.

INQUISITORIAL WITNESS

In 1632 the Inquisition had arrested Bartolomé Febos, a wealthy
young merchant then residing in Madrid as representative of his
father, Rodrigues Lamego, who lived in Rouen in France. The latter
was bound up with other Portuguese merchants of that city in an
extensive network of commercial interests.

Febos had been trapped through a chain of unfortunate circumstances. It appears that in Rouen there were, in effect, two groups
of Portuguese New Christians. The one with which Rodrigues

Madrid: Fame and Flight

Lamego was associated openly Judaized, while the members of the other, led by one António da Fonseca, considered themselves good Catholics. Some time before, Fonseca's son, a friar, was prosecuted by the Inquisition in Galicia, and denounced his father as a Judaizer. However, his brother Jerónimo, a merchant in Madrid, decided to clear the father's reputation. To do so, he paid an inquisitor, Juan Bautista de Villadiego, to travel to Rouen and investigate the matter personally. Villadiego took the opportunity to draw up a detailed report on the religious situation among the New Christians in Rouen and in several other French cities. As a result, a number of Portuguese merchants in Madrid were gravely compromised, Febos among them. He was accused of Judaizing, and of being in correspondence not only with the Judaizers in Rouen, but with certain Jews in Amsterdam.[1]

Imprisoned in Toledo, Febos naturally gave the inquisitors a list of friends and acquaintances who, he felt, would testify in his behalf and help to clear him of the charge. One of those to be summoned was Fernando Cardoso.

On March 7, 1634, Cardoso appeared in Madrid before an inquisitorial tribunal of investigation presided over by the commissioner Dr. Juan de la Peña y Nisso. He was the tenth witness to be called, and his testimony is included in Febos' dossier in the usual summarized form. I have already made some use of the information contained therein concerning Cardoso's age, place of birth, and residence in Madrid. The rest of the testimony follows:

Asked if anyone had advised him beforehand to make a statement in favor of any prisoner of the Inquisition, he said no.

To the first question of the interrogation, he replied that he does not know the advocate of the Inquisition, that it is about four years that he has known Bartolomé Febo the Portuguese defendant, because he cured his illnesses and was frequently in touch with him, and that he has no other knowledge of this case beyond the fact that the aforesaid has

---

[1] On Febos see Caro, *Sociedad*, pp. 45–47. The case is preserved in AHN, *Inq. de Tol.*, Leg. no. 4 (cf. *supra*, ch. II, p. 00, n. 13). Though Febos was twice tortured, Caro says his final sentence was not severe.

138

been imprisoned. [He declares] that he is legally competent to be a witness, and is thirty years old.

It was made known to him that the said Bartolomé Febo had presented him as a witness for his defense, that he should wait for that which was asked of him, and answer that which he knows.

To the eighth question of the interrogation for which he had been summoned, he said that he does not know that the said Bartolomé Febo had received or lodged Jews in his house, nor has such a thing come to his notice, and that many times this witness had entered his house at dinnertime and other times, that he dined with him, and always he saw that his guests were honorable people, musicians, poets, ladies, and persons of good taste, and he never saw that there should be ten or twelve strangers, or less in number, dining with him, but rather that they were always well-known persons; and in particular, Pero Méndez the poet . . . Don Juan de Quesada of the Order of Santiago, Don Jacinto de Lemos, and others, and that the house of the said Bartolomé Febo was always one of good conversation, where usually day and night friends gathered to play and be entertained and, as stated, never did this witness see nor hear anything said to the contrary, and this is the truth by the weight of his oath.

His statement was ratified and he signed it, as did the aforesaid commissioner, and he was told, under pain of major excommunication, to keep it secret.[2]

To appear as a defense witness before the Holy Office, and to admit a friendly relationship with a prisoner prior to his arrest, did not mean, of course, that one was implicated in the crime. True, one of the other witnesses had stated, in passing, that he had seen Febos eating meat during Lent on the advice of Dr. Cardoso and another physician, but their counsel had been purely medical, since Febos was then afflicted with a malady of the eyes.[3] There was nothing unusual in all this. Cardoso was dismissed after signing his deposition, and was not troubled further in the case.

---

[2] The text (AHN, *Inq. de Tol.*, Leg. no. 4, fols. 173r-174v) is published in Caro, *Judíos*, III, pp. 330 f.

[3] Testimony of Simon Faia (Faya), a native of Alemtejo, (AHN, *Inq. de Tol.*, Leg. no. 4, fol. 176r): "y no se acuerda de otra cosa, y que la mitad de la quaresma comio carne por q̄ se lo mando asi el D.ᵒʳ Tamaio y el D.ᵒʳ Cardoso q̄ le curaban."

Madrid: Fame and Flight

Nevertheless, in seventeenth-century Madrid it was preferable, if possible, to have no contact at all with the Inquisition. Once a name had entered the inquisitorial records, no matter how casual the context, the person could never be quite certain of the use that might be made of it later. One may imagine that Cardoso did not feel quite comfortable about the incident. And indeed, although he could not have known of it, his name was copied shortly afterwards into another record, for the inquisitorial bureaucracy was nothing if not thorough. Culling through the dossiers of various cases investigated that year, the inquisitors compiled, undoubtedly for future reference, a "Record of various Portuguese who live in Madrid and who have testified in favor of Portuguese defendants imprisoned by the Holy Office, with their places of residence and of birth, in the year 1634." Cardoso's name appeared in the list of those who had testified for Bartolomé Febos.[4]

That this list could prove more than a routine formality may be deduced from the fact that of the other Portuguese defense witnesses in the Febos case, at least three were eventually prosecuted by the Inquisition.[5] Only a year later, in 1635, a Jesuit writing from Madrid observed that Judaizers were being caught so often that it was no longer considered a novelty.[6] Throughout this time, and in the succeeding years, Cardoso remained unmolested.

---

[4] AHN, *Inq. de Tol.*, Leg. 189 no. 35, fols. 1r-2r (cf. *supra*, ch. II, p. 54, nn. 11, 14). Published in Caro, *Judíos*, III, 326–29. A complete list of witnesses in the Febos case is to be found in Leg. 146 no. 4, fols. 203r-204r.

[5] In the margin of the list, next to the name of Simón Faya, is added the note "reconciliado." For the later prosecution of two of the other witnesses mentioned in the list, Francisco Enríquez of Talavera and his brother Gabriel, see *Catálogo de . . . la Inq. de Toledo*, p. 177.

[6] "Antes de ayer, el teniente de la villa, el licenciado Ramos, como ministro de la Inquisición, fué por su orden á buscar un delincuente en casa de unos portugueses, al cual no halló; mas con esta ocasión se llevo el dueño de la casa y otras siete personas ú ocho las mas de ellas mujeres que estaban actualmente judaizando, cogiéndolos con las manos en el hurto. No hace novedad esto, que hay tanto, después que esta gente vino á Castilla, que ya no se repara como es tan ordinario" (*Mem. hist. esp.*, XIII (1861–62), p. 294). The letter is dated Oct. 2, 1635.

SOCIAL AND ARTISTIC CIRCLES

However, Cardoso's testimony is interesting not only as an encounter with the Inquisition, but also for what it reveals of his life in society. His brief description of the gatherings in Febos' home must hold true as well for other houses he frequented in Madrid. The scene he depicts is engaging: A rich house always filled with guests, its owner a young merchant who is obviously a man of fashion, a brilliant company, sophisticated conversation, poetry and music. Here mingle men of commerce, artists, members of the great chivalric orders of Spain, and aristocratic ladies. The young physician is obviously at home in their midst.

The dossier of Bartolomé Febos also leads us to meet other acquaintances and friends of Cardoso.

A frequent guest at Febos' salon was Dr. Miguel de Silveyra, who was also called as a witness in his behalf.[7] In the document he is described as a native of Celorico in Portugal. fifty-four years old, a physician to His Majesty, "and he was master of mathematics to the kings his fathers."[8] Silveyra's testimony generally paralleled that of Cardoso. He had known Febos for some six or seven years and, especially during the last two, he would come to his house in the evening, "because they played there, and there was conversation about music." Of course he knew Febos only as a Catholic Christian, and in fact they had often attended mass together. Shortly after delivering this testimony to the Holy Office, Silveyra left Spain and settled in Naples. There, in 1638, he published his epic poem *El Macabeo*.[9] In the Peninsula and elsewhere the work was hailed as a masterpiece.

---

[7] AHN, *Inq, de Tol.*, Leg. 146 no. 4, fols. 185v-186r; Caro, *Judíos*, III, 331 f.

[8] On Miguel de Silveyra (Port., da Silveira) see Kayserling, *Sephardim*, pp. 182–88; Amador, *Estudios*, pp. 534–46; Caro, *Sociedad*, pp. 93–101. See also Joaquín de Entrambasaguas y Peña, *Una guerra literaria del Siglo de Oro: Lope de Vega y los preceptistas aristotélicos* (Madrid, 1932), p. 273 n. 61.

[9] *El Macabeo, poema heroico* (Naples, 1638). Another edition appeared in Madrid in 1731, and an Italian translation in 1810.

Madrid: Fame and Flight

Despite a considerable difference in age, Silveyra and Cardoso had been friends. In his treatise on Vesuvius the latter had cited Silveyra's opinion on the origin of earthquakes, calling him "a friend for whom Fame already prepares an immortal laurel, more acclaimed for his *Macabeo* than Vergil for his *Aeneid.* . . ."[10] Some forty years later, in a discussion of astrology, Cardoso was to recall this friendship. His esteem for the poet is obvious, despite some good-natured jibes at his astrological prowess, and the passage incidentally adds some colorful details to our picture of the social milieu in which they used to meet:

Two very outstanding astrologers were friends of ours. One was Silveira, whom we knew in Madrid, Royal Mathematician and a poet of great worth, who loftily sang the renowned poem of the Maccabees in Spanish verse. We used to come together with him from time to time at the home of a certain very beautiful Portuguese lady who was abounding in wealth, eager for literature, cultivated in Rhetoric and Poetry. She lost a female puppy whom she considered among her favorite delights, and lamented over its theft. The hour of the theft having been revealed, we asked Silveira to note the stars and to compose a celestial scheme.

He, very quickly indulging the woman with whom he was uniquely, platonically, but desperately in love, and whom he used to woo with innumerable poems, now contemplates the stars, arranges the celestial houses, and afterward, arising happy and joyful, firmly declares that the puppy is being kept in one of the neighboring houses. But good God, with what remarkable untruth! The dog, as was subsequently discovered, had already traveled more than a hundred miles, taken by the man who had stolen her to a certain high-born woman. At that point I said to him: "O most excellent Astrologer, who miss your aim by no less than a hundred miles, were you as good a birdcatcher or hunter as you are an astrologer, you would never have tasted a partridge or a deer, but would always be hungry. . . ."[11]

In view of this relationship, it would be interesting to know something of Silveyra's own religious attitudes. Unfortunately the

---

[10] Cardoso, *Discurso sobre el monte Vesuvio,* fol. 12v.

[11] Cardoso, *Philosophia libera,* p. 181. The other "astrologer" was Manoel Bocarrro Francês, on whom see *infra,* ch. VII.

142

problem still awaits a definitive solution. That Silveyra was a New Christian may be regarded as certain since, as we will recall, he was a relative of Tomás de Pinedo.[12] His abrupt departure from Spain after 1634 leaves little doubt that the move was precipitated by fear of the Inquisition. Still, neither of these circumstances can be adduced as proof that he ever Judaized. He was surely not an active Judaizer, for then he would not have gone to Naples, a city which at that time harbored no Jewish community, and in which he had perforce to continue to live as a Christian. Furthermore, it has been demonstrated convincingly that the *Macabeo* could have been written by a believing Catholic, for neither in Silveyra's selection of details nor in his treatment is there any special emphasis which must necessarily be regarded as "crypto-Jewish."[13]

Yet there is also some slight weight to place on the other side of the balance. Silveyra's initial choice of the Maccabean Revolt as the theme for his epic is of some moment and should not be entirely discounted. He could not have been blind to the fact that, while the so-called Maccabean saints were venerated by the Church, in essence the story of the Maccabees was one of a great moment in Jewish history. Again, while among medieval Jewry the Maccabean Revolt had been generally quite underrated (except by the author of the *Yosippon*), among the Marranos themselves, perhaps because of their reliance on the Apocrypha, the Maccabean tradition seems to have played a certain role.[14] It should also be noted that the

---

[12] *Supra*, ch. II, p. 61, n. 27. Silveyra was also to be lauded in 1645 by Rodrigo Méndez Silva in his description of Celorico: "Ha procreado señalados hombres en Letras, como el Doctor Miguel de Silveyra, canoro cisne de Europa, bien conocido por su Poema Heroyco del Macabeo" (*Población general de España*, fol. 190v).

[13] See Edward Glaser's examination of "Miguel da Silveira's *El Macabeo*," *Bulletin des études portugaises et de l'Institut Français en Portugal*, XXI (Coimbra, 1959), 5–41.

[14] See, e.g., Caro, *Judíos*, I, 401 f., for a Marrano woman of Trancoso in the 17th century who was considered a "saint," and was held to be a descendant of the Maccabees. A similar instance is recorded in Brazil in 1591, of a mother and two daughters known as "Machabeas" (D'Azevedo, *Christãos Novos*, p. 226). Among the Judaizing rites charged against António Homem and his circle in

Madrid: Fame and Flight

biblical epic in the Iberian Peninsula was a genre cultivated almost exclusively by authors of Jewish ancestry.[15] As for the Maccabean revolt itself, besides Silveyra only one other Iberian writer, an anonymous poet who called himself "Estrella Lusitano," wrote on this theme.[16] The latter, indeed, displayed pronounced Jewish nuances which are absent in Silveyra's epic. But may this not have been precisely because "Estrella Lusitano" published his poem under a pseudonym, while Silveyra, using his own name, was more cautious? Perhaps this might also help to explain the curious fact that although the manuscript of the *Macabeo* had already been circulating privately for years, Silveyra did not actually publish it until he left Spain.[17] Finally, let us consider also that Miguel de Barrios saw fit to include Silveyra in his enumeration of Hispano-Jewish poets. Since De Barrios wrote this work for the Sephardic Jewish community of Amsterdam, and was himself a former Marrano, it seems unlikely that he would have placed Silveyra's name on an illustrious roster of Jewish men of letters if he were known to have been a sincere Christian. Any further elucidation of the riddle of Silveyra's inner feelings must be postponed until additional information is uncovered.

We are in a position, however, to trace the relationships of both Silveyra and Cardoso to other New Christians in Madrid who certainly Judaized at some point in their lives. For example, when De Barrios later mentioned Silveyra in his pamphlet, he put him with Jacob Uzziel and Antonio Enríquez Gómez.[18] It is clear that

---

Coimbra was a vestigial observance of Hannukah, called there "a Paschoa das Candelilhas" (Texeira, *António Homem*, p. 157).

[15] Glaser, "Miguel da Silveira," p. 31.

[16] *La Machabea, dividida en dose cantos, compuesta por Estrella Lusitano* (Leon, 1604). Cf. Glaser's remarks, "Miguel da Silveira, pp. 21, 29.

[17] That the manuscript, in whole or in part, was circulating privately long before Silveyra left Spain may be seen from a reference to it as early as 1623 (Glaser, "Miguel da Silveira," p. 35). Cardoso, as we have seen, praised it in 1632. So also Juan Pérez de Montalvén in his *Para todos*, written in 1633.

[18] Daniel Levi (Miguel) de Barrios, *Relación de los poetas y escritores de la nación judayca amstelodama*, ed. Kayserling, "Une histoire de la littérature juive," *REJ*, XVIII (1889), 285 f: "Entre otras celebras Poesias el Doctor Miguel de Silveira

he associated these three because each had written a Biblical epic. However, there is an additional reason for us to link the latter with Silveyra.

Antonio Enríquez Gómez was also a member of the group that met in the home of Bartolomé Febos and, like Silveyra and Cardoso, was called upon to testify in the case in 1634.[19] His own life illustrates some of the more glaring contradictions in the career of certain New Christians. Born in Cuenca, he had married a woman of Old Christian stock. He went into business, established relations with certain commercial figures in Rouen, and apparently began to Judaize during his trips to France. Between 1642 and 1649 he was to publish a series of Spanish works in Rouen, and, in 1656, his epic poem *Sansón Nazareno*.[20] In this work he consciously modeled himself after Silveyra and betrayed unbridled enthusiasm for the *Macabeo*.[21] Until quite recently it was believed that he was burned in effigy in 1660 at an *auto* in Seville while he was safe in Amsterdam. However, it has been discovered that this was far from being the case. Enríquez Gómez was to return to Spain with the assumed name of Fernando de Zárate, settling in Seville, and publishing a number of plays on Christian hagiographical themes. The Inquisition discovered his true identity, and prosecuted him for having Judaized in Peyrehorade, Bordeaux, and Rouen. He died in the dungeons of Seville while waiting to appear at the *auto* of 1660.[22]

Of the three persons whom Cardoso mentioned by name in the course of his own testimony, it may be possible to identify one.

---

haze el Poema de los Machabeos, Jacob Uziel el de David, y Antonio Enríquez Gómez el de Sanson . . ." The second reference is to Jacob Usiel, *David, Poema eroïco* (Venice, 1624). See Kayserling, *BEPJ*, p. 106.

[19] Caro, *Sociedad*, p. 119. His testimony was adverse to Febos.

[20] *Sansón Nazareno, poema heroico* (Rouen, 1656). For his other works see Kayserling, *BEPJ*, pp. 49–51. An elegy by Enríquez Gómez on the martyrdom of Don Lope de Vera y Alarcón, burned at the stake in Valladolid in 1644, is mentioned by De Barrios, and is extant is manuscript. See A. Neubauer, *Catalogue of the Hebrew Mss. in the Bodleian Library*, no. 2481.

[21] *Sansón Nazareno*, fol. 3r-v of the preliminary material.

[22] Révah, *Les marranes*, pp. 50 f.

Madrid: Fame and Flight

Jacinto de Lemos is most probably the person whom Pellicer was to mention seven years later in this vivid anecdote:

This afternoon, while Don Francisco de Meneses was riding in a coach with Don Jorge Manuel to see the procession, there passed by close to them two Portuguese, Don Jacinto de Lemos, of the Order of Santiago of Portugal, and a brother of his, Fernando Manuel, a financier. Because the latter did not lift his hat to him, he [Meneses] called him, among other insults, a Jew. Fernando Manuel drew his sword, and the two hurled themselves out of the coaches. Meneses dangerously wounded Fernando Manuel and, placing his foot on the latter's face, and wishing to wound him again, he pierced his foot with his own sword. . . . The pride with which these Portuguese businessmen go about Madrid is incredible. Those who in Portugal would not even dare to look at *caballeros* desire here, not only to equal them, but to exceed them.[23]

Having caught a partial glimpse of Cardoso's mode of life and milieu by means of the Febos case, we must turn now to other aspects of his activity which fall into the same period. Several bibliographical notices on Cardoso list among his works one entitled *Panegyrico y excelencias del color verde*, said to have been published in Madrid in 1635.[24] I have searched in vain for this book in praise of the color green, in libraries both here and abroad. Nevertheless, the facts we do possess about the work permit us to learn a good deal about it.

In 1637 there appeared in Madrid a little book entitled *Color verde*

---

[23] Pellicer, *Avisos* (June 26, 1641), cited by Domínguez, *Política y hacienda*, pp. 132 f.

[24] De Barrios, *Relación*, p. 284: "El Doctor y Poeta Ishac Cardoso, que en Madrid se llamó Fernando Cardoso, hizo con notable elegancia y erudición los libros que intitulo el primero Del color verde, dedicado a Doña Isabel Henríques . . ."; Bartolocci, *Bibliotheca magna rabbinica*, III, fol. 921, refers to it as: "Tractatu de colla verde. Excus. Madriti 1635." See also Kayserling, *Sephardim*, pp. 191, 344, n. 238; *BEPJ*, p. 34, listing it as: *Panegyrico y excelencias del color verde, symbolo de esperança, hieroglifico de victoria. Madrid, Fr. Martins, 1635. 8.* From this elaborate indication it would appear that Kayserling saw a copy, but he did not say where. It is not to be found in Madrid or Lisbon. My correspondence with libraries in Germany and Austria has so far yielded no results.

a la divina Celia, by Manuel Fernández Villareal.[25] The author has long been known as a figure of some importance in Marrano history. Born in Lisbon in 1608, he had served in the army in Tangiers, where he rose to the rank of captain. Upon his return to Portugal he engaged in various financial enterprises in Alemtejo, Lisbon, and Coimbra. Then he went to Spain, where he lived at various times in Seville, Madrid, and Malaga. Although, in the period under discussion, he was in the Spanish capital, he eventually left the Peninsula and settled in France. In Rouen, Le Havre, and Paris he pursued an active career as a diplomatic agent in the service of the House of Braganza, and also became a political writer. He finally decided to return to Lisbon, presumably in order to receive the reward and recognition due him for his services. Instead, on October 30, 1649, he was to be imprisoned by the Inquisition, and was even subsequently alleged to observe Jewish rites in his cell. On December 1, 1652, he was burned at the stake as a Judaizer.[26]

The circumstance which prompted Fernández Villareal to write his book on the color green in 1637 is stated in his prologue to the reader: "This discourse is a reply to another on the color blue, which was written by Doctor Fernando Álvarez Brandon (Brandam), a distinguished jurist, an illustrious Lusitanian talent, and an intimate friend of mine."[27] Turning to the text itself we find a statement, written near the very beginning, that "the advantages of the color green are already known today in all their elegance from learned discourses," and in the immediate margin the reference

---

[25] *Color verde a la divina Celia, por el Capitan Manuel Fernandez Villareal, Gratiam & speciem desiderabit oculus tuus, et super hoc Virides Sationes. Ecclesiast. cap. 40. Con licencia. En Madrid, por la viuda de Alonso Martin, Año de 1637.* 4 fols. of preliminary material + fols. 1–32, numbered recto.

[26] Various aspects of his life and work are treated in Barbosa Machado, *Bib. Lus.*, III, 264; Kayserling, *Sephardim*, pp. 229–32; *BEPJ*, p. 109; José Ramos-Coelho, *Manoel Fernandes Villa Real e o seu processo na Inquisição de Lisboa* (Lisbon, 1894); Caro, *Judíos*, II, 128 f. See now especially I. S. Révah, "Manuel Fernandes Villareal, adversaire et victime de l'Inquisition portugaise," *Ibérida* (Rio de Janeiro), no. 1 (April, 1959), pp. 33–54, no. 3 (December, 1959), pp. 181–207.

[27] Fernández Villareal, *Color verde*, fol. 2v of the preliminary material.

reads: "Doctor Cardoso in his elegant and learned panegyric on the color green, which he dedicated to Doña Isabel Henríquez."[28] This is interesting, but there is yet another piece of information to be fitted in with the rest. In his brief entry on Fernando Alvares Brandam in the *Biblioteca Lusitana*, Barbosa Machado states that the latter had originally written his defense of the color blue "in competition with Doctor Fernando Cardoso who had written of the excellences of the color green."[29] The triangle is thus complete. Cardoso had first praised the green, Alvarez Brandam the blue, and Fernandez Villareal the green again. An odd rivalry indeed!

One can hardly avoid the conclusion that we have been plunged here into the atmosphere of the contemporary literary academies of Madrid. Only such a setting would explain the preciousness and baroque quality of a competition between several important writers on so ephemeral a theme as the virtues of the various colors. In the only one of the three works available to us, that of Fernández Villareal, we feel very well the attitude of mock solemnity with which the members of the *academias literarias* would gather of an evening to hold their courtly and poetic tournaments.[30] This impression is heightened by the fact that both Cardoso and Fernández Villareal dedicated their works to ladies. It is confirmed, when we discover that an analogous theme was actually treated in a Spanish literary academy, though not in Spain itself. In 1683 there was

---

[28] *Ibid.*, fol. 1v: "El Doctor Fernando Cardoso en su florido y docto Panegyrico del color verde, que dedicó a la señora Doña Isabel Henríquez." Menéndez y Pelayo (*Heterodoxos*, IV, 297, n. 1A) thought, erroneously, that the work contained a *poem* by Cardoso.

[29] Barbosa Machado, *Bib. Lus.*, II, 17: "Fernando Alvares Brandam, douto medico e muito perito nas letras humanas, a quem o Capitão Manoel Fernandes Villa Real no Discurso del color verde intitula: Insigne y ilustre ingenio. Compoz em competencia do Doutor Fernando Cardozo que escreveo as excellencias da cor verde, *Tratado em defensa da cor azul*. Ms., em cuja obra mostra muita discrição, sciencia, e galantaria."

[30] On the academies see most recently José Sánchez, *Academias literarias del Siglo de Oro español* (Madrid, 1961), and Willard F. King, *Prosa novelística y academias literarias en el siglo XVII* (= *Anejos del Boletín de la Real Academia Española*, X; Madrid, 1963).

Social and Artistic Circles

published in Antwerp the *Rumbos peligrosos* of Joseph Penso de la Vega. Its three novels were based in part on materials which had been presented in one of the literary academies of the Sephardic diaspora.[31] In the third narrative we are introduced to a typical scene in an academy. The princess "Aurora of Thrace" has four suitors who must prove themselves in a contest for her hand. Each of them delivers a discourse on "which is the color most appropriate for a lover to wear if he wishes to express his affection through the color itself."[32] The praise of the colors in the *Rumbos peligrosos* and that of Fernández Villareal in his *Color verde* betray a common background.

If we may assume, therefore, that Cardoso belonged for a time to one of the literary academies in Madrid, we can perhaps better evaluate another reference to a work of his which has not been found. It is listed as *Origen y restauración del mundo*, and according to Kayserling it was published in Madrid in 1633.[33] This appears to be an error. We believe that no work by Cardoso with this title was ever published. It is not mentioned by Nicolás Antonio, De Barrios, Bartolocci, or Barbosa Machado. Kayserling may have simply confused Cardoso with Isaac de Castro, who wrote a book with a similar title.[34]

But in his *Discurso sobre el Monte Vesuvio* Cardoso himself refers

---

[31] *Rumbos peligrosos, por donde navega con titulo de novelas la Çosobrante nave de la temeridad, temiendo las peligrosas escollas de la censura* (Antwerp, 1684). Two other works of Penso de la Vega with a background of the academies are the *Discurso académico, moral, y sagrado, hecho en la insigne Academia de los Sitibundos* (Amsterdam, 1683), and his *Discursos académicos, morales, retóricos, y sagrados, que recitó en la florida Academia de los Floridos* (Antwerp, 1685). Both these Sephardic academies, modeled after those of Spain, were founded in Amsterdam by Isaac Núñez (Baron Manuel) de Belmonte. Another Academia de los Sitibundos was established by Penso de la Vega in Leghorn.

[32] *Rumbos peligrosos*, fol. 168. Cf. King *Prosa novelística*, pp. 187 f. Miss King is unaware of the Sephardic academies, which are discussed by Kayserling, *Sephardim, passim*, and Roth, *Marranos*, pp. 337 f.

[33] Kayserling, *Sephardim*, p. 344.

[34] Kayserling seems to have caught his own error, for he does not mention the work in his final list of Cardoso's writings in *BEPJ*, p. 34. Isaac de Castro's work,

to a work of his own, obviously composed prior to 1632, which may be the work in question. Attacking Pliny's negation of immortality, he adds "as we have stated against the Atheist in our work of the Six Days in defense of the soul" and quotes from it two verses of a poem.[35] This work, then, was at least partly in verse, but there is no indication that it was a published book or pamphlet. We suspect that it too was a discourse delivered in a literary academy. While it is possible that the "Six Days" to which he alludes formed the theme of the work, which may therefore have dealt with the creation of the world, we should guess it might equally refer to a division of the work itself into "six days," in the manner of various other compositions which were destined for the academies.[36]

Be that as it may, Cardoso's dedication of his "panegyric on the color green" to Isabel Henríquez is of overriding interest. This woman was eventually to occupy an honored position in the Sephardic community of Amsterdam, and in the light of our discussion thus far it is significant that in 1684 De Barrios was to describe her in these words: "Doña Isabel Henríquez, *celebrated in the academies of Madrid for her rare talent*, came to the Judaism of Amsterdam. . . ."[37] We shall have occasion to see that Cardoso resumed his contacts

---

entitled *Sobre o principio e restaoração do mundo* (Amsterdam, 1612) is cited in J. Mendes dos Remédios, *Os judeus portugueses em Amsterdam* (Coimbra, 1911), p. 71.

[35] *Discurso sobre el Monte Vesuvio*, fol. 5r-v.

[36] Such, for example, is the division of Juan Pérez de Montalván's *Para todos: ejemplos morales, humanos y divinos. En que se tratan diversas ciencias, materias y facultades. Repartidos en los siete días de la semana* (Huesca, 1633). On Montalvan cf. *infra*, n. 70. There exists, to be sure, a work by Jacob [Francisco] de Cáceres entitled *Los siete dias de la semana sobre la creacion del mundo* (Amsterdam, 1612), listed in *BEPJ*, p. 32. But according to Rodríguez de Castro (*Biblioteca Española*, I, 571) this was merely a translation of a French mystical work.

[37] De Barrios, *Relación de los poetas*, p. 285 (italics mine). Several women bearing this name appear in the inquisitorial archives. A certain Isabel Henríquez escaped to Bayonne and arrived in the Amsterdam Jewish community sometime before 1655. See the information contained in the case of her son Fernando (alias Benjamin) Gil de Espinosa in Caro, *Judíos*, I, 475–77. Another, the wife of Andrés Fonseca, appeared at an *auto* in Cuenca on June 28, 1654 (*Ibid.*, II, 79). She is mentioned also in a list of confiscations in *AHN*, *Inq. de Cuenca*, Leg. 1931 no 21, paragraph 42. It is possible that either of these two women may be the

with her after he had himself departed from Spain.[38] But of the group we have discussed it was not only Cardoso who maintained a friendship with her. A sonnet by Doña Isabel Henríquez was printed at the beginning of Miguel de Silveyra's poem *Partenope orante*, which appeared in Naples in 1639.[39] Obviously they had known each other well prior to his departure for Italy, and one wonders whether she was not the "Portuguese lady" with whom, as Cardoso has informed us, Silveyra was in love. In any case, this information serves to round out the picture I have hitherto attempted to sketch. We see once more how the lines interweave constantly among the intellectuals, many of them New Christians, to whom Cardoso was close in Madrid. That a number of them later Judaized, or were hounded by the Inquisition, is a marked feature in the lives of these men and women with whom he shared his esthetic interests, and engaged in "buena conversación."

AT THE TOMB OF LOPE DE VEGA

We must now extend our view to another circle into which Cardoso had entered, one not unrelated to that which we have just encountered, but which reveals more fully the success he had achieved in the space of but a few years.

On Monday, August 27, 1635, Lope de Vega died in Madrid at the age of seventy-three. The sad event stirred the entire city, and especially Lope's many friends and admirers. Though his body was interred in the Church of San Sebastian the next morning, the funerary solemnities continued for no less than nine days. During this time three memorial sermons were preached in this and other

---

person to whom Cardoso dedicated his work, but a positive identification cannot be made at this time. She is definitely not to be equated with an Isabel Enríquez who was prosecuted in 1638–49 (*AHN, Inq. de Toledo*, Leg. 189 no. 862), and again in 1658 (*Ibid.*, Leg. 170 no. 613).

[38] See *infra*, ch. VII.

[39] Gallardo, *Ensayo*, IV, no. 3943. Cf. Caro, *Sociedad*, p. 100.

churches and were subsequently published.[40] Within three months after the great playwright's death, Cardoso also published his own eulogy, an *Oración funebre en la muerte de Lope de Vega*.[41] Shortly afterward there appeared a commemorative volume by Lope's disciple Juan Pérez de Montalván, entitled *Fama pósthuma a la vida y muerte del Doctor Frey Lope Felix de Vega Carpio*, which, like Cardoso's work, was dedicated to Lope's longtime friend and patron the Duke of Sessa.[42] In addition to other materials, the *Fama pósthuma* contained compositions by 153 persons in honor of Lope. Among them was a sonnet by Cardoso.[43]

These bare facts are already sufficient to establish Cardoso's connection with the circle of "Lopistas" in Madrid, and his deep feelings at the passing of the master. There is, of course, nothing intrinsically surprising in all this. Lope's art had been admired by many, even from afar. In 1636 a collection of Italian eulogies was published in Venice. It is only when we read Montalván's account of Lope's last days that we encounter the unexpected. By a rather

---

[40] These sermons were by Dr. Francisco de Quintana, Fray Ignacio de Vitoria, and Fray Francisco de Peralta. They are described by Cayetano Alberto de la Barrera, *Nueva biografía de Lope de Vega* (= *Obras de Lope de Vega publicadas por la Real Academia Española*, Vol. I; Madrid, 1890), pp. 502–4. All three sermons are reprinted in Lope de Vega, *Obras sueltas*, XIX, 317–466.

[41] *Oracion funebre/ en la muerte de Lope de Vega/ ingenio laureado de las musas/ prodigiosa maravilla de España/ eterna admiracion de las edades/ Al Excelentissimo/ Señor Duque de Sessa, Conde Cabra, y/ gran Almirante de Napo-/ les, & c./ El Dotor Fernando Cardoso/ dedica, consagra, ofrece./ Con licencia/ En Madrid, por la viuda de Iuan/ Gonçalez. Año 1635.* Fol. 1: Full page engraved arms of the Duke of Sessa, with the motto "Tuis auspiciis", + fols. 2–28, numbered recto.

The *Oración* is reprinted in Lope de Vega, *Obras sueltas*, XIX, 467–92. All citations that follow are from the first edition.

[42] *Fama pósthuma a la vida y muerte del Doctor Frey Lope Felix de Vega Carpio y elogios panegyricos a la inmortalidad de su nombre. Escritos por los mas esclarecidos ingenios solicitados por el Dr. Juan Perez de Montalvan que al Excelentissimo Señor Duque de Sessa, heroyco, magnifico y soberano Mecenas del que yaze, ofrece, presenta, sacrifica y consagra. En Madrid, en la Imprenta del Reyno. Año 1636.* A costa de Alonso Perez de Montalvan, Librero de su Magestad. 12 fols. of preliminary material + fols. 1–211. Reprinted as vol. XX of Lope de Vega, *Obras sueltas*.

[43] *Fama pósthuma*, fol. 55r.

dramatic coincidence, the death of Lope de Vega was to be linked in an unusual way with Cardoso's name. Montalván writes:

On Friday, Saint Bartholemew's Day [August 25], he arose early in the morning, prayed the Divine Office, recited mass in his oratory, watered the garden, and shut himself in his study. At midday he felt himself catching cold, perhaps because of the effort he had made in refreshing the flowers, or (as the members of his household affirm) because of another, more lofty exercise, made while scourging himself (a custom he observed every Friday in memorial of the passion of Christ our Lord) and verified by there being seen, in a room where he had retired, that the walls were flecked and the whip had traces of recent blood. . . .

In the afternoon he was present at a lecture on certain theses of medicine and philosophy which were being sustained for three days by Doctor Fernando Cardoso, a great philosopher and very learned in the higher disciplines, in the Scottish Seminary (*Seminario de los Escoceses*). While Lope was there, he suddenly became faint, and it was necessary to carry him between two gentlemen to the quarters of his good friend Don Sebastián Francisco de Medrano, which were located within the Seminary, and where he rested a bit until they took him in a sedanchair to his house.[44]

Three days later Lope de Vega was dead. In his *Oración fúnebre* Cardoso referred to the same incident:

But let us ponder his death which, like his life, was mysterious. On St. Bartholemew's Day, when my modest attainments were able to earn some luster in lectures which continued for four days on various sciences, he came, an illustrious listener, to honor me among that most grave audience of the great and the erudite . . . when, either because of the odors in the church, or the density of the crowd, the famous man fainted, and, taken to his house, died on the third day. Intellectual events claimed his attention to the last, and the discursive arenas attracted his ultimate steps. It is a debt which I shall always owe to his memory. . . .

His illness began in the view of princes and sages, and in all of them already commenced the sorrow of losing him. On the very night he died the moon was eclipsed, so much shadow can be cast by such a corpse.

---

[44] *Fama pósthuma*, fol. 6v. Montalván erroneously places St. Bartholemew's Day on the 18th of August.

Madrid: Fame and Flight

In that darkness Spanish poetry itself appeared eclipsed, and in that dimness, eloquence put on the veil of mourning.[45]

Lope de Vega's last public appearance had thus taken place at a lecture by Cardoso. We now understand perhaps more fully how strong and immediate was the motive which impelled him to write his funeral oration. Other significant details emerge as well. Montalván's allusion to Cardoso as "gran filósofo y muy noticioso de las buenas letras," Cardoso's own references to the large and distinguished audience which was present when he defended his medical and philosophic theses, combine to indicate the esteem which the thirty-one-year-old physician now enjoyed. The fact is that Lope himself, though already feeling ill earlier in the day, made the effort to come to hear him. It was indeed a signal honor for Cardoso, and points to some prior contact between the two.

The extent of their relationship is difficult to determine. In his *Laurel de Apolo*, written in 1628-29 and published in 1630, Lope did not mention Cardoso among some 280 Spanish and Portuguese writers whom he praised. This is certainly understandable since at that time Cardoso had but recently come to Madrid. Nevertheless, it must have been shortly after the publication of this work that Cardoso's name first came to Lope's attention. The circumstances are somewhat curious. In 1631 there appeared in Lisbon a slim volume entitled *Elogio de poetas lusitanos* by one Jacinto Cordeiro, of whom little seems to be known beyond the fact that he was an ensign, a poet, and had lived for some time in Spain.[46] The work

---

[45] Cardoso, *Oración funebre*, fols. 21v-22r.

[46] *Elogio de poetas Lusitanos; Al Fenix de España Fr. Lope Felix de Vega Carpio, en su laurel de Apolo, por el Alferes Iacinto Cordero, con una carta en repuesta al Autor, del mismo Fenix de Espana. Dirigido a la Señora Doña Cecilia de Meneses. Año 1631. En Lisboa con todas las licencias necessarias por Iorge Rodriguez*. Fols. 1-16, numbered recto. The work seems to be of the utmost rarity. In the HSA copy which I have used, a notation on the flyleaf states: "Sólo existe otro ejemplar de este folleto. . . ." It is listed in Domingo García Peres, *Catálogo razonado biográfico y bibliográfico de los autores portugueses que escribieron en castellano* (Madrid, 1890). However, I was somewhat surprised to find no mention of the work in any study of Lope which I have consulted, including those of Rennert-Castro and La Barrera. The latter does cite Cordeiro's name among those whom Lope should have included in the *Laurel*,

is, in essence, a grieved but respectful reply to Lope's *Laurel de Apolo* of the previous year, chiding him for having omitted a number of Portuguese poets "whom with much justice he could have named."[47] Cordeiro goes on to rectify Lope's omissions by praising 62 Portuguese poets in a series of more than 70 octaves.[48] One of these is devoted to Dr. Fernando Cardoso.[49]

It is not really necessary to speculate as to which writings Cardoso could possibly have produced by 1631 to merit being considered a poet by Cordeiro. The Portuguese patriot was anxious to expand his list to the utmost, and even a few occasional poems by Cardoso, of the type included in Pellicer's *Anfiteatro*, sufficed.[50] Similarly, Cordeiro's conception of Cardoso as a Lusitanian poet has reference only to the latter's birth in Portugal, and not to the length of time he had lived there. In any case, Lope de Vega took sufficient notice of the *Elogio* to send an epistle in reply.[51] His personal acquaintance with Cardoso may have begun shortly thereafter.

---

but gives nothing further about him (*Nueva biografía*, p. 423). There is only a very brief notice in the *Enciclopedia Luso-Brasileira*, *s.v.* Cordeiro.

[47] In his Portuguese preface addressed to the poets of his native land, Cordeiro writes: "Senhores Poetas: Este Elogio escrivi em Tercetos, ao Fenix de Espanha Lopo de Veiga Carpio, pera q̄ tivesse noticia de v. ms. aviendose esquesido no seu laurel de Apolo de muytos que aqui vão, que con muyta justicia pudera nomear . . ." (*Elogio de poetas Lusitanos*, fol. 2r).

[48] The verses are in Spanish. In a play on his own name, Cordeiro includes himself, but says he is a "lamb" among lions (fol. 16r).

[49] Luego el doctor Cardoso en el desgarro
con prevenida accion al premio asiste
que a darle Febo el luminoso carro
no lloraras lampecie al caso triste,
del hermano Faeton quando bizarro
muerte a tus ojos con un rayo viste
que el Doctor con su ingenio le domara,
y el, ALTAPETIS, sin vigor quedara.

(*Ibid.*, fol. 12v)

[50] Cordeiro's Lusitanian pride is well illustrated when he says (fol. 5v): "Honrar la patria en mi, no. es desatino/ que es ley, y obligación. . . ." After the Portuguese revolt of 1640 he wrote a *Silva a el rey Dom Ioam IV* (Lisbon, 1641).

[51] This is evident from the title page of the *Elogio* (*supra*, n. 46). Unfortunately, it is missing from the HSA copy.

ORACION FVNEBRE

En la muerte de Lope de Vega.

Ingenio laureado de las Musas,

Prodigiosa marauilla de España,

Eterna admiracion de las Edades.

AL EXCELENTISSIMO

Señor Duque de Sessa, Conde Cabra, y
gran Almirante de Napo-
les, &c.

El Dotor Fernando Cardoso
Dedica, Consagra, Ofrece.

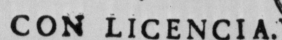

CON LICENCIA.

En Madrid, Por la viuda de Iuan
Gonçalez, Año 1635.

Cardoso's own feelings toward Lope find their fullest expression in the *Oración funebre*. From the very first lines it is clear that his admiration for Lope's genius was boundless:

Lope de Vega has died! The name alone suffices to evoke admiration and feeling! The delights of the Muses will now be lacking! The laurel remains without a triumph, and the ivy without glory! Withered is the fertile plain which he inundated with fruits and flowers! Sorrow pours itself out in tears, and anguish in laments! Other dear friends hear and bewail the death of this prodigy of Spain, while I, with even more loving obligation, owe to his final passage the first acclamation. Like a humble listener he carefully heard me speak of the virtues of the human heart; let me now repay his last attentions with eulogies more felt than expressed. . . . Dead do we see the splendor of poetry, the father of the theater, the symbol of fertility, and the honor of eloquence . . .![52]

Lope, writes Cardoso, encompasses more subtleties than all the poets of antiquity together.[53] Scripture attributes 5,000 verses to Solomon; Lope wrote more *scenes* than that, and his prolific output in no way impaired the quality of his work.[54] As for his style:

He devoted himself to the study of languages in order to discover the treasures in their mines. Expert in Latin and in the vernaculars, Italian, French, and Portuguese, he was so mellow in his own Castilian, that, just as the pagans said that had Jupiter spoken Greek he would have spoken it like Plato, and the Muses would have spoken Latin like Plautus, so, in speaking Spanish, they would have spoken like Lope.[55]

How much dost thou owe, Madrid, to thy son?! How much, O Court, to thy courtier?![56]

The very rivers, the Tajo and the Manzanares, together with the vegetation on their banks, join in commemorating the poet:

Lope is written in the trees, where he celebrated the delights of the grove; *Lope* in the plants, where he painted the lushness of their flowers; *Lope* in the sands, where he stamped the imprint of his footsteps. The entire river bank adorns itself with epigrams and epitaphs. On the leaves of certain plants can be read: 'Here he sang the loves of *Angélica*;' 'here

---

[52] Cardoso, *Oración funebre*, fols. 5r-6r.   [53] *Ibid.*, fol. 9r.

[54] *Ibid.*, fol. 12r.   [55] *Ibid.*, fols. 17v-18r.   [56] *Ibid.*, fol. 15r.

Title page of Cardoso's oration on the death   157
of Lope de Vega (Madrid, 1635)

Biblioteca Nacional, Lisbon

the tenderness of *Arcadia'*; 'here the captious cunning of *Circe'*; 'here the repeated complaints of *Philomena.*' There we discover the valors of *Dragontea* and the *Triumphos de Jerusalem*, while here are seen portrayed a *Peregrino*, and a grateful *Isidro*. On the violets are inscribed the sorrows of the *Rimas humanas*, and on the lilies, those of the *divinas*. . . .[57]

Interspersed between such affectionate hyperboles we find Cardoso's serious defense of the theater. Attacks on the pernicious effects of both plays and performers on public morals had been frequent in Spain since the end of the sixteenth century. The Church in particular was often opposed. In 1598, 1600, 1603, and 1615, royal decrees had been promulgated which aimed at the stringent surveillance and reformation of the stage, but these had no lasting effect. The reign of Philip IV was more favorable since the king himself, like the mass of his subjects, was a passionate devotee of the theater. But, though Philip encouraged and patronized the playwrights, often for private theatricals in his own palace, criticism did not subside. In the years following Lope's death the theaters were to be closed on a number of occasions, and in 1646 a council of theologians would advise the banning of nearly all the *comedias* which had been produced until then, "especially those of Lope de Vega, which have worked such harm in the customs of the people."[58]

Cardoso defends Lope's plays for their realism, their essential morality, and, as might be expected, by an appeal to the example of the ancients:

His comedies were an illustration of our customs, a mirror of life, a disclosure of the times, and a persuasion to virtue. What does it matter that the severe Lacedaemonians did not welcome poets, and exiled Archilochus for wanting to settle within their walls, or that Plato did not allow them in his Republic, when the more sensitive Aristotle not only does not exclude them, but sets down rules whereby they may attain eminence? . . . The Greek and Roman states, which were known throughout the world for their polity, admitted comic and tragic playwrights, and constructed opulent theaters in which were often present

---

[57] *Ibid.*, fol. 25r-v.

[58] Rennert, *Spanish Stage*, p. 246. For a general discussion of opposition to the theater, see *ibid.*, ch. X.

Augustus in his grandeur and other emperors. . . . In the theater are depicted human passions which temper us by their very excess. To see in the theater the actions of the violent, the disobedient, the avaricious, the lascivious—what are these if not exemplary documents for a withdrawal from these transgressions, and a vivid representation of the miserable end to which they lead?[59]

The entire *Oración funebre* ends on a triumphant note:

O courageous champion of the theater! . . . A pilgrim through all ages, the world admires thee, reaps thy eloquence, honors thy thoughts . . . Comedians and tragedians celebrate the day of thy birth, as of old Silius Italicus honored that of Vergil. Immortality acclaims thee Phoenix of Spain. . . . O abundant field (*Vega*) where the fruits competed with the flowers, the ripe with the beautiful, felicitous (*Felix*) in a genius which merited so much, and in a melodiousness which was able so to resound, adorned now with glories whose luster fortune cannot dim! Repose with these celestial sapphires: that Spain dedicates to thee its reverent cult; the world, well-earned eulogies; Fame, loud trumpets; princes, immortal purples; the talented, eternal inscriptions; and the heavens, sacred splendors.[60]

Such is Cardoso's tribute to that same Lope de Vega who was also the author of the poem on the *Cristo de la Paciencia* which we examined earlier. This alone sufficiently indicates the complexities of Cardoso's personal relationships in Madrid. The dualities inherent in New Christian life crop up at every turn. Different levels of awareness intertwine, coexist, contradict each other, and the psyche manages to separate them, at least temporarily. In the *Oración funebre* Cardoso is able to see only the genial aspects of a great artist, and to ignore the rest.

But this is a duality which, in an analogous way, extends also to Lope de Vega himself, and to others like him. Even a cursory study of Lope's works and letters will reveal a full measure of the prejudice and hostility of his age against "Jews" and New Christians. That Lope was a familiar of the Holy Office has already been stated.

---

[59] Cardoso, *Oración funebre*, fol. 18r-v.   [60] *Ibid.*, fols. 27v-28r.

Madrid: Fame and Flight

In a letter written to Góngora in 1617 he boasts of a relative who had a reputation for burning heretics.[61] His plays are perhaps the best examples of his attitudes. *El Brasil restituido* revolves around the treacherous collaboration of the Jews with the Dutch in Pernambuco.[62] The famous *El niño inocente de la Guardia* is based on the notorious trial for ritual murder held in 1490, and offers a justification for the expulsion of the Jews.[63] The latter theme also appears in *El mejor mozo de España*, which deals with the engagement of Ferdinand and Isabella, and the consequent union of Aragon and Castile.[64] At the end of one of Lope's *autos sacramentales*, entitled *La siega*, and written during the reign of Philip IV, "Hebraismo" is cast into the eternal fires.[65] In general, Lope's views seem to be

---

[61] Cited by Caro, *Sociedad*, p. 55. Some ambivalence in Lope's attitude to the *autos de fe* may be gathered from a letter written to the Duke of Sessa in 1615: "Aqui se esta esperando el Auto, fiesta de quien dice el Cardenal que es como la mar, que, pasada la primera admiración, entristece . . ." (*Cartas completas* I, no. 194, p. 255). On the other hand, the *auto sacramental* entitled *"La santa Inquisición"* is attributed to Lope (*Obras*, ed. Real Academia, Vol. III). For some doubts as to the authorship see Rennert-Castro, *Vida de Lope de Vega*, p. 322.

[62] *Obras*, ed. Real Academia, Vol. XIII. Cf. the remarks of Glaser, *Invitation to Intolerance*, p. 360.

[63] *Obras*, ed. Real Academia, Vol. V. For Lope's sources see M. Menéndez y Pelayo, *Estudios sobre el teatro de Lope de Vega* (Madrid, 1949), II, 85 ff. The play has been analyzed by Edward Glaser in his "Lope de Vega's El Niño Inocente de la Guardia," *Bulletin of Hispanic Studies* (Liverpool), XXXII (1955), 140–53, which also contains ample bibliographies.

[64] *Obras*, ed. Real Academia, Vol. X. In Act I, Spain, personified as a woman dressed in mourning, is held between a Moor and a Jew. She turns to Isabella and says: "Y quien librar/ puede mi cuello, tú eres,/ del moro y del fiero hebreo/ que has de desterrar de España . . ." (*ibid.*, p. 331). M. Herrero García has observed, with some justification: "Inútil sería encontrar en el siglo XVII español un solo autor contrario al extrañamiento de los judíos" (*Ideas de los españoles*, p. 619).

[65] *Autos sacramentales desde su origen hasta fines del siglo XVII*, ed. by E. Gonzáles Pedroso (= *B.A.E.*, LXVIII; Madrid, 1924), pp. 171–81. At the end of the drama, after "Herejia," "Seta," and "Idolatria" have submitted to Christ, the latter turns to Hebraismo:
(*Señor*): Y tú, que dices?/ (*Hebraismo*): Que aguardo el Mesías prometido./
(*Señor*): Oh rebelde porfiado! Tú solo me niegas, tú,/ que has visto tantos milagros/

well summarized in the words of his character Ruperto, in the comedy *San Nicolás de Tolentino*: "No Jew can do anything good. How hateful to me is this line of men!"[66]

And yet Lope was capable of maintaining close literary and personal friendships with a number of known New Christians. He thought highly enough of Silveyra to praise him in the *Laurel de Apolo*.[67] Antonio Enríquez Gómez was certainly part of the circle of Lope's admirers, as was the playwright Dr. Felipe Godínez. The latter, to be sure, sometimes became the butt of Lope's jokes because of his ancestry, but this did not interfere with their relations. Like Cardoso, Godínez published an *Oración funebre* on Lope's death.[68]

Moreover, Lope's favorite disciple, Juan Pérez de Montalván, was himself the subject of repeated rumors concerning his Jewish descent.

---

las profecías cumplidas,/ y que vives desterrado/ sin templo, ni sacerdote,/ sin rey, sin amoro humano?/ Echadle en el fuego eterno!

In general the *autos sacramentales* were a major vehicle for attacks against Judaism. The volume just cited contains several examples by other writers, including Calderón de la Barca. On antisemitism on the secular Spanish stage, see Edward Glaser, "Referencias antisemitas en la literatura peninsular de la Edad de Oro," *Nueva revista de filología hispánica*, VIII (1954), 39–62, *passim*.

[66] *Obras*, ed. Real Academia, IV, 340.

[67] *Laurel de Apolo*, Silva III, in *Obras sueltas*, I, 56. Lope also praised Silveyra in his epistle to D. Francisco de Rioja, entitled "El jardín," and published in 1621 as part of the volume containing *La Filomena* (see *Obras sueltas*, I, 487).

[68] Antonio Enríquez Gómez' poem on Lope's death appears in Montalván's *Fama póstuma* (*Obras sueltas*, XX, 146), as does Felipe Godínez' *Oración* (*ibid.*, pp. 147–65). The latter was born *ca.* 1585 in Moguer, of New Christian parents. He was known as a preacher in Seville, and later as a playwright. Having expressed some vaguely unorthodox ideas in his sermons, he was arrested by the Inquisition and reconciled at an *auto* in Seville in 1624. (See Adolfo de Castro, "Noticias de la vida del doctor Felipe Godínez," *Memorias de la Real Academia Española*, VIII (1902), 277–83.) Soon thereafter he came to Madrid. Among his plays there are several on Old Testament themes (printed in *Dramáticos contemporáneos de Lope de Vega*, ed. R. Mesonero Romanos, II, [*B.A.E.* XLV (1853), pp. 199 ff]). See on him Caro, *Sociedad*, pp. 115–18.

Lope's pun, occasioned by a new play of Godínez which appeared in 1628, occurs in a letter to D. Antonio de Mendoza: "La comedia que llamavan La Godina, por ser su autor el dotor Godínez . . . se representó ayer. Dízenme que es más judía que de los Godos . . ." (La Barrera, *Nueva biografía*, p. 654).

Madrid: Fame and Flight

On at least two separate occasions he was attacked on this score by Quevedo.[69] We have already seen Montalván's high estimate of Cardoso, and we may assume they were friends. The appearance of Cardoso's sonnet in the *Fama pósthuma* was undoubtedly by invitation. Yet if Montalván may have been a New Christian, he was also a convinced Catholic. This may be seen most vividly in an *auto sacramental* which he wrote around 1628, entitled *El Polifemo*. For a further understanding of Cardoso's environment, it may be appropriate to summarize Montalván's rather crudely allegorical plot: Polifemo is the Devil, and has as his servants four Cyclops: Judaism, Mockery of God, Deception, and Natural Feeling. He wants to avenge himself on Ulysses (Christ) because the latter had sought him out in his cave (Hell), had put him to sleep with the odor of a strong wine concocted out of His blood, and had then gouged out his eye with a glowing staff shaped in the form of a Cross. Polifemo has now learned that Ulysses, disguised as a Shepherd, is wooing Galatea (The Human Soul), whom he also covets. Appetite, a servant of Galatea, persuades her to accept Polifemo. As he serenades her, the Shepherd appears and they begin to fight. A blow of the Cross fells the attending Cyclops, but Polifemo will renounce Galatea only if the Shepherd buys her from him. The latter agrees, and offers to sell his blood so that he may redeem her. As the Shepherd goes off, there ensues a dialogue between Galatea, Polifemo, and Judaismo, in which she upholds the divinity of the Shepherd, the argument following the outlines of the life of Christ. In a mechanical alteration of the stage an altar with a Cross appears. When Galatea and Appetite approach, the Cross is transformed into a chalice, and a Host. A child (the risen Christ) emerges from the chalice, offers his hand to Galatea, and they pledge themselves to one another. As Polifemo moans, "Therefore I suffer and

---

[69] Quevedo, *Poema heroyco de las necedades y locuras de Orlando*, referring to Montalván as a *marrano*. See *Obras de d. Francisco de Quevedo Villegas*, in *B.A.E.* LXIX [1877], 287; and again in *La Perinola* B.A.E., XLVIII [1859], 467), where he also attacks Godínez (*ibid.*, p. 469). Cf. Caro, *Judíos*, I, 291.

hurt," and Judaismo responds, "Therefore I sigh and weep," the sacred drama is ended.[70]

We are now perhaps even better equipped to appreciate how far the social reality of the New Christian in seventeenth-century Madrid transcended any strict categories which might be delineated simply on the basis of avowed beliefs and attitudes. If, for the moment, we look upon the many contributors to Montalván's *Fama pósthuma* as providing a microcosm of that society, we have a case in point. The editor himself, said to be a New Christian, is also the author of the *Polifemo*, whose anti-Jewish character needs no further comment. In the memorial volume are mingled, in addition to Cardoso's sonnet, verses and compositions by clerics, government officials, scholars, artists, soldiers, and nobles. Some of the contributors bear the most irreproachable pedigrees in Spain; others are New Christians. A considerable number of persons have appeared with Cardoso in other volumes. Pellicer has submitted a eulogy in prose, a "Sacred Urn Erected to the Immortal Ashes of Frey Lope Felix de Vega Carpio." Even Don Juan de Quiñones is present, with a poem in Latin, the first letters of each verse forming an acrostic of Lope's name.[71] Whatever their private feelings and hates they are all here, gathered together and bowed in homage to the "Phoenix

---

[70] *El Polifemo, auto sacramental del Dotor Iuan Perez de Montalvan,* incorporated afterwards as part of the fifth day's entertainment in his *Para todos.* I have used the copy of the *Polifemo* in the HSA Library which, though carrying no date on the title page, appears to be the original edition. It is paginated fols. 118r (read 214r)–226v. At the end: "Tocan y buelvese a cerar todo, cõ que se da fin al Auto de Polifemo. Madrid y Abril de 1628."

Quevedo, who must have seen the actual performance, was revolted. He writes in *La Perinola* of Montalván's representation of Christ as Ulysses: "Esta no es alegoría sino algarabía; no hiciera cosa tan mal sonante ni indecente un moro buñolero . . ." (*B.A.E.,* XLVIII, 474). The *Polifemo* has been analyzed by Hiram Pflaum, *Die Religiöse Disputation in der Europaischen Dichtung des Mittelalters. Erste Studie: Der allegorische Streit zwischen Synagoge und Kirche* (Geneva, 1935). pp. 87–91. For a comprehensive study of Montalván, see George William Bacon, "The Life and Dramatic Works of Doctor Juan Pérez de Montalván (1602–1638)," *Revue hispanique,* XXVI (1912), 1–474.

[71] *Fama pósthuma* (*Obras sueltas,* XX, 85): "Dominus D. Ioannes de Quiñones, Magni Philippi IV Curiae Domusque Regiae Praetor."

of Spain." It is, in its own way, an interesting assembly of mourners, incongruous only if we choose to ignore the many other incongruities in the normal life of Madrid.

UNDER THE PATRONAGE OF OLIVARES

Though by 1636 Cardoso's career displays no mean accomplishments for so young a man, it was in the decade following the death of Lope de Vega that he came into the plenitude of his powers.

In 1637 he published a book which was to give him a secure place of honor in the annals of Spanish medicine. This work, entitled *Utilidades del agua y de la nieve*, was a treatise on the medicinal uses of water and melted snow, and on certain related subjects.[72] It was by far the most ambitious work he had yet undertaken and at the same time it was linked to an important change which now occurred in his own life.

The book is dedicated to the "Conde-Duque," who is of course Don Gaspar de Guzmán, Count of Olivares, Prime Minister of Spain, and whose arms are engraved on the title page. In the elaborate dedication Cardoso calls him "a prince who is equally attentive to arms and to letters." It is doubly appropriate, he writes, to offer him a work on such a theme, for not only does a minister who works so hard during the summer months require a flask of cold water, but also water is the symbol of purity, and the Psalmist has written that the pure of hand and of heart shall ascend the mountain of the Lord. With another metaphorical turn, Cardoso provides Olivares with an obvious hint as to his own expectations

---

[72] *Utilidades/ del agua i de la nieve/ del bever frio i caliente/ al Ec^mo Sor Conde Duque/ El Dotor Fernando Cardoso/* [arms of Olivares]/ *ofrece, dedica consagra./ Con privilegio/ En Madrid, por la viuda de Alõso Martin, año 1637.* 7 fols. of preliminary material, including: *Aprovación* of Fr. Ignacio de Vitoria (Jan. 29, 1637). and of Dr. Juan Gutiérrez de Solórzano, "medico de camara de su magestad" (March 26, 1635); an engraved page showing a hand holding a heart over a body of water, with the motto: "Quis ascendit in montem Domini? innocens manibus & mundo corde"; Dedication to Olivares; etc. The text: fols. 1–108, numbered recto.

of reward. At the time of the Creation, before even there was light, the Spirit of God hovered over the waters to make them fecund. Similarly, whatever coldness there is in the book will be diminished when it has a spirit which moves it, and a warmth which foments it. He excuses himself for writing the book in the vernacular rather than in Latin, explaining that it is because he wanted it to be of use to all, "and in this way the toughness of its scholarship shall be softened by the smoothness of the reading."[73]

It is clear that between 1635, when the book was completed, and 1637, when it was published, Cardoso had sought and found in Olivares a new patron. Two years later, when he published his treatise on fevers, this patronage was confirmed. As we have seen, however, Cardoso had earlier enjoyed the patronage of Enríquez de Cabrera, the Admiral of Castile. While it was not uncommon in Madrid to change one's patron, or to seek the favor of several simultaneously, Cardoso's step was more serious. The Admiral was a mortal enemy of Olivares, and, in soliciting the patronage of the Prime Minister, Cardoso must necessarily have broken with his former benefactor.[74]

In approaching Olivares, Cardoso could well have shared the motives which prompted many others to do the same. Though already surrounded by foes, the Count-Duke in 1635 was still secure in his power, and his, not the king's, was the real power in Spain. He was also known widely as a great patron of art and literature, and the creator of a magnificent private library.[75] For Cardoso, however, such attractive considerations may have been outweighed by an even more decisive factor. Olivares had already become notorious in the eyes of many, as a protector of New Christians, and even as sympathetic to professing Jews. Satirical poems, often anonymous, repeatedly hurled such charges against him.[76] Quevedo

---

[73] *Utilidades*, fol. 6r of the preliminary material.

[74] On the Admiral's hostility to Olivares see Gregorio Marañón, *El Conde-Duque de Olivares: La pasión de mandar* (4th ed.; Madrid, 1959), p. 254, n. 41.

[75] Olivares' cultural pursuits are discussed by Marañón, *Ibid.*, ch. XII ("El Intelectual"), esp. pp. 144–66.

[76] See the examples cited by Domínguez, *Clase social*, pp. 115 f.

in particular would go so far as to depict him in 1639 as taking part in a council of Salonikan Jews, meeting to discuss the steps by which they might appropriate the wealth and power of Spain, and would insinuate that important offices were already in Jewish hands.[77] Of course such extreme statements were the product of sheer malice. Nevertheless, other rumors are so persistent that they cannot be attributed to enmity alone. Though the relations between Olivares and the New Christians require further research and evaluation, the available data are sufficient to show that behind the accusations there lay a reality.[78]

It is not at all necessary to assume that Olivares had any personal love for *conversos* nor even a benevolent interest in their condition. His actions, such as they were, derived from his general tendency to subordinate domestic affairs to the exigencies of foreign policy. Absorbed in his goal of assuring Spanish hegemony in the world, he was ready to adopt any internal measures he felt necessary, regardless of their unpopularity. Olivares knew that the bankers, contractors, and farmers of royal rents which the treasury required could not be recruited in Spain alone. There was no alternative but to enlist the services of Germans, Italians, or—Portuguese New Christians. The latter had a singular advantage. Since Spain and Portugal were still united, and the "Portuguese" were thus vassals of the same monarchy, the money they made could not be considered lost. Olivares was also very much aware that the New Christians, and the Marranos among them, were an important factor in international affairs and commerce. Especially vital was their influence in the Low Countries, then one of the most sensitive spots in Europe.

---

[77] Quevedo, *Isla de los Monopantos*, written in 1639, later inserted in his *La hora de todos* (*B.A.E.*, XXIII [1852], 415 f.).

[78] The first modern scholar to draw attention to Olivares as a protector of *conversos* was Adolfo de Castro, in his *El Conde-Duque de Olivares y el rey Felipe IV* (Cádiz, 1846), esp. pp. 133 ff. Among other instances, he states that Olivares clashed with the Inquisitor-General by asking him to hand over the records of various prisoners. Unfortunately De Castro did not cite the documentary sources from which he drew much of his information. See also his *Historia de los judíos de España* (Cádiz, 1847), pp. 219 f.; Marañón, *Olivares*, p. 180; Caro, *Judíos*, II, 42 ff.

He desired, naturally, to harness this potential for the Spanish side.[79]

Such considerations provide the background for the curious mélange of events and rumor in Madrid between 1634 and 1641. On August 4, 1634, the Jesuits reported that actual negotiations were in progress to allow Jews to enter Spain, and that one Jew dressed in a white headdress, apparently oriental, was seen at the door of the king's quarters.[80] Similarly, Matías de Novoa, the king's chamberlain, wrote that he had heard of a plan to bring professing Jews from Oran and other North African localities and to allow them, in exchange for a vast sum of money, to live in a special suburb of Madrid with freedom to practice their religion openly.[81] According to one report the negotiations broke down because of the intervention of the papal nuncio, Cardinal Monti.[82]

Whatever the actual details, one thing is certain: During the premiership of Olivares there were individual Jews who came to Madrid sporadically and with impunity, and who had dealings with him. The most striking case is that of Jacob Cansino, a Jew whose family was in the Spanish service in Oran, and whose career has yet to be fully elucidated. Cansino is known to have been in Madrid in 1625, 1637, and, although imprisoned in 1646, again in 1656. In 1637, at least, Cansino had in his possession a special license

---

[79] See Domínguez, *Clase social*, pp. 110–12.

[80] "Valido anda que entran los judíos en España; lo cierto es que entran y salen á hablar al Rey y darle memoriales, y hoy vi uno con toca blanca á la puerta del cuarto Rey; pena me dió" (*Mem. hist. esp.*, XIII, 85).

[81] "He oído decir que los judíos de Orán y los que habitan la tierra adentro del Africa tienen aqui sus pretendientes para que los admitan a los contornos de Madrid y les den tierra y suelo en que viven a su libertad y en su ley y a todos los demás que quisieron habitar con ellos, y se empadronarían y darían muchos millones por la permisión ... Ay de las familias nobles de Castilla ... !" (*Memorias de Matías de Novoa, ayuda de cámara de Felipe IV*, II (= *Colección de documentos inéditos para la historia de España*, LXXVII, 380). Cf. Lea, *Inq. of Spain*, III, 292 f.; Domínguez, *Clase social*, pp. 114 f.; Caro, *Judíos*, II, 42 f.

[82] De Castro, *El Conde-Duque de Olivares*, pp. 133–34; Domínguez, *Clase social*, p. 115.

from the Holy Office, and was in close contact with Olivares.[83] Perhaps even more remarkable is the book he published a year later. He had abridged a description of Constantinople by the sixteenth-century Salonikan Rabbi Moses Almosnino, written in Judeo-Spanish, and transcribed it into Roman characters. In 1638 he offered to the Madrid public a book with this fascinating title page: The Extremes and Grandeurs of Constantinople, Composed by Rabbi Moses Almosnino, a Hebrew, and Translated by Jacob Cansino, Vassal of His Catholic Majesty, and His Interpreter of Language in the Places of Oran. This book is dedicated to Olivares, and contains a full-page engraving of the minister piercing with his sword the dragon of his enemies.[84] In such an atmosphere we are not at all surprised to find a rumor current in Madrid, in August

---

[83] These and other data on Cansino have been assembled by Caro Baroja (*Judíos*, II, 110 f.) mostly from the testimony of Luis de Acosta in the case of the widow of Manuel Cortizos (A.H.N, *Inq. de Toledo*, Leg. 148 no. 5; *Catálogo*, p. 182). The comings and goings of individual professing Jews in Madrid and elsewhere during the reign of Philip IV still await a comprehensive study, for which both inquisitorial and Jewish materials are available. It is interesting to note, for example, that in 1649 the famous Rabbi Jacob Sasportas was sent on a diplomatic mission to Spain by the king of Morocco. See the introduction of Abraham Sasportas to his father's responsa, *Ohel Ya'akob* (Amsterdam, 1737). Jacob Sasportas was himself a native of Oran. Graetz (*Geschichte*, X, p. 422, n. 2), has plausibly identified him with the Jaho Çaportas who competed with Jacob Cansino for the post of interpreter for the Spanish crown in that city after the death of the latter's brother, Aron Cansino, in 1633. It was to claim the position for himself as a hereditary right that Jacob Cansino came to Madrid in 1636. The affair is described by him in the prefaces to his edition of the *Extremos y grandezas de Constantinopla* (see the following note), in which he also includes an order of Philip IV restoring the post to him.

[84] *Extremos y grandezas de Constantinopla, compuesto por Rabi Moysen Almosnino, Hebreo, traducido por Iacob Cansino Vassallo de su Magestad Catolica, interprete suyo, y Lengua en las Plaças de Oran. Al Exc. Senor Conde de Olivares, Duque de Sanlucar la MAYOR, camarero MAYOR, y cavallerizo MAYOR de su Magestad, y de su Consejo de Estado, & co. (Filium triplicatum non rumpetur, & c. Eccles. cap. 7. 12.) Con privilegio. En Madrid. En la imprensa de Francisco Martinez. Año de M.DC. XXXVIII.* Further data on the original work, of which Cansino's transcription is an abridgment, will be found in my "Moses Almosnino's Mission to Constantinople," now in preparation.

of 1636, that no less a personage than the Duke of Medinacelli is studying Hebrew with a "rabbi" whom he lodges in his house, and that he has progressed to the point of reading without vowels.[85] In 1641 another project was to be discussed, similar to that of 1634, but this time to bring Jews from the Low Countries into Spain, which failed because of the opposition of the Holy Office.[86]

From the very outset the Inquisition kept its finger on the pulse of events, alarmed at the gossip, and equally upset at the further immigration of Portuguese New Christians into the Spanish capital. In 1637, when Cardoso's *Utilidades* was published, the Jesuits reported that a plan had been presented to establish a complete inquisitorial tribunal in Madrid which would be independent of Toledo.[87] Though nothing came of this, it does reveal that the position of the New Christians remained, potentially at least, quite precarious.

In the light of all these factors it is not difficult to surmise that, by offering his work to Olivares, Cardoso was seeking not merely a patron, but a protector. The book itself was fully worthy of the minister's attention and, indeed, evoked great admiration in Spain well into the nineteenth century.[88] Though we cannot pause to analyze the work in detail, it may be of interest to summarize the various themes which Cardoso discusses:

---

[85] "El Duque de Medinaceli estudia valientemente la lengua hebrea, teniendo en su casa un rabi para este efecto, y ha hecho tan grandes progresos que ya sabe leer sin puntos" (A. Rodríguez Villa, ed., *La corte y la monarquía de España en los años de 1636 a 1637* ([Madrid, 1886], p. 38).

[86] "He sabido por cosa cierta que se trata de restituir y traer los judíos que estan en las sinagogas de Holanda y otras partes; para lo qual se han propuesto en un papel veinte y ocho medios. Oponese á ellas constantemente la Santa Inquisición" (Pellicer, *Avisos*, in *Semanario erudito*, XXXII, 16).

[87] "Dícese por muy cierto se pone tribunal de Inquisición aquí, particular, por las muchas causas que cada día hay de cristianos nuevos venidos de Portugal.... Mucho lo sentiran los de Toledo, si esto tiene efecto ..."(*Mem. hist. esp.*, XIV (1862), 6).

[88] See, e.g., Anastasio Chinchilla, *Historia de la medicina española*, I, 86: "Este libro en mi concepto no tiene igual, ni en mérito, ni en filosofía, ni en crítica, ni en erudición, ni en hechos. Creo que si se reimprimiera, no desmereceria de los libros que se han publicado sobre el agua en los siglos posteriores."

VTILIDADES
DEL AGVA I DE LA NIEVE,
DEL BEVER FRIO I CALIENTE.
AL ECmo Sor CONDE DVQVE
El Dotor Fernando Cardoso

Ofrece, Dedica, Consagra.
CON PRIVILEGIO.

En Madrid por la viuda de Alóso Martin, Año 1637.

1. "The utility of water and its excellences, collected from various writings." (fols. 1r–7r.)

2. "Of thirst, and whether it kills more quickly than hunger. That many have remained 'naturally' many months and years without eating or drinking." (fols. 7r–12r.) Cardoso argues that thirst is more serious, and that the exaggerated accounts of years without food and water are likely the tales of superstitious women.

3. "Whether it is correct to drink water abundantly during fevers." (fols. 12v–21r.) We tend to doubt the most certain remedies and search for the most difficult. Water alone during some fevers can effect more than four concocted medicines.

4. "At which times, whether ordinarily or during fevers, should one drink copiously." (fols. 21r–27r.)

5. "Whether boiled water is finer than crude water." (fols. 27r–28v.) Cardoso recommends that water be boiled.

6. "The necessary conditions which water must have in order to be good." (fols. 29r–32v.)

7. "Which is healthier, rain water or water of the fountain?" (fols. 33r–39r.)

8. "On the water of rivers, and whether the Nile has the virtue of turning to blood." (fols. 39r–41v.)

9. "The marvels of water, and the cause of the flux and ebb of the sea. On the rare secret of the tides. That people die only when the tide ebbs." (fols. 42r–51r.)

10. "On the antiquity and use of snow among the Romans, Greeks, and Hebrews, and the praises of cold drinks collected from the physicians." (fols. 51r–60v.)

11. "On the different methods for making a drink cold, and the instruments employed." (fols. 61r–68r.)

12. "On the persons for whom snow is useful or dangerous, and whether he who has never drunk cold may drink so during illness." (fols. 68r–76v.)

13. "On the abuses of [melted] snow, against those who forbid it in summer. against those who drink it in winter, and those who drink it very cold." (fols. 77r–81v.)

Title page of Cardoso's treatise on the uses   171
of water and snow (Madrid, 1637)

14. "Objections against snow." (fols. 82r–93r.)

15. "On the use which the ancients made of drinking hot drinks, and that many persons in our time are accustomed to it." (fols. 93r–100v.)

16. "Whether it is healthy to drink hot drinks. Chocolate is discussed. What is the drink most natural to man, the hot or the cold?" (fols. 101r–108v.)

The book must have been very well received by Olivares, for less than two years later Cardoso dedicated to him another medical treatise, this time in Latin, from whose preface we learn that the relationship between them was by now fixed. This work, entitled *De febre syncopali*, appeared in Madrid in 1639, and Cardoso's dedication is worth quoting in full:

After having been (most excellent Sir) Professor of Philosophy in Valladolid, and having offered in the chair of *Prima de Medicina* the greatest demonstrations which have ever been witnessed in that University, I presented in this Court theses in various sciences on four consecutive days with the approval of the learned, dedicated to you last year the book on snow, and now I devote to you this treatise on Intermittent Fevers. . . .

Whoever once chooses such a good patron knows that the choice itself involves also constancy, for it would be frivolous to exchange a master toward whom one's affection has not changed, and when it has been the good fortune of our age to have a Minister with whom the most dedicated masters of the sciences can speak, and whose sleepless vigil often owes more to the school than to the palace. Much happiness was in store for the monarchy when it found such a counselor, who united personal disinterest with his talent, and who is the greatest joy of the Prince who sees, better than all, that we have a king's favorite with whom the theologian delights to discuss his purity, the jurist his justice, the philosopher his problems, the humanist his erudition, the physician his care of health, the politician the health of the republic, and finally, all the arts the best of their virtues.

We see fulfilled Plato's wish that the realm shall be fortunate when the philosophers govern, or the governors philosophize. Influenced by example, the nobility of Spain has already begun to shine in Letters and to form libraries, so that those hot and fervid talents of the Spaniards (as Lipsius says) may revive the sublime in their erudition. As Cassiodorus has stated, it is easier for Nature itself to go astray than for Republics to keep from imitating the customs of their rulers.

Recently the Court has been infested with fever, to the dismay of many, and the confusion of all. The physicians are at variance in its diagnosis and cure, some believing the fever to be Intermittent, and others, Malignant. And so, having examined its nature, observed various cases, and discussed it with our own frail talent, we desire to devote to Your Excellency this Discourse, which can merit the praise of being the first, though not the most polished.

Small is the work, great the subject, greater still the intention which dedicates it. I know of nothing more useful to offer, though in the resolution of these doubts many mortal risks may be incurred. If the arrangement, the style, and the fact of having treated anew this dreaded and obscure fever are not sufficient to gain renown, at least we shall have pleased by leaving the field open to greater minds. Other writers treat it very casually, forgetting the many difficulties which time and the experts have raised. We have always based ourselves on the princes of the art, since it would be childish to deviate from them except with proofs. But we have done so in such a manner that, as Seneca says, to them we owe the major part of judgment, while reserving something also to our own. *Multum magnorum virorum iudicio credo, aliquid et meo vindico.*

May God watch over Your Excellency, for the honor of letters, and the glory of arms.

Doctor Fernando Cardoso[89]

The circumstances under which the book was written are stated by Cardoso at the very beginning. In the autumn of 1637 Madrid was struck by an epidemic of fever which continued into the

---

[89] *De febre/ syncopali/ tractatio noviter discussa,/ utiliter disputata./ Controversijs, observationibus, historijs referta./ Ad excelentissium* [sic] *heroem/ Comitem de Olivares, Principum exemplar, Hispa-/ norum lumen, & numen./ Ferdinando Cardoso authore./ olim professore Pintiano./* [Arms of Olivares]/ *Superiorum Permissu./ Matriti, Ex Typographia Didaci Diaz de la Carrera/ M.DC.XXXIX.* 2 fols. of preliminary material: Approbation of "D. Petri Cortesij Regij Medici"; engraved page showing a hand holding a heart over a body of water, with motto "Quis ascendit in montem . . ." (etc.); Dedication to Olivares. The text: fols. 1–40, numbered recto.

The date 1634 given by Kayserling (*Sephardim*, p. 344) and obviously based on Nicolas Antonio, *Bib. Hisp.*, II, 371, is incorrect.

DE FEBRE

SYNCOPALI,

TRACTATIO NOVITER DISCVSSA,
Vtiliter disputata.

Controversijs, observationibus, Historijs referta.

AD EXCELENTISSIMVM HEROEM
Comitem de Olivares, Principum exemplar, Hispanorum lumen, & Numen.

FERDINANDO CARDOSO AVTHORE,
Olim professore Pintiano.

SVPERIORVM PERMISSV.

MATRITI, Ex Typographia Didaci Diaz de la Carrera.
M.DC.XXXIX.

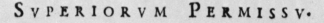

following year and attacked people of all classes and ages.[90] The bulk of the work is concerned, of course, with the description, diagnosis, and cure of the disease. But Cardoso also saw fit to include three case histories. In the first, that of a young man of twenty-four, he relates how Dr. Santa Cruz was called in for consultation. This can refer only to his former teacher at Valladolid, whom he describes as being now an octogenarian, and who died shortly after.[91] The second case was that of one Joseph Belardo, a public notary of whom we have no further information. The last, however, concerned the illness of Simón Tinoco, whom Cardoso describes as a beloved friend, a member of the Order of Christ, forty-two years of age.[92] Such a friendship is perfectly in accord with what we already know of Cardoso's connections in Madrid. The Tinoco family, though stanch Catholics, were apparently of Portuguese New Christian stock. Along with his brother and two relatives, Simón Tinoco had been, at least since 1637, one of the most important financiers of the realm.[93]

With the publication of his *Utilidades del agua y de la nieve* and *De febre syncopali* under the sponsorship of Olivares, Cardoso had reached the summit of his career in Madrid. In fact, there are reports that in 1640, a year after the appearance of the latter work,

---

[90] *De febre syncopali*, fol. 1r: "Anno millesimo trigesimo septimo cum aestas esset fervida, & Autumnis ardēs grassata est Matriti Epidemica Febris Syncopalis, pernitiosa, mortifera, quae plurimos utriusque sortis homines illustres, & vulgares iugulavit; subsequēti anno trigesimo octavo eadem, vel maiori strage persistens acutie tanta, & immani clade saevijt, ut multi quarta, vel quinta accessione perierint. Praecesserat anno antecedenti ingens morbillorum, & Variolarum copia, quae non solū infantes, & pueros, sed virilis solidiorisque aetatis homines affecit. . . ."

The gravity of the epidemic is underscored in a letter written by the Jesuit Sebastián González to Padre Pereyra in October of 1637: "Muertas violentas tenemos cada día además de las enfermedades que este año han sido tantas que ha muchos que tal cosa no se ha visto en Madrid. Dicese por cierto, han llegado á ser los enfermos veinte mil . . . " (*Mem. hist. esp.*, XIV [1862], 203).

[91] *De febre syncopali*, fols. 35v-36v. On Dr. Ponce de Santa Cruz see *supra*, ch. II, n. 62.

[92] *De febre syncopali*, fol. 38r.

[93] See Domínguez, *Política y hacienda*, p. 139, n. 17.

Title page of Cardoso's treatise on intermittent fever   175
(Madrid, 1639)

his achievements were crowned by an appointment as royal physician.[94] In that year, too, he published another medical work, on pregnancy.[95] He was still only thirty-six years old. Some eight years later he would flee Spain forever.

THE MARRANO

At no time in his later works does Cardoso mention the reasons which induced him to abandon the Peninsula, nor does he even refer directly to the move itself. Yet, although we shall probably never know the full story, it is possible to reconstruct at least some of the circumstances which preceded so drastic a step.

Certainly the general situation of the Portuguese New Christians living in Spain began to deteriorate after 1640. In that year Portugal revolted successfully and cast off the Spanish rule which it had endured for six decades. The repercussions in Spain were immediate. Anger and frustration at so grievous a loss expressed themselves in widespread resentment of the Portuguese immigrants, especially the New Christians. Not long after the revolt, on December 28, 1640, a royal decree took note of sporadic outbreaks against the Portuguese "of the Nation" in Seville, Bilbao, and other places. Clearly concerned lest further violence spark a mass exodus of Portuguese which might result in a grave economic collapse, the king ordered

---

[94] So Francisco António Martins Bastos, *Nobiliarchia medica. Noticia dos médicos e cirurgiões mores da real câmara, dos physicos mores do Reino, Armada, Exercito e Ultramarinos, etc. desde os tempos mais remotos da monarchia* (Lisbon, 1858), p. 42, and the references cited there. While I have been unable to corroborate this by documentary evidence from Spain, see the information contained in the Venetian archives, *infra*, ch. V.

[95] This work is usually listed as *Si el parte de 13 e 14 mezes es natural y legitimo* (Madrid, 1640). See Kayserling, *Sephardim*, p. 345; *BEPJ*, p. 34. I have not succeeded in locating a copy. The work is not mentioned by Nicolás Antonio, Bartolocci, or Barbosa Machado. Some of the material may be incorporated in Cardoso's *Philosophia Libera* (Venice, 1673), Lib. VI, especially Quaest. XCIX, fol. 689.

all authorities to protect them from vexation and molestation.[96] On April 2, 1641, Pellicer reported a rumor in Madrid that a "Portuguese" cleric had whipped a child, and that because of the ensuing scandal the Portuguese contractors in the city had prudently stayed away from their usual places of business.[97] Though in the decade 1640–50 the influence of the Portuguese in the chaotic Spanish economy became even more marked than before, a great number went bankrupt.

Meanwhile, other developments contributed to render the position of the New Christians less secure than it had been in recent years. In 1643 Olivares, whose policies had long been heavily attacked, was finally dismissed. At about the same time the Inquisitor-General Antonio de Sotomayor was replaced by the much harsher Diego de Arce Reinoso, who was to hold office until 1665, and whose biographer claimed that because of his zeal 12,000 families of Jewish origin left Spain. During his term no less than 17 *autos generales* were held, and a most rigorous reaction set in favoring the enforcement of the statutes of *limpieza*.[98]

Yet, although the fall of Olivares, the increased hostility to New Christians, and the acceleration of inquisitorial activity must have made Cardoso uneasy, and may even have combined to serve as a catalyst in his final decision to depart, we cannot explain his behavior simply as a negative reaction stemming from fear of the Inquisition. He does not exhibit any of the patterns that can be observed in those New Christians who did flee the Peninsula merely out of fear for their persons. Had we no other information, his subsequent Jewish career alone would incline us to assume that he had already Judaized to some extent in the Peninsula. The fact is, however, that on this point we need not even speculate. Evidence exists that prior to his departure Cardoso was actively propagandizing for Judaism in Madrid.

This information, so important for a proper evaluation of the great

---

[96] Domínguez, *Política y hacienda*, p. 133.

[97] Pellicer, *Avisos*, in *Semanario erudito*, XXXII, 22 f. See also Caro, *Judíos*, I, 175, 202.

[98] See on this period Caro, *Sociedad*, pp. 60 ff.; Domínguez, *Clase social*, p. 121.

turning point in Cardoso's life, was revealed in testimony given to the Inquisition more than a decade after he had left Spain.

In 1659 Diego Gómez de Salazar, a wealthy financier and tax farmer, was imprisoned by the Inquisition of Toledo on a charge of Judaizing. Though considered a "Portuguese" he was born in Ciudad Rodrigo in 1606, began to make his fortune in Andalucía, and came to Madrid in 1637. After a series of false starts in the capital, including a term in prison because he had been bondsman for another financier who had gone bankrupt, he devoted himself to farming various royal rents and taxes. During the ministry of Luis de Haro he was part of a group which advanced between seven and eight million ducats to the government. At the time of his arrest in 1659 he was *administrador general del tabaco* for Castile and León and held, in addition to this monopoly, that of the *alcabala* and *millones* of Granada. The Inquisition, which had been surveying him for many years, charged Gómez de Salazar with the observance of Jewish fasts, holidays, and other rites. It was further alleged that for a long time the family ambition had been to increase its fortune and go to a country where Judaism could be practiced freely. After he had married off his fourth daughter, he made concrete plans to transfer his rents for a good price and then to depart.[99]

Among those whose depositions were used in evidence against him was Rodrigo Méndez Silva, whom we have already encountered as a compatriot of Cardoso, and who had himself been arrested for Judaizing on May 11, 1659, by the Inquisition of Cuenca.[100]

---

[99] For details of the case see Caro, *Judíos*, II, 84–91, and III, App. xliv, pp. 365 f.; *Sociedad*, pp. 81–84. The dossier of Gómez de Salazar is incomplete. On the cover it is noted that he was reconciled, but in reality the case dragged on long after 1659. He appeared at an *auto* in Valladolid on Oct. 30, 1664, and was sentenced to irrevocable life imprisonment. His daughters appeared at another *auto* in Toledo on Oct. 31, 1667. Somehow Gómez de Salazar and other members of his faily were released from prison and reunited. They fled to Bayonne where, at the end of 1671, he died, apparently as a professing Jew. At the great *auto* held in Madrid on June 30, 1680, he was burned in effigy.

[100] On Méndez Silva see the information assembled by Caro, *Judíos*, II, 97–102, 348–50. The record of his torture was transcribed and placed in the dossier of Diego Gómez de Salazar, and is published *ibid.*, III, App. xliii, pp. 359–65. During my stay in Spain I suspected that the original dossier of Méndez Silva's

Méndez Silva was born in Celorico da Beira around 1606, and was thus only slightly younger than Cardoso.[101] Like the latter he had left Portugal and settled in Madrid, where he rose to become Royal Chronicler to Philip IV. He had held this position since 1635, and since 1640 had also been a member of the royal council. Between 1635 and 1659 he published many works on Spanish and Portuguese geography, history, and genealogy.[102] In addition he engaged in various financial ventures, and appears to have gathered a small but comfortable fortune. From the lists drawn up when his goods were confiscated we can form an idea of his library and especially his extensive collection of paintings. The latter included a large number of canvases on Christian religious themes, as well as a portrait of Olivares, sixteen of various members of the House of Austria, and one which the Inquisitors described as depicting a "Jew."[103] Since the dossier of Méndez Silva's own case has not been available to us, we do not know the sequence of events which led to his arrest. The fact that he had been in close relation with the immensely wealthy Manuel Cortizos may have contributed to his downfall, for after the latter's death in 1651 inquisitorial proceedings began against his widow and other members of the family.[104]

---

own case might still be extant in the archives of the Cathedral of Cuenca, but was told that due to a process of reorganization they were inaccessible. Since then a catalogue has appeared (Sebastián Cirac Estopañan, *Registros de los documentos del Santo Oficio de Cuenca y Siguenza, I: Registro general de los procesos de delitos y de los expedientes de limpieza* [Cuenca-Barcelona, 1965]). The dossier is listed here as included in Legajo 511 (Cat. no. 6692, p. 355.) For reasons which remain obscure, all my efforts through various channels to secure a microfilm have failed.

101 When he first testified in 1659 he gave his age as fifty-three. He also claimed to be of Old Christian stock, but this was patently false. Méndez Silva himself had earlier no compunction in attesting to the *limpieza* of the son of Manuel Cortizos for entry into the Order of Calatrava. See the documents in Caro, *Judíos* III, App. xxxiv, pp. 347 f. On Silva as a common converso name, and its derision on the stage, see Glaser, *Referencias antisemitas*, p. 49.

102 For his works, see Nicolás Antonio, *Bib. hisp.*, II (s.v.), and *HSA List*, II, 401 f.

103 For further details, see Caro, *Judíos* II, 99, n. 119.

104 On Cortizos see *supra*, ch. I. Méndez Silva dedicated to him his *Población general de España* (Madrid, 1645).

Méndez Silva was perhaps also compromised when, in 1658, two women imprisoned for Judaizing in Toledo addressed to him a letter in which they begged him to aid in obtaining their release.[105]

The extract from the dossier of Méndez Silva which was placed in that of Diego Gómez de Salazar informs us that some two weeks after his arrest, on May 14, 1659, he voluntarily requested an audience and confessed that he had indeed observed the Law of Moses. Though he repeated this on May 19, in the following months he did not add enough new information to impress the inquisitors. Therefore, on February 27, 1660, he was brought to the torture chamber, and it is the record of the torture which occupies the bulk of the document. While the interrogation, as we have it, is necessarily divorced from its original context in Méndez Silva's own case, it is clear that the inquisitors wanted more facts about other persons with whom he had Judaized.

We are intrigued to find that the very first name which Méndez Silva mentioned when he had been stripped and threatened with the rack was none other than that of Doña Isabel Henríquez. He described her as a widow, and said that some eight or ten years earlier (i.e., in 1650–52) they had revealed themselves to one another in his house, along with others, as followers of the Law of Moses.[106] This was surely the same Isabel Henríquez to whom Cardoso had earlier dedicated his *Panegyrico del color verde*.

Once upon the rack, and exposed to the torture itself, Rodrigo Méndez Silva began to give further information:

His right hand was tied.

He said: "Ay, *Dios mío*, ay, watch out! Ay, *Dios mío*, Señor Don Gregorio, now I remember! Ay, unhappy me, a wretched paralytic, ay!"

He was told to tell the truth, and he need not see himself in such trouble.

He said: "I remember and it is true that there were two persons there," and that he was ill, and he doesn't know who they are, although it seems

---

[105] Caro, *Judíos*, III, App. xli, pp. 356 f.

[106] "Dijo que estaban alli dos mugeres la una D.ª Isabel Henriquez viuda que vivia al Carmen y abra que se declaro con ella en casa de este presente su mug.ʳ abra ocho o diez años por obserbantes de la ley de Moyses . . . " (Caro, *Ibid.*, III, 360 f).

to him they were present there, but not who they were. And that he thinks one day, about ten or twelve years ago, he communicated with Diego Gómez de Salazar in the Prado, and he is a short thin man, a rentor of tobacco who lived in the Calle de Alcalá. And presently he said that he remembers well that he reached an understanding with Diego Gómez de Salazar about ten or twelve years ago, and it was around the time that Doctor Cardoso persuaded him to be a follower of the Law of Moses, Diego Gómez de Salazar first having spoken to him that they avow themselves to one another as followers of that Law, holding it to be the best through which one may be saved. All this while they were walking alone in the Prado. But the said Diego Gómez de Salazar had not told him who had taught him that Law. And all this came to pass because they were good friends. And this one [Méndez Silva] told him that he will keep it because Dr. Cardoso had taught it to him.[107]

And again, some minutes later, after further threats:

He said that he remembers the two persons were two men, one of them Manuel de Amezquita, and that it was at the time of Dr. Cardoso, in his [Méndez Silva's] house, and he said to [Amezquita] that the afore-mentioned Dr. Cardoso had told him that the Law of Moses was good. And the said Manuel did not reveal himself to him, although there entered another brother of his, Diego de Amezquita, and it seems to him that he did not reach an understanding with him. And he thinks that when that which he has said of Manuel de Amezquita came to pass, his [Méndez Silva's] wife was present and declared herself and confided in the said Manuel de Amezquita because he often visited their house and was a Portuguese, and well known, and he knows no more, by the exalted God! And he said to the aforementioned Manuel de Amezquita, when he revealed himself to him, that the said Dr. Cardoso had told him that for the observance of the said Law it would also be good to undertake a fast, but the said Manuel de Amezquita did not divulge his thoughts to him.[108]

---

[107] *Ibid.*, p. 361.

[108] *Ibid.*, p. 362. For a Francisco de Amezquita, a native of Trancoso, and perhaps of the same family, see *supra*, ch. II, p. 59 n. 23. Manuel de Amezquita's dossier appears to be extant at Cuenca. See Cirac, *Registros*, p. 355, leg. 510, no. 6687: "*Amezquita, Manuel de.* Portugal. Madrid, 1659. Judaismo; relapso. Suspenso. Fue reconciliado en la Inquisición de Logroño en 1635."

Madrid: Fame and Flight

Despite the somewhat garbled manner in which the notary recorded this information, it is obvious that Rodrigo Méndez Silva claimed he was first persuaded to follow the "Law of Moses" by Cardoso. This occurred, according to his own recollection, ten or twelve years before, that is, between 1648 and 1650. Since, as we shall see, by 1649 Cardoso had already left the country, it must have been shortly before his departure. The details of this "Law" which Cardoso taught Méndez Silva are not specified, with the single interesting exception of the advice to begin a fast, undoubtedly as a preliminary penance for having lived hitherto as a conforming Christian. Probably Méndez Silva more than once regretted having listened to Cardoso. After being tortured quite severely on the rack, he was remitted to the dungeons. On June 25, 1662, he appeared together with his wife, Doña Clara Feijoo, at an *auto* held in Cuenca, and they were both formally reconciled to the Church. We shall have occasion to meet Méndez Silva again, in Italy.[109]

But let us return to Cardoso himself. The information just elicited concerning his attempt to win over the Royal Chronicler to the "Law of Moses," sparse as it is, puts his entire departure into a perspective it might otherwise lack. If Méndez Silva was telling the truth, then patently Cardoso was already an active Marrano before his flight, and was even ready to incur the gravest risk by persuading others to Judaize. It could be argued, of course, that Méndez Silva implicated Cardoso under torture knowing, in any case, that the latter was long out of the country and therefore safely out of reach. Such an objection cannot be completely dismissed. We can only state that Cardoso's whole subsequent career is in perfect harmony with what his unfortunate friend revealed on the rack. There is no reason to impugn Méndez Silva's information, if we consider that the person of whom he spoke was no ordinary Marrano, but the future author of *Las excelencias de los Hebreos*. If Cardoso's departure was at all due to fear of the Inquisition, it was a fear which resulted from his Judaizing. He does not belong to that type of New Christian who, after living as a good Catholic, suddenly finds himself harassed by the Inquisition, flees abroad, and only then begins to Judaize.

---

[109] See *infra*, ch. V, pp. 205 f.

In fact, there is not the slightest sign that Cardoso was ever prosecuted by the Holy Office. There is rather some indication that he was able to depart without undue haste, and even to take some of his possessions with him.[110] Curiously, in later decades he seems never to have been mentioned or burned in effigy at any of the numerous *autos* held in Spain.

The real problem concerns his development as a Marrano. Cardoso had known Rodrigo Méndez Silva at least since 1637. In that year he had contributed to the latter's *Chatálogo real de España* a sonnet in honor of Prince Baltasar Carlos.[111] Now if the Royal Chronicler's recollection was accurate, it was not until a decade after this that Cardoso induced him to Judaize. Was Cardoso's own belief in the "Law of Moses" then of only recent origin, or had he been a Marrano all along, perhaps ever since, as we have concluded, his father divulged his Jewish ancestry to him? Were there any important fluctuations in his beliefs between the time he left his father's house and his departure from Spain? And if he had long been a Marrano, what personal circumstances or hesitations had delayed that departure for so long?

Some of these questions cannot be answered, for we possess no open window to Cardoso's soul during the decades in Spain, no private diary or personal letters in which to trace his inner thoughts. All we can do in order to cast some light on the problem is to turn back to the works Cardoso published in Madrid, and seek some clue by scanning them closely for whatever hints they may contain. Perhaps in this way we may deduce, however tentatively, something of his beliefs and attitudes. The method admittedly entails its own perils, but it is the only one at our disposal. Remarkably, such a survey proves more fruitful than we have anticipated, and yields some very important results. In brief, we find that those Christian

---

[110] See *infra*, p. 198.

[111] *Chatalogo Real de España, Al Serenissimo D. Baltasar Carlos de Austria, Principe de las españas y nuevomundo, dedica, consagra y ofrece Rodrigo Mendes Silba lusitano, becino de esta corte. Anno 1637.* Cardoso's sonnet is printed on fol. 5r of the preliminary material (fol. 6r in the augmented ed. of 1639, entitled *Catalogo real genealogico de España*).

elements which one would normally expect to abound in any work of a seventeenth-century Spaniard, are in general conspicuously absent, or significantly altered, in the books which Cardoso published in Madrid.[112]

The investigation must be pursued on several related levels. We have found, to begin with, that in the four major works which Cardoso produced in his Spanish period there are, by actual count, a total of twenty-three direct quotations of verses from the Old Testament, and only three from the New. In such a work as the *Discurso sobre el monte Vesuvio* (1632) there are fully ten verses cited from the Old Testament without even a single reference to a verse from Christian Scripture. These computations do not include illustrative material taken from the Old Testament but without the quotation of a particular verse.

Of course such statistics would, in themselves, prove little. However, they assume an added significance when viewed in conjunction with other characteristics. When we pause to analyze the three direct scriptural references to the New Testament, all of them contained in the *Utilidades del agua y de la nieve*, we find the following features:

Two of these passages are cited in a completely neutral context, with no religious overtones at all. Thus, discussing the benefits to be derived from drinking cold water, Cardoso writes: "Its praises are sealed by Christ's promising happiness to him who shall give

---

[112] Cardoso's normal citations from Christian writers may be disregarded as irrelevant to this analysis, since they are merely drawn from the common store of Iberian erudition, and involved philosophic or scientific points with no specifically religious color. If, for example, he cites Petrus Hispanus, "that famous Portuguese physician . . . who became Pope John XXI" (*Utilidades*, fol. 35v), it is only for a scientific opinion the latter expressed in his commentary on the medical works of Isaac Israeli. In other words, we must be careful to emphasize, not the provenance of a particular authority, but the content of the statement itself, and the use Cardoso makes of it. Thus I have also refrained at this point from deducing anything as to Cardoso's religious sympathies from similar citations of *Jewish* authorities, e,g., *Filon Hebreo* (*Utilidades*, fols. 4v. 8v, 95v), Amatus Lusitanus (esp. *De febre syncopali*, fol. 40r-v, in which he cites Amatus' case history of the grandson of Judah Abravanel), or even Maimonides' *Aphorisms according to Galen* ("Rabbi Moyses in suis aphorismis," *ibid.*, fol. 24r). For the significance of such citations in another context, see *infra*, ch. VI, p. 293.

184

His disciples a cup of cold water. *Et quicumque calicē dederit aquae frigidae, non perdet mercedem suam.*"[113] Again, while rejecting those who are opposed to the drinking of hot water, he writes:

To those who say that the ancients were not accustomed to drink hot water, and to the reasons they give, we reply that such drinking does not induce vomiting, but rather lukewarm water does so because it tends to relax the stomach, which retains much better either the very cold, or the very hot. And so it is written in the Apocalypse: *Utinā frigidus, aut calidus esses, sed quia tepidus, neq. calidus neq. frigidus, incipiam te evomere ex ore meo.*[114]

It is evident that Cardoso is bringing both these citations merely to round off a scientific argument, and not to express a religious idea or feeling. This is particularly striking in his use of the latter verse which, in its original context in the Book of Revelation, records the words addressed to the Angel of the Church of Laodicea, and in which the "lukewarm" refers not to tepid water but to those who were indifferent to Christ.

In only one of the three solitary New Testament passages is there some real religious use made of the verse. But this use is singular indeed. While discussing the virtues of myrrh wine, supposed to be a delicacy in ancient times, Cardoso states:

To this idea there may be opposed several verses in Scripture which seem to prove that myrrh wine was neither delicate nor enjoyable. For Saint Mark says that the Jews gave Christ myrrh wine, and Saint Matthew, wine mixed with gall.[115] But as Padre Maldonado has learnedly com-

---

[113] Cardoso, *Utilidades*, fol. 6ov., citing Matt. 10: 42.

[114] *Ibid.*, fols. 101v-102r, quoting from Apoc. 3: 15–16: "I would thou wert cold or hot. So, then, because thou art lukewarm, and neither cold nor hot, I will spew thee out of my mouth."

[115] Mark 15: 23 ("And they gave him to drink wine mingled with myrrh (*myrrhatum vinum*), but he received it not"); Matt. 27: 34 ("They gave him wine mingled with gall (*vinum . . . cum felle mistum*), and when he had tasted of it, he would not drink"). Since both verses deal with the same event, it seemed obvious to most that the two verses were to be equated, and that the myrrh wine mentioned in St. Mark must have been as bitter as the wine mixed with gall in St. Matthew.

mented, these were different drinks, one of them with myrrh before he was placed on the Cross, which they used to give to those whom they executed so that, the senses transported by the ardor of that wine, the pain would be less felt. The second drink was wine, or vinegar, with gall. But the interpreters concede that the first wine (which was offered by the charity of certain men, or of the women who, piously moved, accompanied Him) was in order to strengthen and fortify, so that with senses less aware of the pains, the severity of the torment would be diminished. . . .[116]

In other words, in the one New Testament passage which he does treat in its original context, Cardoso seizes the opportunity to point out that at the Crucifixion those Jews who gave Christ wine with myrrh were not evil torturers, as the verse clearly implies and as was commonly assumed, but, rather, merciful and compassionate! We cannot very well expect more than this from a Marrano in a published work in Madrid. Short of an attempt to exonerate the entire Jewish people, which would have been suicidal, this is surely the utmost liberty which Cardoso could allow himself.

But let us go on now to some other intriguing facets of his writings. It is surely significant that, whenever Cardoso mentions a miracle, it is invariably a miracle from the Old Testament. Thus in the work on Vesuvius, when he wishes to demonstrate that prodigies of earthquake, fire, and similar catastrophes are often God's means of punishing men or instilling awe in them, he mentions in succession the overthrow of Sodom, the earth swallowing Korah and his band, the destruction by divine fire of the captains of Ahaziah when they doubted the prophet Elijah (I Kings 1: 10), and the death of Aaron's sons at the altar.[117] One might, of course, object that such examples are more readily found in the Old Testament than in the New. But this argument is not really satisfying. For Cardoso ends the series with the example of God having revealed Himself to Israel at Sinai amid thunder and lightning. He could just as easily have continued into the New Testament and chosen, for example, Christ's own description of His future return: "For as the lightning cometh out of the east . . . so shall also the coming

---

[116] *Ibid.*, fols. 98r-99r.   [117] *Discurso*, fols. 10v-11r.

of the Son of Man be. . . . Immediately after the tribulation of those days shall the sun be darkened, and the moon shall not give her light, and the stars shall fall from heaven. . . ."[118] Or perhaps the apocalyptic vision: "And there were voices, and thunders, and lightnings; and there was a great earthquake, such as was not since men were upon the earth, so mighty an earthquake, and so great."[119] Surely, with such materials readily available, there was no technical need to stop at Sinai. If he did so, it must have been by choice, and out of an inner necessity.

To be sure, in another place Cardoso does once mention a miracle from the New Testament, but on this single occasion his presentation of the miracle is couched in somewhat paradoxical terms. We have already noted his argument in the *Discurso* that a general flood or conflagration cannot take place naturally, but rather only by supernatural means. In this vein he concludes:

Similarly the second one philosophizes badly when he says that there can occur naturally a universal earthquake; for *besides the fact that this would remove the luster of the miraculous which the common agreement of authors places at the death of Christ (since a miracle must exceed the limits of Nature)*, it is also against the view of the Philosopher, who only admits particulars. . . .[120]

Cardoso is referring, of course, to the earthquake which "rent the veil of the Temple" after Christ expired on the Cross. One is struck first by Cardoso's curiously bland manner in pointing to the miracle as a matter of "la comun de los autores," as though it were merely that, when in fact it is a firm statement of revealed Christian Scripture. But beyond this there is something else which eludes one at first glance and then proves to be even more significant. In effect,

---

[118] Matt. 26: 27, 29. Cf. Mark 13: 24–26; Luke 17: 29–30, 21: 25–27. Cardoso could also have referred to the earthquake which accompanied the opening of Christ's tomb. See Matt. 28: 2: "And behold there was a great earthquake; for the angel of the Lord descended from heaven, and came and rolled back the stone from the door. . . ."

[119] Apoc. 16: 18.

[120] *Discurso sobre el Monte Vesuvio*, fol. 13r. (Italics mine.)

when Cardoso simply wanted to illustrate seriously the divine intervention into the natural order he chose, as we have seen, all his examples from the Old Testament. But now when he is raising, however indirectly, the problem of a possible *rational* explanation of miracles, he suddenly chooses as his example, the upheaval which followed the Crucifixion. It does not matter that technically he rejects this rational interpretation; he could hardly have done otherwise in print. There is, at the very least, a psychological mode revealed to us here. Of a devout Christian we would have expected the very converse: to illustrate divine intervention—in addition to Old Testament miracles—at least a listing of some miracles from the New Testament, including the earthquake after the death of Christ. And then, when stating that a universal upheaval of natural origin would diminish the stature of biblical miracles, he could have chosen any of the examples from the Old Testament. Why, when in essence he is raising a momentary doubt in the reader's mind, does Cardoso focus on the one miracle which is linked directly to the Crucifixion?

But our analysis can proceed even further. It could be maintained that the themes of Cardoso's works were such that they simply did not lend themselves to the inclusion of much specifically Christian material, and that to emphasize the absence of such elements is to present an *argumentum ex silentio*. Fortunately, in the case of two of these works we can directly compare Cardoso's treatment with those of other writers on the very same subjects, and so feel the full difference.

Cardoso's funeral oration finds its exact parallel in occasion, theme, and even title, in Dr. Felipe Godínez' *Oración funebre en la muerte del Doctor Frey Lope de Vega Carpio*, to which I have already alluded.[121] In Cardoso's *Oración* there is only one reference which has any Christian character at all. He merely says of Lope that "being Christian, being loyal, being moral, he directed his intentions to the most worthy and the most just."[122] But this statement occurs in the context of his defense of the morality of Lope's plays,

---

[121] *Supra*, n. 68.   [122] Cardoso, *Oración funebre*, fol. 19v.

and is addressed to a Christian audience. Other than a passing
reference to the "holy pastor" Pope Urban VII having granted Lope
the Order of St. John, which simply reports a fact of Lope's life,
we hear nothing more of Christianity.[123]

It is hard to imagine a greater contrast than that provided by
Godínez' *Oración*, all the more striking when we remember that the
author was also a New Christian. To see in what terms someone
other than Cardoso could praise Lope de Vega, we have only to
read this characteristic passage:

The Eternal Word which was hidden in the thought of the Father
was articulated temporally in the flesh, and soon revealed itself to simple
shepherds. All flesh must see him, says Isaiah, for so clearly does God
manifest his thought that all see it. Before incarnation, says St. Ambrose,
He was a perfume in the mind of God, as in a hidden vessel, and in
becoming Christ, who is God and man, the Church in the Songs of
Solomon called Him a "wafted perfume," and then the great Archbishop
of Milan added elegantly: "The mouth of the Father exhaled, and gave
forth this prepared perfume."

The Son was incarnated, and communicated His fragrance to human
nature; the Holy Spirit blew, and scattered over all the earth the
sweetness of this confection, all things being filled with the scent of its
perfume. For the word of God, when it is pronounced, is so perceptible,
is so much for all, that it can be smelled, touched, seen, heard, and so
that no sense be deprived, He even wished that they taste it in the
Eucharist. Let those who desire to do so speak obscurely. To express
concepts clearly is the style of our Lope, of the heavens, of the angels,
of God Himself.[124]

What is Cardoso's passing allusion to Lope's Christian morality
in comparison to this?

Similar results await us when we compare Cardoso's treatise on
Vesuvius with that of Juan de Quiñones. Both works contain a
section describing the great eruption of 1632. In his *El monte Vesuvio*
Quiñones devotes a major part of his description to a detailed and
enthusiastic account of the miracles which took place in Naples

123 *Ibid.*, fol. 14 v.
124 Godínez, *Oración funebre*, in Lope de Vega, *Obras sueltas*, XX, 161.

and its vicinity: the Church of the Annunciation in Trochia was reduced to ashes, but a priest found the casket containing the Sacrament despite the appearance of the Devil to prevent it, and the casket contained one large host and twelve smaller ones; in another church an image of the Virgin prevented the flames from entering, and thereafter the people would not depart until they could take her with them; the Virgin also saved a woman in her own house; a gentleman left his home and later found the house intact, because he had placed a statue of the Virgin at the door; a poor woman put an image of the Virgin of Constantinople on her bundle of cloth, and it was not burned; a physician found his house unscathed because of his Rosary; several other churches were miraculously saved; at the Church of San Anielo the fiery torrents reached their terminal point, unable to pass farther into Naples, because relics of San Gennaro turned the lava back.[125]

There is not one word of a miracle, nor even a mention of any church that was saved, in Cardoso's *Discurso*. This is doubly revealing. I have already emphasized that since neither Cardoso nor Quiñones had witnessed the eruption of Vesuvius, they must have both relied on the many printed reports which had been received from Naples. Such reports were generally replete with miraculous tales, and were as available to Cardoso as they were to Quiñones. Yet Cardoso supressed any mention of them, and gave in his description only the facts concerning the eruption and the havoc it caused. His silence on the other aspects must surely be regarded as deliberate.

We find other meaningful silences in Cardoso's works. Stock phrases which abound in the books of his contemporaries are entirely absent. We have seen that Christ is mentioned only twice, and have analyzed the context. It should be added that on neither occasion does Cardoso employ such standard expressions as "Christ our Redeemer," or "Christ our Lord." The Virgin is never mentioned in his books at all, even in passing. He never uses such phrases as "Catholic Spain" or "The Catholic Monarchy." When Quiñones gives the date of the eruption in which Pliny died, he states it as

---

[125] Quiñones, *El monte Vesuvio*, fols. 23v-28v.

"año de Christo 81," while Cardoso merely states "año de 81," and this omission of Christ from the date is consistent throughout his writings. More striking still, in attempting to establish the first eruption of Vesuvius, Quiñones and Cardoso both base themselves on a report by Berosus that it occurred in the time of "Alarius, seventh king of Assyria." But while Quiñones fixes it as "in the year of the Creation 2,159, *which is 1,894 before our Redemption*," Cardoso presents it as "in the year of the Creation 1,857, *which coincides with Abraham.*"[126]

Taken in their totality we find it impossible to regard the elements enumerated as merely coincidental. The books Cardoso wrote in Spain do not betray any Christian feeling. On the contrary, there is a marked reluctance even to employ the conventional Christian terminology which appears in other Spanish writers as a matter of course.

In the final analysis one can discover perhaps only two points at which Cardoso made statements that might prove exceptions to this overriding impression. In the poem written in 1631 for Pellicer's *Anfiteatro*, when Philip shot the bull in the arena, Cardoso called him the "Christian Mars." But this was at best a poetic conceit written to flatter His Catholic Majesty. The other passage is more important. In the *Oración funebre* Cardoso writes: "Stammering, the Castilian tongue began to loosen itself after the time of the Catholic Kings (those who corrupted its purity and our customs being expelled)."[127] How seriously are we to take this reference to the expulsion of the Jews by Ferdinand and Isabella as an expression of Cardoso's real feelings? In view of all we know about him, we find it incongruous to believe that Cardoso meant to malign his forefathers out of Christian convictions. We should rather hazard the guess that this single isolated sentence represents a concession to the universal prejudice of his contemporaries, and was probably

---

[126] Quiñones, *El Monte Vesuvio*, fols. 6v-7r; Cardoso, *Discurso sobre el Monte Vesuvio*, fol. 4v. Both are citing Berosus, *De regibus Assiriorum*. (Italics mine.)

[127] "Balbuciente la lengua Castellana començó a desatarse desde los Reyes Católicos (expulsos los que corrompian su pureza, y nuestras costumbres)" (Cardoso, *Oración funebre*, fol. 6v).

intended to safeguard himself. Such concessions on the part of a New Christian were sometimes necessary if one was to survive. Indeed, in a passage written after he had left Spain, Cardoso's brother Miguel (Abraham) recalled:

> The Christians worship the woman Miriam, whom they call Maria . . . and they mention her more than the Lord. For while I was in Spain among the Christians it was their practice that when a man entered his fellow's house he should not say "Praised be God" ("Alabado sea Dios"), to remove any suspicion that he is Jewish, but rather "Ave Maria." . . .[128]

Whether Miguel exaggerated or not is unimportant in comparison with the general atmosphere he evokes. It is in terms of such an atmosphere, with its perennial demands for proofs of orthodoxy, that we can understand Fernando Cardoso's statement on the expulsion. This concession is not surprising. We are rather amazed that he did not make such concessions more frequently.

In sum, a close scrutiny of all Cardoso's works in Spain reveals nothing that we would not expect to find in a committed Marrano who practiced elementary caution. While he may have begun to proselytize only shortly before his departure, consistent indications of his own Marranism may be traced through the writings of almost two decades. We cannot even venture to speculate as to the actual character of his Judaizing, or the specific reasons which kept him in Spain those many years. I affirm only that there are good grounds for regarding his proselytizing of Rodrigo Méndes Silva, and his subsequent departure, as the culminations of a long and steady inner process.

The date of Cardoso's flight from Spain can be fixed with some precision. We have seen that Méndez Silva placed his discussions with Cardoso concerning the Law of Moses in 1648–50. Miguel Cardoso informs us definitely that he was already in Venice in 1649, and it is practically certain that the two brothers left Spain to-

---

[128] The text from which this quotation is taken has been published by Gershom Scholem, "Contributions to the History of Sabbatianism from the Writings of [Abraham] Cardoso" (Hebrew), *Zion*, VII (1942), 26.

gether.[129] They must therefore have departed sometime in 1648.[130] Fernando Cardoso was then a mature man of forty-four. He left at the very height of his fame, though with his two greatest works yet to be written. As had happened repeatedly during the previous 150 years, the Peninsula now lost another gifted son, soon to be reclaimed by the Jewish people. In a bygone age, both might have claimed him equally. That he, and others like him, had to choose decisively between the two is of the essence of the Ibero-Jewish tragedy. On August 24, 1650, the great Portuguese writer and diplomat Francisco Manuel de Mello wrote to the Vicar General of Lisbon of a project for a bibliography of modern Portuguese authors, a *Biblioteca Lusitana*, which would show to the world the achievements of writers born in Portugal in every field of learning, and gave short exemplary lists of those to be included. In medicine, the second name he mentioned was that of Fernando Cardoso.[131] One wonders if he knew, at the time he wrote the letter, that Cardoso was already in the Ghetto of Venice, and had begun a new life. . . .

---

[129] Abraham Cardoso gives the date in his letter to the rabbis of Smyrna written in 1669 (text in *Zion*, XIX (1954), 15). From the autobiographical sketch published by Bernheimer (*JQR*, (N.S.), XVIII (1927–28), 115, we know that at this time he made use of Isaac (Fernando) Cardoso's library. For further details, see *infra*, ch. V, where these matters will be discussed in their proper context.

[130] By an interesting coincidence, two other Cardoso brothers, both businessmen and financiers, and therefore not to be confused with Fernando and Miguel, fled from Madrid seven years later, in 1655. See *Avisos de D. Jerónimo de Barrionuevo* (*1654-1658*), ed. A. Paz y Mélia, I (Madrid, 1892), 325–26, 332. It was said they had departed because enemies were blackmailing them with threats to denounce them to the Inquisition. They made their way first to France, and subsequently to Amsterdam. Unfortunately, Barrionuevo did not record their first names, and we cannot determine if there was any family relationship.

[131] Immediately after Estêvão (Stephen) de Castro. See Francisco Manuel de Mello, *Cartas familiares*, ed. M. Rodrigues Lapa (Lisbon, 1942), p. 231.

Chapter v

ITALY: RECLAIMING A BIRTHRIGHT

In Italy the Jews are generally protected
by all the Princes. Their principall residence is in the most famous City of Venice;
so that in that same City alone they pos-
sesse about 1400 houses; and are used
there with much courtesy and clemency.
Many also live in Padoa and Verona. . . .
—Manasseh ben Israel, *Humble Addresses*

TOWARD the mid-seventeenth century, a Marrano who left
Spain intent on practicing Judaism fully in an open
Jewish community would normally proceed to one of
several areas. He could undertake the long journey to
Turkey or some other part of the Ottoman Empire; or, if he desired
to remain in Western Europe, he generally had the option of going to
Holland, to Hamburg, or to Italy. Cardoso chose the latter course,
perhaps because he felt it more congenial to reside in another Latin
country or, as seems more likely, because he already had contacts
or relatives in Italy itself.[1]

---

[1] Though many of the Marranos who had settled in France were already living
as Jews, they were not yet officially recognized as such by the government, and
Cardoso could well have hesitated to make his home there. Manasseh b. Israel's
appeal for Jewish readmission to England was not to take place until several years
later, and for the time being Marrano life in that country was still clandestine.
Hamburg and its satellites already had flourishing Sephardic communities, but
the largest by far were to be found in Holland and Italy.

Several Cardosos, related to those of Hamburg, resided in Venice in the first

HAVEN IN VENICE

He arrived in Venice in 1648, apparently together with his brother. To any who may have seen them when they came, Fernando and Miguel Cardoso must have appeared, in dress and manner, as merely two more Spanish travelers. As they made their way to the Ghetto over the innumerable tiny bridges which span the watery thoroughfares of the city, they alone must have realized that with each step they were also approaching the lost world of their forefathers.

They were not the first to come in this way and for this purpose. Venice in 1648 harbored one of the most important Jewish communities in the world. It was still a center of Jewish learning, of Hebrew printing, and of international Jewish philanthropy. Within the Ghetto itself there were several autonomous congregations which remained distinct and worshiped in their own synagogues according to their own rites. The first Sephardim to take their place alongside the already established Italian and German communities had been the "Levantine" Jews, Sephardic merchants from Turkey who came in 1540. At about the same time, Marranos fleeing from Portugal also began to arrive in Venice, but these came as individuals, and were sometime vexed by the Venetian authorities. Late in the sixteenth century, however, the situation changed decisively. With the dissolution in 1581 of the Ferrara community, hitherto the most important Marrano refuge in Italy, the influx of Marranos into Venice accelerated. In 1589 a considerable number of Portuguese Marranos were authorized to establish themselves in the city for the purpose of trade. Shortly afterwards they created in the Ghetto

---

half of the 17th century (see Kellenbenz, *Sephardim an der unteren Elbe*, p. 115). The Bibliotheca Marciana in Venice possesses a medical manuscript of the sixteenth century in which treatments and medicines of various physicians have been assembled. One of these is inscribed: "Ex magistro Cardoso portugesi, Medicina mirabile provata alla spilentia." (MS It. III, 10. (5003), Libro de arti segretti, fol. 30v).

a formal congregation of their own, which came to be known as Talmud Tora. These Ponentine Jews, as they were called, worshiped in the most opulent of the Venetian synagogues, the Scuola Spagnuola, built in 1584, and enlarged in 1635. It was in this synagogue that most of the Marranos who fled the Peninsula had their first experience of authentic Judaism.[2]

By the time Fernando and Miguel Cardoso arrived, the Marrano origin of many of the Ponentine Jews was no longer a secret. Though the Papacy had tried to force the Venetian Republic to take action against these apostates, the *Serenissima* paid little heed. In this way Venice became known among the Marranos themselves as one of the more liberal cities for those who wished to return to Judaism. As early as 1607 we hear of a Marrano woman from Portugal who, when she arrived in Florence, was told "that she ought to go to Venice, where she could live better and more freely."[3] By 1651 a Venetian curate would point out, in vain, that there were in the Ghetto many Portuguese Jews who had even been priests in their native land.[4] A document in the archives of the Venetian Inquisition illustrates vividly the audacity with which some persons flaunted their Marrano past. In 1654 a friar, Giovanni Battista Palliani, deposed that on the 16th of April he and a colleague were passing near the Ghetto when a Jew, speaking Spanish, approached them and asked if they wanted to buy anything. In the ensuing conversation it was ascertained that he had come from Madrid. When they asked him the reason, he replied, with delicious irony: "I have come to this city in order to put on my head this Cardinal's hat, for in Spain this was prohibited."[5] He was referring, of course, to

---

[2] On the development of the Sephardic community of Venice and Marrano immigration to the city, see Cecil Roth, "Les marranes à Venise," *REJ*, LXXXIX (1930), 201–23; *idem*, *Venice* (Philadelphia, 1930), pp. 63–71.

[3] She was the mother of Hector Mendes Bravo, who gave this information to the Inquisition of Lisbon ten years later. See Roth in *HUCA*, XVIII, 229 f.

[4] Roth, *Marranes à Venise*, p. 210.

[5] Archivio di Stato di Venezia, Santo Uffizio, Busta 107 (dossier of Pietro d'Acosta; no pagination). When the friars suggested to him that his original baptism was still valid, he vehemently denied it, pointing out that in Spain those priests who baptized his people were themselves Jews, and, though they performed

the red hat which all the Jews of the Venetian Ghetto were required to wear.

For the Marranos who came to Venice, as well as for the Jewish community, the problem of their transition to Judaism was more immediate than the question of the attitude of the Venetian authorities. Direct information on the initial period following the arrival of the Cardosos is provided by Miguel. He writes: "In the year 5,409 [1648–49], in the city of Venice, I was occupied with the Torah, for there was the beginning of my studies."[6] It is clear, then, that his formal Jewish education only began at this point. This must have been true also of Fernando. In another passage, Miguel offers a fuller account of what occurred, and incidentally sheds some light on his older brother as well. After giving some details on his childhood in Spain which we have examined earlier, he states that when he came to Venice he studied "Bible, Mishna, and Gemara" with the rabbis Abraham Valencia, Samuel Aboab, and Moses Zacuto.[7] Then, however, he began to be tormented by doubts, especially concerning the duality which seemed to be implied in God by the terms *'Elohim* and *YHWH*, and by some of the anthropomorphisms in the Talmud. To add to his confusion, he attended a conversionist sermon by a Catholic priest, in which the latter taunted the Venetian rabbis with another duality, that of God and the *Shekina*. Miguel Cardoso was impressed with the argument and felt, at the time, that "there was no one to resolve these problems among all the rabbis of Venice."[8] At this point his account becomes confused in its chronology. He writes that he went to Egypt, whereas it is known from other writings of his that he first spent several years in Leghorn. Farther on he states that in one of his efforts to resolve his doubts,

---

the ceremony, did so without intention ("lui mi rispose padre il n̄ro: nō é vero battessimo, p̄ che [li] ministri, et sacerdoti, che si battezzano sono pure delli nostri Hebrei, quali non intendono battezzarssi . . . et p̄ consequenza noi non siamo christiani ma hebrei . . .").

[6] Abraham's letter to the rabbis of Smyrna. See Scholem, *Zion*, XIX, 15.

[7] See Bernheimer, *JQR*, XVIII, 113.

[8] *Ibid.*, p. 114. The priest was probably a Jewish convert, since he made ample use of rabbinic sources.

he "returned to read in the books of the gentiles," adding: "for my brother had six thousand books in Venice."[9]

There is no question but that Miguel could have made use of Fernando's library only before 1653 for, as we shall see, in that year the latter himself left Venice. In the first few years, therefore, the two must have been together. Now even if the figure of six thousand books is not to be taken seriously, Fernando's library must have been large enough to give rise to such an exaggeration. This casual detail is of some importance. For if Fernando Cardoso had in his possession a large collection of books while he was in Venice, he could not have accumulated it in the short time since his arrival, but must have transferred the bulk of it from Spain. This, in turn, was possible only if the move had been carefully calculated and planned for some time, and tends to confirm our impression that Cardoso's departure from the Paninsula was not a panicked flight from the Inquisition.

Since both brothers arrived in Venice together, they most probably began their Jewish instruction under the same teacher. Fernando may therefore have been taught by any of the three rabbis whom Miguel mentioned. Certainly in the case of one of these, Rabbi Samuel Aboab, it would seem most likely. We shall see that there was a close relationship between them even decades later.

Aboab was one of the more remarkable spiritual leaders of Italian Jewry in the seventeenth century. From 1637 to 1650 he lived in Verona, and in the latter year he was called to become the rabbi of the Ponentine community of Venice. He already had a reputation for both his scholarship and his deep ascetic piety. For Fernando Cardoso he may have been an ideal instructor, since he was also acquainted with secular culture and knew several languages.[10] Moreover, he seems to have had an abiding concern for the reintegration of Marranos into the Jewish community. In an ethical treatise published in 1650, after dealing with the necessity for every man

---

[9] *Ibid.*, p. 115.

[10] On Samuel Aboab (1610–94), see Leopold Löwenstein, "Die Familie Aboab," *MGWJ*, XLVII (1904), 674–77, and M. Kayserling in *JE*, I, 75.

to counsel his fellow and direct him to righteous ways, Aboab wrote:

And how much more so with our brothers the Children of Israel who come from the lands of the dispersion, who have neither known nor seen the path on which any person who is called by the name of Israel should walk! For these above all require many teachers and exhorters who shall set the truth before them and teach them the road in which to tread and the deed to be done. And I have heard many God-fearing, wise, and understanding men, who are grieved at the insufficient enthusiasm for this task among this wise and understanding nation. For to tell the truth, there should be in each and every city in Israel a special brotherhood for this purpose, and just as there are brotherhoods for every other holy task, so there should be none lacking for this. And this one is really the cornerstone.

For what shall they do, those who come from servitude to spiritual liberation, and from pitch and utter darkness to the pure light of the Torah which enlightens the eyes (May the Redeemer and Savior be exalted!), and when they arrive, there is no one there to teach them adequately the principles of the faith and the commandments of God's law? And this is equally true of those [precepts] which require constancy, such as . . . forbidden foods, and the garments one wears, and the observance of Sabbath and festival, and the holiness and purity pertaining to them. . . . And the inquirer asks of his nearest neighbor that which he requires, and the woman inquires of her neighbor, but these are commandments taught by men and women, and sometimes there is little distinction between the knowledge of him who asks and him who is asked. And there are a number of matters of which they are innocent, and they do not even know what to ask, for they believe them to be permitted, since they were not raised to regard them as forbidden. . . . But it would be fitting for them to ask and ask, each one of the great scholars of his city, for such is the duty of each and every man in Israel. However, the greatest punishment is placed, and the collar hangs, on the neck of anyone who can teach and encourage, but does not do so, who sees and hears, but retires to his house. . . .

And why should there not be a holy brotherhood of scholars to aid in redeeming the souls of their brethren whom the Holy One has drawn up from slavery to freedom, and from anguish to joy; and let them also have one book in which there will be written both the principles which are the foundation of the faith, and the general and detailed laws which every man requires, with which they may be taught, each one according to his capacity, from day to day, until he may be made aware of the essence of these matters. . . .

One must also remove from them the vain idea which has spread among almost all the sons of our people who come from the servitude of the soul, and which has become for them a snare and a trap, for they think that so long as a man is not circumcised he is not a part of Israel, that his sins are no sins, and his transgressions as though nonexistent. . . . Consequently there are those who have prolonged this transgression . . . and I have seen one who was already in the place of freedom, who erred in his foolishness with the argument that he was going to bring his family, and therefore he didn't return, for he drowned in the sea, and that was his punishment. . . .

And some claim that the day of their circumcision is, according to them, the first day on which their sins begin to count, and so no one regrets his past evils, and that with which he angered the Lord for many years, except perhaps one out of a city, and two in a family. But this opinion is erroneous and against the principles of our holy faith, for it is clear that "even though he has sinned, he remains a Jew" with regard to all penalties and prohibitions, for circumcision is a commandment like all the rest in the Torah, and even though "this is the gate of the Lord through which the righteous enter," and it is the sign of the convenant with God's congregation, the rest of the Torah does not depend upon it. And if so, he who is of the seed of Israel and is not sealed with this sign cannot, because of its absence, be rid of the other commandments of the Torah. . . .[11]

It is not known whether Aboab ever put into effect his plan for a brotherhood devoted to the reeducation of Marranos, but in any case, he himself had a special solicitude for such instruction. He was also, as we see, very aware of some of the specific difficulties involved. These were real enough. The case which Aboab mentions, of the Marrano who postponed his circumcision because he wanted to return to the Peninsula and bring his family, has its parallels. In a seventeenth-century responsum we hear of a Marrano who

---

[11] *Sefer ha-zikhronot* (n.p., n.d. [*ca.* 1650]), fol. 75r-v. The author's name is not given, but the book is generally ascribed to Samuel Aboab. See *Sefer ḥemdat yamim*, ed. Leghorn, 1762–64, II, fol. 110r-v, and the responsa of Samson Morpurgo, *Sefer shemesh ṣedakah* (Venice, 1743), Yoreh de'ah, no. 61.

returned to Judaism in Italy but stipulated that he could not yet be circumcised because he must go back and collect his debts.[12] The reluctance of some Marranos to be circumcised gave rise to various means of inducement and coercion. There was, for example, a tendency to bar them from certain religious rites, such as putting on the phylacteries, until they had submitted to it.[13] Nor were ideological problems wanting. The Italian Jewish convert Giulio Morosini, who became a zealous missionary to his former coreligionists, reports a discussion which took place in Venice in 1649 in the presence of Rabbi Simone (Simha) Luzzato. A Marrano who had returned to Judaism and his brother, who had remained a Christian, were arguing the meaning of the "seven weeks" in the Book of Daniel, an interesting example of intense religious conflicts within the same family.[14]

However, while the problem of reintegrating the Marranos was certainly serious, one wonders if Aboab was not unduly alarmed.

---

[12] The problem was whether he is to be allowed to raise the Torah scroll in the synagogue. Jacob b. Moses Senior of Pisa, along with several other rabbis, replied that he may. Rafael Meldola later disagreed. See the latter's collected responsa, *Mayim rabbim*, II, fols. 51–53.

[13] *Ibid.* In the latter part of the 17th century the new Sephardic community of London adopted an ordinance not to bury an uncircumcised male in the communal cemetary except by special dispensation of the Mahamad. See Lionel D. Barnett, *El libro de los acuerdos* (Oxford, 1931), p. 23.

[14] Morosini's introduction to his *Via della fede mostrata a'gli Ebrei* (Rome, 1683). Cf. Roth, *Marranes à Venise*, p. 216, n. 3. Morosini's original name was Samuel Nahmias. He states that his final decision to convert came as a result of this incident. In the Venetian archives I found a deposition which he gave to the Inquisition in 1661, in which he states that his baptism took place on Dec. 22, 1649 (Archivio di Stato di Venezia, Busta 106, dossier of Fra Raimondo Tasca, unpaginated).
Regrettably, Morosini failed to record the names of the two Marrano brothers. Could they have been Fernando and Miguel Cardoso? In 1649 they had indeed just arrived in Venice. Miguel himself has informed us of religious doubts aroused by a Catholic priest. Perhaps he has not disclosed the full extent of those doubts? We shall see that on another, not unrelated plane, the brothers later clashed violently over messianic interpretation. For this, as well as for latent and sublimated Christian elements in Miguel's thinking, see *infra*, ch. VII.

Italy: Reclaiming a Birthright

There is, after all, no clear evidence that such Marranos as he describes constituted more than a minority of those who came. The heretic will invariably draw more attention to himself than the believer, and dissidents will always achieve a notoriety which is out of proportion to their number.

It is to be assumed that, like most returning Marranos, both Cardosos underwent circumcision shortly after their arrival. Otherwise Fernando's later panegyric of the rite, and Miguel's frequent allusion to gentiles as "the uncircumcised," would be hard to explain.[15] Probably at this time they also began to use the Jewish

---

[15] Concerning Miguel, however, there are some unresolved problems. In later years rumor had it that he remained uncircumcised. In the polemical *Sefer meribat kodesh*, ed. A. Freimann (*Inyeney Shabbetay Ṣebi*, p. 32) we read that he had "a fleshy wart (*yabelet*) on his foreskin . . . and he admits part of the charge that he has a foreskin, rather than being without one since birth." Such an allegation from an extremely hostile source might of itself be readily dismissed. But in a Hebrew letter written by Miguel sometime after 1687, he tells a bizarre story. Once (in Constantinople?) a woman came to him from Adrianople and asked him if he were circumcised. "I told her," Miguel writes, "in order to get rid of her, that I have something like a lentil [Heb. *'adashah*] or a tiny wart [Sp. *varruga*]." But the woman insisted that in a vision Moses and Aaron had sent her to tell him to "correct" his circumcision so that the redemption of Israel might begin. From this, according to Miguel, the entire confusion arose. The woman continued to proclaim him uncircumcised, and when he came to Adrianople she shouted to him in the market place: "Until when shall you detain the Jewish people in Exile? Circumcise yourself and have pity on this people!" So rampant had the rumor become that once, while debating in public, he asked three *mohalim* to examine him in private, but they, he claims, refused. Miguel's own explanation to his correspondent is as follows: "I was born without a foreskin (*noladeti mahul*) and when I came from Spain to Leghorn the *Mohel* Joseph Gabbai maimed me, for he circumcised me, when he had only [i.e., by Jewish law] to take some blood. And when I was healed there remained some scar tissue in one place, about the size of a lentil, far from the crown [*sic!*] and near the body, and I thought it was about this that the woman had asked." See Isaac Molkho and Abraham Amarilio, "Autobiographical Letters of [Abraham] Cardoso" (Hebrew), *Sefunot*, III-IV (1960), 220 f. The entire account must, of course, arouse some suspicion. It is strange that, as he claims repeatedly, Miguel could not persuade some *mohel* to examine him and give his testimony. And even if his basic anatomical claim were correct, why did he not simply reject at the very outset any aspersions concerning his circumcision, instead of entering into convoluted explanations? One gets the uneasy feeling that he protests too much.

names by which they were henceforth to be known. Fernando and Miguel became, respectively, Isaac and Abraham. It is to be remarked that this choice of Jewish names is somewhat odd. Considering the fact that Fernando was by far the older of the two, it might be expected that he, and not Miguel, would have assumed the name Abraham. We must reckon with the possibility that these may already have been their clandestine names in the Peninsula although, to be sure, there is no way to prove this.[16]

Aboab definitely exaggerated the lack of available resources for the instruction of Marranos, especially when he lamented the absence of a book which could convey to them religious laws and principles. Indeed, not only one but a number of such books already existed. Beside the productions of the Amsterdam press, the returning Marrano had at his disposal a series of works printed in Venice itself. In the early seventeenth century two Spanish condensations of the great legal code of Joseph Caro were published in the city. The first, entitled *Sefer shulkhan ha-panim*, or *Mesa de el alma*, was printed in vocalized Hebrew characters (Ladino), and appeared in 1602.[17] The other, which was printed in 1609, was the work of Rabbi Moses Altaras, and was called *Libro de mantenimiento de la alma*. Unlike the previous work, it was printed entirely in Roman characters.[18] Furthermore, in 1627, Rabbi Isaac Athias published in Venice his

---

[16] In the autobiographical account published by Bernheimer (*JQR*, XVIII), Abraham Cardoso writes: אני המכונה פעם מב׳׳א, ר׳׳ת מיכאל בן אברהם. Unfortunately we cannot deduce from the abbreviation that his father's name was Abraham, for he may here be hiding the other meaning of מב׳׳א — "Mashiaḥ ben Efraim."

[17] The full title: ספר שלחן הפנים ליברו ליבירו לייאמאדו אין לאדינו מיזה די איל אלמה קונפואישטו די טודוש לוש דינים ניסיסאריאוס פארה איל אומברי טיראישלאדאדו פורקי איש דיל ליברו דיל גאון כמוהרר יוסף קארו זל׳׳הה···שנת שסב לפ׳׳ק, על יד זואן דגארה ובביתו·

This was a new edition by R. Isaac Gershon, of a work which first appeared in Salonika in 1568. See Kayserling, *BEPJ*, p. 34.

[18] *Libro de mantenimiento de la alma en el qual se con-tiene el modo con que se a de regir el Iudio en todas sus actiones traduzido dal hebraico al spagnol por Mose Altaras. Con Licencia dei Superiori. Año 5369* (Venice, 1609). Cf. Kayserling, *BEPJ*, p. 11. The book has also been described by Moses Bensabat Amzalak, *A tradução espanhola do livro de Joseph Caro . . . feita por Mosé Altaras . . .* (Lisbon, 1927).

Thesoro de preceptos which, in the manner of the age-old genre of the *Sefer ha-miṣvot*, gave the full list of the 613 biblical commandments, together with an explanation of each in the light of rabbinic tradition.[19] In his introduction Athias had stated the purpose of his work quite explicitly, and it is interesting to compare his remarks with those of Aboab. After pointing out that, in the past, various authors had already composed similar works in Hebrew, Athias writes:

> However, God having castigated the most noble nation of Spain with expulsions, calamities, deaths, and extreme troubles, there remained, as we all know, a great part of it miserably entombed in the darkness of perdition; until the Lord delivered them with the rod of His compassion, and they turned to adore His blessed cult, and served His most holy Name. But, as they emerged from such a bitter captivity, without having been instructed since childhood in the discipline of the Law and the doctrine of the Holy Tongue—they remained, even up to now, deprived of its treasures, lacking its mysteries, and, most important, not knowing in particular the wisdom of the commandments, and being consequently unaware of the highways and roads to their happiness. And until now they have enjoyed only the Bible, with no commentary whatever, and the holy prayers, and some few other compilations. But never have they had someone to point out to them this great foundation of the commandments, making these known to him who, for lack of the language, cannot see them in their original source. . . .
>
> All of which, being considered by me, made me zealous for the Name of the Lord of Hosts, zealous for the good and happiness of my maternal and natural nation, and, finally, I felt myself obligated by the essential and true love which I owe to my fellow. And so, confiding myself in the Mighty One of all worlds, I decided to imitate those pious men and, with their method, to write a book of the commandments, together with their entire explanation, in the vernacular. . . .[20]

---

[19] I have used the second edition: *Thesoro de preceptos adonde se encierran las joyas de los seis cientos y treze preceptos que encomendo el Señor a su Pueblo Israel. Con su declaracion, razon, y dinim, conforme a la verdadera tradicion, recibida de Mosè: y enseñada por nuestros sabios de gloriosa memoria . . . por el excelente y doctissimo señor R. Ishac Atias su memoria para bendicion . . . En Amsterdam, Año* 5409 [1649]. For the Venice ed. see *BEPJ*, pp. 14 f.

[20] Athias, *Thesoro de preceptos*, Preface (fols. 2v-3r of the preliminary material).

When Abraham Cardoso recalled the beginnings of his studies
in Venice as being in Bible, Mishna, and Gemara, he actually
glossed over the first stage. For until competence could be acquired
in the original languages, each of the brothers must have commenced
his study of traditional Judaism in such works as we have mentioned.
Indeed, in the case of the *Thesoro de preceptos* we know definitely
that Isaac Cardoso had studied it, since he later alluded to it, and
it retained its influence over him.[21] Perhaps even the first Jewish
prayers they offered in Venice were in the Spanish language.[22] The
Judeo-Spanish literature was thus the vehicle for their immediate
transition into Jewish life. Once that had been accomplished, it was
a matter of deepening further both knowledge and awareness. But
here, at an early juncture, the brothers parted and went their
separate ways. There is absolutely nothing to indicate that Isaac
Cardoso's confrontation with the normative Judaism of Venice was
in any way violent or particularly problematic. Had he shared any
of Abraham's initial doubts, the latter would not have failed to
mention it in his later polemics. This in no way lessens the drama
of Isaac's leap from the Spanish to the Jewish milieu, and it remains
to be seen how his background colored in specific ways his understanding of Judaism. It merely indicates that, unlike Abraham,
whatever difficulties he encountered were of detail, and did not serve
to obstruct his remarkably successful adaptation to a life so radically
different from that which he had known.

One may well ponder, however, if this was due so much to the
quality of the instruction Isaac received as to the determination and
mental preparation he had already brought with him from Spain.
A poignant contrast to Cardoso's adjustment is provided by Rodrigo

---

[21] E. g., in *Las excelencias de los Hebreos*, fol. 155. See *infra*, ch. VIII.

[22] For Spanish translations of the liturgy, see *BEPJ*, pp. 59–64. Samuel Aboab
was once sent a question which had first been addressed to Solomon Ayalon in
Leghorn: "Concerning ten vernacular-speaking Jews (*yehudim lo'aziim*) who do
not know the holy tongue and live in a place where no one knows the holy tongue,
whether, to fulfill their obligation, they can pray together in the vernacular and
recite the *Kaddish* and the *Kedusha* in the vernacular?" Aboab was inclined to
permit it. See his *Debar Shemuel*, no. 321, fol. 84r-v.

Méndez Silva, who was himself to come to Venice sometime after 1662. Here, to be sure, he was circumcised and took the name Jacob. But he was never seen in the synagogue, and he never wore phylacteries. Out of long habit, he continued to lift his hat at the mention of Jesus or Mary, and kissed the robe of any priest with whom he spoke. He soon became known as a skeptic, and it was bruited about that he doubted the immortality of the soul.[23] Ridiculed for marrying in his old age a girl of eighteen, obviously uncomfortable as a Jew, and yet, out of his bitter experience with the Inquisition, unable to be a Christian either, Méndez Silva in Italy is a pathetic figure, fleeing his past, and yet enmeshed in it. Abraham Cardoso would find the resolution of his own doubts in Jewish mysticism and a heretical messianism, and would ultimately be hounded in every Jewish community to which he came. Isaac's life would ply a more direct and unwavering course.

HOME IN VERONA

He remained in Venice less than five years. On August 25, 1652, in response to prior negotiations which had been initiated on his behalf, the *Va'ad* or governing body of the Jewish community of Verona granted him permission to come and settle in their midst. The document stated:

There have come before their aforementioned excellencies, his honor Moses Cohen, and his honor Jacob Navarro, representing the doctor, his honor R. Isaac Cardoso, and have requested from their excellencies that they should consent for him to come to live here in the holy community of Verona, him and his wife.

And as they have heard these things from the aforementioned men, they issue a decision that the aforementioned doctor (may his Rock and Redeemer guard him) may come to dwell here, as stated; and he shall pay for the right of settlement only twenty-five ducats, for they are

---

[23] All this information is given by the missionary to the Jews, Luigi Maria Benetelli, in his *I dardi rabbinici infranti;* cited by Roth, *Marranes à Venise*, p. 222.

certain that his honor will show his benevolence to the sick poor; and he shall be obliged to come before the assessors like all the other inhabitants of the holy community of Verona, and defray his share for the debts of the holy community which have accumulated because of conflicts with the merchants and speculators, etc.; and similarly he obliges himself, to observe, to do, and to uphold, all decisions, decrees, and agreements of the holy community, both old and new.[24]

The Sephardic community of Verona was of relatively recent origin, and had developed in a rather interesting way. Though the first Sephardic Jew had come in 1587, until 1625 the Jewish community had consisted almost exclusively of Germans and Italians. In the latter year, and especially after 1630, when Venice was struck by plague, the immigration of Sephardic Jews increased. These joined the Ashkenazic community. In so doing, they had necessarily to forego any special claim for the retention of their own corporate identity. They had to conform to Ashkenazic custom, worship together with the German Jews in their synagogue, and be represented in all communal decisions merely as individuals, rather than as an ethnic group with a collective voice. Their very presence in Verona, however, prepared the way for a new development. In 1637 yet another group of Sephardim contracted to come and settle in Verona. These were led by the Aboab family, which included Jacob Aboab, the father of Samuel, and his sons. Unlike the previous immigrants, however, these were not prepared to compromise their Sephardic traditions. They demanded the right to form a distinct congregation, with a Sephardic synagogue, a school, and a communal autonomy of their own. In view of the wealth of some of these families, and the distinguished scholarly reputation of others, the Ashkenazic Jews were not loath to admit them on these terms. Nevertheless, in the agreement which was drawn up in 1638, the Ashkenazic Jews still found it possible, while granting communal recognition to the newcomers, to deny them a vote in the affairs of the community at large. Thus there now existed two separate

---

[24] The document is one of several published by Isaiah Sonne from the communal archives. See his "Sources for the History of the Jews of Verona" (Hebrew), *Zion*, III (1938), 153.

strata of Sephardic Jews in Verona, with the new arrivals forming a genuine Sephardic community, while those who had come between 1625 and 1638 were still absorbed in the general community and subject to its sway.

Such an anomalous situation could not long endure. In effect it meant that the original Sephardim had equal but not ethnic rights, while the later arrivals had ethnic but not equal rights. The latter were the first to begin the struggle with the Ashkenazim by demanding their due representation in the general community, and in this they were able to enlist powerful support from outside. For, just as the city of Verona was under Venetian hegemony, so the Sephardim of Verona were a "colony" of the Ponentine community of Venice from whence most of them had come. They turned now to their Venetian brethren with an appeal for aid, and the latter used their considerable connections with the Venetian government to good effect. In 1644 the authorities in Venice ordered that the Veronese Jewish community grant the Sephardim the voice they had sought. This accomplished, it was now the turn of the original Sephardic settlers to demand the right to withdraw from the Ashkenazic community, and to join the Sephardic community. In this struggle, as well, the Venetian Jews rendered their assistance, and on July 27, 1653, the agreement was formally ratified between the Sephardic and Ashkenazic communities. There would now exist a threefold division: an Ashkenazic, a Sephardic, and a general community, the latter to include representatives of both. Henceforth any Sephardic Jew who lived in Verona, or who would come in the future, would belong to the Sephardic community, which thereby achieved its final crystallization.[25]

As we have seen, Isaac Cardoso had received his residence permit

---

[25] These developments are treated by Sonne, "Sources," pp. 145–54. Cf. also Shlomo Simonson, "The Communal Registers of Verona" (Hebrew), *Kirjath sefer*, XXXV (1959–60), especially pp. 133–36. Subsequent relations between the Ashkenazic and Sephardic communities remained calm until the very end of the century, when a new dispute broke out. For the latter see Salo W. Baron, "A Communal Conflict in Verona" (Hebrew), in *Sefer ha-yobel le-Prof. S. Kraus* (Jerusalem, 1937), pp. 217–54.

in October of the previous year. However, he did not come to Verona immediately. We know only that he was in the city by mid-July, shortly before the final agreement between the communities was about to be promulgated. In an entry preserved in the Jewish registers of Verona, dated July 17, 1653, we find that Cardoso and several others had not affixed their signatures to the document which had authorized the representatives of the Sephardic community to ratify the pact with the Ashkenazim. Obviously he was not yet in Verona when that document was drawn up. Now, in the presence of three witnesses, he expressed his accord with the authorization. In turn, he and the others were assured that, despite the absence of their signatures, they were included in the terms of the agreement, and that neither they nor their successors would ever be vexed on this score by the Ashkenazic community.[26] Since Cardoso must have made his declaration shortly after his arrival, we may place his settlement in Verona sometime in July of 1653.

From the residence permit itself we see that Cardoso was married, and came to Verona with his wife. There is no mention of children. A certain nuance which we shall later find in Abraham Cardoso's polemic leads us to believe that the couple may have always been childless.

The terms under which Cardoso was accepted are significant. A community which was constantly pressed for funds, and in which tax assessments were always a major source of friction, saw fit to

---

[26] "A. di 17 luglio 413, Verona 653: Alla presenza di noi sotto scritti testimoni confessorono in modo valido e sufitiente l. ecc:mo D. Abraham Israel de Vega Passarigno et l. ecc: mo D. Isach Cardoso et il S. Iacob navarro, et il. s.r Iosef Israel Forti hebrei che ancor che non habiano sotto scritto l.autorita datta dall. hon:da natione ponentina abitanti qui in Verona all ecc.mo S.r D. Abraham Cabezon et il s.r moise Gaon di concluder confermar conventioni con l. hon.da natione Tedesca in virtu dell. autorità datoli delli ss.ri del mahamad de l. c.c. de ponentini di Venetia, che sono prontissimi e dispostissimi alla ratefic:ne de capitoli contenuti [in] d.ta conventioni ne mai inquietar non loro ne sucesori la d.ta natione Thedescha e sucesori di esta per diffetto della loro sottoscritione." (Signed)

הצעיר יוסף אלקלעי הצעיר אברהם חי אורטונה ז' דוד הצעיר שאול מררי.

— Jewish National and University Library, Jerusalem: MS Heb. 4° 551 (Pinkas Verona, 1653-1706), fol. 3r.

reduce considerably the sum which he must pay for the right of settlement. It was understood, in return, that Cardoso would provide his medical services to the indigent for small fees or none. We shall yet see that he more than kept his side of the bargain.

But Cardoso was, after all, too famous a personality to slip into Italy entirely unnoticed. On October 16, 1657, Jacopo Zachios de Zarbona, a friar, appeared before the Venetian Inquisition to enter a voluntary deposition. To the comissioner of the Holy Office, Fra Raymondo Maria da Vicenza, he related that the week before, traveling from Verona to Venice, he had met a Jew named Joseph, who holds a concession on tobacco in the *terra ferma*. He took the opportunity to ask him about the many Spanish Jews who live in the Ghetto of Verona, and the latter replied that they were all baptized in Spain. On the basis of the information he was able to elicit he now wished to inform the Inquisition of several facts: That "Dr. Pinto" has died in Verona, and that a son of his lives in Amsterdam; that the Veronese physician Dr. Castro, "a Jew who became a Christian," had been in Spain a pupil of Dr. Cardoso; and, finally, "that the physician Dr. Cardoso was for many years a Christian in Spain . . . that in Madrid he had been physician to the royal court of His Majesty, and that at present this Doctor Cardoso is in the Ghetto of Verona, where he is living as a Jew."[27]

Had such a deposition been given to the Inquisition in Spain, the results would inevitably have been disastrous. In Venice it was different. There is no sign that this information ever led to the

---

[27] Archivio di Stato di Venezia, Santo Uffizio, Busta 106 (Dossier of Fra Raimundo Tasca):

"P⁰ Che il Dottor Pinto era morto in Verona, e c'havia un figlio in Absterdam. . .

2⁰ Ch'il Dottor Castro medico Veronese ebreo fatto xno. fù in Spagna scolaro del Dottor Cardoso.

3⁰ Ch'il Dottor Cardoso sud:⁰ fosse visciuto molt'ani xno. in Spagna et qui vi battezato; et che in Madrid fosse Medico della Corte Reale di sua maestà, et q.ᵗᵒ Dottor Cardoso al presente e in Verona, ove vive da ebreo."

I wish to thank Professor Cecil Roth for directing my attention to Busta 106 prior to my departure for Venice. He earlier had used this information to establish the identity of Pedro de Castro (see *infra*, n. 31), but did not publish the text.

initiation of inquisitiorial proceedings against Cardoso, or that any further action was taken. Already in the Middle Ages the Venetian state had consistently circumscribed the powers of the Holy Office, and in the seventeenth century its power declined even further.[28] Besides, unlike the situation in Spain, Judaizers seem to have been among the least of the concerns of the Venetian inquisitors.[29]

But although Zarbona's deposition had no practical consequences for Cardoso, the information it contains about him is valuable. It provides a contemporary confirmation of the report that Cardoso had been court physician in Madrid, and it draws our attention to two significant figures. The deceased Dr. Pinto to whom the friar referred was Antonio Dias Pinto, a Portuguese New Christian who had been brought to Italy in 1609 by the Grand Duke of Tuscany. At the University of Pisa he had lectured on both canon and Roman law, and was later transferred to Florence as a member of the ecclesiastical court of appeal. Around 1630 he suddenly went to Venice, professed Judaism, and subsquently settled in Verona. An inquisition was instituted against him in 1651, which apparently led to no conclusion.[30]

Since Dr. Pinto could have died at any time between 1651 and 1657, we cannot establish whether Cardoso had the opportunity to know him when he arrived in Verona. However, in the case of the other person mentioned in the deposition, there is no doubt whatever. Dr. Pedro de Castro, a famous physician in his day, was long an enigma to scholars. The available information is still rather meager. It has been reasonably proposed that De Castro was born

[28] See Henry Charles Lea, *A History of the Inquisition of the Middle Ages* (London, 1888), II, 249 ff.; Roth, *Marranes à Venise*, p. 214.

[29] In the index volume to the records of the Santo Uffizio in the Venetian archives I counted a total of 1,447 cases for the 17th century, of which only 28 were for Judaizing. Of the latter, only ten are persons listed as natives of Spain and Portugal, or bearing Iberian names.

[30] On Pinto, see Roth, *Marranes à Venise*, pp. 220 f. His case is extant in Santo Uffizio, Busta 106 no. 1. Two relatives in Venice, Giorgio and Franco (Francisco) Díaz, had been condemned as Judaizers in 1621, but were shortly afterward absolved by the Venetian Senate (Roth, *Ibid.*, p. 214). Their case is found in Busta 77, n. 7.

Italy: Reclaiming a Birthright

in Bayonne in 1603, and was the son of a New Christian physician, Luis de Castro. He went to the Peninsula to study, and later practiced medicine in the South of France, especially at Avignon. Around 1639 he came to Verona and avowed himself a Jew. After a decade or so, however, he reverted to Catholicism, as the deposition indicates. As a Jew he signed his published works with the name Ezechiele de Castro. After he returned to Christianity, he resumed the name Pedro (or Pietro).[31]

The three medical works which De Castro published as a Jew appeared in 1642 and 1646. His next work, *Imber aureus*, was completed in 1651, and published in 1652. Here he again began to employ the name Pedro, and dedicated the book to the College of Physicians of Verona, of which, as a Christian, he could now be a member.[32] His reversion to Catholicism must have occurred shortly before this, perhaps around 1650.

We may now better appreciate the circumstances which brought Cardoso to Verona. His private reasons for leaving Venice can only be surmised. It may be that after the very active life he had led in Spain he now wished to live more quietly than would be

---

[31] De Castro was at one time believed to have been born in Coimbra. That he practiced medicine in Avignon was shown by Alfonso Cassuto in his "Notes sur Pedro alias Ezechiele de Castro," *REJ*, XCIII (1932), 215–17; that he was born in Bayonne in 1603, and was the son of a Dr. Luis de Castro, was suggested by Ernest Ginsburger, "Pedro alias Ezechiele de Castro, *REJ*, XCIV, (1939), 90–95. Cecil Roth established that De Castro had indeed lived as a Jew by publishing a document from Verona in which, in 1640, the physician rented a house in the Ghetto ("Encore un mot sur Pedro (Ezekiel) de Castro," *ibid.*, pp. 96 f.). Finally, Roth confirmed Ginsburger's hypothesis by his discovery that in one of his works De Castro referred to himself as "Petri a Castro Bayonatis." He also brought from the Venetian archives the information that De Castro had subsequently returned to Christianity, and had become a member of the College of Physicians in Verona. See his "Un dernier mot sur Pedro alias Ezekiel de Castro," *REJ*, XCIV, 82–85. Incidentally, from the fact that De Castro had been a pupil of Cardoso Roth had already raised a doubt that the latter was born in 1615 (*ibid.*, p. 84, n. 3).

[32] A complete list of De Castro's works is given by Friedenwald, *Jews in Medicine*, II, 452 f. In 1643 he appeared as signatory to a document in which various Sephardim demanded a vote in the general community in Verona. See Sonne, "Sources," pp. 141–51.

possible in the larger community. Perhaps, too, he had some relatives in Verona. In a list of Sephardic householders in 1660 we find an Abraham Aboab Cardoso, who obviously belonged to the same family which included Samuel Aboab, and to whom Isaac Cardoso may also have been related.[33] But whatever his own motives for wishing to settle in Verona, the move would have been difficult, if not impossible, unless there was a real opportunity for him to practice medicine. It would seem that this opportunity presented itself largely as a consequence of De Castro's apostasy. The order of events would thus be as follows: In the decade 1640–50 Ezechiele de Castro served the Sephardic community of Verona as their physician. When he abandoned the Jewish faith and left the Ghetto, the community required a new physician to replace him. At about the same time, Cardoso, perhaps already informed of what had occurred in Verona, began to contemplate leaving Venice. Negotiations were begun and, as we have seen, the *Va'ad* in Verona eagerly accepted his services.

The irony implicit in the entire situation should not be missed. From Zarbona's deposition it is clear that De Castro was known to have been at one time a pupil of Cardoso. This could only have occurred at the University of Valladolid, during the years 1624–27, when Cardoso was teaching there. An indirect corroboration of a period of study at that university comes to us from De Castro himself. In 1652 he published a medical work of Dr. Antonio Ponce de Santa Cruz which he edited and emended.[34] We will recall that Ponce de Santa Cruz was himself professor of medicine at Valladolid, and was probably Cardoso's teacher as well.[35] Obviously, in editing a book of his, De Castro was repaying a debt which harked back to his own student days. Now, in 1653, De Castro and Cardoso were both in Verona, after not having seen one another for some

[33] The list in Sonne, "Sources," p. 155. On Aboab-Cardosos in Hamburg and Brazil, cf. *supra*, ch. II, n. 17.

[34] Antonius Ponce de Santacruz, *De impedimentis magnorum auxiliorum in morborum curatione libri III . . . Secundis curis emendationes e museo Petri a Castro* (Padua, 1652). See Friedenwald, *Jewish Luminaries*, p. 136.

[35] *Supra*, ch. II, n. 62; cf. ch. IV, n. 91.

twenty-seven years.[36] But under what paradoxical circumstances! In effect, Cardoso had come to Verona to replace, as physician to the Jewish community, a former pupil who had gone from Christianity to Judaism and then reversed himself once more. Cardoso had made his home in the Ghetto, while De Castro was living in the Christian community, enjoying all the prerogatives to which his professional stature entitled him, and was a member of the College of Physicians from which Cardoso, as a Jew, was barred. But Cardoso had made his choice, and it was a final one. One can imagine that each time the two met in the streets Cardoso must have been reminded anew of what his choice had entailed.

He had come to the end of all his journeys. For the next thirty years he lived and worked in the Ghetto of Verona, an honored member of the Sephardic community. Something of the great esteem in which Cardoso was held among his fellow Jews may be seen from the manner in which he is recorded in the list of tax assessments for the entire community in 1660, which included both the Sephardim and the Ashkenazim. The list enumerates 104 taxable householders, and both the Hebrew and vernacular names of each are recorded. Aside from one of the two rabbis, Cardoso's is the only name which is preceded by the honorific *Eccellentissimo* and, in Hebrew, by an even more elaborate equivalent.[37] Next to his Hebrew name we find the added note: "and he has taken it upon himself to visit the sick among the poor in the Ghetto square for nothing."[38]

We should like, of course, to learn more such details about

---

[36] Cardoso later mentioned De Castro in his *Philosophia libera* (Lib. IV, quaest. vii, fol. 204), but merely to cite the latter's book *Ignis lambens*, which had been published in Verona in 1642.

[37] Sonne, "Sources," p. 155. The rabbi is Nathan Pincherle (p. 156). The other rabbi, Mordecai Bassan, has the honorific title only in Hebrew (p. 157).

[38] *Ibid.*, p. 155. This also explains why Cardoso's tax was fixed at the unusually low rate of only 2 ducats, when the other assessments ranged up to 75. Rabbi Pincherle was assessed for 2 ducats but, even so, "only on condition that he shall have no other claim on anything for the next two years."

In 1664 another physician, Dr. Isaac López, took up residence in the Sephardic community, together with his children (*ibid.*, p. 158).

Cardoso's ordinary activities in Verona, but here we encounter an insurmountable obstacle. In Spain, where Cardoso had lived as a Christian and had mingled constantly in high society in Madrid, it was possible to trace many of his activities through Spanish documents and sources. In Verona, however, his life was lived within the confines of the Ghetto. The only documents in which we could have expected to find real information about him are those which were kept in the Jewish communal archives. Indeed, well into our own time the registers of the Sephardic community of Verona were still extant, but these are now lost.[39]

There is every reason to believe that the last three decades which Cardoso spent in Verona were, with one major exception which we shall consider in chapter VII, passed in peace. How he spent his time when he was not performing his medical duties, or taking part in communal affairs, becomes evident only when we open the remarkable work which he completed some fifteen years after his arrival.

---

[39] Most of the registers disappeared during the Second World War. Nothing is left in Verona itself. Eight registers (*pinkasim*) which survived have been transferred to the Jewish National Library in Jerusalem, and are described in detail by Simonson in his aforementioned article in *Kirjath Sefer*. Unfortunately for us, these registers are either of the Ashkenazic or of the "general" community. Not one register of the Sephardic community is extant, and even those which Sonne saw have perished.

There is a great deal of Jewish material in the Archivio di Stato di Verona, and I have examined that which pertains to the latter half of the 17th century. However, these documents generally deal with the Jewish community as a whole, and rarely with individuals. A very useful index to the documents dealing with Jews was compiled some years ago by an archivist in Verona, and is found in the Jewish Historical General Archives in Jerusalem (No. R 8/I-1).

PHILOSOPHER IN THE GHETTO

> Ipse enim dedit mihi horum quae sunt,
> scientiam veram, ut sciam dispositionem
> orbis, terrarum, & virtutes elementorum,
> initium, & consummationem, & medieta-
> tem temporum, vicissitudinem, permuta-
> tiones, & commutationes temporum, anni
> cursus, & stellarum dispositiones, naturas
> animalium, & iras bestiarum, vim vento-
> rum, & cogitationes hominum, differen-
> tias virgultorum, & virtutes radicum.
>
> —*Liber Sapientiae*, 7:17–20

IN 1673 there appeared in Venice a sumptuous Latin tome of more than 750 folio pages entitled *Philosophia libera*, by "the most distinguished physician and philosopher, Isaac Cardoso."[1] From the approbation of the Paduan censors we learn that the book was ready for the press in 1670. Obviously individual sections had been written long before. One has only to leaf through

---

[1] *Philosophia/ Libera/ in septem libros distribvta/ In quibus omnia, quae ad Philosophum naturalem spectant,/ methodice colliguntur, & accurate disputantur./ Opus non solum medicis, & philosophis, sed omnium disciplinarum/ studiosis vtilissimum:/ Auctore Isac Cardoso/ medico, ac philosopho praestantissimo:/ Cum duplici Indice, Quaestionum, ac Rerum Notabilium,/ Ad Serenissimvm Venetiarvm/ Principem/ Amplissimosque & Sapien-tissimos/ Reipvblicae Venetae/ Senatores./* [Engraving: Pastoral scene with fish, animals, and birds, flanked by two female figures, "Philosophia," holding a globe, "Liber-tas," holding a dove. Verses: above, Eccles. 3: 11, below, Job, 36:25]/ *Venetiis, Bertanorum sumptibus, MDCLXXIII/ Superiorvm permissv, et privilegio.* 7 unnumbered preliminary fols. + pp. 1–758 + 10 unnumbered fols.

216   Title page of Cardoso's *Philosophia libera* (Venice, 1673)

PHILOSOPHIA LIBERA

IN SEPTEM LIBROS DISTRIBVTA,

In quibus omnia, quę ad Philosophum naturalem spectant,
methodicè colliguntur, & accuratè disputantur.

Opus non solùm Medicis, & Philosophis, sed omnium disciplinarum
studiosis vtilissimum :

AVCTORE

ISAC CARDOSO

Medico, ac Philosopho præstantissimo :

Cum duplici Indice, Quæstionum, ac Rerum Notabilium.

AD SERENISSIMVM VENETIARVM

PRINCIPEM,

Amplissimosque, & Sapientissimos

REIPVBLICAE VENETAE

SENATORES.

de Scala

Et mandum tradidit disputationi eorum. Ecles. 3

PHILOSOPHIA   LIBERTAS

Omnes homines Vident eum, unusquisq; intuetur procul. Iob 36

VENETIIS, Bertanorum Sumptibus, MDCLXXIII.

SVPERIORVM PERMISSV, ET PRIVILEGIO.

this voluminous book, printed in double columns, to realize that Cardoso must have been fully engaged in writing it at least ever since coming to Verona, if not even earlier.

The *Philosophia libera* may be aptly characterized as Cardoso's *Summa*. Completed when he was about sixty-five years old, it embraces the final conclusions of a lifetime of thought in science, medicine, philosophy, and theology. There is a sense of symmetry and comprehensiveness about this work which marks it as his intellectual legacy.[2]

But it also displays another quality. Being, as it were, an ingathering of Cardoso's entire intellectual past, it also represents his valediction to that past. It is as though there, in the Ghetto of Verona, having made the fateful transition from Christian Spain, he could not fully rest until he had somehow bridged and unified past and present. A Jew at last, he must nonetheless salvage his prior intellectual development and reintegrate it. Thus we encounter in this book almost all the subjects he had already treated in the works published in Madrid, often in an expanded form.[3]

If, however, Cardoso has incorporated his past into this book, he has done so with a major difference. Here, for the first time, he is writing as a Jew, and this is always manifest, beginning with the title page itself. He proudly gives his name as *Isac* Cardoso, no longer Fernando, and, as we shall see, it is with the voice of Isaac that he speaks throughout.

Cardoso dedicated the *Philosophia libera* to the Doge and Senate of Venice. His profound gratitude to the city which had granted him asylum is expressed in glowing words of praise:

---

[2] The book has been often mentioned, sometimes described, but never really studied. See on it, for example, Zeferino González, *Historia de la filosofía*, III (Madrid, 1886), 81–84; Menéndez y Pelayo, *Heterodoxos*, II, 595 ff.; Thorndike, *Magic and Experimental Science*, VII, 683–88; Caro, *Sociedad*, pp. 107–12.

[3] E.g., *Discurso sobre el Monte Vesuvio* = *Phil. lib.*, IV, xi ("De ventis"), xii ("De terraemotu"), xiii ("De iride"), pp. 215–30; *Utilidades del agua* = *Phil. lib.*, I, xii ("De aqua"), pp. 36 f., xvi ("De fluxu & refluxu maris"), pp. 45–51, and especially xviii ("De aquarum bonitate & praestantia"), pp. 57–65; *Panegyrico del color verde*, cf. *Phil. lib.*, p. 312; *Si el parte de 12 y 13 meses es natural y legitimo*, cf. *Phil. lib.*, VI, xcix ("De partu undecimestri, annuo, & c."), pp. 689–91.

218

To the Most Serene
Prince
and to the Most Honorable and Wise
Senators
of the Venetian Republic

Free Wisdom befits a Free Republic, most Serene Prince, most honorable Senators, whom Freedom of their spirits has rendered outstanding for preserving the security of their Fatherland. The same freedom, seated in noble minds, will open the way to dig truth out of the pit and to free the sciences from the yoke of slavery, so that not a sect, but Reason, may promote assent, and judgment, not preconceived opinion, may confirm truth.

There are indeed two marvelous things which greatly exalt your most Serene and outstanding Republic and are celebrated by the commendations of all men: Wisdom, and Liberty. It is they which laid the foundations of the renowned city, they which formed the increases of her empire, and which now hold her firm as the marvel of the world. The wisdom of the Senators and the prudence of the Nobles, proclaimed for so many generations, glorious in so many praises, gleam like a most shining radiance, are worshiped, venerated, looked up to by all, in such a way that the Venetians seem to have been born for counsel, for governing, to be just appraisers of things. Whence it occurs that they have always been suited by their own nature for empires, illustrious in peace, vigorous in war. A city—either the avenger or the rival of Roman Liberty—Queen of the Sea, marvel of the world. She is in command of waters and lands, flourishing in Counsel, prominent in Forces, never violated, always untouched, tireless champion of Christians,[4] placed in the middle of Europe so that she might repress the inroads of Barbarians and balance the power of others by arms and judgment. A city of whom the Psalmist seems to have sung the verse *Thou hast founded her upon the seas*,[5] as though, elevated above the swelling pots of the seas, she casts

---

[4] This phrase is obviously intended to please the Venetian authorities. For Cardoso's real views on Christianity see our analysis of *Las excelencias de los Hebreos*, *infra*, chs. VIII and IX.

[5] Ps. 23 in the marginal notation, which corresponds to the Vulgate (Ps. 24 in the Hebrew Bible). Cardoso has changed the reading of the verse from the third to the second person.

down the proud spirits of the exalted. Moreover, *the waters stood above the mountains*, that is, above the highest mountains of virtue and nobility the clear waters of purity, wisdom, splendor, and health will most fully persist.

Deservedly, therefore, are Free Wisdom and Philosophy dedicated to the Free Prince and wise and free Leaders, so that those who in political matters are outstanding defenders of liberty may be also in natural matters splendid guardians of the same. For so the sciences grow and put forth pleasant and most sweet fruits: not by slavishly following in the footsteps of their elders without choice, but by freely and wisely winnowing the decisions of Ancients and Moderns. Therefore, Most Serene Prince, receive our efforts with a merry brow as illustrious signs of good will, and an eternal monument of allegiance. And may lovers of Liberty and truth always call upon the most flourishing Republic for refuge, and may the learned forever revere a Maecenas.

At Verona, 28 June 1673.

> Of your Serenity
> The Most Humble Servant,
>
> Isac Cardosus

For one who, while in Spain, was accustomed to offer his works to the high and the mighty, who had already dedicated books to Olivares and to Philip IV, this dedication to the Doge and Senate of Venice seems part of a familiar pattern. However, considering the rather special circumstances which had brought Cardoso to Venice, and the fact that he was now writing as a professing Jew, we must wonder if this dedication does not also reflect some special relationship to the Venetian authorities. The reference to a "Maecenas" may be merely a flattering cliché, but it may also indicate some actual patronage of the book. In short, if the dedication be taken in earnest, it is possible that Cardoso had some access to the very highest Venetian circles. This would explain not only the ease with which he first obtained asylum in the city, but also the fact that although the Venetian Inquisition had taken cognizance of him, he was left unmolested.

PHILOSOPHUS DOCTISSIMUS

But let us turn to the book itself.

The Introduction (Prohaemium) to the *Philosophia libera* brings us into immediate contact with some of the most vital centers of Cardoso's thought. It is, in essence, a schematic survey and critique of the history of philosophy and, as such, a key to his own attitudes and assumptions.

Cardoso begins by positing the Jewish origins of philosophy and science. Philosophy began with Adam, was carried forth by Noah after the Flood, and thereafter was cultivated only by the Hebrews. The Greeks, Egyptians, and Chaldeans were not its founders. Abraham first taught the Egyptians mathematics, and later Joseph educated them. Jewish philosophic and scientific endeavor continued up to the Babylonian Exile. At that point, "with the aging of the sciences among the Hebrews, they began to stammer among the Greeks."[6]

Now, while such notions are to be found in Jewish literature, it is significant that Cardoso has taken them directly from Clement of Alexandria and Eusebius of Caesarea, as he himself declares. What is more astonishing is the very extent to which he is indebted to the Church Fathers. As one reads the *Prohaemium* one begins to realize that it is saturated with Patristic materials even when Cardoso does not cite the Fathers by name. The full implications of this dependence will emerge only later, when we shall have reviewed some of the Jewish elements scattered throughout the book.

Cardoso continues his survey by noting that, after philosophy had passed to the Greeks, two schools arose, the "Ionian" and the "Italian." The former was founded by Thales, who was succeeded by Anaximander, Anaximenes, Anaxagoras, Archelaus, and Socrates. Pythagoras was the founder of the Italian school. He is not

---

[6] Fol. 1r of the Prohaemium. That Abraham taught mathematics and astronomy to the Egyptians is stated by Josephus, *Antt.*, I, 8:2, and is cited by Eusebius, *Praeparatio Evangelica*, IX:14.

to be identified with the prophet Ezekiel.[7] Socrates, "whom the Pythian oracle judged most wise, spurning natural philosophy as uncertain, embraced moral philosophy." According to Augustine, Plato studied with the prophet Jeremiah in Egypt.[8] This, Cardoso asserts, is chronologically impossible, but Plato could have learned much about natural and divine matters from other Jews who were there.[9] Plato was "outstanding in all disciplines" and endowed with great eloquence. "He wrote divinely and learnedly about divine things . . . and what some authors have revealed seems certain, that he leafed through the sacred volumes of Moses and watered his gardens from those fountains." Pythagoras also read them.[10]

The scope and method of teaching in the Academy are followed by a review of Antisthenes and the "Cynic Sect," Aristippus and the "Cyrenaic Sect," Zeno and the "Stoic Sect," with a list of famous Stoics culminating in Seneca. We are then introduced to the Epicureans. Epicurus was "an outstanding natural philosopher" who followed Democritus in the principia, that is, concerning atoms and the void. But Lucretius praises him too extravagantly, for he was a philosopher "who cared neither for gods nor for the immortality of the soul." "The most learned Gassendi illustrated the philosophy of Epicurus with most erudite commentaries, diligently refuting the errors into which he had fallen."[11]

---

[7] On the Ionian and Italian schools cf. Clement of Alexandria, *Stromata*, I, 14, 6 et seq. That Pythagoras is not to be identified with Ezekiel is stated by Clement, *Ibid.*, I, 15, 70.

[8] Augustine, *De Doctrina Christiana*, II, 28, 43, citing Ambrose. The same idea in Abravanel, Commentary on Jeremiah 1: 6; Gedalyah ibn Yahya, *Shalshelet ha-kabbalah* (Venice, 1586), fols. 99v-100r.

[9] So Augustine, *De Civ. Dei*, VIII, 11, retracting his earlier opinion.

[10] On Plato as influenced by Jewish Scripture, see especially Eusebius, *Praep. Evang.*, Bks. XI-XII, *passim*. For Pythagoras' appropriation of Jewish doctrines see Josephus, *Contra Apionem*, I, 163.

[11] Pierre Gassendi's most important works on Epicurus were his *Animadversiones in decimum librum Diogenis Laertii* (3 vols.; Lyon, 1649), and his *Syntagma philosophicum complectens logicam, physicam et ethicam*, published posthumously in vols. I-II of his *Opera omnia* (Lyon, 1658). Cf. the study of Bernard Rochot, *Les travaux de Gassendi sur Épicure et sur l'atomisme (1619–1658)* (Paris, 1944).

After a brief description of the Skeptics, founded by Pyrrho and represented notably by Sextus Empiricus, Cardoso turns to the Peripatetics. He gives the main outlines of Aristotle's life and praises him elaborately. Quoting the famous passage from Clearchus of Soli in Josephus' *Contra Apionem*, Cardoso avers that Aristotle was taught by a Hebrew sage.[12] Indeed, some maintain that at the end of his life Aristotle became a proselyte.[13] Aristobolus has shown that the entire Peripatetic philosophy was taken from the Law of Moses, and asserts that Plato and Pythagoras both borrowed heavily from the Hebrews. As a matter of fact, Numenius even referred to Plato as a Greek-speaking Moses.[14] More praises of Aristotle are brought forth, from Plato, Cicero, Plutarch, Pliny, Apuleius, Quintilian, Averroes, Maimonides, and Aquinas. Having mentioned Maimonides, Cardoso seizes the opportunity to laud his achievements as well, noting that the scholastics themselves had utilized his works, and citing the well-known Jewish maxim that "from Moses to Moses there arose none like Moses." The passage on Aristotle from Maimonides' *Guide for the Perplexed* is quoted in Buxtorf's Latin translation.[15]

---

[12] Josephus, *Contra Apionem*, I, 176.

[13] "Porro eruditus Gafarellus in suis annotationib. desumptis ab Hispano quoddā Rab. in sua Catena Cabalistica inquit, Aristotelē se ipsum in fine dierū suorum fecisse proselytum iusticiae, et ad primam causam conversum coactum fuisse fateri in ultima vitae suae periodo verissima omnino esse ea omnia, quae scripta sunt in libro legis Moysis, transisseque ad partes peregrinorum iustorum . . . quae omnia late prosequitur Lycetus lib. de pietate Aristotelis erga Deum" (Fol. 2r-v of the Prohaemium; cf. pp. 121, 605). On Jacques Gaffarel see *infra*, n. 186. "Catena Cabalistica" is clearly the *Shalshelet ha-kabbalah* of Ibn Yahya (on Aristotle's conversion see fol. 102b of the Venice ed.). Cardoso later returns to the subject in *Las excelencias de los hebreos*, p. 363. For "Lycetus," as well as further references, see my remarks *infra*, ch. IX, n. 85.

[14] Aristobolus and Numenius in Clement, *Stromata*, I, 22, 150, cited again by Eusebius, *Praep, Evang.*, IX, 6.

[15] Fol. 2v of the Prohaemium: "Rabbi Moyses eodem fere tempore aut paulo post Averroem uterq; Cordubensis in omnib. scientiis clarissimus eximius, Theologus, Philosophus praeclarus, Medicus insignis, in lege, ac iure Civili, & Canonico Haebreorum consultissimus, & quem saepe citant Scolastici Thomas, Albertus, Henricus, & de quo illud vulgare proverbium circumfertur apud

Philosopher in the Ghetto

Discussing the fate of Aristotle's works, Cardoso observes that many were lost in the course of time. He traces Aristotle's successors and some of his interpreters up to Boethius of Sidon. Thereafter the Peripatetic philosophy "became silent" for several centuries until it revived with Alexander of Aphrodisias. Later Peripatetics were Themistius and, in Justinian's reign, Simplicius.

But the Arabs, after their invasions of Greece in the time of Leo the Isaurian, appropriated the Greek books, and under this impetus they began to study Greek philosophy themselves, especially in Tunis, Fez, and Córdoba. From Spain the Aristotelian philosophy was carried over into France. The books of Aristotle and Averroes were eagerly received in Paris, where Alexander of Hales and Albertus [Magnus] were the first to cultivate them, and later Thomas Aquinas, Duns Scotus, and "an infinite number of monks in the cloisters." These finally divided into "Thomist, Scotist, and Nominalist sects," but without retreating from the Peripatetic philosophy itself.[16] With a brief discussion of the Eleatics the historical portion of the Prohaemium is concluded, and Cardoso passes on to a critique of the "errors of the philosophers."

The keynote is sounded in the opening sentence: "All those sects, and the philosophers their leaders, have their own peculiar errors and, deprived of the light of true religion, they fell into many absurdities. . . ." Thus it is essentially a religious critique which is to be offered at this juncture. Philosophic and scientific strictures are reserved for the main body of the work although even there, as we shall see, religious and scientific criticisms often mingle with one another.

Haebreos, *a Mose usque ad Mosem non surrexit alter Mose,* id est a Mose prophetarum Principe, usque ad Rabbi Mosem, non surrexit alter sapiens, sicut iste Moses, de quo multa Bustrofius in praefatione ad librum Directorij dubitantium R. Mosis quem ex Haebreo in Latinum Sermonem noviter post alias translationes vertit." The younger Buxtorf's translation of the *Guide* had appeared in Basel in 1629 under the title *Doctor perplexorum.* The title Cardoso cites here is essentially that of the translation which was published a century earlier, entitled *Dux seu Director dubitantium aut perplexorum* (Paris, 1520). He obviously knew both.

[16] Fols. 2v-3r of the Prohaemium.

224

The errors of Pythagoras are the doctrine of the transmigration of souls,[17] as well as the Pythagorean numbers "which obscure philosophy." Democritus erred in thinking the world was made by accident from the concourse of atoms, that infinite worlds come into being when the atoms unite, and that the atoms themselves are eternal.[18] Although Plato thinks the world has a beginning, he "constructed it from a certain eternal matter, or foundation, or Chaos." He embraced the Pythagorean transmigration of souls. In his *Republic* he asserted that women ought to be held in common. He affirmed that God is the soul of the world, that our knowledge is reminiscence, and believed in a revolving time cycle of ten thousand years, "so that Achilles would again assemble at Troy, and Plato teach in the Academy."[19]

Cardoso's more elaborate censure of Aristotle follows along the same lines. Aristotle was wrong in maintaining the eternity of the world, in fixing the prime mover to the East and claiming that it operates out of necessity, as well as in denying the immortality of the soul and divine providence. (On the latter score he cites the *Stromata* of Clement of Alexandria, and Epiphanius' *Adversus haereses*.) Referring to various Aristotelian works Cardoso notes also that the philosopher denies the divine origin of dreams, that he regards divine reward and punishment as fables invented for the common people, that in the *Politics* he advocates euthanasia and abortion, and that he does not admit the resurrection of the dead.[20]

Epicurus displays three significant errors: that the world was not created by God, that it is not governed by Him, and that the soul of Man is mortal. Zeno the Stoic commits similar errors. In his Republic, like Plato, he advocates a communality of wives and children, as well as other such matters which are described by Diogenes Laertius.[21]

---

[17] Cf. Cardoso's detailed arguments against transmigration, *Phil. lib.*, lib. VI, quaest. lxxviii, "De transmigratione animarum," pp. 616 ff.

[18] Cf. the very similar discussion of the Greek atomists by Dionysius of Alexandria, preserved in Eusebius, *Praep. Evang.*, XIV, chs. 23–26.

[19] Fol. 3r of the Prohaemium.   [20] *Ibid.*   [21] *Ibid.*, fol. 3r-v.

Philosopher in the Ghetto

Which school, then, among the many that have existed, should one follow? The fact is that "the sects have their own times and fates, just as empires, for when some are overturned others begin to dominate." But it is specifically with Aristotle that Cardoso is most concerned, and it is against the Aristotelian philosophy that most of his barbs are aimed:

From the time of Averroes up to our generation—five hundred years, forsooth!—the Peripatetic sect has acquired great authority, and Aristotle is preferred to all philosophers, the discipline of all the [other] ancients being less esteemed. Only Aristotle is listened to, he alone is interpreted . . . his dogmas are received as oracles with miraculous approbation, and he is thought to have surpassed all men in genius. . . .[22]

The verbal assault grows in intensity. Although Aristotle was indeed a man of the highest genius, he handled many things "with the obscurity of Heraclitus." His ambiguity is often such that "like a waxen nose, he can be turned in any direction." He has been compared to "a cuttlefish which mocks and blackens fishermen by pouring out ink or a blackening fluid lest it be caught." Moreover, "corrosion from dampness and moths increased the obscurity of his writings as they lay hidden," as did the versions of interpreters and the emendations of inexperienced editors. Many works, written either by his pupils or others, were wrongly attributed to him. Nor is his genius, however great, sufficient to place him before all others, "for, although he went beyond Plato in natural matters, he is far surpassed by him in things divine." Even in the investigation of nature Democritus is either his equal or his better. Cardoso reiterates the praises of Democritus by Hippocrates, Seneca, Eustathius, Cicero, and Aristotle himself. In proposing atoms as the principles of natural things Democritus "discoursed more subtly and truly than did Aristotle with his matter, form, and privation. . . ." Nor was Aristotle truly original. Patrizi has written that he derived his entire natural philosophy from Hippocrates and Ocellus Lucanus.[23]

---

[22] *Ibid.*, fol. 3v.

[23] *Ibid.* On Francesco Patrizi (1529–97) see Thorndike, *Magic and Experimental Science*, VI, 373–77.

The endorsement of Aristotle by the Christian scholastics, by Aristobolus and Maimonides among the Jews, and by Averroes among the Arabs, is no validation of his philosophy. Others no less wise, and of equal or superior authority, felt differently about him. The early doctors of the Church were little attached to him. Augustine, in Book VIII of the *City of God*, preferred the Platonic philosophy. Jerome preferred the Stoic, because in most respects it agrees with true religion, and in his work against Pelagius he says that the heretics have set up their seat among the thorns and thickets of Aristotle and Chrysippus. Aristotle is censured also by Gregory of Nazianzus, Tertullian, and Justin.[24] Similarly, against the Jewish Aristotelians, Cardoso ranges Philo, Hasdai Crescas, and, rather irrelevantly, "the Talmudists, who have a great silence about Aristotle, although they discourse at length about natural, moral and divine matters. . . ."[25]

Writing in the latter half of the seventeenth century it is still possible for Cardoso to state flatly that a majority clings to Aristotle, and to warn that numbers in themselves are no recommendation.

What sect, then, ought to be embraced? None. Which philosopher ought to be followed? None, and all. For it behooves a wise man to swear to the words of no master, but to choose out of all what appears better, what appears nearer to reason and more probable, lest we seem slavish rather than free minds.

These are bold words indeed, and they are followed by others in the same vein. There are two hindrances, we are informed, to the search for truth. The first is to devote oneself entirely to one school of thought:

What liberty is it to run about through the opinions of the Thomists, Scotists, and Nominalists, if they are detained in the workhouses of

---

[24] Prohaemium, fol. 3v.

[25] *Ibid.*: "Aristobulo & Rabi Mosi opponimus Philonem disertissimum Platonis aemulum, Talmudistas, qui de Aristotele magnum habent silentium, cum tamen in opere vastissimo, & multiplicis doctrinae, de rebus naturalibus, moralibus, & divinis fuse diesserant, Rabi Xasdai doctum valde inter Haebreos Recentiores (& quem interdum citat eruditus comes Mirandulus Franciscus Picus) Aristoteli & Rabi Moysi parum affectum, qui quaedam Aristotelis dogmata evertit."

227

Philosopher in the Ghetto

Aristotle, like those who can run about anywhere they like—within the prisons—and boast that they are very free; while Aristotle always keeps them beneath his rod and allows them, like birds shut in a cage, to dance about through twigs, but does not permit them to unfold their wings in a free sky?

The second obstacle to truth is "the handling of useless and most vain questions":

They argue anxiously whether a form of corporeity exists, what properties it has, whether the form of a corpse exists and what it's like . . . whether a visive power placed in a stone elicits the act of vision. All the questions they inanely mix in about the possible, whether matter through the absolute power of God is able to exist without form, whether form without matter! With their "subsistential relations," "formalities," "modes," "this-nesses" (*haecceitatibus*) . . . they have disfigured universal philosophy, and of them Isaiah (59: 5) says: *they weave the spider's web*, and Job (8: 14): *as the web of the spider so is his trust. . . .*[26]

The emancipation from old patterns of thought which such passages so resoundingly proclaim must inevitably arouse high expectations for the independence and novelty of the work itself. However, the attentive reader of the Prohaemium will already be forewarned by certain nuances to temper these expectations in advance. We have noted Cardoso's heavy reliance on the Church Fathers and his essentially religious strictures against the philosophers in general and Aristotle in particular. Now, as the task of natural philosophy is defined, we hear that "it contemplates the visible world and seeks into the hidden causes of the effects which it sees, and from the operations of Creation, its appearance, beauty, and variety, it celebrates with marvelous praises God as the Creator of Nature." Significantly, Cardoso chooses two scriptural texts to describe the ideal philosopher. The first, which I have used as a superscription for this chapter, is from the Book of Wisdom: ("For He has given me the true knowledge of the things that are, that I may know the disposition of the whole world and the virtues of the elements, the beginning, end, and middle of times, the alterations of their courses

---

[26] *Ibid.*, fol. 4r.

and changes of seasons, the circuits of the year and dispositions of stars, the natures of animals and anger of beasts, the force of winds and thoughts of men, the diversities of plants and virtues of roots . . .") ; the other is taken from ch. 5 of I Kings ("and he spoke of trees, from the cedar that is in Lebanon to the hyssop which comes out of the wall; he spoke also of beasts and of fowl, and of creeping things, and of fishes"). It is by no means coincidental that both passages were quoted long ago by Eusebius in his chapter on the natural science of the Hebrews.[27]

Cardoso complains that the "modern philosophers" (by which he means the medieval writers as opposed to the ancients) neglected the study of nature, and that even in approaching Aristotle they largely ignored those of his works which concentrated on the natural sciences. They also despised the mathematical disciplines. But in recent generations some men had freed themselves from the "Peripatetic slavery." They selected the more probable opinions of Democritus, Empedocles, Plato, and other ancients, "sweated over the investigation of natural things," shattered many doctrines, and "renewed" others.

Cardoso's list of these innovations is again interesting for what it reveals about his own mentality. Thus: "Count Franciscus Picus Mirandulanus, illustrious in birth and learning," confutes many of Aristotle's "dogmas" in his book on the consideration of the vanity of the doctrines of the nations.[28] Petrus Dolese, "a doctor in Spain and Valencian knight," published a *summa* of philosophy and medicine, in which he follows the philosophy of Democritus.[29] Franciscus Patritius, both in his own philosophy and in his Peripatetic Discussions "fiercely tears Aristotle apart."[30] Bernardinus Telesius

---

[27] *Ibid.*; cf. Eusebius, *Praep. Evang.*, XI, 7.

[28] Giovanni Francesco Pico della Mirandola, *Examen vanitatis doctrinae gentium et veritatis Christianae disciplinae, distinctum in libros sex, quorum tres omnem philosophorum sectam universim, reliqui Aristoteleam et Aristotelis armis particulatim impugnant, ubicunque autem Christiana et asseritur et celebratur disciplina* (Mirandola, 1520).

[29] I am, unfortunately, unable to identify Pedro Dolese. Cardoso regards him as the first of the modern atomists (*Phil. lib.*, p. 10).

[30] Patrizi's "own philosophy" probably refers to his *Nova de universis philosophia*

introduced a new philosophy.[31] Gomezius Pereira in his Antonian Pearl deserts Aristotle and betakes himself to Democritus' camp.[32] Bassonus is completely absorbed in assaulting Aristotle,[33] and Magnenius in his book on atoms defends Democritus.[34] Gassendi, in his philosophy of Epicurus and in the Aristotelian exercises "follows the ancient philosophers, censures Aristotle, and abundantly teaches and extols freedom of philosophizing."[35] The Dominican Tomasso Campanella, "remarkable for his erudition," very often assails Aristotle's philosophy.[36] Beligardus, a Frenchman by nationality but a distinguished professor of philosophy at Padua, published a Pisan Circle and worked out a new philosophy in accordance with Democritus' opinions, rejecting Aristotle.[37] Stephanus Cosmus, "noted for his eloquence and philosophy, and a noble defender of freedom,"

(Ferrara, 1591). Vol. I of his *Discussionum Peripateticarum tomi iv* appeared in Venice in 1571, all four volumes in Basel, 1581.

[31] Bernardino Telesio (1508–88), *De natura iuxta propria principia* (Rome, 1565). Augmented editions, Naples, 1570 and 1586.

[32] Gómez Pereira, *Antoniana Margarita, opus nempe physicis, medicis et theologis, non minus utile quam necessarium* (n.p., 1554). It should be noted that Gómez is the author's personal name, not his surname. On the book, see Menéndez y Pelayo, *La ciencia española*, II, 277 ff.

[33] Sebastien Basso, *Philosophiae naturalis adversus Aristotelem libri XII, in quibus abstrusa veterum physiologia restauratur et Aristotelis errores solidis rationibus refelluntur* (Geneva, 1621).

[34] Jean Chrysostome Magnen, *Democritus reviviscens, sive de atomis; addita Democriti vita et philosophia* (Pavia, 1646).

[35] Gassendi, *Exercitationum paradoxicarum adversus Aristoteleos libri septem* (Bk. I, Grenoble, 1624; Bks. I and II in vol. III of his *Opera omnia*, Lyon, 1658). Both books have now been edited with a French translation by B. Rochot, *Dissertations en forme de paradoxes contre les Aristoteliciens* (Paris, 1959). For the works on Epicurus see *supra*, n. 11.

[36] Campanella (1568–1639) sharply criticizes Aristotle in his *De sensu rerum et magia libri quatuor* (Frankfurt, 1620). On the work itself, see Thorndike, *Magic and Experimental Science*, VII, 292 ff.

[37] Claude Guillermet de Bérigard (1591?–1667?), a Frenchman called to Pisa in 1628 and to Padua in 1640. His anti-Aristotelian work, *Circuli Pisani, seu de veterum et peripat. philosophia dialogi*, appeared in Udine, 1643–47, and in Padua, 1661. Earlier, in 1632, he had published a refutation of Galileo.

230

published a universal physics and, disapproving of Aristotle's doctrines, illustrated those of Democritus.[38] Cardoso goes on to laud Descartes and Digby for promulgating "a new philosophy relying on mathematical principles." Galileo "subtly and most earnestly treated of many things concerning motion and the stars." Vives and Ramus are mentioned together with Giovanni Francesco Pico and Gassendi as having pointed out many philosophical abuses.[39]

In his own work, Cardoso promises, many of the abuses of the past will be rectified. He will gather together all things pertaining to natural philosophy, many of which philosophers tend to omit. He will not devote himself exclusively to the opinions of any school, nor will he receive any opinions as articles of faith or as demonstrated proofs. As far as possible he will flee from purely dialectical discussions which are "trifles and subtleties similar to spiders' webs." His goal is stated in more positive terms as follows:

We shall investigate Nature and its Founder, so that from the world and its multitude of things, as if by a ladder, with enlightened and instructed mind, we may be lifted to God its Maker; for His creatures are the ladder by which we ascend to God, the organ with which we praise God, and the school in which we learn God.

The themes of the seven books of the *Philosophia libera* are then briefly sketched, beginning with the principles of natural things, and ending with God, the latter to be treated with "humility, brevity, and reverence." Generally it is the physicians who appropriate the greater part of philosophy in dealing with "the elements, tempera-

---

[38] I am unable to identify this person. A Stefano Cosmi, Archbishop of Spalato in the 17th century, published several funeral orations which are listed in the catalogue of the Bibliothèque Nationale, Paris, but he hardly fits Cardoso's description.

[39] Cardoso probably has in mind the *Two Treatises* of Sir Kenelm Digby (1603–65) of which the Latin translation appeared in Paris in 1655 as *Demonstratio immortalitatis animae rationalis sive Tractatus duo philosophici* (see Thorndike's analysis, *Magic and Experimental Science*, VII, 498 ff.). Needless to say, Cardoso has vastly overrated Digby's originality. Petrus Ramus (d. 1572) published two works against Aristotle in 1543: *Dialecticae partitiones ad academiam Parisiensem*, and *Aristotelicae animadversiones*.

ments, humors, the admirable fabric of man, and the economy of all nature," whereas the theologians "snatch the more divine and sublime part," debating about God, albeit too profusely. Cardoso intends to overcome this dichotomy, for "it behooves the philosopher to handle both, the human things, that is, and the divine, so that from the visible to the invisible, from the perishable to the immortal, from the temporal to the eternal, we may train, uplift, and kindle the mind."

We are suddenly on familiar terrain. The very arrangement of the books of the *Philosophia libera* points to its ultimate source in the intellectual tradition which Cardoso had absorbed in his youth. The order is hierarchical, ascending from physics to metaphysics, just as it had been long ago in the Valladolid curriculum. The statements concerning the ultimate aims of philosophy were obviously acceptable to the censors of Padua who allowed the work to be published. They would have been approved in Madrid as well.

OF ATOMS AND UNICORNS

Like any other scientific work of the age, the *Philosophia libera* can be approached in two ways. One may consider it vertically, in terms of its position within the history of science, and inquire whether it contains any innovations of significance to future scientific progress. Viewed thus, Cardoso's effort falls short of the mark. It is simply not in a class with the work of such true seventeenth-century pioneers as Galileo, Descartes, Harvey, Pascal, Huygens, or Newton. No major discovery is announced or anticipated in the *Philosophia libera*, no new path in scientific method is blazed in its pages. Indeed, some recent discoveries are either ignored or rejected. Cardoso's own proclaimed independence from any particular "sect" tends to lead him into eclecticism, while his vaunted liberation from Aristotle often means a license, not to strike out on a new course of investigation, but rather merely to choose the view of another ancient instead. Nor, as we shall see, has Cardoso entirely abandoned Aristotle himself. Finally, despite his promise not to become entangled in "vain" discussions, many of the problems treated in the *Philosophia libera* must strike us now as so much tilting at windmills.

But then—almost three centuries have passed since the book appeared. Posterity has inevitably been highly selective in the elements of seventeenth-century thought which it has chosen to remember and preserve. Topics which were of vital concern to the men of that age, raging controversies long since resolved or proved irrelevant, have been forgotten. Indeed, posterity shows little concern even for the archaic elements which were still an integral part of the thought of the innovators themselves. Who chooses to recall today that Kepler was a practicing astrologer, or that Newton performed alchemical experiments? To judge the *Philosophia libera* solely in its vertical relations is to succumb to historical "precursorism," and thereby to miss an important dimension.

Examined horizontally, the *Philosophia libera* offers us a broad view, not only of Cardoso's private intellectual world, but of that age of transition which witnessed the birthpangs of modern science. As such the book has even a certain poignancy, reflecting, beneath its stately Latin prose, the tensions between the claims of the past and the lure of a barely visible future. If, time and again, the "Free Philosophy" returns to the lecture hall of the Spanish university, if, while obviously yearning for the new, Cardoso persists in clinging to the old, he is perhaps on that very score more representative of his age than were the innovators.

Book I of the *Philosophia libera*, devoted to an analysis of the principles of natural things (*De principiis rerum naturalium*) opens with three chapters on the elements. Cardoso still accepts the traditional four, but with several differences. He lashes out against the Aristotelian postulates of primal matter, form, and privation.[40] The elements are simple bodies composed, not of matter and form, but of *atoms*.

Although it had been adumbrated earlier, the revival of atomism was a significant feature of seventeenth-century science, and an important expression of its anti-Aristotelian trends. Cardoso's espousal of atomism would thus seem to range him squarely on the

---

[40] *Phil. lib.*, I, quaest. i, p. 2.

side of the "new."[41] However, we must not overestimate the novelty of his position. By the time the *Philosophia libera* was completed, various atomic theories had already been propagated by a number of thinkers, among whom Gassendi had undoubtedly the widest impact. It is therefore unfortunate that, although Cardoso's brief references to the principal expounders of atomism reveal something of his own indebtedness, we cannot know how early he came to hold such views. After relating that the reputed inventor of the theory was Moschus the Phoenician,[42] who lived before the Trojan War (and learned it from the Hebrews), Cardoso mentions some of the Greek atomists, and later names some of those who have revived atomism in modern times. In addition to Pedro Dolese, Basso, Gassendi, Magnen, and Bérigard, all of whom had figured prominently in the Prohaemium, he lists also Rodrigues de Castro and Sennert.[43]

---

[41] On the history of atomism the basic work is still Kurd Lasswitz, *Geschichte der Atomistik vom Mittelalter bis Newton* (2 vols.; Hamburg, 1892). Suggestive treatments of various aspects of 17th-century atomism are also to be found in E. J. Dijksterhuis, *The Mechanization of the World Picture* (Oxford, 1961), pp. 418–30, and in Andrew van Melsen's compact survey, *From Atomos to Atom* (New York, 1960), chs. II and III. Cardoso is nowhere mentioned in these or similar works, but this is hardly surprising when we consider the omission of many other figures. In this respect, the recent remarks of Robert Hugh Kargen are particularly apt: "In the light of its undisputed importance, it is surprising that the historians of atomism are almost all 'ahistorical'. They tend to remove the ideas and concepts of atomism from their historical context. . . . In these works atomism is treated as an ideological development of a few major figures. . . . The secondary figures who were crucial to the reception and dissemination of atomistic doctrines are either ignored or mentioned only in passing" (*Atomism in England from Hariot to Newton* [Oxford, 1966], p. viii).

[42] *Phil. lib.*, I, quaest. iv ("De atomis et illarum natura"), p. 9. Cardoso's attribution of atomism to Moschus is taken from Sextus Empiricus.

[43] *Phil. lib.*, p. 10. Cf. *Stephani Roderici Castrensis Lusitani medici ac philosophi praestantissimi et in Pisani schola meaicinam primo loco docentis, De meteoris microcosmi libri quatuor* (Florence, 1621). At the end of Bk. I he argues for atoms but, unlike Cardoso, rejects the four elements. See, on him, Friedenwald, *Jews in Medicine*, II, 453 ff. Cardoso's other reference is to the German Daniel Sennert (1572–1637), *Hypomnemata physica*, first published in 1636 and reprinted in Vol. I of his *Opera omnia* (Paris, 1641). Sennert essentially attempted to adapt a modified atomism

According to Cardoso the atoms are "solid, individual, indivisible, insensible, and invisible corpuscles." As the unit is the principium of number, the point that of a line, the moment that of time, so the atoms are the principia of bodies and composites. They have varying figures, those of fire most resembling a spherical shape. But having made this beginning, Cardoso does not carry it forth with any real consistency into his treatment of natural phenomena. His atomism is almost exclusively philosophical, with no real application to mechanics. Its point of departure is the postulate that "nihil faciat ex nihilo, neque redigat in nihilum." The atoms are thus for him primarily an explanation of generation and degeneration. However, like most of the atomists of the time, Cardoso is also careful to divorce himself from the atheistic implications of Greek atomism. In this he follows a path which had been cleared by Gassendi, who was a Jesuit. Like the latter, Cardoso departs from the atomism of Democritus and Epicurus by denying both the infinity and eternity of atoms, their accidental conjunction, and the possibility of infinite worlds. The atoms were themselves created by God, and did not exist before. These themes are further amplified in other sections of the book.[44]

The chapter on atoms is followed by two on the primary and secondary qualities. As in the elements, Cardoso still recognizes four primary qualities and argues against Girolamo Cardan's rejection of cold as being mere privation of heat. The qualities are not accidents,

---

to an Aristotelian framework. Lasswitz (*Gesch. der Atomistik*, I, 441) sees in him the renewer of atomism, a view roundly criticized by Thorndike (*Magic and Experimental Science*, VII, 206). See further, Van Melsen, *Atomos to Atom*, pp. 81–89.

[44] *Phil. lib.*, p. 10: "Sed Atomorum doctrina ut sana euadat, et a calumnijs liberetur, debet aliter explicari ac Democritus et Epicurus sentiebant, illi enim atomos infinitas existimabant, aeternas, et fortuito casu coniunctas elementa conflare, et oberrantes per inane infinitū, infinitos mundos conficere, et seiunctas dissolvere, quae omnia falsa sunt, absurda, et a vera fide aliena, cum nihil sit infinitum ac aeternum praeter Deum, et si atomi aeterne essent, atq. a se ipsis et non ab alio haberent esse tot essent Dij. quot atomi, neq. mundus casu, aut fortuito fuit atomorum concursu productus, sed providentia & potentia Dei, ex nihilo creatus, illa atomos, & elementa produxit, in quo non minus aberrarunt alij veteres philosophi. . . ." Similar statements are made by Gassendi, *Animadversiones*, I, 725–28.

as Aristotle thought, but substances.[45] The rest of Book I is devoted successively to detailed discussions of the four elements, each consisting of several or more chapters. The internal arrangement is somewhat arbitrary, Cardoso using each element almost as a pretext to treat any topic which may in some way be associated with it.

With reference to earth, for example, we have chapters on the element proper, on the shape and size of the globe, its immobility, its division into zones and climates, and the habitability of its various parts.[46]

Of these the chapter entitled "De terrae immobilitate" is of surpassing interest, as it offers a particularly telling illustration of the mélange of old and new in Cardoso's thought. As the title indicates, we have here a rejection of the Copernican theory. This should not, of itself, surprise us. Although, following the work of Kepler and Galileo, the heliocentric theory was by now widely accepted, its victory among both Christians and Jews was far from complete. Particularly in Italy, the censure of Galileo by the Church had created an atmosphere in which his successors either took issue with the new astronomy, or else confined themselves to less controversial matters. If Giovanbattista Riccioli's *Almagestum novum*, published in 1651, was the last great defense of the older system, it was certainly not the last word on the subject. In Italy the latter half of the seventeenth century saw repeated attacks and criticisms leveled against the Copernican world view. A few examples will suffice. In his *De triplici philosophia* (Bologna, 1653), Benedetto Mazzotta maintained the immobility of the earth at the center of the universe "against what Copernicus said and the Church condemned." Orazio Maria Bonfioli published in Bologna in 1667 a work entitled plainly *De immobilitate terrae*. Honoratus Fabri in his *Physica* (Lyon, 1669–71) conceded the ingenuity of the Copernican system but stoutly maintained that the earth did not move. It is to be noted

---

[45] *Phil. lib.*, I, quaest. v ("De calore, & frigore, humore & siccitate"); quast. vi ("De secundis qualitatibus"). The criticism of Aristotle and Cardan, pp. 11 f.

[46] *Ibid.*, pp. 16–36, as follows: Quaest. vii ("De terra"); viii ("De figura & magnitudine terrae"); ix ("De terrae immobilitate"); x ("De terrae divisione"); xi ('De terrae habitatione").

that publication of this work was completed only two years before that of the *Philosophia libera*. A quarter of a century after Cardoso's book appeared, Antonio Francesco Bertini wrote an important, sane, and generally progressive review of the progress of medicine, *La medicina difesa dalle calumnie degli uomini volgari e dalle opposizioni de' dotti* (Lucca, 1699). But the Copernican system, he insisted, is justly condemned by the Holy Office and rejected by many philosophers.[47]

There is no indication that Cardoso's own rejection of the Copernican theory was due to fear of the Church. On the contrary, his treatment of the subject bears every mark of genuine conviction.

At the very outset Cardoso takes a firm stand in favor of the primacy of the experience of the senses, and marshals Aristotle to his aid:

Aristotle wisely says (*De Caelo*, 2: 72) that certain men do not accommodate theories and causes to things that are seen, but force experiences and senses to fit certain theories and opinions of their own. . . . It is indeed the height of madness to entangle the evidences of the senses with sophistic reasonings and empty subtleties. Zeno denied motion, Heraclitus and Cratylus denied rest, and they are refuted by no stronger argument than that rest and motion are perceived by the senses.

The theory of the earth's movement, he avers, is not really new. Despite our manifest experience of its perpetual rest at the center of the universe, a diurnal rotation was already posited by some of the ancients, such as the Pythagoreans, Philolaus, Heraclides Ponticus, Nicaeas of Syracuse, Aristarchus of Samos, Seleucus, and Cleanthes. The opinion of Philolaus and Aristarchus was revived by "two Nicholases"—i. e., by Nicholas of Cusa in his *De docta ignorantia* and later, with great acclaim, by Nicholas Copernicus.[48]

---

[47] On Mazzotta, Bonfioli, Fabri, and Bertini, see Thorndike, *Magic and Experimental Science*, VII, 644, 666 f., VIII, 622, respectively. The list is by no means exhaustive. Nor were anti-Copernican stances confined to Italy. As late as 1690 Pierre Sylvain Regis, who taught Cartesian philosophy at several French universities, published a *Système de philosophie* based on Descartes, in which he also offered to explain the universe on the assumption of either the immobility of the earth or its revolution around the sun (Thorndike, VIII, 614).

[48] *Phil. lib.*, p. 21: "Hanc Philolai & Aristarchi opinionem de motu terrae

Philosopher in the Ghetto

After enumerating some of the more prominent Copernicans, Cardoso gives a fairly detailed twelve-point exposition of their views. Of interest here is the fact that, while philosophical and even mathematical arguments for the heliocentric theory are well summarized, we hear almost nothing of the actual experimental data which had been accumulating in favor of it. And this, even though Cardoso knows and quotes Galileo's *Dialoghi* directly! To complete the exposition he adds the views of the Copernicans on the fallibility of human vision, as well as two scriptural verses which seem to allude to the movement of the earth.[49]

Cardoso opens his own presentation with the terse statement that the immobility of the earth is confirmed by Scripture, reason, and the senses. He cites the Hippocratean maxim that it is far better to trust the eyes than opinions. But his discussion of the evidence of the senses is only a preamble to his actual proofs, of which there are thirteen (as opposed to the twelve attributed to the Copernicans). Significantly, what had been a mere appendage in his exposition of the latter becomes for him the very first proof: the evidence from Sacred Scripture, "in which the highest truth shines, and many arcana of natural things are hidden." We need not review the actual verses (a total of nineteen) which he musters to his cause. So far as he is concerned, "all of sacred letters recall the earth's immobility." Nor, within the framework of our study, must we concern ourselves with his scientific proofs, which range from the incompatibility of linear motion on a rotating globe, through proofs from the motion of birds and projectiles, to the argument that no living creatures or plants could sustain themselves on a moving earth. A further point-

---

plurimis iam saeculis emortuam suscitarunt duo Nicolius. . . ." According to Nicholas of Cusa, judgments about motion are relative. Every point in the world may, with equal right, be called the center, or placed on the periphery. "The earth, which cannot be the center, cannot be without motion." See his *De docta ignorantia libri tres*, ed. P. Rotta (Bari, 1913), Bk. II, pp. 11–12. Though he does not say explicitly that the earth revolves around the sun, he does maintain that both earth and sun move, each with a different velocity.

[49] *Phil. lib.*, p. 23. In the Vulgate, which Cardoso quotes, Job. 9: 6 (*Qui commovet terram de loco suo* . . .) and Ps. 113: 7 (*A facie Domini mota est terra*).

by-point refutation of the Copernican system leads him to conclude that it is more absurd than the Ptolemaic.[50]

In sum, the order in which Cardoso presents his proofs is perhaps more significant than the proofs themselves. The religious factor, exemplified in the scriptural argument, remains the motive force behind the scientific and philosophic criticisms. But if, in the Copernican controversy, Cardoso is to be found on the same side as the Holy Office, it should be stressed that most Jews shared the same opinion. In a work published more than thirty years after the *Philosophia libera* the famous Jewish physician Tobias Cohen assured his readers that Copernicus is "in the caldron of Satan." Indeed, as late as 1714 David Nieto, Haham of the Sephardic community of London, a man of broad culture and sophistication, rejected the Copernican system *in toto*. Cardoso's stand would undoubtedly have been endorsed by most of his Jewish contemporaries.[51]

The chapters devoted to "earth" are followed by nine on water and all that pertains to it. Cardoso examines the seas, tides, islands, as well as marvelous springs, rivers, and fountains.[52] Throughout we find a curious mixture of archaic notions and empirical observations. He is firmly convinced, for example, that the tides are to be attributed to the action of the moon, but he is not sure as to the exact nature of its influence; and so he entertains various possibilities, among them, that the moon somehow acts to arouse the "spirits" in the waters themselves.[53] That men die at ebb tide is something he has

---

[50] *Phil. lib.*, pp. 24–27.

[51] Tobias Cohen, *Ma'aseh Tobiah* (Venice, 1705), Pt. II, entitled '*Olam hagalgalim* (The world of the spheres), chs. 2–4, fols. 49v–53r. The fourth chapter bears the heading:

מביא כל הטענות והראיות אשר לקופרניקוס וסיעתו על עמידת השמש ותנועת הארץ, ודע מה שתשיב לו כי בכור שטן הוא•

For David Nieto's views, see his *Matteh Dan y segunda parte del Cuzari* (London, 1714), pp. 143 ff.: "Pero no nos es permitido seguir esse Sistema, en la Circunstancia de negar el Movimiento del Sol, leyéndose que Yehosuah dixó al Sol que *Parasse en Guibhon....*" See also *ibid.*, pp. 197, 199 ff.

[52] *Phil. lib.*, Lib. I, quaest. xii-xx, pp. 36–70.

[53] *Ibid.* quaest. xvi ("De fluxu & refluxu maris"), pp. 50 f.: "Effectus cognoscuntur Lunae, quamvis modus influendi ignoretur...."

often witnessed, a correspondence voiced decades earlier in his *Utilidades del agua y de la nieve.*[54] It should be noted, however, that some of the foremost scientists of the seventeenth century were in error concerning the tides. Galileo attributed them to the movement of the earth itself, and did not even refer to the phases of the moon.[55]

We gain in perspective, too, when we set some of Cardoso's more exotic digressions against the preoccupations of his contemporaries, and realize they are not digressions at all. His two chapters on air are followed by three on fire, in the last of which he argues vehemently against the notion of a fire that is inextinguishable. Specifically, he rejects the tales of perpetually burning sepulchral lamps cited by Augustine and others, claiming that those are either works of the Devil or exhalations which are ignited suddenly when the tombs are opened. But even Descartes dealt with this problem, and in 1684 a paper on the subject was published in the *Philosophical Transactions* of the Royal Society. Similarly, if Cardoso devotes space to the question of whether the salamander can extinguish fire, and concludes that it may temporarily extinguish nearby coals by its own humidity but must ultimately die, it is useful to remark that exactly a decade later a German savant found it necessary to devote an entire tome to "Salamandrologia," in order to lay this type of lore to rest.[56]

Book II, "De affectionibus rerum naturalium" (on the affections of natural things), begins with a chapter on space and another on the problem of two bodies in one place or one in two, both latter notions being rejected.[57] Next we have a discussion of the vacuum in which there is no reference to Torricelli's experiment, but others against the existence of a vacuum are mentioned, among them one demonstrated to the king of Poland in 1647.[58] There follow eight

---

[54] *Utilidades*, fol. 47r-v.

[55] See his *Discorso del flusso e reflusso del mare*, in *Le opere di Galileo Galilei*, V (Florence, 1895), 378–95.

[56] *Phil. lib.*, p. 80. On Descartes, see Thorndike, *Magic and Experimental Science*, VII, 556 f.; on the paper of 1684, see *ibid.*, VIII, 395. Johann Wurffbain's *Salamandrologia, descriptio historico-philologico-philosophico-medica* (Nürnberg, 1683) is described *ibid.*, VIII, 47.

[57] Quaest. ii ("De duobus corporibus in uno loco, & uno in duobus"), pp. 84 f.

[58] Quaest. iii ("De vacuo"). pp. 85 f.

chapters on various aspects of movement in which, especially on falling bodies, Cardoso displays more accurate information. He knows that both heavy and light bodies increase in velocity, and cites Galileo and others to the effect that the increase is in the proportion of odd numbers.[59] Despite his avowed emancipation from Aristotle he explains the motion of projectiles as produced by the air.[60] Moreover, after completing his survey of motion he continues in an essentially Peripatetic order, with chapters on time, the infinite, the composition of a continuum, whether quantity is to be distinguished from substance, alteration, the action of natural bodies, the necessity of contact between agent and patient, resistance and reaction, and rarefaction.[61]

The very title of Book III, *De coelo et mundo*, is, of course, Aristotelian, but this does not reflect its variegated contents. The first five chapters deal with the creation and duration of the world. In ch. 1 ("De Auctore mundi") Cardoso argues against the mechanistic implications of atomism. This develops, in the next chapter, into a refutation of the eternity of matter. According to Cardoso, Aristotle vacillated but upheld its eternity until, at the end of his life, and as a result of Hebrew teaching, he came to admit creation *ex nihilo*.[62] Ch. 3, on the uniqueness and perfection of the world, asserts that monsters do not impair that perfection, nor do worms, scorpions, or spiders deform its beauty. But it is mainly devoted to a rejection of the existence of prior worlds as claimed by the ancient atomists. "Unus Deus unum mundum creavit," Cardoso insists; had there been another world before ours, Moses would have taught it to us.[63]

---

[59] Quaest. vi ("De velocitate & tarditate motus"), pp. 91 f. In the next chapter ("Utrum omnia gravia aequaliter descendant") he presents both Arriaga's experiments in favor of the equal descent of all weights, and Riccioli's experiment at the Asinelli Tower in Bologna to the contrary.

[60] Quaest. viii ("De motu proiectorum, seu violento"), p. 95.

[61] Quaest. xii-xx, pp. 99–117.

[62] Lib. III, quaest. ii ("De mundi principiis"), p. 121. Cardoso also cites Maimonides, *Guide*, II, ch. 15, to the effect that, in any case, Aristotle did not claim to have proved the eternity of matter (pp. 121 f.).

[63] Quaest. iii ("De mundi unitate, & perfectione"), p. 124. Cardoso shows no awareness of midrashic speculations concerning the creation of prior worlds. Cf.

Philosopher in the Ghetto

Inevitably, the borderline between religious and scientific interests remains somewhat arbitrary, especially in questions of cosmology. In a chapter inquiring as to when the world was created, Cardoso refers to the Talmudic dispute between Rabbi Eliezer, who claimed it occurred in the month of Tishri, and Rabbi Joshua, who maintained it was in Nisan. Following the consensus of later Jewish tradition, Cardoso adopts the former view and places it "in September." Characteristically, he finds support in the fact that other nations seem to have preserved such a tradition, and are alleged to begin their year in September. Such were the Persians, Chaldeans, Indians, Egyptians, as well as the Etruscans (citing Festus Pompeius and Livy), the Ethiopians (citing Damião de Goes), and the Muscovites (citing Mercator's *Muscovia*).[64]

In an interesting discussion of the duration of the world Cardoso rejects various Greek theories of its progressive degeneration or ultimate destruction and conflagration. For the incorruptibility of the world he cites the Bible, Philo's *De aeternitate mundi*, and Maimonides' *Guide*, besides adding "rational reasons" of his own. He claims, for example, that the minerals of the earth "have the virtue of replenishing themselves." The human race itself has not degenerated in the last three thousand years. The span of human life is the same. He recently knew two Jews aged, respectively, one hundred and ten, and one hundred and fifteen. To prove that the world is just as populous as it ever was, he presents both biblical and recent statistics. Man is no less strong nor large than before. Even if the *'Anakim*, *Refaim*, Goliath, and Gog lived long ago, there are also

---

the statement of R. Abbahu in *Bereshit Rabbah*, 3: 7 and 9: 2, that God created and destroyed many worlds before creating this one. Judah Halevi entertains the possibility in *Kuzari*, I, 67. Cardoso's firm rejection of the idea may have been influenced by his reading of Bk. XII of Augustine's *De civ. Dei*.

[64] Quaest. iv ("De anni tempore quo fuit creatus mundus"). p. 126. The dispute between R. Eliezer and R. Joshua is recorded in *TB Rosh ha-shanah*, 10b–11a. Cardoso also uses this occasion to explain the Ten Days of Penitence of the Jews, and the Day of Atonement. Further proofs for the creation in Tishri are sought in alphabetical permutations, e.g., that *Tishri* can be transposed into *reshit* (beginning), an idea common among medieval Jewish writers (cf. *Pa'aneaḥ raza* [Prague, 1607], ad Gen. 1: 1), or into *tirosh* (new wine).

giants today among the Patagonians in the Straits of Magellan, in Sumatra, and in China.[65] The Golden Age of which the classical poets spoke is a myth. It was really the age of Cain. One can only apply the term, if at all, to the brief sojourn in Paradise before Man sinned. Cardoso quotes Ecclesiastes: "Say not how was it that the former days were better than these, for it is not out of wisdom that thou enquirest concerning these."

The sixth chapter, which denies the existence of a world soul, is followed by thirteen on the heavens and their bodies. Cardoso deals with the sun, moon, planets, new stars, and galaxies. He shows himself well aware of the new discoveries made by the telescope, such as sunspots and lunar mountains, and notes that this instrument has finally settled the controversy over the nature of the Milky Way.[66] He denies the existence of men or creatures on the moon, and dismisses various ancient superstitions concerning eclipses. We find now that the works and observations of Tycho Brahe, Kepler, and Galileo are quite familar to him, but that his own geocentric presuppositions prevent him from drawing the logical conclusions from the latter. Interspersed among his more sober reflections are chapters and passages which could easily have been written a century before, with discussions of whether the stars are moved by Intelligences, and whether the heavens are animated. Both are denied. The stars move, but of themselves.[67] In addition to the Hebrew names of the planets, Cardoso sees fit to give also the names of the seven angels who preside over them.[68] A good example of Cardoso's predilection for analogic

---

[65] Quaest. v ("De mundi duratione"), pp. 129 f. On the incorruptibility of the world and on the equal span of human life, cf. Maimonides, *Guide*, II, chs. 28–29 and 47. However, Maimonides does not regard the eternal duration of the world as an essential axiom, though he believes it. Those who hold that it will someday be destroyed are at liberty to think so (*ibid.*, ch. 27).

[66] On sunspots, quaest. xiv, p. 150; lunar mountains, quaest. xv, p. 155; the Milky Way, quaest. xviii, p. 170.

[67] Quaest. x ("An sydera moveantur a se, vel ab intelligentijs"), p. 139; quaest. xii ("An coeli sint animati"), p. 142.

[68] Quaest. xvi ("De reliquis planetis"), p. 160: "Septem planetas tradunt generatim sapientes illisq. assignant septem alios Angelos praesides, quorum typus

thinking is his chapter on the number of the heavens. After reviewing various theories he notes that some modern astronomers claim one heaven which is continuous and fluid. Though the problem is difficult the Bible, after all, uses the phrase "heaven of heavens," and also distinguishes between "heaven" and "firmament." From this he proceeds to the analogy between the cosmos and the Tabernacle. Just as the latter had ten curtains, so there are ten heavens, while the seven planets correspond to the seven-branched candelabrum. Finally, he approves the opinion of Ibn Ezra that the verse "When I see the heavens, the work of Thy fingers . . ." hints at the ten spheres.[69]

Such passages, however, serve to render all the more striking Cardoso's discussion of heavenly influences. Ancient philosophy, he observes, spoke only of the light and motion of the stars, and did not use the term "influence." But "now we take frequent refuge in these occult virtues as at a sacred anchorage." He readily admits that the heavenly bodies exert myriad influences on the earth, and even speaks of the heavens as a "universal cause." But he denies the occult character of such influences. To be sure, his catalogue of heavenly effects is inflated and often distorted. Not only does the moon, for example, affect the tides, but it also causes changes in plants and induces lunacy. The long list continues down to the proposition that from the varied influence of the heavens come the various conditions and temperaments of men and regions. But all this proves merely that the heavenly bodies act on inferior ones. It does not prove that these effects are the result of anything more than the motion and light of the heavenly bodies themselves. Light in particular, whether solar, lunar, or stellar, can have the most

---

fuit candelabrum septem lucernis distinctum exod. 26 nominaq. illorum descri-
bunt Micael, (qui sicut Deus), Gabriel (fortitudo Dei), Rafael (medicina Dei),
Uriel (ignis Dei), Saaltiel (oratio Dei), Yeudiel (laus seu confessio Dei), Baruchiel
(benedictio Dei)." A similar tradition, though without the analogy to the candelabrum, and with some different names, is recorded by Yehudah b. Barzilay
al-Barceloni. See his *Perush Sefer Yeṣirah*, ed. S. Z. H. Halberstamm (Berlin, 1885),
p. 247.

[69] Quaest. viii ("De numero coelorum"), p. 136. Cf. Ibn Ezra ad Ps. 8: 4.

ramified effects on different substances. There is no need, therefore, to speak of occult virtues.[70]

The way is thus prepared for Cardoso's fierce attack against the "vanity of the astrologers," a theme which already figured in his *Discurso sobre el Monte Vesuvio* of 1632, but which is now greatly elaborated and sharpened.[71] The intervening forty years have, if anything, removed any ambiguity or hesitation on the subject. His condemnation of astrology is now unequivocal, and inevitably contains some new nuances. Writing now as a professing Jew, Cardoso cites Isaac Israeli and Maimonides among the opponents of astrology.[72] He dismisses Kabbalists (and alchemists) along with the astrologers, and we shall return to this point when we examine his relations with his brother. His tone throughout is one of sheer scorn. Navigators, he states caustically, do not prognosticate storms out of Jupiter or Saturn, but from the winds, clouds, and condition of the air. As for physicians, their diagnosis is based not on the stars, but on pulse and urine. If we consider the hold that astrological medicine still had on so many of his contemporaries, the statement is one of genuine emancipation.[73] The details of his argument need not be repeated here. Cardoso is well versed in the antiastrological literature from Pico della Mirandola's *In astrologiam* to Gassendi's *Syntagma philosophicum*, and draws heavily on his sources both for his reasoning and for his catalogue of false predictions.[74]

---

[70] Quaest. xx ("De coelorum influentijs"), pp. 173–76. Thorndike (*Magic and Experimental Science*, VII, 686) conveys the erroneous impression that Cardoso accepts occult heavenly influences. He is therefore suprised that in the next chapter Cardoso attacks astrology. But he has missed the point. Concerning the heavenly influence on the diversity of men, which Thorndike cites as his example, Cardoso writes explicitly on the very next page: "Ex diverso coelorum influxu varios esse hominum et regionum status verissimum est, sed id non occultae influentiae tribuendum, sed calori aut frigori," etc.

[71] Quaest. xxi ("De astrologorum vanitate"), pp. 176–89. On the criticism of astrology in the *Discurso*, see *supra*, ch. III.

[72] "ex Haebreorum Isac Israelita & Rabi Moyses astrologicas observationes contempserunt . . ." (*Phil. lib.*, p. 177).

[73] *Ibid.* On astrological medicine in the seventeenth century see Thorndike, *Magic and Experimental Science*, VII, ch. 5, and VIII, ch. 32, *passim*.

[74] *Phil. lib.*, pp. 18 f.

Philosopher in the Ghetto

As subsequent sections of the *Philosophia libera* reveal, other antiquated but still cherished notions are not so easily discarded. In Book IV, devoted to "mixed" bodies, we find chapters on their generation; their affections, crudity, and putridity; on meteors, thunder, and lightning; comets, winds, earthquakes, the rainbow, and other meteorological as well as many mineralogical matters.[75] But between a chapter on the corona and other luminous phenomena, and one on clouds, there is a chapter on "prodigious aparitions." Cardoso gives both modern and ancient references to the sight of men fighting in the sky, such as the appearance of cavalry over Jerusalem while Antiochus Epiphanes was in Egypt, and accepts the reports at face value. He dismisses those "atheists" who claim that these are merely reflections on the clouds of battles actually taking place on earth.[76]

It has been observed by historians of science that in the seventeenth century the Bible was not only accepted by many as authoritative in scientific matters but to some extent even guided scientific curiosity. Cardoso is no exception to this tendency. Part of one chapter is devoted, along with an examination of honey and sugar, to a "scientific" analysis of the nature of the manna which the Israelites ate in the wilderness.[77]

Alchemy in general is attacked, and its claims dismissed. The alchemists cannot produce gold, the philosophers' stone, though ever sought, is never found.[78] Nevertheless, gold itself possesses marvelous properties, and in the following chapter Cardoso embarks on a ramified discussion of the curative virtues of gems and precious stones, still an accepted part of medical lore.[79]

---

[75] Lib. IV, De mixtis, pp. 190–268.

[76] Quaest. xv ("De prodigiosis apparentijs"), pp. 232 f. On the cavalry over Jerusalem see II Macc. 5: 1–4. Cardoso also speaks of the "arcana of nature" (p. 233) which exceed the forces of nature itself, and are the product of some directing Intelligence. Examples of this are strange rumblings and birds fighting in air, which usually presage slaughter and wars.

[77] Quaest. xxiii ("De melle, manna, & saccaro"), pp. 244 f.

[78] Quaest. xxviii ("De transmutatione metallorum"), pp. 260–62.

[79] Quaest. xxix ("De lapidibus"), pp. 262–68.

Book V, "On the Soul and on Living Things," brings us to the world of plants and animals. Characteristically, it opens with four chapters on the soul—its nature, the different kinds of soul (vegetative, sensitive, and rational), its "seat" (he places it in the heart), and the question as to whether its potentialities are separable from itself (he denies this).[80] The three categories of soul provide the organizing structure for the rest of Book V. Thus Cardoso first presents a botany, with chapters on the vegetative soul, on the parts and species of plants, and on the "marvels of plants." The latter includes a section on analogies between plants and animals, descriptions of exotic plants and herbs, and a discussion of chocolate, coffee, and tea.[81] Concerning spontaneous generation Cardoso is somewhat equivocal. He is willing to admit it, but with the major qualification that it all derives from seed, whether conspicuous or latent, "for seminal virtues are hidden in the earth itself, and in water."[82]

With the sensitive soul as a point of departure Cardoso treats of animal nutrition, the humors, blood, phlegm, bile, melancholia, and vital spirits.[83] These are followed by eight chapters on the external senses and seven on the internal, including discussions of hunger, thirst, and prolonged abstinence.[84] The rest of Book V is devoted to such physiological topics as perspiration, sleep and wakefulness, insomnia, respiration, pulse and movement, as well as detailed classifications of animals, fish, birds, and insects. Scattered throughout are advanced observations, but as always they compete with regressive ones. Cardoso knows, for instance, that color does not reside in objects, but is merely "light refracted, reflected, and

---

[80] Lib. V, *De anima, & viventibus*, quaest. i-iv ("De natura animae"; "Quotuplex sit anima"; "De animae sede"; "An potentiae distinguantur ab anima"), pp. 269–73.

[81] Quaest. vii ("De mirabilibus plantarum"), pp. 278–81. As he had done almost forty years earlier, Cardoso warns against overindulgence in drinking chocolate (pp. 279 f.). Cf. his *Utilidades del agua*, fols. 106r-107v.

[82] *Phil. lib.*, p. 281.

[83] Quaest. ix-xix, pp. 282–304.

[84] Quaest. xx-xxxiv, pp. 304–51. Hunger, thirst, etc., had been dealt with in the *Utilidades* (*supra*, ch. IV).

distributed."[85] But he is very far from an understanding of the real nature of perception. In Book II he had put forth the notion that a lion is terrified by a crowing cock, and an elephant by a grunting sow, because the discrepancy between the corpuscles of sound and their organs of hearing causes the latter to be irritated.[86] Similarly, the difficulties which seventeenth-century scientists still encountered in attempting to systematize the seemingly endless and bewildering variety of nature are well reflected in Cardoso's own classification of animal species. He feels constrained to employ no less than 60 classifying principles, from generation, habitat, movement, and size, through modes of vision, types of tails, milk, sounds emitted, diseases, nutrition, "fortitude," all the way to longevity and "purity."[87] Moreover, in common with so many men of his time, he is quite preoccupied with the "arcana" of nature, and pauses continually along the way to point them out. To be sure, we have already seen that he is capable of dismissing specific myths and fables. But a discussion of the rhinoceros is followed by a sober note on the unicorn, and he does not confuse the two.[88]

The sixth and longest book in the *Philosophia libera*, comprising 108 chapters, is devoted to Man. It begins, appropriately, with a disquisition "On the Dignity and Excellence of Man," in which Cardoso hymns the praises of the human being and lauds his achievements. Both the title and the symbolism he employs are replete with echoes of the Renaissance. Man is the microcosm of the universe. He shares many attributes with the animals, and yet far transcends them. He is, as Scripture indicates, the image of God. As God is the "infinite circle," the center of the universe from whence

---

[85] "Lux refracta, reflexa ac disposita" (*Phil. lib.*, p. 311).

[86] *Phil. lib.*, p. 114. Gassendi explained the fright of the lion by proposing that the corpuscles emitted by the cock hurt his eyes (Thorndike, *Magic and Experimental Science*, VII, 453).

[87] Lib. V, quaest. xli ("De differentijs animalium"), pp. 370–78.

[88] Quaest. xlii ("De natura animalium"), p. 378: "Monoceros atrocissima bellua longe diversa a Rhinoceronte equi magnitudine. . . . Cornu unum ingens e media eius fronte protenditur cubitorum duum. . . . Vivus non capitur." Cardoso does add that "multa de unicornu praedicantur, sed plura animalia unicornua sunt." The statement itself is a direct paraphrase of Pliny, 8.21.31.

all proceeds, so Man is the "finite circle," the center of the world. God is the supreme monarch of all things; Man is His vicar and legate, a kind of earthly god (*deus terrenus*). He was produced unarmed and naked, so that he might make us of all arms, and clothe himself with all garments. Two things have rendered him admirable: his reason and his hand, which excel those of all other animals. Cardoso lists some of the most remarkable human achievements, from the Colossus of Rhodes and the Pyramids, to more "recent miracles" such as the invention of printing and various mechanical models of astronomical phenomena.[89]

Twenty-four chapters now deal with pregnancy, birth, and related gynecological subjects such as menstruation, conception, sterility, the formation of the fetus, twins and multiple conceptions. But interspersed among these are some more exotic topics. In the eighth chapter, for example, Cardoso takes up the question as to the precise time when the soul enters the fetus. After reviewing the opinions of Hippocrates, Empedocles, Aristotle, Galen, Avicenna, and more recent writers (most of them Spaniards), he quotes the Talmudic anecdote in the tractate *Sanhedrin* in which Rabbi Judah the Prince learns from the Emperor Antoninus that the soul enters at the time of conception. He goes on to cite Rashi's commentary on Genesis, in which it is indicated that the fetus is formed in forty days, and a sermon of the Amsterdam rabbi Saul Levi Morteira which states that the soul does not enter until the moment of birth. With all these conflicting opinions, it is difficult to determine the exact date and hour. If he must give an opinion, Cardoso feels that the soul probably enters within the first three days after conception, in accordance with the Talmudic passage cited earlier.[90] The fourteenth chapter deals with mutations of sex, followed in succession by

---

[89] Lib. VI; *De homine*, quaest. i ("De hominis dignitate & excellentia"), pp. 409–12.

[90] Quaest. viii ("De foetus animatione, seu tempore quo anima rationalis in corpus infunditur"), pp. 436–44. Cf. *TB Sanhedrin*, XI, fol. 91b; Rashi, commentary ad Gen. 7: 4; Saul Levi Morteira, *Gib'at Sha'ul* (Amsterdam, 1645), no. xxxiii, entitled "Nishmat 'adam" (fol. 108r-v in ed. of Warsaw, 1912, which I have used).

chapters on the hermaphrodite, giants, pygmies, and monsters, the latter with the admonition that "our stupidity admires not the order but the error of nature."[91] Chapter 19 discusses "Satyrs, Fauns, Centaurs, Tritons, etc." While accepting the descriptions reported of these creatures, Cardoso tries to explain them in "natural" terms. They are either demons (the satyrs may be the *se'irim* mentioned in Lev. 17: 7) or abnormal animals and men.[92] Chapter 20 deals with monsters produced by the unnatural crossbreeding of different species, something which Scripture has forbidden the Jews to allow among their own animals.[93] To the question of whether the human being can be generated except through the union of a man and a woman, Cardoso replies firmly in the negative.[94]

Chapters 26 through 69 offer a complete human anatomy, with a separate discussion of every limb and organ. Chapters 70 to 75 deal with the human body as a whole, focusing on the body as a microcosm, on its proportions and its beauty.[95] The next 16 chapters may best be characterized as a "psychology," in the old comprehensive sense of all that concerns the soul, its activities, and even its somatic effects. Here are included chapters on the rational soul and on immortality, one chapter devoted to a categorical denial of the transmigration of souls, others on intellect and will, memory, natural and diabolical divination, prophecy, speech, language, laughter, weeping and tears, and even graying and baldness. Of these, the chapter on prophecy will prove to be of central importance when we come to examine Cardoso's conflict with his brother over the

[91] Quaest. xviii ("De monstris"), p. 473.

[92] Quaest. xix ("De satyris, faunis, centauris, tritonibus, & similibus"). See especially p. 477.

[93] Quaest. xx ("De monstris ex diversae speciei animalibus"), pp. 478–82.

[94] Quaest. xxi ("Utrum homo possit aliter generari quam ex coniunctione maris & foeminae"), pp. 482–89. In a work completed after the *Philosophia libera* and published posthumously in 1709, Christian Friedrich Germann claimed that Augustus Caesar was born of a woman and a serpent, and reported the same of Luther and Scipio Africanus. See Thorndike, *Magic and Experimental Science*, VIII, 632.

[95] See especially quaest. lxxi-lxxiii ("De analogia hominis ad mundum"; "De proportione corporis humani"; "De pulchritudine corporis humani"), pp. 576–87.

messianic claims of Sabbatai Zevi.[96] Chapters 92 to 101 deal with
various aspects of obstetrics.[97] Finally, chapters 102 to 108 survey
the stages of man's existence on earth: the span of life, the number
of ages, puberty and adolescence, youth, maturity and old age,
natural death, whether the term of life may be prolonged or diminished, and finally—the Resurrection.[98] From this, the transition to
Book VII, devoted to God, is both logical and inevitable. The
correspondence of the sevenfold division of the *Philosophia libera* to
the seven days of Creation, while not strictly applied, is obvious
nonetheless. Man, created on the sixth day, has been discussed in
the sixth book; God, who rested on the Sabbath, in the seventh book.
The symmetry is complete.

Before we go on to examine Cardoso's view on matters divine, we
should consider one salient point which emerges from our survey
thus far. Whatever else his transition from Spanish Marrano to
Italian Jew may have involved, it is clear that from Valladolid to
Verona his intellectual world is a continuum. His science and his
philosophy are basically what he acquired in Spain and carried with
him from Spain. As we shall see when we analyze his *Excelencias de los
hebreos*, he may have arrived at a different evaluation of his Iberian
intellectual heritage. But he has had to relinquish none of its
contents. His scientific views were as compatible with the Judaism of
Italy in 1673 as they had been with the Catholicism of Spain four
decades earlier.

THEOLOGY

Nor did the theological views expressed in the *Philosophia libera*
contain anything which might unduly upset the Paduan censors. To
be sure, Cardoso presents a theology which is thoroughly Jewish,
appeals often to Jewish authorities, and illustrates a number of his

---

[96] See *infra*, ch. VII.
[97] *Phil. lib.*, pp. 671–95.
[98] *Ibid.*, pp. 695–725.

theses from Jewish sources. But given the initial recognition that the author is a Jew, that he limits himself largely to those aspects of Jewish theology which are common also to Christianity, and that he refrains from any active anti-Christian polemic, the book could not be considered dangerous. For example, to extol the unity of God is of itself, after all, not anti-Christian, unless it be accompanied by specific or implied derogations of the Trinity. Here, undoubtedly, caution played an important role. In the *Philosophia libera* Cardoso consciously repressed anti-Christian elements which would come to the fore six years later in *Las excelencias de los hebreos*.

To sequester Cardoso's views concerning God and other religious questions in a separate section under the rubric of "theology" is, of course, to violate his own scheme. The dichotomy is not his, but ours. For him these theological elements are all a part of "natural philosophy," and if we isolate them now, it is only for analytic purposes. It has already become apparent that the entire *Philosophia libera* is permeated by a religious outlook. We shall confine ourselves here to an examination of his views on immortality, resurrection, and God.

Cardoso's views concerning immortality have recently come into question through the publication of a polemical tract by Orobio de Castro against the Amsterdam heretic Dr. Juan de Prado. There, Orobio cites a reference by De Prado to a "Dr. Cardoso" who maintains that the human soul is no different from that of the animal, and that hence it is mortal.[99] Professor Révah, who published this text, suggests that the reference is apparently to Isaac Cardoso, though he is somewhat surprised that such a view is here attributed to so orthodox an apologist as the author of *Las excelencias de los hebreos*.

---

[99] "Pesame de que solo Escoto le persuada a Vmd. la immortalidad del alma y mas me pesa que confiesse Vmd. que la consequencia sacada por el Doctor Cardoso de que su alma no se distingue de la *rugible* sea solo contra Escoto. Es decir que solo Escoto defiende su alma de Vmd. de brutal, pues solo contra el milita la opinion contraria de Cardoso. Yo no sé como diablos se ha communicado tanto con Escoto, sino es que ha cobrado amistad con algun frayle franciscano y le ha encajado esso en los cascos" (I. S. Révah, *Spinoza et Juan de Prado*, appendix B, p. 139).

"If Prado's reference is exact, it shows how great was the diffusion of heterodox tendencies in Marrano circles."[100]

It is almost certain, however, that Isaac Cardoso never held such a view, and that some other explanation must be sought for this passage in Orobio de Castro's epistle. If indeed Juan de Prado had Isaac Cardoso in mind, he was surely misinterpreting him. On the other hand, Orobio may have misread what De Prado had written. We do not possess the latter's original text, and thus have our information at third hand. But the most logical assumption is simply that the Dr. Cardoso mentioned without further specification was another physician of that name.

That Isaac Cardoso never questioned the immortality of the soul is fairly demonstrable. Certainly the chapter "De immortalitate animae" in Book VI of the *Philosophia libera* is, as we shall see presently, a thorough *defense* of the doctrine. The chapters on the soul itself also show a clear distinction between the animal and the human soul. It could be argued, of course, that these represent views at which Cardoso arrived late in life. But fortunately we also possess direct evidence from his early writings as well. We will recall now that in the very first of his published books, the *Discurso sobre el Monte Vesuvio*, which appeared in Madrid in 1632, Cardoso fiercely attacked Pliny for his rejection of the soul's immortality. He also included a poetic epitaph for Pliny, written even earlier, again criticizing the latter's error. Moreover, in the same book Cardoso cited several verses from yet another work which he had written "against the atheist . . . in defense of the soul."[101] When the *Discurso* was published Cardoso was some twenty-eight years old; when the *Philosophia* appeared he was close to seventy. The view of the soul's immortality is the same in the one as in the other. There is no reason to suppose that his opinion on the matter was anything but consistent throughout his life.[102]

---

[100] Révah, *Spinoza*, p. 45. He adds parenthetically: "Il écrivit aussi un ouvrage, *Philosophia libera*, qui semble important, mais qui n'a jamais été convenablement étudié."

[101] *Discurso sobre el Monte Vesuvio*, fol. 5r-v.

[102] Caro Baroja (*Sociedad*, p. 108) suggests that Cardoso may have denied immortality when he was a student, "con el radicalismo propio de la juventud."

Philosopher in the Ghetto

Contrary to the assertion of Menéndez y Pelayo, Cardoso never wrote directly against Juan de Prado, and there is no indication that they even knew one another.[103] But his chapter on the immortality of the soul certainly had in mind the Prado type, which he must have encountered both within and beyond[104] the Peninsula: "The assertors of the mortality of the soul, whom I have myself known, were wicked men, devoted to vices, and bound to no law. . . ."[105] According to Cardoso the certain knowledge of the soul's immortality which Adam possessed was lost in the course of time, recovered by the Hebrews, and subsequently taught by Moses to the other nations. As a result, there has been among them an almost universal consensus on the subject. The immortality of the soul has been accepted by the Chaldeans, the ancient Hermetics, the Egyptian kings and

---

In view of what we know of Cardoso's attitude as early as 1632, this explanation also seems unlikely. Besides, Juan de Prado, whose polemic with Orobio de Castro took place in 1663–64, was hardly referring to the *student* opinions of "Doctor Cardoso." The possibility remains that De Prado may be alluding to Isaac's brother Abraham who was, after all, also a physician. Was the immortality of the soul among the theological problems with which Abraham wrestled when he arrived in Venice? Did Juan de Prado pass through Italy while the latter was still there, and could they have met? We know little of De Prado's whereabouts between 1638, when he received the doctorate in medicine at Toledo, and 1657, when he asked the Sephardic community of Hamburg to intervene on his behalf with that of Amsterdam. See Révah, *Spinoza*, pp. 24 f.

[103] Menéndez y Pelayo, *Heterodoxos*, II, 601. The error is noted by Révah, *Spinoza*, p. 46, n. 1.

[104] For Spain, see Quevedo's attacks against the "ateístas" cited by Caro, *Sociedad*, pp. 112 f. We recall the rumors in Italy concerning Rodrigo Méndez Silva's denial of immortality (*supra*, ch. V, n. 23). The problem had agitated Sephardic Jewry especially since the early 17th century, largely as a result of heterodox currents among the Marrano emigrants, of whom Uriel da Costa is only the most famous example. Two Sephardic works devoted to the subject stand out: Samuel da Silva's reply to Da Costa, the *Tratado da immortalidade da alma* (Amsterdam, 1623), and Manasseh b. Israel's *Nishmat hayyim* (Amsterdam, 1651). Though certain of Cardoso's arguments are inevitably similar, he does not display any direct acquaintance with either of these works. Da Silva's treatise, now of the most extreme rarity, is excerpted, along with other pertinent materials, in Carl Gebhardt's *Die Schriften des Uriel da Costa* (Amsterdam, 1922).

[105] *Phil. lib.*, VI, quaest. lxxvii ("De immortalitate animae"), p. 611.

254

priests, the Druids of Gaul, Persian Magi, Indian Brahmins, Thracians, Arabs, Romans, and Goths, as well as by the poets. Beginning with Thales, most of the Greek philosophers have maintained it. Aristotle knew it, and admitted it at the end of his life.[106]

The doctrine is proved by Scripture, of which Cardoso discusses 30 verses, often employing Jewish midrashic interpretations.[107] Significantly, he also utilizes three verses from the Second Book of Maccabees,[108] although the Apocrypha are not part of the Jewish canon. On the other hand, he never cites the New Testament. It is a pattern that we might perhaps expect of a former Marrano.

Immortality of the soul can also be proved "rationally." Among the 12 rational proofs that are offered, our attention is caught not merely by philosophical ones, but by such arguments as the universal human craving for immortality which expresses itself in the erection of pyramids, obelisks, mausoleums, and statues; the great care which all peoples lavish on the dead; the visitations of the spirits of the dead recorded both in Scripture and among the nations; and—not least—the proof "out of human misery," for, unless the soul be immortal, then Man is surely the most miserable of all the animals.[109]

Those so foolish as to reject immortality, and thereby to "forget the dignity of man," are few, and they deviate from the norm of humanity. The first to do so was Cain in his argument with Abel prior to the murder.[110] Later impugners of the doctrine were Epicurus, Dicaearchus, the Sadducees, Lucretius, Pliny, Protagoras, and finally (leaping to the Renaissance) Pietro Pomponazzi.[111] Ten

---

[106] *Ibid.*, pp. 604–6.

[107] E. g., on Gen. 2: 7: "*Et formavit Deus hominem de terra rubra* . . . ubi notandum est, quod pro illo verbo *formavit* hebraice positum est *Vayser* cum duplici *Iod* seu *I* cum in formatione ceterorum animantium unicum tantum *I* apposuisset ad demonstrandum ut annotarunt Haebreorum sapientes duplicem vitam homini fuisse concessam hanc caducam, & aliam immortalem" (*Phil. lib.*, p. 606). The interpretation is to be found in *Bereshit Rabbah*, 14: 8.

[108] II Macc. 6: 26, 7: 9, 12: 43–45.

[109] *Phil. lib.*, pp. 609–11.

[110] *Ibid.*, p. 613. Cardoso cites the "Paraphrastes Caldeus Ankelos." It is, however, not Targum Onkelos, but Targum Jonathan (ad Gen. 4: 8).

[111] *Ibid.* Protagoras is included because "he reduced the soul to the senses, which

arguments against immortality are reviewed in order, and refuted. At the very end of the chapter Cardoso comes to grips with the basic problem as to why there is apparently no explicit discussion of immortality in Scripture. This, he notes, has given weapons to the atheists and Epicureans. To solve the problem he cites the opinions of three Jewish authorities. Maimonides wrote that the true recompense of the soul is entirely spiritual, and God did not explain the details, for He did not desire that men serve Him out of desire for reward. Also that, though the prophets describe the messianic era, they did not depict the future glory of the soul, for it is truly indescribable, and any metaphor would diminish it.[112] Ibn Ezra claimed that Scripture was written in such a manner as to be comprehensible not only to the learned, but to ignorant women as well. Hence temporal rewards were made explicit, while the rest could be inferred by the wise.[113] Finally, Joseph Albo explained that the promises expressed in the Torah were addressed to the entire people collectively, whereas immortality of the soul concerns only the individual as such.[114]

As enthusiastic as Cardoso shows himself in upholding the immortality of the soul, he is equally firm in rejecting metempsychosis. He observes that, unlike resurrection and immortality, transmigration of souls is not an essential article of Jewish faith, even among those "Kabbalists and Talmudists" who believe in it.[115] Although, from a

---

are perishable." (Cardoso is referring to the discussion of knowledge and perception in Plato's *Theaetetus*.) The attack against Pomponazzi is occasioned by the views expressed in his *De immortalitate animae* of 1516.

[112] *Phil. lib.*, p. 616. Cardoso refers, respectively, to chs. 9 and 8 of Maimonides' "Tractatus de penitentia" (i.e., *Mishneh Torah*, "Hilkhot teshubah"). A Spanish translation had appeared in 1613 (*Tratado de la thesuvah o contrición compuesto por Rabbennu Moseh Egypcio, traduzido palabra por palabra de lengua hebrayca en Español, por el Doctor Samuel da Sylva, portugués. En Amsterdam, Anno 5373 de la creación del mundo*). The translator is the same Da Silva who polemicized against Uriel da Costa (*supra*, n. 104).

[113] Cf. Ibn Ezra ad Gen. 32: 39.

[114] Cf. Albo, *Sefer ha-'ikkarim*, IV, ch. 40.

[115] *Phil. lib.*, VI, quaest. lxxviii ("De transmigratione animarum"), p. 616: "Invaluit etiam haec opinio apud nonnullos Haebreos Cabalistas & Talmudistas.

purely formal point of view, there is some truth to this assertion, Cardoso's negative attitude to transmigration still merits attention. We shall find in his *Excelencias de los hebreos* that he accepts with equanimity quite a number of other Jewish doctrines which are no more central than this. Moreover, in the seventeenth century belief in transmigration was so widespread among Jews that, whatever its status as an article of faith, any direct attack on it could be regarded as somewhat suspect. It had become, in Gershom Scholem's words, "an integral part of Jewish popular belief and Jewish folklore."[116] Manasseh ben Israel certainly treated it as a basic dogma, in both his treatise on the soul, and on resurrection.[117] Conversely, the opponents of the doctrine in the seventeenth century were often those whose views in general were considered radical or even heterodox. Cardoso's rejection of metempsychosis thus ranges him curiously on the side of figures with whom he otherwise has little real affinity—for example, with Leone Modena and even Uriel da Costa.[118] It may be that Cardoso's attitude flowed from his avowed antagonism to the Kabbalah as a whole. It is also possible that he was already strongly predisposed against metempsychosis by reading some of the Church Fathers while still in Spain.[119] If this be so, then

---

nam inter illos solum resurrectio & immortalitas animarum est de fide, animarum vero transmigratio nihil apud illos ad fidem pertinet. . . ."

[116] *Major Trends in Jewish Mysticism*, p. 283.

[117] See his *Nishmat hayyim*, Pt. IV, chs. 6–23, fols. 155r-174r; cf. his *De resurrectione mortuorum libri III* (Amsterdam, 1636), II, 18.

[118] For Leone's attack on metempsychosis see especially his *Sefer Ben David, ve-hu ma'amar neged 'emunat gilgul ha-nefashot*, first published in Eliezer b. Solomon Ashkenazi's *Ta'am zekenim*, ed. R. Kirchheim (Frankfurt, 1854), fols. 61r-64v. Da Costa regarded the doctrine as one of the evils resulting from belief in the soul's immortality: "os Phariseos que somente a çertas almas deram immortalidade, bem aventurança eterna & tambem males eternos para nam condenarem essas almas facilmente aos tormentos disseram & dizem que quando acontecia fazer hũa alma num corpo obras por onde merecia ser condenada, ou faltandolhe para cumprir algũ mandamento, a tornava Deus a mandar em segundo e terceiro corpo ganhe como elles dizem o pam que no ceo ha de comer" (Gebhardt, *Die Schriften des Uriel da Costa*, p. 61).

[119] E. g., Augustine, *De Trinitate*, XII, 151; *De civ. Dei*, X, 30; XII, 21.

his rejection of the idea after becoming a professing Jew was merely facilitated by his discovery that Jewish tradition was itself far from unanimous on the subject.

In brief, Cardoso presents metempsychosis as a Pythagorean and Platonic doctrine, though he also alludes to other sources and quotes, at one point, a passage from the Hermetic *Poimandres* on the soul's ascent and liberation from the body. He notes that among the Jews the transmigration of souls is known as *gilgul*, which he renders as a "rotation" or "circumgyration," the soul revolving from one body to another, just as a perpetually rotating heavenly sphere is called in Hebrew *galgal*. It is not known whether the Pythagoreans took the notion from the Hebrews, or vice versa. The first indication of such a belief among Jews occurs before the Maccabean age, when the Sadducean and Essene sects first arose. The Essenes did derive their notion of transmigration from the Pythagoreans. Josephus relates that the Pharisees also adhered to it.[120]

Against transmigration Cardoso invokes the authority of Saadia Gaon, Joseph Albo, and David Kimhi.[121] It is possible, he observes, to interpret the Pythagorean or Platonic doctrines metaphorically, as referring to the fact that men often assume animal characteristics and so can be said to be changed into brutes. But even this type of direct metaphor has little basis in Scripture, which tends merely to use comparatives, e. g., "Man abideth not in honor; he is like the beasts that perish" (Ps. 49: 13). Among the more "recent" Jewish

---

[120] *Phil. lib.*, p. 616: "Vocant illi hanc animarum migrationem *Gilgul*, id est rotatio vel circumgiratio quia de corpore in corpus circumvoluuntur. . . ." The analogy between the doctrines of Essenes and Pythagoreans, as well as the reference to Pharisaic belief in transmigration (*ibid.*, p. 617) are taken from Josephus, *Antt.*, XV, 10; *Bell. Jud.*, II, 8.

[121] *Phil. lib.*, p. 617: "Saadia Gaon Princeps Academiarum Haebreorum in Persia [*sic*], & eximius sacrorum Bibliorum interpres, qui Arabicam paraphrasim ex Haebreo doctissime conscripsit . . . Iste igitur Philosophus & Theologus *lib. de fide* improbat eos qui animas ante corpora praeexistere affirmant & transmigrationem, quod etiam faciunt Ioseph Albus & David Kimchi Theologi praestantissimi." Cf. Saadia, *'Emunot ve-deot*, VI, ch. 8; Albo, *'Ikkarim*, IV, ch. 29. Kimhi's remarks on *gilgul* occur in his commentary on Ps. 104: 30, but the passage appears only in the *editio princeps* of 1487.

writers, Abravanel cites various reasons and scriptural verses in confirmation of metempsychosis, "but this is neither the time nor place to refute them."[122]

The chapter on the resurrection of the dead[123] defends a doctrine which was, unlike metempsychosis, fundamental to both Judaism and Christianity. Within the Jewish community itself, however, resurrection was as much impugned by the skeptics as the immortality of the soul. Against these "Sadducees" Manasseh ben Israel had already been impelled to write a special treatise on the subject.[124]

Cardoso's treatment of the problem betrays some curious features. To begin with, some of the most salient elements in Jewish discussions of resurrection down through the ages are entirely absent. We hear nothing on such questions as whether Israel alone will be resurrected, or all mankind. There is no mention of Maimonides' reinterpretation of the doctrine nor, indeed, of the classic problem of the relation between resurrection and the immortality of the individual soul. Cardoso says nothing on the nature of life during the period of the Resurrection, nor does he discuss any possible limit to its duration. He completely glosses over the nexus between resurrection and the redemption of Israel. His silence on these and similar matters may be attributed in large measure to the fact that he was writing for a gentile audience, but we must also bear in mind the character of the *Philosophia libera*. As has been emphasized, Cardoso is dealing with theological problems within the framework of natural philosophy. Because his overwhelming concern at this point is to prove the very

---

[122] *Ibid.* Abravanel argues for the transmigration of the human soul into a human body in a lengthy discourse on the mystical meaning of levirate marriage. See his *Commentary* on Deut. 25: 5. However, he rejects transmigration into the body of an animal. See the discussion of Daniel 4: 29 ff. in his *Ma'ayene ha-yeshuah* (Amsterdam, 1647), VI, 5, fols. 33v-34r.

[123] Lib. VI, quaest. cviii ("De resurrectione"), pp. 719–25.

[124] *De resurrectione mortuorum libri III. Quibus animae immortalitas & corporis resurrectio contra Zaducaeos comprobatur; caussae item miraculosae resurrectionis exponuntur; deque judicio extremo, & mundi instauratione agitur; Ex Sacris Literis, & veteribus Rabbinis* (Amsterdam, 1636). In general, "Sadducees" in 17th- and 18th-century Sephardic literature is a term applied to contemporary deniers of the Oral Law and, in particular, of immortality and resurrection.

possibility of bodily resurrection, he is inevitably more intent on the process than on the state of being after it has been achieved. In taking this course, however, he is not the first to become embroiled in the dilemma of simultaneously defending the supernatural character of resurrection while seeking proofs through analogies in nature itself.

Cardoso defines resurrection succinctly as "the recalling to life of the same body and soul at the same time." He is careful to distinguish this from the cyclical *annus magnus* of the ancient philosophers, an idea which he attacks on several occasions.[125] Two opinions on resurrection are reviewed: a) that it can occur naturally, and b) that through Divine power it can occur only in Man. Both are rejected. Cardoso asserts that resurrection is a Divine work, and brings biblical verses to prove it. It is, in fact, the peculiar province of God, and is accomplished directly by Him, though other miracles need not be. There are those who argue that the soul can "naturally" return to the body because, being immortal, it survives the body, and the two have a mutual longing for one another. But all such arguments are dismissed. "We must say that the soul of Man was freely introduced by God into the body, is freely recalled only by Him, and only the Will which created it can bring it back."[126] The opinion that resurrection is possible only in Man asserts that his soul alone, being immortal, is not corrupted. Corrupted things cannot be revived, because the same things cannot have a double existence and double duration, "since if it were reproduced it would now begin to be in another duration . . . and hence would not be the same, but similar." To which Cardoso replies that, while the same thing cannot have a double duration and existence at the same time, it will be able to do so at different times. This leads to a discussion as to whether resurrection necessarily involves the return of past time. Cardoso maintains that reproduction of time is not required for the reproduction of a thing. Time will not return with the Resurrection. Things themselves do not depend upon time for their existence. In any case such objections are really groundless, for "it must be held as certain that all things, corrupted or permanent, or successive, as motion and

---

[125] *Phil. lib.*, p. 719. Cf. p. 724, cols. a and b.   [126] *Ibid.*, p. 721.

time, *can* return the same through the power of God, since it is easier to recall what was, than to produce what never was."[127]

Cardoso proceeds to present some curious analogues to resurrection in the natural world. Drowned flies revive if buried in warm ashes or exposed to the sun for a short time. Lucian affirms the soul of a fly to be immortal, though he mocks the immortality of the human soul. Some people concede only that the fly is asleep. Others maintain that a new soul has been produced, since flies are easily born from rotting matter, water, and dust. However, though the soul of a fly be dissolved, its parts are not corrupted, just as the boards, stones, and bricks of a house fall apart when it is destroyed, but can be rebuilt into a house. Paradoxically, certain living things are revived because of their own imperfection, while others which are more perfect do not return to life.[128]

Resurrection is reasonable. Both body and soul should receive punishment or reward for vice or virtue. Christians, Jews, and Muslims believe it. The Jews say that three classes of men have no share in the world to come: those who deny the existence of God, the Divine Law, or the Resurrection.[129] For his solace, God has already given Man some prototypes of resurrection: Enoch, Elijah, and Moses, who was not dead, but "was taken body and soul into the paradise of immortality."[130] Quotations from Scripture follow, to

---

[127] *Ibid.* The argument that the restoration of something which has once existed is more plausible than *creatio ex nihilo* had already been voiced by Saadia (*'Emunot ve-deot*, VIII, 3).

[128] *Ibid.* Ideas on the resuscitation of the fly and other insects were widespread in th 17th century. Cf. Thorndike, *Magic and Experimental Science*, VII, 413.

[129] *Phil. lib.*, p. 722, paraphrasing the famous statement in Mishna *Sanhedrin*, 10: 1.

[130] *Phil. lib.*, p. 722. The assumption of Enoch and Elijah is of course indicated in the Bible, though we shall have occasion to take note of the Rabbinic reticence concerning it. The legend that Moses too entered heaven alive is reported or hinted in a number of Rabbinic sources. See, e. g., *TB Sotah*, 13b ("Some maintain that Moses did not die"). It is far more likely, however, that Cardoso first learned this tradition from the quotations of the Greek fragments of the *Assumption of Moses* preserved by the Church Fathers. See, e. g., Clement, *Stromata*, VI, 15; Origen, *In Josuam homiliae*, II, 1.

show that resurrection is possible, has already been performed for some, and will be performed again at a time determined by God. Because the Sadducees and Samaritans accepted only the Law of Moses and not the other writings of the prophets, the Jews proved the Resurrection from the Pentateuch.[131]

In a rather rhapsodic passage Cardoso speaks of the alternation of death and rebirth in nature. As trees seem to be dead in the winter months, without fruit and leaves, and yet are easily revived from dry seeds "dead" in the earth, so can be the bodies of men. Mixing metaphor, myth, and scientific "fact," he speaks of bulls and oxen "degenerating" into bees, horses into beetles, the phoenix renewed from its ashes, the silkworm stirring from a tiny lukewarm egg. Why, then, cannot Man revive? The Scriptures speak of death as sleep. The Greeks call tombs *cemeteria*, that is—"dormitories." But "the Jews even more appropriately and divinely call the place of tombs *bet ha-ḥayyim*, literally 'the house of the living,' indicating that souls are immortal and that bodies will again return to life."[132]

How does resurrection occur? Does God create new bodies similar to the first, or do all the parts which belonged to a body reunite? For the first opinion Cardoso refers to Hasdai Crescas, Kimhi, and Abravanel. For the second he cites Saadia Gaon.[133] Cardoso opts for Saadia's view, and explains the process in some detail. Bones are the solid foundation of the human edifice, and in the Resurrection, as in the first creation, the forming of bodies will begin from them. There

---

[131] *Phil. lib.*, p. 722. Cf. *TB Sanhedrin*, 90b: "The heretics asked Rabban Gamliel: From whence [do you know] that the Holy One revives the dead? He replied: From the Torah, the Prophets and the Hagiographa. And they did not receive [his proofs]." Cardoso's proof texts are to be found in the subsequent Talmudic discussions, e. g. (Exod. 15: 1): "*Tunc cecinit Moses & filij Israel etc.*, ubi in Haebreo est pro *cecinit*, cantabit, *yasir* in futuro, significans quod adhuc in tempore resurrectionis iterum cantabit Moses mirabilia Domini. . . ." This is the proof brought by R. Meir (*Sanhedrin*, 91b).

[132] *Phil. lib.*, p. 722: "sed proprius & divinius Haebrei appellant locum sepulchrorum *Betaxaim.* . . ."

[133] *Phil. lib.*, p. 723. See Abravanel's remarks on the "fourth principle" of the Resurrection in his Introduction to his Commentary on Isaiah. There he also quotes Crescas' view in support of his own. For Saadia, see *'Emunot ve-deot*, VII, 7.

is, in fact, a Jewish tradition concerning a bone called *Luz* which is indestructible.[134] The body, even if eaten by beasts, or cremated and scattered, shall return to its original flesh, through the power of God. All this will happen, not gradually and successively, but in a moment of time. Origen erred in thinking that resurrected men might be round, for that would be indecorous. Man is to have an erect figure when he is raised, just as before, so that his head shall aim toward heaven, his feet toward earth. Impious and wicked men will be resurrected, along with the righteous, not for salvation and life, but for punishment and death.[135]

Returning to the question of natural resurrection Cardoso asserts that this is impossible for man and the "perfect" animals, since by nature they come to life only through generation. Less perfect creatures can, however, be aroused. He denies the tales of lion cubs and weasels being roused from death by their fathers' breath; they may simply be asleep. Marvelous stories of men who have slept for months and years may well be true. There are many miracles of nature which foolish men ridicule because they have no knowledge of nature's virtues or the disposition of natural causes. But the ancient pagan stories of dead men brought back to life are fictions. Similarly, the rebirth of the phoenix is either a fable, or else it is not a real resurrection but a new bird. Nothing can be deduced concerning natural resurrection from the rejoining of a severed ear, since here the soul is still extant in the body.[136]

Finally, two symbols of resurrection are noted: mercury, because it scatters into tiny parts and reunites, and seed, which lies dead in the ground and sprouts forth again.

And it is a greater miracle for Man to be born than to rise again, since it is more miraculous for the soul to be created out of nothing and

---

[134] *Phil. lib.*, p. 723. The legend concerning the *luz*, the nucleal bone from which the resurrection of the body will commence, is found in a number of rabbinic sources, as well as in the *Zohar*. It was widely accepted by Christian and Arab theologians and anatomists. See the references cited in *JE*, VIII, 219, and Ginzberg, *Legends of the Jews*, V, 363. Cardoso himself refers to *Bereshit rabba*, the *Zohar*, and *Pirke de R. Eliezer*, though it is to be suspected that he does so at second hand.

[135] *Phil. lib.*, pp. 723 f.   [136] *Ibid.*, p. 724.

introduced into the body, than for it to be called back to the body after it is already created. And yet we marvel that Man is revived, since it is unusual; we do not marvel that he is born, since it is frequent. Thus we admire eclipses of the sun and moon because they do not commonly occur, but forget their perpetual motion, outstanding speed, and the skillfully arranged order of the stars. We do not care for them with such eagerness since, continually appearing before our eyes, they keep us less in suspense.[137]

Book VII of the *Philosophia libera* is, as has been indicated, devoted entirely to a discussion of God.[138] No philosophical innovations are to be found here. Cardoso's approach to God is thoroughly traditional, his arguments are culled largely from medieval Jewish and Christian philosophy. Here above all he stands revealed before us as a man of the most firm and intense faith. His philosophical attitudes are easily integrated with his religious beliefs. I shall summarize the general thrust of his argument, pausing only occasionally to take note of specific nuances.

The first of the 11 chapters into which the seventh book is divided deals, inevitably, with the existence of God, for which Cardoso presents ten proofs. He begins with an argument from consensus. All men, however fierce or uncivilized they may be, have in their hearts a presentiment of some divinity.[139] The existence of God is also manifest from the marvels and awesomeness of the universe itself. Cardoso offers data on the sun (it is 166 times bigger than the earth, and covers more space in one hour than could a bullet in five thousand). Among the fixed stars some are 50 to 100 times bigger than the earth. With the aid of the telescope we now know of the phases of Venus and four satellites of Jupiter.[140] The third proof is the argument from the design and order of the universe; the fourth, from the beauty and sublimity of creatures; the fifth, from the need for a First Cause. In the sixth we are informed that spirits and demons

---

[137] *Ibid.*, p. 725.   [138] Lib. VIII, *De Deo*, pp. 726–58.

[139] *Ibid.*, p. 726. The ninth proof (p. 729) is again an argument from consensus, the natural fear of some divinity implanted in all men. However, it was love, not fear, which first led men to a knowledge of God.

[140] *Ibid.*

exist; there must therefore be one supreme power to govern them all, else they would make a shambles of the world.[141] Other proofs are those miracles which could have no natural origin, the phenomenon of prophecy, and, of course, the Scriptures. However, Cardoso insists that God is not merely a proposition of faith, but a "universal axiom of nature."[142]

Since knowledge of God is implanted in all men, and since His existence is far more self-evident than that every whole is greater than its part, anyone who is an atheist is insane and ought to be tied up, flogged, cured with drugs, and banished from the consort of men until he regains his senses.[143] In view of the widespread abhorrence of the atheist, even among tolerant men of the age, Cardoso's remark hardly comes as a surprise. The apparent harshness of his stance is somewhat mitigated by the fact that he would have the atheist regarded merely as a lunatic. It is further softened when, after giving a list of ancient atheists, he suggests that they were called so, not because they denied a supreme divinity, but because they rejected the polytheistic faiths of the time. Similarly, the gentiles labeled the Jews and Christians as atheists.[144]

For no one really denies God. To demonstrate this, Cardoso cites Strabo's reference to the Galicians, Asturians, and Cantabrians, who feared a god whose name they did not know, as well as a report of a cannibalistic Brazilian tribe, the Tapuya, said to be utter barbarians, who nonetheless recognize in thunder a manifestation of divine power. One can encounter those who deny or doubt the immortality of the soul, but not true atheists who deny God. Even Epicurus, Lucretius, Pliny, and the Sadducees were not atheists in that strict sense of the term.[145]

The second chapter, on the Essence of God, is mainly concerned

---

[141] *Ibid.*, p. 728.   [142] *Ibid.*, p. 729.   [143] *Ibid.*

[144] *Ibid.*, pp. 729 f., quoting Pliny, Tacitus, and Juvenal, on the charge of Jewish and Christian "atheism."

[145] *Ibid.*, p. 730. As further proof he cites Ps. 14: 1 ("The fool hath said in his heart, 'There is no God' "), noting that here the Hebrew word for God is not the Tetragrammaton, but *'Elohim*, which also signifies "judge." Hence, not God Himself, but rather His providence, is being denied.

to show that this aspect cannot really be known. "God, insofar as He Himself is concerned, is light itself, but insofar as we are concerned, is darkness itself. There is nothing more clear than He, yet nothing more obscure, supremely knowable unto Himself, and supremely unknown to us."[146] Yet any knowledge of God, however slight, is most pleasing and noble. The *via negativa* is outlined, mainly along Maimonidean lines, followed by a long discussion of the incorporeality of God. Included here is a long list and elaborate praise of those who believe God should not be adored in the form of any image, of temples without statues, and of worship without temples.[147] Among almost all nations the name of God contains four letters, because the ineffable Name which signifies His essence has four letters in Hebrew. Cardoso presents a list of them which, if not entirely accurate or germane, is at least impressive.[148]

The Unity of God is the subject of the third chapter, six proofs being offered in its support. A list is given of ancient philosophers who realized the unity of God, beginning with Hermes Trismegistus, and extending through the Pythagoreans, various Pre-Socratics, and Orpheus.[149] After discussing the meaning of God's unity Cardoso analyzes the origin of polytheism and idolatry in the world, beginning in the time of Enosh.[150] The short fourth chapter on God's immutability offers the classic proofs, and advances the Maimonidean etymology of the Hebrew *Shadday* as "sufficient unto Himself."[151]

---

[146] *Ibid.*, p. 731.   [147] *Ibid.*, pp. 733 f.

[148] *Ibid.*, p. 735: "Apud Graecos dicitur Teos, apud Assirios Adad [*sic*], id est unus, Latini vocant Deus, Persae sire, Magi Orsi, Arabes Alla, Turcae Agdi, Indi Zimi, Etrusci Esar . . . Goti Thor, Germani Gott . . . Aegiptij nomen summi Iovis Amun, quod corrupto vocabulo dicitur Amon, Itali Idio [*sic!*], Galli Dieu, Hispani Dios, Lusitani Deus. . . ."

[149] Quaest. iii ("De unitate Dei), p. 737. For Orpheus, see Eusebius, *Praep. Evang.*, XIII, 7.

[150] *Phil. lib.*, pp. 738–40. In his *Excelencias de los Hebreos* the history of idolatry is linked to a discussion of Israel's mission in the world. Cf. *infra*, ch. IX.

[151] Quaest. iv ("De immutabilitate Dei"), p. 741: "Saddai hoc est sibi sufficiens, & abundantissimus." Cardoso does not indicate his source, which is obviously Maimonides, *Guide*, I, ch. 63: "The name Shadday, therefore, signifies 'He who is sufficient'. . . ."

The Infinity of God is treated in chapter 5. Since the essence of God is infinite, so are His attributes. Immensity is infinity as to place, eternity as to duration, omnipotence as to power, and omniscience as to knowledge. Although the divine perfections are intrinsically one and the same, they are conceived by us as distinct and separate because of the weakness of our minds, which must operate by analogy to created things.[152] Four chapters now follow, each devoted to one of the infinite attributes. Thus infinity as to place means an infinite diffusion in every dimension, through essence, and not through parts. If there existed an immeasurable body it would indeed exist everywhere, but only through its parts, and it would not exist totally in every place. However, in all individual points of space God's total essence, His power, wisdom, and every perfection, are present. Nor does diffusion imply an expansion, but rather an indivisible and continuous presence everywhere. Among the Jews God is therefore called *Makom* (Place), for He is indeed the Place of all things.[153] Is God, then, also outside the world in imaginary spaces? Beyond the heavens there are no corporeal spaces or intervals, but there are found uncreated and spiritual intervals, not to be distinguished from the infinity of God Himself. When we say that God is outside the world diffused through infinite spaces, or that He is in imaginary spaces, we mean neither that He is in some fictitious place nor that He is in some space distinct from Himself, but that He is in space which is an extension of His own "immensity." Created space exists through corporeal extension; uncreated space is the very immeasurability of God. It is "imaginary" only because our minds cannot conceive it other than by imagining an infinite space essentially similar to our own. On the other hand, some people, thinking they honor God thereby, actually diminish His immensity by claiming He cannot be present in unseemly places. But the sun's rays are not befouled by shining on unclean things. God, being everywhere, is immobile. To speak of His "descent," as does Scripture, is to speak metaphorically.[154] The chapters devoted to

---

[152] Quaest. v ("De infinitate Dei"), p. 741.
[153] Quaest, vi ("De immensitate Dei"), p. 742.
[154] *Ibid.*, pp. 743 f.

God's eternity, power, and wisdom, as well as that which concerns His truth, life, goodness, and other attributes, employ the same general approach and need not detain us here. Like the discussion of immensity they consist in the main of philosophic arguments for the infinity of each attribute, with digressions into scientific and classical literature.[155]

The longest chapter in Book VII is the very last, which deals with the Providence of God.[156] This is to be expected. A perennial religious problem, the question of Divine Providence continued to exercise the minds of men, especially at a time when it was perhaps more openly attacked than before. Not a few seventeenth-century Sephardic works in the vernacular were entirely devoted to sustaining the belief in the face of those who denied it.[157] But these were largely concerned with the problem of God's providence in relation to the Jewish people and its tribulations. This aspect is absent in the chapter under review. Cardoso deals here only with the general problem of God's justice toward humanity, and especially the individual human being. He will take up God's unique relation to Israel only in his "Jewish" book, *Las excelencias de los hebreos*.

Twelve reasons are advanced to justify belief in Divine providence, and they are fairly standard. Even stupid animals, for example, do not neglect their young. How much more so God, who created everything, and loves his works. The sea keeps the same measure, and does not overflow the land. From Synesius of Cyrene, Cardoso brings the amusing tale of the man who complained that large fruits like gourds and melons grow on the ground, while small ones like pears, apples, and almonds, grow on high trees. But lo, as he was speaking a little pear fell on his unsuspecting head, and he realized

---

[155] Quaest. vii-x: "De aeternitate Dei" (pp. 744 f.); "De potentia Dei" (pp. 745 f.); "De sapientia Dei" (pp. 746–48); "De veritate, vita, bonitate, & alijs attributis Divinis" (pp. 748–50).

[156] Quaest. xi ("De providentia Dei"), pp. 750–57.

[157] E. g., Daniel Levi (Miguel) de Barrios, *Providentia particular de Dios sobre el Pueblo de Israel*, in *Arbol de la vida* (Amsterdam, 1689) (*BEPJ*, p. 25); Saul Levi Morteira, Providencia de Dios con Ysrael (in manuscript; *BEPJ*, p. 74); Isaac Jesurun, *Livro da Providencia Divina* (Amsterdam, 1663) (*BEPJ*, p. 53). Cf. also David Nieto, *De la Divina Providencia* (London, 1704, 1716).

that had it been a melon his wound would have been far more serious![158] The "standard-bearer" of the enemies of providence was Epicurus. He did not utterly deny the existence of God, but argued that He has no care for His creatures. Lactantius traces this doctrine back to Democritus. But in any case, an improvident god is not God, and so some men accuse Epicurus of atheism, and from his ideas some rush headlong into it. Epictetus distinguished among the various errors which have sprung up concerning God. Some say that no divinity exists, others that He exists, but rests and cares for nothing; others that He cares only for the celestial things, not for the terrestrial; others that He even cares for the latter, but only collectively. Some deny providence only over human affairs, in order to maintain human freedom; others assert, on the contrary, that God cares only for men.[159] Cardoso next reviews the arguments of the opponents of divine providence, from the unjust differences among men, to the question of why there are so many poisonous things on earth, and the utility of moths, mice, and serpents. It is said that a viper burned to ashes is a cure for the bite of the same beast. How much better it would have been for it not to have existed at all, than for a remedy against it to be sought from itself![160]

But "all the weapons with which the Epicureans and atheists besiege the divine citadel of providence are weak and fragile." Men deny providence because they do not know the deepest secrets of God. Far from diminishing it, the inequality of degrees strengthens providence. As a sculptor does not make everything in his statue to be eyes, so God does not make all to be angels or men. A painter does not paint equally beautiful colors everywhere on his canvas, but gives to each part one which is suitable to it. Who would criticize a comedy or a tragedy because all the characters are not heroes? No state would be more unfortunate than one in which everyone were equal, rich and noble. Furthermore, in the truly essential things everyone *is* almost equal. Rich and poor alike breathe the air and feel the heat of the sun; no less rain falls on the fields of either. God permits evil and sin for the exercise of human freedom. In a blacksmith's shop, even if not understanding the reason for all the

---

[158] *Phil. lib.*, pp. 750 f. [159] *Ibid.*, p. 752. [160] *Ibid.*, p. 753.

bellows, anvils, and hammers, we would not find fault with the craftsman; yet in the world we dare reproach God! He was at liberty to create man or not. Had He refrained, it would have been no great injury. But it would be a very great injury indeed to have created him and then to show no concern for him. The complaints about the troubles of the righteous and happiness of the wicked arise out of the perversity of human judgment, which considers only perceptible goods to be good, and tangible evils to be evil. Seneca has shown that true felicity lies within. It is often useful for good men to suffer, since wealth would corrupt them. Nothing is truly good except virtue, and the observance of the Law of God. The wicked are tortured by conscience, which is far worse than corporal punishment. It may be that even the impious, or their parents, have done some good, and are being rewarded in this life with a fragile and perishable convenience, while God reserves eternal good for the pious. The impious are often the rod and scourge of God to try the righteous in constancy, patience, and virtue.[161]

And so on, right to the very end. For the modern reader all this hardly constitutes an answer to Job. But then, which theodicy shall? Cardoso stands squarely in the mainstream of a venerable tradition. If he has nothing new to add, that is because, given the presuppositions of a God who is both omnipotent and perfectly just, the arguments have long been exhausted. Of the radically new solution to the problem of evil advanced by sixteenth-century Lurianic Kabbalah, Cardoso may have had no knowledge, or else he wanted no part of it. In closing, he suggests the following works for further reading: The selections from Philo concerning providence which are quoted by Eusebius;[162] Epictetus, as cited by Arrian; Plutarch's *De sera numinis vindicta;* Seneca's *De providentia;* Photius' citations of Himerius; Synesius' *De fato;* Boethius' *De consolatione philosophiae;* Book IV of Joseph Albo's *'Ikkarim;* and Maimonides' *Guide*, Bk. III, chs. 17 and 18. The juxtaposition of classical, Christian, and Jewish authors is characteristic. And with this the *Philosophia libera* is concluded, "ad Laudem et Gloriam Omnipotentis Dei."

---

[161] *Ibid.*, pp. 754-58.   [162] *Praep. Evang.*, VIII, 14.

JEWISH STRANDS: A BACKWARD GLANCE

There is thus no hint in the *Philosophia libera*, nor in any of his earlier works, that Cardoso was ever susceptible to the new skeptical currents of the age. We must conclude that in those elements of religious faith which are common to Christianity and Judaism his transition from Marrano to professing Jew must have posed no particular difficulties. The significance of this continuum in smoothing his path to Judaism is surely not to be underestimated. On the other hand, such particular dogmatic points of contention between the two faiths as the Trinity, the Messiahship of Christ, the chosenness of Israel, and the validity of the Law had certainly demanded of him a clear choice. In our analysis of Cardoso's flight from Spain we have found good reason to suppose that he had already made such choices quite some time before his actual departure. But, as has been stressed, it is precisely the conflicting claims of Judaism and Christianity which are not discussed in the *Philosophia libera*, being reserved for Cardoso's Jewish book, *Las excelencias de los hebreos*.

And yet the *Philosophia* is, in its own way, also a "Jewish book." It is so as much by what it chooses to omit as by what it includes. Even if he were initially unaware of the identity of "Isac" Cardoso, no gentile reader could have failed to note the absence of any mention of Jesus or, indeed, any reference to the New Testament, in the theological discussions, while the frequent interspersing of allusions to Rabbinic literature would have dispelled any lingering doubts as to the author's religious allegiance. We have observed such Jewish strands all along. Now we must take a closer look at them, for they may offer us a new insight, not only into Cardoso, but into a crucial aspect of the entire Marrano problem in the seventeenth century.

We shall choose our examples at random, without attempting a comprehensive catalogue.

Throughout the book Cardoso is fond of using Hebrew words, which he transliterates, and of offering Hebrew etymologies. Some of this is merely playful. In his discussion of animals he notes that the Jews are careful to employ four different Hebrew words for

271

the lion, depending on his age: *gur, kefir, 'ari*, and *labi*.[163] Speaking of the dog, he observes that its loyalty is already indicated in the etymology of the Hebrew word *keleb*, which can be vocalized as *ka-leb* and translated as "like a heart."[164] He is equally fond of citing maxims from Rabbinic literature. Thus, while commenting on Psalm 115: 7 ("The dead praise not the Lord") in his discussion of immortality, he writes: "And the Hebrew sages observe that one hour of contrition in this world is better than a thousand in the world to come."[165] In dealing with astral influences on the span of human life, Cardoso cites the Talmud, Rabbi Solomon ben Abraham ibn Adret (*"Arisba"* = ha-RaShBA), and Ibn Ezra, to the effect that Israel is not subject to the constellations.[166] Aggadic explanations also abound. The word *'ish* (man) contains the letter *yod*, while *'ishah* (woman) contains the letter *heh*. The two letters form the name of God. When God is not

---

[163] *Phil. lib.*, p. 379. He also cites yet another word: *layish*.

[164] *Ibid.*, p. 380: "Hebraice canis dicitur *keleb*, id est quasi cor, *caleb, leb* enim cor significat."

[165] *Ibid.*, p. 615. See also *Kohelet Rabb.*, 4: 10.

[166] *Phil. lib.*, p. 714: "& sapienter inquit Arisba in suis consultationibus, *Adebaquim bamisvot em le maala min amazal*, id est, qui adhaerent praeceptis, sunt super planetas, & Thalmudistae illam proferunt praeclaram sententiam, *En mazal le Israel*, id est, non est planeta Israeli; tollitur vero repugnantia cum Abenesra supra cap. 34 Exodi, *En mazal le Israel col zeman se em somerim a tora, veim lo ismerua, islot baem amazal*, hoc est, non est planeta Israeli omni tempore quo legis sunt observantes, at si legem non obseruauerint, dominabitur illis planeta". Cf. Solomon b. Adret, *Responsa*, V, 48; *TB Shabbat*, 156a; Ibn Ezra, Commentary ad Ex. 34: 21.

It seems most probable, however, that Cardoso derived this information from Manasseh b. Israel, who writes as follows: "omnes uno ore asserunt cum Arisba הדבקים במצות הם למעלה מן המזל *qui adhaerunt praeceptis sunt supra planetas*... Hinc Thalmudici doctores alicubi ajunt אין מזל לישראל, id est, non est planeta Israeli; & alio rursus in loco contrarium dicunt יש מזל לישראל, id est, Est planeta Israeli. Quorū facta distinctione, liquet utrumque verum esse; nam uti inquit doctus Aben Esra super cap. xxxiv Exodi לא אם ,התורה שומרי שהם זמן כל לישראל מזל אין ישמרוה בהם ישלוט המזל id est, non est Israeli planeta, omni illo tempore quo legis sunt observantes; At si legem nõ observaverint, dominatur illis planeta" (*De termino vitae, libri tres. Quibus veterum Rabbinorum, ac recentium doctorum, de hac controversia sententia explicatur* [Amsterdam, 1639], p. 18).

272

present in the relations between man and woman, all that remains
in each is the word *'esh* (fire), by which they are consumed.[167]

When the occasion presents itself, Cardoso also displays an eagerness to discuss certain aspects of Jewish law and practice. In
analyzing the various calendars among the nations, he can hardly
refrain from stating that the Jews were the first to reconcile the solar
and lunar years, and then proceeding to explain certain aspects of
the Jewish calendar.[168] In this instance the Jewish material is at
least placed in an organic context. At other times, however, the
theme which is treated serves merely as a pretext for the insertion of
Jewish matters. Such is very often the case in passages which deal
with purely medical topics. On the subject of Caesarian section, for
example, Cardoso gives as the Hebrew equivalent the term *yoṣe dofen*
from the Mishnah.[169] He also cites two Mishnaic passages, one which
suspends the ordinary period of purification after childbirth in the
case of a woman who gave birth "from the side," the other denying
rights of primogeniture to one so born.[170] While discussing virginity,
Cardoso cites two cases from the Talmud. One concerns a Jerusale-

---

[167] *Phil. lib.*, p. 447. Cf. *TB Sotah*, 17a, and Rashi ad loc.

[168] *Phil. lib.*, pp. 148 f. The reconciliation was first effected by Moses and then
"infallibly arranged by Hillel." The Hebrew word "year," *shanah* (sanna),
indicates "mutavit, iteravit repetijt." There is also a discussion of the four *tekufot*
of the year (*ibid.*, p. 149).

[169] *Ibid.*, lib. VI, quaest. c ("De partu Caesareo"), p. 691: "Yose dofen, hoc est
extractus a latere, de quo in Misna seu traditionibus Hebraicis fit mentio." The
phrase occurs in Mishnah *Zebakim* 8: 1, where it is applied to animals; in Mishnah
Bekorot 7: 7, referring both to animals and to the High Priest; *ibid.*, 8: 2, referring
to male children; *Niddah*, 5: 1, referring to children of both sexes. In the latter,
both Rashi and Obadiah of Bertinoro explain the birth as induced by drugs
(על ידי סם), but cf. Maimonides ad loc.: «והוא שישוסע חלצי האשה». That the term
was used in the 17th century by Jewish physicians as the literal equivalent of
Caesarian section is clear from the discussion of Tobias Cohen. See his *Ma'aseh
Tobiah*, "Gan na'ul," ch. 18, p. 138 ff.

[170] *Phil. lib.*, p. 692. Cf., respectively, Mishnah *Niddah* 5: 1, and *Bekorot* 8: 2.
Cardoso also relates here that he observed what appears to have been a hysterec-
tomy performed in Verona. The fifty-year-old wife of Isaac Carpi had her
uterus removed by the surgeon Paulo Cortesio, and had lived so for the past
five years.

mite family whose women neither menstruated nor bled when the hymen was ruptured. The other tells of a complaint once brought before R. Judah by a husband who claimed that no tokens of virginity had appeared on his wedding night. It was a time of drought, and the couple was told merely to bathe, eat, and drink, and all would be well.[171] In this connection, too, Cardoso notes that the verse "and they shall spread the garment before the elders of the city" (Deut. 22: 17) was interpreted metaphorically by Rabbi Ishmael. This, in turn, gives him the opportunity to point out also the rabbinic interpretation of the biblical *lex talionis*.[172]

More significantly, despite Cardoso's general restraint of his Jewish passions in the *Philosophia libera*, there are passages in which we can already detect an anticipation of *Las excelencias de los hebreos*. For example, the praise of Palestine will be taken up again in the *Excelencias*, where an entire chapter will be devoted to it. Indeed, some lines in the latter are direct quotations from the *Philosophia libera*, rendered into Spanish. The major difference, characteristically, is that in the *Excelencias* there will be much on Palestine belonging forever to the Jewish people, while this note is entirely absent in the *Philosophia*.[173] At one point, in his survey of the animal kingdom, Cardoso offers to classify them also by their "purity" and "impurity," and enters into a discussion of the Jewish dietary laws, another major theme in the *Excelencias*.[174] At times a seemingly casual Jewish reference in the *Philosophia* proves, in retrospect, to contain important overtones. Thus, in the discussion of virginity to which we referred above, Cardoso cites the injunction that the High Priest must marry a virgin (Lev. 21: 13). This is, of itself, innocuous enough. But then he proceeds to note that the Vulgate has a somewhat different reading from the Hebrew, a theme to be expanded at great length in the *Excelencias*. Moreover, he takes pains to specify that in

---

[171] *Phil. lib.*, p. 567. Cf. *TB Ketubot*, 10b.

[172] *Phil. lib.*, p. 568. For R. Ishmael's opinion see *Mekilta*, Nezikin, VI, 45 and XIII, 16; *Sifre*, Deut., 237.

[173] *Phil. lib.*, pp. 34 f. Cf. *Excelencias*, Pt. I, ch. 9.

[174] *Phil. lib.*, pp. 375–78, quoting Maimonides, *Guide*, III, ch. 48. For Cardoso's treatment of the dietary laws in the *Excelencias*, see the discussion *infra*, ch. VIII.

Hebrew a girl up to the age of twelve is called *na'arah*, afterwards *bogeret*, and that the word for "virgin" is *betulah*.[175] No conclusions are drawn from this exercise in philology. But it may very well be an oblique reference to that classic crux in Judaeo-Christian polemic, the Vulgate reading of Isaiah 7: 14 as *ecce virgo concipiet*.

Finally, in rare instances we encounter a passage which is evocative of the very tone of the *Excelencias*. In the midst of a discussion of the Hebrew language, Cardoso pointedly observes that while an independent Jewish kingdom existed Jewish children spoke Hebrew and "imbibed it with their milk." Once carried off into captivity, the Jews necessarily adopted the languages of the nations they served. But even now the first thing they teach their children is the Hebrew verse "Shema Yisrael, Adonay 'elohenu, Adonay 'eḥad!", and it is with these words that Jews also die.[176] Similarly, in his attack on astrology Cardoso seizes the opportunity for a thrust, not only against the belief itself, but against those who have persecuted his people. As one of the many fallacies of astrology he offers the fact that the English, the Germans, and the Jews are all placed by many astrologers under the sign of Aries. "But what," he cries, "have the English and the Jews in common, save the love of the wolves for the lambs?!" And he proceeds to tell of the expulsion of the Jews from England.[177]

These examples could be easily multiplied, but in essence they all lead us to the same basic problem: From whence did Cardoso derive his Jewish information?

---

[175] *Phil. lib.*, p. 565. The discrepancies between the Vulgate and the Hebrew text are the subject of *Excelencias*, Pt. II, ch. 8, to be discussed *infra*, ch. IX.

[176] *Phil. lib.*, p. 649: "Pueri Haebrei dum stetit eorum respublica, & Regnum, Haebraice loquebantur, & cum lacte eam linguam a nutricib. sugebant, at vero in captivitates abducti, perdita libertate, & servituti addicti, linguis gentium quibus serviunt ab initio propter necessitatem imbuuntur, verum tamen est quod prima verba quibus edocentur sunt illa Haebraica *Semach Israel A. eloenu A. Eiad* [*sic*], id est *audi Israel, Dominus Deus noster Deus unus est*, eisdemque ultimis moriuntur omnes Haebrei inviolabili more, vel moribundis proferentibus, vel assistentibus dictantibus."

[177] *Ibid.*, p. 178. Shortly afterwards he attacks Cardan (for whom he generally displays the highest respect) because he places the Jewish Law under the sign of Saturn.

275

It is obvious that the more than twenty years which had elapsed between his arrival in Italy and the completion of the *Philosophia libera* provided ample time for Cardoso to have acquired a fund of Jewish knowledge directly from Jewish books. In this case the question still remains whether he had access to primary Jewish sources in the original Hebrew and Aramaic, or whether he drew his information from Jewish books available in the vernacular languages. We shall return to this question more appropriately when we analyze the *Excelencias*.

In the *Philosophia libera* the problem assumes a different and even more intriguing aspect. For it is obvious, almost from the very beginning of the work, that at least *some* of his Jewish materials are drawn from non-Jewish sources. At times Cardoso himself supplies the reference; at other times we can trace the source ourselves.

Most impressive, initially, is the reliance on Jewish motifs drawn from the writings of the Church Fathers. This is the case, as we have seen, with Cardoso's discussion of the Jewish origins of philosophy. We have also observed several instances in which what would appear to be an *aggadah* drawn directly from Rabbinic literature is actually taken from Patristic writings. Is it possible to determine when Cardoso first came across such information?

I think we may reasonably assume that Cardoso did not spend his time reading the Church Fathers in the Ghetto of Verona in order to glean Jewish data from their works. As a professing Jew he could now go directly to Jewish sources, or consult one of the local rabbis. Indeed much of the Jewish information in the *Philosophia libera*, and certainly in the *Excelencias*, bears witness to his Jewish reeducation since leaving Spain. His deep acquaintance with Patristic literature is obviously the result of his former education in Spain itself.

Nor is it to be argued that in the *Philosophia libera* Cardoso cites Jewish themes from Christian sources merely because he is writing for a gentile public. At no time in the book does he display the least hesitation in recording direct Jewish references, where these are available to him. We must rather conclude that when he presents non-Jewish references for Jewish materials it is because he himself first learned them from Christian sources, most probably while still in Spain.

Jewish Strands: A Backward Glance

In this connection, let us pause to examine some further illustrations.

In Book VI of the *Philosophia libera* an entire chapter is given over to the problem of language. It opens with a general discussion in which Cardoso affirms that, although no language is natural to man, none is preternatural either. While none is native to him, Man has a propensity for all, and can acquire them through industry and labor. Just as he is born unarmed and naked, but acquires weapons and clothes, so he is born deaf and mute, but can acquire all sounds. After reviewing an experiment, reported by the Jesuits, of raising a child in silence, he notes that God taught Adam the Hebrew letters and roots, but that Adam derived from them expressions for all natural things. At this point Cardoso begins a praise of the Hebrew language (*encomia linguae hebreae*) in which several details are relevant to our inquiry. Among the singular qualities of the language, Cardoso stresses that not only nouns but even letters in the Hebrew language have a meaning. *Alef* signifies "doctrine"; *bet,* "house"; *gimel,* "retribution"; *dalet,* "door."[178]

Now certainly the meaning of the Hebrew letters plays an important role in both Rabbinic and Kabbalistic literature. But there is absolutely no reason to suppose that Cardoso first learned of this interpretation from Jewish sources. His Portuguese contemporary Francisco Manoel de Mello is equally aware of it.[179] Furthermore, the *mode* of interpretation had found its way into Christian literature ever since the Church Fathers. With only slightly different etymologies, Eusebius writes that

each letter among the Hebrew has its name from some significant idea, a circumstance which it is not possible to trace among the Greeks; on

---

[178] *Ibid.,* lib. VI, quaest. lxxxvi ("De linguarum diversitate & praestantia"), p. 649: "Tandem illud habet singulare lingua sancta, quod in illa non solum nomina sed etiam littere aliquid peculiare significant, ut Alef doctrinam, Bet domum, Ghimel retributionem, Dalet portam, & sic de ceteris. . . ."

[179] See his posthumously published *Tratado da sciencia Cabala* (Lisbon, 1724), pp. 128–30, with only a slight variation: "Mas os Rabinos com singular erudição das Escrituras Sagradas explicão assim seu Alphabeto . . . & dizem: Aleph sit *via, seu Institutio* . . . Beth, *Domus* . . . Ghimel, *Retributio* . . . Daleth, *Ostium, fores, vel Janua.* . . ." He continues thus through the entire alphabet.

which account especially it is admitted that the letters are not originally Greek. Now the Hebrews have, in all, twenty-two letters, of which the first is *Alph*, which translated into the Greek language would mean "learning"; and the second *Beth*, which is interpreted "of a house"; the third is *Gimel*, which is "fullness"; the fourth *Delth*, which signifies "of tablets." . . .[180]

Further on Cardoso posits that one of the important factors in the perfection of a language is its economy, rather than a superfluous multiplication of synonyms. In this respect, too, Hebrew is superior, for what appear to be synonyms are really quite different words with precise nuances of their own. Thus the various terms for "man" are not at all the same. *'Adam* is "Man" proper; *'ish*, an illustrious man; *'enosh*, a sick man; *geber*, a strong man. Parallel distinctions in the terms for "man," though again with different etymologies, are to be found in Eusebius.[181]

When we turn to another genre, we are faced with equally interesting configurations. For example, in a discussion of Palestine Cardoso introduces a well-known *aggadah* which relates that Adam, Abraham, Isaac, and Jacob, together with their wives, were all buried in Hebron. That is why it is called *Kiryat-'Arba*, the "City of the four." But while the legend is found in several places in Rabbinic literature, it is also recorded in Jerome's Commentary on Genesis, and that may very well be where Cardoso first encountered it.[182]

---

[180] *Praep. Evang.* X, 5 (cf. also XI, 6). Jerome discusses the meaning of the Hebrew letters in several places, and attempts to extract a Christian sense from them. So in his letter to Paula he writes: "Aleph interpretatur 'doctrina,' Beth 'domus,' Gimel 'plenitudo,' Deleth 'tabularum'. . . . Post interpretationem elementorum intelligentiae ordo dicendus est. Prima conexio est 'doctrina domus plenitudo tabularum ista,' quo videlicet doctrina ecclesiae, quae domus Dei est, in librorum repperiatur plenitudine divinorum . . ." ("Ad Paulam", in *Lettres*, ed. and tr. by J. Labourt, II (Paris, 1951), 33). Cf. his even more elaborate comments on the Hebrew alphabetical acrostic in the Book of Lamentations (*In Lamentationes Jeremiae Tractatus*, Migne, *PL*, XXV, 787–92). The acrostic was, of course, retained in the Vulgate itself.

[181] See *Praep. Evang.* XI, 6, distinguishing between *'adam*, *'enosh*, and *'ish*.

[182] *Phil. lib.*, p. 34. Cf. Jerome, *Quaestiones in Genesim*, 23: 2 (Migne, *PL*, XXIII, 1022): "hoc est quatuor, quia ibi Abraham, & Isaac, & Jacob, conditus est;

Jewish Strands: A Backward Glance

That Patristic literature is replete with motifs from the Jewish *aggadah* is a fact too well known to require further demonstration here. But what of other types of Jewish material scattered throughout the *Philosophia libera*, such as citations of Talmudic law, or medieval Jewish philosophy and biblical exegesis?

Here too, if one looks closely, some very revealing references are to be found. It is no accident that, whenever Cardoso cites Maimonides' *Guide for the Perplexed*, he gives the precise reference to book and chapter, and often quotes substantial passages from the text. The *Guide*, of course, was available in Latin translation, and it is clear throughout that Cardoso knew the work intimately. His references to Maimonides' *Mishneh Torah*, however, present a different problem. Only some sections of it had been translated into Latin, and one, by a Jew, into Spanish. We may assume that Cardoso could have read these parts only after leaving Spain. And yet—citations from the *Mishneh Torah* were also to be found in Catholic works available within Spain itself. Indeed, on one occasion Cardoso gives us the source from which he drew his information. Discussing the relative distances covered by the daily movement of the sun and the stars, he cites not only Maimonides' code, but other Jewish writers such as Abraham Zacuto, Ibn Ezra, and Gersonides. But Cardoso has not consulted these works directly. He himself informs us that his source for all these opinions is Augustinus Ricius' *De motu octavae spherae*.[183]

& ipse princeps humani generis Adam. . . ." For the Jewish sources, see *Bereshit Rabb.*, 58: 4; *TB 'Erubin*, 53a; *Sotah*, 13a.

[183] "At vero Albategnus cap. 51 affirmat stellas fixas conficere unum Gradum non centum sed sexaginta sex annis, eandemque sententiam habet Abraham Zacutus ut refert eius discipulus August. Riccius tract. de motu octavae spherae cap. 5 & 43 quem docentem audivit Salmanticae anno 1474 hoc est 223 post Alfonsum, ipseque Riccius citat Rabi Moysem in lib. Misnetora seu iteratae legis, Abenesra in lib. Taanim (sic) seu rationem dixisse fixas annis 70 Gradum unum peragere . . ." (*Phil. lib.*, p. 168). Maimonides' statement is to be found in *Mishneh Torah*, "yesodey ha-Torah," 3: 7.

Ricius was a 15th-century convert to Christianity. The work to which Cardoso refers was first published in 1512 as *De motu octavae spherae, opus mathematica atque philosophia plenum. Ubi tam antiquorum quam iuniorum errores luce clarius demonstrātur, in quo & quam plurima Platonicorum & antiquae magiae (quam Cabalam Hebraei dicunt)*

We are thus led in yet another direction, for quotations from Jewish literature were by no means restricted to Christian theological or even philosophical works. As in the case of Ricius' treatise, such materials can be found scattered throughout the scientific literature of the sixteenth and seventeenth centuries, and indeed sometimes in the most unlikely places. In his chapter on hermaphrodites, Cardoso devotes a paragraph to the status of the *androgynos* in Jewish law, and refers the reader to Gaspard Bauhin's *De hermaphroditorum natura*. This is of itself sufficiently interesting. But, when we turn to the actual work, we find that Bauhin not only discusses Jewish law; he quotes in Latin part of a *baraita* which often appears in printed editions of the Mishnah as Ch. 4 of the tractate *Bikkurim*.[184]

We have already had occasion to note that when Cardoso cites the sixteenth-century Jewish chronicler Gedalya ibn Yahya's *Shalshelet ha-kabbalah* (*Catena cabbalistica*) it is from the writings of Jacques Gaffarel.[185] We cannot be certain whether Cardoso was generally acquainted with Gaffarel's works. However, having cited one, he may well have known others. All contain a plethora of quotations from Rabbinic and Kabbalistic literature.[186]

---

dogmata videre licet intellectu suavissima. A second edition appeared in Paris in 1521. See M. Steinschneider, *Catalogus Librorum Hebraeorum in Bibliotheca Bodleiana*, cols. 2143–45. Ricius himself speaks of studying with Zacuto not only in Salamanca but later in "Carthage" (apparently Tunis, to which Zacuto came after fleeing from Portugal). Ricius' work was known in Spain in the 17th century, being cited by Antonio de León Pinelo in his *Epitome de la biblioteca oriental i occidental, nautica i geografica* (Madrid, 1629).

[184] *Phil. lib.*, p. 466. See Bauhin, *De hermaphroditorum monstrosorumq. partuum natura ex Theologorum, Jureconsultorum Medicorum, Philosophorum, & Rabbinorum sententia* (Oppenheim, 1614), lib. I, cap. xxix ("De Hermaphroditorum apud Judaeos Jure"), pp. 388 ff. The *baraita* is given on p. 392: "Rabbi Meir dixit: Androgynus est creatura per se ipsa ac specialis, neque voluerunt sapientes definire ac statuere, an vir, an mulier judicari deberet. . . ."

[185] See *supra*, n. 13.

[186] For a sketch of Gaffarel's life, concentrating on the largely ineffective condemnation of his *Curiositez inouyés* by the University of Paris, see Thorndike, *Magic and Experimental Science*, VII, 304–9. Among his works, the *Abdita divinae cabalae mysteria* (Paris, 1625) seems to be important, but has been unavailable to me. It was Gaffarel who published the unauthorized first edition of Leone

Jewish Strands: A Backward Glance

Data from medieval Jewish philosophers whose works had not been translated were also available to Cardoso in Christian sources. We recall his mention of Hasdai Crescas' critique of Aristotle, in which he himself remarks that Crescas "is occasionally cited by Count Franciscus Picus Mirandulus."[187] In fact, the latter cites Crescas no less than five times in his *Examen vanitatis doctrinae gentium*, including a separate chapter on Crescas' argument in favor of the vacuum.[188]

Perhaps a uniquely instructive example of Cardoso's use of Jewish material embedded in Christian sources may be seen in his citation of the *aggadah* concerning the 6,000 years' duration of the world. In this instance, it is important to examine the full text of the passage in the *Philosophia libera*. Cardoso writes:

> Some people indeed, with deeper speculation, contemplate the renovation or end of the world; for, since the world was created in six days and God rested on the seventh, so the world will last for six thousand years, and in the seventh thousand there will be rest, and the Sabbath of the earth. So say the Talmudists in the book Sanedrim [*sic*], that is, "Of the Judges," from the tradition of Elijah, that the world will be of six thousand years: two thousand of emptiness, two thousand of law, two thousand of the days of the Messiah. . . . They prove also that the first six parents, Adam, Seth, Enos, Cain, Malalael, Iared, are dead, but the seventh, Enoch, was translated into heaven. Therefore, after six millenia in which there are toil and death, there will be a seventh of immortal life. And just as a thousand years are the same with God as one day, according to the verse in Psalm 79, "a thousand years before Thine eyes are as yesterday which has passed," and just as He rested after six days of the world, so after six thousand years' rest will be the reward of the just and the good.

Modena's *Riti* (Paris, 1637), as well as a catalogue of the Kabbalistic MSS in Pico della Mirandola's library (Paris, 1651). An ample list of his writings may be found in J. A. Fabricius' preface to the Latin translation of the *Curiositez* which I have utilized, entitled *Curiositates inauditae, sive selectae observationes de variis superstitionibus, veterum, orientalium maxime, Judaeorum, Persarum & c.* (Hamburg, 1706).

[187] Cf. *supra*, n. 25.

[188] Giovanni Francesco Pico della Mirandola, *Examen vanitatis doctrinae gentium et veritatis Christianae disciplinae*, lib. VI, cap. 6, fol. 179r: "Quid pro vacuo adversus Aristotelem attulerit Rabi hasdai." See also fols. 95r, 175v, 176v, 184v.

Justin, *Contra gentes*, 7, mentions the same opinion, as do Lactantius, Bk. 2, ch. 2, Augustine, *De civit.*, 20: 7, Genebrardus in his *Chronolog.*, Sixtus Senensis, *Bibliotheca*, Bk. 5, annot. 190; and Lactantius relates that, among the gentiles, Hidaspes, Trismegistus, and the Sybils handed down the same opinion about the duration of the world.[189]

Upon close analysis, this passage betrays several interesting characteristics. To be sure, the *aggadah* itself is found in the tractate *Sanhedrin* of the Talmud, but Cardoso has specified neither folio nor chapter.[190] This already indicates that he has taken it from some secondary source. The first clue as to what that source might be is provided by the references to Patristic literature. In Lactantius and in Augustine we do find the tradition of the six thousand years to be followed by the "Sabbath" of one thousand, but there is no mention of the three periods of two thousand years each.[191] On the other hand, the analogy with Enoch's translation into heaven in the seventh generation is entirely absent in the Talmudic passage. As a matter of fact, in the whole Tannaitic literature and in the two Talmuds Enoch is not even mentioned, while in the Midrash there are attempts to deny his translation altogether.[192] The comparison to Enoch is drawn by Augustine in another passage. In effect, what we have in the *Philosophia libera* is a weaving together of the Talmudic *aggadah* with the Augustinian analogy, but of course without the Christological context of the latter.[193]

---

[189] *Phil. lib.*, p. 131. Psalm 79 should read Psalm 89 (in the Vulgate; Psalm 90 in the Hebrew).

[190] See *TB Sanhedrin*, ch. XI ("Helek"), fol. 97a: תנא דבי אליהו ששת אלפים שנה הוי עלמא שני אלפים תהו שני אלפים תורה שני אלפים ימות המשיח. The "Sabbath" of 1,000 years is not mentioned in this statement, but in that which immediately precedes it.

[191] See Lactantius, *Divinae Institutiones*, VII, 14; Augustine, *De civ. Dei*, XX, 7 (where the tradition is mentioned in the context of an attack on the "carnal" views of the millenarians). The reference to Justin does not seem to be correct. The millenium is dealt with in his *Dialogus cum Tryphone Judaeo*, lxxx, but with no mention of 6,000 years.

[192] See especially *Ber. Rabb.*, 25: 1.

[193] See Augustine, *De civ. Dei*, XV, 19 ("De significatione quae in Enoch translatione monstratur").

It is a combination which Cardoso did not create himself. The tradition recorded in *Sanhedrin* was sufficiently diffused in later Christian sources, and Cardoso has indicated two, at least, with which he was familiar.

His reference to the *Chronographia* of the sixteenth-century French Hebraist Gilbert Genébrard already supplies us with an ample source.[194] On the very first page of this work, while surveying different schemes for the periodization of world history, Genébrard points out that the tradition of six thousand years' duration is found in the Talmudic tractate *Sanhedrin*, and even gives the title of the chapter. He then goes on to present the analogy with Enoch.[195] The only element missing in the *Chronographia*, namely, the actual quotation of the Talmudic text, is supplied in the other sixteenth-century work to which Cardoso has referred, the *Bibliotheca sancta*, by the Italian Jewish convert Sixtus Senensis.[196] Indeed, Sixtus quotes the passage not only in Latin, but in the original as well, and even adds a transliteration![197]

---

[194] The work appeared in 1580 and 1585. I have used the third, augmented edition, *Gilb. Genebrardi Theologi Parisiensis Divinarum Hebraicarumque literarum professoris regii, Chronographiae libri quatuor . . . subiuncti sunt libri Hebraeorum Chronologici eodem interprete Genebrardo* (Paris, 1600).

[195] *Chronographia*, p. 1: "Mundum sex mille annis duraturum non est Elie Tesbitis Prophete vaticinatio, sed cuiusdam Eliae Rabbini Iudaeorum Cabbalici commentum, in Talmud, *tractatu Sanedrin, cap. Helec. . . .*" On p. 2 he writes: "Deus sex diebus absoluit mundum, septimo quieuit, ac sabbatum consecrauit. Iam mille anni sunt apud Deum sicut dies hesterna quae praeteriit. Postremo sex primi parentes . . . mortui sunt. Septimus Enoc vivus in coelum translatus est. Post igitur millenarios sex, quibus labor & mors viguerit, septimus initium erit quietae & immortalis vitae."

[196] Sixtus Senensis (1520–69) was deeply involved in conversionist and anti-Talmudic activity. He was largely responsible for the burning of the Talmud in Cremona in 1559, though he claims to have saved the Zohar from the flames. See, on him, Graetz, *Geschichte*, IX, 343–45. The *Bibliotheca* was first published in Venice in 1566. I have used the third edition, *Bibliotheca sancta a F. Sixto Senensi, Ordinis Praedicatorum, ex praecipuis Catholicae Ecclesiae authoribus collecta, et in octo libros digesta . . .* (Cologne, 1586). For the Cremona book-burning see *ibid.*, p. 313; for the rescue of the Zohar, p. 315.

[197] *Bibliotheca sancta*, lib. V annot. cxc, p. 400: "Apud Hebraeos vero antiquissima Heliae prophetae traditio habetur in Thalmudicis voluminibus, ordine

Nor do Cardoso's explicit references exhaust the possibilities. The text from *Sanhedrin* is quoted in other Christian works of the sixteenth and seventeenth centuries. And lest we entertain any doubts as to the currency of such an *aggadah* in books available in the Iberian Peninsula, we have only to contemplate its appearance in a "conversionist" work aimed at the New Christians, written in Portuguese, and published in Lisbon in 1621: the *Diálogo entre discípulo e mestre catechizante* of João Baptista d'Este.[198]

What we have learned thus far brings our initial question into even sharper focus. Having sampled some concrete instances in which Cardoso draws his Jewish information from Christian sources, we must again ask why, after having lived as a Jew in Verona for so many years, he should do so at all. Why cite the *Mishneh Torah* from an astronomical work by a Jewish apostate? Why introduce Hasdai Crescas through Pico della Mirandola, Gedalyah ibn Yahya through Gaffarel, a Talmudic passage through Genébrard or Sixtus Senensis?

I believe only one answer can be adequate. When Cardoso records Jewish data from Christian sources, it is primarily because this is how he first became aware of such data. Happily for us, in writing the *Philosophia libera* he did not bother to check every Jewish item for its authentic source with the Veronese scholars and rabbis. He was content, as in the examples we have reviewed, to cite the sources which he had known before coming to live among Jews. In short,

---

quarto, tractatu 4, cui titulus est SANEDRIN, hoc est, Iudicium, in haec verba: [there follows the original quotation in Hebrew characters, but the lines have been confused in the type-setting. Then:] *scitta alphe sene leheue alma, vechad chareb, be alaphim tohu, be alaphim tora, be alaphim iemot Hamasciach,* hoc est, Sex millia annorum erit mundus, & iterum destruetur: duo millia inanitatis, duo millia legis, duo millia dierum Messiae." The same passage is also quoted on p. 65.

[198] Fol. 164r: "No tratado dos Sanhedrin cap. Chelec, diz assi: Sentença da casa de Elias. Seis mil annos permanecera o mundo, & mil estara posto em ruina, dous mil estar vazio, ou sem ley, & dous mil com ley, & dous mil annos seraõ os dias do Messias." On the book and its author see *infra*, ch. IX, n.4. It is to be noted that the *aggadah* also appears in Gaffarel's *Curiositez* (p. 44 in the Latin ed. of 1706), and in one of the Iberian anti-Jewish works which Cardoso cites elsewhere, Jaime Pérez de Valencia's *Tractatus contra Iudaeos* (Valencia, 1484), unpaginated, quaest. 2.

these are the shards of his Marrano experience in Spain, and with a keen and vigilant eye we can still find them strewn about on the surface of the *Philosophia*. A thorough archaeology, alas, is beyond our reach. It would require that we should have read all that Cardoso read while still in Spain. Were it possible to do so, I have no doubt that we would find a fund of Jewish information quite beyond our expectations.

As it is, though we are unable to recapture Cardoso's entire "library" prior to his flight from the Peninsula, we can proceed somewhat farther than we have done. We can peruse some of the Christian works to which Cardoso directly refers and, not contenting ourselves with his actual citations, we can see what else they contain.

Genébrard's *Chronographia*, for example, includes a host of the most varied kinds of Jewish information. Beyond the biblical period, there is a good deal on the transmission of the Oral Law among the rabbis of the Mishna and the Talmud.[199] Occasionally Genébrard pauses to explain a Jewish custom.[200] An entire page is devoted to the Kabbalah.[201] Above all, there are numerous references to events in medieval Jewish history. [202] These are usually quite succinct, in common with the general style of the work, but they are drawn directly from authentic Jewish sources, and they are presented in a straightforward manner. For his notes on the intellectual history of medieval Jewry Genébrard's most frequent source is the *Sefer ha-kabbalah* of Abraham ibn Daud, while for the history of persecutions he relies on Joseph ha-Kohen's *Dibre ha-yamim le-malke Ṣarfat u-malke bet Ottoman ha-Togar*.[203] The interest evinced in Jewish

---

[199] E. g., *Chronographia*, p. 229. Cf. the Index, *s.v.* "Talmud."

[200] *Ibid.*, p. 221, on the construction of an *'erub* for the Sabbath.

[201] *Ibid.*, p. 317. Genébrard is hostile to it. For a partial change in his attitude, see Francois Secret, *Le Ẓôhar chez les kabbalistes chrétiens de la Renaissance* (Paris, 1964), pp. 88-91.

[202] In general, see the Index *s.v.* "Iudaei," "Iudaeorum," etc., but even here the listings are incomplete.

[203] E. g., p. 567: "R. Abraham in Cabbala" (on the Geonim Hai and Sherira); p. 590: "R. Ioseph Sacerd. in Chro. regum Franciae & Turciae" (on the Crusader massacres).

literary history is certainly not what one would expect from a chronicle of the history of the world. We can only try to imagine what it could have meant to an active Judaizer in Spain, eager for any scrap of Jewish information, to be able to read an account, however brief, of the flowering of Hebrew poetry among his fore-bears. And if, in another passage, he found a note on "Iudaeorum fabulae & mendacia contra Christum," surely that was not unwelcome either.[204]

Was the *Chronographia* available and known in the Iberian Peninsula? A glance at the Spanish editions of the Index of Prohibited Books may prove helpful in this as in other instances.

Although the French editions of the *Chronographia* carried the approbation of the Theological Faculty of the University of Paris, the work is already listed in the Index published in Madrid in 1583 by the Inquisitor-General Gaspar de Quiroga. However, it was by no means to be prohibited absolutely; only certain passages were to be purged.[205] What those objectionable passages might be is seen in the supplementary *Index expurgatorum* which Quiroga published the following year. Though two appendices (which will be discussed later) were expunged, only the mention of Ulrich von Hutten was to be eliminated from the text of the *Chronographia* proper. Significantly, none of the Jewish information in the book was touched.[206] Two other minor expurgations from the text were ordered in the *Index* edited in 1612 by Bernardo de Sandoval y Rojas, and again, neither of these concerned the Jewish materials.[207] Nothing more was added

---

[204] On Hebrew poetry in Spain, see *Chronographia*, p. 573; for the "Jewish fables and lies against Christ," see p. 203 (with references to the Talmudic tractates).

[205] *Index et catalogus librorum prohibitorum, mandato Illustriss. ac Reverendiss. D.D. Gasparis a Quiroga, Cardinalis Archiepiscopi Toletani, ac in regnis Hispaniarum Generalis Inquisitoris, denuo editus, Cum Consilio Supremi Senatus Sanctae Generalis Inquisitionis* (Madrid, 1583), fol. 19v: "Chronographia Genebrardi, nisi repurgetur."

[206] *Index librorum expurgatorum ... D.D. Gasparis Quiroga ...* (Madrid, 1584), fol. 120v: "Ex Genebrardi Chronographia: Pag. 406 ubi nomerantur Theologi catholici, expurgetur nomen Huldrichi Hutteni, equitis Germani."

[207] *Index librorum prohibitorum et expurgatorum Ill^{mi}. ac R^{mi}. D.D. Bernardi de*

by the time the Madrid *Index* of 1640 appeared, some eight years before Cardoso's departure from Spain.[208] In sum, Genébrard's *Chronographia* could be read virtually intact, and indeed the work is cited by Spanish writers of unimpeachable orthodoxy in the seventeenth century.[209]

Jewish information is scattered also through the pages of the *Bibliotheca* of Sixtus Senensis, a work which never even appeared on the *Index*. Here, certainly, the animus of the apostate against his former faith, and especially against the Talmud, is very apparent. Nevertheless, the Jewish materials are there. The work contains a discussion of "true" and "false" Kabbalah, an entire section devoted to a description of Talmudic literature, and a catalogue of Rabbinic writers.[210]

In order better to appreciate the significance of such works for Spanish Marranos, some remarks of Orobio de Castro are relevant.

Sandoval et Roxas . . . Archiepisc. Toletani Hispaniarum Primatis . . . Generalis Inquisitoris . . . auctoritate et iussu editus (Madrid, 1612), p. 364, referring to the edition of the *Chronographia* published in Lyon, 1609.

[208] I have used the edition of 1667 which is an exact reprint of that of Madrid, 1640: *Index librorum prohibitorum et expurgandorum novissimus, pro Catholicis Hispaniarum Regnis Philippi IV, Regis Cathol., Ill. ac R. D.D. Antonii a Sotomaior . . .* (Madrid, 1667), p. 461. (Though bearing "Matriti" as its place of publication, this reprint may have been made outside the Peninsula. See F. H. Reusch, *Der Index der Verbotenen Bücher* [Bonn, 1883–86], II, p. 50). In the Portuguese Index of 1624 we have substantially the same minor expurgations. See *Index auctorum damnatae memoriae . . . editus auctoritate Illmi. Domini D. Ferdinandi Martins Mascaregnas, Algarborum Episcopi. . . ac Regnorum Lusitaniae Inquisitoris Generalis* (Lisbon, 1624), pp. 125 and 624.

[209] E. g., Fray Benito de Peñalosa y Mondragón, *Las cinco excelencias del español* (Pamplona, 1629), p. 25. On the book, see *infra*, ch. VIII.

[210] On the Kabbalah see *Bibliotheca*, p. 90, and Index *s.v.* For the Talmud see pp. 122 ff. (*s.v.* "Traditiones"); pp. 126–28 ("Catalogus voluminum totius Thalmud"), listing and describing each Talmudic tractate; pp. 128–30 ("Index errorum aliquot, quos ex innumeris stultitijs, blasphemijs, & impietatibus Thalmudici operis collegimus"), beginning with "Adversus Christum Deum nostrum." It was apparently the wide currency of Sixtus' work in the 17th century which prompted Saul Levi Morteira to write a *Repuesta a las objeciones con que el Sinense injustamente calumnia al Talmud* (1646), available in several MSS. See Kayserling, *BEPJ*, p. 75.

Philosopher in the Ghetto

In his *Carta apologética*, addressed to Juan de Prado, Orobio observes:

> In Spain I read with deep attention the *Fortalitium fidei*, an old and very erudite book against Judaism and Mohammedanism . . . then, *el Burgense*[211] . . . as well as the *Bibliotheca* of Sixtus Senensis with its invective against the Talmud, and many others of this type, both printed and in manuscripts, which we call *reconditae eruditionis*, and it would be too much trouble to refer to them all. This has always been my concern, this the greates anxiety of my deliberations, not in order to investigate what faith may be, or in what it may consist, for this was not (or did not appear to me) necessary, but rather whether this or that dogma of the Christian was believable, whether his doctrines were credible. . . .[212]

Orobio thus informs us that in Spain he had read the books of Alonso de Espina, Paul of Burgos, Sixtus Senesis, as well as other anti-Jewish and Christian theological books, "in order to know how the others believe, and to know how I must believe" (para saber como creyan los otros y saber como yo havia de creer). This was, of course, hardly the intention of the authors themselves. It is essentially a highly selective and specialized reading of the anti-Jewish literature, in which the Christian assault is not taken for granted, but rather in which the very doctrines attacked are pitted against the attacker in an effort to weigh the truth of each.

We must bear in mind that Orobio's remarks are not intended to give an account of his Jewish *knowledge* in Spain, but occur almost parenthetically in an attempt to convince Juan de Prado that the real issue is not faith per se, but the claims to truth of particular revealed religions. We should remember, too, that there were some significant differences in the careers of Cardoso and Orobio. The latter fled abroad after his imprisonment by the Inquisition. Cardoso was never prosecuted. Before his departure he was secretly proselytizing for the "Law of Moses." It is quite possible that at some time Cardoso too wavered between Christianity and Judaism and read the anti-Jewish literature in the manner which Orobio has described.

---

[211] I. e., the *Scrutinium scripturarum* of Pablo de Santa Maria (Solomon ha-Levi), the 15th-century convert who became bishop of Burgos.

[212] For the Spanish text see Révah, *Spinoza et Juan de Prado*, p. 132.

But given that at some point this particular problem had been solved, that a firm choice had been made in favor of Judaism, could not this same literature (and other genres as well) yield something further, with only a slight additional focus on the part of the reader? Committed in his heart to Judaism, could not a Marrano now also find, in these very works, some substantive information about the doctrines and practices of Judaism itself?

Of course he could—if he so desired. And in books circulating in Spain and Portugal. We have already examined some particular instances in detail, and may now summarize more broadly the different genres in which Jewish information was available. Restricting ourselves to those which are represented in works actually cited by Cardoso, we have: a) the Jewish literature of the Hellenistic period, notably the Apocrypha, Philo, and Josephus; b) the *Targum* (available in both Aramaic and Latin in the Complutensian and Regian polyglot Bibles); c) Patristic literature; d) the ramified anti-Jewish literature; e) the works of Catholic Hebraists, notably, but not exclusively, the Spanish; f) various general works of the sixteenth and seventeenth centuries on history, theology, philosophy, and science, which, though not primarily concerned with Judaism, contain remarks on Jews and Jewish rituals as well as quotations from Rabbinic and medieval Jewish literature.

Ironically, we can enhance our understanding of the potential for Marranism in two of these genres, by turning again to the Spanish Indices.

All the editions of the *Index* in Spain to which we have referred are, of course, unanimous in prohibiting the Talmud, its commentaries, and any other Rabbinic works considered inimical to Christianity. However, they also agree in exempting the *Targum* from this prohibition.[213] But this is not all. In the Madrid edition of the *Index* in 1640, the exemption is coupled with an added proviso that "at the beginning of it there be placed, as an antidote, that which is noted in the *Expurgatorio* of this Index under the word

---

213 "Y no por esto se entiende ser prohibido el Thargum, que es la Paraphrasis Chaldaica" (*Index*, [1583], fol. 2v). Cf. ed. of 1612, p. 2; ed. of 1640 (1667), p. xii.

Thargum. . . ."[214] Turning to that rubric we find the text of the proposed preface, as follows:

We warn the orthodox reader [of] a fact which has been noted by many pious and learned men, that the *Thargum* . . . which is circulated into almost all the books of the Old Testament and which, it is certain, arose from various Jewish and not Christian authors, is corrupt and depraved, and in most cases is sprinkled with Jewish fables and nonsense of the Talmudists, contains praises and eulogies of the treacherous people of the Jews, twists not a few testimonies of Sacred Scripture from the true and Catholic sense, sometimes even mixes in perverse dogmas, and sometimes disagrees with the true and genuine reading and interpretation which the Church approves. Therefore it should neither be considered of such great importance, nor from its authority should a sufficiently firm argument be derived, but it ought to be read everywhere cautiously and with judgment.[215]

There can be little doubt that such an "admonition" would be regarded by a Marrano intellectual almost as an *invitation* to study the *Targum*, indeed, "cautiously and with judgment!" We have here another illustration of that paradoxical Spanish tendency to keep Jewish elements alive through the very process of combating them.

That the anti-Jewish polemical literature might similarly subvert its own purposes is something of which the Indices, at least, do show some awareness. All the various editions contain a general rule which prohibits the reading of books of "controversy" or "disputation" with heretics which are written in the vernacular (*en lengua vulgar*), except by pious and learned men (*hombres píos y doctos*), presumably clerics, who must obtain for this a special written license from the Inquisitors.[216] Apparently books in Latin, being innaccessible to most, were considered less dangerous. Yet the fact remains that polemics in the vernacular continued to be published in Spain and Portugal, and that they bore the approbations of the Holy Office.

---

[214] *Index* (1640), p. xii.

[215] *Ibid.*, p. 945.

[216] *Index* (1583), fol. 3v; ed. of 1612, p. 4; ed. of Lisbon, 1624, p. 82; ed. of Madrid, 1640, p. ix.

However it may have been justified, this was one rule in the *Index* which was observed most often in the breach.

I have thus far deliberately postponed the most difficult and tantalizing question of all—the possibility of a direct confrontation in Spain, not merely with Jewish fragments embedded in Christian works, nor with the *Targum*, but with any of the integral Jewish texts which had been translated into Latin by the seventeenth century. Even if, a priori, we were to rule out those translations which were the work of Protestant Hebraists, the number extant in Cardoso's time was still considerable. Unfortunately, so far as I know, the availability of such Latin translations in the Peninsula has never been seriously investigated. Within the limited scope of this study and of the materials available to us we cannot hope to find a definitive solution to the problem. However, certain considerations move us to propose that, in this regard as in others, the situation in Spain was far more complex than is generally conceded. We must reckon with the possibility that at least some Latin versions of authentic post-biblical Jewish texts were accessible to those who wished to consult them.

We may well begin, as a case in point, with the aforementioned work of Genébrard. The various French editions of the *Chronographia* contain at the end a separate series of his Latin translations of Jewish texts. These include: the *Seder 'olam rabba* and *Seder 'olam zuta* ("Chronologia Hebraeorum maior . . . et minor"); Ibn Daud's *Sefer ha-kabbalah* (Historica cabbala . . . Rabbi Abraham Levitae Davidis filii") up to the Geonic Period; Eldad ha-Dani's account of the Lost Tribes ("Eldad Danius Hebraeus historicus de Iudaeis clausis"); Chapters 11–12 of "*hilkhot melakhim*" from Maimonides' *Mishneh Torah*, dealing with the Messianic era; the discussions of the advent of the Messiah in *Sanhedrin*, fol. 97a-b; Maimonides' analysis of the thirteen principles of the faith in his Commentary to the Mishnah; various prayers from the liturgy of the Roman *Maḥzor;* and Maimonides' enumeration of the 613 commandments.[217]

The *Chronographia* itself was, as we saw above, only lightly censored,

---

[217] In the *Chronographia* (Paris, 1600), these texts are placed at the end with a separate pagination and frontispiece.

and none of its Jewish materials were thereby affected. What was the fate in Spain of the "appendices"?

Already in the Madrid *Index* of 1584 we find a demand for the total elimination of two of the appended texts: the chapters on the Messianic Kingdom from the *Mishneh Torah*, and the report of Eldad ha-Dani.[218] Eight years later we encounter, in an inquisitorial document, an interesting judgment by Fray Hernando de Castillo on the *Cronologia de los hebreos del libro de Gilber* [*sic*] *Genebrardo*. "It is," he writes, "a dangerous book, so that the *confesos* in whom the blood [of their Jewish ancestors] still churns, may know new prayers, rites, etc. taken from the Talmud. . . ."[219]

We could ask for no keener assessment. But although, given such an awareness, we might have expected all the appended Jewish works to be expunged forthwith, the Indices reveal that this was accomplished neither immediately nor thoroughly. To the provisions of the *Index* of 1584, that of 1612 adds only a call for the expurgation of a marginal note from the *Seder 'olam rabba*.[220] Only in later editions is there finally a supression of all the texts.[221]

In essence, however, the Indices are really more useful in determining the availability of certain works than their unavailability. Even in Spain, and despite the Inquisition, the mere listing of a book as forbidden by the *Index* was far from an absolute guarantee that it would not be read. The inquisitorial archives themselves contain numerous documents of cases in which prohibited books were found in private libraries confiscated from owners who had been arrested for other causes, or simply in libraries about to be sold after their

---

[218] *Index* (1584), fol. 120v.

[219] A. Paz y Mélia, *Papeles de Inquisición: Catálogo y extractos*, ed. Ramón Paz (Madrid, 1947), p. 419, no. 1.256, dated Valladolid, October 15, 1592.

[220] *Index* (1612), p. 364: "Ex eiusdem Gilberti Genebrardi, Chronologia Hebraiorum maiore quae *seder olam Rabba* inscribitur (Lugduni . . . 1608) . . . dele notum marginalem, *Mendose in nostra*, & c." The note in question reads: "Mendose in nostra editione bibliorum Latina annis."

[221] *Index* (1640), p. 461: "Quia vero in fine eiusdem Chronographiae, habentur nonnulla Opuscula Iudaica, quae Genebrardus Latinitati donavit, & fere ad nullum usum fidelium, videntur quoque expungenda . . ." (there follows a list of the Jewish texts). Cf. also *Index*, ed. of Lisbon, 1624, p. 624.

owners had died.[222] Rodrigo Méndez Silva, for example, was found to have possessed a manuscript copy of the *Tizón de la nobleza española* as well as other forbidden works.[223] Among the 2,424 books left by the deceased D. José Antonio de Salas, a knight of the Order of Calatrava, the Madrid Inquisition in 1651 discovered no less than 250 prohibited works when it inspected the library prior to its sale.[224] Surely it is possible that some complete and unexpurgated copies of Genébrard found their way into private hands, the *Index* and the inquisitors notwithstanding.

Nor should it be assumed that those who might have most reason to fear the Inquisition necessarily shunned any contact with prohibited books or works of suspect authors. An interesting sidelight is provided in the case of Cardoso himself. The works of Amatus Lusitanus, the great Portuguese Marrano physician of the sixteenth century, were heavily censored in the various editions of the *Index*.[225] The author was known throughout Europe as one who had openly reverted to Judaism after leaving the Peninsula. His *Centuria* contained a physician's oath of a definitely Jewish character, its fifth book was dedicated to Don Joseph Nasi, the powerful ex-Marrano at the Turkish court, and in fact these were among the Jewish materials ordered expunged by the *Index*. But since the work *as a whole* was not prohibited, Cardoso had no hesitation in citing the *Centuria* while still in Spain, in his *De febre syncopali* of 1639. In the same book Cardoso also cited Maimonides' *Aphorisms*.[226] Both works, of course, were of a medical nature, and therefore innocuous in themselves. Their provenance, however, might have inspired greater caution in a Marrano. I suspect that their open citation by Cardoso is to be seen as resulting from his relative sense of security during the ministry of Olivares. Thus even fear of the Inquisition seems to have varied in different periods.

---

[222] For such cases in the 17th century see Paz y Mélia, *Papeles*, pp. 463–65.

[223] In the list of property confiscated from Méndez Silva after his arrest in 1659, cited by Caro, *Judíos*, II, 100.

[224] Paz y Mélia, *Papeles*, p. 463, no. 1.455.

[225] See, e. g., the *Index* (1640), pp. 43–45.

[226] For Amatus see *De febre syncopali*, fol. 31r; for Maimonides, *ibid.*, fol. 24r.

At any rate, we obviously face a much graver problem than that of Maimonides' *Aphorisms* when we inquire whether Cardoso could have had access in Spain to Maimonides' *Guide for the Perplexed.*

At the outset, such a possibility seems almost inconceivable. We are accustomed to think of seventeenth-century Spain as completely quarantined, by the diabolical efficiency of the Inquisition, from contact with anything that possessed the faintest Jewish echo, let alone such a work as the *Guide.* But just as we may sometimes overestimate the totalitarian successes of the Inquisition, we tend, perhaps even more often, to ignore its complexities. On the question of the *Guide* in Spain, albeit in Latin translation, we must again have recourse to the *Index.*

As we have observed, all editions of the Spanish *Index* absolutely prohibit the Talmud and Rabbinic literature generally. The *Index* of 1612 also adds Kabbalistic works (*los Cabalísticos, i los otros impíos i nefarios libros de los Hebreos*).[227] Exemption is made for the *Targum.* In addition, "learned and pious men" may apply to the inquisitors for permission to consult Rabbinic commentaries on the Bible (though not on the Talmud).[228] However, in the Madrid *Index* of 1640 we find, for the first time, a further clause which we would hardly expect. As with the aforementioned exemptions from the ban on Rabbinic literature, so also the following works are not forbidden: those which are "merely historical or grammatical," such as Masoretic works of the type published by Johann Buxtorf; the biblical concordances of Mordecai Nathan, "and other similar works of philosophy, dialectics, or grammar, which Sebastian Munster has translated from Elias Levita, Rabbi David Kimhi,

---

[227] *Index* (1612), p. 2. Curiously, there is no mention of Kabbalistic works in the corresponding rule of the *Index* of 1640.

[228] *Index* (1583), fol. 2v: "Pero bien se podran permitir a hombres doctos, assi estos, como algunos Rabbinos, q. escriven sobre la divina Escriptura, aviendo para ello expressa licêcia in scriptis de los Inquisidores." Cf. *Index* (1612), p. 2; *Ibid.* (1640), p. xii. In the Lisbon *Index* of 1624 we have a somewhat different text in the "regras geraes" (no. 1, p. 81). In accordance with the Roman *Index* it specifically prohibits *Commentaria Rabbi Salomonis* (i.e., Rashi), *Chimi* (i.e., David Kimhi), and others, whether in Hebrew or Latin. The writings of no Rabbi can can be kept, "sem licença in scriptis."

and others"; the *Book of the Roots* of Rabbi David; and the "*Ductor* or *Doctor Dubitantium* of Rabbi Moses the Egyptian, and other similar works which treat neither of religion, nor of the Jewish sect, nor of its ceremonies."[229]

Though we might have thought that such a singular provision was merely copied mechanically from some Roman *Index*, this was not the case. The clause was really indigenous to Spain. In general, it should be noted, the Spanish Indices exhibit a suprising independence from the Roman editions, in both their inclusions and their omissions. Only the Spanish *Index*, and not the Roman, was authoritative for Spain and its territories. Besides, according to Spanish law the decrees of the Holy Office in Rome, and the Roman Congregation of the Index, were subject to review by the Spanish Inquisition. Even when the latter accepted them, the decrees were promulgated in its own name.[230]

It does not matter that this provision does not seem to accord with some actual prohibitions listed in the very *Index* in which it is

---

[229] *Index* (1640), p. xii: "Como no tampoco se entiende estar prohibidos los libros de los Rabinos que meramente son Historiales, o Gramaticales, como son los Masoretas, y la *Masora magna y Parva*, con algunas otras Anotaciones de Rabinos, que hizo imprimir y publicar Ioan Buxtorfio; las Concordancias Hebraicas de Rabbi Mardocai Nathan, y otros semejantes de Philosophia, Dialectica, o Grammatica, que traduxo en Latin Sebastiano Munstero, de Elias Levita, Rabbi Salomon, R. David Kimhi, y otros; El libro de las Raizes de R. David; el *Ductor* o *Doctor Dubitantium*, de R. Moyses Aegyptio, y otros semejantes, que no tratan de Religion, ni de la secta Iudayca, ni de sus Ceremonias."

Mordecai Nathan (Isaac b. Kalonymos Nathan) is the author of the biblical concordance *Me'ir netib*, which was published several times in Latin, and served as the basis of Buxtorf's Concordance of 1632. The "Libro de las Raizes" is Kimhi's *Sefer ha-shorashim*. The title by which the *Index* here refers to the Latin version of Maimonides' *Guide* is essentially a conflation of that published in Paris in 1520 and Buxtorf's translation of 1629. Cf. *supra*, n. 15.

[230] The clause exempting the *Guide* is not to be found in any of the 16th- and 17th-century Roman Indices which I have consulted, nor in any of those analyzed by Reusch, though he is aware of its presence in the 1640 Madrid edition (see *Der Index*, I, 53). The only exemption which the Spanish Indices appropriated from the Roman is, oddly enough, the Hebrew *Maḥzor*, forbidding only vernacular translations of it. On the general independence of the Spanish Indices see Reusch, *Der Index*, I, 2; II, 21, 55.

found. For example, if "historical" works were to be allowed, why should Genébrard's translation of Ibn Daud have been expunged? The fact is that inconsistencies in censorship were ever present. They in no way alter the central datum, that in a Spanish *Index* published in Madrid while Cardoso still lived in the city, it is explicitly stated that the Latin translation of the *Guide* is a permitted book. Nor is the contradiction as blatant as may appear at first glance. The rationalization offered is apparently to be interpreted as meaning that the *Guide* belongs in the category of general religious philosophy or biblical exegesis.[231] Whatever the merits of such a rationale, we still have to reckon with the permission of the book itself. Farther than this we cannot proceed. We have, at present, no way of knowing to what degree practice corresponded to theory, whether the book actually circulated, and if so, among whom it was to be found. But at least we must henceforth seriously entertain the *possibility* that Cardoso read the *Guide* in Spain. This must, for the moment, suffice us.

Our basic contention, however, remains, Even without Maimonides' *Guide* or any other integral Jewish works such as those contained in Genébrard's appendices, we have seen how a seventeenth-century Marrano like Cardoso could, while reading non-Jewish works, and without danger to himself, glean much more Jewish information than might be suspected in a Spain devoid of open Jewish life since 1492. As such, it was a kind of study of Judaism by retrieval, a garnering of lost elements from alien and often hostile sources. But then—this method, if such it may be called, would not be so far removed from that employed long ago by some of the Church Fathers in ransacking pagan literature for Jewish references suited to their own purposes. Eusebius is himself a prime example. Indeed, for a man who, like Cardoso, was steeped in Patristic literature, this approach may even have been particularly congenial.

Of course, even such information was not accessible to all. It should be perfectly clear that only the Marrano intellectual, the

---

[231] Part III of the *Guide*, which deals with the significance of the biblical commandments, could also be considered, from a Christian point of view, as "historical." On the other hand, Ibn Daud's *Sefer ha-Kabbalah* is not merely an historical chronicle, but contains some anti-Christian polemic.

university graduate, is being considered and, even among this group, only the highly motivated. The mass of Marranos, those of the lower classes, were hardly equipped to read such books in the first place. Nor can we assume necessarily that Cardoso himself devoted his time to systematic "research" along these lines, though he may well have done so. Generally the information came in the course of wide reading, almost incidentally, but its impact was surely felt by those who were already predisposed to be sensitive to it. We must also be wary of exaggerating the scope and content of the Jewish knowledge thus acquired. By its very nature such knowledge would be fragmentary, an incomplete mosaic of bits and pieces gathered over the years. A Jewish "reeducation" would still be necessary once one fled the Peninsula.

But let the importance of such knowledge not be underestimated either. One thing should be emphasized above all. The common view of the Marranos a century or more after the Expulsion as hermetically sealed off from any but the most vestigial notions of the reality of Judaism is in need of revision. It is a view which tends to generalize about the entire Marrano situation from the all too notorious case of an Uriel da Costa. Carl Gebhardt, with Da Costa in mind, neatly defined the third generation Marrano as "a Catholic without faith, and Jew without knowledge, though a Jew by desire."[232] It is the middle clause which is troublesome. Gebhardt made his meaning plain. He wrote that Da Costa had "a fixed picture of Judaism solely from the Law and the Prophets. The post-biblical religious sources were inaccessible to him because of his unfamiliarity with the Hebrew language. However, the Judaism which he found in Amsterdam was the Judaism formed through a two thousand years' tradition."[233]

It is not clear, however, why a Marrano such as Uriel da Costa, who had studied canon law at the University of Coimbra, had to limit his Jewish knowledge to the Bible once his curiosity about Judaism had been aroused. To be sure, it is easy to conclude from

---

[232] Gebhardt, *Die Schriften des Uriel da Costa*, p. xix: "Der Marrane ist Katholik ohne Glauben, und Jude ohne Wissen, doch Jude im Willen."

[233] *Ibid.*, p. xxvii.

Philosopher in the Ghetto

Da Costa himself that all he encountered in the Judaism of Amsterdam was a complete novelty, and therefore a traumatic shock to him who knew Judaism only from Scripture. But if we closely examine his so-called theses against the Tradition[234] we find ourselves increasingly perplexed. Certainly some of the ritual and legal details, which he uses to demonstrate his contention that the Rabbinic tradition had distorted biblical law, may have come to him only through direct observation of Jewish life after his flight. But was there nothing in Christian works available in Portugal on the very practices which he later impugned? Indeed, was there not a venerable tradition of Christian attack against these very elements of the Oral Law of the Jews, and even utilizing a similar argument? Surely one can find the details of the phylacteries (the substance of Da Costa's first "thesis") in Christian sources.[235] The same is true even of so esoteric a detail as the "Chair of Elijah" used at circumcisions.[236] The criticisms of Jewish tradition by an Uriel da Costa are not those of one who necessarily knew nothing of it before, but rather of one who could not free himself from the Christian view of that tradition. For Da Costa is not content with internal criticisms. At one point he adds the chagrined exclamation: "And with this we give the gentiles occasion to ridicule us" (*e que damos com isto aos gentios de zombarse de nos*).

All of which suggests that the Da Costa case could bear some reexamination. To put it bluntly, why should the erstwhile student

---

[234] "Propostas contra a tradição," *ibid.*, pp. 22–26.

[235] See, for example, the comprehensive description of the phylacteries in Sixtus Senensis, *Bibliotheca*, pp. 92 f.; *s.v.* "Phylacteria Scribarum & Pharisaeorum."

[236] Da Costa (Gebhardt, *Die Schriften*, p. 23): "diz: que se offende a Ley, com preparar hũa cadeira para Eliau, sendo cousa acressentada. . . ." See Sixtus Senensis, *Bibliotheca*, p. 591; "Hunc Iudaei Heliam esse putant: quia ille zelum habuit pro foedere circuncisionis, proindeque semper cum puerum circumcidunt, in omni circuncisione adornant Heliae sellam. . . ." See also Jaime Pérez de Valencia, *Tractatus contra Iudaeos*, quaest. 5: "unde quando circuncidunt pueros in synagoga, praeparant duas sedes, unam pro helya quem credunt venire et ibi adesse in circuncisione, et alteram sedem praeparant pro rabino qui exercet actum circuncisionis."

of canon law have been so shocked to find that the Judaism of Amsterdam was not quite that of Moses, when he was quite aware that the Catholicism of Coimbra was hardly the Christianity of Jesus? On the other hand, if his rejection of Catholicism itself had been even partly due to a realization that it was not New Testament Christianity, then his "biblical" stance vis-à-vis Judaism was essentially a consequence of a mentality which he had developed while still in Portugal. The attitude with which he came, rather than his alleged ignorance, would thus prove to have been far more the decisive factor.[237]

Be that as it may, for us Da Costa is important only insofar as he has been presented as something of an archetypal Marrano. Certainly Cardoso's remarkable adjustment to normative Jewish life would be almost inexplicable if he had come to Italy a postbiblical *tabula rasa.* As we indicated in our introductory chapter we really have, at present, no way of knowing which type predominated, nor how many other variations were present. Cardoso may well have been an exception to the rule, and he even shows marked differences from his brother Miguel. More intensive investigation of individual Marrano figures may eventually pave the way toward a synthesis. The task, as may be readily seen, is fraught with difficulties. At no time did Cardoso himself set down a forthright account of his Jewish knowledge in Spain. When he was living as a Marrano he could not do so. Once he was living as a Jew it may have seemed pointless. As a result, we have had to attempt a reconstruction out of hints which he only inadvertently left behind.

---

[237] I now find my intuition concerning Da Costa partly confirmed in an important article by I. S. Révah which had hitherto escaped my attention ("La religion d'Uriel da Costa, Marrane de Porto," *Revue de l'histoire des religions,* CLXI (1962), 45–76). He too has concluded that Da Costa's notion of Judaism while still in Portugal was not limited to Scripture. However, while I have raised the question of the knowledge which Da Costa could have derived from books, Professor Révah has approached the problem from a different angle. As a result of his researches in the Portuguese inquisitorial archives concerning various members of Da Costa's maternal family, he is able to show that the Marranism which the latter knew in Porto contained a number of postbiblical Jewish practices. See especially the summary of these rites, *ibid.,* p. 74.

Philosopher in the Ghetto

Cardoso published the *Philosophia libera* as a Jew and, for all that the public was meant to know, as one who had lived all his life as a Jew. The novelty in this respect must finally be appreciated. Viewed in perspective, the book marks a certain milestone. With the exception of the works of Elijah del Medigo at the end of the fifteenth century, consisting mainly of translations and commentaries, and the *Dialoghi d'amore* of Leone Ebreo, which appeared posthumously in 1535, the *Philosophia libera* is the first major work in general philosophy to be written and published by a professing Jew in a secular language, and intended from the outset to reach a wide European audience.[238] Quite apart from its merits, the very appearance of this book must have had an impact on both Jews and Christians, if only as a phenomenon.[239] That its author grandly claimed his share as an equal in the common intellectual tradition, while by choice he was living the restricted life of a ghetto Jew with all its disabilities, was an incongruity which could not have escaped his contemporaries.

Cardoso, however, could not have paid much attention to such apparent paradoxes. Considered subjectively, his life must have seemed to show in retrospect a consistent, almost providential pattern. By coming to Italy he had at last unified his inner and his outer existence. At the same time that he was broadening his knowledge of Judaism, he had also harvested the fruits of all his speculations in the wisdom of the gentiles. From his former life he had salvaged everything that was of value to him. Now, having set his spiritual house in order, he could look forward tranquilly to the sunset of his years.

And yet he was not to enjoy the full measure of peace which he had earned. Just in the period when the *Philosophia libera* was nearing its

---

[238] I am, of course, discounting Spinoza, whose work on Descartes appeared in 1663, some seven years after his excommunication.

[239] For citations of the *Philosophia libera* by Christians, see the Epilogue, *infra*. A copy of the book in the Biblioteca Comunale of Verona contains an inscription in Cardoso's hand, apparently to a fellow physician who is not named: "Comiti Illustrissimo, Medico excellentissimo, Philosopho doctissimo, Auctor Donat Ex Animo." I have thought it fitting to apply one of the dedicatory phrases to the author himself; hence the title of the first section of this chapter.

completion, the Jewish world was being shaken by events which could not but affect Cardoso as well, especially when his brother became one of the leading protagonists. From the point which we have reached we must now retrace our steps a few years in time, and direct our attention to this central episode.

ABRAHAM, ISAAC, AND THE MESSIAH

Tañe con *sophar* grande para nuestra al-
forria, y alça pendón para apañar nuestros
captiverios, y apáñanos a una ayna de
quatro partes de toda la tierra a nuestra
tierra. Bendito tú A[donay] apañan der-
ramados de su pueblo Ysrael.

—Orden de oraciones

Ya viene *mashiaḥ*
de los altos cielos,
shofar d'oro en mano
lo viene tañendo. . . .
—From an old Ladino folksong
(M. Attias, *Romancero Sefaradi*, no. 136)

T HE YEAR 1666 witnessed the climax of the greatest
messianic movement in Jewish history. Led by Sabbatai
Zevi and his prophet Nathan of Gaza, it unleashed a
messianic passion among the Jewish people which knew
no bounds of geography or class. And then, at the very height of
the frenzied expectation of an imminent return to the Land of Israel
and the establishment of the messianic kingdom, with brutal
suddenness the *annus mirabilis* became for many an *annus terribilis*. In
September of the same year, the Messiah himself converted to Islam.

The history of the Sabbatian movement has already been unfolded
in magisterial detail by Professor Gershom Scholem.[1] Our concern

---

[1] Gershom Scholem, *Shabbetai Ṣebi veha-tenuah ha-shabbetait bi-yemei ḥayyav* (2 vols.;

here is not with the movement as such, but rather with Isaac Cardoso's attitude toward it, as revealed in his conflict with his brother Abraham.

MARRANISM AND MESSIANISM

In a now classic pioneering essay on Sabbatian ideology which appeared in 1932, Scholem drew a fruitful parallel between the crisis which followed the apostasy of Sabbatai Zevi, and that which had ensued immediately after the Crucifixion. In both instances the believers were faced with a tormenting choice. Having experienced briefly, but intensely, the full reality of the messianic presence, they had now either to accept the verdict of "history" and regard that presence as having been an illusion, or to insist on the validity of their innermost spiritual experience, and to reinterpret history in its light. In the case of the believers in Sabbatai Zevi the paradox to be dealt with was even more grim than that which had faced the nascent Christian community, for, as Scholem pointed out, the paradox of a crucified messiah can be exceeded only by that of an apostate messiah. Yet, although the majority became disillusioned in the shock that followed the news of Sabbatai Zevi's conversion, others, and they were by no means few, continued to believe. His tragic step was soon interpreted as a preordained act of divine necessity. Ultimately, evil could not be conquered from without. Before the final salvation of the world could be accomplished, the Messiah, with great risk and immense sacrifice, had himself to plunge by his conversion into the realm of darkness and evil, so that he might deliver the holy sparks which are embedded therein. With the emergence of this profound, but explosive, rationalization of the catastrophe, Sabbatianism was transformed from a messianic mass movement into an esoteric "mystical heresy."[2]

Tel-Aviv, 1956–57). Forthcoming volumes on the course of the movement after Sabbatai Zevi's death will undoubtedly include a comprehensive discussion of Abraham Cardoso.

[2] See Scholem, "A Commandment Which Is Fulfilled through Its Violation" (Hebrew: "Misvah ha-ba'ah ba-'aberah"), in *Knesset*, II (1937), 347–92. See also

Abraham, Isaac, and the Messiah

The prime architect of postconversion Sabbatian ideology, after Nathan of Gaza himself, was Abraham Cardoso. Indeed, he later became its most prolific and passionate spokesman. Until his death in 1706, Abraham poured forth a veritable flood of letters and tracts which amount, in sum, to an entire mystic theology of vast boldness and power. For our limited purpose, the point of departure must be to consider his activity, not so much within the framework of Sabbatianism, as within that of Marranism. It is under the latter aspect that his clash with Isaac reveals its particular problematics.

That Sabbatianism, especially after the conversion, found a particularly strong response among former Marranos, was already underscored by Scholem in his aforementioned essay. In fact, it was from a letter sent by Abraham to Isaac Cardoso, which we shall consider presently, that Scholem sought to demonstrate an intimate correlation between the heretical ideology of Sabbatianism and the spiritual preparation afforded by the Marrano experience. A former Marrano would be particularly receptive to the rationalization of the Messiah's conversion. Marranos could understand, perhaps better than other Jews, that conversion might simply be a mask for an inner existence of a radically different order. Moreover, if the Messiah himself had to convert to another religion and live, in effect, the life of a "Marrano," then by extension their own past as Marranos seemed susceptible of a new and positive reevaluation.

These points are indeed well taken, and can even be elucidated further. Along with the "Marrano" psychology which is revealed in postconversion Sabbatianism, we must also take into account the powerful strain of messianism which always existed among the Marranos. This can be documented even before the Expulsion of 1492. Throughout the sixteenth century messiahs, prophets, and prophetesses continued to appear among the Peninsular Marranos. One need only cite the response in Portugal to the arrival of David Reubeni in 1525, and the emergence of the truly messianic figure of Solomon Molkho, in order to appreciate how readily some Marranos were swayed by messianic impulses.

---

his *Major Trends in Jewish Mysticism*, 3d rev. ed. (New York, 1954), ch. 8 ("Sabbatianism and Mystical Heresy"), especially pp. 307 ff.

304

Less known, perhaps, is the fact that in the seventeenth century a perceptible current of Marrano messianism still existed. Marrano credulity and ready acceptance of "false messiahs" comprised a theme which contemporary Spanish and Portuguese antisemites did not cease to emphasize.[3] On the stage and in literature the same was true, so much so that ultimately the verb *esperar* (to hope) became a catchword with which to identify the character who is of Jewish descent. *Esperanza* is the Jewish characteristic *par excellence*, and the satiric use of such terms is a leitmotiv in the Spanish drama of the Golden Age.[4] Now and again among the Marranos of the seventeenth century there are obscure echoes of the birth of a presumed Messiah.[5] Of equal interest are the messianic myths which continued to circulate among them. A particularly touching example is a Marrano legend of the coming of the Messiah which expresses well their pent-up longing for deliverance. When the Messiah comes to Spain, it is said, he will arrive in the guise of a fish for, if he appeared as a man, the inquisitors would catch and burn him. As a fish, he will enter by swimming up the river Tajo (or the Guadalquivir), and then accomplish the redemption.[6] While such notions provided ample opportunity for ridicule, we can perhaps distinguish two important features which, compressed in the legend, also serve to illustrate the Marrano mentality. The obvious is that so overwhelming was their fear of the Inquisition that finally they could only conceive of the Messiah himself as having to enter the Peninsula surreptitiously. But the choice of the fish is also interesting, for it

---

[3] E. g., Costa Mattos, *Discurso*, fols. 47v-49r, mainly on 16th-century messiahs among the Marranos. Cf. Torrejoncillo, *Centinela*, fol. 138 and *passim*.

[4] See the quotations from Lope de Vega, Tirso de Molina, Quevedo, Calderón, etc., in Herrero García, *Ideas de las españoles*, pp. 626–31. Additional data from Portuguese writings appears in Glaser, *Invitation to Intolerance*, p. 329, n. 5; see also his *Referencias antisemitas*, pp. 55–61.

[5] E. g., in Antequera, in 1642. See Caro, *Judíos*, I, 481.

[6] The legend appears, with variations, in the following: Lope de Vega, *El niño inocente* (Act I), where one of the Jews says a relative told him the story; in Torrejoncillo, *Centinela*, fol. 103: "Dizen otros, que ha de venir en figura de peze por el río Guadalquivir, temeroso de que los inquisidores le cojan, le prendan, y le quemen." For a 16th-century reference, see Sicroff, *Controverses*, pp. 161 f.

seems to fuse a Christian symbol with a dim recollection of the ancient Jewish folk motif of the messianic Leviathan.[7] Similarly, it can be shown that myths concerning the messianic role of the Lost Tribes were also current among the Marranos. To choose but one example, there was a tradition concerning the *pueblo cerrado*, which is none other than the Lost Tribes of Israel, enclosed now in a remote land, and waiting to emerge in the time of the Messiah to aid in the redemption of their brethren. In the confessions of the physician Felipe de Nájera (1607), such ideas were most prominently displayed. He avowed that the nine and one half tribes whom Shalmanessar exiled are still living in an area near the Ganges, or in the empire of the Grand Turk, together with the prophets Enoch and Elijah, ready for the advent of the Messiah. Even more interesting is Nájera's insistence that they shall liberate not only the Jews, but Portugal itself.[8]

SABBATIANISM AND SEBASTIANISM?

This raises also the vital question of the confluence of Marrano messianism and Portuguese messianism. The Portuguese people became, in the sixteenth century, as fervently "messianic" as the Jews themselves. In its most important form, this messianism arose after the death of the young king Dom Sebastian in 1578 at the Battle of Alcazarquivir in Morocco. This terrible finale to Sebastian's rash crusade against Islam cost Portugal the flower of her manhood, and enabled Spain to assume control less than two years later. After the battle, however, the few survivors could not recover the king's body, and in Portugal itself there were many who simply would not

---

[7] That the Leviathan motif was still remembered among some of the Marranos is indicated by satires on the subject in sermons preached by the Portuguese inquisitors. See Glaser, *Invitation to Intolerance*, p. 349.

[8] See the excerpts from Nájera's dossier in Caro, *Judíos*, I, 414. Nájera himself believed that he was of the tribe of Zebulun. There may be a connection between such ideas and the Prester John legends which were very widespread among the Portuguese.

accept the fact that he had died. A belief arose, which was to grip the Portuguese until well into the nineteenth century, that Sebastian would return to liberate his people. Time and again imposters emerged, each claiming to be Sebastian, but, despite repeated disillusionments, faith in him survived. In the eighteenth century the great Sephardic rabbi of London, David Nieto, would write in his reply to a sermon preached at an *auto-da-fé* by the Archbishop of Cranganore, a remarkably telling retort: a nation like the Portuguese, who still await the return of King Sebastian, should better understand the Jewish willingness to accept a few false messiahs![9]

The Portuguese historians of Sebastianism have stressed how much Marrano messianism contributed to its development.[10] However, the possible subsequent effects of Sebastianism in preparing the mentality of some of the Marranos who later embraced the messianic movement of Sabbatai Zevi have yet to be explored. The parallels between Sebastianism and postconversion Sabbatianism are manifest. We may even note, parenthetically, that shortly before 1666 the appearance of Sebastian and the messianic transformation of the world were eagerly anticipated by Padre António Vieira.[11]

---

[9] Cited by Glaser, *Invitation to Intolerance*, p. 335, n. 44.

[10] The most comprehensive study is that of J. Lúcio d'Azevedo, "A evolução do sebastianismo," *Arquivo histórico português*, X (1916), 379–473 (reprinted separately, Lisbon, 1918).

[11] D'Azevedo, *Christãos-Novos*, p. 285. On Vieira's messianism, see his *História de António Vieira* (2 vols.; Lisbon, 1918–21). Vieira's messianic writings are available in the edition of A. Sérgio and H. Cidade of his *Obras escolhidas*, vol. VI, which contains the important "Esperanças de Portugal, quinto imperio do mundo" (pp. 1–66). See also *Cartas do P.e Antonio Vieira*, ed. Mario Gonçalves Viana (Porto, n.d.), pp. 135–64.

Scholem (*Shabbetai Ṣebi*, I, 122 ff.) has emphasized that the initial messianic awakening among the Jews in 1665/6 need not be attributed to Christian influence, but can better be explained as the result of internal Jewish development, even though that year was also the focus of the hopes of a number of Protestant chiliastic groups. (On the latter see also *ibid.*, pp. 74–82.) With this approach we are in complete agreement. But while the *origins* of Sabbatianism are not to be sought in the Christian sphere, once the movement began certain Christian influences did come to the fore, as Scholem himself pointed out with reference to Marrano participation. In that case, however, I deem it more important to focus on con-

Abraham, Isaac, and the Messiah

Though it may seem virtually impossible to establish just how much awareness there was in the Cardoso family of Sebastianism, or other forms of Portuguese messianism, certain facts should be brought to the fore which may prove a lead for future research. The most important antecedent of Sebastianism in Portugal was a messianic movement which swept through the province of Beira in the third decade of the sixteenth century. Its leader was a rustic cobbler of Trancoso, Gonçalo Eannes Bandarra. His prophetic verses were later subjected to an exegesis which made it seem that he had foretold the death of Dom Sebastian and his subsequent return, and so, in the seventeenth century, they remained a classic text of Sebastianism. Though Bandarra was accused of Judaizing by the Portuguese Inquisition, there is no real evidence that he did so. The fact remains, however, that he was in close contact with many New Christians, and produced a tremendous enthusiasm among them.[12]

Now Trancoso, Bandarra's home, was also the birthplace of Isaac Cardoso, and one small detail captures our attention beyond the mere coincidence. In the trial of Bandarra by the Inquisition of Lisbon in 1540, he avowed that whenever his memory failed him he would have recourse to the aid of two educated men of the town: Father Bartholomeu Rodrigues, and *Doctor Alvaro Cardoso*.[13] This was some sixty-four years before Isaac Cardoso was born. Was this Dr. Alvaro Cardoso an ancestor, or at least a member of the family? If, as seems likely, he was a physician, the possibility must be entertained, for in a town the size of Trancoso there must have been few physicians to begin with. Once again, in the absence of Cardoso's genealogy, we cannot decide.[14] We do know, however, that among

---

temporary Portuguese messianism than on Protestant chiliasm. No Jews had gone through a Protestant experience, but many had lived as Iberian Catholics.

[12] D'Azevedo, *Evolução*, pp. 380 ff. For Bandarra's verses concerning the Jews, see the facsimile reprint of the edition of 1603 of João de Castro's *Paraphrase et concordancia de alguas propheçias de Bandarra, çapateiro de Trancoso* (Porto, 1942), pp. 73 f.

[13] The document in D'Azevedo, *Evolução*, p. 440.

[14] All efforts to locate the baptismal registers of Trancoso for the period of Issac Cardoso's birth have failed. A note from the Conservatoria do Registro Civil de Trancoso, dated July 7, 1965, informs me that no one there knows what

the Marranos of Trancoso the memory of Bandarra remained very much alive. Felipe de Nájera, who was also a native of Trancoso, related in 1607, when he was forty-five years old, that in his youth his parents had often spoken of Bandarra, that the latter's verses were sung by children in the streets, and that they contained much about the lost tribes. He stated further that Bandarra was held among them to be descended from the Jews whom Ferdinand the Catholic had expelled from Spain. Nájera himself had copied Bandarra's verses, and could still remember a great number by heart after so many years.[15]

It is certain, at least, that Isaac Cardoso was well aware of the figure of Bandarra, for he wrote a fairly detailed passage concerning him in the *Excelencias*. While discussing the fact that true prophecy is a unique prerogative of the Jews, he mentions several famous gentile oracles. Significantly, perhaps, Bandarra is the only one to whom he devotes more than a passing mention.[16]

---

happened to them. Dr. Carlota Gil Pereira of the Lisbon Library reports that there is no record of them with the Inspecçao Superior das Bibliotecas e Arquivos, which is in the process of gathering old baptismal registers from all localities in Portugal.   [15] Caro, *Judíos*, I, 414, n. 37.

[16] *Excelencias*, fols. 292 f.: "Al Bandarra alega el Covarruvias en su tratado de la verdadera, y falça Prophecia, este no sabiendo escrivir havrá 150 años pronostico muchas cosas de los Portuguezes en sus coplas que van en sueños, y dialogos, y que el año de quarenta se levantaria un Rey nuevo en Portugal, como assi fue, porque el año de 1640 levantaron los Portuguezes al Rey D. Joan el IV, y dixo tambien muchas cosas en sus versos de la venida de los Tribus de Reuben, Simhon, y Levi, y cosas grandes de un gran Pastor, y Rey. Este aunque no sabia leer las Sacras Escrituras hazia que se las leyessen, y principalmente de los Prophetas, de los quales segun parece juntando, mudando, trasponiendo, imitando, componia sus sueños, y prophecias. Era çapatero de viejo, como el mismo de si confiessa, y está en grande veneracion entre los Lusitanos, que admirados de algunas predicciones, que salieron verdaderas, le levantaron un honesto, y honrado tumulo, en la Villa de Trancoso, donde era natural, y adonde murio."

We may note that a work on one of the false Sebastians had been earlier written by the Marrano physician Estêvão Rodrigues de Castro, and published posthumously by his son (*De simulato rege Sebastiano poemation, olim iuvenali aetate conflatum . . . ed. a Franc. de Castro eius filio*, Florence, 1638). See Friedenwald, *Jewish Luminaries*, p. 55. Cf. Theophilo Braga, *História de Camoēs Parte II: Eschola de Camoēs* (Porto, 1874), ch. VI, pp. 173–87.

Abraham, Isaac, and the Messiah

Cardoso's awareness of Sebastianism can also be demonstrated from a personal anecdote. His description of Miguel de Silveyra's astrological pretensions has already been recorded in chapter III. In the same passage of the *Philosophia libera* he goes on to mention another acquaintance from bygone days:

The second was Bocarro, by another name Rosales, a man of renown among the Hamburgians and the Portuguese, of whom they say that he predicted a new king, and that they would escape from the yoke of Castile into freedom and sovereignty. But he had predicted many things to the Governor of Belgium Francisco de Mello[17] who trusted him too much, including a happy outcome in that famous battle in which he was defeated by the Prince of Condé, by whose prowess the great battle line of Spaniards fell.[18] The same astrologer had promised safety from the stars to his own only son when he was sick, and a long life. Nevertheless, in the very flower of his youth, he died from the severity of the disease at the age of seventeen or thereabouts, against the opinion of his father, who was willing to trust neither other doctors nor the lethal signs, and, when he was already about to die, cared more for stars than for drugs. There are numberless fallacious predictions which can be collected, but that saying of Marlianus is most certain: if you wish to divine, say precisely the opposite of what astrologers either promise or threaten. . . .[19]

The allusion is to Manoel Bocarro Francês, another highly interesting figure in seventeenth-century Marranism. Born around 1590 in Lisbon, he studied at Coimbra, Alcalá, and Montpellier, and became a physician. In 1624 he was implicated in the testimony of a brother before the Inquisition of Goa. Sometime later he left the Peninsula forever. He went to Rome, then to Amsterdam, where he emerged as a professing Jew under the name Jacob Rosales, and finally settled in Hamburg. There he practiced medicine, produced several astrological works, and, in a curious shift of allegiance,

---

[17] Not to be confused with the Portuguese writer Francisco Manoel de Mello.

[18] A reference to the Battle of Rocroy (May, 1643) in which the pride of the Spanish army under Francisco de Mello was annihilated by the French under the Duc d'Enghien, eldest son of the Prince de Condé.

[19] *Philosophia libera*, p. 181.

310

became involved in various political intrigues in the service of Spain. In 1658 he was denounced to the Holy Office in Lisbon as living in the Sephardic community of Leghorn. In 1660 he was a member of its Hebra de Casar Orfãs. He died in 1662, on the way to Florence.[20]

We are here concerned with only one aspect of Bocarro's career which Cardoso has mentioned: his prediction of "a new king" to the Portuguese. This is undoubtedly a reference to Bocarro's *Anacephaleoses da Monarquia Lusitana*, the first part of which was printed in Lisbon in 1624.[21] Though nominally dedicated to the king of Spain, this work, a poem of 131 Portuguese octaves which mixes ecstatic glorifications of the Portuguese past with messianic prognostications of its future restoration, places Bocarro squarely in the camp of the "Sebastianists." Another part of the poem, unpublished for obvious reasons, was dedicated to the duke Teodósio of Braganza, whom the author apparently regarded as the long-awaited *Encoberto*, the "Hidden One" who will be the future savior of Portugal.[22] We do not know when, nor under what circumstances, Cardoso knew Bocarro. It must suffice us to recognize that Cardoso's own knowledge of Sebastianism came not merely from books, but from contact with one who was, at least for a time, a well-known Sebastianist.

One other scrap of information, itself rather cryptic, should at least be mentioned here. It is known from several sources that in Smyrna Sabbatai Zevi appointed a Jewish physician of that city to be the king of Portugal in his impending messianic world-empire. In one account this physician is described as a former Portuguese Marrano who spent much of his life in France, "and many of his relatives are still there, attempting to conceal their Judaism; and he

---

[20] For his career see Hermann Kellenbenz, "Dr. Jacob Rosales," *Zeitschrift für Religions- und Geistesgeschichte*, VIII (1956), 345–54; *idem, Sephardim an der Unteren Elbe*, pp. 338–44; I. S. Révah, "Une famille de Nouveaux Chrétiens: les Bocarro Francês,: *REJ*, CXVI (1957), 73–89.

[21] *Anacephaleoses da Monarchia Luzitana, pello Doutor Manoel Bocarro Francês, Lisboa, por Antonio Alvarez, 1624.* The work was ordered confiscated shortly after publication. A copy, formerly in the Palha Collection, is now in the Houghton Library at Harvard.

[22] Excerpts from this part have been published by D'Azevedo, *Evolução*, App. VIII, pp. 229 f.

believed with perfect faith that in a little while he will rule over Portugal, for so the Messiah promised him when crowning him shortly before he left Smyrna." To be sure, this appointment was by no means unique. It must have taken place in the great ceremony held on the Sabbath of the 4th of Tebet in one of the Smyrna synagogues, when Sabbatai Zevi ordained many of his closest followers to be "kings" of various parts of the world. Still, one may well wonder if this former Portuguese Marrano's own faith in his imminent rule over Portugal may have derived, not only from his belief in Sabbatai Zevi, but also from some Sebastianist strain in his own thinking. His name, unfortunately, has not been accurately transmitted. He is certainly the same Smyrna physician who later hid Nathan of Gaza in his home after the Messiah's conversion, and whom Jacob Sasportas calls Cardoso. As Scholem has shown, he cannot have been Abraham Cardoso, for the latter was in Tripoli at the time. Other Cardosos, however, are known to have lived in Smyrna, and perhaps there was some family relationship.[23]

To try to deduce more than this would be to exceed the few facts that have been outlined and presented in all diffidence. We have no direct information at all as to Abraham Cardoso's own cognizance of Sebastianism. But whether or not there was some influence in the Cardoso family of the Portuguese messianic tradition, Scholem's basic point remains. There certainly seems to have been an experiential and psychological predisposition among many Marranos to follow Sabbatai Zevi, and to accept the mystical interpretation of his conversion. Against this background, the respective attitudes of Isaac and Abraham Cardoso to Sabbatianism stand out in the very sharpest relief, and confront us with an interesting case study of Scholem's thesis. Here are two brothers, both having emerged out of a common Iberian matrix, both of them former Marranos, and yet their responses to the Sabbatian movement were diametrically opposed. While Abraham became its most fervent apostle, Isaac was

---

[23] For the episode of the "king of Portugal" see Scholem, *Shabbetai Ṣebi*, I, 351. The ceremony in the synagogue and the list of other kings are discussed, *ibid.*, pp. 320 f., 348 ff. On the concealment of Nathan of Gaza see Jacob Sasportas, *Sefer Ṣiṣat Nobel Ṣebi*, ed. I. Tishby (Jerusalem, 1954), p. 200.

one of its vehement antagonists. How is this to be explained? Scholem has analyzed the nexus between Marranism and Sabbatianism. Perhaps, out of the conflict between Abraham and Isaac Cardoso, we may also find a link between Marranism and *anti*-Sabbatianism.

BROTHER AGAINST BROTHER

News of Sabbatai Zevi had begun to race through the Jewish communities of Italy at the end of 1665. By December the rumors had already generated enough enthusiasm among the Jews of Verona for one of its rabbis, Saul Merrari, to write to Samuel Aboab in Venice and ask his advice as to what course of action to follow. Aboab's reply shows the ambivalence which a number of Jewish leaders must have felt at this early stage. While he voiced his misgivings at the possible effects which any messianic manifestations might have among the gentiles, he also emphasized the positive value of the awakening of repentance among the Jews themselves. For the rest, he advised a cautious policy of silence until future events should clarify the situation.[24] As it turned out, Verona subsequently became one of the strongholds of Sabbatianism in Italy and, even after the conversion of Sabbatai Zevi, many believers were to be found there.[25]

---

[24] The letter was published by Meir Benayahu, "News from Italy and Holland on the Beginning of Sabbatianism" (Hebrew), *Ereṣ Yisrael*, IV (1956), 200. On the fantastic mixture of fact and fancy in this early stage, cf. the documents assembled by a Jew in some community between Venice, Verona, and Trieste, published by Scholem, "An Italian Note Book on the Sabbatian Movement in 1666" (Hebrew), *Ẓion*, X (1945), 55–66.

[25] The movement was strong enough in the city to attract the attention of a Christian chronicler: "Gl'Hebrei quest'anno (1666) credettero, che venisse il loro Messia, per molti segni seguiti, col mezzo di uno, che si fece chiamare Nataan Profetta Levi. Questo haveva un seguito di numero infinito d'huomini, perciò molti Hebrei di diverse luoghi, havendo venduto quant' haveuano di buono, s'incaminarono à ritrovare il Profetta, e in ogni luogo, com'anco in Verona fecero Orationi, sperando certo vedere il loro Messia" (Lodovico Moscardo, *Historia di Verona* [Verona, 1668], p. 546).

Abraham, Isaac, and the Messiah

Isaac Cardoso thus had the opportunity to observe closely the messianic upheaval in his own city. Indeed, if a passage in his account of the movement is a reflection of what actually took place in Verona, then he even saw, at the height of the enthusiasm in 1666, the abolition of the great fast of the Ninth of Ab, in token of the advent of the messianic age.[26]

When the Sabbatian movement erupted, Abraham Cardoso was no longer in Italy. The brothers must have bidden each other farewell when Isaac settled in Verona, or perhaps even earlier. Abraham had gone first to Leghorn, where he remained until 1658–59, and then had spent several years in Egypt. In 1663 he settled in Tripoli as physician to the Bey, on the recommendation, it was said, of the Duke of Tuscany.[27]

The conflict between Isaac and Abraham Cardoso over the messiahship of Sabbatai Zevi occurred entirely in the years 1666–68, while Abraham was still living in Tripoli. Our information concerning this episode centers around a correspondence between the two, of which only the letters of Abraham have been preserved, and even in these there is a gap. It is possible, however, to reconstruct practically the entire sequence of this correspondence, taking into account also the missing letters on either side.

The first extant letter written by Abraham to Isaac was included among many other primary documents in the famous anti-Sabbatian collection of Rabbi Jacob Sasportas, *Ṣiṣat nobel ṣebi*, and can be dated shortly after April of 1668.[28] Somehow this letter came into the hands

---

[26] *Philosophia libera*, fol. 641. See translation, *infra*, p. 345.

[27] For some difficulties in the chronology of his stay in Egypt and arrival in Tripoli, see Bernheimer, *JQR*, XVIII, 114, n. 8; Scholem, *Zion*, XIX, 15, n. 51. In 1675 he was again in Leghorn where, the following year, he was excommunicated by the Mahamad. (The ban is printed by Bernheimer, pp. 127–29). Several other questions remain unresolved. Where and when did he study medicine? Who were the "relatives" who came from Leghorn to join him in Tripoli in 1663? (The latter are mentioned in his letter to the rabbis of Smyrna, *Zion*, XIX, 13).

[28] Jacob Sasportas, *Sefer Ṣiṣat nobel Ṣebi* (hereafter referred to as *ṢNṢ*), ed. I. Tishby, pp. 289–97. The letter was printed earlier with several omissions and corruptions by A. Freimann in his *Inyene Shabbetai Sebi: Sammelband kleiner Schriften*

of Abraham de Sousa, one of the stanchest opponents of Sabbatianism in Amsterdam. We owe its preservation to the fact that De Sousa forwarded it to Sasportas in Hamburg so that he could write a refutation.[29]

However, before we examine the contents of this letter, we must recognize that it does not represent the real beginning of the correspondence. For at the very outset, Abraham Cardoso writes to Isaac: *"I have received your letter,* and because you have believed that *what I wrote to you concerning our Messiah* is true . . . I shall tell you everything you have asked of me."[30] There was, then, a prior exchange of letters between the two. Obviously Abraham had written earlier to Isaac, informing him of the news of the Messiah, and the latter had requested further information. Those first letters have been lost, but we must try to determine when they were sent.

It seems likely that Abraham first wrote to Isaac in 1666, and that it was sometime before the conversion of Sabbatai Zevi. The burden of the letter we have begun to consider is an attempt to convince Isaac of the reasons for the apostasy, and Abraham's explanation exudes an air of novelty, as though previously he had not dealt with this theme at all. Furthermore, in a Spanish letter to Isaac which we shall examine later, and which was written in the fall of 1668, Abraham says explicity that it is about two years since he wrote to him for the first time. Apparently in that first letter the conversion was not yet an issue, but only the question as to whether Sabbatai Zevi was truly the Messiah. Shortly after receiving that letter, Isaac may have heard of the conversion, and in his reply to Abraham he must have questioned him as to whether he could still retain his faith in this man. The letter in *Ṣiṣat nobel ṣebi* is thus to be regarded as Abraham's somewhat delayed response to this query, a delay undoubtedly occasioned by his own gropings towards a solution.

über Sabbatai Ẓebi und dessen Anhänger (Berlin, 1912), pp. 87–92. For the date see Tishby's remarks, *ṢNṢ*, p. 308, n. 2.

[29] Sasportas' reply: *ṢNṢ*, pp. 297–308. On Abraham de Sousa see his remarks, *ibid.*, p. 260. A "Menasa de Susa" settled in the Sephardic community of Verona in 1664 (Sonne, "Sources," p. 158).

[30] *ṢNṢ*, p. 289. (Italics mine.)

Now in two anti-Sabbatian sources it is implied that from the very beginning Isaac Cardoso was inimical to the Sabbatian movement and thoroughly hostile to his brother. In his acrid prefatory remarks to Abraham's letter, Sasportas writes:

And while he [Nathan of Gaza] was there in Leghorn, there came a letter from a certain man, an idolatrous physician, who lives in Tripoli. And he had come from Spain, grown in years, his belly filled with forbidden foods, conceived and born in unholiness, having transgressed and defiled, and afterwards he had come to Judaism. He went to Leghorn, and to Egypt, and from there he wandered until he made his home in Tripoli, and when the rumors began he made himself a prophet with words of vanity, and fulfilled the prophecies of Nathan and his messiah.

But his brother in Verona, also a physician, was one of the unbelievers. When he heard of the ravings of his brother in Tripoli, he wrote him a letter making sport of him, his dreams, and his words, and reminded him of bygone days when they were in Spain and this soothsayer was enmeshed in the toils of lust, and roamed the streets of Madrid with harp and timbrel, accompanied by others like him. And he told him in his letters that perhaps the musical instruments induced in him this gift of prophecy, and other such comic jibes. And in sum—that he should send him proof of these rumors, and what evidence that they are true. . . .[31]

Again, in the absolutely violent tract against Abraham Cardoso entitled *Sefer meribat kodesh* we read:

There is in him yet another established flaw: that his brother, the great rabbi and divine philosopher, his distinguished honor R. Isaac Cardoso . . . never liked him, and could never wish him well, for he knew that the thoughts of his heart were only toward evil. And this, as is well known, is a clear sign of a false prophet: that his own brother does not believe in him.[32]

Unquestionably, however, both sources have telescoped the actual facts, attributing to an earlier period an attitude which developed later. Sasportas wrote his words in 1669. By that time Isaac Cardoso had broken decisively with Abraham and, as we shall see, had

---

[31] *Ibid.*, p. 270.   [32] Freimann, *Inyene*, p. 32.

really made the remarks which Sasportas ascribed to him. But this was not yet the case in 1666/67, when Isaac replied to Abraham's first letter. At that time, as Sasportas himself inadvertently indicates at the end of his statement, Isaac must have asked about proofs and evidence. For how else are we to explain the fact that in the letter in *Ṣiṣat nobel ṣebi* Abraham treats the reply which he had received from Isaac not as a mockery of himself but as a serious inquiry to be answered in full? Moreover, there is in this letter no trace of a strained relationship between the brothers. This the author of the *Sefer meribat kodesh*, writing decades later, could not have known, or chose to ignore. We have noted that in Venice Abraham made use of Isaac's library, surely an indication of an amicable relationship. In his letter Abraham is friendly throughout, even intimate. At one point he writes: "And if some of these matters reach you, and they say of me that I dreamed such and such, then know that I wanted to hide many things, and so in a modest way I said of them that they are dreams; *but to you I write these things as they really are.* . . ." And he closes the letter: "And peace to you, and to your house and all that is yours, peace!"[33]

No, there was no enmity between the two up to this point. The rift developed subsequently. We must infer that initially Isaac had not quite made up his mind on the Sabbatian question. After Abraham's first letter reached him he may already have been skeptical, but drew no final conclusions. His attitude at that time must have been similar to that which Samuel Aboab expressed to Saul Merrari. While he did not participate in the movement, he was apparently willing to stand aside and see what would develop. Only after the conversion did his doubt become absolute, and only when he had read Abraham's letter defending it did he become openly hostile toward him.

We may now examine the contents of the letter itself. Abraham's impassioned effort to convince Isaac that Sabbatai Zevi is the Messiah rests on several distinct foundations. He points first to his personal experience. There have been divine revelations and authenticating miracles in his own household. Already in 1664 he

---

[33] *ṢNṢ*, pp. 291, 297. (Italics mine.)

had heard from heaven that the Messiah would be revealed the next year. One night it was disclosed to him that one of his wives, who was pregnant, would bear a son who would die shortly after the Messiah came, and this was fulfilled. The sister of his wife Judith saw many visions which he alone could interpret. Miraculous healings were vouchsafted to him and to other members of the family. Judith also began to communicate with a heavenly messenger, who still visits them at the present time. One day, while he was pondering some mysterious visions of the night before, his three-year-old daughter Rachel explained them. She had been told the interpretation by a man who was standing near him, but whom he could not see. In the month of Adar, 1667, he was informed that another son would be born to him on a Sabbath, to be called Ephraim, but that this child would not die like the other. This, too, accompanied by other signs, has come to pass.[34]

But Abraham by no means limits himself to the miraculous. At the heart of his argument lies a radical reevaluation of the conception of the Messiah in Jewish tradition. "Most people, and the sages of our time, have thought that the Messiah is destined to come with sovereignty, with signs, miracles, and wonders; in this they have greatly erred." For the very opposite is true. Abraham marshals all the traditional midrashic and aggadic passages which refer in any way to the sufferings of the Messiah, in order to demonstrate that, when he first appears, he must rather be plunged into the deepest misery. He insists that there is no contradiction between this and the prophecies of the Messiah's glory, for they are consecutive stages.

First he shall be low, and regarded by the Jews as an abominable evildoer, and he shall take upon himself the sufferings and all that has been decreed upon him for the sins of Israel, for on this condition he came to the world, and for this he was created, and only afterward shall he rise . . . until there shall be realized for him all the greatness of which the prophets and sages spoke.[35]

---

[34] *Ibid.*, pp. 289–91. These elements recur in many of Abraham Cardoso's writings. His children later died.

[35] *Ibid.*, p. 292.

It is no wonder, then, that he finds his most powerful support in the fifty-third chapter of Isaiah. In Abraham's exegesis, all the sufferings of the Servant of the Lord forecast the actual experience of the Messiah. "If anyone should come who is not despised, cursed, and abhorred, then it is impossible that he should be the Messiah . . . for all that the prophet Isaiah said in chapter 53 must be fulfilled. . . ."[36]

This, then, is the messianic pattern which has hitherto been ignored. However, the ultimate depths of the messianic agony have not yet thereby been fathomed. Abraham now reaches what he terms "the great secret." Though Isaiah and others had hinted at it, the explicit meaning of the Messiah's travail has only become clear in retrospect, with Sabbatai Zevi's conversion to Islam. Only the conversion of the Messiah could fulfill all the terms of the prophecy and make him the despised of men. Mere departures from the Law, such as had occurred at the height of the movement, were insufficient, "since all Jews know that the prophets may do and ordain things which are not according to the Torah and commandment . . . and how much more so the Messiah." When Sabbatai Zevi was brought before the Sultan he only sought a martyr's death. He was forced instead to convert to Islam, against his will. But in fact, this was inevitable. Abraham finally reveals the reason in a manner which leaves no doubt as to the profoundly personal roots of his new theology. His own words convey the full force of what his understanding of the Messiah's conversion meant for him. He says: "The Messiah was destined to become a Marrano (*'anus*) like me!"[37]

And the essence of the mystery is that we were all obliged, according to the Torah, to become Marranos before we could emerge from the Exile, for so it is written in the Torah (Deut. 28: 37): *and there shalt thou serve other gods, wood and stone*—measure for measure, because we desecrated the Torah and voluntarily practiced idolatry, and caused the desecration of the Name, for His blessed Name was defiled among the nations on account of our transgressions. Therefore justice requires, and so it was expressly decreed in the Torah, that we should become idolators and desecrate the Torah in the midst of the nations, despite ourselves

---

[36] *Ibid.*, p. 293.   [37] *Ibid.*, p. 291.

and against our will, and that we be defiled and constrained, and that from there we should cry out to God. . . .[38]

The burden of this terrible punishment which was reserved for the entire Jewish people has now been assumed for them by Sabbatai Zevi:

And because they abandoned the Torah, defilement was decreed upon the Messiah son of David, that he should become a Marrano against his will, so that he should not be able to fulfill the Torah. . . .

And God *hath made to light on him the iniquity of us all* (Is. 53: 7), for all of us were obliged to be Marranos, *and he was numbered with the transgressors* (v. 12) for only those are called transgressors of Israel who leave the faith . . . and the Jews number him now among the transgressors, but he *made intercession for the transgressors*, that is, for those who were obliged to abandon true religion for gentile faiths, *although he had done no violence, neither was there any deceit in his mouth* (v. 9).[39]

Finally, relying on an exegesis long current among the Peninsular Marranos:

Similar to this is that which happened to Esther, for through her a great deliverance was accomplished in Israel. And certainly most of the ignorant must have loathed her for having been married to a gentile idolator, which is a stringent prohibition of the Torah, but the sages who knew this secret and recognized the truth of the matter, did not regard her as a sinner. . . .[40]

Evidently when he wrote this letter Abraham still assumed that Isaac would share his faith. Especially in such passages as those just cited, he was appealing not just to his own, but to their common experience as Marranos. This remarkable interpretation of Sabbatai Zevi's entry into Islam provided at the same time the most potent justification of the years during which they had themselves lived as Christians in Spain. Indeed, why should not also Isaac be expected to succomb to its fascination?

But whatever hopes Abraham Cardoso may still have entertained on this score were soon utterly shattered. This may be seen most

---

[38] *Ibid.*, p. 293.   [39] *Ibid.*, p. 294.   [40] *Ibid.*, p. 295.

vividly from two Spanish letters of his, written from Tripoli in October of 1668, and extant in an Oxford manuscript. Both letters are focused on the conflict which had by now developed between the brothers. The first letter is addressed directly to Isaac. The second, which amplifies a number of details, was written to Abraham's brother-in-law in Amsterdam, Abraham Baruch Henríquez, who remained a firm believer in Sabbatai Zevi.[41]

---

[41] Bodleian Library, Oxford, MS Opp. Add. 4⁰ 150 (Cat. Neubauer no. 2481). The letter to Isaac: fols. 1r-11r. To Henríquez: fols. 12r-17v. Though unsigned, the contents and style, as well as the provenance, leave no doubt that the writer is Abraham Cardoso, and that the recipient of the first letter is Isaac. This was already indicated to me by Kayserling's notation (*BEPJ*, p. 71), itself taken from Neubauer: "(Messia). Tripoly de berberia anno 5429," giving the first line of each letter, and adding: "L'auteur inconnu n'est pas d'accord avec Yshac Cardoso et Orobio de Castro concernant ses opinions sur le messie." I subsequently found that Professor Scholem had cited a passage from the MS (fol. 12r-v) in another context in *Zion*, VII, 23, n. 46. The manuscript itself is a copy of the original letters. Regrettably, the copyist was extremely careless, and in several places he apparently did not quite understand what he was copying. The orthography is haphazard throughout, and sometimes absolutely anarchic, so that even the same word will be spelled in different ways. I am preparing an edition of the entire text which I hope to publish shortly.

Another letter from Abraham Cardoso to Henríquez is included in *ṢNṢ*, p. 361, though without mentioning his name. It is not known on which side Henríquez was his brother-in-law, but Abraham was apparently in the habit of sending copies of his epistles to him. Thus he also sent him a copy of his letter to the rabbis of Smyrna (cf. Scholem's remarks in *Zion*, XIX, 1–3) which was then recopied and forwarded from Amsterdam to Hamburg. Henríquez is mentioned by De Barrios (*Relación de los poetas*, p. 289) as a member of the Academia de los Floridos in Amsterdam. He seems also to have had an interest in Judeo-Christian polemic. A MS copy which he made of Abraham Gómez Silveira's *Entretenimientos gustosos o diálogos burlescos entre un Judío, Turco, Reformado, y Católico* is in the JTS library. (See A. Marx, "The Polemical Mss. in the Library of the Jewish Theological Seminary of America," in *Studies in Jewish Bibliography . . . in Memory of Abraham Solomon Freidus* [N.Y., 1929], p. 264). Henríquez' continuing messianic preoccupations decades after the Sabbatian episode may be inferred from a MS in his hand dated 1703, entitled *Sefer 'abkat rokhel* (Columbia University Library, MS X93/H39). It is a copy of a work of that name comprising various apocalyptic and mystical writings which had earlier been published in Augsburg (1540) and Venice (1566).

Abraham, Isaac, and the Messiah

From the very beginning of Abraham's letter to Isaac it is clear that something drastic has occurred since he last wrote to him several months earlier. The tone of conciliation has entirely disappeared. Dating his letter in the Jewish manner, Abraham quotes a verse from the weekly reading of the Torah: "And it came to pass that when Isaac was old, and his eyes grew dim, so that he could not see . . ." (Gen. 27: 1). Immediately afterward, he adds another verse: "Have we not one father? Hath not one God created us? Why do we deal treacherously every man against his brother, profaning the covenant of our fathers?" (Mal. 2: 10). Both verses presage the mixture of bitterness and anguish which informs almost every page of the letter itself. Abraham states that about two years earlier he first wrote to Isaac "with the love of a brother and the obedience of a son," informing him of his bodily infirmity and spiritual joy, giving him good tidings of divine favors, and advising him that no matter what "extravagances" he may hear about Sabbatai Zevi, he is the true Messiah. Isaac, however, had responded with public insults against him, which he had disseminated in Flanders. When Abraham sent him a modest reply, showing him "what his studies could not have enabled him to know," Isaac had reacted with even worse attacks, without really answering any of his substantive arguments.[42]

What particularly galled him was the nature of Isaac's assault, which contained personal allegations about him. He says that, although he never claimed the gift of prophecy, Isaac had made it seem as though he had. Out of hatred for him, Isaac had written to Doña Isabel Henríquez in an attempt to discredit him as a prophet by describing the sins of his youth, to wit: "that I played guitars, sang villancicos, and composed comedies, and that it was only through the merit of my fathers that I didn't disgrace them completely."[43]

Thus Sasportas' account of Isaac's satirical remarks was essentially correct, except for the fact that they were not made at the very

---

[42] MS Oxford, fol. 1r-v. It is obvious that Abraham chose to ignore an earlier stage in the correspondence when Isaac asked him for more information, and thus contradicts his own statement in the letter in *SNS* (p. 289):

» ויען אשר האמנת שמה ששלחתי אליך על עניני משיחנו אמת, אמלא משאלות לבך וחסרונך ואגיד לך כל מה ששאלת ממני «.

[43] *Ibid.*, fol. 1v.

beginning of the correspondence. Isaac broke decisively with Abraham only after receiving the letter which Sasportas included in his *Ṣiṣat nobel ṣebi*. He then launched his open campaign against Abraham and wrote to his old friend Isabel Henríquez in Amsterdam, knowing well that his letter would be widely circulated.[44] A copy of Isaac's letter, perhaps sent by Abraham Baruch Henríquez, found its way back to Abraham in Tripoli, and occasioned the rejoinders now under consideration.

Significantly, Abraham makes no attempt to deny the truth of what Isaac had written about his past in Madrid. Rather, while tacitly admitting it, he upbraids Isaac for thinking it at all relevant to the issue:

There is a notable difference between us. For if you had indicated to me that an angel of the Lord has revealed any mystery to you, I would have believed its truth without inquiring into your merits, nor imagining you to be a prophet.[45]

In other words, the granting of a divine revelation is independent of the worth of the recipient, and, to prove it, Abraham cites the examples of Manoah, of Hagar, of David after his sin with Bathsheba, and of the rebellious prophet Jonah.[46] The note of personal indignation is evident throughout, and the mark of Abraham's anger is to be found in the violence of his own remarks. Turning to the "turbid waters" of Isaac's letter, calling him a "sick physician," he asserts that it is his pious obligation to open the latter's eyes to the truth.

The best offense, of course, is to launch a frontal assault, and one can only marvel at the thoroughness with which Abraham tries to turn the tables on Isaac. His general theme is audacious and simple. He adopts a tone of perfect orthodoxy. The Law, both written and oral, is perfect, and we owe complete obedience to the sages of Israel who have preserved it from one generation to the next,

---

[44] On Isaac Cardoso's friendship with Isabel Henríquez in Madrid, see *supra* ch. IV. For some information on her activity in Amsterdam, see De Barrios, *Relación de los poetas*, pp. 56 f., and Kayserling, *Sephardim*, pp. 250 f. Was she related to Abraham Baruch Henríquez?

[45] *MS* Oxford, fol. 1v.   [46] *Ibid.* See also fol. 9v.

so that, my dear Sir, we do not believe in the sages of Israel because of the prophets, but rather we believe them for themselves, in conformity with the precepts of the Law; and we do not believe the prophets because they are prophets, but because the sages of Israel have approved them for us, and have said that we should recognize them as such. And similarly, since the words of the prophets are subject to various interpretations, and are far from our limited understanding, in no manner can we negate the sayings of the sages of Israel. . . .[47]

Thus Abraham seems to speak as a pious, tradition-minded Jew, squarely within the four ells of the Law—except for the paradoxical conclusion which he reaches. It is not he, but *Isaac*, who is the heretic. Isaac and others like him flout both Scripture and the Sages. He writes:

you deserve the most severe punishment of the divine rod, first, because you falsely depict the Messiah according to your mistaken blindness, negating the sages of Israel, *tannaim*, and *amoraim*, and second, because you infuse the Jewish people with the deceptive hope and barbarous faith in an imaginary Messiah. . . .[48]

And why is this so? Abraham's argument constantly resumes his favorite theme: that all of Jewish tradition, from the prophets to the sages, teaches us that when the Messiah comes he must be afflicted and degraded, maligned, spat at, apparently rejected by God, imprisoned. There must be a thousand doubts as to whether he should be believed or not. According to Abraham, all the sages agree "that there must come to pass all that Isaiah says in chapter 53 . . . *literally*, and that only after seven years of torment and afflictions will there commence his prowess, prodigies, triumphs, and victories. . . .[49]

I do not speak out of my own opinion, but out of the verdict of sages and prophets. And of him who speaks out of his own caprice, like you and Doctor Orobio y Silva [*sic*], the verse says *they have set up kings, but not from me* (Hos. 8: 4), that is, out of their own opinion. Unhappy Verona, and miserable age, in which there is present a messenger neither heard of nor expected![50]

---

[47] *Ibid.*, fols. 2v-3r.   [48] *Ibid.*, fol. 3r-v.
[49] *Ibid.*, fols. 3v-4r.   [50] *Ibid.*, fol. 3v.

The "Doctor Orobio y Silva" whom Abraham mentions is certainly Isaac Orobio de Castro, the former Marrano who settled in Amsterdam and became the most prolific Sephardic polemicist of the seventeenth century. His polemics were not confined to Christianity alone. He attacked also the philosophy of Spinoza and his partisans, as well as the various heterodoxies which were then to be found among the Sephardim of the Dutch capital. Here he emerges as an anti-Sabbatian as well, and Abraham singles him out repeatedly, together with Isaac Cardoso, as the special object of his scorn.[51] Most ironic, perhaps, is the fact that in his letter to Abraham Baruch Henríquez, Abraham Cardoso analyzes the Marranos who returned to Judaism almost in the same terms as did Orobio, in a passage which was quoted in the introductory chapter. Here is Abraham:

Of our brothers who have come from Spain there are three classes: some are philosophers and scientists; others are naturally wise, some of them bachelors [of the universities]; and others attach themselves to every saying of the sages, because they do not consider themselves to be such [sages].

Of the first, the majority are philosophers and metaphysicians, and when they hear the sayings of the sages of Israel, these being without [philosophical] proofs and demonstrations, they judge ill of them, and from then on they do not even bother to understand them. Now since the Law is translated and explained by the sages, and they do not accept them, they remain bad Jews, though not Christians. Some, who place their necks under the yoke of the legal maxims, and study them, emerge

---

51 Most of Orobio's writings are still extant in numerous manuscripts. A convenient list of his works will be found in M. B. Amzalak's edition of his reply to a treatise against the Law by a French Reform minister, under the title: *La observancia de la divina ley de Mosseh* (Coimbra, 1925), pp. xviii-xxxix. Orobio's imprisonment and torture by the Inquisition are related in Limborch, *Historia Inquisitionis*, II, fols. 158, 322 f. The latter's disputation with him is analyzed by Hans Joachim Schoeps, "Isaak Orobio de Castro's Religionsdisput mit Philipp van Limborch," *Judaica*, II (1946–47), 89–105, and in his *Israel und Christenheit* (Munich-Frankfort, 1961), pp. 97–113. The most important treatments of his relations to Spinozism are Révah, *Spinoza et Juan de Prado*, and Joaquim de Carvalho, "Orobio de Castro e o Espinosismo," offprint from *Memorias da Academia das Ciencias de Lisboa*, II (1937), which contains a Spanish version of Orobio's *Certamen philosophicum adversus Joh. Bredenburg.*

wise and obedient. Others cast themselves in the middle, and remain neither Jews nor Christians, but rather naturalists. Against these I have become a fierce fighter, and if the imminent time of salvation were not approaching, I should have to publish a work showing that this sect is the most vile, and they are the most ignorant, all with efficacious arguments, for just recently I convinced someone from these parts who became intoxicated with naturalism.

The second are haughty people, and for everything they ask a verse in Scripture, which, according to them, has until now never been well understood or explained by any sage of Israel, and they wish it to be according to their own explanation. The affairs of the Messiah are not presented literally in Scripture, since there is not a verse which cannot be interpreted in another sense by him who would deny the sages.

It is necessary to announce that I do not treat of the Messiah except with those Jews who are perfectly within the obedience due, according to the Law, to the prophets and the ancient sages of Israel, whose waters we drink, and in whose light we walk. With the result that I do not treat of the messiah written or imagined by Doctor Cardoso, nor by Doctor Orobio, nor by anyone else; but of the Messiah of Israel, conforming to sages and prophets of truth. . . .[52]

Abraham has thus placed his brother Isaac, as well as Orobio de Castro, in roughly the same category as that which Orobio assigns to the heretic Dr. Juan de Prado! He has used the very arguments of his opponents against them, almost, at times, to the point of parody. It is clear that Isaac Cardoso and Orobio de Castro had attacked Abraham's Messianic teachings as heresy, and as flying in the face of Jewish tradition. Abraham has hurled the charges back at them.

Some of the details of Isaac's arguments can also be deduced from Abraham's letter. He is, for example, at great pains to explain why Nathan of Gaza was unable to present evident and universally convincing signs to authenticate his prophecy. According to Abraham, if Nathan had given completely convincing proofs, then of course everyone would have believed. But, paradoxically, it is precisely this which would have denied the tradition of the sages that the appearance of the Messiah must engender innumerable doubts and dis-

---

[52] *MS* Oxford, fol. 12r-v. Cf. Orobio's account of Marrano heterodoxy quoted *supra*, ch. I.

putes.[53] The very ambiguities are part and parcel of the "signs" of the Messiah. "There must be," Abraham writes to Isaac, "believers like me, and detractors like you."[54] The crux of the matter is that the beginning of the messianic age is the time when the faith of Israel is tested. So important is this element that Abraham is prepared to say: "Whoever does not believe that Sabbatai Zevi *can* be the Messiah, *even if he is not*, does not believe in the Messiah of Israel![55]

That is why Abraham also returns several times to combat various Maimonidean opinions, which had obviously been used by Isaac, such as the notion that we are not required to believe a messiah until he rebuilds the Temple.[56] Nor does the prophet Elijah have to precede him. Were such things to occur, our choice would no longer be one of faith, for this would be not to "believe," but to "know."[57]

Another important argument which he combats in great detail is the idea, ultimately derived from Jeremiah, that God repents himself only of promises of doom, but not of blessing, and that the fulfillment of the latter is a criterion of true or false prophecy. Abraham insists that this is no test at all, for God has also left good promises unfulfilled, and any number of examples can be found in Scripture itself.[58] However, when he comes to apply this analysis to Nathan of Gaza, Abraham is a bit hard pressed. It is true that Nathan had announced that the Redemption would come in a year and a half, and that this did not take place. But Nathan had only heard it from the "heavenly academy," and not directly from God, and he never even used the standard prophetic phrase "thus saith the Lord."[59]

One area is evidently a source of particular embarassment to Abraham. Except for one or two curt statements, he is reluctant to discuss the antinomian acts which Sabbatai Zevi performed and decreed at the height of the movement. It must be understood that

---

[53] *MS* Oxford, fol. 5v, and *passim*.   [54] *Ibid.*, fol. 6v.   [55] *Ibid.*, fol. 7r.

[56] *Ibid.*, especially fols. 5v, 15v. Cf. *ṢNṢ*, p. 292.   [57] *Ibid.*, fol. 6r.

[58] *Ibid.*, fol. 8r-v: God did not bring those who emerged from Egypt into the Promised Land; King Josiah was killed in battle, though Hulda had prophecied that he would come to the grave in peace, etc.

[59] *Ibid.*, fol. 10r.

by the time he wrote this letter, Abraham himself had returned to a full observance of the traditional precepts, including the fast of the Ninth of Ab.[60] Certainly with regard to Sabbatai Zevi's conversion he drew a sharp line, seeing it as a necessary act for the Messiah alone, and for years he fiercely polemicized against those who saw themselves bound to emulate him. As for the earlier breaches of the Law, in his letter to Isaac Abraham can only say that Nathan's character was sufficient to authenticate his discovery that Sabbatai Zevi is the Messiah, "and if it came about that for a limited time we changed the Law, *at that time* it was good. . . ."[61] To Abraham Baruch Henríquez he writes more explicit, even of the conversion itself:

[He who] abandons the faith he formerly held that the prophet Nathan was a true prophet because Sabbatai Zevi has been clothed or has become a Turk, sins by pride, or error, or mortal transgression, *for God is not subject to the Law*, or Nature, since He is absolute Lord of all, and can require or command that the Messiah make himself such, just as He commanded Abraham that he sacrifice Isaac. . . .[62]

We have yet to consider what is perhaps the most revealing highlight in Abraham's letters, but at this juncture we must pause to take stock of Isaac. Hitherto we have been able to form some idea of the issues around which the conflict developed by citing Abraham alone. Though Isaac's letters to him are lost, and we therofore miss the personal immediacy of the heat of the conflict, we can turn to Isaac's other writings for information as to his views toward Sabbatianism. For this purpose we have three interrelated sources at our disposal:

1. The chapter on Prophecy in the *Philosophia libera*.
2. The section on the history of the Sabbatian movement which closes this chapter.
3. The chapter on Prophecy in *Las excelencias de los Hebreos*.[63]

---

[60] Letter to the rabbis of Smyrna, *Zion*, XIX, 5.

[61] *MS* Oxford, fol. 10v. (Italics mine.)

[62] *Ibid.*, fol. 16r. (Italics mine.).

[63] *Phil. lib.*, VI, quaest. lxxxiii ("De prophetia"), fols. 636–42; *Excelencias*, pp. 286–301 ("Octava excelencia de los hebreos: La prophecia").

Obviously these chapters will be of real use to us in understanding the conflict only if they reflect Isaac Cardoso's views around the time of the conflict itself. The *Philosophia libera*, as we have seen, was published in 1673, and the *Excelencias* in 1679. However, we can easily establish that the relevant sections were written earlier.

A textual comparison of the two works shows that, with minor revision, practically the entire chapter on prophecy in the *Philosophia libera* was merely translated by Cardoso into Spanish and then incorporated into the *Excelencias*.[64] This means that the chapter on prophecy in the latter work was already completed in its Latin form by 1670, when the entire *Philosophia libera* received the censors' approval.

The major omission in the chapter on prophecy in the *Excelencias* is the account of the Sabbatian movement which closes the corresponding chapter in the *Philosophia libera*. But the very fact that in the *Philosophia* the discussion of prophecy culminates in a description of the Sabbatian episode is a clear indication that Cardoso's analysis of prophecy is by no means academic; it has a distinct bearing on his view of Sabbatianism itself. The time in which he composed that final section is, fortunately, also revealed to us. Cardoso writes of the examination of Nathan of Gaza by the Venetian rabbis as having

---

[64] One example will suffice to illustrate the correspondence.

Phil. lib., fol. 636:

"Quare vera prophetiae ratio in illustratione quadam divina collocabitur, sic enim propheta apud Haebreos vocatur Roe, et Xoseh, hoc est videns, et prophetia dicitur Xason id est visio . . . et prophetae saepius incipiunt visio Amos, Isaiae & c. ac si praecipua, et essentialis ratio prophetae in visione statuatur . . . . Igitur prophetia poterit definiri: Illustratio mentis divina, qua res secretiores cognoscuntur."

Excelencias, p. 288:

"La verdadera razon de la Prophecia se funda en una vision Divina, y illustracion de la mente con que se conocen las cosas ocultas o futuras, y por esso el Propheta se llama en hebraico Roe y Joseh, que significa veyente, y los Prophetas comiencan muchos vezes sus Prophecias diziendo Vision de Amos, de Iesayahu & ct. Como la verdadera razon de la Prophecia consista en la vision . . . y segun esta dotrina podemos difinir, que la prophecia es una ilustracion de la mente con que percibe las cosas ocultas."

occurred "last year." Since that event is known to have taken place shortly after Passover of 1668, the *terminus ad quem* for the completion of Isaac Cardoso's chapter on prophecy is April, 1669.[65] In sum, whether we draw from the material in the *Philosophia libera*, or in the *Excelencias*, the views expressed are roughly contemporaneous with his clash with Abraham, and were written down, at the latest, a few months after Abraham wrote to him in October of 1668.

Before we approach this material directly, we should note that a personal element must also have played a certain role in the conflict. Several differences between the brothers are manifest from the very beginning. Isaac was fully twenty-three years older than Abraham. At the time they left Spain Isaac was famous, and had already achieved a glittering career, while Abraham was barely on the threshold of maturity. Some of Abraham's most biting remarks inadvertently reveal how sensitive he still was to the rather overwhelming shadow of his brother. "Accept, hear, and understand," he writes to Isaac, "that neither science nor years are the important thing. . . ."[66] He knows that in at least one area of knowledge, the Kabbalah, he has far outstripped Isaac. The latter's negative judgment on this discipline is to him a personal affront, a sign that Isaac deprecates his talent and studies. A profound desire that Isaac give him his due is easily discerned, as he continues caustically:

When a layman says that such and such a medicine suits a patient, or that this bloodletting was not done well, you would not alter anything because of what is said out of scientific ignorance. So then why do you discuss what you neither know nor believe. . . .? Finally, sir, a doctor of Hippocrates and Galen cannot pretend to be anything else. . . .

Are all of you these days wiser than the doctors Samuel, Rashi, and Rabbi Moses of Gerona? Then from whence does it arise that all those theologians, metaphysicians, philosophers, mathematicians, astrologers, and physicians exalted and revered the sages of Israel, while those of today wish themselves to be the sages? Señor Doctor Isaac Cardoso will not be satisfied to be a Rabbi Moses bar Nahman, nor Doctor Orobio to be a Doctor Rabenu Moses of Egypt, but they must be giants and *nefilim*. . . .[67]

---

[65] See *infra*, n. 87.　　[66] *MS* Oxford, fol. 4v.　　[67] *Ibid.*, fols. 10v-11r.

Keen personal competition is also visible when Abraham boasts on several occasions of the number of his children. If Isaac was indeed childless, then this must have constituted a particularly wounding barb. The height of asperity is reached in Abraham's closing recommendation that, if Isaac still desires to reply, let him not inscribe the name of God in his letter, for Abraham intends to burn whatever he receives of him.

In his own published works, Isaac did not once refer to his brother by name. Nevertheless, at least one passage in the *Excelencias* may well have Abraham in mind, for although it is ultimately derived from Rabbinic literature, the fact that he chose to cite it may reflect the intensity of his own feelings. Praising the commandment not to hate one's brother, he observes:

What can be more abominable than for brothers to hate one another. . .? But such love should be extended only to those who by their deeds deserve the name of brothers. The impious, however, who have estranged themselves from their God and their people, it is permitted to abhor, learning this from David: *Do I not hate them, O Lord, that hate Thee? . . . I hate them with utmost hatred* (Ps. 139: 21–22).[68]

Though we have seen that such hatred was late in coming, the seeds of conflict were present long before. In addition to differences in age and accomplishment, there was also a glaring difference in temperament between the two. Just as Abraham was an ecstatic, a visionary, always turbulent, so Isaac impresses us as calm, methodical, always in control of himself. As the *Excelencias* will reveal to us, he is at the same time capable of great passion, but it is a passion tempered by sobriety. Nothing is more illustrative of the contrasts than the ease, almost the compulsion, with which Abraham intimately reveals himself, so that there is hardly a work of his which is not exuberantly autobiographical. Isaac's reticence in this regard is almost total, to such a degree, as to frustrate his biographer at every turn. One may wonder, finally, if the very fact of their being brothers

---

[68] *Excelencias*, p. 219. The statement is found in *'Abot de R. Nathan*, Version I, ch. XVI. Isaac Athias, on whom Cardoso so heavily depends in his exposition of the commandments, does not mention it. See his *Thesoro de preceptos*, fol. 58v.

did not make it difficult for Isaac to accept Abraham's claims. He knew him too well. Others could be impressed by the great mystic Abraham Cardoso. Isaac, who remembered his brother's youthful escapades in Madrid, could perhaps not take him as seriously.

But while we should recognize the personal factor, we must beware of explaining the conflict in purely subjective terms. Substantive ideological differences were involved here. Let us now examine some of Isaac's own views on the issues which we have already noted.

Just how much of an impression was made upon Isaac by Abraham's recital of the miracles in his household and especially of the many visions which had been received by the women, may be gauged from the following passage:

It should be noted that among the Hebrews more prophets were men than women, and that among the gentiles more women than men, for since men are ordinarily wiser, stronger, and endowed with other virtues than are the women, the divine spirit better infuses them; while women, being weaker, more credulous, and less wise, are inspired by the devil in order to evoke greater admiration and marvel.[69]

Isaac's opinion of the Kabbalah was, as we have seen, equally low, and Abraham certainly had reason to take offense. In the section of the *Philosophia libera* entitled "De astrologorum vanitate", he writes:

There are three silly and foolish types of whom I do not know whether they are worthy of great laughter or pity: Alchemists, Astrologers, and Kabbalists. Whichever way you please, each is mad in his own realm. The Alchemist in the realm of the elements, the Astrologer in the celestial realm, the Kabbalist in the angelic or intellectual realm, [all] obstinately and absurdly rave.[70]

---

[69] *Excelencias*, p. 292; *Phil. lib.*, fol. 638. A similar judgment on the female imagination had been expressed by him years before in the *Utilidades del agua* (fols. 10 f.), referring to exaggerated stories of abstinence from food and drink: "Mas es de ponderar, que todas estas historias admirables que ponen los autores, son por la mayor parte de mugeres, o porq. su calor menor . . . o porque dadas a la supersticion, y ambiciosas del aplauso, nos engañan facilmente. . . . "

[70] *Phil. lib.*, fol. 176.

However, it would also be an error to predicate his opposition to Sabbatianism merely on the ground that he was a "rationalist." It must be abundantly evident by now that Isaac Cardoso had his own predilections for the fabulous. Furthermore, when it suited his purposes he was not loath to quote even the Zohar. It was not the "irrationality" of Sabbatianism which was uppermost in his mind, but something more vital.

The point of departure for Isaac's attack on the Sabbatian movement was the question of the validity of the Law. We shall see in the next chapter how fervidly he embraced the totality of the Jewish halakhic tradition. Here let us remark only that, while discussing the Law in the *Excelencias*, he raises the all-important problem of the force it will have in the messianic era, and leaves no doubt as to his opinion:

The third point will be to prove that the Law of Moses is eternal, and that Israel must observe it perpetually, without exchanging it for another law, and this truth is clearly demonstrated in Sacred Scripture. . . . Speaking of the Messiah, Isaiah says: *and the government is upon his shoulder*, and the Chaldean explains: *And he shall receive the Law upon himself, to guard it.*[71]

This theme is fully taken up in the chapter on prophecy. Much of this chapter is devoted to a thoroughly Maimonidean analysis of true and false prophets, in which the Sabbatian movement is not named. Yet all the arguments are patently applicable to Sabbatianism and, on one level, it is apparent that this is what Isaac had in mind. In the following important passages we have but to substitute, for "the prophet," Nathan of Gaza, and we immediately understand their relevance:

[When] the prophet is already recognized by his works, his saintliness, and wisdom, God commands that he be obeyed, *provided that he does not speak against the Law*, for the Law is the rule of the prophets, and they must be directed by it, and not the Law by the prophets.[72]

---

[71] *Excelencias*, p. 142 (citing Isa. 9: 5 and Targum *ad loc.*).

[72] *Ibid.*, p. 293. For these, as well as many of Cardoso's subsequent ideas on the criteria for true and false prophecy, see especially Maimonides' *Epistle to Yemen*

Despite a superficial similarity, this statement is really quite different from Abraham's assertions that the prophets are to be understood in the light of the interpretation of the sages, for, as his exegesis shows, Abraham was referring to certain *aggadic* interpretations. Isaac, on the other hand, stands firm on one criterion alone: does the prophet demand an alteration in the Law itself? He is even willing to concede that

The prophet may very well, for some reason, transgress a certain precept of the Law, so long as it is not idolatry, and violate it for a certain time, such as breaking the Sabbath, sacrificing away from holy ground (as did Elijah on Carmel in order to convince the prophets of Baal, and for the greater glory of God). But this can only be so for that single time and occasion, leaving the precept itself forever after firmly in its observance and in its inviolable force. . . .[73]

Patently, the transformation of fasts into feasts, and the other antinomian manifestations of 1666, do not fit into this category:

But if a prophet should arise and say that God commanded him to add a precept to the Law, or to diminish another, or to expound it by a different exposition than that which tradition teaches, or that the precepts of Israel are temporary and not obligatory forever—then we have to understand that he is a false and lying prophet, because he falsely argues the Law, and he deserves death by strangulation. For the good Lord gave His holy Law to Moses and Israel so that we should guard it forever, we and our children. And God is not a man who lies, or deceives, and thus it is written: *All this word which I command you, that shall ye observe to do; thou shalt not add thereto, nor diminish from it.* And in Deuteronomy: *It is not in heaven,* as if to say: once only did the Lord give us the Law from the heavens and told us to observe it perpetually, through all our generations. It is already no longer in the heavens, but rather in our hearts and in our hand, to do it. Nor should we believe him who wishes us to depart from it, or make innovations in it, even though he be a prophet, or an angel. And if all the prophets together were to command that we violate a single precept, we should forever regard them as false

---

(*'Iggeret Teman*), ed. A. Halkin (New York, 1952), as well as *Mishneh Torah*, "Yesodey ha-Torah," 7: 7–10. See also *infra*, n. 89.

[73] *Ibid.*

prophets, and we would not obey them, and they would be worthy of death. For the Law is the norm and the guide of the prophets.[74]

Other points which were fiercely contested by Abraham crop up. Isaac insists, for example, that the moral character and personal qualities of a man are decisive in determining whether God will reveal Himself to him. The accurate prediction of the future, especially in a prophecy of good tidings, is certainly a test of a prophet. Despite some vacillations, Isaac also concludes that a prophet with a mission to the people at large must present universally recognizable signs.[75]

There is, however, another dimension to this discussion of false prophets, and it is equally significant. As we read, we realize that all of Isaac's remarks are applicable, not only to Sabbatianism, but to Christianity as well. Just as the "false prophet" can be interpreted as Nathan, so he can also be read as Jesus. There is here a double polemic. That Christ is not named is due to reasons of prudence, as in many other passages in the *Excelencias* which have Christianity in mind. Here, two levels are intertwined. The emphasis on the eternal force of the Law, the necessity for visible signs, and similar arguments are simultaneously a rejection of Christian and Sabbatian claims.

This confluence of anti-Sabbatian and anti-Christian polemic is strikingly confirmed by certain passages in Abraham's two Spanish letters of October, 1668. In his attack on Isaac and Orobio de Castro, Abraham returns time and again to one point with an insistence that reveals to us how important this issue was in the conflict. He charges that both of them really know that the Messiah must first be thoroughly afflicted and despised. If they do not admit it, this is only out of cowardice, *because they are fearful that such an admission will play*

---

[74] *Ibid.*, p. 294. For another passage in this vein see *ibid.*, p. 398, quoted below, ch. IX, p. 431.

[75] It is interesting to see how the two brothers often use the same proof-text for their opposing views. Thus, Isaac cites the signs which Moses requested God to give him when he returned to Egypt, to show that signs are necessary to the prophet (*Excelencias*, p. 299). Abraham, on the other hand, deduces from the same incident the primary importance of faith, else why did Moses care whether the Jews would believe him or not? (*MS* Oxford, fol. 8v).

into the hands of the Christians. Abraham knows full well that his major proof-text, Isaiah 53, is also a classic crux of contention between Judaism and Christianity, and that to read it as a description of the person of the Messiah is to come perilously close to the Christian exegesis. But he is willing to run the risk. Thus, after reiterating to Isaac that the Messiah can triumph only after he is degraded, he adds:

And anyone who otherwise conceives or pretends the Messiah to be is nothing but an idiot, or ignorant of the teachings of the sages. *And if the Christians say the same, what harm can come to us from the truth?* They took it from the sages of Israel. To that extent it is entangled in Augustine's book on the City of God, being a contemporary of the sages of the Gemara, with whom he conversed and from whom he learned. Shall we abandon the truth for fear of the lie? No benefit at all shall emerge for our opponents by conceding that which is certain. Shall it be better, in order not to give arms to the Christians, to depict a Messiah contrary to the prophets. . .?[76]

Isaac must have presented an array of Jewish commentators who refused to interpret Isaiah 53 as referring to the Messiah. Abraham counters:

The sages of Israel say that the Messiah has to reveal himself in the Holy Land, that he must be afflicted and profaned because of the sins of Israel, based on the verse of chapter 53 of Isaiah, and they received and taught, by common agreement, that this entire chapter speaks of the Messiah. And from them the Christians drew. And the later commentators, such as Don Isaac Abravanel . . . Ibn Esra, Rashi, Saadia Gaon, *in order to flee from Idumean arguments,* some explain it as the Jewish people, others as Josiah or Jeremiah, as any righteous man, or as the Messiah son of Ephraim. . . .[77]

---

[76] *MS* Oxford, fol. 4r. (Italics mine.)

[77] *Ibid.,* fol. 13r. "Idumean" means Christian, in accordance with the medieval Jewish usage.

A veiled polemic against the Christian interpretation of Isa. 53 is found in Isaac Cardoso's comparison of the Hebrew text of certain verses with the Vulgate (*Excelencias,* p. 396). Orobio de Castro was particularly concerned with the exegesis of this chapter, and devoted to it an entire treatise, of which a Portuguese trans-

In the same vein, when denying the argument that the Messiah must build the Temple and be preceded by a general revelation of Elijah:

It seems to me that I am hearing these overscrupulous fools [who claim] that this is to give weapons to the *goyim*, and in so doing they accuse the sages, for it is not my caprice. But neither they [the sages] nor I are afraid of Idumean arguments. . . .[78]

But perhaps the most significant statements of all occur in yet another passage, in which Abraham speaks of the relation between the Messiah's degradation and subsequent triumph.

And in another place it is implied that twice he shall be incarcerated, having to exclaim *My God, my God, why hast thou forsaken me*, for all of Psalm 22, and the end of 89, refer to him; that they shall have to curse him; that God must bring him under severe sentences and troubles never imposed on the ancient fathers; that the enemy must oppose him, and that woe to him who shall be present at that time, because of the great disorders and doubts which there must be concerning the belief [in him]; and that many shall have to abandon the Law; and that afterward he shall ascend to be supreme and elevated with the spirit of the Lord, and with that of his mouth he shall slay evil, cast down idolatry, and triumph in the world.

This is the true Messiah of Israel according to the sages of Israel, of which the Christians avail themselves and say that the Messiah must be humble; and because he must also be triumphant, they affirm that all the prophecies shall not be completely fulfilled . . . until the final coming, when he shall come triumphantly on the clouds of the heavens. And we say that between the abasement and the glory of the Messiah son of David, there must be no death, for the Messiah son of David does not have die. . . .[79]

---

lation, *Explicação paraphrástica sobre o Capitulo 53 do propheta Isaias*, is mentioned by Kayserling (*BEPJ*, p. 82). Most of it was published by A. Neubauer in his *The Fifty-Third Chapter of Isaiah* (Oxford, 1876), pp. 21–118. It also forms the substance of ch. VIII in the anonymous French translation of a number of Orobio's works, entitled *Israel vengé, ou exposition naturelle des prophéties Hébraïques que les Chrétiens appliquent à Jésus leur prétendu Messie* (London, 1770). pp. 108–87. See *infra*, ch. IX, p. 429.

[78] *MS* Oxford, fol. 15r.   [79] *Ibid.*, fol. 13v. (Italics mine.)

Abraham, Isaac, and the Messiah

Abraham has here divulged perhaps more than he himself realized, and the issues in the conflict are now clearer than ever. The verses he applies to Sabbatai Zevi are the very ones which Christian exegesis had always cited for Jesus, and Abraham knew it. He himself relates elsewhere that while in Spain he had studied Christian theology for two years, and from other statements of his we know how deeply this knowledge affected him even later.[80] To underscore this is not to impugn Abraham's conscious Jewish loyalties, which were fierce and total. It is rather to point out that there were important Christian elements from which he never fully succeeded in divorcing himself, but which remained conspicuous even after he had woven them into the complex fabric of his Judaism. This is very different from Isaac's occasional tendency to lapse into Christian terminology and categories in expressing traditional Jewish concepts. In Abraham's Jewish theology not merely the form, but the content itself, betrays how active the Christian elements continued to be within his soul. The passage just quoted explicitly brings Abraham's Sabbatianism and the Christian messianic teaching to their closest point of contact. Here, in the final analysis, the two are separated by

---

[80] On these theological studies see Abraham's remarks in the selection from his *Derush ha-kinnuyyim* published by Scholem, "New Contributions to the study of Abraham Cardoso" (Hebrew), in *Abhandlungen zur Erinnerung an Hirsch Perez Chajes* (Vienna, 1933), Hebrew Section, p. 344:

» ואני שנולדתי ביניהם ראיתי כל מה שהביאו ולמדתי כאנוס חכמת האלהות שלהם הנקראת טיאולוגיי׳׳א, וטעמיהם הבל וראיותיהם רעות רוח... «

Cf. also *Zion*, VII, 25, n. 60, where two years are specifically mentioned. In the *Derush ha-kinnuyyim* Abraham's treatment of the Christian trinitarian dogma is accurate, and he is at great pains to differentiate between it and his own doctrine of the deity which involves "The First Cause," "The Holy One," "The Shekhina." Still, the two triads are close enough for him to be able to say that the Christian idea of the Trinity is only a "corruption" of the "secret of the divinity" which the ancient sages had known but which had subsequently been forgotten among most Jews (p. 336). Many other important Christian elements are revealed in the selections published by Scholem in *Zion*, VII, 22–23. Cf. also the interesting analysis of the beliefs of the "philosophers," Muslims, Christians, and pagans, in his *Derush zeh 'eli va-'anvehu* published by Scholem, "Two New Theological Texts of Abraham Cardoso" (Hebrew), *Sefunot*, III-IV (1960), esp. pp. 281–84. Scholem has also suggested that gnostic ideas may have come to him through his readings about the ancient gnostic heresies in Christian literature.

a hair: the Christians possess the truth in believing that the Messiah must undergo radical suffering; they err only in thinking that he must *die!*

Is it any wonder, then, that Isaac Cardoso, Orobio de Castro, and others, attacked Abraham's views not merely in substance, but as a teaching which gives "arms" to the Christians? These men realized instinctively that to concede a suffering Messiah is already to grant the overwhelming portion of the Christian messianic claim, and that from thence it is no more absurd to accept the crucified Messiah than the apostate Messiah. Indeed, it was perhaps easier.

The very nature of the messianic promise was bound up in this issue. Is the Redemption to be, from the very outset, terrestrial? Here again we see how the lines between anti-Sabbatianism and the Judeo-Christian polemic tend to blur. Isaac Cardoso had taken his stand squarely on the immediate temporal fulfillment of all the messianic prophecies. Abraham hurled back this sarcastic reply:

Let us return to the aforementioned messiah of Doctor Cardoso and his capricious companions: he is neither Christian nor Jew, but imaginary; he must come casting rays of light . . . and then, all at once, in a twinkling, he has to ingather the tribes, and the wheat from the chaff; he must come on a cloud of sugar candy, his body of butter paste, his garment of soft bread. And for support they drag in the great Rabbi Moses of Egypt, whom they see but do not understand even in the light, and they have thrust upon him the opinion that perforce Elijah must first come, and that there must be blown a shofar as huge as their own simple imaginations, without which not only the doctrine of the sages, but even Sacred Scripture, cannot be fulfilled![81]

To Isaac Cardoso, as to any Jew who had lived as a Marrano in Spain, this gross ridicule of age-old Jewish hopes for the material and concrete realization on earth of the messianic promise, in favor of a suffering messiah, must have had an uncomfortably familiar ring.

---

[81] *MS* Oxford, fol. 14r. Abraham must have seen in Maimonides both a stumbling block and an ally. For while the Maimonidean insistence that the Messiah cannot violate the Law is difficult for him, Maimonides' own radical attenuation of traditional eschatological conceptions (e.g., *Guide*, II, 29; *MT*, Teshubah, 8: 2 ff., Melakim, 12: 1 ff.) plays into his hands.

Abraham, Isaac, and the Messiah

Such burlesques of the alleged vulgarity of the Jewish conception of the Messiah, regarded as a result of Jewish inability to understand the spiritual sense of Scripture, were a stock in trade of Peninsular antisemites. To take but one example from many, how different is Abraham's statement from the following characteristic passage of the Spaniard Torrejoncillo?

There is no way to make them [the "Jews"] believe that the true Messiah has arrived, although all their anxieties are that the Messiah, whom they are always awaiting, should come! And I ask: How do they imagine him to be? Very rich. How greedy! With great pomp and secular ostentation. How vainglorious! With a very huge household, greater than that of Solomon. What sensualists! With an overabundance of food and delicacies. What gluttons! With much honey and butter. What cravers for sweets. . . .![82]

Though Abraham was speaking in the name of Sabbatai Zevi, and Torrejoncillo in the name of Jesus, the argumentation is essentially the same. We see once again how easily obliterated is the boundary between Abraham's Sabbatian propoganda and that of the Christian *adversus judaeos*. It is therefore no mere coincidence that the two foremost Marrano apologists for Judaism to the Christian world in the seventeenth century are, at the same time, the two leading anti-Sabbatians to emerge out of the Marrano ranks. The one attitude necessarily flowed out of the other.

But if the conflict over Sabbatai Zevi was, for Isaac Cardoso, intimately bound up with the Judeo-Christian polemic, then the entire problem of Marranism and Sabbatianism is unfolded before us in a new aspect. Professor Scholem's thesis concerning the correlation between the two is illuminating, but it is incomplete. If it is true that the Marrano experience converged, on one level, with Sabbatianism, as in the case of Abraham Cardoso, it is equally true that the same Marrano experience could also lead in the very opposite direction. Of this Isaac Cardoso is a prime example.[83]

---

[82] Torrejoncillo, *Centinela contra judíos*, p. 102.

[83] Though they may have been in the minority, insufficient attention has been paid by scholars to former Marranos who were opposed to Sabbatianism, and we

For the former Marrano is not only a man who has lived a double religious life and rationalized his position. The Marrano who returns to Judaism with the wholeheartedness of an Isaac Cardoso is also a man who has consciously and decisively rejected Christianity. What does this mean, if not that he has already firmly rejected the Christian interpretation of the prophets, the Christian abrogation of the Law, and the suffering Messiah who will bring about the earthly kingdom only when he reveals himself again? With the exception of the particular nuance of the Messiah's conversion, and the use of Jewish texts, there was nothing in Abraham's messianic arguments that Isaac had not already known, weighed, and abandoned years before. To say that Isaac Cardoso was gravely concerned lest the Sabbatian ideology give weapons to the Christians in their mission to the Jews is really to point to this more profound and personal level on which the conflict was waged. In essence the drama of Isaac's clash with Abraham was a repetition of one whose final act he had already resolved within himself before he left Spain. The issues which Abraham now raised in connection with Sabbatai Zevi were essentially the same that Isaac had already hammered out with regard to Christ, and on which he had staked his existence. To accept Abraham's reasoning would have meant for him to deny the very ground of his life, which had brought him from the Spanish court to an Italian Ghetto. This he could not do.[84]

---

really know very little on this score. Yet here, for example, is Tomás de Pinedo: "In ea anno 1666 surrexit pseudopropheta ille Nathan, qui una cum suo pseudo-masiach Sebathai Sebi decepit stultos Judaeos, non eos quibus *Ex meliore luto finxit praecordia Titan.* Facile homines praesertim stulti credunt quae desiderant" (*Stephanus de Urbibus*, p. 193, n. 20; *s.v.* "Gaza"). For his life see *supra*, ch. II, pp. 59 f.

[84] Perhaps, finally, we may now also better understand Isaac's rejection of the Kabbalah. It could be demonstrated quite easily that unlike Abraham, who studied the Kabbalah in depth after his return to Judaism, Isaac largely obtained his rather superficial knowledge of it while still in Spain, and from *Christian sources*. We have already stressed that his attitude toward Kabbalah cannot be attributed to "rationalism." But if his primary encounter had been with *Christian kabbalism*, with its generally positive evaluation of the Kabbalah as supporting the Christian faith, his rejection may well have been motivated, at least in part, by the "Christian" overtones and associations with which it was still linked in his mind. That antipathy to Kabbalah may partly derive from such considerations is seen clearly

Abraham, Isaac, and the Messiah

In a final desperate effort to convince, Abraham abandoned exegesis, theology, and theory, and directed a passionate appeal *ad hominem:*

Here enter Doctor Cardoso of Verona, Doctor Orobio of Amsterdam, and a conglomeration of rabbis, saying that the Messiah must be holy and not an apostate, a Jew and not a Mohammedan. [But] it is known that anyone who becomes a *goy* for fear of death is called, and is, a Jew by the entire Law; and it is clearer than the sun that by force the Sultan put the turban on Sabbatai Zevi. Therefore by divine law he is perfectly Jewish, and by the law of Moors or Christians he has not even emerged from Judaism, since one and the other hold that the terrorized, or the forced, does not yet enter their community. . . .

I ask these doctors and the majority of those who have come from Spain, who, while there, prostrated themselves to strange gods, without circumcision, without the Law, nor Jewish works—whether they were Christians or Jews? For if they were not [Jews] in Spain, they shall be so as little in Flanders, from which it follows that neither here nor there are they Jews nor Christians, since he who is not a Jew while he doesn't circumcise or immerse himself is in any event a *goy gamur.* . . .

And if they shall say to me that we *were* Jews in Spain, and that such are all the Marranos who remain there, and so I too believe, then are they not ashamed to open their mouths and call Sabbatai Zevi an unfaithful apostate? Especially when they, and their fathers, grandfathers, and great-grandfathers, abandoned the Law . . . some by force, and others by spontaneous choice, and entertained themselves among the *goyim* for 180 years, without circumcision, marriage ritual, menstrual purity, without the Law, for mundane interests and vain glories, and most come fleeing from the whip—and yet call themselves perfect Jews in Spain, and a holy people! And Sabbatai Zevi, who devoted himself since childhood to the Lord, with study, abstinence, and continuous sanctity,

---

in these remarks of Leone Modena: "I have told you more than once that it [i.e., the Kabbalah] affected me badly. For I was accustomed since my youth to debate with the apostates from our people who are never silent, and on this I prided myself, that I was the most expert of my contemporaries. But whenever I wanted to read or peruse these books, immediately there came before my eyes words and themes which support them [i.e., the apostates to Christianity] . . ." (*'Ari nohem*, ed. Julius Furst [Leipzig, 1840], ch. III, p. 9; cf. also Modena's remarks on Christian Kabbalah, *ibid.*, p. 7).

but was forced to don a turban, shall not have the right to call himself a Jew?![85]

But even this argument would not really impress Isaac, although he too was quite aware that by no means all of his brethren in Spain were "Jews." For him, as we shall see in the *Excelencias*, the Marranos are, nevertheless, *testigos de la unidad de Dios*—witnesses to the Unity of God. . . .

THE AFTERMATH

After October of 1668 all relations between the brothers came to an end. There is no indication that they ever again communicated with one another. Some months later, Isaac wrote his own account of the Sabbatian movement, and inserted it in the *Philosophia libera*.[86]

As in all his published works, the autobiographical element is submerged, and one would be hard put to divine from its contents that during the previous two years he had been personally touched by the events he describes:

But we ought not to pass over in silence the history of a certain false Messiah and fictitious prophet in our time who rose up a few years ago and thoroughly upset the situation of the Jews. There was a certain Hebrew born in Smyrna named Sabbatai. He had a fine and handsome appearance, was zealous of the Law, but indulged too much in the study of Kabbalah, weakened his body with prolonged prayers and fasts, bathed himself in the waters of the sea almost every day, though it was the heart of winter or the heat of summer, prayed with excessive superstition, and, being very haughty, displayed excessive piety before the masses. Believing that he had been endowed with prophetic spirit and was the Messiah, and that he would lead back the Hebrews from their widespread and long captivity into the Promised Land, he promised that

---

[85] *MS* Oxford, fols. 16v-17r. If Abraham had knowledge of his sufferings at the hands of the Inquisition, "fleeing from the whip" may well be a jibe against Orobio de Castro.

[86] *Phil. lib.*, fols. 641–42.

he would cross the sea with his disciples and that, embracing the book of the Law, he would arrive with dry feet. His piety turned to madness, and the haughty man was warned by the elders to take care not to presume so many and such deep mysteries about himself, since otherwise he would pay the penalty and be treated as if he were insane. He, having great confidence in himself, despised the warnings and had little regard for the counsels of the elders. Therefore, after he had been warned rather often and had been summoned, and since he never listened to their words, they faced him with his deeds, chided and cursed him, and cast him out of the congregation.

He departed in flight to Thessalonica and wandered through the cities of Greece, uplifted with no less presumption and disdain, and was cast out; and finally he came to the Holy Land and Jerusalem, where, concentrating on the study of the Law, he unraveled books, and especially the Zohar, which explains the five books of the Law in a mystic and allegorical sense, and he was regarded as the Prince of Kabbalists. He also studied the commentators of that type, and, keeping himself at home, he obtained a great reputation for piety, not only among the Hebrews, but also among the Turks, by praying, fasting, reading, and teaching. The more prudent regarded him as a hypocrite, while the masses thought that he was pious.

Among others who were either his pupils or companions of his studies he held in intimacy a certain young man named Nathan of Gaza. Moved by frequent conversation and unusual ambition, he secretly declared himself the Messiah and proclaimed the prophet Nathan as his precursor. A plan was entered into between them that each commend the other, and other profligate companions were joined to them. A letter was sent to Egypt and other regions that the Messiah had arrived, and they were applauded joyfully by the simple folk. Meanwhile, he left the Holy Land and returned to Smyrna, where he was revered by his brothers and kinsmen, and by the masses, as a holy man and as the Messiah. The credulous declared that his face shone with unusual splendor and that when he prayed he breathed forth a most pleasant odor upon the bystanders, that he partook of food only from Sabbath to Sabbath and passed six days without nourishment (as if those things would bring forth either the Messiah or a prophet). He contrived all this with skill and deceit, for he made his face to shine through rouges, waters and pigments; while praying he exhaled an odor, since his hands and face were saturated with musk and amber; and he ate bread and sweets that were secretly hidden in his pocket. Those of the Jews who did not believe those imposters were chided and falsely accused, and attacked physically by the malicious ones.

Sabbatai, elated by the acclamations of the ignorant masses, thought that he was permitted to do many things. He transgressed a number of precepts of the Law, violated the Sabbath, uttered the ineffable Name of God, offered sacrifices outside the Temple and the Holy Land, profaned the fasts instituted by our ancestors, and converted into a festival the celebrated fast of the month of July which was instituted in memory of the overthrow of Jerusalem by Titus and was wont to be observed by wailing, grief, and tears, because he had been born on that day. His pupils and followers immersed themselves in banquets. While others sat, praying and beating their breasts, affected by the fast, and showed the greatest sadness, they gave themselves sumptuously to meals and banquets; while others, who were overwhelmed by hunger and thirst, showed their bitterness, they (about whom Jeremiah, chapter 11, says: *And you exult when you do wrong*) danced and joyously played instruments.

What save sadness did Sabbatai, who was born on a funereal day, predict? He was unfortunate in his very name, since, in the Hebrew language, Saturn is called Sabbatai, a sad and malignant star regarded as a rather great misfortune by the astrologers. Rumor increased, and talk began to multiply as it proceeded. There was a tumult, and he was accompanied by a great throng of men. Those who were more prudent feared an insurrection through the new movement. He set out to Constantinople, and on the way was detained by the governors of Turkey in fortresses which are very strong citadels, two hundred miles distant from the palace. While detained in prison he was visited by a large number of Jews, and nothing save gold or silver was shown to the guard. Meanwhile, the governor feared that some uprising might arise from the tumultuous crowd, and when a report was sent to the Vizier in Adrianople, where the king was, he sent for Sabbatai. When he had been brought before him, he asked him whether he was the Messiah awaited by the Jews and whether he knew miracles and prodigies. He denied that he performed miracles or was the Messiah, but stated that he was a Jew zealous in the Law. Rebuked by the king because he was arousing tumults among the people, he was threatened that either he must lose his head or become a Mohammedan; and he, overcome by fear of death, embraced Mohammedanism, and, becoming an Ishmaelite instead of a Jew, he changed the Law of Moses into the Koran. He who professed the Law, transgressed the Law, about whom the prophet says, *Those who handle the Law did not know me, and the shepherds walked crookedly against me.*

345

Abraham, Isaac, and the Messiah

Meanwhile, that other seducer, the false prophet Nathan who proclaimed Sabbatai the Messiah, predicted that, on the twenty-seventh day of the month of October (others say of February) in the year 1667, would come the redemption of the Jews from misery and long captivity; but an utterly vain outcome corresponded to this insane prediction. Finally, both were held in hatred and contempt by the Jews, according to the statement: *The fools will not stand in the sight of your eyes, for you hate all who work vanity.* The false messiah, having become a Turk, served the Turks; and the false prophet, leaving Palestine, wandered through various provinces, but nowhere established himself.

When, imbued with certain Kabbalistic inventions and figments, he came to Venice last year, he was summoned by the rabbis and leaders.[87] In an examination of prophecy he was found to be a simple and foolish man, fearful, and hardly versed in the Law. They discovered that his prophecy was vain and false. He boasted that he had looked into the Chariot, that wondrous vision of the prophet Ezekiel, and that an angel was announcing the future to him; however, when examined, he admitted that it was not a prophetic vision, but the fault was closer to ambition, hypocrisy, pride, and ignorance.[88] Afterwards he visited Leghorn, where he was also recognized and ejected. Finally he wandered through the states of the Turks, and mad, he paid the penalty for insanity; for he who wished to gather together the scattered Hebrews was himself exiled, and he wandered and roamed.

Rabbi Moses mentions certain similar messiahs and false prophets in Cordoba, Spain, and Africa, in a letter which he wrote to Teman, or the Southern regions, where a certain seducer who arose in the name of sanctity drew to his opinion several celebrated men who believed that he was the Messiah.[89] He was mad and silly, although he preached repentance, contrition, and piety, and Rabbi Moses himself advised the Hebrews of that region that they should treat that Messiah as though

---

[87] On the examination in Venice, see Scholem, *Shabbetai Ṣebi*, II, 649 ff.

[88] His "confession" is preserved in the letter entitled *Ẕikron li-beney Yisrael* which was circulated afterwards by the Venetian Jewish authorities. It is printed in *ṢNṢ*, pp. 267 f. See also Scholem, *Shabbetai Ṣebi*, II, 650–52.

[89] Maimonides' *Epistle to Yemen* was first printed in Basel in 1629, in *Ta'alumot ḥokhmah*, a selection of the writings of Joseph del Medigo. But Cardoso did not necessarily read it in Hebrew. A Latin version (*Epistola ad Meridiem*) by G. H. Vorstius was appended to his translation of David Gans' *Ṣemah David* (*Germen Davidis*) (Amsterdam, 1644).

he were insane, that they expose him and torment him a little, and that they detain him for so long a time that he should return to his senses and not declare himself the Messiah. Arisba[90] and other authors also mention others who paid the penalty for seducing some, or who were reduced to the number of the insane, and of them the prophet says: *They walked after emptiness and became empty.* The wise men of the Hebrews say that after prophecy ceased in olden times, a certain part of it is found only among children and madmen, indicating that sometimes they predict by chance things that will definitely happen.

But it is necessary to test pseudo prophets diligently through their life and habits, inasmuch as they often deceive by feigned consecration and piety; and they show themselves through no indication better than through that feeling which, according to Aristotle, is to us a source of scandal and disgrace, namely, the pleasures and fornications of love[91]; in the same way that Zedekiah the son of Maaseiah and Ahab the son of Kolaiah were detected at Babylon, who considered themselves masters of prophecy and under the veil of holiness, until finally their falseness was detected, and they were burned by King Nebuchadnezzar because of an accusation which was proved, as is said in Jeremiah 29: *May the Lord make you like Zedekiah and like Ahab, whom the King of Babylon burned in fire. Likewise they have also committed adultery with the wives of their friends, and have falsely spoken a word in my name.* And almost all who have boasted of false prophecy, says Rabbi Moses, have betrayed themselves by their lust, since it is the first step and first sign of wise men and of prophets, to despise corporeal pleasures, and afterwards to deal with divine matters.

With the writing of this account, the Sabbatian episode in Isaac Cardoso's life may be regarded as closed. And yet, events were to add to it a strange postscript. We will recall that already in 1665 Samuel Aboab had expressed his concern lest the Sabbatian movement prove a tool in the hands of the gentiles,[92] and we have seen to what extent the Judeo-Christian polemic loomed in Cardoso's own thinking. As it turned out, such fears were fully justified.

---

[90] Cardoso is referring to Responsum no. 548 of R. Solomon b. Adret, occasioned by a false messiah in Ávila in 1295.

[91] It may be that in this and the succeeding lines Isaac has his brother Abraham in mind. The latter had two wives, Judith and Sarah. See *Sefunot*, III-IV, 207, 209.

[92] See *supra*, n. 24. See also his *Debar Shemuel*, n. 371, fol. 97r.

Abraham, Isaac, and the Messiah

Following the collapse of the movement, antisemites and missionaries to the Jews made ample use of the messianic debacle for their respective purposes. The latest frustration of Jewish hopes provided a marvelous occasion to heap ridicule on the Jews, to offer new proof of their rejection by God, or a wedge with which to drive home the Christian message. On its simplest level, the argument suggested that, if the Jews were ready to accept such an obvious impostor as Sabbatai Zevi, surely they must now finally realize that the true Messiah, Christ, had been awaiting them all along. Others, more subtle, retold the story of the movement in such a way as to put into relief those aspects which offered Christian parallels, convinced that these had already paved the way for an acceptance of Christ.[93]

To the end of the seventeenth century and beyond, this mode of attack continued.[94] In fact, in a work by Benetelli published in 1704,

---

[93] So, e. g., Lodovico Maracci, *L'ebreo preso per le buone* (Rome, 1701), pp. 267–79. After treating previous false messiahs, he begins: "Ma niuno di questi vostri Gabbamondi hà fatto più romore e più bruttamente ha ingannato et vituperato la vostra gente, che quel Sabbatai Tsevi. . . ."
See also the analysis of I. Sonne, "New Material on Sabbatai Zevi from a Notebook of R. Abraham Rovigo," *Sefunot*, III–IV (1960), 52 ff. He chides Scholem for underestimating the seriousness of the report (*Shabbetai Ṣebi*, II, 648) that, immediately after the conversion in 1666, Jesuit missionaries baptized over a thousand Jews. The exaggerated figure is unimportant; what matters is, rather, the efforts of the missionaries to manipulate the messianic apostasy for their own goals (Sonne, p. 54).

[94] To the treatment of the Sabbatian movement by Maracci, one may add, in Italy alone: Giulio Morosini, *Via della fede*, I, 76–78; Bartolocci, *Bibl. magn. rabb.*, IV, 48–51; Carlo Giuseppi Imbonati, [*Shema Yisrael*]: *Adventus messiae a Iudaeorum blasphemiis, ac haereticorum calumniis vindicatus*, fol. 116 (printed at the end of his bibliography of Latin writers against the Jews, which forms vol. V of Bartolocci's *Bibliotheca* [Rome, 1694]).
Perhaps the most dramatic description of the effects of the Sabbatian and post-Sabbatian movements on Christian missionary propaganda is given by the physician Tobias Cohen in his *Ma'asseh Tobiah* (Venice, 1707), pp. 25 ff., e.g.: "And see how the nations, and especially the Christians, open wide their mouths against us without end, and deride us, and rebuke and curse us, saying all the day: Where, then, is your king the Messiah for whom you hope? Surely all the calculated times have already passed by, the harvest is gone, the summer is over, and you have not been redeemed! And why do you spin idle dreams, saying he

the source of the author's information on the Sabbatian movement was the *Philosophia libera!*[95] We may well suspect that a similar use was already being made of the work shortly after its publication in 1673, and that Cardoso must have regretted more than once that he had placed his account in a Latin work for all to read. This must have been for him a crowning, bitter irony. He, who had been so concerned lest weapons be given to the enemies of Israel, had himself unwittingly played into their hands. Six years later, in publishing the *Excelencias*, he would suppress this section entirely. And in that work he would finally take up his own weapons, to defend his faith and his people against a hostile world.

---

will surely come and not tarry? But do you not see that so many false messiahs have led you astray in your foolishness! ... And indeed several of the false messiahs have misled some of the Children of Israel, and they have given an opportunity to our enemies to mock us and to abuse us, and it is almost a sword in the hands of the gentiles with which to kill us!"

[95] Luigi Maria Benetelli, *La saetta di gionata scagliate a favor degli Ebrei* (Venice, 1704), pp. 506-7: "L'istoria che qui ristringo è prolissamente riferita da Isac Cardoso." It should be observed that Maimonides' own survey of pseudo messiahs in the *Epistle to Yemen* had already been utilized earlier by Christian polemicists for the same purposes.

SPOKESMAN FOR JUDAISM

> Negra yo y hermosa. . . . No me miredes
> porque yo denegrida, que me ennegreció
> el sol. . . .
>
> —*El Cantar de los Cantares*

I have termed the *Philosophia libera* Isaac Cardoso's "summa." *Las excelencias de los Hebreos* is his apologia, and it is so in a double sense: a vindication of Judaism and Jewry before the nations, and a culminating justification of his own life and the choice he had made.

The book appeared in Amsterdam in 1679, and was published at the famous Sephardic press of David de Castro Tartas.[1] Cardoso dedicated it to the wealthy Jacob de Pinto, one of the founders of the "Yeshiba de los Pintos," who probably paid the cost of the printing. In the dedication, dated Verona, March 17, 1678, he stated the purpose of his work:

The Jewish people, as much beloved of God as persecuted by men, has been, for two thousand years, since the time of Nebuchadnezzar,

---

[1] *Las/ excelencias/ de los Hebreos/ por el Doctor/ Yshac Cardoso/* [woodcut: hand gathering flowers, with motto: "El que me esparsio me recogera]/ *Impresso en Amsterdam en casa de/ David de Castro Tartas/ El año de 1679.* 3 pp. of Dedication + pp. 1–431.

Some copies contain an additional title page placed between pp. 332 and 333, headed: *Las excelencias y calunias de los Hebreos.* See Alvaro Néves, *Bibliografía Luso-Judaica: Noticia subsidiaria da colecção de Alberto Carlos da Silva* (Coimbra, 1913), p. 18.

scattered among the nations, expiating its sins and those of its fathers against the Holy Law, maltreated by some, afflicted by others, despised by all, so that there is no state or kingdom which has not unsheathed its sword against it, shedding its blood, consuming its substance, as the Psalmist says: *Who eat up my people as they eat bread.* This people was specially created to praise the Lord. . . . God took it for His inheritance, and exalted it with illustrious titles, of "servant," of "son," of "firstborn," of "betrothed," of "beloved," and other proofs of inseparable and perpetual love. . . .

The nations who see Israel brought low, despised, and without any human succor, judge it abhorred and rejected by its God. They see it externally disfigured, but it is beautiful within, like the tents of Kedar and the curtains of Solomon, as the Betrothed herself sings: *Black am I, but comely: do not look at me that I am swarthy, for the sun has darkened me.* Its beauty is unknown because of its troubles, and the afflictions of its captivity; it is punished, but never abhorred, loved forever, and castigated temporarily. *With an everlasting love have I loved thee,* the captivity being but a moment in respect to the Redemption. *For a small moment have I forsaken thee, but with great compassion will I gather thee; with a little wrath I hid my face from thee for a moment, but with everlasting kindness will I have compassion on thee.*

Its separation makes it abhorred by the nations, but the very same fact makes it most endeared to its Creator. All conspire against it and afflict the afflicted, leveling upon it a thousand calumnies, intriguing against their lives and their goods, so that, were they not sustained by the Divine hand, they would already have been engulfed by the wolves and the lions who so pant after their blood.

In all centuries past and present, horrible accusations are raised in order to consume them, without allowing them a brief respite in their tribulations. It was necessary to minutely relate these slanders in the face of the virtues which reveal them for what they are, so that truth may shine forth all the more, and the lie may be confounded.

When the book appeared, Cardoso was somewhat disappointed with the printing itself. He sent a copy to Samuel Aboab in Venice, and in the accompanying letter, dated July 23, 1679, he observed:

It contains many errors which the printer discovered too late in time, and rushed through, not reflecting well the original [manuscript], both in the orthography, and in the substance of the text, as well as forgetting

351

in the margin many references which I had placed there. When an author is not present, there are always many errors in the printing. You must supplement with your learning, our roughness, and with your goodness, our defects. . . .

Aboab sent his reply a week later and, after reading it, Cardoso need not have worried further about the reception of the *Excelencias* among the Jews. In a graceful and subtle allusion to the fact that Cardoso,who had come to Judaism so late in life, was now expounding it to others, Aboab wrote:

It is worthy recompense to God for His singular favors, when he who has been worthy to receive them tries to imitate Him by communicating their benefits to others. You have followed this precept by enabling us to share the light of your rare erudition in the excellent book on the excellence of Israel against our slanderers. . . .[2]

Cardoso could well appreciate the force of these words. The course that had led from Trancoso to this day was singular indeed. At the age of seventy-five, his life had finally achieved its destiny.

THE PLACE AND SCOPE OF THE EXCELENCIAS

Las excelencias de los Hebreos stands firmly within the tradition of Sephardic apologetics and polemics written in the vernacular tongues. If any fruitful comparison is to be made, however, we must first distinguish broadly between those works which were printed and those which remained in manuscript.

Cardoso's decision to print his work in Amsterdam may well have been due to significant hesitations at having it published, like the *Philosophia libera*, in Venice. Despite the vaunted freedom of the

---

[2] Both letters, as well as another from Cardoso to Aboab on the Hebrew derivation of the names of Spanish cities, were published by Marco Mortara, "Isaac Cardoso et Samuel Aboab," *REJ*, XII (1886), 301–5.

latter city, he may have felt that a book of this character had best see the light of day in the Dutch capital where, presumably, a greater range of expression was possible. Indeed, he had ample reason to act in this manner. Some four decades earlier, Leone Modena had presented himself before the Venetian Inquisition to forestall any embarassment that might arise because of the publication, in Paris, of his relatively innocuous description of Jewish customs and beliefs, the *Historia dei riti Ebraici*.[3] A year later there had appeared in Venice Simone Luzzato's important *Discorso circa il stato de gl' Hebrei*, arguing the usefulness of the Jews to the Venetian Republic.[4] The measure of Luzzato's own qualms concerning the gentile reaction may be seen in the exaggerated humility with which he often presses his case. Equally revealing, perhaps, is the fact that the printed *Discorso* constituted only a part of a more comprehensive work which was to include a detailed exposition of Judaism, but which Luzzato decided, probably out of prudence, not to publish.[5] The Venetian atmosphere is perhaps best reflected in a letter of Leone Modena to Rabbi Gershon Cohen, in which he describes his own polemical discussions with Christians:

These days I often attend the discourses of a group of [Christian] scholars and, as you know, much of the talk revolves among us concerning their

---

[3] See Cecil Roth, "Léon de Modène, ses Riti Ebraici, et le Saint-Office à Venise," *REJ*, LXXXVII (1929), 83–88.

[4] *Discorso circa il stato de gl' Hebrei, et in particolar dimoranti nell'inclita Città di Venetia* (Venice, 1638). It has been translated into Hebrew by D. Lattes, with introductions by M. A. Shulwass and R. B. Bacchi, as *Ma'amar 'al Yehudey Veneṣia* (Jerusalem, 1951). All future references are to this edition.

[5] The title page of the *Discorso* refers to it as "un apendice al trattato dell'opinione e Dogmi de gl'Hebrei dall'universal non dissonante, e de Riti loro piú principali." Though noting that Luzzato alludes to this treatise again in the text, and that De Rossi mentioned it, Bacchi asserts that it was never written (*Ma'amar*, pp. 30 f.). But there may well be an allusion to a manuscript of it in Samuel Aboab's discussion of books which are useful in combating those who doubt the Oral Law, and which are written in the vernacular. After citing Imanuel Aboab's *Nomologia* and Manasseh b. Israel's *Conciliador*, he adds: דברי הקונטרוס כתיבת יד הנמצא בינינו מאת במוהר״ר שמחה לוצאטו ז״ל... (*Debar Shemuel*, fol. 52v). One of the Inquisitors' demands of Leone Modena was that he inform them of any work similar to his own which another may have written. (See Roth, *Léon de Modène*.)

questions and our replies, and behold, were I to write you a third part of them I know that they would be sweet to your taste, *but you are aware that they cannot be committed to writing, for they are only to be communicated orally.*[6]

Nor was there a feeling of complete security in this regard even in Amsterdam. Sometime between 1631 and 1642 the Lithuanian Karaite Zaraḥ ben Nathan wrote to Manasseh ben Israel, whose Amsterdam press was well known, asking him to publish two Karaite works: the great anti-Christian polemic *Hizzuk 'emunah* of Isaac b. Abraham Troki, and Joseph Malinowski's hymn, *Ha-elef lekha.* Manasseh's reply is not preserved. Significantly, however, while the latter work was actually published through Manasseh's instrumentality, Troki's polemic was not.[7] To take yet another example, in 1667 Jacob Abendana published in Amsterdam his Spanish translation of Judah Halevi's *Kuzari*, together with a commentary.[8] In the famous dialogue between the Khazar king and the representatives of the various religions, the conversation with the Christian is radically abridged, and he is simply called a "wise man of Edom." The presentation of specifically Christian dogma is completely eliminated, although it constitutes more than half of the Christian scholar's statement in Halevi's original text.[9]

This points to a more general phenomenon. A survey of seventeenth-century Jewish apologiae in Spanish, Portuguese, and Italian

---

[6] *Kitbe ha-Rab Yehudah Aryeh mi-Modena* (*Leo Modena's Briefe und Schriftstücke*), ed. Ludwig Blau (Budapest, 1905), Hebrew section, no. 47, p. 48. (Italics mine.)

[7] Zaraḥ's letter is printed in Jacob Mann's *Texts and Studies in Jewish History and Literature*, II: *Karaitica* (Philadelphia, 1935), no. 134, pp. 1225–28. For the printing of Malinowski's poem see *ibid.*, p. 730, n. 174. Characteristically, Troki's work, written in the 16th century, was first printed in 1681 in Wagenseil's anti-Jewish *Tela ignea Satanae*. A Spanish translation (*Fortificación de la Ley*) made in 1621 by Isaac Athias remained in manuscript and was never published.

[8] *Cuzary, Libro de grande sciencia y mucha doctrina. Discursos que passaron entre el Rey Cuzar y un singular Sabio de Ysrael llamado R. Yshac Sanguery. Fue compuesto este libro en la lengua Arabiga por el Doctissimo R. Yeuda Levita, y traduzido en la lengua Santa por el famoso traductor R. Yeuda Aben Tibon, En el año de 4927 a la Criacion del mundo. Y agora nuevamente traduzido del Ebrayco en Español, y comentado, por el Hacham R. Jacob Abendana, con estilo facil y grave. En Amsterdam, Año 5423.*

[9] See *ibid.*, p. 8.

reveals that they can be roughly grouped into two categories. Apologetic works which merely concentrated on defending Judaism or explaining it to the gentiles were printed, and this was indeed one of the marks of the new age. However, active polemics which directly assailed Christianity were copied and recopied in manuscripts, and circulated privately. This was so in Amsterdam, let alone elsewhere, and it explains, for instance, why none of Orobio de Castro's tracts were published by him. In fact, the only overt anti-Christian polemics which appeared in print were brought to the press by *Christian* polemicists, who published them side by side with their own refutations. Thus it was Philip van Limborch who was to publish his "friendly disputation" with Orobio in 1687.[10] Earlier, in 1669, Anton Hulsius, professor of Hebrew at Leiden, printed his exchange of letters with Jacob Abendana on Haggai 2: 9 ("The glory of this latter house shall be greater than that of the former").[11]

There were, then, limitations which had to be observed in a published work even under the most favorable of circumstances. References to Christianity had to be oblique and circumspect. We shall not expect to find in the *Excelencias* the same uninhibited attacks upon Christianity that are contained in the polemical manuscripts of the time. Rather, we shall be surprised to find Cardoso as outspoken as he is.

When we turn for comparison to the printed apologetic literature, we find several differences in both the aim and the achievement of the *Excelencias*. It is, to begin with, the most comprehensive of them all. The *Flagellum calumniantium* of the Hamburg physician Dr. Benedict de Castro, which appeared in 1631, was limited to the refutation of charges which had been hurled against other members of the medical profession who were of Marrano origin.[12] Such works

---

[10] Limborch, *De veritate religionis Christianae amica collatio cum erudito Judaeo* (Gouda, 1687).

[11] *Disputatio epistolaris habraica, inter Antonium Hulsium, linguae S. Professorem, et Jacobum Abendanah Rabbinum Amsterdamensem super loco Haggaei cap. 2. v. 9 . Major erit gloria domus hujus posterioris quam prioris. Addita versione Latina, In usum Collegii Rabbinici.* (Leyden, 1669).

[12] Benedict (Baruch Nahmias) de Castro, *Flagellum calumniantium, seu Apologia* (Amsterdam, 1631). There is a good summary in Friedenwald, *Jews in Medicine,*

of Manasseh ben Israel as his *Esperanza de Israel,* his *Humble Addresses* to Oliver Cromwell, or the *Vindiciae Judaeorum,* were all geared to the immediate purpose of gaining the readmission of the Jews to England.[13] Although these books are full of important apologetic materials, the emphasis is pragmatic, dwelling heavily on the benefits which will accrue to the Commonwealth by the presence of the Jews, and attempting to allay English fears concerning their loyalty and reliability. This, in a different setting, is also the burden of Simone Luzzato's more original and incisive *Discorso.* One may finally look for a precedent for Cardoso's work in the *Nomologia* of Imanuel Aboab, published in Amsterdam in 1629.[14] But although many of its arguments are relevant also to Judeo-Christian polemics, the book remains essentially a defense of the Oral Law against those who impugned it among the Jews themselves. Its historical notes, and the occasional fierce indictments of the Iberian treatment of the Jews, are subsumed to this central theme.

We shall see that Cardoso drew heavily on all these works, and that in a sense his book sums up the entire chain of Sephardic apologetics. There is hardly a topic in the aforementioned books which is not treated in the *Excelencias* in one form or another. Yet none of the earlier writers had attempted so bold and sweeping an *apologia pro Israel* as did Cardoso, nor one on so sustained and lofty a plane. In the *Excelencias* he steps forth to defend not merely the Oral Law, but the whole of Judaism; not only Jewish beliefs and practices, but the Jewish people; and in so doing, he takes it upon himself to refute systematically almost all the charges which have been cast at both Jews and Judaism in his time. Moreover, his championship of Jewry is not tied to special circumstance, as was the case with

I, 53–67. An earlier edition in Portuguese, *Tratado da calumnia* (Antwerp, 1629), is mentioned by Kayserling, *BEPJ,* p. 36.

[13] For editions and translations see *BEPJ,* pp. 69 f. The English texts have been reproduced by Lucien Wolf in his *Menasseh ben Israel's Mission to Oliver Cromwell* (London, 1901).

[14] *Nomologia o discursos legales, compuestos por el virtuoso Haham Rabi Imanuel Aboab de buena memoria. Estampados a costa, y despeza de sus herederos, en el año de la creacion 5389.*

Mannasseh and Luzzato. He is therefore free to rise above special pleading, and to avoid many of the compromises which they were forced to make. The *Excelencias* is a proud and impassioned outcry to the entire world for justice to Israel and its faith, made all the more intense and compelling by Cardoso's own experience of years spent among the gentiles.

That experience makes it imperative to view the *Excelencias* not only in a Jewish context, but against the Iberian background as well. No matter what transformations Cardoso may have undergone, the forty-four years in Portugal and Spain could never quite be effaced.

Not the least fascinating aspect of *Las excelencias de los Hebreos* is that its very title points back to the Peninsula, and the same is true even of the first "excelencia": *Pueblo escogido de Dios.* "A people chosen by God"—that is what the Spaniards of the seventeenth century literally felt themselves to be.[15] It was a common thing to hear in Spain that the biblical prophecies for Israel had been fulfilled in the Spanish people, and there was a spate of books on the Spanish "excelencias" to prove it.[16] For our purpose it will be sufficient to choose one vivid example. In 1629 there was published in Pamplona a work by the Benedictine Fray Benito de Peñalosa y Mondragón, entitled *Libro de las cinco excelencias del Español.*[17] In one chapter ("How the Spaniards spread the Catholic Faith, a mission and prerogative of the chosen people of God") he deals with the promise given by

---

[15] "España se creyó, por decirlo así, el pueblo elegido de Dios, llamado por El para ser brazo y espada suya, como lo fué el pueblo de los judíos." M. Menéndez y Pelayo, *Calderón y su teatro* (Madrid, 1910), p. 65.

[16] See Herrero García, *Ideas de los españoles,* pp. 13 ff., citing, among others, Dr. López Madera, *Excelencias de la monarquia y reyno de España* (3d ed.; Madrid, 1625).

[17] *Libro de las cinco excelencias del español que despueblan a España para su mayor potencia y dilatacion. Ponderanse para que meior se adviertan las causas del despueblo de España, y para que los lugares despoblados della, se habiten, y sean populosos. Por el M. Fr. Benito de Peñalosa y Mondragon, monge Benito Professo de la Real Casa de Nagera. Dedicado al Rey nuestro Señor Filipo IIII* [arms] *Año 1629. Con licencia. Impresso en pamplona, por Carlos de Lebayen, Impressor del Reyno de Navarra.* The five *excelencias* form the first part of the book (fols. 1r-162v). The rest discusses the depopulation of Spain.

Spokesman for Judaism

God to Jacob (Gen. 28: 14): *And thy seed shall be as the dust of the earth, and thou shalt spread abroad to the west, and to the east, and to the north, and to the south, and in thy seed shall all the families of the earth be blessed.* Here is how Fray Benito understands the verse:

> To better advantage we see today the Spanish nation exercising this ministry and obtaining the blessings which God cast to Abraham and Jacob, the spiritual fathers of its intense and widespread faith. For in all the kingdoms of the earth an infinite number of Spaniards are preaching the Gospel, and showing the nations the Law of Grace. And in this work they are superior to the ministries of the Hebrew people, as the spirit is superior to the flesh. Because although [the ancient Hebrews] had already been spread through all three parts of the world, Asia, Africa, and Europe, none of them reached or knew of America, the fourth part, which, together with its islands, is vaster than the other three. Today the Spaniards are spread out and numerous in all four parts, and preach the Roman Catholic Faith with such great fruit as to die for it, while in this respect the Hebrews were rarely martyrs for the defense of the Law of God. . . .
>
> The second reason we are superior to the Hebrews in this dispersion is that they preached the written law, while we preach the Law of Grace. . . .[18]

It is not necessary to suppose that Cardoso had read Peñalosa's book. The genre is important. "Las excelencias del Español" and "las excelencias de los Hebreos," each insisting on his election. But with what a difference! The Spaniard of the seventeenth century can still buttress his chosenness by pointing to a vast empire extending throughout the world, visible proof of God's favor. With the same pride, and an even greater certainty, Isaac Cardoso will undertake to show the glory of the most abased and vilified of peoples.

---

[18] *Ibid.*, first *excelencia*, ch. viii ("Como los españoles dilatan la Fe Catholica por todo el mundo, oficio y prerrogativa que tenia el Pueblo de Dios escogido"), fol. 23r. It is odd to find the Spanish conquests and missionary activities in the New World praised also by the 17th-century rabbi of Ferrara, Judah del Bene, in his *Kis'ot le-Bet David* (Verona, 1646), ch. 44, fol. 83r-84r. See the analysis of Isaac Barzilay, *Between Reason and Faith: Anti-Rationalism in Italian Jewish Thought 1250-1650* (The Hague-Paris, 1967), pp. 214 f. Cardoso's attitude is diametrically opposed. See *infra*, p. 393.

The Place and Scope of the Excelencias

The organization of the book is relatively simple. The entire work is divided into two parts. The first consists of ten *excelencias* of the Jews, and presents in great detail Cardoso's positive exposition of the nature of Judaism and of the Jewish people. To some extent this plan is arbitrary, and was merely chosen for the sake of convenience. Thus the fourth *excelencia* alone comprises three sections, and certain themes which are treated in one chapter sometimes recur in others. On the whole, however, the headings of each are a fair indication of their contents. The *excelencias* occupy fully three quarters of the book, in the following order:

I.   "A People Chosen by God."

II.   "One People."

III. "Separated from all the Nations."

IV.   "Three of their natural characteristics."
      A. Compassionate.
      B. Charitable.
      C. Decent and modest.

V.   "Circumcision."

VI.   "The Sabbath."

VII. "The Divine Law."
      (Consisting of a general introduction, followed by an analysis of ten classes of precepts: (a) divinity; (b) sanctuary and priesthood; (c) purity and impurity; (d) dietary laws; (e) women and married life; (f) festivals; (g) deeds of compassion and almsgiving; (h) justice and government; (i) civil law; (j) criminal law. There follows a listing of the 613 commandments, and a final section on revelation.

VIII. "Prophecy."

IX.   "The Holy Land."

X.   "Witnesses to the Unity of God."[19]

---

[19] *Excelencias*, pp. 1–331: I. "Pueblo escogido de Dios"; II. "Gente una"; III. "Separados de todas las naciones"; IV. "Tres propriedades naturales suyas"; V. "La circuncición" [*sic*]; VI. "El Sabath"; VII. "Ley Divina"; VIII. "La Prophecia"; IX. "Tierra Santa"; X. "Testigos de la Unidad de Dios."

Similarly, Part II consists of ten *calunias*, each chapter being devoted to the refutation of a specific slander against the Jews:

I.   They adore false gods,

II.   They exude a bad odor.

III. Jews have tails and Jewish men menstruate.

IV.   They pray three times daily against the gentiles.

V.   They persuade gentiles to accept Judaism.

VI.   They are unfaithful to the Princes.

VII. They are wicked and cruel.

VIII. They corrupt the Sacred Scriptures.

IX.   They desecrate images, and are sacrilegious.

X.   They kill Christian children in order to use their blood in their rites.[20]

SOURCES AND METHOD

More than 100 different authorities are cited by name in the *Excelencias*, and a considerable number of others can be identified.

The largest single category is represented by Greek and Roman writers, just as in the works he had published previously, but with the obvious difference that here they are generally employed either to bolster his arguments for Judaism, or as objects of attack for their antisemitic statements. Thus Strabo is invoked, on the one hand, to prove that the Jewish diaspora antedates Christ, and on the other, to refute his statement that Jews circumcise their women.[21] When repeating the rabbinic dictum that the 248 positive precepts of the Torah correspond to the number of organs and members in the

---

[20] *Excelencias*, pp. 333–431: I. "Falsas adoraciones"; II. "Mal olor"; III. "Cola y sangre"; IV. "Orar tres vezes al día contra las gentes"; V. "Persuadir las gentes al Hebraysmo"; VI. "Infieles a los Principes"; VII. "Impios y crueles"; VIII. "Corruptores de los libros sagrados"; IX. "Dicipadores de Imagenes"; X. "Matar niños christianos para valerse de su sangre."

[21] *Ibid.*, pp. 16, 95.

human body, Cardoso points out that Galen was close to that figure, having counted 242.[22] Solomon's vast work-projects are lauded not only in themselves, but as conforming to Aristotle's recommendation that a nation is most felicitous when it is largely composed of laborers.[23] Jewish modesty in dress is supported by Tacitus' reference to Roman sumptuary laws.[24]

After our examination of the *Philosophia libera* we are not surprised to find that Cardoso makes use of the Church Fathers when it suits his purpose, though in the *Excelencias* this is not frequent. He cites Origen, Clement of Alexandria, Eusebius, Augustine, and Jerome, the latter two, as we shall see, in order to vindicate the Hebrew text of the Bible.[25] That he knows intimately the works of Renaissance humanists as well as seventeenth-century writers is even more evident in the *Philosophia*. In the *Excelencias* we find, on the rite of circumcision among the Abyssinians, Sebastian Muenster's *Geographia*, Paolo Giovio, and Pierre Belon;[26] Julius Scaliger and Erasmus in connection with the *foetor judaicus*;[27] and, somewhat unexpectedly, even Thomas More's *Utopia*.[28] However, with the exception of the classical authors, the bulk of Cardoso's non-Jewish citations are from Peninsular writers of every type: the Portuguese chronicler Damião de Goes, José de Acosta's *Historia natural y moral de las Indias*, the jurist Diego de Villalpando, the historian Padre Juan de Mariana, the *Gobernador Christiano* of Fray Juan Márquez, the *Historia Pontifical* of Gonzalo de Illescas, the Polyglot of Benito Arias Montano, etc. Of Iberian antisemites he particularly singles out Lucas of Tuy, Alonso de Espina, Fray Vicente Ferrer, Jaime Pérez de Valencia, and a seventeenth-century work on the *Niño Inocente de la Guardia*. It need hardly be added that he has obviously read many more such books which he does not name.

The preponderance of classical and hispanic erudition is, after all,

---

[22] *Ibid.*, p. 154.   [23] *Ibid.*, p. 79.   [24] *Ibid.*, p. 81.

[25] *Ibid.*, pp. 94, 326, 393 f. For Cardoso's discussion of the biblical text see *infra*, ch. IX.

[26] *Ibid.*, p. 95.   [27] *Ibid.*, pp. 340, 344.

[28] *Ibid.*, p. 274, taking issue with both More and Plato on the desirability of a society in which women and property would be held in common.

to be anticipated. The vital question concerns Cardoso's use of Jewish sources.

In our analysis of the *Philosophia libera* in chapter VI we took stock of the Jewish materials which Cardoso had derived from non-Jewish sources, and proposed the thesis that information of this type was available to him while he was still in Spain. Now, with the *Excelencias* before us, we are finally in a position to examine the Jewish knowledge he had acquired since he came to live as a Jew in Italy. That he had learned much is obvious. Indeed, Kayserling was so impressed that he spoke glowingly of the "deep and astounding erudition" displayed in the book. But we must seriously inquire as to just how deep it really was. Had Cardoso, in the years in Venice and Verona, achieved a sufficient mastery of rabbinic Hebrew and Aramaic to study the great Jewish classics directly, or did he have access essentially to that which was available in vernacular translations?

Most easily perceived, of course, is his use of Jewish literature in Spanish and Portuguese, for a number of such works are mentioned directly, either by title or by the author's name. Thus he cites Isaac Athias, whose *Thesoro de Preceptos* was an important source for his own section on the commandments.[29] Samuel Usque's *Consolaçam as tribulacoens de Israel* serves him for certain historical events, as does Aboab's *Nomologia*.[30] He quotes from a poem by Jonah Abravanel on the martyrdom of Isaac de Castro Tartas.[31] Since he is writing in Spanish, his verbatim quotations from Scripture are drawn from the Ferrara Bible. In addition, he has read in Italian the *Discorso* of Simone Luzzato.[32]

From this list, one may suspect that he has drawn upon other Jewish works in the vernacular without giving the reference (or perhaps, as he complained, his marginal indications were omitted in the printing). It is certain that he has closely read Manasseh b. Israel's *Esperanza*. His discussion of the River Sambation is derived from there, though he has amplified the account considerably.[33]

---

[29] *Ibid.*, p. 155.   [30] *Ibid.*, pp. 380, 384.
[31] *Ibid.*, p. 325. For the passage itself, see my translation, *infra*, p. 398.
[32] *Ibid.*, p. 337.   [33] *Ibid.*, pp. 109–11. Cf. *Esperanza*, X, 39.

Manasseh also proves to be a prime source for his reports of episodes in the history of the Spanish and Portuguese Jews, especially of the martyrs to the Inquisition. There is, finally, an extensive use of Josephus and Philo, and, occasionally, of the Apocrypha.

Still, such sources account for only a relatively small portion of Cardoso's Jewish material. The overwhelming bulk of Part I of the *Excelencias* purports to present Judaism out of the standard fonts of postbiblical Jewish tradition. It is precisely here that the question of Cardoso's sources is most difficult to resolve. The book offers a profusion of Talmudic, Midrashic, and other rabbinic elements. In particular, Cardoso displays a wide grasp of the entire range of aggadic literature, and almost every page bristles with rabbinic homilies and parables. One would be prone, at first glance, to conclude that he has drawn them all from the original texts, especially since he cites some by name, e.g., "Misna Sanhedrin," "Abot, o capítolos de los padres," the "Rabot," "Yalcut," "Guemara de Ros Asana."[34]

But to take even these explicit references at face value is to ignore how much Talmudic and Midrashic lore was already available by this time in the Judeo-Spanish literature itself. Such works as Athias' *Thesoro*, or the *Mesa de el alma*, condensed and digested a great deal of halakhic and aggadic information and made it readily available, occasionally even citing the source. The Spanish translation of *Pirke Abot* was to be found in every Sephardic household, often bound together with the *Paraphrasis caldaica* to the Song of Songs.[35] There certainly existed abundant opportunities to cite the rabbinic literature from these secondary sources.

We can probe even farther. On several occasions Cardoso quotes a Talmudic passage verbatim. For example, in his discussion of the Day of Atonement he offers a literal translation of Mishnah *Yoma*, 8:9: "If a man says 'I will sin and repent' . . . he will be given no chance to repent [etc.]." Here, then, we would seem to have definite evidence that Cardoso had gone to the Mishnah itself. But this is not

[34] *Ibid.*, pp. 5, 83, 109, 160.
[35] I.e., the Spanish translation of the Targum to the Song of Songs. For editions see *BEPJ*, p. 30.

at all the case. It can be proved conclusively that in this instance Cardoso was not translating directly from the Mishnah, but had actually taken the passage from the *Menorat ha-ma'or* of Isaac Aboab. That famous ethical compendium of the Middle Ages; filled with Talmudic quotations, had been translated into Spanish by Rabbi Jacob Hages as the *Almenara de la luz,* and appeared in Leghorn in 1656.[36] A textual comparison shows that not only the Mishnah itself but even Cardoso's remarks which immediately precede and follow it are taken from this work.[37] There is no doubt that the *Almenara de la luz* also furnished him with many other rabbinic passages.

[36] *BEPJ*, p. 51. I have used the second edition: *Almenara de la luz. Tratado de mucho provecho para benefiçio del alma. Compuesto en lengua Ebraica por el gran sabio Yshac Aboab, traducido en lengua bulgar para benefiçio comun por el Haham Iahacob Hages. Impreso en Amsterdam. En casa de Iahacob alvares sotto, Moseh abenyacar brandon, y Benjamin de yongh. Año de la Criacion del mundo 5468.*

[37] *Excelencias*, pp. 309 f.: "Y si bien Dios nos assegura de perdonar nuestros pecados en este día, ha de ser con que nos dispongamos a dexar los malos caminos, y arrepentirnos de lo passado, pues no valdra el santo día al que tuviere pensamiento de bolver a pecar, y dizen los Sabios, *El que dize pecaré, y tornaré en contrición, no le conceden del cielo lugar de hazer penitencia; pecaré, y el día de Quipur me perdonara, no le perdonara el Santo día.* No es la intención del ayuno affligir el cuerpo, y quedar immundo de los pecados, que la voluntad del Señor no es sino dirrigir [*sic*] el hombre sus obras, que assi responde el Propheta a los que se quexavan, diziendo que se affligian, y ayunavan, y Dios no les respondia ni mirava a sus ayunos, y les dize de parte de Dios Bendito: *Como ha de hazer cuenta de vuestro ayuno, si en el vos estais deleytando, y hazeis vuestra voluntad para pleyto, y para contienda ayunais, este es el verdadero ayuno, soltar los ataderos de malicia, dar limosna, vestir al desnudo, recoger al pobre, repartir al hambriento su pan. . . ."*

Almenara de la luz, fol. 140r: "Si bien que en este santo día nos aseguro el Criador del mundo de perdonar nuestros pecados, ha de ser con que se disponga el hombre a dexar sus malos caminos y arrepentirse por lo passado y recebir sobre si de no bolber mas a pecar, y la penitencia se entiende desta suerte por que por otro modo mientras tuviese pensamiento de querer bolver a pecar, no le valera, ni el santo día de kipur le perdonera, y assi dizen nuestros Sabios en el ultimo capitulo de Yoma estas palabras, *el que dize pecaré y tornaré . . .* [*etc.*]. Consta de aqui que no perdona el D. Bendito sino a los que tornan como es la razon, tambien sabemos que no es la intencion del aiuno el affligir su cuerpo solamente y quedar ymmundo en los pecados que esto aborece el Santo B., y no es su voluntad sino que enderece el hombre sus obras como lo dize el Propheta Ysayas en repuesta de lo que quexaban Ysrael diziendo por que ayunamos y no biste, afligimos nuestras almas y no sabes,

In essence, all that can be established with any certainty from the *Excelencias* is Cardoso's knowledge of biblical Hebrew. His close study of the text of the Hebrew Bible is apparent from his numerous philological observations. But there is no real evidence that he had, at best, more than a rudimentary ability to read postbiblical Jewish texts in the original language. His quotations of such texts are either derived from translations existing in Spanish and Portuguese (or, as in the case of Maimonides' *Guide*, in Latin), or else they are taken from citations found in other Jewish works written in the Iberian vernaculars. This phenomenon cannot be explained merely by the fact that he is writing in Spanish for a Spanish-reading public. We have only to turn for comparison to the Spanish works of Manasseh b. Israel to feel the difference. In the latter, the rabbinic sources are cited with an amplitude and specificity which we largely miss in Cardoso. Some significance may also be seen in the fact that, in the exchange of letters between Cardoso and Samuel Aboab, both wrote in Spanish, and that, when Rabbi Judah Brieli sent him his Hebrew poem in praise of the *Excelencias*, Cardoso replied in Italian.[38]

We should not be surprised. Isaac Cardoso had left Spain in middle age. His brother Abraham, who was then in his early twenties, still had the time and the youthful energy to become a Kabbalist. But forty-five is an age at which it is difficult to become a Talmudist, especially when one is absorbed in writing a *Philosophia libera* while ministering to the sick. Over the years Isaac must have read every Jewish book he could lay his hands on in the languages he knew, discussed the finer points of Judaism with the rabbis and intellectuals of the Ghetto, listened avidly to the sermons in the synagogue, perhaps even frequented the House of Study to hear a lecture on some problem in *halakhah*. But it was too late to acquire the tools for independent rabbinic study.

To be sure, this means that Cardoso's Jewish scholarship was not really original, and the book itself bears out this conclusion. Yet, in a real sense, this is inconsequential. The *Excelencias* claims to be not a

---

responde el Propheta en nombre del D.B. *como a de hazer quenta de buestro ayuno* . . . [etc.]."

[38] See *REJ*, pp. 301–5, and *Ozar Nechmad*, III, 167 f.

work of Jewish scholarship, but a defense of Jews and Judaism, for which Cardoso's equipment proves more than ample. Kayserling and others have thus missed the point. What is truly astounding in the *Excelencias* is not its erudition per se, but *the manner in which that erudition was acquired*. If, in analyzing its sources, we find that the majority are in the vernacular, we should be all the more impressed by the phenomenon itself. For we see here how, largely be means of translations, a man like Cardoso was able to receive not merely the content but the very texture of Jewish tradition. Regarded from this vantage point, *Las excelencias de los Hebreos* attests to the success of the great effort of Sephardic Jewry in the sixteenth and seventeenth centuries to recast that tradition into the Iberian idioms. However, he derived it, Cardoso shows a very competent mastery of the *aggadah*. He can himself spin a Jewish homily as well as if he had spent his youth in an Italian yeshiva, rather than at a Spanish university. His work achieves its distinction not so much in original Jewish erudition as in its enormous pathos. Were we merely to abstract and list the Jewish information it contains, we should entirely miss its particular contribution. It is the firing of all its many elements in the crucible of Cardoso's profound identification with his people's sufferings, his eloquence, and his towering indignation at the tormentors of Israel, which makes the *Excelencias* a masterpiece of Jewish apologetics.

The means Cardoso employs are varied. In his exposition of Judaism his general approach is first to allow the tradition to speak for itself, to explain it, and to stress its truth, its rationality, and—not least—its beauty. If he can utilize a scientific or medical argument, or if he can find a friendly statement in a gentile author, he will do so eagerly. He will often make use of the same opportunity to take issue with a false or erroneous opinion which he feels may be due, if not to malice, then to ignorance of the reality of Jewish life. His refutations of antisemitic charges are thus by no means restricted to the ten *calunias* of Part II.

Some of his methods reveal also the strong influence of his immediate Jewish environment. Such, for example, is his fondness for allegory, so common in the Italian Jewish homiletics of the time. Cardoso, however, is more restrained than many of his contemporaries. He does not generally offer his allegories as primary explanations, but adds them in order to enhance the argument.

More serious, and most noticeable, is his extensive use of letter-symbolism and *gematria*. The lengths to which this is sometimes carried can be illustrated from his discussion of circumcision. Thus: when God instituted circumcision He changed Abram's name by adding the letter *he* from his own Ineffable Name, and added it also to Sarai. In this way He united husband and wife, for together they now constituted the perfect number ten.[39] The incision itself has the form of *yod*. The *he* in Abraham's name, and the *yod* in his flesh, make up *YaH*, which is half of the Ineffable Name of God. It has been noted by the *investigadores de misterios* that in a circumcised Jew the Lord's name *SHaDaY* is manifest: *Shin* is represented by the nose, *dalet* in the arm doubled at the breast, *yod* in the sign of the covenant; but without the latter you have the word *SHeD*, which means "demon."[40] *Berit* (covenant) has the numerical value 612; this, plus the word itself, adds up to 613, the number of the precepts in the Torah. But *TORaH* yields 611 and, with the word itself, makes 612; therefore *torah* and *berit* are equal. *Milah* (circumcision) numerically equals 85, which, plus the word itself, yields 86. This is also the numerical value of *'Elohim*. In the verse *"Mi Ya'aleh Lanu Ha-shamaymah"* (Who shall ascend for us to heaven), the first letters of each word form the word *Milah*, while the last letters form YHVH. *Milah* is itself numerically equal to *PeH* (mouth). This teaches that the mouth should not speak obscenities, nor the genital commit illicit acts.[41]

Cardoso's attitude is summed up in such statements as these:

The Law commences with "in the beginning" and concludes with "Israel," as if it were the intention and goal of the creation of the world; for in the Holy Law the names, the letters, and the vowels are full of profound mysteries.[42]

In the Hebrew letters, as they enclose great mysteries, so there can be derived from them marvelous concepts.[43]

---

[39] *Excelencias*, pp. 88 f.   [40] *Ibid.*, p. 89.

[41] All the above, *ibid.*, pp. 91 f.   [42] *Ibid.*, p. 7.   [43] *Ibid.*, p. 23.

Now in an ordinary Jewish author of the seventeenth century we should find nothing remarkable in such elements. They are to be encountered throughout the Jewish literature of the age, deriving in part from ancient sources, and largely attributable to the extensive popularization of kabbalistic ideas since the end of the sixteenth century. *Gematria* such as Cardoso employs are also a marked feature of the vernacular compendia of Jewish law and custom from which, as we have observed, he first obtained his formal Jewish knowledge.[44]

It is precisely the fact that Cardoso came so late into the Jewish community which raises some questions. What enabled him to embrace these seemingly exotic methods so wholeheartedly? And what personal need, if any, did they serve?

The first question dissolves if we simply recognize that letter and number symbolism were by no means so alien to him as we might initially suppose. They were widely employed in Christian theological and even profane literature from the time of the Church Fathers through the Middle Ages and the Renaissance.[45] Indeed, the ease with which such techniques could be assimilated to both Jewish and Christian materials, and a measure of how congenial they could be to the temper of both Christians and Jews, may best be illustrated by two Iberian examples. When Cardoso's Portuguese contemporary Francisco Manoel de Mello encountered the letter-symbolism of the Kabbalah, it immediately struck a familiar chord, and he could write with equanimity that "this is the grammer, or, to express it better, the mystical exposition, origin, and derivation of the Hebrew

---

[44] For *gematria* in connection with circumcision see Athias, *Thesoro de preceptos*, fols. 60v–61r. In Manasseh b. Israel's Portuguese compendium, *Thesouro dos Dinim que o povo de Israel he obrigado saber e observar* (Amsterdam, 1645), p. 152, we read: "Finalmente he o preceito da circunção de tanta excelencia, que contrapeze como toda a Ley. E como doctamente advirtem os Antigos, naquellas palavras do Deut. cap. 30 מי יעלה לנו השמימה, quem subira a nos ao Ceos? as ultimas letras destas 4 palavras fazem o nome Tetragramaton e inefavel de el Dio bendito; e as primeyras fazem *Mila*, circuncição. . . ."

[45] For rich examples see V. Hopper, *Medieval Number Symbolism* (New York, 1938). especially pp. 62–135; Etienne Gilson, *Les idées et les lettres* (Paris, 1932); E.R. Curtius, *European Literature in the Latin Middle Ages*, tr. W. R. Trask (New York, 1963), Excursus XIV and XV.

letters, whose venerable mystery the Church observes. . . ."[46] Conversely, when the Jewish apostate João Baptista d'Este wrote his *Diálogo*, he inserted an entire chapter ("On the Name of Our Lady, Deduced from the Words of Isaiah [9: 6], Conforming to the Hebrew Style, and from the Mystery of the Closed Letter *Mem*. . .") in which, by means of anagrams, he elicited "Maria Princesa" from the Hebrew *le-marbeh ha-misrah*, her virginity from the closed *Mem*, and, by *gematria*, the year of Christ's advent.[47]

Far from constituting a complete novelty with which Cardoso had to wrestle when he came to Judaism, the various forms of letter-symbolism were rather a familiar technique which had only to be applied to new materials. Cardoso's use of these methods may thus be viewed in a triple aspect. It represents at once a bridge from the past, a reflection of the Italo-Sephardic Judaism of his day, and—it sometimes does serve a serious personal purpose. For the attentive reader of the *Excelencias* will not fail to notice that the allegories, and especially the *gematria*, tend to cluster together at particular points in the book. A second glance will show that this generally occurs when Cardoso is discussing those Jewish ideas or precepts which are most refractory to rational explanation, and which seem to cause him some difficulty or discomfort. The *gematria* then become not mere embroideries, but a means by which to surmount the hurdles.

Before proceeding to analyze the major themes of the *Excelencias*, we must therefore first examine the book to see what it reveals of Cardoso himself. To the extent that it is possible we must try to determine what changes are reflected in his own outlook, and what influences his own past may have exerted on his understanding of Judaism. In all this there is, of course, a severe limitation. The book was published three decades after he began to profess Judaism openly. We have, in a sense, a "before" and an "after," without the transition itself. Yet, even so, a comparison of the two yields some interesting facts which will aid us in understanding the work as a whole.

---

[46] *Tratado da sciencia Cabala*, pp. 130 f., giving as one example the chanting of the first three chapters of Lamentations, with their Hebrew acrostic. See also p. 115, on the etymological and numerical mysteries of the name Jesus.

[47] *Diálogo entre discipulo e mestre catechizante*, ch. XXI, pp. 38–40.

PERSONAL ORIENTATIONS AND MARRANO ECHOES

That Cardoso has embraced the whole of traditional Judaism down to its most minute details, and without reservation, is evident throughout the *Excelencias*. There is not a single precept of the Law which he is not prepared to defend and extol.

No less obvious is the fact that this passionate acceptance of Judaism has also involved, on certain levels, a reevaluation of his own past. This seems to emerge in the very sharpest relief when we ponder that the author of the *Utilidades del agua* and the *De Febre syncopali* writes now:

This Divine Law is the true wisdom which unites the souls with their Creator. It is this which makes the Hebrews wiser and greater than the other nations, for so God says: *This is your wisdom and your understanding in the sight of the peoples, that when they hear all these statutes shall say—surely this is a wise and understanding people* (Deut. 4: 6). . . . So that the Lord predicts that through the Law, and its righteous judgments, the Jews are called wise.

And in truth, Israel does not cultivate human sciences, nor treat of uncertain Philosophy, nor of doubtful Medicine, nor of false Astrology, nor of fallacious Chemistry, nor of secret Magic. It does not care to know the histories of the nations, nor the chronologies of the times, nor the politics of the rulers. All of its intent and desire is to study the Law, and to meditate on its precepts, in order to keep and to do them. . . .[48]

Such a passage, however, should not mislead us. Were we in possession only of the scientific works which Cardoso had written in Madrid, we would surely interpret this extreme statement in the *Excelencias* as a radical, even brutal, rejection of his entire intellectual past. But after all—the *Philosophia libera* had appeared only six years before! Both books were completed after he had lived for several

---

[48] *Ibid.*, p. 135.

decades as a Jew, and it is hard to imagine that in the short interval between the two he suddenly disavowed the former. To grasp properly this and similar passages, we must take into consideration two dimensions of the Judaism which he came to know: the Sephardic and the Italian.

Merely in contemplating the two books which Cardoso wrote as a Jew one can hardly refrain, I think, from seeing in the background two archetypal polarities of the Sephardic intellectual tradition. Behind the *Philosophia libera* there looms, ultimately, the figure of Maimonides; behind *Las excelencias de los Hebreos*, that of Judah Halevi. This is not to say that the system in the former is "Maimonidean," or that the latter is a restatement of Halevi, though the influence of each can certainly be found at specific points. Rather, it concerns the very nature of Cardoso's respective endeavors in the two works, and the assumptions and attitudes they embody. If only symbolically, the *Philosophia* stands in the Maimonidean tradition to the extent that it admits the claims of both Faith and Reason, and assumes a harmony between the two. The *Excelencias*, on the other hand, is Cardoso's *Kuzari*. It is so not merely for the obvious reason that, like Halevi, he has here undertaken a "Book of Argument and Proof in Defense of the Despised Faith," but because of its emphases: the religious significance of Jewish peoplehood, its chosenness, its preeminence, the centrality and uniqueness of Jewish prophecy, the special virtues of the Land of Israel. All these and others are Halevian themes and, as though Halevi's conclusions are taken for granted, no attempt is made to explain them in philosophical categories. In the passage just quoted, we seem to hear the distant echo of Halevi's own admonition to a Spanish contemporary:

> See now, yea, see, my friend, and understand,
> And turn away from the lure of thorns and snares,
> And let not the wisdom of the Greeks beguile thee,
> Which hath no fruit, but only flowers. . . .

But the apparent inconsistency between the *Philosophia* and the stance taken in the *Excelencias* can be elucidated more directly if we consider the Italian Jewish milieu in which Cardoso lived.

Italian Jewry had long been engaged by the claims of both secular knowledge and Jewish tradition. Always particularly receptive to the cultural influences of its environment, yet firmly anchored in its Jewish learning and piety, it was able to accommodate the two, sometimes by separating their respective spheres of influence, at other times by achieving a precarious balance between them. The common notion that it was only the advent of the Catholic Counter Reformation in Italy which engendered a corresponding Jewish reaction against humanistic concerns is certainly untrue. Even at the height of Renaissance influence, humanistic learning was not absorbed by Italian Jews without serious misgivings. Moreover, those who entertained such reservations were not necessarily mere obscurantists, but often men who themselves possessed broad secular culture, and were yet concerned over its potential dangers to Jewish faith and tradition.

Nor, by the same token, did the Counter Reformation put an end to the humanistic pursuits of Italian Jews. Such impulses carried well into the seventeenth century and beyond. What occurred was rather more complex. In the wake of the proliferation of the Italian ghettos, the burning and censorship of Hebrew books, the oppressive anti-Jewish legislation, the inner tensions which had existed all along now became accentuated, and former doubts returned with renewed force. Interest in secular culture and its acquisition continued, but in the face of an increasingly inimical gentile world, the *value* of the knowledge of the gentiles could not but appear more problematic than ever. The relation between Jewish and secular learning continued to preoccupy Italian Jewish intellectuals throughout the late sixteenth and seventeenth centuries with special urgency, and the disparagement of secular studies is a major strand in the literature of the age.

Thus Judah Moscato (1532–90), deeply imbued with Renaissance learning, declares himself opposed especially to natural philosophy and metaphysics.[49] The physician Abraham Portaleone (d. 1612?)

---

[49] See his *Nefuṣot Yehudah* (1st ed., Venice, 1588; I have used ed. Warsaw, 1871), Sermon 13, and especially Sermon 14, captioned "Distinguishing between the Sacred and the Profane." On Moscato's attitudes see Barzilay, *Between Reason and Faith*, ch. IX.

berates himself, in the preface to his voluminous treatise on the ancient Temple, for having so long neglected Jewish studies in favor of the sciences, a trend which was allegedly reversed only when he suffered a stroke and subsequently repented.[50] Judah del Bene (1618?–78) urges his contemporaries to "study only the Torah, and dispense with the multitude of Arabic, Chaldean, or Greek books."[51] Azariah Figo (1579–1647), who had served as rabbi in Venice along with Leone Modena and Simone Luzzato, and who died only a year or so before Cardoso's arrival, preached as follows to his congregation:

Know that unlike the gentile sciences, which depend upon one another, is our holy Torah. For not one of them can justify itself unless the other be justified, since no one can become an astronomer who has not acquired knowledge of geometry and algebra, and no one can be a physician who has not first occupied himself with natural philosophy, and he will not know anything if he has not studied logic. . . . But our Torah does not require any science or study outside itself, for all is in it and of itself.[52]

On another occasion Figo pointedly compared the astronomical lore of the Talmud, which is merely a means toward the proper fixing of the Jewish calendar and its festivals, with profane astronomy, which seeks to know the universe as an independent goal:

Thus the sages of Israel are very remote from it, for all the corners to which they turn are only a path and an avenue toward the soul's success in obtaining eternal felicity through everlasting immortality. It is for this that we were created, and not for anything that is not directed to this purpose. And that is why they received from Him, may He be blessed, the precept of computing the periods and constellations, not in order to acquire the science itself so as to know everything in the heavens above, but for what may be derived from it in action here on the earth below. . . . From which it may be seen without doubt that [the sages] did not learn it from the scientific books of the nations, and that they had no need

---

[50] *Shiltey ha-gibborim* (Mantua, 1612), preface to his sons.

[51] *Kis'ot le-Bet David*, ch. III, fol. 10v.

[52] *Binah le-'ittim* (1st ed.; Venice, 1648; I have used ed. Lemberg, 1858), Pt. II, Sermon 43, fol. 28r (cf. 34r).

for the geometry of Euclid nor the Almagest of Ptolemy and their ilk. But they received that science by tradition, one man from the other unto Moses our master, who was taught by Him, may He be blessed. . . .[53]

But forceful as the views and statements we have cited may seem, they display only one side of the coin. The other is revealed by the very same figures. His protestations notwithstanding, Portaleone's *Shiltey ha-gibborim* is filled with long excursuses, each constituting, on the slightest pretext, a veritable Renaissance treatise on such a subject as music, precious stones, and even the arts of warfare. Despite his mistrust of specific disciplines, Moscato vigorously defended the value of secular studies, while even Del Bene was jealous of the achievement of gentile scholars. The attitude toward the wisdom of the gentiles is thus riddled with ambivalence, and we can ask for no more poignant example of this than to turn once more to Figo. In the introduction to his halakhic work *Gidduley terumah* he describes, perhaps more candidly than Portaleone, his own turn of heart:

God knows and is my witness . . . that barely had I passed the days of my youth, at which time, as if to confirm the vanity of this stage of life, I passionately pursued the vain secular studies of the gentiles, as soon as I began to reach manhood . . . my foolish eyes, previously blinded, were opened through the grace of God. I saw the shame of my youth in making the peripheral essential and the essential peripheral. I was abashed and mortified for having relaxed my interest in the basic Jewish studies, the Talmud and all that is linked to it. . . . My spirit melted within me in regretting this past weakness, *and in worrying about the future, lest I again be overcome by the desire to embrace the bosom of the foreign enchantress, and that she will completely deprive me, Heaven forbid, of my priceless beloved.* . . . Therefore I resolved to expel this handmaid, and admonished my soul: "Return to thy true mistress, the *Gemara*. . .!"[54]

Though consistency might appear to demand it, the *Philosophia libera* and the attack on the profane sciences in the *Excelencias*

---

[53] *Ibid.*, Sermon 46, fol. 35r.

[54] Figo, *Sefer gidduley terumah* (1st ed.; Venice, 1643; I have used ed. Zolkiew, 1809), Introduction, fol. 3v. (Italics mine.)

represent neither consecutive nor mutually exclusive attitudes on Cardoso's part. Both were coeval in him, for both were crosscurrents in an Italian Jewish society which provided warrants for each. All the figures mentioned oscillated between attraction and resistance to gentile wisdom. In Cardoso we merely find the two attitudes more neatly polarized between his two Jewish books. If Figo managed to renounce the foreign seductress, he had reason nonetheless to fear her continued blandishments. In writing the *Philosophia libera* Cardoso had already satisfied her to the full.

But the measure of the changes which had occurred since Spain is certainly manifested in other statements, which stand in direct contrast to what we already know of his early years. We will recall the *fiesta agonal* celebrated in Pellicer's *Anfiteatro*, and Cardoso's sonnet in praise of Philip IV when he killed the bull. Here is Isaac Cardoso in the *Excelencias*, refuting the charge that the Jews are cruel:

> From this entire discussion we may gather how false is the slander which alleges that the Jews are cruel and inhuman, for they are, on the contrary, compassionate and benign to men and beasts, as much by nature as by divine precept. It is rather the Nations who are cruel and inhuman. . . . They sacrificed men to their gods, threw them to wild beasts . . . set up those infernal games of the gladiators who killed one another in the circuses and amphitheaters, in order to give pleasure to those who looked at such doleful spectacles . . . regarding the dead with exhilaration, and cruelty with joy. . . .
>
> Never among the Jews have there been such delights, nor such barbarous and cruel festivities, nor did they go to the hunt or the chase in order to kill animals for pleasure. . . .[55]

Even more striking is another passage, written by the same man who, years before, had passionately defended the staging of *comedias* in his funeral oration for Lope de Vega:

> Books of comedies and amorous novels, with their sweet words and poetic fictions, are a strong indication of lasciviousness, and a deceitful instrument of perdition, troublers of the soul, violators of purity in which time is wasted, teachers of vanities and vices. Comedies and tragedies

---

[55] *Ibid.*, p. 389.

were invented by profane nations, not by the holy people Israel, whom the Lord chose to sing His divine praises, and not lascivious loves and vicious inventions. . . .

What are comedies, if not mainly examples of vices, leading to lusts and sensual indulgence? What are novels and romantic fables, if not a school in which sins are learned and virtues are corrupted? And it matters not if one says that they contain also many good things and moral judgments which can reform life and benefit customs, because there are asps hidden among the flowers. . . .

Plato banished the poets from his Republic, as well as books which deal with poetry, because under the pretext of fiction they contaminated the youth with their teaching. The same was done by the Lacedaemonians, who exiled the poet Archilochus and his works, though they were so esteemed in other places, because their reading contaminated the good behavior of the young.

It is the sacred books which should be read, for in them is the true doctrine, the most sublime rhetoric, and the most supreme delight.[56]

This passage illustrates how deep a transformation Cardoso had really undergone. By its very terminolgy and examples it completely reverses the views he had once expressed in the *Oración funebre*. This about-face on comedies cannot be ascribed merely to the sobering effects of old age. Such a passage could easily have been written by Samuel Aboab, or some other ascetically inclined rabbi of the time, and is an indication of how thoroughly Cardoso had absorbed the more austere aspects of the ethos of rabbinic Judaism.[57]

The same desire to detach himself from the past is obviously behind much of that reluctance to speak about his life which we have noted repeatedly. It is as though by his silence Cardoso would, if it were possible, blot out that past entirely. With the exception of

---

[56] *Ibid.*, p. 76. Cf. the excerpt from Cardoso's *Oración funebre, supra,* ch. IV, pp. 158 f.

[57] A minor point, but interesting and somewhat amusing, is the change in his attitude toward the drinking of wine. In the *Utilidades del agua*, Cardoso had categorically opposed it. Now, in connection with the Sabbath *kiddush*, he writes: "Kidus quiere dezir santificación, y se toma en él por instrumento el vino, por ser el licor que *alegra el coraçón del hombre,* como dize el Psalmo, y es el que despierta y fortifica los espíritos vitales . . ." (*Excelencias*, p. 116).

the story about the illness of Don Juan de Quiñones, and a very brief anecdote about a madman in Madrid who thought he was the king,[58] he never alludes in the *Excelencias* to the fact that he had lived in Spain. Sometimes, to be sure, it is possible to catch a glimpse behind the curtain. For example, there is certainly a reference to Marranism in Spain when Cardoso, emphasizing the voluntary character of God's covenant with Israel, states: "because the cruelty of tyrants was seen, and the barbarity of those depraved souls who unjustly oblige and force others to follow their laws, human understanding being free to follow that which appears best to it."[59]

Similarly, Cardoso says nothing explicit about his return to Judaism. But at one point he delivers a powerful indictment of those Jews who live among the gentiles and do not come to live as Jews in free lands. Though they are not named, the entire tenor of the passage makes it clear that he has the Peninsular New Christians in mind. The desire of the Jews, he says, to live like the nations of the world was always abhorrent to God, but He shall rule over them despite their desire. Echoing Abravanel, he continues:

> But soon He predicts: *And I will cause you to pass under the rod, and I will bring you into the bond of the covenant, and will purge out from among you the rebels and them that transgress against me. I will bring them forth out of the land where they sojourn, but they shall not enter into the land of Israel* (Ezek. 20: 37 f.). As if to say, that He shall chastise those obstinate sinners who want to live among the nations, enjoying their merchandise and honors, adoring sticks and stones, leaving the company of their brothers who are serving God in free lands. Of those He says that, since they have rebelled against His holy Name, in the future general redemption of His people He will take them out of captivity, but they shall not come to the Land of Israel, indicating that He will slay them on the way, as the Sages say occurred in Egypt during the plague of darkness to those impious and perverse ones who, sunk in their idolatries, did not desire their liberty. For it is not just that the Redemption be seen by him who

---

[58] *Ibid.*, p. 233.

[59] *Ibid.*, p. 124. Cf. Aboab, *Nomologia*, p. 298: "O qual ley Divina, o Humana, Gentilica, o Moderna, permite que se fuercen los animos (que el summo Señor crió libres) a creer lo que no creen, y amar lo que aborrecen!"

has no concern for redemption, nor that he should enjoy the happiness of Israel who does not join himself to the community of Israel.

Balaam wished to die as an Israelite and to live as a gentile, and so he said: *Let me die the death of the righteous, and let mine end be like his* (Num. 23: 10). This is the case with those who live in lands far from ours, following the rites and vanities of the nations, or even those who, placed in our midst, are oblivious of their obligations, and wish to die as Jews and live as gentiles. But these two extremes cannot meet. For death must correspond to life, and he dies well who has lived well. . . .[60]

Cardoso's impatience with those who have remained behind in the Peninsula "adoring sticks and stones" makes us want to know why he himself delayed so long in leaving, but we receive no answer. On the other hand, that "death must correspond to life" is the closest to a statement of his own motive for taking the step which we shall ever hear from him.

Yet as much as he succeeds in covering up his tracks, he also betrays himself indirectly in other ways. For example, the fifth *excelencia*, one of the most glowing panegyrics of circumcision to be found in Jewish literature, appears in a new dimension when we consider the age at which Cardoso himself underwent the rite in Venice. Except for the Sabbath, this is the only Jewish observance to which an entire chapter is devoted. Such disproportion makes real sense only in terms of the subjective meaning which this particular rite had for him. It is not difficult to perceive the personal force of Cardoso's words when he says that, because of the pain involved, circumcision was always an obstacle to the acceptance of Judaism by the gentiles, and adds:

For it is not like some light wound in the leg, or an easy bruise on the arm, but rather something hard and difficult which no one would resolve to undertake, unless he were moved by great awareness and zeal to embrace the Law of the Lord. This is also the reason why it is done at the tender age of eight days, when the pain is not so great as later . . . and the imagination is still weak. But all this increases with maturity, when a man becomes apprehensive, and fears things before they happen. . . .[61]

---

[60] *Excelencias*, p. 48.   [61] *Ibid.*, p. 90.

Moreover, the influence of Cardoso's Marrano past is woven into the very fabric of the work itself. It is first evident in the repeated references to *misterios* which run like a leitmotiv throughout the book, and which seem to hover somewhere between the Jewish concept of the "secrets" of the Torah and the Catholic mysteries. Thus, not only does God call Israel His betrothed in the Song of Songs *con sentido espiritual y místico*, but the Song of Moses is also a *cántico misterioso*.[62] The Hebrew letters, various elements in the ancient sacrifices, are all mysteries, as are the thirty-nine stripes of the flogging in Jewish law.[63] The lifting of the hands in the priestly blessing is an *acto misterioso*. Anything which involves combinations of the number seven, or fifty, is mysterious, as witness the Jubilee or the Feast of Weeks.[64] The latter example is interesting because Cardoso first gives eminently rational reasons for its observance, but he still insists that "[God] commanded us to count seven weeks, which make 49 days, and the holiday falls on the fiftieth, a most mysterious number, which comprises the 50 gates of Divine Wisdom, of which 49 were opened to Man, and the last was reserved to the Lord." And again: "the truth is that the Divine mysteries are very hidden from us even in natural things, and how much more in matters as profound as the commandments of the Lord."[65]

To be sure, such details as the 49 gates of wisdom are to be found in Jewish sources,[66] but it is the overtones of the "mysteries" as Cardoso uses the term which catch the attention. Our impression is confirmed by certain terms and phrases which, even when employed to express Jewish concepts, leave no doubt as to their derivation from the Christian milieu which Cardoso had known so intimately.

Thus, emphasizing the unity of the Jewish people, their unanimous acceptance of the Law at Sinai, and their responsibility for one another, he states that they constitute a *cuerpo místico*, a term reminiscent of the Church as the mystic body of Christ.[67] Similarly, in

---

[62] *Ibid.*, pp. 4, 6. [63] *Ibid.*, pp. 23, 177, 254.

[64] *Ibid.*, p. 211. [65] *Ibid.*, pp. 202 f.

[66] See the references in Louis Ginzberg, *The Legends of the Jews* (Philadelphia, 1928), VI, 284, n. 25.

[67] *Excelencias*, p. 26. Cf. *infra*, n. 77.

speaking of circumcision, he characterizes the rite as follows: "Not only is circumcision a perfection of the body, but of the spirit as well, God ordaining it so as a mysterious sacrifice (*como sacrificio misterioso*), to mortify the flesh and lessen the sensual impulses. . . ."[68] Again—"without this covenant of the *berit*, or circumcision, the Jew cannot be saved" (*no se puede salvar el Judío*).[69] "This commandment is of such high status that it makes satisfaction for the original sin (*al peccado original*), Adam's sin of disobedience."[70] It is also interesting to note the terminology and tone of his description of the ancient Sanhedrin. It was "the fount of the Law, and the fount of doctrine (*fuente de la doctrina*), and all that issued forth from this consistory (*consistorio*) . . . we must believe, receive, and observe promptly, without any reply whatever, under penalty of death, as may be seen in the case of the Rebellious Elder. . . ."[71]

But, in sum, these and similar lapses into Christian phraseology do not really alter the thoroughly Jewish character of the book. They are but the natural results of habits of thought and expression acquired through decades of living as a Christian, the ghosts of a past that was dead, but not forgotten.

With this in mind, we shall now begin to examine the *Excelencias* as a whole. The contents of the work itself are so rich and varied that any attempt to provide a consecutive summary of details would be inadequate, and would in any case not add much to our understanding. I have chosen rather to analyze the book in terms of its central themes, and to group around each what seems most relevant or characteristic.

----

[68] *Excelencias*, p. 90. Cf. Athias, *Thesoro*, fol. 60v: "Mas no fue esta señal una divisa corporea simplexmente [*sic*] sin otro misterio, sino una obra tan insigne, que aunque hecha en la carne, diesse (con su divino secreto) al cuerpo de Israel, perfeccion corporal y espirituel."

[69] *Excelencias*, p. 91. For a more balanced statement on the place of circumcision in Judaism, see the remarks of Samuel Aboab in his *Sefer ha-zikronot*, quoted *supra*, ch. V, p. 200.

[70] *Excelencias*, p. 92. On the passage as an anti-Christian polemic see the discussion *infra*, p. 409.

[71] *Excelencias*, p. 226.

THE JEWISH PEOPLE

Both the *Excelencias* and the anti-Jewish literature with which Cardoso was acquainted share a common theological framework. While opposite conclusions are drawn, and the nuances are specific to the age, there were certain constants in the Judeo-Christian polemic with which Cardoso had to cope.

Foremost among these was the Christian dogma that the Jewish people was rejected by God, and it is therefore to the election of Israel that the first *excelencia* is devoted.

This election of Israel to be the people of God, this sacred betrothal, was neither temporary nor conditional, but eternal and absolute, for so the sacred verses confirm, and reason persuades. God is not like earthly rulers who at one time choose a favorite or minister, and at another time repudiate him because of some dereliction he has commited. . . .[72]

He is especially concerned to refute three classic Christian proofs of the rejection of Israel. To the argument from the fact of the dispersion and debasement of Jewry, he replies with the traditional theodicy, that these are but a temporary punishment meant to purify them from their sins. God's favors have been withdrawn, but not His love, for "many waters cannot quench love" (Cant. 8: 7). To the corollary notion that the absence of miracles also signifies God's repudiation of Israel, he has this to say:

However, if they consider it well, they shall find that, in this very abasement and general degradation of the Jews, the Lord has performed more miracles with them, and more continuously, than in ancient times. . . . What greater marvel than to see a lamb among seventy wolves, as the people of Israel is among the seventy nations of the world, who like carnivorous wolves or rapacious lions desire to tear them to pieces and swallow them alive, but God, like a true shepherd, does not allow it. . . ?

What greater miracle than to see a people persist for two thousand years among the nations with its name and its Law, when of other nations

---

[72] *Excelencias*, p. 5.

there is hardly a trace? Where are the Moabites, the Ammonites, the Tyrians, the Phoenecians, the Carthaginians? Where are the Lacedaemonians, the Athenians, the Assyrians, the Greeks, the Romans? All have become extinct, or their name has perished, and they are transformed into other nations, without their name, their kingdom, or their ancient laws. Only among the Jews do the name, the Law, and their succession endure, without being changed to other rites, and even though various Princes wanted to blot out their memory. . . .[73]

The second gentile argument concerns the length of the exile. Cardoso himself notes that according to the Talmud there was no idolatry in the period of the Second Temple. If so, why has this exile been so much longer than the others? The gentiles say

that such a long captivity must be due to another sin, greater and more serious than idolatry . . . and this sin they call Deicide, because of the death of Christ. This argument is the Achilles' heel, and the principal weapon with which the Jews are attacked, both by strangers and by those who have converted from Judaism to other religions. . . .[74]

Cardoso's main argument here is that the Jewish diaspora antedates the death of Christ, and that therefore the Exile cannot possibly be regarded as a punishment for the Crucifixion. To prove this, he cites references to the Jewish dispersion in Strabo's *Geography*, in the *Antiquities* and *Contra Apionem* of Josephus, and in Philo's *Legatio ad Gaium* and *In Flaccum*. He also elaborates on the old Sephardic tradition that captive Jews from Jerusalem had been taken by Nebuchadnezzar to Spain. There they built various cities, including Toledo, which some derive from the Hebrew *toledot*.[75] The captivity and exile are because of our sins and those of our fathers, and if the Jews turn to the Lord in penitence, they will be redeemed. They have not been replaced in God's affections by any other people,

---

[73] *Ibid.*, pp. 13–14. [74] *Ibid.*, p. 16.

[75] *Ibid.*, p. 17. Similar ideas were expressed by Abravanel at the end of his commentary to the Book of Kings. For other references to the antiquity of Jewish settlement in Spain see F. Baer, *Untersuchungen über Quellen und Komposition des Schebet Jehuda* (Berlin, 1923), pp. 58–60. See also Cardoso's letter to Samuel Aboab in *REJ*, XII, 301–5.

for no one since has received a new law as on Sinai, or kings and prophets from God's own hand. The nations are fond of quoting only the biblical prophecies of calamity for Israel, and not the prophecies of consolation and future greatness.

More significant is Cardoso's reply to the taunt that all sovereignty has departed from the Jews, hinging on the famous verse "the scepter shall not depart from Judah . . . until Shiloh come" (Gen. 49: 10). He grants that "Shiloh" is the Messiah. But, while many Jewish commentators in the past had interpreted the "scepter" as any specific form of supracommunal Jewish leadership in the diaspora such as the Exilarchate or the Negidut, or had pointed to the Khazar Kingdom while it still existed, Cardoso gives the very broadest definition possible. For him *any Jewish community* is proof that the "scepter" has not departed:

And it elicits no little admiration to see a people dispersed and scattered among the nations, and exiled for so many centuries, guarding its rites and ceremonies, and being like a Republic apart, governing itself by the Law which God gave it, and by its sages who are its Ministers and Governors, God having desired to give us this consolation in the midst of the nations by means of the princes in whose lands we are.

Thus the prophecy of Jacob is marvelously explained, that the scepter shall not be taken from Judah . . . until Shiloh (Messiah) comes. That is—the scepter of dominion shall not be taken from the Jews until the coming of the Messiah. They shall always rule and govern themselves by their sages in their rites, ceremonies, marriages, funerals, feasts, traditions, all in conformity with the Law which God has commanded us. The verse does not say "crown," but "scepter," and that signifies any form of rule. . . .[76]

Though the hegemony of the commandments over Israel is an idea of old vintage, Cardoso has in mind something more tangible. He has pointed to the reality of Jewish life as he knew it, with its

---

[76] *Excelencias*, p. 22. On the interpretation of Gen. 49: 10 through the ages see Adolf Posnanski, *Schiloh, ein Beitrag zur Geschichte der Messiaslehre* (Leipzig, 1904). See also Cardoso's discussion of Jewish servitude, *infra*, ch. IX. Costa Mattos alludes to the fact that the Jews thought they possessed the scepter of Judah in Castile, but now, he complains, they really have it in Portugal! (*Discurso*, fol. 144v).

large measure of internal independence, regulating its life under its own recognized leaders, formulating its own ordinances, adjudicating its cases in its own courts on the basis of Jewish law. In essence he has emphasized what he himself saw in Venice and Verona—the universally acknowledged corporate status of Jewry and their communal autonomy—and has thus been able to represent even the local community as a "republic" in miniature. At the same time, he is also keenly aware of the worldwide unity of the Jewish people, so much so that the second *excelencia* extols them as *Gente una—one* people.

Here, as elsewhere, Cardoso is not speaking in a vacuum. Initially, his stress on the unity of Israel appears to be directed against the constant harping of their enemies on the fact of their dispersion. But there are also other levels to the argument. Iberian antisemites were themselves fond of emphasizing the solidarity of the Jews whenever they conjured up the spectre of universal Jewish plots to subvert Christendom. Torrejoncillo, for instance, has an entire chapter to show "how the Jews, wherever they live, are each for the other, like a mystic body."[77] In this sense, Cardoso is attempting to show the virtue of what the enemy proclaimed a vice. But it is also worth observing how the very same claim for unity was made by Iberian writers for Christendom itself. Costa Mattos writes in his tract against the Jews:

The Catholic Church, militant spouse of Christ, forms the spiritual union of the faithful. Although they are physically scattered through various parts of the world they are joined together in precepts and in religion, with one Lord, one Faith, one Baptism, one God, and one head—Christ. . . .[78]

Cardoso ironically cites as his text Haman's ancient formulation, that "there is a certain people scattered about and dispersed among

---

[77] Torrejoncillo, *Centinela*, p. 113; "Como los Judíos, donde quiera que estan, son unos para otros, como un cuerpo místico." Cf. Cardoso's remark (*Excelencias*, p. 26), speaking of Israel's unanimous acceptance of the Law at Sinai: "y desta union y conformidad nació el ser los hijos de Ysrael fiadores unos de otros, todos hazen un cuerpo místico. . . ."

[78] Costa Mattos, *Discurso*, fol. 10r.

the peoples . . . and their laws are diverse from those of every people, neither keep they the king's laws" (Esther 3: 8), and continues:

[The verse] announces this people's unity and separation from all in order thereby to render it more abhorred, while for the same reason it is most singular and marvelous. . . .

In a nation or territory like Italy, France, or Spain, there are many nations in each one, so intermingled with each other because so many came to live there, that the true and original one can no longer be recognized. While Israel, by contrast, is one people among many, one even though scattered, and in all places separate and distinct, its Law diverse from others. . . .[79]

There are three main reasons for the unity of Israel: their common descent; their common and fervent adherence to the Law; and the love and brotherhood they hold for one another. While Cardoso discusses each of these features in detail, it is the first which is most engrossing in the light of his background:

No nation in the world can say it is one, except Israel, for only to it did the Lord communicate this preeminence—*Who is like Thy people Israel a nation one in the earth* (II Sam. 7: 23)—because as regards the body they have one single father, and one single Law as regards the soul. . . .

The peoples of the world do not proceed from one father, nor do they follow one law. Since in their lineage all are intermingled with one another, none can say that he is an Italian, Frenchman, Spaniard, German, or Greek, and so with the other peoples, because all are confused and mixed together. There came to Italy and Spain Tyrians, Phoenicians, Chaldeans, Egyptians, Arabs, Goths, Iberians, Vandals, Carthaginians, Alemani, and many others who intermingled, so that they cannot trace their ancestry, and since the nations of the earth do not separate themselves in foods or in women, they cannot attain the same separation and distinction as the sons of Israel, who are apart from all. . . .[80]

The full force of such a passage can be felt only if we try to imagine how for decades in Spain, especially in the arstocratic circles which he had frequented, Cardoso must have encountered all the extravangances of Spanish pride. The preoccupation of the

---

[79] *Excelencias*, p. 24.   [80] *Ibid.*, p. 72.

Spaniards with *limpieza* and *hidalguía*, with "Gothic" ancestries and genealogical investigations, could not but have impressed itself upon him during those many years. As a New Christian he had known, even if he did not suffer, all the slanders of tainted blood which his brethren had to endure. In the seventeenth century, Spanish writers themselves went to the most absurd lengths to prove the immaculate lineage of their nation to the rest of the world. To appreciate what Cardoso has said of the Jews, let us once more call to witness Peñalosa's work, where the fourth *excelencia* bears the heading: "Among the Spaniards is found the most ancient nobility of any of the nations, retaining always the blood of their first progenitor, Tubal." According to the author, Tubal had come to Spain in the year 2,163 B.C. From him were descended the Asturians and Cantabrians, as well as other peoples of the mountainous north and west of Spain, "and they did not mingle with the Goths, nor with the Moors from Africa, nor any other nations which at any time possessed these realms but were unable to subject that fierce mountainous region." Then, Peñalosa continues:

From these most ancient mountain peoples are descended all the Spaniards with whom Spain was populated. . . . To these was promised the empire of the world, and not to the progeny of Greeks, Carthaginians, and Romans, who inhabited these realms before Christ was born. And so that those might perish, the Divine Majesty permitted the Arabs to lay waste the entire kingdom, and then it was repopulated anew by these small remnants who had maintained themselves in the mountains of Spain since the time of Tubal. . . .[81]

Against such a singular recasting of Spanish history, Cardoso's emphasis on the ethnic purity of Israel stands out in greater relief. In that very people whose blood the Spaniards regarded as a stain on their own, he has found the true *hidalguía*, and a real *limpieza*, which he now holds up for all to see. He can point for the ancestry of his nation, not to Tubal, but to Abraham:

The unity of [Israel's] descent shows itself in that all are descendants of Abraham, of Isaac, and of Jacob, the three distinguished patriarchs

---

[81] *Las cinco excelencias del español*, fols. 75v-76r.

who merited the particular favor of being chosen, and that the Lord should call himself their God. . . . This unity is indicated by the prophet Isaiah (51: 2)—"Look unto Abraham your father . . . for one have I called him, blessed him, and multiplied him. . . ." Of this progeny of Abraham he chose Isaac, and not the sons of Hagar and Keturah; and of Isaac he chose Jacob, and not Esau. . . .[82]

But, as Cardoso has already adumbrated, the Jews are not only united among themselves; they are also separated from all the other surrounding peoples. That this in itself should be considered an *excelencia* (the third) is significant. Since Hellenistic times, Jewish separation had been thrown up as proof of Jewish misanthropy, of an *odium humani generis*. Cardoso will deal specifically with that charge in the seventh of the *calunias*. For the moment he is concerned only with the positive aspects of this separation.

The Jews are separated above all in being a *guided* people, governed by God with special providence, and not by a "presiding angel," as is the case with the other nations. This is also why the sages have said that "Israel has no planet." They are dominated, not by astral powers, but by God alone.[83] Since Israel is to be a holy people, it must of necessity be separated, for the word *Kadosh* already implies both aspects. The two primary means whereby the Jews are separated are abstention from prohibited food and from forbidden women. Here Cardoso gives an elaborate explanation of the dietary laws, which we shall consider later. In general the Lord took particular care to separate His people in body (by circumcision), in soul (by the Law), in dress (by the wearing of fringes), in houses (by the *mezuzah*), in fields (by the prohibition of mixed sowing), and even in animals (by not mating diverse species). All this together comprises *santidad* (holiness).

Thus far there is nothing unusual in the doctrine which he expounds. It is when we reach the discussion of the Ghetto and the Badge that we become increasingly amazed at how far-reaching his ideas on the subject of separation really are. Cardoso is fully prepared

---

[82] *Excelencias*, p. 24. "The sons of Hagar" = Muslims; "Esau" = Christians.
[83] *Ibid.*, pp. 36 f.

to hold up as a model, not merely voluntary separation, or that which is necessitated by observance of the Law, but enforced segregation as well:

In their habitations in almost all cities, they are separated in quarters and locations apart; in others they wear a sign, either in the hat or on the shoulder, all in order to be distinguished and separated. As the prophet says (Isa. 61: 9), *And their seed shall be known among the nations, and their offspring among the peoples; all that see them shall acknowledge them, that they are the seed which the Lord had blessed.* For their being marked and distinct, as well in their dwellings as in their dress, is not so much due to the deprecation of the nations as it is the particular providence of their separation. . . .[84]

To gloss the verse in Isaiah as forecasting the Ghetto and the Badge is, in its own way, as paradoxical an exegesis as any through which Abraham Cardoso found his apostate messiah in Scripture. We could, of course, dismiss this passage as a mere instance of making a virtue out of necessity.[85] However, the rest of the chapter shows that Cardoso truly believes a total separation from the gentiles to be a blessing. One has the impression that these uncompromising terms are but the repercussions of his own leap from the Spanish Court into the Ghetto, and that in order to achieve it he had been not only

---

[84] *Ibid.*, p. 47.

[85] In a sense this is what happened in Verona itself, where the Jews observed an annual celebration commemorating the establishment of the ghetto. It was first described by Cecil Roth in his "La fête de l'institution du ghetto. Une célébration particulière à Vérone," *REJ*, LXXIX (1924), 163–69. Sonne has shown, however, that this celebration was not due to an initial Jewish desire to have the ghetto, but to the fact that the Jews of Verona were saved thereby from a worse fate. They had already begun to be threatened with a ghetto before 1585, but were dismayed to learn that the place set aside for this purpose was outside the city in one of the foulest locations available. The mob, at the same time, was urging their expulsion. Only after years of the most arduous efforts were they able to secure from the Veronese authorities a place near the center of the city, and it is therefore no wonder that, when the ghetto was formality established in 1599, they hailed it as a deliverance. (See Sonne's remarks and documents in *Zion*, III, pp. 126–29.) It is possible that Cardoso is partly reflecting a general feeling in the community that the ghetto is a blessing in disguise.

prepared, but psychologically compelled, to develop so extreme an attitude. At the same time it is clear that he is also arguing with those Jews who had begun to ape gentile customs while still within the Jewish community. It is with them in mind that he speaks of "the error of some of the ambitious and ignorant who acquire the liberty of the gentiles and walk like them. . . . That which is really an infelicity appears to them a privilege, and that which is a disgrace seems a favor."[86] What he naturally does not choose to consider is the fact that he had already enjoyed the privileges which these Jews now sought, and that perhaps because of this he could now more easily renounce them.

To the gentiles, he addresses this resounding justification:

> If we could see today those ancient philosophers, whether Platonists in their Academy, or Stoics in their Portico, retiring from the crowd, lovers of virtue, preaching right conduct, would we not take great notice of them and admire their way of life, although they possess neither the true religion nor the light of the most holy Law? Then with how much more reason should esteem be given to the Jews who, separated from all peoples in their foods, in women, in customs, guard the Divine Law which the Lord has commanded them to observe perpetually. . . .[87]

Despite the apparent confidence with which these words are uttered, there is something plaintive in this attempt to portray the Jews as Stoics, and the Ghetto as a latter-day Academy. Cardoso is stronger when he leaves such hyperbolic analogies and simply describes the inner beauty of ordinary Jewish life. In the third *excelencia* he illustrates Jewish compassion with examples of the duty to visit the sick, to bury the dead and comfort the mourner, to rejoice the bride and groom, to slaughter animals humanely, all taken from the life around him, as well as by references to Bible and Talmud.[88] The Jews are charitable, being descendants of Abraham. He takes the opportunity to answer the old canard that the Law of Christ is the law of love, while that of the Torah is based on terror and rigor:

---

[86] *Excelencias*, p. 48. It may be that a few individual Jews in Verona had acquired an exemption from wearing the Jewish hat.

[87] *Ibid.*, pp. 50 f.   [88] *Ibid.*, pp. 51–57.

Charity is so proper to the Children of Israel, and it is so natural to them to succor the poor, that the entire Law leads to the fear of God and to charity towards one's fellow. For it is a law of love, and of benevolence, not of terror and burden as is alleged by those with bad intentions, who either lie, or do not wish to recognize its compassion because of the innate hatred which they harbor against the Jews.

Similarly, examples are given of Jewish modesty and sobriety in dress, in sexual mores, and in speech.[89]

Though following Maimonides in his exposition of details, Cardoso's insistence on prophecy as a unique prerogative of the Jewish people (8th *excelencia*) is strongly reminiscent of Judah Halevi.

These nations that thou art to dispossess hearken unto soothsayers and unto diviners; but as for thee, the Lord thy God has not suffered thee to do so. A prophet will the Lord thy God raise up unto thee from the midst of thee, of thy brethren, like unto thee. . . . As if to say—magic, astrology, superstition, auguries, divination are proper to the nations . . . but to you I give the admirable gift of prophecy with particular grace and favor, and not to the idol-atrous. . . .[90]

That prophecy is the possession of Israel is already indicated by the fact that Abraham, the first Jew, the first to be circumcised, is also the first to be called *nabi*. Moreover, prophecy is a virtue of the Land of Israel. If Ezekiel, Daniel, and, to some extent, Jeremiah prophesied outside the Holy Land, their prophecies were nonetheless concerned with it.[91] If Balaam, being both a gentile and impious, seems to be an exception, that is only apparent. He was a prophet by "accident" rather than intention, and, although his prophecy was meant to be evil, he was forced in any case to proclaim the glory of Israel.

In the same manner as Balaam we must discuss others who are reputed to be prophets among the gentiles, such as the Sibyls, Orpheus, [Hermes] Trismegistus, Zoroaster, and Zamolxis, among the Greeks, Egyptians, Persians, and Dacians; also the Sages count seven prophets of the nations:

---

[89] *Ibid.*, pp. 83–86. In the course of his discussion, Cardoso also goes to some lengths to explain why Jews allow their beards to grow, and compares this with the customs of other nations.

[90] *Ibid.*, p. 286. [91] *Ibid.*, pp. 290 f. Cf. Halevi, *Kuzari*, II, no. 14.

Balaam and his father, Job, and his four friends. But if these enjoyed the heavenly dignity of prophecy, it was also by accidental encounter, nor were they required to have those dispositions of virtue and wisdom which were found in the true prophets of Israel. And mostly those seers were able to predict some future events when they were seized by fury or inspired by some spirit, as we see when Vergil depicts his Cumaean sibyl prophesying in a frenzy, and beside herself, and seers have been similarly described by Seneca, Lucan, and others.[92]

Cardoso similarly dismisses the gentile oracles who have arisen in later times:

Among the nations certain predictions are celebrated with the name of prophecies, as are those of the abbot Joachim in Italy, Isidore in Spain, Merlin in England, Nostradamus in France, and Bandarra in Portugal. But these are for the most part equivocal, enigmatic, obscure, as well as being culled artificially from Sacred Scripture, transposed, augmented, confused. And their devotees explain them [each] in their own way, and, when events occur, they subsequently accomodate the predictions to them.[93]

The bulk of the section on prophecy is concerned with the distinction between true and false prophets, the relation of the prophet to the Law, and other details already discussed in connection with the Sabbatian movement. We have seen that, in a seemingly theoretical dissertation on the nature of prophecy, there is really a two-pronged rejection of the messiahship both of Jesus and of Sabbatai Zevi.

The same theoretical air seems initially to pervade the ninth *excelencia*, in praise of the Holy Land, until we examine it also within a polemical framework. The absence of a land or territory to call their own was another perpetual means for denigrating the Jews. Cardoso is therefore obviously concerned to show that the loss of the land is no sign of God's disfavor, and here too we encounter the

---

[92] *Ibid.*, p. 292. On the seven gentile prophets see the references in Ginzberg, *Legends*, VI, 125, n. 27. That Isaac Cardoso had Hermetic writings in his library may be seen from the remarks of Abraham, who had read several of them in Venice. See Bernheimer, *JQR*, XVIII, 116.

[93] *Excelencias*, p. 292. The passage on Bandarra, quoted *supra*, ch. VII, n. 16, follows immediately after this.

traditional theodicy of the Exile as an expiation for sin. But we soon notice that there is something more at stake. In the first place, Cardoso tries to demonstrate that the Jewish claim on Palestine is qualitatively different from that of other nations on their own lands, for Israel alone was granted its land by God:

Just as God chose one nation as His people, so also He chose one land for its habitation, and for the indwelling of His divinity among the nations. He did not grant dominion simply, but under oath, so that it be understood that it is the proper inheritance of the Hebrews, given by the Creator of the world and Lord of all lands. This is a privilege and distinction which no other nation has, since not one of them can say that the land it inhabits was given to it by God, but rather by the conquering sword, or by deceitful cunning, or by voluntary surrender....[94]

But it is when we pass the biblical praises of the Holy Land and come to Cardoso's detailed descriptions of its fertility, climate, topography, and even its ancient demography, that we realize he is writing his account very much in the manner of the sixteenth and seventeenth-century Spanish encomia of Spain itself. That he is attempting to describe a land which he has never seen, and which was certainly unreal to him, should not distract us. One may perhaps smile today at his list of fruits and vegetables, his grave delineations of latitude and longitude, or his solemn demarcation of the territorial boundaries of each of the Canaanite nations. But we understand very well his attempt to set up his people's land as the rival, and in many respects the superior, of the other countries of the world. Since he knows full well that in agricultural or mineral produce other countries easily have the upper hand, he finally turns to the resources of the spirit:

As, of necessity, the child takes nourishment from its mother, so the nations suckled from Judea the milk of faith, of wisdom, and the true knowledge of one God. . . . As man is a microcosm of the world, so is the world a macrocosm of man, whose limbs are the provinces and the nations, and whose head is Jerusalem. . . .[95]

---

[94] *Excelencias*, p. 302.　　[95] *Ibid.*, p. 304.

Paraphrasing the Talmudic adage that "the atmosphere of the Land of Israel makes wise," he writes:

Because of the subtlety of the air, and the disposition of the Land, the sages say that the Holy Land infuses wisdom and saintliness, and that in it alone can there be prophecy. There are various cities which have especially produced wise men, such as Athens in Greece, Córdoba in Spain, and Jerusalem—in the universe. . . .[96]

He is perhaps most affecting when he speaks of the small size of the country. We must bear in mind the Spanish boast of the grandeur of empire to sense the full contrast:

But it is very worthy of note that the Lord did not give His cherished people a large realm and such extensive provinces as we know were held by the Assyrians, the Persians, and the other great monarchies and kingdoms, but rather enclosed them in such narrow boundaries as those of the Holy Land.

To this we respond that the Lord wished to show that great realms are great plunders, and that the domination of foreign territories is more the result of violence and force than of justice and equity. . . . It closed the doors to ambition, and opened them to rectitude and temperance. *For all the earth is mine,* says God. The nations usurp it, but the earth is God's. His divine goodness gave the Promised Land to His people with repeated oaths, unlike the other nations of the world, who cannot say that the land they inhabit is theirs and that God gave it to them, but rather that some took it from others. . . .

The Promised Land was small, and given to Israel so that it might understand that it should pay more attention to the divine service than to the extension of the covetousness of man. Great empires are not acquired by equity and justice, nor are they sustained by truth, for the desire to dominate narrows the limits of reason, and distends the bounds of arrogance. . . .[97]

In this entire discussion of the Land of Israel, as throughout the book, the Messiah is never explicitly mentioned. This may well be regarded as a conscious reticence on the part of Cardoso in the wake of the messianic catastrophe through which Jewry had but recently

---

[96] *Ibid.*, p. 308.   [97] *Ibid.*, pp. 314 f.

passed. However, the messianic hope itself is never absent. Israel, Cardoso affirms, "persecuted, chastised, scattered among the nations, has lost the land, but not the promise, has lost possession, but not ownership. . . ." The title page of the *Excelencias* bears an emblem showing a hand emerging from heaven, gathering flowers, with the motto: "He who has scattered me, shall gather me. . . ."

Until that time, it is the vocation of Israel to be "witnesses to the Unity of God."[98]

The wise men of the nations and the ancient philosophers, after many years of study and long contemplation, came to know that there is only One God, creator of the world. In the midst of so much idolatry and adoration of false deities, because of their moral virtues and intense awareness, they came to notice a First Cause.

But hardly are the Jews born and nourished with their mothers' milk, barely are they able to speak, when the first words they are taught are the *Shema*, and they proclaim that there is only One God who is to be worshiped. The children begin where the philosophers leave off. . . .[99]

As the Lord is One in heaven, He desires that His witness be one on earth. . . . Together they testify to Unity: Israel—that God is One; God —that Israel is one. . . . Israel declares: *Shema, Hear O Israel;* God declares: *Hear, O my people;* Israel recites: *And thou shalt love thy God;* He proclaims: *With an everlasting love have I loved thee.*[100]

The highest form of witness is, of course, martyrdom itself. Cardoso begins by briefly citing the ancient examples: Hananiah, Mishael, and Azariah; Daniel in the lions' den; Hannah and her seven sons; those who were slain in Roman times.[101] But the cases

---

[98] The tenth *excelencia*. It opens with an attack against atheism, presenting both the teleological argument, and the argument from design.

[99] *Excelencias*, p. 319. Cf., in a different context, *Phil. lib.*, p. 649, quoted *supra*, ch. VI, n. 176.

[100] *Excelencias*, p. 321.

[101] *Ibid.*, p. 323. He calls Hannah *aquella valerosa Macabea*, and adds that of her and the other Maccabean martyrs "haze un docto y elegante libro Iosepho, llamandole el imperio de la razón." The reference is of course to *IV Maccabees*. That Josephus was the author was already held by Eusebius, who writes in the *Ecclesiastical History* (III. 10): "The man [Josephus] has also produced another work of a lofty character on the Supremacy of Reason. . . ."

he unfolds in the succeeding pages constitute, almost without exception, a Marrano martyrology.

In the Inquisitions of Spain, since their foundation unto this day, they have burned alive many Jews, men and women, for being constant and firm in the religion of their fathers. Only a few years ago, in Córdoba, in Coimbra, and in Lisbon, they burned women alive for following and proclaiming with great constancy the Law of Moses. As far as the Indies, in the New World, in New Spain, in Peru, they burned alive various men for not being willing to exchange their Law. . . .[102]

He goes on to cite the case of Dr. Tomás (Isaac) Trebiño de Sobramonte, burned at the stake in Mexico City, but without any comment. This detail was taken by him from Manasseh b. Israel's *Esperanza de Israel*, where Trebiño is also mentioned only in passing.[103]

But while he is indebted to Manasseh's work for some other examples as well, it is obvious that Cardoso must have had access to independent sources of information, for his reports contain elements not found in the earlier work. Thus, while Manasseh speaks quite briefly of Francisco Maldonado da Silva, Cardoso gives this more elaborate account:

And in Lima a physician, Silva, a great preacher of this Law, who was imprisoned for thirteen years and ate no meat during that time, except some maize flour in small quantity, undertaking great fasts and abstinences. He allowed his beard and hair to grow like the Nazirites, and circumcised himself with a knife, managing to complete the cutting of the praeputium with scissors. He changed his name from Maldonado de Silva to Eli Nazareno, and when he signed, he wrote: "Eli Nazareno, unworthy servant of God, alias Silva."

---

[102] *Ibid.* Immediately before this passage Cardoso writes that the sermons of Fray Vicente Ferrer caused many Jews to be killed. It may be, however, that he really has in mind Ferrand Martínez, whose role in instigating the Spanish massacres of 1391 is well known.

[103] Cardoso calls him simply "Trebiño." Cf. *Esperanza*, p. 100. For his story, see George Alexander Kohut, "Jewish Martyrs of the Inquisition in South America," *Publications of the American Jewish Historical Society*, IV (1896), 124, and Boleslao Lewin, "Tomas Trebinio de Sobramonte: the 'Saint of the Jewish Faith' in Mexico" (Yiddish), in *Davke*, IV (Buenos Aires, 1953), 166–204.

The theologians and inquisitorial officers summoned him many times in order to convince him, but he disputed with them by word and in writing. He wrote many treatises in his cell, joining together many old pieces of paper from various wrapped items which he asked for, and he did it so ingeniously that they seemed all of one piece. The ink he made from charcoal, the pen out of the bone of a chicken which he cut with a knife formed out of a nail, and he wrote a calligraphy which seemed as though printed.

They burned him alive at the end of thirteen years, and the *Auto*[104] which was printed in Madrid in 1640 stated . . . that after the announcement of the crimes of the relaxed was completed, there arose so fierce a wind, that the residents of Lima affirmed they had not seen one so strong in many years. It violently rent apart the canopy over that part of the platform where this condemned man stood, and he, seeing the sky, said: "This has been done by the God of Israel, so that He may see me face to face from heaven."

This *auto* took place in Lima on the 23d of January, 1639.[105]

Not mentioned at all in the *Esperanza* nor, for that matter, in any Jewish source known to us, is the following:

Another singular event occurred in Coimbra about a hundred years ago. They arrested as a Jew one Diego Lópes de Piñancos in a place near the city of La Guardia in Portugal, and the Sierra de Estrella, and, from the time he was taken, he began to announce that he was a Jew, and wished to live and die in the Law of Moses. When he was brought before the Inquisition, although the theologians tried to convince him, he always remained firm in his resolve. They sentenced him to be burned alive. When he was placed upon the stake, tied with its chains of iron, and raised high, the fire began to touch him. But then a great portent took place, for the chains fell into the fire, but he disappeared and was no longer to be seen. All of which caused enormous consternation among

---

[104] The text has "el *Autor*," an obvious misprint.

[105] *Excelencias*, pp. 323 f. Manasseh merely records the date, that he ate no meat, was imprisoned for 14 years, and circumcised himself (*Esperanza*, p. 100). The *auto* was the greatest held in Lima up to that time. On Maldonado da Silva, and on the *auto* itself, cf. Kohut, *Jewish Martyrs*, p. 113; José Toribio Medina, *Historia del Tribunal del Santo Oficio de la Inquisición de Lima (1569-1820)* (Santiago de Chile, 1887), pp. 146 ff.

the multitudes of people who were present, and they said that the demons had such a craving and desire for him, that they snatched him away body and soul, and in this way they eased their suspense and astonishment. To this day, in the Convento de la Cruz in Coimbra, he is painted, among others being burned, with two demons at his shoulders, and with the name of Diego Lópes de Piñancos. And aged Old Christians used to relate that they themselves had seen him, and had been present at the event.[106]

It may well be that Cardoso had heard this story years ago in his own family. "La Guardia" is certainly the city of Guarda, in the *Serra da Estrela*, and Trancoso itself is not far from it. Perhaps it was one of the tales that circulated among the Marranos of the region. In any case, his next illustration concerns one of the most famous Marrano martyrs of the seventeenth century, Isaac de Castro Tartas. Cardoso's description is especially interesting because it also shows the impact which such events had upon the Sephardic diaspora:

Certainly marvelous and worthy of contemplation is that which occurred in our time (for it was on December 22, 1647), to a lad named Isaac de Castro Tartas, twenty-five years of age, born in France in the province of Gascony, in a tiny but noble town called Tartas. When the Portuguese had begun their campaign in Brazil, at the time that it was in the hands of the Dutch, he was in Bahia. Being recognized there as a Jew of Parahiba, where various Jews lived, he was arrested, and brought to the Inquisition in Lisbon. He soon admitted he was a Jew, and wished to live and die as such. Seeing his great constancy, the inquisitors sent him theologians and learned men to see if they could persuade him to abandon the Law of Moses. But he, like the true sage and great theologian and philosopher that he was, also knew how to dispute and argue with them. . . .

It must also be revealed that . . . when he left Parahiba for Bahia, his relatives and friends told him that he should watch what he did, for if the Portuguese recognized him as a Jew, they would carry him off as a prisoner to the Inquisition. To which he replied that if they caught him, he would sanctify the name of the Lord.

But we should consider that before he departed from that city, he wrote

---

[106] I know of no other reference to this martyr. Roth's account (*Hist. of the Marranos*, p. 149), is obviously derived from Cardoso.

to his parents in Amsterdam, telling them that he was going to Rio de
Janeiro to see if there he could lead some of his relatives to the fear of
God, and that they should not expect a letter from him for four years.
When the four years were up, a letter came, informing them that he had
been burned alive in the city of Lisbon.

There was now a greater marvel. . . . In Amsterdam it is the custom
not to sell *miṣvot* (i. e., congregational honors), but rather to place the
names of the *kahal* or congregation in two caskets, one for going up to
the Torah, the other for opening the doors of the *hekhal* (i. e., the Ark),
and lifting out the Scroll . . . so that all may participate by lot . . . and
when the *parnasim* know that someone has left the city to live in another
land, they take his card out. That had been done in the case of this
divine youth when he left Amsterdam for Brazil. But then it happened
later, when his parents and brothers received the news that he had been
burned alive in Lisbon, that on the first Sabbath of his funerary honors,
the *Haham* Rabbi Saul Levi Morteira, peace be unto him, devoted his
sermon to the blessed martyr. When they went to draw the lots, the
first which emerged for the opening of the doors of the *hekhal* was that
of the glorious Isaac de Castro Tartas. . . .

Among the elegies which certain poets wrote for him, there are some
verses of Señor Jonah Abravanel, as follows:

> These are certain signs
> That sacred was thy story,
> For when the pious celebrated
> The remembrance of thy death,
> Upon thee emerged the lot
> To open the portals of glory.

Since this valiant man was burned in Lisbon, they have resolved no
more to burn anyone alive, because after burning for a long time in the
flames, his voice was heard calling out and invoking the name of the Lord
Adonay, saying: "*Shema Yisrael, Adonay Elohenu, Adonay Ehad!*"[107]

---

[107] On Isaac de Castro Tartas see Wiznitzer, *Jews in Colonial Brazil*, pp. 110–19.
He was the brother of David de Castro Tartas, the printer of the *Excelencias* (see
BEPJ, p. 37). According to the French ambassador, who was present at the *auto*,
his last words were "Eli Adonay Sebaot"; Cardoso may be ascribing the *Shema* to
him because that is the theme he is discussing.

Jonah Abravanel was a nephew of Manasseh b. Israel (*BEPJ*, p. 7). Among
others who wrote poems for the occasion were an Abraham Cardoso (not to be

Cardoso mentions briefly also the terrible Chmelnitzki pogroms of 1648–49: "These past years, during the wars of the Poles and the Tartars, there were Jews without number who were slain because they did not wish to give up the Law."[108] Other references to Ashkenazic martyrdom are found, not here, but in the section on the blood-libel.

Finally, we must not close this survey of Cardoso's exposition of the virtues of the Jewish people without taking account of one all-important factor: his *style*. It is this which gives the work its power even when Cardoso is drawing on the material of others. We can perhaps best appreciate this quality by an example. As we have noted, Cardoso often uses the midrashic interpretation of the Song of Songs in praise of Israel. But in many instances he then elaborates a "midrash" of his own, and writes passages of considerable poetic beauty. Here is Cardoso in a very characteristic expansion of the comparison of Israel to the dove:

Israel is compared to the Dove, for so the Song says: *One is my dove, my perfect one, one is she . . . pure is she to her that bore her*. Three names He gave [to Israel]: Perfect, One, and Pure. It is compared to the dove for her purity, her whiteness, and her timorousness, for she is persecuted by all the birds, by all clawed asunder. She eats only the pure grain, loves the dovecot and the nest, and although other birds overtake her, she turns away and separates herself from them, flying off with great speed to her own kind when she is given liberty to do so. And so doves are used between cities as couriers and post-bearers, for though they be separated by a hundred miles from the dovecot, if they are allowed to fly off from that place, then soon, whether by instinct or sense of smell, they return to the nest within a few hours, and the flight is direct, and unwavering. Thus Israel, the persecuted dove among the nations . . . returns to her nest, to her God, to her Law. She flies directly to Him, constant, and loyal. . . .[109]

---

confused with Isaac's brother), and João Pinto Delgado. See Cecil Roth, "An Elegy of João Pinto Delgado on Isaac de Castro Tartas," *REJ*, CXXI (1962), 355–66.

[108] *Excelencias*, pp. 325 f.   [109] *Excelencias*, p. 330.

THE LAW

Cardoso's exposition of Jewish law is contained in the chapters on circumcision and the Sabbath, and most systematically in the seventh *excelencia* ("Ley Divina"). These cover minutely the entire gamut of Jewish practice, and constitute a veritable manual. For our purposes it will be more fruitful to seek out general principles rather than to dwell on details which are, after all, common elements of the halakhic tradition.

That he accepts the entire corpus of Jewish law as binding has already been indicated. The intensity of his acceptance is perhaps best revealed in such a statement as this:

The Divine Law is an article of our Faith, and foundation of our belief, whether we reduce them to thirteen [principles] as does Rabbi Moses, or to six as Rabbi Hasdai, or to three as Joseph Albo: The Unity of God, the Divine Law, and Reward and Punishment. Although divergent in their number, they are uniform in their result and substance, and we could even reduce them all to one, which is—to believe in the holy Law, for in this single article are included the three, the six, and the thirteen.[110]

However, in this, as in other passages, it is not always easy to determine specifically how Cardoso is using the term "Law" (*la Ley*). The Spanish word itself is resonant with various nuances, and so it is when Cardoso and other Sephardic writers employ it. *Ley* is elastic enough to be synonymous with "religion," and indeed, when Cardoso writes repeatedly of *las leyes de las gentes* he usually means "other religions." When he prefixes the definite article, capitalises the word, and certainly when he adds the adjective "Divine," he has in mind only the Jewish "Law." But even then we must try to determine whether he is restricting the term to the *halakhah* alone, or if he means Judaism in the wider sense of both practices and beliefs.

---

[110] *Excelencias*, p. 128.

The fact that in the above passage Cardoso speaks separately of "Law" (*Ley*), "Faith" (*Fée*), and "belief" (*creencia*), would seem to limit the first term to *halakhah* in the strict sense. From this it might seem that Cardoso's view of Judaism is such that he defines it as law, and regards ideas and beliefs to be of secondary importance. But this is not the case. What Cardoso seems to be saying is that *functionally* no other "article" is necessary. The very acceptance of the Divine Law as binding presupposes having accepted other cardinal beliefs as well, while all of Jewish theology is already implicit in the various laws themselves. In reducing the various creedal formulations to one, Cardoso is not taking issue with the importance of having correct beliefs. For him those beliefs are *comprised* in the "Law."

That he has in mind the wider connotation of the *Ley Divina* is made very explicit several pages later, in these words:

The Law, perfect and divine, consists in holding true opinions concerning God, and just relations with one's fellow; these are the two foundations on which it is based, and the two signs by which it is distinguished from human [laws]. In that which concerns the Divinity, it holds as certain that there is one God, Eternal, Immutable, Infinite, Incomprisable; that His unity is incomparable, with no admixture of another godhead, nor any other accompaniment; that He is absolute lord of all creation; that He governs His creatures with infinite wisdom and providence; that He is Immense, Omnipotent, and imposes reward and punishment on men according to their merits; and all these attributes and propositions are embraced by human reason with evident proofs. Many of the gentile philosophers knew this through speculation, and, abandoning their idolatries, arrived at the recognition of one infinite God, Creator of the Universe.

As for one's fellow, [the Law] disposes absolutely perfect judgments and statutes, conforming to reason, and established with equity, which human laws do not have, for they do not know exactly the magnitude of the sin, nor the correct proportion and measure of the penalty. . . .[111]

The notion that the *halakhah* embraces not only deeds, but ideas as well, is of itself quite unimpeachable. Upon reflection, what is

---

[111] *Excelencias*, p. 131. On gentile philosophers reaching a knowledge of the One God, cf. *Phil. Lib.*, p. 737.

striking in the passage with which we began is the sharpness of Cardoso's statement that all creedal principles of Judaism can be reduced to one: "belief in the Holy Law." I know of no antecedent for such a formulation in Jewish literature. The very phrase is interesting. When Maimonides, or Albo, included an article concerning the Law, it was couched in terms of belief in its divine *revelation*. No one phrased it as belief *in* the Law itself. While the practical difference here may well be only a semantic one, it is still worthy of attention. To "believe in the Law" is not a normal Jewish phrase; it is, however, quite distinctly a Marrano phrase. To "believe in the Law of Moses" or to "save oneself" in that Law are common expressions in the inquisitorial dossiers of Judaizers. It is probable, therefore, that Cardoso's terminology derives from his own Marrano past.

In the introductory section of the seventh *excelencia* Cardoso undertakes to show that the Law is of divine origin, that it is perfect, and that it is eternal. Of these the last is the most relevant to his apologetic task, for, just as he has argued against the Christian dogma of the repudiation of Israel, he must also counter the very possibility of an abrogation of the Law. Resuming a classic contention of Jewish apologetics, he emphasizes that such an abrogation, or the giving of a new law, would have to be executed is the same manifest and prodigious manner as the granting of the Torah at Sinai, which he describes in rhapsodic detail. In fact, it would require even more signs than before. Since such a new revelation has not taken place, nothing is changed:

But let us now extend the discussion even further. Let us suppose that God with His absolute power should desire to abrogate the circumcision of His people and replace it by immersion [i.e., baptism], or that He should want to annul the Sabbath and substitute for it Friday, like Ishmael, or Sunday, like Edom—something which He will not do, because He has assured us that His Law will not be changed—but suppose this impossibility. How can the Jews be expected to believe that God has changed the Sabbath and circumcision, unless it were with the same marvels by which the Law was given? And even these would not suffice, for He has told us that we should keep it through all our generations. In order to remove from us all suspicion or shadow of hesitation, it would be necessary to impress in the souls of all Israel a supernatural illumination and divine evidence that it was His will to change the Law or that precept for another, and forever, for in no other manner would we be obligated to follow it.[112]

Many gentiles try to prove the imperfection of the Law and its temporary duration by pointing to three laws which seem particularly flawed: usury, polygamy, and divorce. Usury, Cardoso notes, is of course forbidden among Jews, but it may be given to gentiles and taken from them. This should not shock the gentiles so, since their own imperial and royal laws now permit it among their own subjects with moderate use. If they also permit it to the Jews, that is because in this way they compensate them for the landed property and other business which they forbid them to have, thus giving them some means of subsistence among the miseries of captivity. Polygamy is not a commandment but a permission, and there is no doubt that the Law holds monogamy to be more perfect. As for divorce, it is allowed in order to avoid intolerable hatreds, occasional murders, and perpetual quarrels among some married couples.[113]

Another alleged proof of the imperfection of the Law is the statement in Ezekiel (20: 25): *Wherefore I gave them also statutes that were not good, and ordinances whereby they should not live.* But this verse must be seen in the context of the entire chapter, for it is stated earlier (vv. 11–13) that they didn't observe His laws which had been given so that they might "live by them." Therefore, God gave them the bad laws of kings, and the cruel laws of princes. Another interpretation of those "bad laws," following the Targum, Rashi, and Abravanel, is that they refer to such curses as are contained in chapter 26 of the Book of Leviticus.[114]

The final proof adduced to show that God had to grant a new Law is the thirty-first chapter of Jeremiah, which speaks of the New Covenant. However, this is "like searching for bumps on the bullrushes and spots in the sun," because the chapter as a whole revolves around the future redemption of the Jewish people. As for the New Covenant, the real meaning of it is that He will put the

---

[112] *Excelencias*, p. 144.   [113] *Ibid.*, pp. 148–50.   [114] *Ibid.*, p. 151.

same Law in their hearts so that *all* shall be wise and God-fearing. The novelty is not in the Law, but "the method."[115]

As one reads Cardoso's discussions of the Law it becomes clear that he is attempting to vindicate it not only before the gentile world, but also to those Jews who had become lax in its observance, as well as to those returning Marranos who found it burdensome. He himself alludes to Jews who only keep the Law externally and surreptitiously violate the dietary laws. These hypocrites are like swans, seemingly white, but inside their flesh is black:

They say also that the Law is heavy and ponderous, since it consists of 613 precepts, a load so great that it is impossible to observe and hard to remember, and that laws should be few, the better to be obeyed. To which we reply that the Law is most soft, most sweet and gentle. . . . It is light and smooth to the virtuous, and tough and burdensome to the indolent and the forgetful. To those who fear the Lord, six hundred precepts seem like six, while to the impious and the neglectful, six seem like six hundred. . . .[116]

The Law is "sweeter than honey, smoother than wine, more fragrant than amber and musk, richer than gold and jewels, and more luminous than the sun." The Sabbath is an example:

All the nations of the world have their festive days, but these are ordained by men in honor of their gods or their saints. So we see that the ancients had their festivals dedicated to Ceres, to Jove, to Mars, the Saturnalia, the Bacchanalia, those of Flora; Edom has Sunday; Ishmael, Friday; but all these are human institutions, not commanded by God, but by princes or councils. . . . But the Sabbath and holidays of the Jews were not ordained by them, but by the Divine Majesty . . . and from this it results that . . . the Jews feel on this day an internal delight, a refreshed spirit, a new soul . . . and even though the nations have tried to imitate this precept, ordaining festive days, they could not follow this exact observance, nor do they have the inner joy which the Jews feel on this sacred day. . . .[117]

---

[115] *Ibid.*, p. 512. Cardoso also insists on the necessity of the Oral Law, and gives the calendar as an example. So also Aboab, *Nomologia*, Part I, chs. 16–20, pp. 76–101. For Cardoso's further treatment of the abrogation of the Law and of Christian exegesis, see *infra*, ch. IX, pp. 431 f.

[116] *Excelencias*, p. 150. On the hypocritical Jews, see pp. 38 f.

[117] *Ibid.*, p. 104.

The contrast between divine and human law is constant. All the world's lawgivers have tried to validate their laws by claiming they had received them from their gods. So, for example, Minos from Jupiter, Solon from Minerva, Lycurgus from Apollo, Numa Pompilius from the nymph Egeria. But these were only stratagems. Such laws were really created by men, invented out of their own heads, and no *people* saw or heard the deity speaking to them. "Not like this was the Law of Moses, which was given by God *publicly* at Sinai to millions of souls."[118]

If the emphasis on the public character of the Sinaitic revelation was at least as old as Saadia, the quest for the *ta'ame ha-miṣvot* (the "reasons for the precepts"), has been a perennial Jewish concern. Most of Cardoso's discussion of the Law takes its place within this tradition, and makes use of all its various instruments, rational, symbolic, philsophic, even mystical; all with an added strand of Cardoso's own secular erudition.

A somewhat unusual example is Cardoso's analysis of the dietary laws, a category of precepts which has always been refractory to rationalization, and which, understandably, causes him particular difficulties.

In its general aspect Cardoso treats the prohibition of certain foods as part of God's desire to separate Israel from the gentiles. The laws forbidding certain specific foods also have a reason, which only divine wisdom knows, and Jewry is only obliged to observe these commandments because they were given by God, for He values obedience more than speculation. However, since human understanding naturally desires to know reasons and causes, because in this way it finds its repose and satisfaction, he will investigate the matter further.[119]

There are, he notes, three opinions concerning the dietary laws. The first holds that the forbidden foods are unhealthy, and this is the opinion of Maimonides.[120] The second opinion maintains that

---

[118] *Ibid.*, pp. 126 f.

[119] The discussion of the dietary laws appears on pp. 39–45.

[120] See Maimonides, *Guide*, Pt. III, ch. xlviii.

certain animals were prohibited for symbolic reasons. Thus Eliezer the High Priest answered Aristeas, the legate of Ptolemy.[121] Finally, it has been suggested that the forbidden foods engender in man a bad temperament which leads in turn to grossness and obscurity of the understanding, a contamination of thought by an unclean spirit, and a resulting concupiscence and propensity for sin.

The most arresting feature of the discussion is Cardoso's rejection of the medical justifications. To suggest that these foods were forbidden because they are injurious to health would be to demean the Law, for any good medical textbook deals minutely with all foods and their physiological effects, while the Law of God contains wisdom which cannot be found elsewhere. Here, then, we hear the voice of Cardoso the physician. But, he continues, most pagans and gentiles are no more sick than the Jews, though they eat these prohibited foods; they are, indeed, healthy and robust. Here we may also detect the voice of the former Marrano who knows this from his personal experience. In any case, he goes on to note that certain foods such as cucumbers, mushrooms, and onions, which the physicians consider detrimental, are permitted by the Law, and that the converse is also true. Besides, God did not call any of the foods unhealthy, but simply *unclean.*

Despite the seeming assurance of this argument, Cardoso subsequently vacillates among all three explanations, adding one example after another, and obviously dissatisfied with any single reason. At one point he is even willing to combine the three, but he eventually manages to settle upon one idea. The prohibited foods possess a secret harmfulness, not manifestly physiological, which is known only to God. Since food is assimilated and becomes a part of man, if it is "unclean," then that part of man is also unclean; and since there is a conjunction of body and soul, the latter too suffers. Thus God commanded all these prohibitions in order to keep the soul pure.

In the last instance, however, Cardoso shows that he is well aware

---

[121] The symbolic meaning of the dietary laws in discussed in the *Letter of Aristeas*, 11. 139 ff.

of the weaknesses in all the explanations he has presented, and emphasizes that they do not affect the imperative itself:

The Law does not say speculate on the reasons for my commandments, but rather—do them and keep them. The obedient patient does not speculate with his physician on the reason for the salutary potion which the latter gives him in order to cure his illness. For if the physician should reply, and the patient be dissatisfied with the reason for the medicine, he might not take the remedy and thus not be cured of the sickness. But after having imbibed it, he can consider it and its ingredients. So the wise and virtuous who wish to keep the spiritual health of their souls take and observe the divine commandments as true antidotes for their own deeds, and heavenly elixirs for achieving the highest good; and then, if they wish, they may speculate and indulge their curiosity, so long as they have preceded this with faithful observance.[122]

Cardoso certainly followed his own injunction. Whatever his intellectual difficulties with specific details of the Law, he laid his life under its yoke completely and without qualification. Thoroughly convinced of its absolute religious validity, he was now equally persuaded that it contains the highest wisdom attainable by man. He could write:

Finally, the Jews put all their study in the Law. It is their theology, their philosophy, and their true wisdom. In it they sharpen their wits and discover marvelous secrets and concepts, for which God commanded us that we meditate on it day and night. In the theorems of Euclid, the lines of Archimedes, the logic of Crispinus, the metaphysics of Aristotle, the numbers of Pythagoras and atoms of Democritus, there are great subtleties, but they are most unequal and inferior to the debates of law which the Sages disputed, and the admirable meanings they extracted from each verse. Their investigations are divine, and divine their conclusions, compared to which, human subtleties are spiderwebs of little substance. . . .[123]

· [122] *Excelencias*, p. 44.   [123] *Ibid.*, p. 284.

ANTI-CHRISTIAN POLEMICS

But the *Excelencias* are not confined to defense alone. Here and there in the book Cardoso launches active attacks of his own against certain elements of Christian life and belief. I have already stressed the caution which the printed word imposed on Jewish polemicists. Cardoso's solution to the dilemma is interesting. Generally, he will allude to Christianity by name ("the Christians say . . .") only when he is refuting an anti-Jewish charge. But when he is himself assailing some aspect of Christianity, he will usually refrain from identifying it specifically as such, leaving it to the reader himself to make the identification. We must, in short, read between the lines.

This is often easy enough. For example, we understand very well whom he has in mind when he writes: "Prayer is conveyed in the commandment—*And serve the Lord your God*. And this must be offered solely to His Divine Majesty, and not to angels, nor to saints. . . ."[124]

Similarly, but more obliquely, when he writes that the Jews have no "absurdities" in their faith; or when he stresses that, among the Jews, the Law, being of divine origin, is studied by all, and adds a thinly veiled reference to the prohibition of reading the Bible in the vernacular in Catholic Spain:

The difference is that laws of human origin are not taught except to the lawyers, scrupulously insisting that they be studied only by those whose profession they are, forbidding the laymen not only to argue and discuss them, but even to read them in the common language. So, among the Persians the Magi, among the Egyptians the priests, among the Ethiopians the Gymnosophists, among the French the Druids; and among the present nations they put some to the sword and reduce others to silence, although it is natural among all men to desire to know matters of the spirit, and to discuss celestial themes. . . .[125]

These, however, are only barbs. More significant, if we read them correctly, are those passages which actually touch on the essentials of

---

[124] *Ibid.*, p. 158. Cf. also p. 37.   [125] *Ibid.*, p. 134.

Christian faith. An excellent illustration may be found in one of Cardoso's discussions of circumcision:

This precept is of such high rank that it came to make satisfaction for the Original Sin, Adam's sin of disobedience, because of which he became subject to death, he, as well as all of his descendants, being expelled from Paradise, and forbidden the Tree of Life.

By contrast, in Abraham was seen the height of obedience in his sacrifice of his son by divine command, and the same in Isaac, by offering himself for the sacrifice, which God accepted as though he had carried it out. Adam and Eve lost grace through disobedience; Abraham and Isaac recovered it by their obedience. Adam and Eve lost Paradise for an apple; Abraham and Isaac won the Holy Land through the *berit*. Adam and Eve lost the Tree of Life, but it was regained by Abraham and Isaac in the Holy Law, which is the veritable tree of all life, and so the verse says (Prov. 3: 18), *She is a tree of life to them that hold her fast. . . .*[126]

The passage is, at its core, a rejection of Christian redemptive history, with Abraham's circumcision and the sacrifice of Isaac taking the place of the Crucifixion. It reverses the Christian typology which saw in the patriarchal act a prefiguration of God's sacrifice of the Son. If Abraham has already made full "satisfaction" for the "original sin," then the advent of Christ and his death on the Cross are, in effect, both unnecessary and irrelevant. It is to be noted, however, that while rabbinic tradition ascribed many great and marvelous benefits to Abraham's actions, the rabbis were careful not to endow them with such absolute centrality as Cardoso does here. Indeed, they were far from unanimous that death is due to Adam's sin in the first place. The influence of Christian categories, deriving from Cardoso's own past, is evident even in the very moment when he is polemicising against Christianity.[127]

---

[126] *Ibid.*, p. 92.

[127] On Christian typological use of the sacrifice of Isaac, see Shalom Spiegel, "From the Legends of the *'Akedah*" (Hebrew), in *Alexander Marx Jubilee Volume*, Hebrew Section (New York, 1950), especially pp. 507 ff., and the references given there. For the difference in Rabbinic empasis, *ibid.*, pp. 25 ff. That Adam is responsible for his own death alone is stated repeatedly in Rabbinic sources. See the citations in Ginzberg, *Legends*, V, 129.

Spokesman for Judaism

Another device which Cardoso frequently employs when he wants to make an anti-Christian remark is to cite some other religion, either an ancient or an exotic one, as his example:

There is a great difference between that which God has [ordained] in foods and other areas of the Law, and that which men do in order to mortify their desires. For the latter, not being commanded by the Lord, do not have the same perfection as do His commandments. The wearing of sackcloth, not eating meat nor drinking wine, wounding the flesh so that the blood flows, not eating anything that has lived, as do the Brahmins of India and some who wish to withdraw from the common and social life of men, seeking solitude and the desert, all these, since they are not precepts ordained by God, do not really have the holiness which they seem to exhibit, and quite often they cover up great vices under the cloak of virtue. . . .[128]

Since Cardoso could hardly have been concerned with the defects of Hindu religion, we must understand these remarks as aimed at Christian monasticism, and the excesses of asceticism and self-mortification which he had witnessed in the Peninsula.

In one section only, that which closes the discussion of the Law in the seventh *excelencia*, does Cardoso throw most of his caution to the winds:

And if the nations say to us that they also have a revelation from their gods and their laws, then immediately, by reason and argument, it can be proved to them that such revelation cannot be divine. First—because it commands things contrary to the Divine Law, which is the older, and the sacred cannot contradict the sacred, nor can there be a prophet who contradicts the Law of Moses or changes some precepts for others, for God has already commanded us not to believe him; and if there should

---

[128] *Excelencias*, p. 45. In a rather candid note to the reader, Isaac Athias points out in the preface to his *Thesoro de Preceptos* that his use of such terms as "planets and stars" (i. e., "worshipers of planets and stars"), as well as "pagans," is really a screen which he is forced to use, obviously because of censorship: "Los nombres que se hallaran de planetas, Estrellas, y Paganos, son supositos, y los primeros dos significan todo aquello q̃ no es servicio del Culto divino; y paganos por todo el que no es de Isr., y fue forcado usar dellos, no de otras mas proprios, assi como se ve en nuestros libros Hebreos."

be another holy law in place of this one, then God will have deceived us with His own word, since He told us that we should guard it eternally. Second—because other laws contain absurdities and impossibilities which they are obliged to believe, and therefore they cannot be divine; for human reason clearly proves that there cannot be many gods, *nor that God can be a man*, nor that the planets and stars can be gods, all things of which the gentiles have persuaded themselves. . . .[129]

And somewhat later, after discussing the difference between the recognition of One God which some have been able to achieve through speculation, and the specific knowledge of His Law, given to Israel by revelation, Cardoso finally challenges the adversary by name:

The Law of Moses is acknowledged to be divine by all the wisest and most politic of peoples, such as the Christians, the Mohammedans, and the sects into which they are divided, Lutherans, Calvinists, Zwinglians, Arians, and many others, who lean upon it and affirm it as the foundation of their own [religion]. All recognize it as divine, and given by God to His people, while it does not recognize any of the others except as human inventions and political laws of princes and lords, who instituted them as their reason dictated, or their private interest, and changed and transformed them according to the times.

The nations themselves give great proof that our religion is the true one, and that the Law of Moses is the divine, since among themselves each holds the other to be false. The Mohammedans regard the Christian religion as the false one, the Christians the Mohammedan. They oppose and revile each other even in the chief dogmas regarding the Divinity, and the sects into which they are divided are supremely opposed in the most essential matters of faith. But all of them are uniformly agreed that the Law of Moses is divine and given by God—only that the duty of its observance is already past, either *because that man has come*, or the one sent by God to reform the world, according to them, and to give a new law for the salvation of men.

And so they changed the precepts of the Divine Law in their fashion, and invented new rites and ceremonies according to their belief, and they did not make known that God had already proclaimed in His Law that nothing be added to it or eliminated from it, and that no prophet

---

[129] *Ibid.*, pp. 275 f. (Italics mine.)

is to be believed who requires that it be abandoned, or that other gods or laws are to be followed. Everything has been anticipated by God and set forth with His divine foreknowledge, so that we not be deceived by certain appearances and remove ourselves from His holy Law. It is clearly demonstrated that this revelation, this Law, is the only divine one, given by God, immutable and eternal, most perfect in every detail, as we have shown earlier, and this is seen in the righteousness of its precepts. After the Law of God was given with so many miracles and so majestically, in God's presence, it requires no further miracles for its confirmation, for it is its own confirmation. . . .[130]

We shall not find so bold and forceful a statement in any other printed work of Jewish apologetics in the seventeenth century.

---

[130] *Ibid.*, pp. 279 f. "That man" (recalling the medieval Hebrew usage, *'oto ha-'ish*) = Jesus; "the one sent to reform the world" = Muhammad. (Italics mine.)

Chapter ix

DEFENDER OF ISRAEL

No ay maldad que no atribuyen a los
Judíos, luego por ser Judíos son culpa-
dos. . . .
—*Las excelencias de los Hebreos*

T HE second part of the *Excelencias* examines, in ten chapters,
the charges which have been leveled against the Jews.
Up to this point Cardoso has been content generally to
describe and explain both the Jews and Judaism. He is
now concerned with the direct refutation of specific antisemitic
smears. Cardoso's approach to these *calunias* exhibits several
characteristics which must be taken into account before we can
properly assess this section of his book.

IBERIAN FOCUS

We should recognize at the outset that the slanders with which
Cardoso deals here had a wide European diffusion, and can be
documented from the antisemitic literatures of several countries.
Nevertheless, his discussion of these charges is, as may be expected,
suffused with Iberian overtones. In form and texture, if not always in
content, the antisemitism which he combats in the *calunias* is still
largely that of the Peninsula which he had abandoned decades
before, rather than of Italy where he now lived.

Las
EXCELENCIAS
Y CALUNIAS
DE LOS HEBREOS.

Por el Doctor
YSHAC CARDOSO.

This was certainly not because he was unaware of the anti-Jewish literature produced in Italy itself. That Cardoso knew Italian after so long a sojourn in the country may be readily surmised, and is confirmed by his correspondence in that language with Judah Brieli. He actually refers once to an important Italian work, the *Messia venuto* of Giovanni Maria Vincenti, and he surely read others.[1] The relative absence of specifically Italian elements in Part II of the *Excelencias* thus confirms our impression that the rabid hostility to Judaism in the Peninsula was one of the most lingering memories of his Spanish experience. This alone will explain why the bulk of the third *calunia*[2] is a direct retort to the charge of Jewish male menstruation as formulated in Madrid so many years before by Don Juan de Quiñones.

But there was also in the seventeenth century an intrinsic difference between the Italian and Iberian literatures written *adversus Judaeos* which may help to elucidate some of his choice of subjects. The Italian works are, by and large, conversionist in their aim and approach. Their general objective is not to denigrate the Jew per se, but rather to belittle and ridicule Jewish beliefs, in the hope of bringing the Jew to acknowledge Christ as savior, and the Christian faith as superior to his own. If there is a Jewish characteristic which comes under particular fire it is that proverbial "obstinacy" which refuses to recognize the manifest truth that the Messiah has already appeared.[3] In essence Cardoso has already given his reply to such conversionist onslaughts in the first part of his book. The Spanish and Portuguese tracts, however, are not really aimed at conversion, for the "Jews" of whom they speak are already, formally at least,

---

[1] See *infra*, n. 80. [2] "Cola y Sangre," pp. 345–49.

[3] The following Italian books of the 17th century are characteristic: Tommaso Bell'haver, *Dottrina facile e breve per ridurre l'Hebreo al conoscimento del vero Messia e Salvatore del mondo* (Venice, 1608); Pietro Pichi, *Epistola agli Hebrei dell'Italia, nella quale si dimostra la vanita della loro penitenza et aspetazione del Mesia* (Rome, 1622); Aloys. Tineti, *Apologia della Fede contro l'ostinazione Hebraica* (Venice, 1627); Iul. Cesare Misuracci, *Ragionamento della venuta del Messia contro la durezza ed ostinatione Ebraica* (Orvieto, 1629). For other works see Moritz Steinschneider, "Letteratura antigiudaica in lingua italiana," *Vessillo Israelitico*, XXX (1882), 206–8, 244–46, 371–73.

Title page of second part of the *Excelencias*   4I5

In the copy of the Biblioteca Nacional, Madrid

baptized Christians. [4] There it is the very person of the "Jew," his humanity, his racial traits, his biological endowments which are necessarily the objects of attack. Costa Mattos' cry—*Pouco sangue Judeo he bastante a destruyr o mundo* (A little Jewish blood is enough to destroy the world!)—is characteristically Iberian. The only other anti-Jewish literature of the time which, though for different reasons, approached the Hispano-Portuguese in its virulence, was the German, and of the German vernacular literature Cardoso had no firsthand knowledge.

Nowhere is the Iberian emphasis in Cardoso's analysis of the *calunias* more apparent than in his selection of historical examples. The overwhelming majority are from Spain and Portugal. It will therefore come as no surprise that Cardoso's apology often shares with the Iberian antisemitic literature a common universe of discourse. Each moves from scriptural argument to the same arsenal of Hispano-Portuguese learning, selecting weapons which, though aimed at different targets, bear all the marks of having been forged in the same foundry.

At times, indeed, it is fascinating to observe how Cardoso will ingenuously muster the identical historic fact which has been utilized by an Iberian antisemite in order to make the very opposite point. A vivid example of this is the interpretation of the death of Affonso, the eldest son of King John II of Portugal. Both Cardoso and Vicente da Costa Mattos mention the event, and both are agreed

---

[4] Genuinely conversionist tracts were sometimes written by Jewish apostates who came to the Peninsula from abroad. The outstanding example is João Baptista d'Este, who published an edition of the Psalms with a conversionist commentary (*Consolaçam christãa e luz para o povo hebreo* [Lisbon, 1616]), as well as a catechistic work directed to the "Jews" (*Diálogo entre discipulo e mestre catechizante, onde se resolvem todas as duvidas que os Iudeos obstinados costumão fazer contra a verdade da Fé Catholica* [Lisbon, 1621]). His name would indicate that he came from Italy. He himself alludes to his Jewish origin, when speaking of the Jews, as follows: "E como meus irmãos, que são em quanto ao sangue, posto que não na fé . . ." (*Diálogo*, fol. 3r of the preface to the reader). On rare occasions one also finds a work from the pen of an Iberian Christian which, as though oblivious to peninsular realities, is aimed at the conversion of "Jews." Such a book is Fernão Ximenes de Aragão's *Doutrina catholica para instrucção e côfirmação dos fieis, e extincção das seitas supersticiosas, e em particular do Iudaismo* (Lisbon, 1625).

that the prince died because the Lord wished to punish his father. For Costa Mattos, John's sin lay in his admission of some of the Spanish Jewish exiles to his realm in 1492. For Cardoso it was his cruelty in sending the children wrested from the Portuguese Jews to perish on the island of St. Thomas.[5]

Still, though Clio may often seem a fickle muse, wantonly offering herself in turn to each protagonist in a polemic, there is a difference between even a homiletical use of history and its thorough abuse or sheer fabrication. In this respect one must state emphatically that Cardoso's use of historical materials is infinitely more responsible than that of the Spanish and Portuguese antisemites, and therefore doubly effective. We find in Part II of the *Excelencias* nothing comparable to the wildly exaggerated fables and blatant historical forgeries which abound in the Iberian tracts, offering such "authentic texts" as a letter from Pontius Pilate to Tiberius Caesar in which Jesus and his miracles are described, or Pilate's "original" sentence of the Saviour, written in Hebrew (!) and allegedly discovered in Aquilea in 1580.[6]

THE BURDEN OF ANTIQUITY

But there is another facet to Cardoso's discussion of the *calunias* which may initially disconcert the modern reader, and that is the seemingly disproportionate space allotted to truly ancient charges. This is perhaps most obvious in the first two chapters, which combat the accusations that Jews worship false and monstrous deities and exude a bad odor, but it is also manifest in the abundant references throughout the book to ancient pagan antisemitic allegations.

However, what may seem at first to be pedantry or deliberate archaism proves, on closer examination, to be nothing of the sort. We

---

[5] Costa Mattos, *Breve discurso contra a heretica perfidia do Iudaismo*, fol. 161v; *Excelencias*, p. 388.

[6] The letter to Tiberius is given in Portuguese by Costa Mattos (*Discurso*, fols. 36v-37r) and in Latin by Torrejoncillo (*Centinela*, fols. 52 f.). Pilate's sentence of Jesus appears in the latter, fols. 175–78. Both draw on 16th-century sources.

have only to read the antisemitic and apologetic literature of the age in order to appreciate to what degree, in both genres, the ancient is felt to be fully and immediately contemporary. Tacitus remains an important adversary, because any educated person of the time has read his works. Simone Luzzato, for all his "modern" economic arguments, still found it necessary to devote the fifteenth chapter of his *Discorso* to "the accusations which Cornelius Tacitus raised against the ancient Jewish people, and the replies to them."[7] Antiquity is profoundly relevant, because the pagan slanders recur again and again in the latest anti-Jewish works, and because ancient disputes are reenacted in a perennial cycle where time itself seems to be suspended. This may be seen to striking advantage in the publication nine years after the appearance of the *Excelencias*, and four years after Cardoso's death, of a Spanish translation of Josephus' *Contra Apionem* by the former Marrano Joseph Semah Arias. Most revealing of the climate of the times are these words of dedication by Arias to Orobio de Castro: "The excellences of our nation, defended by the illustrious historian Josephus against the calumnies of Apion the Alexandrian, I dedicate to Your Honor, the illustrious Josephus of our time, against the Apions of this era. . . ."[8]

In the first *calunia*, which deals with the charge of false worship (*falsas adoraciones*), not even one postclassical author appears. The discussion revolves mainly around the well-known allegation of Apion, Tacitus, and Plutarch that the Jews worshiped an effigy of the head of an ass in the Temple in Jerusalem.[9] It is interesting to observe how Cardoso's rebuttal is somewhat tempered by his ingrained reverence for the Graeco-Roman writers. Torn between his admiration for

---

[7] Luzzato, *Ma'amar*, pp. 123–37. Cardoso cites his arguments against Tacitus on p. 337 of the *Excelencias* ("Observó sutilmente el Sapiente Luzitano [*sic*] en el discurso que hizo de los Hebreos . . .").

[8] *Respuesta de Josepho contra Apion Alexandrino, traduzida por el Capitan Ioseph Semah Arias, dedicada al doctissimo Señor Yshac Orobio de Castro* (Amsterdam, 1687). I have quoted from p. 1 of the dedication.

[9] Josephus, *Contra Apionem*, II, 7; Tacitus, *Hist.*, V, 4; Plutarch, *Quaestiones convivales*, IV, quaest. v, 2. These texts, as well as many of those cited below, are conveniently assembled in Théodore Reinach, *Textes d'auteurs grecs et romains relatifs au Judaïsme* (Paris, 1895). See respectively, pp. 131, 305, 139.

their general achievements and his manifest abhorrence of the calumnies they have leveled against his people, his indignation remains relatively restrained. He is pained, above all, to find that such great men could have allowed themselves to utter such lies and absurdities. Thus he declares himself surprised that Tacitus, who professes to be a true historian, should have accepted uncritically the account of Apion at a time when the Scriptures were available in Greek, the works of Philo and Josephus could be read, and there were Jews in Rome whom he could have consulted.[10] Reviewing Plutarch's charges, Cardoso notes that he accuses the Jews of adoring not only the ass, but the pig as well, claiming it is out of veneration rather than aversion that they abstain from eating it, offering similarly absurd explanations for their abstention from the hare, and alleging that they worship Bacchus on the Feast of Tabernacles. But, although Plutarch was "a great philosopher and historian," he erred because of his great hatred for Jews and his ignorance of their "mysteries."[11] The next step is simply to enumerate some of the gross factual errors which pagan writers have committed in discussing the Jews. Justin, for example, regarded Moses as the son of Joseph. Alexander Polyhistor, as cited by Suidas, wrote that Moses was a woman. Diodorus Siculus stated that Moses received the Law from a god named Yao.[12]

Cardoso's refutation of both pagan slanders and errors assumes several forms. He holds them up to the mirror of that which Jewish law really demanded, he attempts to show the irrationality of the allegations, and he marshals contradictory statements from pagan literature itself. The Jews, he points out, were stringently forbidden to adore the form of anything in the sky or on earth, and were prohibited by their law to possess any image whatsoever. In order to appreciate the force of such laws among the Jews, one has but to

---

[10] So also Luzzato, *Ma'amar*, p. 123.

[11] *Excelencias*, pp. 334 f.; Plutarch, *Quaestiones*, quaest. vi, 2 (Reinach, *Textes*, p. 143).

[12] Justin's abridgment of Pompeius Trogus, *Historiae Philippicae*, XXXVI, 2 (Reinach, p. 253); the fragment from Alexander Polyhistor quoted by Suidas, *ibid.*, p. 65; Diodorus Siculus, I, 94 (*ibid.*, p. 70).

consider the many calamities which befell them when they refused to worship the statue of Caligula. Furthermore, when Pompey, Crassus, and Titus despoiled the Temple, they found no image within. Neither Polybius, Strabo, nor Nicholas of Damascus states that Antiochus found one there. On the contrary, Dio Cassius states explicitly that the Jews are separated from the other nations not only in their entire mode of life, but principally in their denial of all other gods, and that in Jerusalem they have never had an image.[13] Tacitus himself admits that the Jews have an imageless god, "and he who discredited them with the worship of the head of an ass, in another part of his book, either because he became better informed, or was moved by some sacred impulse or by conscience, came to admit that the Jews know only one God in the mind. . . ."[14] Strabo states that Moses censured the Egyptians for worshiping gods in animal form, and the Greeks for doing the same with gods in human form. Hecataeus, cited by Eusebius, asserts that the Jews have no image in their Temple.[15]

The fact is that the gentiles simply did not realize that the true God is really the God of the Jews. In a sense this is understandable, for they didn't know His Name, which was ineffable. Isaiah himself called Him the "hidden God" (*Dios escondido*), and the poet Lucan wrote: "Incerti Iudaea Dei" (Judea of the uncertain God . . .).[16]

Here Cardoso elaborates the theory, already adumbrated in the *Philosophia libera*, concerning the partial and imperfect dissemination of the Jewish concept of the Invisible God among the pagans. The Lord desired that knowledge of Himself be not entirely lacking in

---

[13] The passage as a whole is heavily indebted to Josephus, *Contra Ap.*, II, 7. Cf. also Dio Cassius, XXXVII, 15–18: 9 (Reinach, p. 182).

[14] *Excelencias*, p. 336. See Tacitus, *Hist.*, V, 5 ("Iudaei mente sola unumque numen intelligunt . . .").

[15] Strabo, *Geog.*, XVI, 35 (Reinach, p. 99); Hecataeus of Abdera, *ibid.*, p. 16.

[16] *Excelencias*, p. 336. Cardoso's reference is to Isa. 45: 15 ("Verily Thou art a God that hidest Thyself . . ."). Lucan's phrase occurs in the *Pharsalia*, II, 592–93: "Cappadoces mea signa timent et dedita sacris/ Incerti Iudaea dei . . ." (Reinach, p. 265). Cardoso's translation is not precise. The statement should be rendered: "Judea devoted to the rites of an uncertain god."

the world, "whether confused, as among the nations, or clear, as among the Jews," and this was one of the reasons He dispersed the latter throughout the world. As a result one might say that vestigial notions of the true Divinity remained among the nations. The Romans, for instance, did not pronounce the name of the god who was the protector of the Republic. The Athenians had an altar devoted to the Unknown God. According to Herodotus the gods of the Pelasgians had no name, and Strabo records essentially the same of other peoples who worshiped a god whose name they did not know. Statius and other gentile poets wrote that the Divinity cannot be represented in images. Plutarch stated that the Romans were one hundred and seventy years without images in their Temples although, Cardoso adds, there can be idolatry without idols, as when the sun and stars are worshiped. Indeed, it is through astral worship that idolatry began in the time of Enosh.[17]

Often the remarks of pagan authors about Jewish practices derived from sheer misunderstanding of what they saw. Juvenal insists that they worship the clouds and the sky, and Petronius that they worship the "ears" of the sky.[18] But all this merely stems from the fact that pagans saw Jews looking heavenward while invoking the invisible creator of the universe. As another possible instance of such confusion Cardoso cites with approval an ingenious suggestion of Simone Luzzato. The notion of an image in the Temple may have

---

[17] *Excelencias*, pp. 336 f. (cf. *Philosophia libera*, pp. 738–40). It should be stressed that the passage as a whole is more a theodicy of Jewish exile than an acknowledgment of pagan monotheism. Cardoso here admits at best that the gentiles possessed some obscure fragments of divine knowledge, but these obviously did not amount to very much. In fact, though he follows Maimonides on the origins of idolatry in the time of Enosh (see *Mishneh Torah*, " 'Abodat kokhabim," 1: 1), he is far from endorsing the latter's citation of Jer. 10: 7–8 to assert that "all the nations know that Thou art alone, and it is only their error and foolishness to believe that this vanity springs from Thy will."

Statius ("Estatio") is the 1st-century Roman poet Publius Papinius Statius. For the Rabbinic sources on the beginnings of astral worship in the time of Enosh see Ginzberg, *Legends*, V, 150 f., n. 54.

[18] Juvenal, Satire XIV, 1. 97 (Reinach, p. 292); Petronius, fragm. 37 ("Iudaeus licet et porcinum numen adoret/ et caeli summas advocet auriculas . . ."), *ibid.*, p. 266.

first arisen because of a Jewish practice of preserving as a memorial in their sacred places, certain objects connected with miracles. Such was the case with the Brazen Serpent, and perhaps also with such objects as the vase of the manna, the flowering staff of Aaron, and the sword with which David decapitated Goliath. The charge of adoring the head of an ass would be explained if we presuppose that in a similar way the Jews had merely preserved the jawbone of the ass with which Samson smote the Philistines.[19]

As an analogue, Cardoso finally adduces an example from his own realm of experience. In Portugal, he relates, the ignorant masses are prone to believe that Jews worship the *tora*[20] and keep it hidden in their houses, confusing this with the Hebrew word *Torah*, the Law which Jews revere. This is the only "modern" reference in the entire chapter. It need hardly be added that, if ancient slanders could retain such an undiminished vitality in the seventeenth century, medieval slurs were certainly repeated *ad nauseam* in the antisemitic literature of the age. In sum, if Cardoso's discussions are filled with details from times long past, that was largely due to an adversary who refused to recognize chronological distinctions, mingling at will materials from pagan antiquity, the Church Fathers, medieval Jew-baiters, and the latest rumor.

IN DEFENSE OF THE "HEBRAIC TRUTH"

Even when this is recognized, however, one may still be taken aback to find an entire chapter of the *calunias* (VIII: "Corruptores de los libros sagrados") devoted to the accusation that the Jews have willfully corrupted the text of the Bible. That such a defense should have had to be undertaken in the late seventeenth century seems absurd, until we again confront the realities of the time. The charge itself had a very long pedigree. Echoes of it may already be found in

---

[19] *Excelencias*, pp. 337 f. Cf. Luzzato, *Ma'amar*, pp. 124 f.

[20] Cardoso assumes the reader will understand the allusion. The *tora* (Port. *toura*) to which he refers was an effigy of a bull commonly used in fireworks.

In Defense of the "Hebraic Truth"

Patristic literature. After the rise of Islam, the doctrine of *taḥrif* was invoked to explain both the absence of allusions to the Prophet in the Jewish Bible, and the altered form in which many Old Testament elements appear in the Quran, the dogma of Jewish falsification finding its systematic expositor in the eleventh-century Andalusian theologian Ibn Hazm.[21] Among Christians the accusation becomes fully articulate in the ninth century, in the polemical correspondence of Paulus Alvarus against the proselyte Bodo.[22] For the Christians, of course, the problem was largely one of discrepancies in the reading of certain key words or phrases, especially those considered important for Christological exegesis. In the sixteenth century, before and after the Reformation, the comparative reliability of the Hebrew as opposed to the Vulgate provided one of the battlefields upon which some of the larger issues within Christendom were fought out. The question figured prominently in the Reuchlin–Pfefferkorn controversy, and in the struggle between Protestant and Catholic.[23] Though not directly involved in these conflicts, Jews could not help but be drawn to the defense of their most sacred possession. The reliability of the Masoretic text was upheld in Italy by Elias Levita, and again by the Jewish physician Lazzaro da Viterbo, who wrote a Latin treatise on the subject.[24] Sixteenth-century Spain also had its impugners of the Hebrew Bible, the most important being León de Castro, professor of Greek at Salamanca and persecutor of Arias Montano and Fr. Luis de León, whose writings Cardoso knew well, and who considered all who found fault with the Vulgate in favor of the Hebrew to be Judaizers or Jews.[25]

---

[21] See Baron, *Social and Religious History*, V, 88.

[22] See Peter Browe, *Die Judenmission im Mittelalter und die Papste* (Rome, 1942), pp. 118 f.

[23] See Graetz, *Geschichte*, IX, 99 f., 496.

[24] See C. D. Ginsberg's introduction to his edition of Elias Levita's *Massoreth ha-Massoreth* (London, 1867), pp. 45 f.; David Kaufmann, "Lazarus de Viterbo's Epistle to Cardinal Sirleto concerning the Integrity of the Hebrew Bible," *JQR* (O.S.), VII (1895), 278–96. See, further, Poznanski, *Schiloh*, pp. 66–68.

[25] See Bataillon, *Érasme et l'Espagne*, p. 360; Aubrey Bell, *Benito Arias Montano* (Oxford, 1922), p. 24; Sicroff, *Controverses*, p. 269. In Portugal the charge was

Defender of Israel

It might be expected that by the seventeenth century the issue would already have been settled, but this was far from the case. In Portugal it was a recurring feature of the anti-Jewish literature until well into the eighteenth century.[26] Nor had controversy on the matter died in the rest of Europe. In Amsterdam Immanuel Aboab inserted an entire chapter into his *Nomologia* in the form of a dialogue which, he asserted, had taken place years before in Ferrara between himself and a Christian cleric, on "the many translations and different alterations and corrections of the Greek and Latin bibles, and how in many essential matters they are not in accord with the true and sacred Hebrew text."[27] In 1662 Anton Hulsius, whom we have already noted as engaged in theological discussion with Jacob Abendana, published a book to prove the authenticity of the Hebrew text of the Bible.[28] If this was still necessary in Protestant Holland, we can perhaps understand how much more it was so in Catholic Italy.[29]

Cardoso introduces his own discussion with a flourish:

The Jews are most faithful custodians of the Sacred Scriptures, and most diligent treasurers of those inestimable and precious jewels which the holy books contain, these being an inner consolation and incomparable joy which they possess in this great captivity, availing themselves of the Law and the reading of the sacred writings as a remedy and help through so many tribulations, and believing firmly that just as the prophecies of their misfortunes have been fulfilled, so also shall be infallibly fulfilled the prophecies of their well-being. . . .

It is not permissible to change, add, nor diminish one word, one syllable, one vowel of these divine words; and for this reason, although

---

leveled by João de Barros. See his *Dialogo Evangelico sobre os artigos da Fé contra o Talmud dos Judeus*, ed. I. S. Révah (Lisbon, 1950), p. 51.

[26] For the 17th century see, *inter alia*, João Baptista d'Este, *Diálogo*, fols. 15r-v, 62v-63v; Ximenes de Aragão, *Doutrina Catholica*, fol. 94r.

[27] Aboab, *Nomologia*, pp. 218-45.

[28] Anton Hulsius, *Authentia absoluta S. textus Hebraei vindicata* (Rotterdam, 1662).

[29] Fourteen years after the publication of the *Excelencias* we find the charge again in Tommaso Luigi Francavilla, *L'Hebreo trafito dalla propria penna* (Trent, 1693), p. 75.

424

the Jews are scattered to the four parts of the world, their books are intact and pure, with no variation of any kind. They hold them in supreme veneration, for it is a great prerogative and excellence of the Israelites to keep the most holy Law, written three thousand years ago, while neither time, nor captivities, nor the tyrannies of princes and monarchs have been able to silence this sacrosanct reading. It surpasses all human writings, not only in holiness and purity, but also in antiquity. For among the nations there is not to be found any writing older than that of Homer, as Josephus affirmed and Lucretius pondered, stating that before the war of Thebes and the destruction of Troy the poets did not sing anything; and Homer was in the time of Samson and Eli, and the laws of Solon, Lycurgus, and Minos were instituted and ordained much later, it being a singular providence of the Creator to preserve a most holy, most pure, and most ancient Scripture, for the glory of His Name and the exaltation of Israel.[30]

In his defense of the "verdad hebraica" Cardoso is, as he himself admits, heavily indebted to Aboab. The following arguments, for example, can be traced directly to the *Nomologia:* that the lack of conformity among Greek and Latin bibles is proved by the many conflicting editions banned in the Index of Prohibited Books; most of the criticisms of the extant versions of the Septuagint; and several citations of Augustine and Jerome on the authenticity of the Jewish text.[31]

However, Cardoso's chapter is far from a slavish imitation. At a number of significant points he goes beyond Aboab and advances new arguments and illustrations.

Thus Cardoso notes the meticulous rules observed by Jewish scribes in writing a scroll of the Torah:

The devotion and holiness with which it is written, the purity which governs the writer, the perfection of the parchment on which it is inscribed, the attention and vigilance which he exerts so as not to vary one point of the true originals, are incomparable, and singular is the care which is observed in this task. So that we see that the books of

---

[30] *Excelencias*, pp. 390 f.

[31] On the Index see *Excelencias*, p. 391, and *Nomologia*, pp. 222 f.; on the Septuagint, *Exc.*, p. 392, and *Nom.*, p. 244.

the Law and the Prophets written in the Hebrew language are identical in Persia, in Turkey, in Asia, with those that are in Egypt, in Africa, in Italy, in Germany, and in all the provinces and kingdoms where the Jews dwell, without one point or atom of discrepancy.[32]

His strictures concerning the authorship of the Vulgate are also not to be found in Aboab. He points out, to begin with, that, although the Latin translations which are collectively called the Vulgate are commonly attributed to Jerome, it is no small question among the Catholics themselves as to whether they are really his. That they are not Jerome's has been maintained by Santes Pagninus, though others have claimed they are his either wholly or in part. Cardoso asserts that it can be proved the Vulgate is not the work of Jerome if one merely considers that the latter's translations in his own commentaries often do not conform to it. The real author of the Vulgate is therefore unknown, and there is little sense in using it to emend either the Greek or the Hebrew bibles.[33]

This being the case, and realizing the difference between the Vulgate and the Hebrew original, learned men have undertaken to translate the Bible into a Latin closer to the Hebrew source.[34] Even the Septuagint agrees more with the Hebrew than does the Latin, and the "Hebraizing theologians" mainly make use of it.

For since the Hebrew language is most concise, fecund, and mysterious, some words have various meanings which are most relevant and proper for the allegorical and mystical. The most erudite and wise place these words in their writings according to the Hebraic truth, in order to confirm their thoughts and uncover the true version, and these are called Hebraizers. And since the Hebrew language has no vowels, but only consonants, and for the vowels it utilizes points, making different sense if they are pointed with *Patach* or *Kameṣ*, and at other times [even] without

---

[32] *Excelencias*, p. 391.   [33] *Ibid.*, p. 393.

[34] *Ibid.*, Cardoso cites the following editions: The Complutensian (Alcalá, 1514–17); the "Regia" (i.e., the Antwerp Polyglot of Arias Montano [1569–72], called the Regia because the expenses were defrayed by Philip II); the Pagninus Bible (Lyon, 1527); "Vatablo" (the Latin Bible published by Robert Estienne in 1545 with notes by François Vatable); and the Bible of Sebastien Münster (Basel, 1534–35).

426

varying the points the words have a different meaning, it follows that there are in this language most excellent conceits, and they enclose great mysteries, the Hebrew language being in itself holy and full of secrets.[35]

To the quotations from Christian authorities invoked by Aboab, Cardoso adds others. He cites an important passage from Jerome's commentary on Isaiah, stating that, if anyone claims the Jews have falsified Scripture since the advent of Christ and the Apostles, one cannot contain one's laughter, for Christ and the Apostles quote the text in the very form in which the Jews are alleged to have falsified it.[36] Even the Jewish apostates (*los mesumadim Judíos hechos Christianos*), who are capital enemies of the Jews, agree on this point.[37] So also Tena, Bishop of Tortosa, who upholds the integrity of the Hebrew text, states that if Justin, Origen, and Chrysostom occasionally affirm that the Jews corrupted the Scriptures, they have in mind the translations into Greek made by Aquila, Symmachus, and Theodotion.[38] The necessity of correcting the biblical text on the basis of

---

[35] *Excelencias.* On the secrets and mysteries of the Hebrew language cf. *supra*, chs. VI and VIII.

[36] *Excelencias*, p. 394. Jerome's statement reads: "Sin autem dixerint post adventum Domini Salvatoris, et praedicationem Apostolorum libros Hebraeos fuisse falsatas, cachinnum tenere non potero, ut Salvator, et Evangelistae, et Apostoli ita testimonia protulerint, ut Judaei postea falsaturi erant" (*Commentarium in Isaiam Prophetam*, lib. III cap. vii, in Migne, *PL*, XXIV, 99). Cardoso also refers to Jerome's "Epistola a Sunnita [*sic*] y Fratella" on the need to consult the Hebrew whenever the Greek and Latin are in doubt. See "Ad Sunniam et Fretelam," dealing with the corruptions in the LXX on Psalms in *Saint Jérôme; Lettres*, ed. Labourt, V, 104.

[37] Cardoso cites "Joanes Ysac, en tres libros contra Lindano en defensa de la verdad hebraica." The reference is to Johann Levita Isaac (1515–77), a baptised Jew who became professor of Hebrew at Cologne. See on him Wolf, *Bibliotheca Hebraea*, III, 357; IV, 842, who does not, however, list the work in question. "Lindano" is Guglielmus Lindanus, Bishop of Ruremond in Holland, an adversary of Benito Arias Montano. His *De optimo Scripturas interpretandi genere*, upholding the superiority of the Vulgate over the Greek and the Hebrew, appeared in Cologne in 1558.

[38] The reference is to Luis de Tena, *Isagoge in totam S. Scripturaram* (Barcelona, 1620), a treatise on the integrity of the Hebrew text of the Bible, and on its translations.

the Hebrew has been sustained by Antonio de Lebrixa (*el Nebrissense*) in his Apology to Cardinal Ximénez,[39] and by Calvin and his followers, "for the water of the source is always purer and clearer than that of the tributaries into which it flows. . . ."

Cardoso's specific examples of discrepancies between the Septuagint and the Hebrew Bible are, with one exception, entirely derived from Aboab's *Nomologia*, an indication that he himself may have known little Greek.[40] But with regard to the Vulgate it is otherwise. This was, after all, the version with which Cardoso grew up and which he knew most intimately. Of the eleven instances of textual variants in the Latin which Cardoso discusses, only four (Gen. 2: 18; Isa. 4: 5, 12: 13, 53: 8) are borrowed from the *Nomologia*.

If we pause to analyze the examples which Cardoso himself brings forth, we may conclude that two of them are merely intended to illustrate errors in the Vulgate.[41] The rest, however, were obviously chosen deliberately because the Latin renderings have specifically Christian implications which Cardoso does not even have to make explicit since they are obvious to the reader. These passages are the following:

Daniel 9: 26—an extremely difficult verse in the Hebrew, which the Vulgate interprets to mean that after 62 weeks Christ will be slain, and the people that shall deny him shall not be his. "The author of the translation," Cardoso writes, "wanted to give a sense to these obscure and truncated [Hebrew] words, and supplied it with

---

[39] For his argument see Bataillon, *Érasme et l'Espagne*, p. 31.

[40] *Excelencias*, p. 395. The exception is his observation that in the LXX on Jonah 3: 4 the Greek text has the prophet announce that Nineveh will be destroyed at the end of 43 days rather than the 40 mentioned in the Hebrew text. (The LXX actually reads 3 days.)

[41] Ps. 19: 5 (Vulg. 18: 5), in which the Hebrew states: "Their *line* is gone out through all the earth." The Vulgate: "Their *voice*" (*sonus*), obviously reading קוֹלָם instead of קָו. Cardoso suggests that the Vulgate committed this "error" merely because קוֹלָם occurs in the previous verse.

Exod. 2: 22, where the Vulgate transposes an entire passage, adding (immediately after Tzipporah gives birth to Gershom) "and she bore another son, and called his name Eliezer . . . (etc.)," which is not found in the Masoretic text until ch. 18, v. 4.

additional ones." And he adds drily: "But the divine letters do not require supplementation, only intelligence. . . ."[42]

Isaiah 53: 7—(on the Servant of the Lord), the Vulgate translates "he was offered because it was his own will" although, Cardoso observes, the sense of the Hebrew is that he was afflicted against his will.[43]

Isaiah 53: 10—the Vulgate has "he shall see a long-lived seed," while the Hebrew states "he shall see seed, prolong his days."[44]

Habakkuk 3: 18—the Vulgate: "I shall rejoice in God my Jesus"; the Hebrew: "in the god of my salvation."[45]

Psalm 22: 17 (Vulg. 21: 17)—the psalm which begins "My God, my God, why hast Thou forsaken me?" The Vulgate: "they pierced my hands and feet." The Hebrew: "like a lion [they are at] my hands and feet."[46] Cardoso goes on to say that the psalm really refers to David

---

[42] *Excelencias*, p. 396. The Hebrew reads: ואחרי השבעים ששים ושנים יכרת משיח ואין לו; the Vulgate: "Et post hebdomades sexaginta duas occidetur Christus, et non erit ejus populus qui eum negaturus est. . . ."

[43] Heb.: נגש והוא נענה; Vulg.: "Oblatus est quia ipse voluit. . . ." The point at issue, of course, is Christ's foreknowledge of his death.

[44] Heb.: יראה זרע יאריך ימים; Vulg.: "videbit semen longaevum. . . ." The basic issues are made abundantly explicit in Orobio de Castro's discussion of Isaiah 53: 10 in his *Prevenciones divinas contra la vana idolatria de las gentes*, which I give in Neubauer's translation: "*he will see his seed* cannot fit him, for he died, as they affirm, without offspring or descendants; but to this they answer that he had a spiritual seed by generating the Christian church, and this, not natural children, must be understood by *seed*. This answer is contrary to the sacred text, and is only the means of escaping from the difficulty, because in Holy Scripture the word *semen* never signifies spiritual children, but those after the flesh . . ." (Adolf Neubauer, *The Fifty-Third Chapter of Isaiah* [Oxford, 1876–77], II, 469; for the Spanish text see I, 43).

[45] Heb.: אגילה באלהי ישעי; Vulg.: "et exultabo in Deo Jesu meo."

[46] *Excelencias*, p. 397. Heb.: כארי ידי ורגלי; Vulg.: "foderunt manus meas et pedes meos." It is interesting to compare João Baptista d'Este's discussion of the same verse (*Diálogo*, fols. 104r-105v). The "master," attempting to show that the Crucifixion was foretold in Scripture, declares: "E esta verdade nos manifestou tambem o Propheta Rey no Psal. 21 onde fallando em nome de Christo diz assi: Porque me rodearão os caẽs, a congregação dos malfeitores me poserão em cerco, furarãome as mãos, & pés." When the "disciple" points out that as a child in the Hebrew school the reading given him was not "they pierced" (*furarão*) but "like

when he was persecuted, or to the Jewish people. The proof that the reading of the Vulgate was never in the original lies in the fact that, since both Matthew and John quote from this same psalm the verse "they divide my garments among them and cast lots over them" (*ibid.*, v. 19; cf. Matt. 27: 35; John 19: 24), they surely would not have overlooked so striking a verse as one which spoke of piercing hands and feet. Obviously, then, this reading was not in the text of the Psalms which they had before them.

But after all, is it even reasonable to suspect that the Jews altered the passages of which they are accused?

If, in order to eliminate certain allusions and meanings which are of concern to the faith of their opponents, the Jews had vitiated and changed the sacred Scriptures, they would have more readily excised other verses which appear to show some opposition to their own doctrines. How could they have taken out or altered the places which are less offensive, and left intact others which are more objectionable, such as the prophecy of Jacob *the scepter shall not depart from Judah*, chapter 53 of Isaiah, the "weeks" of Daniel, and other similar ones? What greater affront than the abominable idolatry of the Calf, what greater opprobrium than Isaiah's assertion that they are a sinful nation, rebellious, a people full of evil. . .? They would have eliminated all these things had they innovated anything into Scripture. They would have deleted *the Lord said unto my lord* of Psalm 110, diverting the weapons with which the Christians make war against them, and erasing all which seems to militate against them, taking unto their whim and will the correction and variation of the Sacred Text, since the Christians hardly understand three Hebrew words, as Petrus Cunaeus observes in his *Republica Hebraea*.[47]

---

a lion" (*como hum leam*), the master continues: "Devemos saber, que esta palavra nas suas biblias, he *Chare chetiv*, o que significa, assi está escrito, mas assi se deve ler. E neste lugar dizem: Está escrito furarão, & se ha de ler como hum Leam. . . . Mas porque (dizendo furarão) se mostra mui claro que falla do Messias . . . ordenarão este *Carechetiv*, paraque não se ensinasse nas escolas, a fim que não conheção esta verdade. . . ." Such a *kere u-ketib* is not to be found in the Masoretic text, and is the sheer invention of the author. He concludes: "Por onde he cousa mui clara, que elles corromperam o texto. . . ."

[47] *Excelencias*, p. 397. I have corrected the reference to Ps. 110, which is here printed incorrectly as 120. The verse of course lent itself to a Trinitarian exegesis. Cardoso's final allusion is to Petrus Cunaeus' defense of the Masoretic text in his

In Defense of the "Hebraic Truth"

Had there been any doubt as to the real issue involved in the preceding textual discussions, this unambiguous passage renders it eminently clear. Cardoso has here plunged into the Judeo-Christian polemic with remarkable directness. Certainly, when we consider that the Vulgate had been formally declared the authoritative version of the Church ever since Trent, this open attack against its authorship and authenticity in a printed book must have demanded considerable courage. From here it is natural for Cardoso to turn again to the question of the Christian abrogation of the Law. In a particularly strong and defiant passage he emphasizes that, on this score, all the controversial biblical verses are essentially irrelevant:

Neither the passages they say we have altered, nor those we have mentioned as appearing to cast some shadow upon our firm belief, can ever oppose the Divine Law, or give the most minimal sign of its abrogation, or divert us one iota from observing its precepts. The Law of the Lord, which He gave to His people with so much majesty and greatness at Mount Sinai, in the sight of millions of souls, with prodigious marvels and the divine voice heard from the mouth of God, and which He commanded that we observe through all our generations . . . no prophet, man, nor angel has the authority to alter, exchange, or extinguish it. Neither can we believe the Prophet who wants to change it, be he the greatest saint who ever was, but we must regard him as false and deserving death. For we are warned by the same God, who states it clearly: that if there be a prophet among us who wishes to divert us from the Law, and that we follow another God which neither we nor our fathers have known—that we do not believe him, that he is a false prophet, that we do not revere him, and that we put him to death because he wanted to separate us from our God.

What does it matter, then, that the prophecy of Jacob is obscure, that the weeks of Daniel are confused, that the chapter in Isaiah and certain

---

book on the ancient republic of the Jews, first published in 1617. The statement to which Cardoso refers reads: "Erat igitur illa tempestate penes Iudaeos arbitrium et vis ac norma emendandi Biblicum contextum. Profecto, quam facile illis fuisset, interpolare ea loca, quae redarguere eorum deliria videbantur cum vix tria verba Hebraice intelligerent Christiani? sed obstat pietas, vetabatque moveri, quae sacra essent" (*De republica Hebraeorum libri III* [Leiden, 1631], lib. I, cap. xviii, p. 132).

431

Defender of Israel

Psalms are difficult to explain, if God has commanded us to follow His Law eternally. . .?[48]

Nonetheless, Cardoso still feels obliged to combat specifically some of the Christian interpretations of biblical verses as pointing to Christ or the abrogation of the Law. Thus: the new covenant of Ezekiel does not mean a new Law, nor does the "water" mean baptism (*ni por las aguas entender el baptismo*);[49] "Let us make man" in Genesis does not mean that there are companions to the most simple Unity of God; the denunciations of the festivals in Amos (5: 21, "I despise your feasts and . . . your solemn assemblies") and in Isaiah (1: 14, "Your new moons and your appointed seasons my soul hateth") do not imply their abrogation. Only the transgressions which accompanied these celebrations were attacked, and that is why God does not say "My feasts," but "your feasts." Finally, if Jacob's prophecy states that the scepter shall not depart from Judah until the Messiah comes, we do not infer from this that when he does come it *will* depart!

So much, then, for the charge of corrupting the Scriptures. Within the total context of the *Excelencias* the chapter is certainly important and revealing. In the framework of Part II, however, it is really rather atypical. Although by extension the accusation of falsifying biblical texts also implies Jewish deceit, the charge still moves fundamentally on a theological plane. When it is expressed, it is couched in the relatively restrained language of scholarly and exegetical discourse. It is, in short, a medieval analogue to what Solomon Schechter called in modern times the "Higher Antisemitism." With the rest of the *calunias* it is different. They consist of the most vituperative charges of corruption, not of Jewish texts, but of the Jews themselves. Antisemitism is here unfolded in some of its most demonic manifestations.

---

[48] *Excelencias*, p. 398.

[49] *Ibid.* Cf. Ezek. 36: 25–26: "And I will sprinkle clean water upon you. . . . A new heart also will I give you, and a new spirit will I put within you. . . ."

JEWISH PHYSICAL DEFECTS

Thus two of the chapters are devoted to allegations concerning the biological degeneracy of the Jews.

Of these, the second *calunia* ("Mal Olor") examines the age-old canard that Jews exude a bad odor. Cardoso recognizes, of course, that the notion of a *foetor Judaicus* originated with the classical writers, and points to Martial and Ammianus Marcellinus as the ones from whom everyone else borrowed. He cites Marcellinus' anecdote that when the Emperor Marcus Aurelius traversed Palestine on his way to Egypt he was often disgusted by the stench and tumult of the Jews.[50] Among "modern" authors he singles out Venantius Fortunatus, who relates that the odor leaves Jews after their baptism, "Filelfo," Jacob Gretser, and Simon Majolus, the latter a particular favorite of Iberian antisemites.[51] "Adulation and hate," Cardoso observes ruefully, "blind the eyes of reason." Pliny's admiration for Alexander the Great prompts him to assert

---

[50] *Excelencias*, p. 339. Martial, *Epigrammaton*, IV, 4 (Reinach, p. 287). Ammianus Marcellinus, *Rerum gestarum*, XXII, 5 (*ibid.*, p. 353): "Ille enim cum Palestinam transiret Aegyptum petens, Iudaeorum faetentium et tumultuantium saepe taedio percitus. . . ." According to Reinach this passage was indeed the origin of the accusation. For examples of Iberian treatments of the Jewish odor in the 17th century see Costa Mattos, *Discurso*, fols. 131v ff., Torrejoncillo, *Centinela*, p. 169. Ironically, we hear contemporary complaints that because many Portuguese are regarded abroad as Jews, some foreigners, when speaking to a Portuguese, pretend they have to ascertain if he exudes such an odor. See the references in Glaser, *Invitation to Intolerance*, p. 380.

[51] Venantius Fortunatus' poem celebrating the conversion of the Jews of Clermont in 576 provides the first known reference to the legend that the odor disappears with baptism. (See Israel Lévi, "L'odeur des juifs," *REJ*, XX (1890), 249 ff.) I have not been able to identify Filelfo. Perhaps Cardoso has in mind the 15th-century Florentine humanist Francesco Filelfo. The German Jesuit Jakob Gretser (1562–1625) discusses the Jewish odor in his *De Sancta Cruce* (Ingolstadt, 1598), lib. I, cap. xcviii, reprinted in his *Opera omnia*, I (Ratisbon, 1734), p. 171. Cf. also Majolus, *Dies caniculares* (Mainz, 1614), III, colloq. I ("De Perfidia Iudaeorum"), pp. 812 f.

433

that his sweat was fragrant and aromatic. Hatred of the Jews attributes to them an evil odor. Neither claim is reasonable.

At this juncture Cardoso becomes somewhat enmeshed in the coils of his own erudition. One must ask if it is really necessary for him to enter into a discussion of Alexander's perspiration, to cite Cardan and the Byzantine John Tzetzes on the pleasant odor of Alexander's corpse, Julius Scaliger on an Indian king who examined his prospective brides by their sweat, and Aristotle on the fragrance of the leopard and the panther. The claim concerning Alexander is rejected, for since he was much given to wine and intemperance his body could not have been fragrant.[52]

Obviously tastes and conventions have changed. Where for us a touch of humor would have sufficed, Cardoso has felt the charge to be sufficiently serious as to require "scientific" refutations. Fetid things, he writes, are of two types: those which are so by accident, because of putrefaction, and those which are so by nature, because of a bad mixture of elements. So also with the products of different geographical regions, the dry being aromatic, and the humid, malodorous. Now since the Jews are natives of the dry and hot Syrian region, they do not give off bad vapors. Furthermore, they do not eat blood or unclean animals. Their general abstinence and frugality keep them from eating many types of food which create indigestion. Their habits of purity are such that they wash before prayer and before meals. Finally, circumcision helps them avoid many impurities in the region of the genitals. Cardan, who is an authority in all the sciences (*universal en las ciencias*) says that because of their separated foods the Jews are healthier and live longer, despite their constant cares and troubles.

Much more effective is the following passage, in which Cardoso abandons his scientific ruminations, and recovers his sense of irony:

The illustrious philosopher Zeno denied movement and said that it does not exist; at which, when Diogenes heard it, he refuted him with no

---

[52] *Excelencias*, pp. 340 f. Cardoso suggests that Alexander may have carried some fragrant amber on his person. Cf. his similar explanation of Sabbatai Zevi's alleged fragrance in the *Philosophia libera* (*supra*, ch. VII).

other argument than by strolling before the portico where he was lecturing. On the other hand, Heraclitus and Cratylus denied stillness, and said that all things are in perpetual movement. Diogenes could have ridiculed them also, simply by seating himself. So also those who attribute this evil odor to the Jews, whether by nature or by mystery, can easily verify it by experience among many [Jews] in Italy, Flanders, and Turkey. . . . And some Jews, who change their religion, neither have the odor because of their circumcision, nor free themselves from it by baptism, but remain as they were before. . . .[53]

If the *foetor Judaicus* was a charge which pervaded almost all antisemitic literature, the third of the *calunias* ("Cola y Sangre") brings Cardoso directly back to his Spanish experience. The slander that Jews have tails and that Jewish males menstruate was, as we have seen, the subject of an entire treatise by his close acquaintance in Madrid, Juan de Quiñones, and the very form in which the charge is described by Cardoso immediately betrays its provenance. It was, he writes, first derived from a misreading of several verses in Deuteronomy and in Psalms (he quotes Deut. 28: 13, 27, 43, 44, and Ps. 78: 66) which threaten that if the Jews disobey the Lord they shall be "as the tail" and that they shall be plagued in the posterior parts. These, it will be recalled, are precisely the biblical passages cited by Quiñones in his tract.[54]

Misinterpreting these verses, not realizing that some are metaphoric, people have inferred that this tail, blood, and the sickness of those parts are native to the Jews and originated because of a murder (*de una muerte*) which their ancestors committed in Jerusalem.[55]

In an interesting passage Cardoso attempts to explain that the accusation that Jews possess tails may also have arisen out of a semantic confusion. The Portuguese, he relates, have an idiom: *judío* [*sic*] *rabudo* (long-tailed Jew). But this tail (*rabo*) which they impute to them probably derived from the title *Rabi*, which is "master" among the Jews. Conversely, in Castile they say *portugueses rabudos*, because they ordinarily wear large capes.[56]

---

[53] *Excelencias*, p. 344.   [54] Cf. *supra*, ch. III, nn. 83, 84.

[55] *Excelencias*, p. 345.

[56] Cf. Torrejoncillo, *Centinela*, pp. 169 f.: "Los Judíos de las colillas, o rabillos en

Defender of Israel

For the record he cites various exotic fables of satyrs with tails mentioned by Ptolemy, Pausanias, and Solinus. Moreover, not only Jews are alleged to have tails. Genébrard and Majolus tell of people in England who are so afflicted because their ancestors mocked an Augustinian friar sent to preach to them.[57] Here Cardoso inserts the personal anecdote of his encounter with Don Juan de Quiñones during the latter's illness, already analyzed in detail, and proceeds to his own refutation of the charge that Jewish men exhibit a menstrual flux.

One can only be amazed, he observes, at the defects which the enemies of the Jews attribute to them from no motive but hatred, even though experience shows them to be false. The only foundation for such a charge is the fact that some Jews have hemorrhoids, as do men of other nations, and these sometimes grow so large as to have the appearance of tails. Far from being afflicted with peculiar maladies, Cardoso insists that Jews are generally healthier than gentiles. Johann Buxtorf the Elder ("El Bustrofio") admits that, in the opinion of many, Jews have greater longevity and more health, and are less prone to leprosy, because of the distinction they make in their foods. But he also writes that some die young, and that epilepsy and plague are common among them. Buxtorf, of course, is still hostile to the Jews. He should have realized that their selective diet

---

el remate del espinazo, son descendientes por linea recta de aquellos q̃ eran Maestros entre ellos, a quien llamavan Rabies, acá llamamos Rabinos. . . ." Cardoso's remarks also find substantial support in the dictionary of archaic Portuguese usages published at the end of the 18th century by Joaquim de Santa Rosa de Viterbo, who notes that the Portuguese masses called the Spaniards *rabudos*, while the latter called the Portuguese *judíos*: "Já conta alguns seculos o prejuizo louco, com que o vulgo Portuguez chama aos Castelhanos *Rabudos*, como se nascessem com hum grande, e vergonhoso rabo . . . E se os Portuguezes chamão aos Hespanhoes *Rabudos*, estes os tratão de *Judíos*." He goes on to cite some reported instances of men with tails, notably in the islands of Formosa and Borneo, but concludes that, though monsters may exist, "a sábia Natureza procede invariavel em seguir as Leis Cosmologicas, que recebeo do seu Autor, e pelas quaes o Racional não deve nascer rabudo" (*Elucidario das palavras, termos, e frases, que em Portugal antiguamente se usarão* [Lisbon, 1799], II, 260 f., *s.v.* Rabudos).

[57] Cf. Juan de Quiñones' remarks on the murderers of Thomas Beckett, *supra*, ch. III.

436

also makes them more exempt from the other maladies he mentioned. Even gentiles order meat from the Ghetto markets, because it seems to them healthier, without blood, taken from slaughtered animals rather than dead carcasses, and free of other infirmities. Plague is a general evil, common to all, and when it arrives the best remedy is prayer and charity. Leprosy, however, is definitely to be seen in smaller proportion among the Jews because of their abstention from pork, blood, hare, and other unclean animals and fish. Pigs especially, being "sons of mud and fathers of filth," are subject to leprosy and other contagious diseases. But, in any case, Jews refrain from these foods not because of their evil qualities, but because God has prohibited their consumption.[58]

After a further discussion of leprosy in biblical and in modern times, Cardoso adds this rather poignant remark: "If any infirmity can be said to be most specifically Jewish, it is melancholia, because of the sadness and fear contracted from the injuries and oppressions of exile. . . ."[59]

He continues with an analysis of the real meaning and context of the aforementioned biblical verses, and then notes that the enemies of Israel malign them not only with tails, but about the head as well. Majolus says that Jews walk with the head bent like pigs, a charge remote from reason and experience. Indeed, Cardoso exclaims, it would be more appropriate for the slanderers to tilt their heads like the pig since it is they, and not the Jews, who love it so![60]

The true measure of his rage may best be perceived in the anecdote with which he concludes the discussion. For here, in the one such instance in the book, Cardoso retorts to Quiñones' obscene charge with a vulgar joke: a half-mad Jew met a Christian who began to mock him, calling him a dog. Suddenly a dog chanced to pass between them. The Jew lifted it up by the tail, and pointed out to the Christian that it was not circumcised. . . .[61]

---

[58] *Excelencias*, p. 347. See Buxtorf, *Synagoga Iudaica* (Hanover, 1604), ch. XXXIII ("De morbis Iudaeorum"), p. 494.

[59] *Excelencias, loc. cit.*

[60] *Ibid.*, p. 348. Majolus, *Dies caniculares*, pp. 813 f.

[61] *Excelencias*, p. 349.

JEWISH MISANTHROPY

Two *calunias* may be viewed as variations on the ancient theme that the Jews are possessed of a hatred for all gentiles, which they express both in words and in deed.

The first of these (IV: "Orar tres vezes al día contra las gentes") takes up the specifically Christian accusation that the Jews pray against them thrice daily. Like the charge of falsifying Scripture, this one too has a long history.[62] Among the prayers which Christian polemicists and papal bulls singled out as directed against Christendom were the twelfth benediction of the daily *'Amida* (the so-called *birkat ha-minim*, or prayer against the heretics), and the *'Alenu* prayer. It is with these that Cardoso deals, and he follows mainly in the footsteps of Manasseh b. Israel and Simone Luzzato, themselves continuing a traditional line of Jewish apologetics.

He begins with the affirmation that it is a divine command through Jeremiah (29: 7) to pray for the city in which one lives and for the peace of the kingdom, and cites God's promise to Abraham, "in thee shall all the families of the earth be blessed." Therefore, on the Feast of Tabernacles in the ancient Temple, 71 sacrifices were offered, of which 70 were for the nations. The High Priest prayed not only for Israel, but for the gentiles as well. Israel itself continues to be a "high priest" praying for all men. The kings of the East and the emperors of Rome, at their own expense, would tell the Jews to offer to God prayers and sacrifices for their welfare. Often English and Dutch captains ask the Jews on their ships to pray in the midst of a

---

[62] The accusation that Jews blaspheme against Christ and Christians in their prayers was voiced more than once in ancient times by the Church Fathers. With the exception of Agobard of Lyons nothing further was heard of it in Western Europe until the 13th century, when it reappeared in conjunction with the accusations leveled against the Talmud at the so-called Disputation of Paris in 1240. Thereafter, the charge was repeated incessantly. See my remarks in "The Inquisition and the Jews of France in the Time of Bernard Gui," *Rutgers Hebraic Studies*, I (1965), especially pp. 38–47, and the references given there.

438

tempest. All this would be incomprehensible if they felt that the Jews were praying against them.[63]

Most of the Jewish liturgy came into being long before Christ lived, and therefore could not have applied to Christians. The prayer against the heretics, which Rabban Gamliel instituted shortly after Titus destroyed the Temple, had in mind the Sadducees, heretics who denied the immortality of the soul, angels, and resurrection, "like Epicureans."[64] "I personally confess," he writes, "that I repeat this prayer three times a day . . . and in these words I have no other intention . . . than that they signify generally the impious and perverse." As for the *'Alenu*, which Cardoso records in Spanish translation, and which contains in the Sephardic rite the phrase "for they bow down to vanity and nothingness and pray to a god who does not save," this refers only to idolatrous religions, and such a prayer should be acceptable to all who worship one God.[65]

More forceful is Cardoso's treatment of the seventh *calunia* ("Impios y Crueles") which charges that the Jews behave wickedly

---

[63] *Excelencias*, pp. 350 f. For similar arguments see Luzzato, *Ma'amar*, p. 128; Manasseh b. Israel, *Vindiciae Iudaeorum* (in Wolf, pp. 125–34).

[64] *Excelencias*, pp. 352 f. Cf. Manasseh, in Wolf, pp. 125 f., who gives the reading as "*la-Mumarim*, & c., that is, *For Apostates, let there be no hope, let all Hereticks be destroyed.* . . ." Cardoso offers two alternative readings: "A los *perdidos* no sea esperança, y los *hereges* en un punto serán destruhidos . . ." (p. 352), and "A los *renegados* no sea esperança, y todos los *malsines* en un punto serán destruhidos . . ." (p. 353). (*Malsin*, Heb. "malshin" : "informer.") The Hebrew text of the *birkat ha-minim* has been altered so many times as to make it extremely difficult to determine the original. On the various older readings see my aforementioned study of the Inquisition and the Jews of France, p. 42. In the Spanish prayer book published in Amsterdam in 1648, the benediction begins: "A los *renegados* no sea esperança, y todos los *hereges* y todos los *malsines* como punto serán perdidos" (*Orden de oraciones de mes con los ayunos del solo y congregación y pascuas . . . Amsterdam . . . en casa de Nicolao Ravesteyn, por yndustria del Doctor Effraim Bueno y Ionas Abravanel, 5408*, p. 144).

[65] *Excelencias*, p. 354. Cf. Manasseh, in Wolf, pp. 134–36, giving an English translation. Like Manasseh, Cardoso includes the anecdote that Moses Hamon, the 16th-century physician of Suleiman I, translated the Jewish liturgy into Turkish, whereupon the Sultan singled out the *'Alenu* prayer as surpassing all others. He does not, however, repeat Manasseh's confusion of Suleiman with Selim.

and cruelly towards the gentiles. The accusation is older than Christendom. Cardoso cites the famous passage in Tacitus stating that, although the Jews are inflexibly honest and compassionate among themselves, they regard the rest of mankind with the hatred of enemies, and Juvenal's taunt that they would not point out the road, nor a fountain of water, to one who is not of their faith.[66] Cardoso indignantly rejects these allegations as being "so far from the truth, it is like calling the snow black and the fire cold." When the Gibeonites asked David to kill the descendants of Saul, Scripture notes that "the Gibeonites were not of the Children of Israel" (I Sam. 21: 2), a phrase which Cardoso interprets homiletically to mean that this cruelty was uncharacteristic of the Jews. For the latter are "compassionate with God, with their own, with strangers, with pilgrims, with enemies, with animals, birds, and trees, and in sum—the entire Law is a compendium of compassion and a pattern of love." And he gives examples for each category from Jewish law.

Turning back to Tacitus, Cardoso remarks that, although the Roman historian maintains the Jews hate all others, he also states that they regard it a great sin to kill their relatives. The text reads "necare quempiam ex agnatis nefas." But Justus Lipsius eruditely emends the word *agnatis*, taking *natis* to mean children. For what novelty would it be not to kill relatives? The point is that the Greeks and Romans exposed children to die, and the Jews did not.[67]

This observation leads Cardoso into his main line of attack. Drawing historical materials largely from Usque's *Consolaçām*, and some from Aboab's *Nomologia*, he will use them to hurl the charge back into the teeth of the gentiles by cataloguing some of the enormous cruelties they have perpetrated against the Jews. He begins with the Leper Persecution in France and the accusation of poisoning the wells in Germany in the fourteenth century, claiming that in

---

[66] *Excelencias*, p. 377. Tacitus, *Hist.* V, 5 (Reinach, pp. 306 f.); Juvenal, Satire XIV, lines 103–4 (*ibid.*, p. 292). Torrejoncillo writes that when Jews cannot hurt Christians in any other way, "they trample and spit on our shadow, and derive as much pleasure as though they had spit in our face" (*Centinela*, p. 151).

[67] *Excelencias*, p. 379. "Agnatis" is, technically, any blood relation on the father's side. On the emendation in Tacitus, see Reinach, p. 307, n. 3.

the former alone 5,000 Jews were slaughtered.[68] What simpleminded intelligence or malice so great could bring itself to believe that the Jews in these instances contaminated the wells, as if they did not also have to drink the same water?! Why should they kill their neighbors from whom they derive benefit? But reason is of no avail:

Passion attributes cruelty to the lambs, and mercy and meekness to the wolves and tigers who in all ages tear the Jews to pieces with ferocious fury, God permitting it for the expiation of their sins. The nations deem it meritorious to vent their rage against those on whom God has hurled His chastisement, and to afflict the afflicted. And they do not notice that when a father punishes his son he does not allow strangers to pursue and destroy him. *I was but a little angered, and they were much angered,* says the Lord about the nations who persecute Israel. . . . They impute cruelty to the Jews in order to conceal their own. Let the histories be read, and one will see the tyrannies and cruelties they inflicted upon them throughout the centuries![69]

Cardoso's examples range from the forced conversion of the Jews by Sisebut in Visigothic Spain to the massacre of the New Christians in Lisbon in 1506.[70] Though he does give some instances of persecution elsewhere, the bulk of his illustrations come from Spain and Portugal, in keeping with his general Iberocentric orientation. In

---

[68] On the Leper Persecution see Usque, *Consolaçam as tribulaçoens de Israel*, ed. J. Mendes dos Remédios (Coimbra, 1906–8). III, no. 18, fols. 19v ff., and in Martin Cohen's English translation (*Consolation for the Tribulations of Israel* [Philadelphia, 1965]), pp. 190 f. On the poisoning of the wells see *Consolaçam*, III, no. 19, fols. 20v f. (Cohen, p. 192). Cardoso's date for the latter event is given correctly as 5106 (1436). Usque has 5006.

[69] *Excelencias*, p. 381. The verse, which Cardoso has slightly altered, is Zech. 1: 15 ("And I am angered with a great anger against the nations that are at ease; for I was but a little angered, and they helped for evil").

[70] *Excelencias*, pp. 381–84. As Cardoso himself notes (p. 382), the bulk of his illustrations are derived from Usque, and indeed for certain events he even gives the same erroneous dates. For the Spanish Expulsion, however, his sources are Gonzalo de Illescas, *Historia pontifical y catholica* II (Barcelona, 1589), fol. 122r-v, and Pedro Salazar de Mendoza, *Chronica de el gran cardenal de España Don Pedro Gonçalez de Mendoça* (Toledo, 1625). His material on the forced baptism of the Portuguese Jews in 1497 is largely indebted to Aboab's *Nomologia*, pp. 291–99.

any case, he observes, both Christian and Jewish works are so full of accounts of cruelties against the Jews that merely to give the references would require a separate book.

Let it not be supposed, however, that the tyrants who have persecuted the Jews have emerged unscathed from their evil deeds. They have all, in fact, met with a bad end. Here Cardoso resumes a favorite theme of Usque who, in the *Consolaçãm*, regards God's revenge against the persecutors as the "fourth way" of human consolation. Among the monarchs who were visited with divine punishment Cardoso enumerates, with vivid details, Pharaoh, Nebuchadnezzar, Antiochus, Pompey, the Roman emperors, Heraclius of Byzantium, Sisebut and Reccared of Spain, Philip the Fair of France. Ferdinand and Isabella were punished by dying without a male heir, for the prince Don Juan died earlier, "and thus the line of the Gothic kings in Spain ended, and gave way to the House of Austria." John II of Portugal, who sent the Jewish children to St. Thomas in 1495, died of poison, and his son Affonso was killed at the celebration of his engagement to Isabella, daughter of the Catholic Kings. John III, who introduced the Inquisition into Portugal, died of apoplexy. "There have been many judges, secular as well as ecclesiastical, who have forced this people through torture to confess injustices and crimes which they have not committed, sometimes condemning them to death, and they have themselves been seen to die violent and horrible deaths." In Cardoso's providential view of history, inquisitors too cannot escape the Divine wrath. . . .[71]

---

[71] *Excelencias*, pp. 385–89. Cf. Usque, *Consolaçam*, III, fols. 50v ff. (Cohen, pp. 228 ff.): "The fourth way for you to receive consolation also derives from this mercy. The Lord not only prepared these grades for the great mountain of punishment which you were required to climb, but in order for you to scale it with less hardship, He from time to time consoles you by redemptive acts and taking vengeance on your oppressors for the malice with which they have inflicted the penalty for your iniquities. Jeremiah's words testify to this: 'I will visit upon you nations the wickedness of your thoughts.' You have already witnessed this in the fates of the early nations—the Egyptians, Babylonians, Assyrians, Greeks, and Romans, and in the more modern nations of whom you recently complain." It should be noted that Cardoso's examples of the punishment of Ferdinand and Isabella, as well as John III of Portugal, are not found in Usque.

JEWISH SUBVERSION

In the seventeenth century, as in earlier and more recent times, it was an antisemitic axiom that the Jews actively undermined society and the state. If, in Spain and Portugal, there were no longer any professing Jews, we have had ample occasion to see the same charge hurled incessantly at the New Christians. Within the Peninsula and beyond, the antisemitic literature of the age is filled with denunciations of Jewish subversion, both political and religious.

It is to the charge that the Jews are traitors, and therefore a menace to the security of the state, that the sixth *calunia* ("Infieles a los Principes") is dedicated.[72]

In this chapter Cardoso presents the Jews as faithful everywhere to the rulers of the lands in which they reside, "by nature, by divine command, and out of gratitude." By nature—because of their noble and ancient blood, loyalty being "the companion of nobility." By divine command—through Jeremiah's admonition. From gratitude —because "the noble are the truly grateful." If the emphasis on nobility echoes the pride of the Spaniard, there is a specifically Jewish nuance in the further assertion that the sense of constancy among the Jews has been developed by their unswerving loyalty to God, whereas the nations are wont to exchange their gods with ease. We may well note the contrast between Cardoso and Luzzato. Nowhere do we find a reflection of the latter's more realistic assessment, linking the loyalty of the Jews to their universal lack of power.[73]

---

[72] Although the same charge was also treated by Luzzato (*Ma'amar*, p. 92) and Manasseh b. Israel (*Humble Addresses*, in Wolf, pp. 90 ff.), Cardoso shows no dependence on them.

[73] Luzzato, *Ma'amar*, "Experience teaches us that when difficulties with merchants occasionally arise . . . the members of other alien nations who are under the rule of foreign princes turn to their ambassadors and representatives. . . . Not so the Jewish nation, scattered and separated throughout the world, which has no ruler nor head to defend it. She is ever ready, out of a swift flexibility, to submit

But Cardoso is here more interested in an appeal to the historical record than in theoretical aspects. The loyalty of the Jews, he writes, was already well known to the ancient kings, both Greek and Roman, and because of this they made use of them in important affairs. Leaning heavily on Josephus for his materials, he gives a number of instances: Antiochus, after rebellions in Phrygia and Lydia, sent 2,000 Jewish families to settle there. Seleucus granted the Jews the privilege of citizenship in the cities of Asia, Syria, and in Antioch itself. After the Roman conquest of Jerusalem the Alexandrians and Antiochans asked Titus and Vespasian to revoke Jewish citizenship, but they refused. When Alexander the Great attacked Tyre and demanded that the Jews transfer their loyalty from Darius, they replied that they could not violate the oath they had sworn to the Persian king, although this refusal placed them all in danger. Ptolemy Lagos transferred Jews to Cyrene and other Lybian cities because he was certain of their loyalty. Ptolemy Philometor and his wife Cleopatra had two Jews, Onias and Dositheus, as captains of the army. Jewish fidelity to Rome was recognized by Julius Caesar, who favored them greatly. Various Roman consuls even freed them from military duty so they could observe their rites, as did also the Turkish sultan Suleiman. When the Jews of Asia and Cyrene were molested and maligned by the cities, Augustus Caesar sent a letter in their behalf. In the wars between Augustus and Antony the Jews of the East were faithful to Antony until his defeat, and later equally so to Augustus.[74]

Similar examples abound in "modern times." In fourteenth-century Spain, after Henry of Trastamara killed Pedro the Cruel, the Jews of Burgos fortified themselves and refused to recognize any but Pedro's legitimate heir. Even Henry was impressed by this Jewish loyalty to a dead and vanquished king. During the "German Wars" (i.e., the Thirty Years War) the Jews of Prague valiantly defended their sector of the city against Gustavus Adolphus, and

---

to the decrees of the community, to the degree that if the government comes and imposes special taxes on the members of this nation, we generally do not hear that they should open their mouth or voice any complaint."

[74] *Excelencias*, pp. 368–71.

largely thanks to them the city was not taken. As a result, they were given new privileges by the Emperor Ferdinand. The loyalty of the Jews is also well known to the most wise Republic of Venice, which has had ample proof of it in the war with Turkey over Crete. Awareness of Jewish loyalty is reflected in the words of a Venetian nobleman, which Cardoso cites in a rare personal note. Once the Jews were taking a corpse for burial in the Jewish cemetery on the Lido, the cortege in the canal being made up of many boats. One of a number of gentlemen who observed the numerous red hats of the Jews from the bank rose up, and taking off his own hat, called out: "O nation most faithful to your God, go in peace!" "And we," Cardoso adds, "responded with great courtesy."[75]

He next examines two specific allegations of Jewish betrayal, both of them among the most widely cited in the Iberian antisemitic literatures. The first is the notorious accusation that in the year 714 the Jews opened the gates of Toledo to the Moors, for which Cardoso gives as sources the Archbishop Don Rodrigo and Lucas of Tuy. To refute them he relies on the authority of the great Jesuit historian Mariana, "who wrote dispassionately of the history of Spain," and who states that the Christians themselves surrendered the city.[76]

The other incident is derived from Alonso de Espina's *Fortalitium fidei*, in which it is related that Don Meir, the Jewish physician of Henry III of Castile, bought with some Jews a host from a sacristan in Segovia. They took it to the synagogue and threw it into a kettle of boiling water, whereupon the host raised itself on high. Seeing this,

[75] *Ibid.*, pp. 371 f. On the loyalty of the Jews of Burgos to Pedro in his struggle with his stepbrother see Baer, *Sefarad ha-noṣrit*, p. 219; on Jewish participation in the defense of Prague, and the extension of their privileges by Ferdinand II, see Graetz, *Geschichte*, X, 47; for the Jewish attitude toward the Turkish war, see Roth, *Venice*, p. 304.

[76] Rodrigo Jiménez de Rada, *De rebus Hispaniae*, lib. III, cap. xxiii, in Andreas Schott, *Hispaniae illustratae*, II (Frankfurt, 1603), p. 67; Lucas de Tuy, *Chronicon mundi* (in Schott, *ibid.*, IV [Frankfurt 1608], 70 f.); Juan de Mariana, *Historia general de España*, I (Madrid, 1678), lib. VI, cap. xxiv, p. 227. After noting the opinions of Jiménez and Lucas, Mariana concludes: "Todavía yo mas me allego a los que dixeron que la Ciudad despues de un largo cerco entregaron a partido sus mismos Ciudadanos."

and being afraid, they gave it to the prior of a Dominican convent and told him what occurred. The physician and others were arrested and, while under torture, Don Meir confessed that he had also poisoned the king. They were drawn and quartered in Segovia. Cardoso notes, however, that those who wrote the chronicles of the reigns of Henry and his son John II, such as Alvar García, Pedro López de Ayala, and Fernan Pérez de Guzmán, say nothing of such a murder, nor do Marineo Sículo, "Vasco," or Mariana. Besides, "what intelligent man will not immediately recognize the falseness of the story? What judgment will not perceive it to be an invention born out of hatred and malevolence against this persecuted people?" It is obviously promoted not by responsible historians, but by those ill affected toward the Jewish nation.[77]

Should one require further proof that the Jewish presence is neither subversive nor dangerous, one need only look at the behavior toward them of the supreme leaders of Church and Empire:

The Pope, who is the head of the Catholic Faith, permits the Jews to live in Rome and in the territories of the Church (and so does the Emperor of Germany), because he is the protector of the Church. And it is not religious zeal among the other nations which makes them expel the

---

[77] *Excelencias*, p. 373, and again on p. 405. For the allegation itself see Espina, *Fortalitium fidei*, lib. III, consid. ix. Cardoso also mentions "Garibay" as a source. He has in mind Esteban de Garibay y Zamálloa, *Compendio historial de las chronicas y universal historia de todos los reynos de España* (Barcelona, 1628), ch. LVIII, pp. 422 ff.: "De lo que Alvar Gutierrez y fray Alonso de Espina escriven de la muerte del Rey don Henrique aver resultado de veneno que le dió un Judío médico suyo." Baer has shown the falseness of Espina's tale (*Sefarad ha-noṣrit*, p. 388) and observes (*ibid.*, p. 537, n. 29) that Kayserling was the first to say so (cf. *Sephardim*, p. 53). We see, however, that Cardoso had already dismissed the story long before. On Alvar García see Nicolás Antonio, *Bib. Hisp. Nova*, I, s.v. "Alvarus." Cardoso's other references are: Pedro López de Ayala, *Crónica del Rey Don Pedro* (Seville, 1495); Fernán Pérez de Guzmán, *Crónica del Rey Don Iuan el segundo* (Logroño, 1517); Lucius Marineus, *Opus de rebus Hispaniae memorabilibus* (Alcalá, 1533). I do not know whom Cardoso means by "Vasco." Perhaps we should read *Vaseo*, i.e., Joannes Vasaeus, *Chronici rerum memorabilium Hispaniae* (Salamanca, 1552).

Jews . . . but rather the desire to rob them of their goods and denude them of whatever they possess.[78]

Papal toleration of Jewish residence was, of course, a fact. But Cardoso was also living in a Catholic land, and this may have colored some of his other remarks. He tells with relish that Martin Luther once wanted to extort money from the Jews of Frankfurt in return for withholding his anti-Jewish pamphlet from publication. But they, out of loyalty to Charles V, refused to have anything to do with him.[79] We shall soon see evidence of the same bias when Cardoso discusses the charge of host desecration.

For the Jews are not accused of political subversion alone. Two *calunias* charge them with the religious subversion of Christendom. The Jews, it is alleged, actively proselytize (V: "Persuadir las gentes al Hebraysmo"), and they mistreat images and other sancta of the Christian faith (IX: "Dicipadores de Imagenes, y Sacrilegios").

Cardoso was not the first seventeenth-century apologist to deal with the question of proselytizing, and he begins in a way that is sufficiently familiar. The gentile nations try to spread their religions, either with the sword, or through preaching, or both, and on this pretext they go on to conquer other kingdoms. (The example of Spain itself must have been paramount in his mind.) But not so the Jews. They, on the contrary, hold it a sin to propagate their Law and enlarge their conquests, for to everything God has set a proper limit. The Divine Law was given at Sinai only to the Jews and not to other peoples. Had God wished the latter to have it, He would have given it immediately to Adam or to Noah. But to them He gave only the "natural law," the so-called Seven Precepts of the Sons of Noah." The Jews must observe, beyond the natural law, the

---

[78] *Excelencias*, p. 376.

[79] *Excelencias*, p. 372. Simone Luzzato assured the Venetians that "it is known that the Jewish nation leans, in certain principles, more to the Roman Church than to the sects of those territories which have separated themselves from her" (*Ma'amar*, p. 153). In the Iberian Peninsula, as in other parts of Catholic Europe, the Jews were widely suspected of influencing the rise of the Protestant heresies. For example, Costa Mattos writes: "E assi Calvino pella grande correspondencia que tem em sua seita com elles, se chama pay dos Iudeos . . ." (*Discurso*, fol. 137r).

Law of Moses which they accepted voluntarily. The gentiles can partake of glory merely by following the natural law alone.[80] If the nations claim a wrong was done them by not giving them the divine Law, the Jews reply that this was a gratuitous gift to Israel, and that the nations have sufficient means, through natural law, to enjoy the future messianic age. Besides, if they did not observe even these few precepts in the first age, all the less would they have observed the multitude of laws given to Israel.

Paraphrasing the Talmudic formula for the examination of potential proselytes, Cardoso points out that far from receiving an inducement, the other nations only see Israel afflicted and abhorred. If some accept Judaism, it can only be out of the greatest fervor and devotion, a willingness to abandon all honors and join the despised. If the Jew knows Judaism to be precious, it is still "like a king who has a beautiful, wise, and virtuous daughter. It would be unseemly that he take her around to seek a match." That is why God did not command the prophets to preach the Law throughout the world. If He sent Jonah to Nineveh, it was not to proclaim the Law of Moses, but only the natural law to which all are subject.[81]

The main outlines of the argument thus far can be found also in Simone Luzzato and Manasseh b. Israel.[82] Cardoso's subsequent

---

[80] *Excelencias*, p. 357. Later (p. 364) he combats the notion that anyone can save himself no matter what his religion: "Daquí se colige el error de un autor moderno en su Mesias Venuto que da por cosa averiguada tener los Hebreos por opinión, que cada uno puede salvarse en su Ley, siendo error grande, y que ningún Autor nuestro dize este absurdo, porque solo limitan a la Ley de Moseh, y a la natural, que son los siete precetos de Noah ya referidos, y no a tantas religiones y leyes falsas como ay en el mundo de idolatras, y supersticiones. . . ." The work to which Cardoso refers is Giovanni Maria Vincenti's *Il Messia venuto: Istoria spiegata e provata agli Ebrei* (Venice, 1659), consisting of 100 sermons, and an appendix on whether Christians should retain the Jews or expel them. We cannot infer from Cardoso's remarks, in the passage just quoted, the place which he assigns to Christianity. Let us recall that in the polemics of many former Marranos Catholicism is, in effect, "idolatria."

[81] *Excelencias*, pp. 359–61. The emphasis on "dexando las honras por los desprecios" is, of course, also an echo of Cardoso's own experience.

[82] Luzzato, *Ma'amar*, pp. 118 ff.; Manasseh, *Humble Addresses* (in Wolf, pp. 102 f.); *Vindiciae Iudaeorum* (*ibid.*, pp. 137).

discussion, however, marks a bold departure from that of his predecessors. For they are content merely to prove that Jews do not actively proselytize. Cardoso, having made the same point, goes on to dwell with great pride, and in considerable detail, on the many proselytes who have come to Judaism *voluntarily*. Where Manasseh only mentions casually that "it may happen that some of the Sect of the Papists, of a better mind, embrace the Jewish religion," Cardoso proclaims: "Many of the gentiles came to seek the Law of the Jews without being persuaded by them, but illumined by their own understanding. For the Lord has granted to all sufficient reason and natural light with which to choose the best and recognize the truth. . . ."[83]

As examples of proselytes in ancient times Cardoso points to the royal house of Adiabene; Fulvia, the wife of the Roman senator Saturninus; Flavia Domitella and her husband Flavius Clementus, relatives of the emperor Domitian, who had her exiled and executed him. The presence of many proselytes in the Roman period is attested by Juvenal, and by "Elio Spartiano" (Aelius Spartianus) in his life of the emperor Alexander Severus, telling of the harsh penalties imposed on those who became Jews.[84]

Other ancient proselytes went on to become great sages of the Law. Onkelos, who translated the Scriptures into Aramaic, was the son of Titus' sister. Rabbi Tarfon (!), Rabbi Meir, and Rabbi Akiba were all descendants of proselytes. Culling numerous aggadic examples from Rabbinic literature, Cardoso asserts that many of the greatest enemies of the Jews, or their progeny, became proselytes. It is said even of Aristotle that toward the end of his life he converted to Judaism.[85]

---

[83] *Excelencias*, p. 362.

[84] On Adiabene: Josephus, *Antt.*, XX; on Fulvia, *ibid.*, XVIII; on Flavia Domitella, Dio Cassius (Reinach, pp. 195 f.); on Roman proselytes in general, Juvenal, Satire XIV (*ibid.*, pp. 292 f.); Aelius Spartianus in *Historia Augusta* (Severus, XVIII) (Reinach, p. 346).

[85] *Excelencias*, pp. 362 f. On Onkelos, see *TB Gittin*, 56a; Meir as a descendant of Nero who became a proselyte (*ibid.*). That Akiba was descended from proselytes is not stated explicitly in the Talmud, but see Nissim Gaon ad *TB Berakhot*, 27b, making him a descendant of Sisera. I do not know where Cardoso received the

Defender of Israel

From recent times Cardoso chooses two examples of proselytes who died as martyrs. Fray Diogo da Assumpção and Don Lope de Vera were both Old Christians who had been burned at the stake for Judaizing, the one at Lisbon in 1603, the other at Valladolid in 1644. The cases had caused a scandal in the Peninsula and were, of course, well known in the Sephardic diaspora. They are cited in Manasseh's *Esperanza de Israel*. However, we have here an illuminating instance of Cardoso's different utilization of the same historical material. For while Manasseh had merely recorded the two stories as examples of Jewish martyrdom, and of the cruelty of the Inquisition, Cardoso uses them to prove that important Christians, in this case a friar and a nobleman, have indeed embraced the Jewish faith and were willing to die for it.[86] There is considerable daring in all this since, after all, his prime intent was to refute the charge of proselytizing per se. Luzzato, for example, not only denied categorically any past or present Jewish desire to proselytize, but prudently refrains from mentioning any specific case of gentile conversion. Cardoso's explicit thesis is that while the Jews, it is true, do not seek proselytes, many gentiles have nevertheless become Jews of their own accord. And to this he adds, with characteristic defiance:

---

notion that R. Tarfon's ancestors were proselytes. Such a tradition is ruled out by the fact that he is recorded as being of priestly descent, and he himself states that he officiated in the Temple (*TP Yoma*, III: 7).

The legend of Aristotle's conversion, already mentioned in the *Philosophia libera* (*supra*, ch. VI, n. 13), had wide currency among medieval Jews. For details see Louis Ginzberg, "Aristotle in Jewish Legend," *JE*, II, 98 f.; Baron, *Social and Religious History*, VIII, 63, 306 n. 16. (For similar medieval legends making him a proto-Christian, see Martin Grabmann, *Mittelalterliches Geistesleben*, II (Munich, 1936), 92 ff.). Cardoso also states that Aristotle's conversion to Judaism is proved by "Lyceto, en un libro particular desta materia, que intitula de Pietate Aristotelis erga Deum." The reference is to Fortunio Liceti (1577-1656), *De pietate Aristotelis erga Deum et homines, libri duo* (Ultini, 1645).

[86] *Excelencias*, p. 363. Cf. Manasseh, *Esperanza de Israel* (in Wolf, pp. 97-99). Torrejoncillo, who knew of Don Lope de Vera's case, could not tolerate the idea that he was an Old Christian. His Judaizing propensities must have been due to the fact that his nurse was of Jewish stock ("era de sangre infecta . . ."). See his *Centinela*, p. 214.

Let us, moreover, disabuse ourselves of the thought that the Jews do not induce the gentiles to follow their Law because in promoting such an enterprise (the latter) can acquire neither nobility nor glory. For the Jews are most noble of blood and most ancient of lineage, three or four thousand years old, a people chosen by God among all those in the world. Neither can princes be given greater luster than that which is acquired by those who bring themselves into the congregation of Israel. . . .[87]

But the charge that the Jews *actively* proselytize is merely another product of the mortal hatred which the gentiles have toward them. If any gentile converts of his own volition to the Law of the Hebrews, the latter are immediately held guilty of having influenced him to do so. This was seen in Spain when the Edict of Expulsion specified no important crime other than that of inducing others to Judaize, especially the nobles of Andalusia. If, through their own speculations and sentiments, the Law of Moses seemed preferable to them, the Jews were to blame.[88]

The very suffering and low estate to which the Jews have been reduced is an excellent touchstone for the motives and character of converts, both gentile and Jewish. Those who are still willing to become Jews despite the need to abandon their comforts and liberty, are usually the finest spirits among the gentiles. Conversely, those Jews who abandon Judaism are generally a perverse and greedy sort, seeking only temporal gain. And that is precisely why, at the time of the Redemption, proselytes will no longer be accepted, for then they will come either out of fear, or for convenience, "and he who does not accompany Israel in affliction and calamity shall not accompany them in their felicity. . . ."[89]

Thus far Cardoso's remarks on proselytizing. The other accusation of religious subversion may be more easily summarized. The ninth *calunia* indicts the Jews with sacrilegious acts against Christian holy

---

[87] *Excelencias*, p. 364.

[88] The text of the Edict has been published several times, most recently by L. Suárez Fernández, *Documentos acerca de la expulsión de los judíos* (Valladolid, 19 no. 177, pp. 391–95. While the Jews are blamed for the Judaizing of Chris there is no specific mention of the Andalusian nobility.

[89] *Excelencias*, p. 366.

objects generally, but is mainly concerned with alleged desecrations of the Host. Here Cardoso does not pause to philosophize, but states flatly that such accusations are no more than pretexts for the killing and robbing of Jews.

The Jews do not desecrate Christian images; they simply ignore them. The Lord commanded Israel not to make any image because His sovereign majesty, unique, invisible, and eternal, will brook no comparison to anything else. How can the Infinite be represented in a stone or a painting? If the rational soul, or an angel, cannot be expressed corporeally, how much less so the Divine Essence. After this barely disguised judgment against Christian iconography, Cardoso states that God commanded the Jews not even to look at images, for "the eyes are the ambassadors of the heart and couriers of the soul." Nor should the modes of serving idols be investigated, which means that one should not even read books describing how planets and idols are worshiped.[90]

Only in their own land are the Jews bidden to destroy images; God did not command them to do so in foreign lands. Gideon did not destroy idols on his own initiative, but because the Lord ordered him to do so. Had he been among gentiles, with no power nor dominion, he would not have been obliged to imperil his life in this manner. In any case, it is not the Jews who commit the desecrations, but the Protestants:

The followers of Luther, Calvin, and Zwingli, and all those who call themselves of the Reformed religion are the ones who zealously dare to trample hosts, to demolish images and burn statues, either because living in their own lands they have this liberty without any danger, or because in others they despise all fear through the zeal of their religion. . . . [91]

---

[90] *Excelencias*, p. 401, referring to Maimonides' *Tratado de la idolatria*, i.e., MT, " 'Abodat kokabim," I : 2. Yet Cardoso himself surely read "idolatrous" works. His brother Abraham states explicitly that among the books he read in Isaac's library in Venice were certain "Chaldean" writings (*JQR*, XVIII, 115). In the *Excelencias*, and especially in the *Philosophia libera*, there are enough accounts of heathen practices to show that Cardoso, in common with many of his contemporaries, had a keen interest in such subjects.

[91] *Excelencias*, pp. 402 f. Cf. Costa Mattos, *Discurso*, fol. 138r: "Os Zwinglios,

Cardoso devotes most of this chapter to historical illustrations of real or alleged host desecrations, in support of his twin theses that such acts are often the work of Christians, and that in other instances the Jews are falsely accused of them. Two cases are taken from the *Fortalitium fidei*, one of them concerning a Christian woman who pawned a garment with a Jewish banker. The latter promised her more money if she would bring him a host. When she brought it, he put the host in a boiling caldron with great curses. By a miracle, a child emerged from it and swam in the water, and when the Jew attempted to wound it, he could not.[92] Cardoso offers no comment on such tales, apparently feeling that their intrinsic absurdity is sufficiently manifest. He does analyze again, and at length, the story of the physician Don Meir, but this time dwelling on the element of host-desecration rather than the poisoning of the king.

The incidents he discusses in greatest detail are taken from seventeenth-century Spain and Portugal. In Madrid "about forty years ago," in the Church of San Felipe, Benito Ferrer, a Catalan, took the host from a friar during Mass, crumbled it to bits, and trampled it with his feet. Refusing to repent of his act, he was burned alive at the stake.[93] Later, an Englishman did the same in the royal prison of Madrid, and in 1670 a similar case occurred in the "Domo, or great church of Paris." Again in Lisbon, on May 11, 1671, in the parochial church of Olivelas, an António Fernandes despoiled the images of their vestments, and took the ornaments and crucifixes of gold, as well as the vessels in which the hosts were kept. The prince Dom Pedro attired himself in mourning, inquiries were made, religious processions were held. They arrested "many of the Hebrew Nation" and all were in great danger. Finally the true cul-

---

Anabaptistas, Calvinos, Manicheos, e muitos outros, aborrecem todos o culto dos imagens, e guardão nos casamentos as regras de Moyses."

[92] *Fortalitium fidei*, fol. 185v; Usque, *Consolaçam*, III, 2r-3r (in Cohen, pp. 168 f.).

[93] *Excelencias*, p. 403. The incident actually took place in 1623. See Andrés de Almansa y Mendoza, *Relación del auto público de la Fé que se celebró en esta Corte, Domingo 21 de Enero de 1624* (Madrid, 1624). The *auto* was one of the most spectacular of the time. On the participation of Lope de Vega and Juan de Quiñones see *supra*, ch. III, n. 67.

prit was found and, after confessing, his hands were cut off and he was garroted and burned.[94] Another incident occurred in Lisbon when the host was stolen from the church called "La Engracia." The crime was attributed to a New Christian named Solis, without any proof, only because he was of the Hebrew Nation. He remained steadfast through the cruelest tortures, insisting that on the night the host disappeared he was playing cards with friends. Nevertheless, he was burned alive before the very church where the crime had been committed. Two years later the thief was discovered in Galicia. But at the time, so great was the emotion and outcry against the Hebrew Nation, that all were in the gravest peril. It is well known that the judges who condemned the innocent man soon died themselves in terrible illness and pain.[95] Finally, Cardoso presents his account of the *Cristo de la Paciencia* which was analyzed at length in an earlier chapter.

The Jews, in sum, are made to suffer either for sheer fictions, or for the crimes of others. "Innocence pays for the actions which malice has executed." Thus:

When the Calvinists or the Protestants or the Muslims drag Christs on the ground, trample hosts, destroy images or demolish altars, no miracles are invented claiming that the statues speak or the hosts leap or shed blood, but it is only when these [deeds] are attributed to the Jews, who are like shorn sheep and tame lambs. There is no one to protect or defend

---

[94] *Excelencias*, p. 403.

[95] *Ibid.*, pp. 403 f. Cardoso gives no date. The incident is mentioned as taking place in 1631 in Manasseh b. Israel's *Vindiciae Iudaeorum* (in Wolf, p. 117) but with different details: "A very true story happened at Lisbon, Anno 1631. A certain Church missed one night a silver pixe or box, wherein was the popish hosts. And forasmuch as they had seen a young youth of our nation, whose name was *Simao pires solis*, sufficiently noble, to passe by the same night, not farre from thence, who went to visit a Lady, he was apprehended, imprisoned, and terribly tortured. They cut off his hands, and after they had dragged him along the streets, burnt him. One year passed over, and a thief at the foot of the gallowes confessed how he himself had rifled and plundered the shrine of the host, and not that poor innocent whom they had burnt. This young man's brother was a Frier, a great Theologist, and a preacher; he lives now as a *Jew* in *Amsterdam*, and calls himself *Eliazar de Solis*."

A copy of the sentence is preserved in a manuscript volume of inquisitorial

them, and they lack the power to defend themselves, and the voice with which to complain. . . .[96]

Despite his own repeated assurances that Jews are forbidden even to malign other gods, Cardoso apparently could not resist at least a verbal thrust of his own. The passage with which he closes the section, though mentioning only pagan idols, cannot but be read as a thinly veiled ridicule of Christian images:

Amusing was that act of Dionysius who, seeing Jupiter in a temple with a rich vest brocaded in gold and pearls, and Aesculapius son of Apollo with a great beard of gold, commanded that they be removed and taken home, saying of Jupiter that his golden garment was too heavy for summer and too cold for winter, and of Aesculapius, that it is not good that the son have a beard when the father is beardless, thus gracefully mocking, as he well knew how, these vain gentile deities. . . .[97]

THE BLOOD LIBEL

The tenth *calunia*, with which the book ends, constitutes perhaps the most extensive and systematic survey of the Blood-Libel written by a Jew up to this time.[98] In this chapter Cardoso's sense of outrage reaches its peak:

---

sentences formerly in the Palha Collection (Cat. no. 2433) now in the Houghton Library of Harvard University (MS Port. 4772), pp. 6–10: "Sentença de Simão Solis . . . por haver commettido o execrando roubo da Egreja da Sancta Engracia, etc. Em 15 de Janeiro de 1630." It would seem that subsequently it became an annual custom to hold a special service at the church in honor of the Blessed Sacrament. See Christovam d'Almeida, *Sermam do dezagravo de Christo Sacramentado na solenissima festa que o mes de Ianeiro lhe faz todos os annos a Nobleza de Portugal na Igreja de Santa Engracia* (Lisbon, 1671). Unfortunately the sermon speaks in generalities of the "Jews" and gives no historical details.

[96] *Excelencias*, p. 407.

[97] *Ibid.*, p. 408. The key words are "father" and "son."

[98] So far as I am aware, the following Jewish works, touching on the Blood-Libel in one way or another, were published prior to the *Excelencias:* a) Zalman Zevi of

Defender of Israel

If a child or youngster is missing in any city, if he has been kidnaped, then the Jews have stolen him, if cruel and perverse men have killed him, the Jews are the murderers. There is no crime so atrocious, nor cruelty so wild, but that it cannot be imputed to them. They must always bear the punishment for the crimes commited by the depraved of all sorts. Even if their innocence is manifest, they are the guiity and the punished. They are like the lamb in Aesop's fable, who was met by his enemy the wolf. . . . The latter accused him of having eaten, three months earlier, the grass from his field. The lamb replied that at that time he had not yet been born. . . . And although the cruel wolf recognized the truth of his explanations, he said to him: In any case, I must eat you. . . .[99]

This abominable accusation, Cardoso writes, has caused such untold misery to the Jews that one can readily apply to them the verse in Isaiah 53: "He was oppressed . . . as a lamb that is led to the slaughter, and as a sheep that before his shearers is dumb, he opened not his mouth. . . ." Although the Christians are sufficiently close to the Jews to be aware of their beliefs, instead of reproving such lies, they propagate them.[100]

Cardoso presents a fairly detailed historical account of ritual

---

Aufhausen, *Yudisher Teriak* (Hanau, 1615), a reply written in Judeo-German to a work by the apostate Samuel Friedrich Brenz, *Jüdischer abgestreisster Schlangen-Balg* (Nürnberg, 1614), both books reprinted with an annotated Latin translation of the former by Johann Wülfer in his *Theriaca Judaica* (Nürnberg, 1681); b) Leon Karmi, pseud. (possibly a baptised Jew), *De charitate et benevolentia a Christianis erga Judaeos ab Evangelica lege extractus* (Amsterdam, 1643) [*non vidi*]. This excessively rare work is described in some detail by Wolf, *Bibliotheca Hebraea*, II, 1054, 1131–35; c) Manasseh b. Israel's *Vindiciae Iudaeorum* (1656); d) A defense of Raphael Levi of Metz (see *infra*) entitled *Factum servant de réponse au livre intitulé Abregé du Proces fait au Juifs de Metz* (Paris, 1670) [*non vidi*]. To these one might add several defenses against the specific charge that Jewish doctors murder their Christian patients, e. g., David de Pomis, *De medico hebraeo enarratio apologica* (Venice, 1588), and Benedict de Castro, *Flagellum calumniantium* (Amsterdam, 1631).

[99] *Excelencias*, pp. 408 f.

[100] Cardoso writes that, although ignorant of Jewish customs, the pagan world never leveled such charges against the Jews. He thus chooses to ignore Apion's famous charge that the Jews annually sacrifice a Greek in the Temple in Jerusalem. Manasseh b. Israel does refer to this in his *Vindiciae* (in Wolf, pp. 119 f.).

murder accusations from the twelfth to the seventeenth century. His main sources are the *Fortalitium fidei* of Espina, and Usque's *Consolaçãm*, though he consulted other works as well.[101] In all, he discusses 15 cases, of which fully half are from Spain, and the rest from France, Germany, and Italy.

From Vincent of Beauvais' *Speculum historiale* he cites a ritual murder accusation against the French Jews for which, he believes, they were expelled by Philip Augustus, as well as the latter's order that 84 Jews be burned at the stake on the same charge.[102] In Vienna, during the reign of Frederick III, a large lake froze over, and when three little boys ran out to play on it, the ice cracked and they fell in. The emperor commanded that 300 Jews be burned. At the last moment the ice thawed, and the bodies floated to the surface. "So pernicious are precipitous judgements, for they precede examination with execution, and inquiry with condemnation."[103] Next we have the famous case of Simon of Trent in 1475, and a similar one five years later in the neighborhood of Friuli for which three Jews were brought to Venice and burned.[104] Around 1174 some Jews in Saragossa were accused of sacrificing a Christian boy and hiding his body in a well.[105] Another example of the charge in Spain, this time in 1468, is followed by a lengthy account of the most notorious case of all, that of the *Niño Inocente* of La Guardia in 1491. As late as 1521 Fernando de la Ribera of Tembleque, an Old Chris-

---

[101] *Fortalitium fidei*, lib. III, consid. vii; Usque, *Consolaçam*, III, *passim*.

[102] *Excelencias*, p. 410. Both incidents in Usque, though with fewer details in the first and more in the second. See, respectively, *Consolaçam*, III, 8r f., 4r f. (Cohen, pp. 177 f., 171 f.).

[103] Cf. *Consolaçam*, III, 7v (Cohen, p. 176). Usque derived the tale from Espina.

[104] Neither case in Usque. Cardoso cites "El Bergomense" and "El Surio" as his sources. I am unable to identify them.

[105] If the date is correct, this would mark the first recorded ritual murder accusation in Spain, rather than that of Saragossa in 1250 as cited by Yitzhak Baer. Cardoso's source is "Iacob de Valencia" (i.e., Jaime Pérez de Valencia, *Tractatus contra Iudaeos*) but I have found no reference to the event in this work.

tian, was caught and burned for having played the part of Pilate when the child of La Guardia was murdered.[106]

Cardoso now pauses to discuss an epistle of Johann Lang ("Juan Langio"), a German physician, who cites Giovanni Francesco Pico della Mirandola as believing in the Blood-Libel. Among the latter's alleged views, the Jews are sorcerers who require blood for their sacrifices. They kill a Christian child each year in a subterranean cave, and they joined with the lepers to poison the wells. In Verona they killed a boy named Rosso and bribed the emperor Rudolph to attack the Veronese. But Cardoso dismisses Lang's assertions outright. Pico was so wise it is hardly conceivable that he lent credence to such charges. It is merly a fiction of Lang, who is ill disposed to the Jews, and who rails against the use of Jewish physicians by the German nobility. The two Picos were "two phoenixes among the talents of Italy, who never said such things nor wrote them in their works, who were learned in the Hebrew language and, in order to know it, supported rabbis with large salaries. . . ."[107]

Other cases derive directly from the *Fortalitium fidei:* a Jew allegedly came to Espina and told of witnessing ritual murders in Pavia and Saona; in 1454 near Valladolid, when two Jews charged with ritual murder were tortured by the local lord Don Luis de Almanza, the government had the case transferred to its jurisdiction, and although Espina thundered forth denunciations from the pulpit, the accused were freed; a Jewish father in Tavora, in order to avenge his son who had been executed for a crime, committed monstrous deeds against the Christians. From a book on the *Niño inocente* by Sebastián de Nieva, Cardoso cites an anecdote concerning an impoverished nobleman who was persuaded by some French Jews to sell them the heart of his young son. They were given a pig's heart instead.

---

[106] Cardoso's sources are Rodrigo de Yepes, *Historia de la muerte y glorioso martyrio del Sancto Inocente que llaman de la Guardia* (Madrid, 1583), and a work on the same subject by "Sebastián de Nieva, Commissario de la Inquisición," i.e., Sebastián de Nieva Calvo, *El Niño Inocente, hijo de Toledo, y martir en la Guardia* (Toledo, 1628).

[107] *Excelencias*, pp. 412 f. I have not located the work of Lang to which Cardoso refers.

Having also bought a consecrated host, the Jews pulverized both, mixed them together, and threw the compound into the river in order to kill Christians. The pigs who subsequently drank of the river died, but not the people, and so the Jews were discovered and punished.[108]

What properties, Cardoso asks rhetorically, do a host and a pig contain to kill even pigs, when neither of itself is poisonous? These and similar stories are again the products of a groundless hatred whose object is to destroy the Jews. But that is a vain project, as the Lord has assured (Jer. 46: 28).: "For I will make an end of all the nations . . . but I will not make an end of thee." Other cases of ritual murder are mentioned by Espina, by Majolus in his *Dies caniculares*, and by various authors who uncritically copy from one another.[109]

Cardoso's final example is contemporary, having occurred only some nine years before the publication of the *Excelencias*, and deserves to be quoted in full:

But let us conclude with another tragic story which occurred in the year 1670 in Metz of Lorraine, whose court condemned to be burned alive one Raphael Levi of Boulay, accused of having kidnaped a Christian boy, without sufficient proofs nor definite indications. Nor were the clear defenses of the said Levi enough. Even as he was imprisoned, the body of the child was found devoured by the beasts in a forest, which [should have] sufficed for his release. Since there was an uproar against the Jews, the latter appealed to the king of France, for after having condemned Levi they wanted to proceed against others, and he commanded that the case be brought before him. He bitterly reproved the atrocious and cruel deed, ordering that henceforth all cases against Jews involving such and similar crimes be brought before His Majesty, and he confirmed the Jews in the privileges granted by his father and the kings who preceded him.

They also accused Levi of magic, saying that to this end he pronounced certain Hebrew words during the torture (though he always denied the

---

[108] *Ibid.*, pp. 413–17. A similar case involving a pig's heart is found, as Cardoso notes, in Usque. See *Consolaçam*, III, 5r f. (Cohen, pp. 172 f.).

[109] Majolus, *Dies caniculares*, III, colloq. 1, p. 819, and *passim*.

459

deed), that he was a great rabbi who made trips to Italy, the Levant, Germany, and Holland, as an agent of the Jews, and they spoke of him as a great scholar. All these falsehoods were imputed to him in order to aggravate the crime, while actually he was not a man of letters but an ordinary Jew who had made some trips to Italy in order to bring palm leaves and citrons for the celebration of the festival of *Sukkot*, or Tabernacles, as is the custom. The words he uttered during the torture were his prayers under that rigorous stress, just as the Christians are wont to say theirs. Here in Verona, while the rope was applied to a Jew for a certain disobedience or inadvertence, he repeated that customary prayer *Semah Ysrael—Hear O Israel, the Lord our God is One God*, and the Christians who heard him say *Semah Ysrael* thought he was calling for *Samael*.[110]

The secret enemies of Raphael Levi and of the other Jews drew up their complaints to the Criminal Lieutenant of Metz, saying that he had kidnaped a Christian boy in order to sacrifice him. The case being formed, he came voluntarily to present himself before the magistrates in the prison in order to find himself innocent . . . but it did not avail him, nor did they admit his appeal. By the mere suspicions and conjectures of certain lying witnesses . . . the court condemned him to be burned alive with a hasty execution. To add color to his cruelty, and in order to oppress and condemn the other Jews, they accused him of usury and illicit commerce. And His Most Christian Majesty, now that he could not restore life to a dead man, reprehending the court, and taking the Jews under his protection, arrogated to himself and his council, as supreme judge, all such and similar crimes attributed to them. For if this royal decree had not intervened, all the other Jews would also have been unjustly punished in their lives and property. And this decree went forth from Saint Germain on April 18, 1670.[111]

Having brought the examples of the Blood-Libel down to his own day, Cardoso continues in anguish:

This is the calumny of blood, this the testimony of homicide, which so often their adversaries' hatred and envy have leveled against the Jews at the cost of their lives, without fear nor conscience, according to the

---

[110] My emendation. The printed text has *Samuel*, which does not make sense in the context, while *Samael* would be an invocation to the Devil.

[111] *Excelencias*, pp. 418 f. On the events see Graetz, *Geschichte*, X, 248 ff.

Psalm (54: 5), *strangers are risen up against me, and violent men have sought after my soul; they have not set God before them.* The ages invent each day new motives for our persecution. Loudly did David exclaim against the evil ones, and went on most accurately to portray in his own person the present state of his people, saying that it is for the sake of God that he suffers shame and derision. . . . And then he casts a curse against his tormentors, saying that God should pour His wrath upon them, that their table be a snare unto them, their houses uninhabited, that they be blotted out of the book of the living and not be inscribed with the righteous, that He add iniquity unto their iniquity so that they come not unto His righteousness, and he gives the reason: *for they persecute him whom Thou hast smitten, and they tell of the pain of those whom Thou hast wounded.* . . .

The nations see them innocent, neither assassins, nor homicides, nor profligates, but rather professing a strictly moral life in their retirement, with compassion and love of their neighbors. These things being manifest to all, they accuse them of secret murders, since they cannot point to public ones. . . .[112]

The Blood-Libel actually comprises an accusation of three sins: homicide, the eating of blood, and the practice of magic arts, each of which is for the Jews among the most stringently forbidden practices. Human sacrifices and diabolical superstitions were in use among the Christians by the Gnostic sects of whom Porphyry speaks. On Good Friday they took part in incestuous orgies. The creatures born of such unions were torn from their mothers' breasts, their veins opened, the bodies burned, and the blood mixed with ashes was drunk in order to engender a "prophetic fury."[113] Similarly lurid stories of the rites of other nations are given in detail. Cardoso then utilizes the opportunity to compare, not only the practices of the Jews with those of the nations, but their use of evidence as well, and thus to indict the procedure of the Inquisition:

From these execrable homicides it is clearly seen that they are proper to the gentile nations . . . and not to the Children of Israel whose Law rigorously forbids them. The confessions of some are not sufficient warrant for such severe penalties. Being placed in the rigors of torture, desiring

---

[112] *Excelencias*, p. 419.   [113] *Ibid.*, p. 421.

461

death rather than suffer a prolonged torment, the innocent sometimes confesses the crime committed by the inhuman and is condemned to die, while the wicked denies the sin he committed and his life is spared. That is why the Divine Law does not ordain the torture of the accused, for it is fallacious. Rather, it restricts the knowledge of causes and the verification of crimes to firm witnesses, not vacillating and lying ones, and by their deposition it resolves to free or condemn him. . . . But if they are shown to be false, they are given the same penalty they intended for the innocent.

O Divine and Sacred Law, which does not condemn through circumstantial evidence and conjectures, but by true and faithful testimonies which agree as to the time, the hour, and other conditions they examine, nor does it leave false witnesses without an exemplary chastisement for the falsehood they imputed!

Ulpian, one of the princes of jurisprudence, put little faith in torture for the investigation of crimes, and called it a fragile and dangerous thing which deceives truth, since many with patience and endurance so despise torture that no certainty can be elicited from them, while others have so little patience and are so little able to suffer, that they would sooner die than endure it, and so they not only confess themselves guilty, but even accuse others of that which they never committed. . . .

In the Inquisitions ordinarily the Jews are seen to confess what they never did, because of the intolerable severity of the tortures, attributing to themselves unheard of and absurd crimes for not being able to suffer the violence of the pains. And who doubts that the judges themselves, even though they be innocent and free of guilt, would confess even more than is charged to them if subjected to these terrible punishments?

In the Sacred Law one's own confession does not condemn a man to capital punishment, but only the firm and certain testimony of two or three witnesses. To these is limited the entire verification of the offense. But among the nations the name "Jew" is so discredited and odious that it alone suffices as sign and proof of the imagined crime. . . .[114]

The very last section of the chapter is perhaps the most noteworthy. Having given a survey of ritual murder accusations, Cardoso now reviews the pronouncements of Christian authorities who have come to the defense of the Jews. Where Manasseh b. Israel had only

---

[114] *Ibid.*, pp. 422 f.

noted vaguely in his *Vindiciae Judaeorum* that "this matter of bloud hath been heretofore discussed and disputed before one of the Popes at a full councill,"[115] Cardoso gives ample and concrete details.To be sure, he did not have at his disposal the even more elaborate references which later scholars and apologists have brought to light, but for a Jew writing in the seventeenth century his documentation is remarkably thorough.

Cardoso presents a concise and accurate account of the following:

1. The bull of Gregory IX "directed to all Christians" and citing "the example of his predecessors Calixtus, Eugenius, Alexander, Celestine, Innocent, and Honorius," an obvious reference to the traditional papal bull of protection *Sicut Judeis* as reissued by Gregory on May 3, 1235.[116]

2. The bull *Lachrimabilem Judaeorum Franciae* issued by Gregory on September 9th of the following year (1236) "in which he deplored the miserable estate of the Jews unjustly afflicted by the Christians who, instead of preparing themselves for the holy war . . . invent every kind of malice against the Jews in order to destroy them. . . . Nor do they consider, he says, that the Christians owe to the Jews the foundations of their religion . . . and he reproves them for abusing religion as a pretext for more freedom to rob the goods of these innocents. . . ."[117]

3. After summarizing material from Otto von Freising on the pogroms against the Jews during the Second Crusade, Cardoso cites the epistle of Bernard of Clairvaux against the anti-Jewish excesses of the Cistercian monk Radulph.[118]

---

[115] *Vindiciae*, ed. Wolf, p. 121.

[116] *Excelencias*, p. 424. See A. Potthast, *Regesta Pontificum Romanorum* (Berlin, 1875), no. 9893. Cardoso does not give the date.

[117] Potthast, *Regesta*, no. 10243.

[118] See St. Bernard, *Epistolae*, in Migne, *PL*, CLXXXII, no. 363. Cardoso goes on to state somewhat ambiguously (p. 425): "Tambien Pedro Abad Cluniacense escrive a Luys Rey de Francia, y era el tiempo que los predicadores hazian grandes invectivas contra los Judíos exagerando los pecados de sus padres, que crucificaron a Xpo. y llenas destas calunias todas las Ciudades, tuvieron necessidad los Papas y los Principes de toda su autoridad para reprimir tantas crueldades y

4. The bull of Innocent IV against the Blood-Libel issued in 1247 to the archbishops and bishops of Germany and France.[119]

5. The protective bull issued by Clement VI "in the seventh year of his pontificate" (Sept. 26, 1348).[120]

Thus far only one pronouncement, that of Innocent IV, really concerns the Blood-Libel per se. Obviously Cardoso did not know of the bulls of Gregory X (1272), Martin V (1422), and Paul II (1540), which deal directly with the accusation. Later on he does mention the imperial edicts of Frederick III, Charles V, and Maximilian II, proclaiming the charge to be false.[121] He also relates that once, when the Jews of Constantinople were accused of ritual murder, "the Grand Turk Sultan Amurates" (i.e., Murad) ordered his Pashas and Cadis to make a thorough investigation as to how Jews bake unleavened bread and, as a result, branded the accusation a mere slander.[122]

These edicts, like the aforementioned papal bulls, are merely summarized. But Cardoso also had the felicitous thought to publish in full the original texts of three other documents to which he somehow had access. They appear in the following order:

---

muertes como executavan contra los Judíos." Does he believe that Peter the Venerable of Cluny was friendly to the Jews? On Peter's violently hostile letter on the Jews sent to Louis VII, see Baron, *Social and Religious Hist.*, IV, 122, 301 f.

[119] Potthast, *Regesta*, no. 12596. This seems to have been the first papal bull specifically directed against the accusation.

[120] Issued to protest the massacres of the Jews during the Black Death. See Baronius-Raynaldus, *Annales ecclesiastici* (Lucca, 1738–59), XXV, 455, no. 33. Baronius is Cardoso's major source for papal bulls, and he undoubtedly made use of the 12-vol. Rome ed. of 1588–93.

[121] *Excelencias*, pp. 425 f., 430. For the sources of these edicts see Hermann Strack, *Das Blut* (8th ed.; Leipzig, 1911), p. 185. Cardoso shows no knowledge of the epoch-making proclamation of Frederick II in 1236.

[122] Two sultans bearing this name ruled the Ottoman Empire in the 16th and 17th centuries, Murad III (1574–95), and Murad IV (1623–40). I find no reference to such an event in either reign. Perhaps we have here an echo of the *firman* of Suleiman the Magnificent on the ritual murder accusation leveled against the Jews of Amasia and Tokat by the local Christians in 1545. See Graetz, *Geschichte*, IX, 303 f.; Solomon Rosanes, *Korot ha-Yehudim be-Turkiyah ve-arṣot ha-kedem*, II (Sofia, 1937–38), App. 3, pp. 283–85.

1. An edict of Bona and Gian Galeazzo Maria Sforza of Milan against the ritual murder accusation, issued on May 19, 1479.

After quoting the preamble verbatim, Cardoso gives a detailed description of its contents. It seems that, in the wake of the Blood-Libel in Trent some four years earlier, similar accusations had been leveled in the Duchy of Milan in such towns as Valenza, Monte Castello, Bormio, and Pavia. To these renewed charges the ducal decree reacted with stern firmness. It began by stating that many children are lost and cannot thereafter be traced. No one in his right mind should believe the allegations against the Jews, whose law forbids both murder and the eating of blood. If it is charged that they commit these acts because they despise Christ, that is simply not credible. Many Jews who have become Christians and even doctors of the Church, such as Nicholas de Lyra, Pablo de Santa Maria ("El Burgense"), and others who were well informed as to Jewish rites would surely have written of such practices had they really existed. In Turkey many Jews own Christian children as slaves and could commit this crime without risk, and yet nothing is heard of it. The decree ordains that if some Jews have been accused they and their accusers must be brought before the ducal court, that no riot or injury be inflicted on the others, and warns that, if these be found innocent, the witnesses against them shall be punished under criminal procedure.[123]

---

[123] *Excelencias*, p. 426. The complete text of the original decree, in Italian and Latin, has been published, together with a series of eight other documents which preceded it, by Corrado Guidetti, *Pro Judeis: riflessioni e documenti* (Turin, 1884), pp. 280 ff.; for the decree itself see no. 9, pp. 289–94. Cardoso incorrectly gives the year as 1470, which is intrinsically impossible since the decree mentions the Trent libel of 1475. He was probably misled by the manner in which the date was recorded ("die xviij Maij. MCCCCLXX nono"). Bona Sforza, widow of Galeazzo Maria who had been assassinated in 1476, was nominally regent for her son Gian Galeazzo, only ten years old at the time. In Cardoso's account a few place names are either hispanicized or misspelled, e. g., Valenza is given as "Valencia," Bormio as "Bornio." Cardoso also mentions "Estadella," which does not appear at all in Guidetti's text. The decree was obviously issued at the request of the Jews themselves ("pro parte Universitatis Hebraeorum in Dominio nostro commorantium, acceptimus supplicationem") and undoubtedly they supplied some of the arguments. The notion that Nicolas de Lyra was a convert from Judaism was

2. A decree of Pietro Mocenigo, Doge of Venice, addressed to the Retores, Podestá, and Captain of Padua, April 22, 1475.

Cardoso presents the complete Latin text, followed by his own literal translation into Spanish. This decree was issued in the very midst of the uproar over the case of Simon of Trent. It notes that Jews in the Venetian territories have been mistreated, and that those who pass from one place to another have been attacked and robbed. In particular, various preachers have been responsible for inciting the mob. In a remarkably forthright statement the Doge declares that the Jews must not be molested, and strictly forbids preachers or other persons to arouse the people against them.[124]

3. A notarial transcript of a sentence handed down by Giustiniano Contareno, Podestà of Verona, February 28, 1603.

Cardoso again records the full Latin text with a Spanish translation, the latter omitting only certain Christian turns of phrase. This time, however, the incident is one whose memory must still have been vivid within his own community. We learn from the document that in 1603 a Jew of Verona, Joseph Abrahamini, was accused by Bernardino Bertoro, a shoemaker of St. Marks, of having attempted the abduction of his son. Abrahamini, the charge continued, wanted to take the boy into the Ghetto, either in order to convert him to Judaism, or to kill him and use his blood. One of his alleged motives was the fact that his own daughter had recently become a Christian.

Abrahamini himself denied everything, and he had the good fortune to possess an excellent advocate. The lawyer not only brought forth a convincing defense, but also demonstrated from various passages in Scripture that the Hebrew rite holds the shedding of blood in abomination. He also demonstrated that various princes have held the blood accusation to be false, citing Bona and Gian Galeazzo Sforza of Milan, Pietro Mocenigo of Venice, and the emperors Frederick III and Maximilian II. As a result, "the illus-

---

fairly widespread (see Graetz, *Geschichte*, VII, Note 13: iii, p. 454; cf. Aboab, *Nomologia*, p. 238). Pablo de Santa Maria is not mentioned in Guidetti's text, but rather St. Paul.

[124] *Excelencias*, p. 427 (Latin); p. 428 (Spanish). The original in Guidetti, *op. cit.*, pp. 278 f.

trious lord Podestà, together with his most excellent Consul, released the said Joseph."[125]

The three documents we have just surveyed are unquestionably authentic. Two of them are quoted in the famous memorandum on the Blood-Libel drawn up in 1759 by Cardinal Lorenzo Ganganelli (later Pope Clement XIV),[126] and all three were republished from the archives in 1884. The question remains as to where Cardoso himself obtained them.

So far as we have been able to determine, they do not seem to have appeared in any printed work prior to the *Excelencias*. It is significant, however, that at the end of each text Cardoso also quotes one or several notarizations which had been added in the seventeenth century. The decree of Sforza and the sentence of Contareno were notarized in Verona in 1626, and the decree of Mocenigo was notarized in Padua (which, like Verona, was in Venetian territory) in 1602.[127] We must assume that in those years the Jews of Verona and Padua had themselves requested and obtained from the authorities a revalidation of these older documents, undoubtedly as a result of the recrudescence of the Blood-Libel. After all, Abrahamini's lawyer had already utilized copies of the Sforza and Mocenigo decrees in his defense in 1603. These notarized copies must have been deposited in the archives of the Jewish communities of Verona, Padua, and perhaps other towns of the Veneto, to be used if the occasion again arose.[128] To such copies Cardoso could easily have had personal access while writing the last chapter of his *Excelencias*. If our reasoning is correct, this may well mark the first time a

---

125 *Excelencias*, p. 429 (Latin); pp. 426–30 (Spanish). Guidetti, *Pro Judeis*, pp. 303 f.

126 The decree of Pietro Mocenigo and the Verona sentence of 1603 in Gangaelli's report, ed. by Moritz Stern in his anonymously published work on *Die päpstlichen Bullen über die Blutbeschuldigung* (Berlin, 1899), pp. 53 f., and by Cecil Roth, *The Ritual Murder Libel and the Jew* (London, n.d.), pp. 48 f.

127 The texts of these notarizations agree, except for very minor variations, with those published by Guidetti.

128 This is confirmed at least for the Sforza decree. Guidetti (*Pro Judeis*, p. 289) notes: "Il presente documento si conserva negli Archivii della Comunità israelitica di Verona."

Jew published in a book the actual texts of a series of governmental proclamations in defense of his people.[129]

"A REPUBLIC APART"

The final appeal is thus, inevitably, addressed to the princes. What does Cardoso ask?

To say that he appeals for toleration of the Jews is merely to state the obvious; Manasseh b. Israel and Simone Luzzato had also pleaded for that. It is the proud tone of Cardoso's appeal and the terms in which it is couched which set it apart from the others. Unlike them, Cardoso does not base himself on mercantilistic arguments that the Jews are an economic asset, except for a fleeting

---

[129] It is interesting to observe that some or all of these documents begin to proliferate in other books by both Jews and gentiles immediately after the appearance of the *Excelencias*, though a direct dependence on Cardoso need not always be assumed. Pietro Mocenigo's decree and the Verona sentence appear in Isaac Viva, pseud., *Vindex sanguinis, sive Vindiciae secundum veritatem, quibus Judaei ab infanticidiis & victima humana, contra Jacobum Geusium* (Amsterdam, 1680), p. 17 (reprinted as an appendix to Wülfer's *Theriaca Judaica*). Shortly afterwards Mocenigo's decree was published in a Hebrew translation by Isaac Hayyim (Vita) Cantarini in his account of the attack against the Ghetto of Padua in 1684, entitled *Paḥad Yiṣḥak* (Amsterdam, 1685), fol. 48r-v. In 1705 five Jews of Viterbo were arrested on charges of ritual murder. In their defense the Roman rabbi Tranquillo Vita (Hizkiah Manoah Hayyim) Corcos published three memoranda on the subject addressed to the papal reporter on Jewish affairs. In the third of these, entitled *Alla sagra consulta Illustriss. e Reverendiss. Monsig. Ghezzi ponente per l'Università degl'Hebrei di Roma: Sommario* (Rome, 1706), Corcos prints both the text of Mocenigo's decree (fol. A2 no. 2), and the Verona sentence (fol. A3 no. 3). The German Christian Hebraist Johann Christoph Wagenseil, though otherwise hostile to the Jews, defended them against the Blood-Libel in his *Benachrichtigung wegen einiger die gemeine Judischheit betreffenden Sachen* (Altdorf, 1707), and reprinted Mocenigo's decree (p. 119). The line of defense established by Cardoso's *Excelencias* and the works we have just cited sets the basic pattern for the books against the slander published in the 19th century by Stern, Chwolson, Guidetti, Strack, and others. Indeed, Chwolson refers directly to Cardoso on several occasions. See his *Die Blutanklage und sonstige mittelalterliche Beschuldigungen* (Frankfurt, 1901), pp. 245, 248, 259, 296, 314.

reference to the fact that unlike other foreign groups they do not take their earnings out of the country.[130] Above all, there is not a trace of obsequiousness in what he has to say; what he desires is demanded as a right which justice dictates. It may be argued that he can allow himself this luxury because, again unlike Manasseh and Luzzato, he is not caught up in such practical exigencies as persuading England to admit the Jews or preventing a threatened expulsion from Venice. I suspect rather that the most potent factor at work is his ingrained Spanish pride. In any case, we hear nothing of Manasseh's "how profitable the Jews are," nor is there a vestige of Luzzato's repeated assurances to the Venetians that "the Jewish group is, by its very nature, subdued, submissive, and subjugated, inclined to bow its head before the ruler."[131] Analyzing the status of the Jewish people among the nations, he offers this summary of his views:[132]

The Jews are not the serfs of the nations, but a Republic apart, which lives and governs itself by its laws and precepts which God gave them at Sinai, and which He commanded them to keep forever in all their generations. . . .

And that the Jews who live today are not really the slaves of the princes in whose territories they reside is clearly proved by such important authors as Vásquez, and Márquez in his *Governador Christiano*.[133] If some writers say that they are slaves, they mean it only in the sense that an entire nation may serve, without any individual person being a slave to one or another lord, but as a whole it is subject and detained against its will under the rule of an empire, and is not equal to other citizens. . . .

The majority of the Jews who are in the world were not conquered in just war, because prior to the destruction of Jerusalem by Titus and Vespasian they were already diffused through the kingdoms and provinces of the entire globe, as we have demonstrated in the first *excelencia* from Strabo, Philo, and other authors. . . .

---

[130] *Excelencias*, p. 376.

[131] Manasseh b. Israel, *Humble Addresses* (in Wolf, pp. 81 ff.); Luzzato, *Ma'amar*, p. 100.

[132] The following is a somewhat abbreviated translation of pp. 374–76.

[133] The reference is to Juan Márquez, *El Gobernador Christiano, deducido de las vidas de Moysen y Josue, principes del Pueblo de Dios* (Salamanca, 1612).

Defender of Israel

Nebuchadnezzar and Vespasian reigned and conquered the Holy Land, and Pompey first made it tributory to the Roman Empire, but there was more ambition than right in their conquest, the arrogance to enlarge their kingdoms. God desired to chastise the sins of the Jews, but He did not make their enemies to be their heirs or the just possessors of the land. They acquired the fact, but not the right of ownership of that holy territory, as the prophet Isaiah so gravely pondered: *Where is the bill of your mother's divorcement wherewith I have put her away? Or which of my creditors is it to whom I have sold you? Behold, for your iniquities were ye sold, and for your transgressions was your mother put away!*, as if to assure that not one of the nations can say that it is the creditor of the Jews, or that God has sold the Jews to them. Punished, yes, for their sins, and dispersed for their transgressions; but forever God is their king and their spouse.

That is why, we may well remark, no kings of the world, neither Nebuchadnezzar nor Titus or Vespasian, called themselves kings of the Jews; they either did not desire or were not able to take the title which belongs to God alone. And even more was this singular fact pondered by the famous historian Dio Cassius in his Roman history, saying that although Titus and Vespasian won such a great victory over the Jews, and triumphal arches were erected for them . . . neither called himself *Judaicus*, although it was a custom among the Romans to take as surnames the name of the provinces they conquered. . . . But not one took the name *Judaicus*, for God did not permit that by name they should show themselves the victors of that people, but rather the ministers and executors of the divine vengeance. Nor did He allow them to appropriate the ownership and rule which is specific to God, being king and lord of Israel. . . .[134]

The gentiles should deal with the Jews as the Jews dealt with the gentiles, allowing them to live among them so long as they are not idolatrous. There were two types of sojourners in Israel, some who were called righteous sojourners, and they were those who converted from their gentile estate to Judaism, and they were equal to the other Israelites; and others who were called resident sojourners, who desired and were able to live among them, although they did not follow their Law. . . .

---

[134] Of course the real reason for Vespasian's and Titus' refusal to accept the title was simply that they did not want to associate their names with the Jews or Judaism. (See Baron, *Social and Religious Hist.*, II, 92). We have here a good illustration of Cardoso's ability to turn an adverse historical fact to Jewish advantage and, indeed, to create a "midrash" on an historical event.

In essence Cardoso's argument might almost be styled "juridical," though it is characteristically interwoven with his theology. He has rejected the very notion of the *servitus judaeorum*. While he grants the *de facto* subjugation of the Jewish people, he stanchly insists that *de jure* the Jews belong to no one but God alone. To prove it, he has invoked the concept of the "just war," a medieval idea which was widely discussed by the Jesuits who elaborated the Spanish theory of empire in the sixteenth and seventeenth centuries. Since the Jews had never been conquered in such a war by the nations among whom they now live, it follows that the latter have no right to regard them as their serfs. Indeed, it is not as a servant to his master that Cardoso speaks, but rather as the ambassador of one nation to another. Since the gentiles have effective control, but no intrinsic rights, over the Jews, the least they can do is to leave them alone, free to live their collective life in security, and to govern themselves as a "republic" with a divine constitution.

Did Cardoso really believe that such a singular argument would find a receptive ear among the nations? We may well doubt it. And even if it should? At one point he himself observes wearily: "It is true that various wise men and prudent princes abhor these calumnies . . . but the mob does not believe the wise, nor does the populace obey the princes, when hatred dominates reason, and fury closes the door to supplications."[135] But in sum it does not really matter. Cardoso had stated his credo, and that was sufficient. In the end, everything is left intact. Israel, separated from the nations in its birth, remains so in its life. Its history awaits its fulfillment, not from earthly princes, but from its true king.

If the *Excelencias* is a major work of Jewish apologetics, as in all such works the measure of its success is to be gauged first by its impact upon the Jews themselves. This was immediate. Upon receiving a copy of the book, Rabbi Judah Brieli of Mantua, himself no mean polemicist, wrote these lines to Cardoso:[136]

---

135 *Excelencias*, p. 407.

136 On Judah (Leone) Brieli (1643?–1722), see the notice by I. Broydé in *JE*, III, 385. He was the author of a critique of the Acts of the Apostles, as well as a *Riposta al libro che fue dato alle stampe dal Padre Piñamonti intitolato "La sinagoga*

Defender of Israel

Isaac, in recounting our people's glories
Thou hast traversed the highest spheres of science,
Blacked out the light of the mockers' taunts,
And smashed with thy genius those who rise against us. . . .

---

disingannata," neither of them published. A manuscript of the latter is in the library of the Jewish Theological Seminary of America (see Marx, *The Polemical Mss.*, no. 70, p. 264). A poem of Brieli against the apostate Judah Ancona was included by Hayyim Schirman in his *Mibḥar ha-shirah ha-'ibrit be-'Italyah* (Berlin, 1934), p. 347. The poem to Cardoso was published by Marco Mortara, in *Ozar Nechmad*, III (Vienna, 1860), 167 f.

EPILOGUE

Four years after the publication of *Las excelencias de los Hebreos* Isaac Cardoso died. He was some seventy-nine years old. On October 27, 1683, probably within a few days after he had been laid to rest, the *Vaad* of the Jewish community of Verona met and resolved:

Since it is absolutely imperative to try to find a professional physician in the Holy Community for the poor, as there had been unto this very day the deceased, the distinguished physician, His Honor Isaac Cardoso (may the memory of the righteous be a blessing), therefore let it be decided to empower and permit . . . the treasurers to negotiate in this regard.[1]

The matter was urgent, and the entry in the *pinkas* was, as usual, terse and businesslike. For us, however, it is not without a certain poetic symmetry that both in the document which had permitted him to settle in Verona thirty years before, and in that which now marked his passing, Cardoso is mentioned in the same connection: the healing of the sick poor. We see that, to the very end, the conditions laid down three decades earlier had been fulfilled. That his own long life had found, in so many ways, its complete fulfillment, is abundantly manifest. It remains for us now to inquire into the subsequent fate of his work.

The enthusiasm shown by Samuel Aboab and Judah Brieli for the *Excelencias* was fully shared by other Jews in the years following its publication. Some measure of the powerful impression it had made may be gauged from these words of Moses Hagiz, written more than half a century later:

---

[1] The document was printed by Sonne in *Zion*, III, 153. It is dated 8 Heshvan (5), 444.

Epilogue

If you have any desire to learn and to teach from books which were composed by the perfect sages in the vernacular tongue, then the first is Rabbi Imanuel Aboab, who wrote and explained the basis of the faith of the Sages in the first part of a book known as the *Nomologia*, which was printed in the year 5389. And after it is the book called *Excelencias de los Hebreos* (that is to say, the greatness of the Jews), composed by the distinguished physician, healer of both bodies and souls, the sage who feared the word of the Lord, His Honor our master R. Isaac Cardoso. For from these two it can be demonstrated . . . even to the wise men of the nations, so that they admit and not be ashamed to acknowledge, how very much the true Rabbinic tradition is necessary for everything. . . .[2]

In Spain itself there was, of course, no question of circulating such a work. Yet in the eighteenth century individual copies seem to have found their way into ecclesiastical libraries, and it became known to the bibliographers. Rodríguez de Castro, for example, gave an analytic sketch of its contents from a copy which he had seen in the library of the Discalced Friars of the *Merced*.[3] Towards the very end of the century, in Portugal, Ribeiro dos Santos was able to present a full description of the book in his survey of Portuguese Jewish writers, published in the journal of the Lisbon Academy of Sciences.[4] In these and similar instances, however, the reading of the *Excelencias* in the Peninsula must have been confined to very small circles of bibliophiles and to those who wished to know more about Judaism for polemical purposes.

Elsewhere in Europe the book did find a non-Jewish audience, and some were deeply, though grudgingly, impressed. Thus the great German classical scholar and bibliographer Johann Albert Fabricius

---

[2] Moses Hagiz (1671–1750), *Mishnat ḥakamim* (Wandsbeck, 1733), fol. 120.

[3] Joseph Rodríguez de Castro, *Biblioteca Española*, I, 582–84.

[4] António Ribeiro dos Santos, "Da litteratura sagrada dos judeos portuguezes no século XVII," *Memorias de litteratura portugueza publicadas pela Academia Real das Sciencias de Lisboa*, III (1792), 313–16. Fourteen years later he published there his "Ensaio de huma Bibliotheca Lusitana Anti-Rabbinica, ou Memorial dos escritores portuguezes que escreverão da controversia anti-judaica" (*ibid.*, VII [1806], 308–77).

474

(1668–1736) wrote: "I have seen no one after Josephus Flavius who has argued the praises of the Jews more learnedly and thoroughly than Cardoso, although the Jews are not infrequent in their own praises."[5] Initially, however, it may well have been the *Philosophia libera* which had the wider currency among the gentiles, perhaps because it was written in Latin. In Italy, at any rate, the missionary Benetelli focused all his attacks on the earlier work, calling its author "the baptised Jew and circumcised Christian, Isaac Cardoso."[6]

A curious feature is the career of the *Philosophia libera* in the Peninsula. It is somewhat symbolic of the later development that Nicolás Antonio was aware that Fernando Cardoso had left Spain to Judaize in Venice and knew also of an Isaac Cardoso who had written the *Philosophia libera*, but could not connect the two, and listed them as separate entries.[7] In a sense, a similar separation was to take place with regard to the *Philosophia libera* and the *Excelencias*. At a time when the latter was at best a curiosity, the *Philosophia libera* exerted some influence on Spanish intellectual life. According to Menéndez y Pelayo, in his spirited but tendentious defense of Spanish science, it was to be found in the eighteenth century in many monasteries and universities, and was read freely and extensively.[8]

---

[5] Johann Albert Fabricius, *Bibliographia antiquaria* (Hamburg-Leipzig, 1716), p. 308: "Nullum vidi qui post Flavium Josephum Cardoso doctius et operosius Judaeorum laudes perorasset; licet sint Judaei in laudibus suis haud infrequentes." Fabricius also gives a summary of the *Excelencias* in his *Delectus argumentorum et syllabus scriptorum qui veritatem religionis Christianae adversus Atheos . . . Judaeos et Mohammedanos lucubrationibus suis asseruerunt* (Hamburg, 1725), p. 668.

[6] Luigi Maria Benetelli, *Le saette di gionata scagliate a favor degli ebrei* (Venice, 1704), p. 33: "l'Ebreo sbatezzato, e Cristiano circonciso, Isac Cardoso." He attacks the *Philosophia libera* on no less than ten occasions.

[7] See the second edition of the *Bibliotheca Hispana Nova* (Madrid, 1783), I, fol. 827, *s.v.* "Isac Cardoso": "Si nomen spectamus Judaici erroris assecla, si cognomen Lusitanus, aut e Lusitania oriundus, apud Italos in Veronesi urbe non solum medicam artem professus est, sed & eruditum valde opus foras edidit hoc titulo: *Philosophiam liberam. . . .*"

[8] Marcelino Menéndez y Pelayo, *La ciencia española* (Obras, ed. nacional, LVIII-LX [Santander, 1953]), II, 335. See also p. 309, citing the opinion of the Jesuit Zeferino Gonzáles that the *Philosophia libera* is an "opus sane egregium." His own admiration for the work is very great. He notes that Cardoso shows a

Epilogue

This may very well have been the case, for, with the exception of its Jewish details, the book as a whole was part and parcel of the Spanish philosophic and scientific tradition, and could easily have continued to appeal to the Spanish mind. Moreover, while in the eighteenth century the new experimental science of the seventeenth conquered the field in the rest of Europe, Spain remained largely unaffected, and such a work as the *Philosophia libera* could still receive the attention which it could no longer command elsewhere.

But our chief concern remains with the *Excelencias*, and here we encounter a phenomenon which requires some explanation. The fact is that for all its manifest sweep and power, and despite the initial enthusiasm it aroused, there is little doubt but that from the mid-eighteenth century onward the book sank into relative obscurity. Mentioned later by scholars, it did not exercise any appreciable influence on the Jewish people at large.

In part the lot of the *Excelencias* may be linked to that which befell the entire Hispano-Portuguese Jewish literature. That great corpus of vernacular writings had arisen in the first place largely as a means of meeting a real need, the education of the Marranos who rejoined the Sephardic diaspora during the sixteenth and seventeenth centuries. By the latter part of the eighteenth century its historic task had already been completed. Marrano emigration from the Peninsula had by then slowed to a mere trickle and, in any case, there already existed sufficient books to accommodate the few who still came. It is

---

mastery of all of Spanish philosophy (*ibid.*, I, 265), and refers often to the relative independence of his thinking. Especially significant for him is Cardoso's atomic theory, which he attempts to summarize (*ibid.*, II, 33 f.). He cites with approval Cardoso's distinction between "grace" and "beauty" (*Historia de las ideas estéticas en España*, II, 313). In his *Historia de los heterodoxos españoles* (II, 298 f.) he calls him a "ciudadano libre de la República de las letras," and writes that the *Philosophia libera* is "lleno de sutiles novedades." It is only when he reaches the *Excelencias* that he finds himself at a loss: "Imposible parece que el autor de la *Philosophia libera* y el de las *Excelencias de los Hebreos* sean uno mismo. Esta segunda obra, escrita al gusto de los más fanáticos doctores de la Sinagoga de Amsterdam, rebosa de orgullo judaico y hiel anticristiana, como si hubiesen juntado en el alma de Cardoso todas las furias vindicativas de su raza, exasperada por matanzas, saqueos, hogueras y proscripciones" (*ibid.*, p. 300).

476

true that in Sephardic communities around the world Portuguese, Spanish, or Ladino continued to be spoken and written. In London one may still encounter in Haham David Nieto a major author in Spanish, but he died in 1728, and it is significant that in 1756 his son Isaac already felt impelled to publish a sermon he had delivered in an English translation.[9] Everywhere congregational minute books were still kept in the Iberian tongues, and so were occasional prayers, but this was increasingly out of reverence for the past rather than the demands of the present. In Verona itself, even before the end of the seventeenth century, real ethnic differences between Sephardim and Ashkenazim became blurred. As all became Italianized, each began to give up its own language, so that in the eighteenth century the only real distinction remained in certain synagogal customs.[10] Finally, and perhaps most important, the latter part of the eighteenth century witnessed the worldwide decline of Sephardic Jewry as a whole. The communities in the vast reaches of the Turkish Empire had already sunk into the decadence which had engulfed the entire Near East. In Western Europe the Ashkenazim rose rapidly to a position of leadership in Jewry which was soon to become absolute. The eclipse of the Sephardic vernacular literature was a concomitant of the waning influence of its bearers.

However, the relatively short-lived influence of the *Excelencias* was due also to certain specific factors. It was the peculiar misfortune of the work to appear on the eve of a revolutionary age in Jewish history, but when the nature of the impending transition was still far from apparent.

When Cardoso left Spain and came to Italy to live as a Jew, the order which he so fervently embraced, and which he personally found so fresh, already contained the stresses and strains which were later to burst it asunder. He came, in a sense, to a mansion whose halls enchanted him, but whose foundations, unknown even to most of its own inhabitants, were already seriously weakened. With the

---

[9] Isaac Nieto, *A Sermon Preached in the Jews' Synagogue on Friday, Feb. 6th, being the Day appointed by Authority for a General Fast. Translated from the Spanish Language by the Author* (London, 1756).

[10] Sonne, "Sources," p. 143.

hindsight that only time allows, the historian today can see in the Sabbatian movement an eruption of pent-up Jewish forces, seeking, however blindly and impulsively, a radical "messianic" restructuring and reevaluation of the fundamental patterns of Jewish existence. At the time, however, it is doubtful whether even the participants in the movement could have detached themselves sufficiently from the literal messianic framework in order to sense the deeper currents of which it was the expression. For those who had stood aloof, and for many others who were disillusioned, it was not difficult to conceive after 1666 that what had occurred had been merely an aberration, painful to be sure, but temporary. And so, indeed, it really seemed. The Jewish tradition which Cardoso encountered still offered itself to view as an organic whole, and continued to be lived as such by the mass of Jews. The Jewish community was still in every respect a corporate entity which could be characterized as a "Republic." Antisemitism still expressed itself within its medieval frame of reference. The setting of the *Excelencias* is, in short, very much the real world of Cardoso's time. But in all three respects that world was to change drastically in the course of the next century.

For our own orientation we have but to take notice of a simple but striking fact. Nine years before Cardoso extolled the *Pueblo escogido de Dios*, another scion of the Marranos, Baruch Spinoza, had already observed drily that "at the present time . . . there is absolutely nothing which the Jews can arrogate to themselves beyond other people"[11] Though the fruits will at first be slow in coming, the seeds are already sown. The distance between the *Excelenias* and the *Theological-Political Treatise* is the gulf which separates two distinct worlds. For better or worse, it is Spinoza's book which is the harbinger of that which is to come.

---

[11] See the entire passage in Spinoza, *Tract. Theol. Pol.*, ed. Gebhardt, ch. III, pp. 54 ff., presenting his reply to those "quibus sibi persuadere volunt, Hebraeorum electionem non temporaneam, et ratione solius imperii, sed aeternam fuisse. . . ." The proofs which Spinoza rejects are, incidentally, the very ones which Cardoso sets forth in the *Excelencias*. Interesting too, for the sake of comparison, are Spinoza's remarks concerning circumcision and Jewish separation from other nations, both of which, he charges, drew upon them that hatred which has largely preserved them to the present day.

Indeed, we can find a potent and ironic symbol of the fate of the *Excelencias* merely by glancing at what is perhaps the last important work to make some use of its arguments: the Abbé Grégoire's famous "Essay on the Physical, Moral and Political Regeneration of the Jews," urging the emancipation of French Jewry, and published on the eve of the French Revolution. Grégoire refers several times to the *Excelencias* (once in order to dismiss the charge of Jewish male menstruation). But for him the book is already no more than a rare curiosity. And how could it be otherwise? Grégoire's treatise itself declares all corporate Jewish autonomy and particularity to be anachronisms incompatible with the modern state, and in its pages we hear the death knell of the Jewish society which Cardoso had known and extolled.[12]

Had Cardoso written the *Excelencias* a century before, there could have been time for the work to secure for itself a lasting place in Jewish literature. As it turned out, the hour was very late. In the eighteenth century the vanguard of Jewry in Western Europe begins its headlong struggle for emancipation, no longer satisfied to be a "republic apart." In the intellectual sphere it is no longer mere attacks against the Oral Law or even Scripture itself which are in question, but the very foundations of faith. From without, the nature of the adversary himself is transformed in an increasingly secularized world such as Cardoso could not yet envision, one in which it is idle to argue the exegesis of a verse when the source from which it is taken is no longer regarded as sacred, or to debate who has been chosen when neither gentile nor Jew will believe in Him who chooses.

And yet, paradoxically, it is my conviction that in our time it has become possible once more to read the *Excelencias*, and to do so with

---

[12] *Essai sur la regénération physique, morale et politique des Juifs, ouvrage couronné par la Société Royale des Sciences et des Arts de Metz, le 23 Août 1788, par M. Grégoire, Curé du Diocèse de Metz* . . . (Metz, 1789), p. 35: "Cependant, en général, on ne peut pas reprocher aux Juifs la libertinage qui flétrit et dépeuple nos Villes. Cardoso les loue de n'avoir aucun de ces livres détestables dont le but est d'attiser la luxure; il prétend que la décence est en eux une vertu presqu'innée"; p. 208, n. 10: "V. son traité aussi rare que curieux en Espagnol, Las excellentias [*sic*] de los Hebreos. . . ." For male menstruation see p. 46. On p. 181 Grégoire states that Jews have a low opinion of their wives. "Vainement Cardoso nous assure qu'ils en font estime."

profit. If the eighteenth century found it increasingly irrelevant, for us it is pertinent, for we shall approach it differently than they could. Unlike them, we shall not be thwarted because it offers no solutions to the problems of Jewry as we know them today, for we do not seek such answers in its pages. But we possess something which the men of the eighteenth century did not have—a sense of history; and that is as much our need as it is our possession. We shall read *Las excelencias de los Hebreos* much as we read Josephus' *Contra Apionem*, with the same feeling of distance, and with the same empathy which only distance makes possible. The parallel is a just one. Both of them works written in vernaculars of the Jewish diaspora, each of them passed by in the forward sweep of the people's historic course, Cardoso's work may now also be reclaimed, to be read no longer as apologia but as the response of a great Jewish heart to a perennial hatred.

Before my first research trip abroad, I had hoped one day to bring this study to a close by citing Cardoso's epitaph, but all my efforts to locate his tombstone have failed. As so often in confronting the Jewish past, we are left in the end with a book, and some glimpses of the life out of which it was forged. In Verona, the ancient Roman amphitheater still stands, but the location of the Ghetto, while known, is no longer recognizable as such. Sephardic life in the city had in any case disappeared long ago. The old Sephardic synagogue which used to occupy the fifth floor of a house facing the Piazza delle Erbe was closed in 1759, and its sacred objects removed and kept by the community at large. Today, when one approaches the Tempio d'Israele in which is kept the ark before which Cardoso once prayed, one pauses to read an Italian inscription to the right of the entrance:

BEHOLD THE TEARS OF THE OPPRESSED, AND THEY HAVE
NO COMFORTER (Ecclesiastes 4: 1)
For the defenseless victims
Deported from Verona
A tiny fragment of an immense holocaust
of six million Jews,
prey of the Nazi barbarism.

To the eternal warning of posterity,
The Jewish community of Verona
Dedicates this stone . . .

Classical rabbinic texts as well as medieval Jewish commentaries to the Bible are not listed here. They can be found in the standard editions. Books printed from the fifteenth to the eighteenth century are recorded here under short titles. In the list of secondary sources, titles of Hebrew articles are given in English; titles of Hebrew books are given in the original, with an English translation following immediately in parentheses.

I. MANUSCRIPTS AND ARCHIVAL DOCUMENTS

GREAT BRITAIN

Oxford. Bodleian Library. MS Opp. Add. 4° 151. Two Spanish Letters of Abraham Cardoso.

ISRAEL

Jerusalem. Jewish National and University Library. MS Heb. 4° 551. Pinkas Verona (1653–1706).

ITALY

Venice. Archivio di Stato. Santo Uffizio, Busta 106. Dossier of Fra Raimondo Tasca.

Venice. Archivio di Stato. Santo Uffizio, Busta 107. Dossier of Pietro d'Acosta.

Venice. Biblioteca Marciana. MS It. III. 10. (5003). Libro de arti segretti.

Bibliography

PORTUGAL

Lisbon. Arquivo dos Registros Paroquiais. Conselho de Celorico da Beira:
    Santa Maria, Liv. 1.
    São Martinho, Liv. 1.
    São Pedro, Liv. 1.
Lisbon. Biblioteca Nacional. MS 868 (Collecção Moreira, II). Treatise
of Don Juan de Quiñones.

SPAIN

Madrid. Archivo Histórico Nacional. Inq. de Cuenca, Leg. 1931, no. 21:
Memoria de las personas presas por la Inquisición con sequestros de
bienes que han salido reconciliadas o condenadas por la de Cuenca.
Madrid. Archivo Histórico Nacional. Inq. de Toledo, Leg. 140, no. 4:
Cristo de la Paciencia.
Madrid. Archivo Histórico Nacional. Inq. de Toledo, Leg. 146, no. 4:
Bartolomé Febos.
Madrid. Biblioteca Nacional. MS 2363. Sucesos del año 1631.
Salamanca. Archivo Universitario. Libros de actas de Bachilleramientos
en las diversas Facultades de la Universidad de Salamanca. Lib. 745,
747.
Salamanca. Archivo Universitario. Matrículas de todos los estudiantes
en todas facultades desta Universidad de Salamanca. Lib. 321–25
(1616–21).
Valladolid. Archivo Provincial y Universitario. Leg. 238 (3–7). Provisión
de la cátedra de Filosofía en el Lic. Fernando Cardoso 9 dic. 1623–
7 mayo 1624.
Valladolid. Archivo Provincial y Universitario. Leg. 238 (3–8). Provisión
de la cátedra de Súmulas vacante por ascenso del Lic. Fernando
Cardoso a Prima de Filosofía, en el Lic. Juan Gómez del Pinar, a
4 enero–17 mayo 1625.

UNITED STATES

Cambridge. Houghton Library, Harvard University. MS Port. 4772,
pp. 6–10: Sentença de Simão Peres Solis . . . por haver commettido
o execrando roubo da Egreja de Sancta Engracia . . . Em 15 de
Janeiro de 1630.
New York. Columbia University Library. MS X93/H39. Sefer abkat
rokel. (Copied by Abraham Baruch Henríquez.)

482

II. PRIMARY PRINTED SOURCES

Abendana, Jacob, tr. *Cuzary. Libro de grande sciencia y mucha doctrina . . . por el Doctissimo R. Yehuda Levita.* Amsterdam, 1663.

Aboab, Imanuel. *Nomologia, o discursos legales.* Amsterdam, 1629.

Aboab, Isaac. *Menorat ha-ma'or.* See Hages.

Aboab, Samuel b. Abraham. *Debar Shemuel.* Venice, 1702.

——— *Sefer ha-zikronot.* n.p., n.d.

——— See also Mortara.

Abravanel, Isaac. *Ma'ayene ha-yeshu'ah.* Amsterdam, 1647.

——— *Mashmi'a yeshu'ah.* Offenbach, 1767.

Adret, Solomon b. Abraham ibn. *She'elot u-teshubot.* Pts. I-III, New York, 1958. Pt. V, Leghorn, 1825.

Albo, Joseph. *Sefer ha-'ikkarim,* ed. and tr. by Isaac Husik. 4 vols. in 5. Philadelphia, 1946.

Almansa y Mendoza, Andrés de. *Relacion del auto publico de la Fè que se celebro en esta Corte, Domingo 21 de Enero de 1624.* Madrid, 1624.

Almeida, Christovam d'. *Sermam do dezagravo de Christo Sacramentado na Igreja de Santa Engracia.* Lisbon, 1671.

Altaras, Mosé. *Libro de mantenimiento de la alma, en el qual se contiene el modo con que se à de regir el Iudio en todas sus actiones.* Venice, 1609.

Amarillo, Solomon. *Kerem Shelomo.* Salonika, 1719.

Anguiano, Fray Matheo. *La nueva Jerusalen, en que la perfidia hebraica reitero con nuevas ultrages la passion de Christo, Salvador del mundo, en su sacrosanta imagen del Crucifixo de la Paciencia en Madrid.* Madrid, 1709.

Antonio, Nicolás. *Bibliotheca hispana.* 2 vols. Rome, 1672.

——— *Bibliotheca hispana nova.* 2 vols. Madrid, 1783–88.

Arias, Joseph Semah, tr. *Respuesta de Josepho contra Apion Alexandrino.* Amsterdam, 1687.

Atias (Athias), Ishac. *Thesoro de preceptos, adonde se encierran las joyas de los seys cientos y treze preceptos, que encomendó el Señor a su Pueblo Israel.* Amsterdam, 1649.

Augustine (Aurelius Augustinus), Saint. *La Cité de Dieu (De civitate Dei).* Latin text, with French tr. by G. Combès. 5 vols. (*Œuvres de Saint Augustin,* vols. 33–37.) Paris, 1959–60.

——— *De doctrina Christiana.* In Migne, *PL,* vol. XXXIV.

——— *De Trinitate.* In Migne, *PL,* vol. XLII.

Bibliography

Autos sacramentales desde su origen hasta fines del siglo XVII, ed. E. González Pedroso (*B.A.E.*, vol. LXVIII.) Madrid, 1924.

Ayala Fajardo, Juan de. *Oracion panegirica Christo desagraviado de los oprobrios que unos Hebreos le hizieron en su Sacrosanta Imagen*. Madrid, 1639.

Barbosa Machado, Diogo. *Bibliotheca Lusitana, historica, critica e cronologica*. 4 vols. Lisbon, 1741–59.

Barnett, Lionel D., tr. *El libro de los acuerdos: Being the Records . . . of the Spanish and Portuguese Synagogue of London, 1663–1681*. Oxford, 1931.

Barrionuevo de Peralta, Jerónimo de. *Avisos de D. Jerónimo Barrionuevo*, ed. A. Paz y Mélia. 4 vols. Madrid, 1892.

Barrios, Miguel (Daniel Levi) de. *Arbol de la vida*. Amsterdam, 1689.

———— *Coro de las Musas*. Brussels, 1672.

———— *Relación de los poetas y escritores de la Nación Judayca Amstelodama*. See Kayserling.

———— *Triumpho del govierno popular en la Casa de Jacob*. n.p., n.d.

Barros, João de. *Diálogo Evangélico sobre os artigos da Fé contra o Talmud dos Judeus*, ed. I. S. Révah. Lisbon, 1950.

———— *Ropica Pnefma*, ed. I. S. Révah. 2 vols. Lisbon, 1952.

Bartolocci, Giulio. *Bibliotheca magna rabbinica*. 4 vols. Rome, 1675–93.

Basnage, Jacob Christian. *Histoire des Juifs depuis Jésus Christ jusqu'à présent*. 15 vols. The Hague, 1716–26.

Basso, Sebastian. *Philosophiae naturalis adversus Aristotelem libri XII*. Geneva, 1621.

Bauhin, Gaspard (Caspar). *De hermaphroditorum monstrosorumq. partuum natura, ex theologorum, jureconsultorum, medicorum, philosophorum & rabbinorum sententia*. Oppenheim, 1614.

Bell'haver, Tommaso. *Dottrina facile e breve per ridurre l'Hebreo al conoscimento del vero Messia*. Venice, 1608.

Bene, Judah del. *Kis'ot le-Bet David*. Verona, 1646.

Benetelli, Luigi Maria. *Le saette di Gionata scagliate a favor degli ebrei*. Venice, 1704.

Bérigard, Claude Guillermet de. *Circuli Pisani, seu de veterum et peripat. philosophia dialogi*. Udine, 1643–47.

Bocarro Francês, Manoel. *Anacephaleoses da monarchia Luzitana*. Lisbon, 1624.

Boton, Jacob de. *'Edut be-Ya'akob*. Salonika, 1720.

Brieli, Judah. See Mortara.

Buxtorf, Johann. *Synagoga Iudaica*. Hanover, 1604.

Cansino, Jacob, ed. *Extremos y grandezas de Constantinopla, compuesto por Rabi Moysen Almosnino, Hebreo*. Madrid, 1638.

Cantarini, Isaac Hayyim (Vita). *Paḥad Yiṣḥak*. Amsterdam, 1685.

Cardoso, Abraham (Miguel). See Section III: Bernheimer, Molho, Scholem.

Cardoso, Fernando [Isaac]. *De febre syncopali*. Madrid, 1639.

———— *Discurso sobre el Monte Vesuvio*. Madrid, 1632.

———— *Oración funebre en la muerte de Lope de Vega*. Madrid, 1635.

———— *Utilidades del agua i de la nieve, del bever frio i caliente*. Madrid, 1637.

————, Isaac [Fernando]. *Las excelencias de los Hebreos*. Amsterdam, 1679.

———— *Philosophia libera in septem libros distributa*. Venice, 1673.

———— See also Mortara.

Cartas de algunos PP. de la Compañia de Jesus sobre los sucesos de la monarquia entre los años de 1634 y 1648. In *Memorial Histórico Español*, vols. XIII–XIX. Madrid, 1861–65.

Castro, Benedict de. *Flagellum calumniantium*. Amsterdam, 1631.

Castro, Isaac de. *Sobre o principio e restauração do mundo*. Amsterdam, 1612.

Castro, João de. *Paraphrase et concordançia de algũas propheçias de Bandarra, çapateiro de Trancoso*. Facsimile ed. Porto, 1942.

Clement of Alexandria (Clemens Alexandrinus). *Les Stromates (Stromata)*, ed. and tr. into French by Marcel Caster. 2 vols. Paris, 1951–54.

Cohen, Tobias. *Maʼaseh Tobiah*. Venice, 1707.

Colección de los autos generales y particulares de fe, celebrados por el tribunal de la Inquisición de Córdoba, anotados y dados a luz en 1836 por el Lic. Gaspar Matute y Luquin. Madrid, 1912.

Corcos, Tranquillo Vita. *Alla sagra consulta Illustriss. e Reverendiss. Monsig. Ghezzi ponente per l'Università degl'Hebrei di Roma: Sommario*. Rome, 1706.

Cordeiro, Jacinto. *Elogio de poetas lusitanos, al Fenix de España Fr. Lope Felix de Vega Carpio en su Laurel de Apolo*. Lisbon, 1631.

Costa, Uriel da. *Exemplar humanae vitae*. See Limborch, *De veritate*. . . .

Costa Mattos, Vicente da. *Breve discurso contra a heretica perfidia do Iudaismo*. Lisbon, 1623. See also Gavilán Vela.

Cunaeus, Petrus. *De republica Hebraeorum libri III*. Leiden, 1631.

Digby, Sir Kenelm. *Demonstratio immortalitatis animae rationalis sive tractatus duo philosophici*. Paris, 1655.

Dodici maleditioni quali ereditorno gli Hebrei per la morte da loro procurata e data al nostro Signore Giesù Christo sotto l'Imperio di Tiberio Cesare. Perugia, 1617.

Dramáticos contemporáneos de Lope de Vega, ed. R. Mesonero Romanos. Vol. II (B.A.E., vol. XLV). Madrid, 1853.

Enríquez Gómez, Antonio. *Sanson Nazareno, poema heroico*. Rouen, 1656.

Bibliography

Espina, Alonso de. *Fortalitium fidei contra Judeos, Sarracenos, aliosq. christianae fidei inimicos.* Lyon, 1511.

Este, João Baptista d'. *Consolaçam christãa e luz para o povo hebreo.* Lisbon, 1616.

———— *Dialogo entre discipulo e mestre catechizante, onde se resolvem todas as duvidas que os Iudeos obstinados costumão fazer contra a verdade da Fé Catholica.* Lisbon, 1621.

Eusebius Pamphilius of Caesarea. *Eusebii Pamphili, Evangelicae praeparationis, libri XV,* ed. and tr. into English by E. H. Gifford. 4 vols. Oxford, 1903.

Fabricius, Johann Albert. *Bibliographia antiquaria.* Hamburg-Leipzig, 1716.

———— *Bibliotheca graeca.* vol. III. Hamburg, 1708.

———— *Delectus argumentorum et syllabus scriptorum qui veritatem religionis Christianae adversus atheos . . . Judaeos et Muhammedanos lucubrationibus suis asseruerunt.* Hamburg, 1725.

Fernández Villareal, Manuel. *Color verde a la divina Celia.* Madrid, 1637.

Figo, Azariah. *Binah le-'ittim.* Lemberg, 1858.

———— *Sefer gidduley terumah.* Zolkiew, 1809.

Francavilla, Tommaso Luigi. *L'Hebreo trafito dalla propria penna.* Trent, 1693.

Freimann, A., ed. *Inyeney Shabbetay Ṣebi (Sammelband kleiner Schriften über Sabbatai Ẓebi und dessen Anhänger).* Berlin, 1912.

Gaffarel, Jacques. *Curiositates inauditae.* Hamburg, 1706.

Galilei, Galileo. *Discorso del flusso e reflusso del mare,* in *Le opere de Galileo Galilei.* Vol. V. Florence, 1895.

Garibay y Zamálloa, Esteban. *Compendio historial de las chronicas y universal historia de todos los reynos de España.* 4 vols. Barcelona, 1628.

Gassendi, Pierre. *Animadversiones in decimum librum Diogenis Laertii.* 3 vols. Lyon, 1649.

———— *Dissertations en forme de paradoxes contre les Aristoteliciens,* ed. and tr. by B. Rochot. Paris, 1959.

———— *Syntagma philosophicum complectens logicam, physicam et ethicam.* In *Opera omnia,* Vols. I-II. Lyon, 1658.

Gavilán Vela, Diego, tr. *Discurso contra los judíos, traducido de lengua portuguesa en Castellano.* Salamanca, 1631.

Genébrard, Gilbert. *Chronographiae, libri quatuor.* Paris, 1600.

Gershon, Isaac, ed. *Sefer shulḥan ha-panim. Libro llamado en Ladino Mesa de el alma.* (Spanish in Hebrew characters). Venice, 1602.

486

Godínez, Felipe. *Oración funebre en la muerte del doctor Frey Lope Felix de Vega Carpio.* In Lope de Vega, *Obras sueltas*, XX, 147–65.

Gómez de Mora, Juan. *Auto de la Fe celebrado en Madrid este año de MDCXXXII.* Madrid, 1632.

Gómez Solís, Duarte. *Discurso sobre los comercios de las dos Indias*, ed. Moses Bensabat Amzalak. Lisbon, 1943.

Grégoire, l'Abbé Henri. *Essai sur la regénération physique, morale et politique des Juifs.* Metz, 1789.

Gretser, Jakob. *De Sancta Cruce.* In *Opera omnia*, vol. I. Ratisbon, 1734.

Hages, Iahacob, tr. *Almenara de la luz. Tratado de mucho provecho para beneficio del alma, compuesto por . . . Yshac Aboab.* Amsterdam, 1708.

Hagiz, Moses. *Mishnat ḥakamim.* Wandsbeck, 1733.

Halevi, Judah b. Samuel. *Sefer ha-Kuzari*, tr. Judah ibn Tibbon, ed. A. Tzifroni. Tel-Aviv, 1948.

———— See also Abendana.

Hulsius, Anton. *Authentia absoluta S. textus Hebraei vindicata.* Rotterdam, 1662.

———— *Disputatio epistolaris hebraica inter Antonium Hulsium . . . et Jacobum Abendanah . . . super loco Haggaei cap. 2 v. 9.* Leiden, 1669.

Illescas, Gonzalo de. *Historia pontifical y catholica.* Barcelona, 1589.

Imbonati, Carlo Giussepi. *(Shema Yisrael): Adventus messiae a Iudaeorum blasphemiis, ac haereticorum calumniis vindicatus.* Rome, 1694.

Index librorum prohibitorum (by date):

Index et catalogus librorum prohibitorum, mandato Illustriss. ac Reverendiss. D.D. Gasparis a Quiroga. Madrid, 1583.

Index librorum expurgatorum . . . D.D. Gasparis Quiroga. Madrid, 1584.

Index librorum prohibitorum et expurgatorum Ill^{mi}. ac R^{mi}. D.D. Bernardi de Sandoval et Roxas. Madrid, 1612.

Index auctorum damnatae memoriae . . . editus Illmi. Domini D. Ferdinandi Martins Mascaregnas. Lisbon, 1624.

Index librorum prohibitorum et expurgandorum novissimus, pro Catholicis Hispaniarum Regnis Philippi IV, Regis Cathol., Ill. ac R. D.D. Antonii a Sotomaior. Madrid, 1640. Reprint: "Madrid" (Lyon?), 1667.

Jerome (Hieronymus), Saint. *Commentarium in Isaiam Prophetam.* In Migne, *PL*, vol. XXIV.

———— *In Lamentationes Jeremiae Tractatus.* In Migne, *PL*, vol. XXV.

———— *Lettres*, ed. and tr. by Jérôme Labourt. 6 vols. Paris, 1949-58.

———— *Quaestiones in Genesim.* In Migne, *PL*, vol. XXIII.

Jesurun, Isaac. *Livro da Providencia Divina.* Amsterdam, 1663.

Bibliography

Jiménez de Rada, Rodrigo. *De rebus Hispaniae*. In Andreas Schott, *Hispaniae illustratae*, II (Frankfurt, 1603), 25–148.

Josephus Flavius. *Works*, ed. and tr. by H. St. J. Thackeray and R. Marcus, 9 vols. Cambridge, 1926–58.

——— See also Arias.

Justin Martyr. *The Writings of Justin Martyr and Athenagoras*, tr. M. Dods *et al.* Edinburgh, 1867.

Kayserling, Meyer, ed. "Une histoire de la littérature juive de Daniel Lévi de Barrios," *REJ*, XVIII (1889), 276–89.

Leb, Joseph ibn. *She'elot u-teshubot*. Amsterdam, 1762.

León Pinelo, Antonio de. *Epitome de la biblioteca oriental i occidental, nautica i geografica*. Madrid, 1629.

Liceti, Fortunio. *De pietate Aristotelis erga Deum et homines, libri duo*. Ultini, 1645.

Limborch, Philip van. *De veritate religionis Christianae amica collatio cum erudito Judaeo*. Gouda, 1687.

——— *Historia Inquisitionis*. Amsterdam, 1692.

Lusitano, Estrella, pseud. *La Machabea*. Leon, 1604.

Luzzato, Simone (Simḥa). *Ma'amar 'al Yehudey Veneṣia* (Hebrew tr. by D. Lattes of the *Discorso circa il stato de gl'Hebrei*, with introductions by M. A. Shulwass and R. B. Bacchi). Jerusalem, 1951.

Magnen, Jean Chrysostome. *Democritus reviviscens, sive de atomis; addita Democriti vita et philosophia*. Pavia, 1646.

Maimonides, Moses. *Doctor perplexorum*, tr. Johann Buxtorf. Basel, 1629.

——— *Dux seu Director dubitantium aut perplexorum*. Paris, 1520.

——— *'Iggeret Teman (Epistle to Yemen)*, ed. Abraham Halkin, tr. Boaz Cohen. New York, 1952.

——— *Mishneh Torah*. 5 vols. Vilna, 1928.

——— *Moreh nebukim*. Hebrew text ed. Yehudah ibn Shemuel. Jerusalem, 1947.

Majolus (Maiolus), Simon. *Dies caniculares*. Mainz, 1614.

Manasseh ben Israel. *De resurrectione mortuorum, libri III*. Amsterdam, 1636.

——— *De termino vitae, libri III; quibus veterum Rabbinorum, ac recentium doctorum, de hac controversia sententia explicatur*. Amsterdam, 1639.

——— *Esperança de Israel*. Amsterdam, 1650. See also Wolf.

——— [Libri IV de immortalitate animae.] *Nishmat ḥayyim*. Amsterdam, 1651.

——— *Thesouro dos Dinim*. 5 pts. Amsterdam, 1645–47.

——— *To His Highnesse the Lord Protector of the Commonwealth of England,*

Scotland and Ireland, the Humble Addresses of . . . in behalfe of the Jewish Nation. Amsterdam, 1655. See also Wolf.

———— *Vindiciae Judaeorum, or a Letter in Answer to Certain Questions . . . Touching the Reproaches Cast on the Nation of the Jewes.* London, 1656. See also Wolf.

Maracci, Lodovico. *L'ebreo preso per le buone.* Rome, 1701.

Mariana, Juan de. *Historia general de España.* 2 vols. Madrid, 1678.

Márquez, Juan. *El gobernador Christiano.* Salamanca, 1612.

Mascarenhas, Fernando. See *Index librorum prohibitorum,* 1624.

Meldola, Rafael. *Mayim rabbim.* Amsterdam, 1737.

Mello, Francisco Manoel de. *Cartas familiares,* ed. M. Rodrigues Lapa. Lisbon, 1942.

———— *Tratado da sciencia Cabala.* Lisbon, 1724.

Méndez Silva, Rodrigo. *Catalogo Real genealogico de España.* Madrid, 1639.

———— *Chatalogo Real de España.* Madrid, 1637.

———— *Poblacion general de España.* Madrid, 1645.

Misuracci, Iulio Cesare. *Ragionamento della venuta del Messia contro la durezza ed ostinatione Ebraica.* Orvieto, 1629.

Modena, Leone. *Kitbe ha-Rab Yehudah Aryeh mi-Modena (Leone Modena's Briefe und Schriftstücke),* ed. Ludwig Blau. Budapest, 1905.

———— *Sefer 'ari nohem,* ed. Julius Fürst. Leipzig, 1840.

———— "Sefer Ben-David." In Eliezer b. Solomon Ashkenazi, *Ta'am zekenim,* ed. R. Kirchheim. Frankfurt, 1854.

Morosini, Giulio. *Via della Fede mostrata a'gli Ebrei.* 3 vols. Rome, 1683.

Morpurgo, *Sefer shemesh ṣedakah.* Venice, 1743.

Mortara, Marco, ed. "Isaac Cardoso et Samuel Aboab" (exchange of letters between the two), *REJ,* XII (1886), 301–5.

———— Poem of Judah Brieli on the *Excelencias,* and reply of Cardoso, in: *Ozar Nechmad,* III (1860), 167 f.

Morteira, Saul Levi. *Gib'at Sha'ul.* Warsaw, 1912.

Moscardo, Lodovico. *Historia di Verona.* Verona, 1668.

Moscato, Judah. *Nefuṣot Yehudah.* Warsaw, 1871.

Neubauer, Adolf, ed. *The Fifty-Third Chapter of Isaiah, according to the Jewish Interpreters.* 2 vols. Oxford, 1876–77.

Nicholas of Cusa. *De docta ignorantia libri tres,* ed. P. Rotta. Bari, 1913.

Nieto, David. *De la Divina Providencia.* London, 1704.

———— *Matteh Dan y segunda parte del Cuzari.* London, 1714.

Nieva Calvo, Sebastián de. *El Niño Inocente, hijo de Toledo y martir en La Guardia.* Toledo, 1628.

Novoa, Matías de. *Memorias de Matías de Novoa, ayuda de cámara de Fe-*

Bibliography

lipe IV. 6 vols. (*Colección de documentos inéditos para la historia de España,* LX-LXI, LXIX, LXXVII, LXXX, LXXXVI.) Madrid, 1875 et seq.

Orden de oraciones . . . estampado . . . por yndustria del Doctor Effraim Bueno y Ionas Abravanel. Amsterdam, 1648.

Origen (Origenes), Adamantius, St. *Homélies sur Josué (In Josuam homiliae),* ed. and tr. by Annie Jaubert. Paris, 1960.

Orobio de Castro, Isaac (Balthasar). *Israel vengé, ou exposition naturelle des propheties hebraïques que les Chrétiens appliquent à Jésus, leur prétendu Messie.* London, 1770.

———— *La observancia de la Divina Ley de Mosseh,* ed. M. B. Amzalak. Coimbra, 1925.

Patrizi, Francesco. *Discussionum Peripateticarum tomi IV.* 4 vols. Basel, 1581.

———— *Nova de universis philosophia.* Ferrara, 1591.

Pellicer de Tovar, Joseph (José). *Anfiteatro de Felipe el Grande.* Madrid, 1631.

———— *Avisos históricos que comprehenden las noticias y sucesos particulares ocurridos en nuestra monarquía desde el año de 1639.* In *Semanario erudito.* vols. XXXI-XXXIII. Madrid, 1790.

Peña, Juan Antonio de. *Discurso en exaltacion de los improperios que padecio la imagen de Cristo à manos de la perfidia Iudaica.* Madrid, 1632.

Peñalosa y Mondragón, Fray Benito de. *Libro de las cinco excelencias del Español.* Pamplona, 1629.

Penso de la Vega, Joseph. *Discurso académico, moral y sagrado, hecho en la insigne Academia de los Sitibundos.* Amsterdam, 1683.

———— *Discursos académicos, morales, retóricos y sagrados, que recitó en la florida Academia de los Floridos.* Antwerp, 1685.

———— *Rumbos peligrosos.* Antwerp, 1684.

Pereira, Gómez. *Antoniana Margarita, opus nempe physicis, medicis et theologis, non minus utile quam necessarium.* N.p., 1554. (*Non vidi.*)

Pereyra, Abraham Israel. *La certeza del camino.* Amsterdam, 1666.

Pérez de Montalván, Juan. *El Polifemo, auto sacramental.* N.p., n.d. (Madrid, 1628?).

————, ed. *Fama pósthuma a la vida y muerte del Doctor Frey Lope Felix de Vega Carpio.* Madrid, 1636.

———— *Para todos.* Huesca, 1633.

Pérez de Valencia, Jaime. *Tractatus contra Iudaeos.* Valencia, 1484.

Pichi, Pietro. *Epistola agli Hebrei dell'Italia, nella quale si dimostra la vanita della loro penitenza et aspetazione del Messia.* Rome, 1622.

Pico della Mirandola, Giovanni Francesco. *Examen vanitatis doctrinae gentium et veritatis Christianae disciplinae.* Mirandola, 1520.

Pinedo, Tomás de, ed. *Stephanus de urbibus.* Amsterdam, 1678.

Pomis, David de. *De medico Hebraeo enarratio apologica.* Venice, 1588.

Portaleone, Abraham. *Shiltey ha-gibborim.* Mantua, 1612.

Quevedo Villegas, Francisco de. *Obras,* ed. A. Fernández-Guerra y Orbe (B.A.E., vols. XXIII, XLVIII, LXIX). Madrid, 1852, 1859, 1877.

Quiñones de Benavente, Juan de. *Discurso contra los gitanos.* Madrid, 1631.

———— *El Monte Vesuvio, aora la montaña de Soma.* Madrid, 1632.

———— *Memorial de los servicios que hizo al Rey Don Felipe III nuestro Señor, que santa gloria aya, y que ha hecho a V. magestad, que Dios guarde.* Madrid, 1643.

Quiroga, Gaspar de. See *Index librorum prohibitorum,* 1583, 1584.

Relación del auto de la fe que se celebró en Madrid Domingo a quatro de Julio de MDCXXXII. N.p., n.d. (Madrid, 1632).

Reinach, Théodore, ed. *Textes d'auteurs grecs et romains relatifs au Judaisme.* Paris, 1895.

Ricius, Augustinus. *De motu octavae spherae.* Paris, 1521.

Río, Martin del. *Disquisitionum magicarum, libri sex.* Lyon, 1604.

Rodrigues de Castro, Estêvão. *De meteoris microcosmi, libri quatuor.* Florence, 1621.

Saadia b. Joseph (Gaon). *Sefer ha-'emunot veha-de'ot.* Constantinople, 1861.

Salazar de Mendoza, Pedro. *Chronica de el gran cardenal de España Don Pedro Gonçalez de Mendoça.* Toledo, 1625.

Salucio, Augustín. *Discurso . . . acerca de la justicia y buen gobierno de España en los estatutos de limpieza de sangre.* In *Semanario erudito,* vol. XV. Madrid, 1788.

Sandoval y Rojas, Bernardo de. See *Index librorum prohibitorum,* 1612.

Sasportas, Jacob. *'Ohel Ya'akob.* Amsterdam, 1737.

———— *Sefer Ṣiṣat nobel Ṣebi,* ed. I. Tishby. Jerusalem, 1954.

Sefer meribat kodesh. See Freimann.

Sennert, Daniel. *Hypomnemata physica.* In *Opera omnia,* vol. I. Paris, 1641.

Silveyra, Miguel de. *El Macabeo, poema heroico.* Naples, 1638.

Sixtus Senensis. *Bibliotheca sancta.* Cologne, 1586.

Sotomayor, Antonio de. See *Index librorum prohibitorum,* 1640.

Spinoza, Benedict. *Tractatus Theologico-Politicus,* ed. Carl Gebhardt. Heidelberg, 1926.

Sylva (Silva), Samuel da. *Tratado de la thesuvah.* Amsterdam, 1613.

Bibliography

Telesio, Bernardino. *De natura iuxta propria principia.* Rome, 1565.

Tena, Luis de. *Isagoge in totam S. Scripturaram.* Barcelona, 1620.

Tineti, Aloysio. *Apologia della Fede contro l'ostinazione Hebraica.* Venice, 1627.

Torrejoncillo, Francisco de. *Centinela contra judíos.* Pamplona, 1691.

Trani, Joseph. *She'elot u-teshubot.* Venice, 1645.

Tuy, Lucas de. *Chronicon mundi.* In Andreas Schott, *Hispaniae illustratae,* IV (Frankfurt, 1608), 1–116.

Usiel, Jacob. *David, poema eroïco.* Venice, 1624.

Usque, Samuel. *Consolaçam as tribulaçoens de Israel,* ed. J. Mendes dos Remédios. 3 vols. Coimbra, 1906–8. (English tr.: *Consolation for the Tribulations of Israel,* tr. Martin Cohen. Philadelphia, 1965.)

Vega Carpio, Lope Félix de. *Cartas completas.* 2 vols. Buenos Aires, 1948.

―――― *Colección de las obras sueltas, assi en prosa, como en verso, de d. frey Lope Felix de Vega Carpio.* 21 vols. Madrid, 1776–79.

―――― *Obras . . . publicadas por la Real Academia Española.* 15 vols. Madrid, 1890–1913. New ed., *Obras dramáticas.* 13 vols. Madrid, 1913–1930.

Verga, Solomon Ibn. *Shebet Yehudah,* ed. A. Shohat. Jerusalem, 1957.

Vieira, Padre António. *Cartas do P.e António Vieira,* ed. Mário Gonçalves Viana. Porto, n.d.

―――― *Obras escolhidas,* ed. António Sérgio and Hernâni Cidade. 12 vols. Lisbon, 1951–54.

―――― *Obras inéditas.* 3 vols. Lisbon, 1856.

Vincenti, Giovanni Maria. *Il Mesia venuto. Istoria spiegata e provata agli Ebrei.* Venice, 1659.

Viva, Isaac, pseud. *Vindex sanguinis, sive vindiciae secundum veritatem quibus Judaei ab infanticidiis & victima humana, contra Jacobum Geusium, vindicantur.* Amsterdam, 1681. See Wülfer.

Wagenseil, Johann Christoph. *Benachrichtigung wegen einiger die gemeine Judischheit betreffenden Sachen.* Altdorf, 1707.

Wolf, Lucien, ed. *Menasseh ben Israel's Mission to Oliver Cromwell: being a reprint of the pamphlets published by Menasseh ben Israel to promote the readmission of the Jews to England.* London, 1901.

Wülfer, Johann, ed. and tr. *Theriaca Judaica ad examen revocata, sive scripta amoibaea Samuelis Friderici Brenzii . . . & Salomonis Zevi . . . accessit . . . Isaaci Vivae Vindex Sanguinis contra Jacobum Geusium.* Nürnberg, 1681.

Ximenes de Aragão, Fernão. *Doutrina Catholica para instrucção e cõfirmação dos fieis, e extincção das seitas supersticiosas, e em particular do Iudaismo.* Lisbon, 1625.

Yahya, Gedaliah ibn. *Shalshelet ha-kabbalah.* Venice, 1586.

Yehuda b. Barzilay al-Barceloni. *Perush Sefer Yeṣirah,* ed. S. Z. H. Halberstamm. Berlin, 1885.

Yepes, Rodrigo de. *Historia de la muerte y glorioso martyrio del Sancto Inocente que llaman de La Guardia.* Madrid, 1583.

Zaḥalon, Yom Tob. *She'elot u-teshubot.* Venice, 1694.

III. SECONDARY WORKS

Adler, Elkan N. "Documents sur les marranes d'Espagne et de Portugal sous Philippe IV," *REJ,* XLVIII (1904), 1–28; XLIX (1904), 51–73; L (1905), 53–75; LI (1906), 251–64.

Ajo G. y Sainz de Zuñiga, C. Mª. *Historia de las universidades hispánicas.* 3 vols. Ávila, 1958.

Alcocer Martínez, Mariano. *Anales universitarios: Historia de la Universidad de Valladolid.*

I. *Libro de Bezerro.* Valladolid, 1918.

III. *Expedientes de provisiones de cátedras.* Valladolid, 1921.

VII. *Bio-bibliografías de médicos notables.* Valladolid, 1931.

Alonso Cortés, Narciso. *Miscelánea Vallesolitana.* 3d series. Valladolid, 1921; 5th series, Valladolid, 1930.

—— "Pleitos de los Cepedas," *Boletín de la Real Academia Española,* XXV (1946), 85–110.

Amador de los Ríos, José. *Estudios históricos, políticos y literarios sobre los judíos en España.* Madrid, 1848.

—— *Historia social política y religiosa de los judíos de España y Portugal.* 3 vols. Madrid, 1875–76. Reprint (1 vol.), Madrid, 1960.

Amzalak, Moses Bensabat. *A tradução espanhola do livro de Joseph Caro . . . feita por Mosé Altaras sob a denominação de 'Libro de mantenimiento de la alma.'* Lisbon, 1927.

Archivo Histórico Nacional (Madrid). *Catálogo de las causas contra la fe seguidas ante el Tribunal del Santo Oficio de la Inquisición de Toledo.* Madrid, 1903.

—— *Consejo de Castilla. Sala de Alcaldes de Casa y Corte: Catálogo por materias.* Madrid, 1925.

Asensio, Eugenio. "El erasmismo y las corrientes espirituales afines," *Revista de filología española,* XXXVI (1952), 31–99.

Assaf, Simḥa. *Be-'oholey Ya'akob* (In Jacob's Tents. A collection of scholarly essays). Jerusalem, 1943.

Bibliography

—— "The Marranos of Spain and Portugal in the Responsa Literature" (Hebrew), *Me'assef Zion*, V, 19–61.

Azevedo, João Lúcio d'. "A evolução do Sebastianismo," *AHP*, X (1916), 379–473. (Also published separately. Lisbon, 1918.)

—— *História de António Vieira*. 2 vols. Lisbon, 1918–21.

—— *História dos Christãos-Novos portugueses*. Lisbon, 1921.

Azevedo, Pedro A. d'. "Médicos Cristãos Novos que se ausentaram de Portugal no princípio do século XVII," *Arquivos de história da medicina portuguesa* (N.S.), V (1914), 153–72.

—— "O Bocarro Francês e os Judeus de Cochim e Hamburgo," *AHP*, VIII (1910), 15–20, 185–98.

Bacon, George William. "The Life and Dramatic Works of Doctor Juan Pérez de Montalván (1602–1638)," *Revue hispanique*, XXVI (1912), 1–474.

Baer, Yitzhak (Fritz). *Die Juden im Christlichen Spanien*. Vol. II: *Kastillien/ Inquisitionsakten*. Berlin, 1936.

—— *Galut*. New York, 1947.

—— *Toledot ha-Yehudim bi-Sefarad ha-noṣrit*. Tel-Aviv, 1965. (English tr.: *A History of the Jews in Christian Spain*. 2 vols. Philadelphia, 1961–66).

—— *Untersuchungen über Quellen und Komposition des Schebet Jehuda*. Berlin, 1923.

Baião, António. *Episódios dramáticos da Inquisição portuguesa*. 3 vols. Porto, 1919; Rio de Janeiro, 1924; Lisbon, 1938.

Baron, Salo W. "A Communal Conflict in Verona" (Hebrew), in *Sefer ha-yobel le-Prof. S. Kraus* (Jerusalem, 1937), pp. 217–54.

—— *A Social and Religious History of the Jews*. 1st ed., 3 vols. New York, 1937; 2d, rev. ed. (in progress), 12 vols. New York, 1952– .

Barrera, Cayetano Alberto de la. *Nueva biografía de Lope de Vega* (= *Obras de Lope de Vega*, ed. Real Academia Española, vol. I). Madrid, 1890.

Barzilay, Isaac. *Between Reason and Faith: Anti-Rationalism in Italian Jewish Thought 1250–1650*. The Hague-Paris, 1967.

Bataillon, Marcel. *Érasme et l'Espagne: Recherches sur l'histoire spirituelle du XVIᵉ siècle*. Paris, 1937.

Bell, Aubrey. *Benito Arias Montano*. Oxford, 1922.

Benayahu, Meir. "News from Italy and Holland on the Beginning of Sabbatianism" (Hebrew), *Ereṣ Yisrael*, IV (1956), 194–205.

Bernheimer, Carlo. "Some New Contributions to Abraham Cardoso's Biography," *JQR* (N.S.), XVIII (1927–28), 97–129.

494

Braamcamp Freire, Anselmo. "Tombo da comarca da Beira," *AHP*, X (1916), 209–366.

Braga, Theophilo. *História de Camoes Parte II: Eschola de Camoẽs*. Porto, 1874.

Browe, Peter. *Die Judenmission im Mittelalter und die Päpste*. Rome, 1942.

Brugmans, H. K., and A. Frank. *Geschiedenis der Joden in Nederland*. Pt. I (no more published). Amsterdam, 1940.

Caro Baroja, Julio. *La sociedad criptojudia en la corte de Felipe IV*. Madrid, 1963.

——— *Los judíos en la España moderna y contemporánea*. 3 vols. Madrid, 1962.

Cassuto, Alfonso. "Neue Funde zur ältesten Geschichte der portugiesischen Juden in Hamburg," *ZGJD*, III (1931), 58–72.

——— "Notes sur Pedro alias Ezechiele de Castro," *REJ*, XCIII (1932), 215–17.

Castro, Américo. *The Structure of Spanish History*. Princeton, 1954.

Castro y Rossi, Adolfo de. *El Conde-Duque de Olivares y el rey Felipe IV*. Cádiz, 1846.

——— *Historia de los judíos de España*. Cádiz, 1847.

——— "Noticias de la vida del doctor Felipe Godínez," *Memorias de la Real Academia Española*, VIII (1902), 277–83.

Chinchilla, Anastasio. *Anales históricos de la medicina en general, y biográfico-bibliográficos de la española en particular: I. Historia de la medicina española*. Valencia, 1841.

Chwolson, Daniel. *Die Blutanklage und sonstige mittelalterliche Beschuldigungen*. Frankfurt, 1901.

Cirac Estopañan, Sebastián. *Registros de los documentos del Santo Oficio de Cuenca y Sigüenza, I: Registro general de los procesos de delitos y de los expedientes de limpieza*. Cuenca-Barcelona, 1965.

Cohen, Gerson D. Review of B. Netanyahu's *The Marranos of Spain*, in *Jewish Social Studies*, XXIX (1967), 178–84.

Curtius, E. R. *European Literature in the Latin Middle Ages*, tr. W. R. Trask. New York, 1963.

Deleito y Piñuela, José. *La vida religiosa española bajo el cuarto Felipe*. Madrid, 1952.

Dijksterhuis, E. J. *The Mechanization of the World Picture*. Oxford, 1961.

Domínguez Ortiz, Antonio. "El proceso inquisitorial de Juan Nuñez Saravía, banquero de Felipe IV," *Hispania*, no. 61 (1955), pp. 559–81.

——— *La clase social de los conversos en Castilla en la edad moderna*. Madrid, 1955.

——— *Política y hacienda de Felipe IV*. Madrid, 1960.

Bibliography

Entrambasaguas y Peña, Joaquín de. *Una guerra literaria del Siglo de Oro: Lope de Vega y los preceptistas aristotélicos.* Madrid, 1932.

Esaguy, Augusto d'. *Apontamentos da história da medicina.* Lisbon, 1931.

Farinelli, Arturo. *Marrano: storia di un vituperio.* Geneva, 1925.

Febrero Lorenzo, María Anunciación. *La pedagogía de los colegios mayores a través de su legislación en el Siglo de Oro.* Madrid, 1960.

Friedenwald, Harry. *Jewish Luminaries in Medical History, and a Catalogue of Works bearing on the Subject of the Jews and Medicine from the Private Library of Harry Friedenwald.* Baltimore, 1946.

———— *The Jews and Medicine.* 2 vols. Baltimore, 1944.

Gallardo, Bartolomé José. *Ensayo de una biblioteca española de libros raros y curiosos.* 4 vols. Madrid, 1863–89.

García Peres, Domingo. *Catálogo razonado biográfico y bibliográfico de los autores portugueses que escribieron en castellano.* Madrid, 1890.

Gebhardt, Carl. *Die Schriften des Uriel da Costa.* Amsterdam, 1922.

———— "Juan de Prado," *Chronicon Spinozanum,* III (1923), 269–91.

Gilson, Etienne. *Les idées et les lettres.* Paris, 1932.

Ginsberg, C. D., ed. *Massoreth ha-Massoreth* (by Elias Levita). London, 1867.

Ginsburger, Ernest. "Pedro alias Ezechiele de Castro," *REJ,* XCIV (1933), 90–95.

Girard, Albert. *Le commerce français à Séville et Cadix au temps des Hapsbourg.* Paris, 1932.

Glaser, Edward. "Invitation to Intolerance: A Study of the Portuguese Sermons Preached at Autos-da-fé," *HUCA,* XXVII (1956), 327–85.

———— "Lope de Vega's 'El Niño Inocente de la Guardia'," *Bulletin of Hispanic Studies* (Liverpool), XXXII (1955), 140–53.

———— "Miguel da Silveira's 'El Macabeo'," *Bulletin des études portugaises et de l'Institut Français en Portugal,* XXI (1959), 5–41.

———— "Referencias antisemitas en la literatura peninsular de la Edad de Oro," *Nueva revista de filología hispánica,* VIII (1954), 39–62.

Gonzáles y Díaz Tuñón, Zeferino (Çeferino). *Historia de la filosofía.* 4 vols. Madrid, 1886.

Gottheil, Richard J. H. "The Jews and the Spanish Inquisition (1622–1721)," *JQR* (O.S.), XV (1903), 182–250.

Grabmann, Martin. *Mittelalterliches Geistesleben,* vol. II. Munich, 1936.

Graetz, Heinrich. *Geschichte der Juden.* 11 vols. Leipzig, 1897–1911.

Guidetti, Corrado. *Pro Judeis: riflessioni e documenti.* Turin, 1884.

Herculano, Alexandre. *Da origem e estabelecimento da Inquisição em Portugal.* 3 vols. Lisbon, 1854–59.

Hernández Morejón, Antonio. *Historia bibliográfica de la medicina española.* 7 vols. Madrid, 1842–52.

Herrero García, Miguel. *Ideas de los españoles del Siglo XVII.* Madrid, 1928.

Hirsch, August. *Biographisches Lexikon der Hervorragenden Aerzte aller Zeiten und Voelker.* 6 vols. Vienna-Leipzig, 1884–88.

Hopper, Vincent, F. *Medieval Number Symbolism.* New York, 1938.

Hume, Martin. *The Court of Philip IV: Spain in Decadence.* London, 1907. New ed. New York, n.d.

Johnston-Lavis, Henry James. *Bibliography of the Geology and Eruptive Phenomena of the more important Volcanos of Southern Italy.* 2d ed. London, 1918.

Kargen, Robert Hugh. *Atomism in England from Hariot to Newton.* Oxford, 1966.

Kaufmann, David. "Lazarus de Viterbo's Epistle to Cardinal Sirleto Concerning the Integrity of the Hebrew Bible," *JQR* (O.S.), VII (1895), 278–96.

Kayserling, Meyer. *Biblioteca Española-Portugueza-Judaica.* Strassbourg, 1890.

—— *Geschichte der Juden in Portugal.* Leipzig, 1867.

—— *Sephardim: Romanische Poesien der Juden in Spanien.* Leipzig, 1859.

—— "Thomas de Pinedo, eine Biographie," *MGWJ*, VII (1858), 191–202.

Kellenbenz, Hermann. "Dr. Jakob Rosales," *Zeitschrift für Religions- und Geistesgeschichte*, VIII (1956), 345–54.

—— *Sephardim an der Unteren Elbe: Ihre Wirtschaftliche und Politische Bedeutung vom Ende des 16. bis zum Beginn des 18. Jahrhunderts.* Wiesbaden, 1958.

King, Willard F. *Prosa novelística y academias literarias en el siglo XVII.* Madrid, 1963.

Kohut, George A. "Jewish Martyrs of the Inquisition in South America," *Publications of the American Jewish Historical Society*, IV (1896), 101–87.

Lasswitz, Kurd. *Geschichte der Atomistik vom Mittelalter bis Newton.* 2 vols. Hamburg, 1892.

Le Hon, M. H. "Eruption du Vésuve de 1631," *Bulletins de l'Academie Royale des Sciences des Lettres et des Beaux Arts de Belgique* (2d series), XX (1865), 483–538.

Lea, Henry Charles. *A History of the Inquisition in the Middle Ages.* 3 vols. London, 1888.

—— *A History of the Inquisition of Spain.* 4 vols. New York, 1907.

497

Bibliography

Leite de Vasconcellos, J. *Etnografía portuguesa*, vol. IV, ed. M. Viegas Guerrero. Lisbon, 1958.

Lemos, Maximiano. *Amato Lusitano: a sua vida e a sua obra*. Porto, 1907.

Lévi, Israel. "L'odeur des juifs," *REJ*, XX (1890), 249 ff.

Levita, Elias. See Ginsberg.

Lewin, Boleslao. "Tomas Trebinio de Sobramonte: the 'Saint of the Jewish Faith' in Mexico" (in Yiddish), *Davke*, IV (Buenos Aires, 1953), 166–204.

Lindo, E. H. *The History of the Jews of Spain and Portugal*. London, 1848.

Löwenstein, Leopold. "Die Familie Aboab," *MGWJ*, XLVII (1904), 661–70.

Mann, Jacob. *Texts and Studies in Jewish History and Literature*. Vol. II: *Karaitica*. Philadelphia, 1935.

Marañón, Gregorio. *El Conde-Duque de Olivares: la pasión de mandar*. 4th ed. Madrid, 1959.

Martins Bastos, Francisco António. *Nobiliarchia medica*. Lisbon, 1858.

Marx, Alexander. "The Polemical Manuscripts in the Library of the Jewish Theological Seminary of America," *Studies in Jewish Bibliography . . . in Memory of Abraham Solomon Freidus* (New York, 1924), pp. 247–79.

Médicos perseguidos por la Inquisición Española. Madrid, 1855.

Medina, José Toribio. *Historia del tribunal del Santo Oficio de la Inquisición de Lima (1569–1820)*. 2 vols. Santiago de Chile, 1887.

Mendes dos Remédios, J. "Os Judeus e os perdões gerais, de D. Manoel ao Cardeal-Rei," *Biblos*, I (1925), 631–55.

———— *Os judeus em Portugal*. I: Coimbra, 1895; II: Lisbon, 1928.

———— *Os judeus portugueses em Amsterdam*. Coimbra, 1911.

Menéndez y Pelayo, Marcelino. *Calderón y su teatro*. Madrid, 1910.

———— *Estudios sobre el teatro de Lope de Vega*. Madrid, 1949.

———— *Historia de las ideas estéticas en España*. 5 vols. Santander, 1947.

———— *Historia de los heterodoxos españoles*. 5 vols. Santander, 1947.

———— *La ciencia española*. 3 vols. Santander, 1953.

Mesonero Romanos, Ramón de. *El antiguo Madrid*. 2 vols. Madrid, 1881.

Molho, Isaac Raphael, and Abraham Amarillo. "Autobiographical Letters of [Abraham] Cardoso" (Hebrew), *Sefunot*, III-IV (1959–60), 183–241.

Netanyahu, B. *Don Isaac Abravanel: Statesman and Philosopher*. Philadelphia, 1953.

———— *The Marranos of Spain from the Late XIVth to the Early XVIth Century According to the Hebrew Sources*. New York, 1966.

Neubauer, Adolf. *Catalogue of the Hebrew MSS. in the Bodleian Library.* Oxford, 1886–1906.

Néves, Alvaro. *Bibliografia Luso-Judaica.* Coimbra, 1913.

Paz y Mélia, A. *Papeles de Inquisición; Catálogo y extractos,* ed. Ramón Paz. Madrid, 1947.

Penney, Clara Louisa. *Printed Books 1468-1700 in the Hispanic Society of America.* New York, 1965.

Pflaum, Hiram. *Die religiöse Disputation in der Europäischen Dichtung des Mittelalters. Erste Studie: Der allegorische Streit zwischen Synagoge und Kirche.* Geneva, 1935.

Posnanski, Adolf. *Schiloh: ein Beitrag zur Geschichte der Messiaslehre.* Leipzig, 1904.

Potthast, A. *Regesta Pontificum Romanorum.* 2 vols. Berlin, 1875.

Ramos-Coelho, José. *Manoel Fernandes Villa Real e o seu processo na Inquisição de Lisboa.* Lisbon, 1894.

Ramos de Oliveira, Manoel. *Celorico da Beira e o seu concelho através da história e da tradição.* Celorico, 1939.

Rennert, Hugo Albert. *The Spanish Stage in the Time of Lope de Vega.* New York, 1909.

———, and Américo Castro. *Vida de Lope de Vega.* Madrid, 1919.

Reusch, F. H. *Der Index der verbotenen Bücher.* 2 vols. Bonn, 1883–86.

Révah, I. S. "Autobiographie d'un Marrane, édition partielle d'un manuscrit de João [Moseh] Pinto Delgado," *REJ,* CXIX (1961), 41–130.

——— "La religion d'Uriel da Costa, Marrane de Porto," *Revue de l'histoire des religions,* CLXI (1962), 45–76.

——— "Les Marranes," *REJ,* CVIII (1959–60), 29–77.

——— "Manoel Fernandes Vilareal, adversaire et victime de l'Inquisition portugaise," *Iberida* (Rio de Janeiro), no. 1 (April, 1959), 33–54; no. 3 (December, 1959), 181–207.

——— *Spinoza et le Dr. Juan de Prado.* Paris, 1959.

——— "Une famille de 'Nouveau-Chrétiens': les Bocarro Francês," *REJ,* CXVI (1957), 73–86.

Reynier, Gustave. *La vie universitaire dans l'ancienne Espagne.* Paris-Toulouse, 1902.

Ribeiro dos Santos, António. "Da litteratura sagrada dos judeos portuguezeses no século XVII," *Memorias de litteratura portugueza publicadas pela Academia Real das Sciencias de Lisboa,* III (1792), 227–373.

Riccio, Luigi. "Nuovi documenti sull'incendio Vesuviano dell'anno 1631," *Archivio storico per le province Napoletane,* XIV (1889), 489–555.

Bibliography

Rivkin, Ellis. "The Utilization of Non-Jewish Sources for the Reconstruction of Jewish History," *JQR* (N.S.), XLVIII (1957–58), 183–203.

Rochot, Bernard. *Les travaux de Gassendi sur Epicure et sur l'atomisme (1619–1658)*. Paris, 1944.

Rodríguez de Castro, Joseph. *Biblioteca española: Tomo primero, que contiene la noticia de los escritores rabinos españoles desde la época conocida de su literatura hasta el presente*. Madrid, 1781.

Rodríguez-Moñino, Antonio. "Les Judaizants à Badajoz de 1499 à 1599," *REJ*, CXV (1956), 73–86.

Rodríguez Villa, A., ed. *La corte y la monarquía de España en los años de 1636 a 1637*. Madrid, 1886.

Roth, Cecil. *A History of the Marranos*. Philadelphia, 1947.

——— "An Elegy of João Pinto Delgado on Isaac de Castro Tartas," *REJ*, CXXI (1962), 355–66.

——— "Encore un mot sur Pedro [Ezekiel] de Castro," *REJ*, XCIV (1933), 96–97.

——— "Immanuel Aboab's Proselytization of the Marranos," *JQR* (N.S.), XXIII (1932–33), 121–62.

——— "La fête de l'institution du ghetto: une célébration particulière à Vérone," *REJ*, LXXIX (1924), 163–69.

——— "Léon de Modène, ses 'Riti Ebraici,' et le Saint-Office à Venise," *REJ*, LXXXVII (1929), 83–88.

——— "Les Marranes à Venise," *REJ*, LXXXIX (1930), 201–23.

——— "Neue Kunde von der Marranengemeinde in Hamburg," *ZGJD*, II (1930), 228–36.

——— "Notes sur les Marranes de Livourne," *REJ*, XCI (1931), 1–27.

——— "Quatre lettres d'Elie de Montalto: contribution à l'histoire des Marranes," *REJ*, LXXXVII (1929), 137–65.

——— "The Religion of the Marranos," *JQR* (N.S.), XXII (1931–32), 1–33.

——— *The Ritual Murder Libel and the Jew*, London, n.d. (1935).

——— "The Strange Case of Hector Mendes Bravo," *HUCA*, XVIII (1943–44), 221–45.

——— "Un dernier mot sur Pedro alias Ezekiel de Castro," *REJ*, XCIV (1933), 82–85.

——— *Venice*. (Jewish Communities Series.) Philadelphia, 1930.

Sainz de Robles, Federico Carlos. *Historia y estampas de la villa de Madrid*, Vol. I. Madrid-Barcelona, 1933.

Sánchez, José. *Academias literarias del Siglo de Oro español*. Madrid, 1961.

Saraiva, António José. *História da cultura em Portugal*. 3 vols. Lisbon, 1950–62.

Schoeps, Hans Joachim. "Isaac Orobio de Castro's Religionsdisput mit Philipp van Limborch," *Judaica*, II (1946–47), 89–105.

—— *Israel und Christenheit*. Munich-Frankfurt, 1961.

Scholem, Gershom. "A Commandment which is Fulfilled through Violation" (Hebrew), *Knesset*, II (1937), 347–92.

—— "A Letter of Abraham Miguel Cardoso to the Rabbis of Smyrna" (Hebrew), *Zion*, XIX (1954), 1–22.

—— "An Italian Note-Book on the Sabbatian Movement in 1666" (Hebrew), *Zion*, X (1945), 55–66.

—— "Contributions to the History of Sabbatianism from the Writings of [Abraham] Cardoso" (Hebrew), *Zion*, VII (1942), 12–28.

—— *Major Trends in Jewish Mysticism*. 3d rev. ed. New York, 1954.

—— "New Contributions to the Study of Abraham Cardoso" (Hebrew), *Abhandlungen zur Erinnerung an Hirsch Perez Chajes* (Vienna, 1933), Hebrew Section, pp. 323–50.

—— *Shabbetay Ṣebi veha-tenu'ah ha-shabbetait biyme ḥayyav* (Sabbatai Zebi and the Sabbatian movement during his lifetime). 2 vols. Tel-Aviv, 1956–57.

—— "Two New Theological Texts of Abraham Cardoso" (Hebrew), *Sefunot*, III-IV (1960), 243–300.

Schwarz, Samuel. *Os Cristãos-Novos em Portugal no século XX*. Lisbon, 1925.

Secret, François. *Le Zôhar chez les kabbalistes chrétiens de la Renaissance*. Paris, 1964.

Serís, H. "Nueva genealogía de Santa Teresa," *Nueva revista de filología hispánica*, X (1956), 364–84.

Sicroff, Albert A. *Les controverses des statuts de pureté de sang en Espagne du XVᵉ au XVIIᵉ siècle*. Paris, 1960.

Silva Rosa, J. S. da. *Die spanischen und portugiesischen gedruckten Judaica in der Bibliothek des Jüdischen Portugiesischen Seminars Ets Haim in Amsterdam: eine Ergänzung zu Kayserling's Biblioteca Española-Portugueza-Judaica*. Amsterdam, 1933.

—— *Geschiedenis der Portugeesche Joden te Amsterdam*. Amsterdam, 1925.

Simonson, Shlomo. "The Communal Registers of Verona" (Hebrew), *Kirjath Sefer*, XXXV (1959–60), 127–36, 250–68.

Slouschz, Nahum. *Ha-'anusim be-Portugal* (The Marranos in Portugal). Tel-Aviv, 1932.

Bibliography

Sokolow, Nahum. *Baruk Spinoza u-zemano* (Baruk Spinoza and his time). Paris, 1929.

Sonne, Isaiah. "New Material on Sabbatai Zebi from a Notebook of R. Abraham Rovigo" (Hebrew), *Sefunot*, III-IV (1960), 41–69.

—— "Sources for the History of the Jews of Verona" (Hebrew), *Zion*, III (1938), 123–69.

Spiegel, Shalom. "From the Legends of the '*Akedah*" (Hebrew), *Alexander Marx Jubilee Volume* (New York, 1950), Hebrew volume, pp. 471–547.

Steinschneider, Moritz. "Letteratura antigiudaica in lingua italiana," *Vessillo Israelitico*, XXX (1882), 206–8, 244–46, 371–73.

Stern, Moritz. *Die päpstlichen Bullen über die Blutbeschuldigung*. Berlin, 1899. (Published anonymously).

Strack, Hermann. *Das Blut*. Leipzig, 1911.

Suárez Fernández, Luis. *Documentos acerca de la expulsión de los judíos*. Valladolid, 1964.

Szajkowski, Z. "Trade Relations of Marranos in France with the Iberian Peninsula in the 16th and 17th centuries," *JQR* (N.S.), L (1959–60), 69–78.

Texeira, António José. *António Homem e a Inquisição*. Coimbra, 1895.

Thorndike, Lynn. *A History of Magic and Experimental Science*. 8 vols. New York, 1923–58.

Trachtenberg, Joshua. *The Devil and the Jews*. New Haven, 1943. Reprint, New York, 1961.

Van Melsen, Andrew. *From Atomos to Atom*. New York, 1960.

Vitale, Vito. "Un particolare ignorato di storia pugliese: neofiti e mercanti," *Studi di storia napoletana in onore di Michelangelo Schipa* (Naples, 1926), 233–46.

Viterbo, Joaquim de Santa Rosa de. *Elucidario das palavras, termos, e frases, que em Portugal antiguamente se usarão*. 2 vols. Lisbon, 1799.

Wiznitzer, Arnold. *The Jews of Colonial Brazil*. New York, 1960.

Wolf, Johann Christoph. *Bibliotheca Hebraea*, 4 vols. Hamburg-Leipzig, 1715–33.

Yerushalmi, Yosef. "The Inquisition and the Jews of France in the Time of Bernard Gui," *Rutgers Hebraic Studies*, I (1965). Offprint.

Zedner, Joseph. *Catalogue of the Hebrew Books in the Library of the British Museum*. London, 1867.

Zimmels, H. J. *Die Marranen in der Rabbinischen Literatur*. Berlin, 1932.

ADDENDA

With the exception of chapters VI and IX, which were written later, this book was completed by April of 1966. Some of the following studies were then either unknown or unavailable to me, while some have appeared subsequently. I group them here under the chapters to which they are directly relevant.

Chapter I. Any discussion of the Spanish Inquisition and the converso problem must now take into account the researches of Professor Haim Beinart. His superb Hebrew study of the conversos of Ciudad Real, entitled *'Anusim be-din ha-Inkvisiẓiah* (Conversos on Trial by the Inquisition: Tel Aviv, 1965), is a model of what can be accomplished through the judicious use of fifteenth-century inquisitorial documents for the reconstruction of Marrano life at the time. For later periods see, *inter alia,* his lecture on "The Records of the Inquisition: A Source of Jewish and Converso History," in *Proceedings of the Israel Academy of Sciences and Humanities,* II (no. 11, Jerusalem, 1967), 211-27, and his review of Julio Caro Baroja's *Judíos en la España moderna y contemporánea* in Hebrew, *Kirjath Sefer,* XXXIX (1964), 346-57, and in Spanish, *Hispania,* XCIV (1964), 291-301.

To note 25 add now A. J. Saraiva's *Inquisição e Cristãos Novos* (Porto, 1969).

Chapter IV. The Febos case is the subject of an expanded study by Caro Baroja in his "El proceso de Bartolomé Febos o Febo," in *Homenaje a Don Ramón Carande,* II (Madrid, 1963), 59-92. The dossier of Méndez Silva from the Cuenca archives (see note 100) has been analyzed by I. S. Révah, "Le procès inquisitorial contre Rodrigo Méndez Silva, historiographe du roi Philippe IV," *Bulletin Hispanique,* LXVII (1965), 225-52. The documents apparently contain little more than we already know of Cardoso's activities at the time.

Chapter VI. I have summarized my views on Marrano awareness of postbiblical Judaism in a Hebrew lecture, "Marranos Returning to Judaism in the Seventeenth Century: Their Jewish Knowledge and Psychological Readiness," to appear in the Proceedings of the Fifth World Congress of Jewish Studies, Jerusalem, 1969. On the related

Bibliography

question of the periodic presence of Jews in the Iberian Peninsula see the new materials in my "Professing Jews in Post-Expulsion Spain and Portugal," in the forthcoming Jubilee Volume to be published in honor of Professor Salo Baron by the American Academy for Jewish Research.

Chapter VIII. Note 107, add: J. Cardozo de Bethencourt, "L'Auto da fé de Lisbonne, 15 de décembre 1647," *REJ*, XLIX (1904), 262-69.

Chapter IX. Note 94, cf. also Padre António Vieira's "Papel a favor dos Cristãos-Novos no tempo em que o principe regente D. Pedro tinha mandado publicar uma lei de vários castigos contra eles, movido do roubo que se fez ao Sacramento da paróquia de Odivelas, o qual papel se deu ao principe sem nome, em 1671," in his *Obras escolhidas*, IV, 72-108.

Finally, the reader is advised that the English translation of Américo Castro's *Structure of Spanish History* has been cited solely for the sake of convenience. Further revisions in the original Spanish text have been incorporated into what is now the authoritative edition, *La realidad histórica de España* (México, 1962). Conversely, Bataillon's *Erasme et l'Espagne* was updated with new bibliographical references, prologue and appendix, in the Spanish translation, *Erasmo y España* (México-Buenos Aires, 1950).

Index

Index

Cardona, Thomas de, 92

Cardoso (surname), 56

Cardoso, Abraham, author of poem on Isaac de Castro Tartas, 398n

Cardoso, Abraham (Miguel), brother of Isaac, 64, 254n, 365, 452n; birth, 69; flight from Spain, 192-93; settlement in Italy, 195-98, 201n, 202-3, 205-6; problem of his circumcision, 202n; and the Sabbatian movement, 302-4, 312-42; settlement in Leghorn, Egypt, and Tripoli, 314; writings, 45, 69n, Christian elements in, 337-41

Cardoso, Alvaro, 308

Cardoso, Ephraim, 318

Cardoso, Fernam, see Cardoso, Isaac

Cardoso, Fernando, see Cardoso, Isaac

Cardoso, Fernão, see Cardoso, Isaac

Cardoso, Gonçalo, 56n

Cardoso, Isaac (Fernando)
—life: birth, 51-55, 73; in Beira Alta, 55-65; childhood, 64; family background, 64-65, 69, 209; move from Portugal to Spain, 66, 68, 70; university years, 72-89, chair of philosophy, 72-73, 79-84, *pretendiente* in medicine, 73; degrees, 73, 75, 84; at Madrid, 90-193, and *Cristo de la Paciencia* case, 110-14, and Quiñones, 122-36, as inquisitorial witness, 137-41, social life, 141-51, and Lope de Vega, 151-59, under patronage of Olivares, 164-76, in inquisitorial documents, 180-82; flight from Spain, 192-93; settlement in Italy, 194-215, permit to settle in Verona, 206-10; and the Sabbatian movement, 302-49; death, 473
—literary character and style, 399; Christian terminology in the *Excelencias*, 379-80; citation of Christian sources in Madrid publications, 184-92; citation of Jewish sources, 184-88;

influence of classical authors, 417-22; influence of Spanish background, 413-17; knowledge of Biblical Hebrew, 362, 365; knowledge of Jewish sources, 276-99; knowledge of rabbinic Hebrew and Aramaic, 362, 365; mastery of the *aggadah*, 366; use of allegory, 366-67, 369; use of *gematria* and letter symbolism, 367-69
—the Marrano, 29, 49-50, 176-93; family background, 41, 64-65; influence of Marranism in writings, 357, 379
—the physician, 75-85, 123, 136, 164, 171-76, 181, 210, 213-14, 406, 473
—writings (as Fernando Cardoso):
De febre syncopali, 78n, 85n, 90n, 172-75, 184n, 370
Discurso sobre el Monte Vesuvio, 73n, 85n, 99-105, 142n, 149, 187-88, 189-91, 218n, 253
Oración funebre en la muerte de Lope de Vega, 152, 188-89, 191
Origen y restauración del mundo, 149
Panegyrico y excelencias del color verde, 146-47, 180, 218n
Si el parte de 13 e 14 mezes es natural y legitimo, 176n
sonnet in honor of Prince Balthasar Carlos, 183
sonnet in honor of Lope de Vega, 152
sonnet in praise of Philip IV, 97-98, 375
sonnet on Vesuvius in work by Quiñones, 134-35
Utilidades del agua y de la nieve, 164-65, 171-72, 175, 184-85, 218n, 332n, 370, 376n
—writings (as Isaac Cardoso):
Las excelencias de los Hebreos, 39n, 257, 266n, 268, 271, 274, 350-472; as exposition of Judaism, 350-412,

anti-Christian polemics, 408-12; as refutation of slanders against Jews, 413-72; reception of, 473-80; cited, 112n, 123, 223n, 328-35, 343, 349
Philosophia libera, 142n, 216-301; as scientific work, 232-51; as theological work, 251-70; as "Jewish" book, 271-301; and views on Sabbatianism, 328-30, 332, 343, 349; and views on science, 370-71, 374-75; reception of, 475-76
Cardoso, Judith, 318
Cardoso, Manuel, 37n
Cardoso, Miguel, *see* Cardoso, Abraham (Miguel)
Cardoso, Rachel, 318
Cardoso de Fonseca family, 63n
Cardoso family, 62-63, 69n, 308, 312
Carlos, Infante Don, brother of Philip IV, 121n
Caro, Joseph, 203
Carpi, Isaac, 273n
Castillo, Fray Hernando de, 292
Castro, Benedict de, 78n, 355, 456n
Castro, Ezechiele de, *see* Castro, Dr. Pedro de
Castro, Isaac de, 149
Castro, Leon de, 423
Castro, Luis de, 212
Castro, Dr. Pedro de, physician in Verona, 210-14
Castro, Pedro de, professor of Hebrew at the University of Valladolid, 89
Castro, Stephen de, 102
Castro Tartas, David de, 350, 398n
Castro Tartas, Isaac de, 362, 397-98
Catholic Church, 384; *see also* Church fathers
Celorico da Beira, Port., 55-56, 58, 61-63, 179
Charity of the Jews, 390
Charles V, emperor, 447, 464

Children, inquisitorial testimony of, 115-20
Chmelnitzki pogroms, 399
Chosen People, Jews as the, 381-84; Spaniards as the, 357-58
Christ, *see* Jesus Christ
Christian references in Cardoso's Madrid publications, 184-92
Christian religious celebrations at the University of Valladolid, 88
Christians, and the Divine Law, 411
Chrysippus, 227
Chrysostom, Saint John, 427
Church Fathers in the *Philosophia libera*, 221, 228, 257, 261n, 276, 296; in the *Excelencias*, 361, 368
Cicero, 223, 226
"Ciencia y mar y Casa Real," 72
Circumcision: and Marranos in Spain, 37-38, 133; of Marranos returning to Judaism, 200-2; Cardoso's views on, 367, 378, 380, 387, 409, 434-35; Manasseh b. Israel on, 368n
Cleanthes, 237
Clement of Alexandria, 221, 222n, 225, 361
Clement VI, pope, 464
Clement VII, pope, 67
Clement XIV, pope, 467
Cohen, Moses, 206
Cohen, R. Gershon, 353
Cohen, Tobias, 239, 273n, 348-49n
Coimbra Port., 38n, 67
Colegio de San Bartolomé, 86-87
Colegio de Santa Cruz, 87-88
Colegios mayores, 86-87
Collaço (or Collazos) Pablo, 37n
Comedies: Cardoso's defense of, 158; attacked by him later in life, 375-76
Compassion of the Jews, 186, 389, 440
Condé, Prince of, 310
Contareno, Giustiniano, 466-67
Conversos, *see* New Christians

Index

Index

Index

514

Index

Maimonides, Moses *(Continued)*
—writings, 184*n*, 293-94, 452*n*; *Aphorisms according to Galen*, 184*n*, 293; *Epistle to Yemen*, 346*n*, 349*n*; *Mishneh Torah*, 279, 291-92, 421; *Moreh nebukim (Guide for the Perplexed)*, 223, 241*n*, 242, 270, 279, 294-96, 365, 405
Majolus, Simon, 433, 436, 437, 459
Malachi, Book of, cited, 322
Maldonado, Padre Juan, 185
Maldonado da Silva, Francisco, 395-96
Malinowski, Joseph, 354
Man, Cardoso on the dignity of, 248-49
Manasseh ben Israel, 257, 259, 354, 365, 398*n*, 438, 439*n*, 468-69
—writings, 254*n*, 272*n*, 353*n*, 368*n*; *Esperança de Israel*, 121*n*, 356, 362, 395-96, 450; *Humble Addresses*, 194, 356, 443*n*, 448, 469; *Vindiciae Judaeorum*, 356, 454*n*, 456*n*, 462-63
Manoah (Biblical), 323
Manoel I, king of Portugal, 5
Manuel, Fernando, 146
Manuel, Jorge, 146
Maracci, Lodovico, 348*n*
Marcus Aurelius, 433
Mariana, Juan de, 361, 445, 446
Marineus Siculis, Lucius, 446
Mark, Gospel of, cited, 185*n*, 187*n*
Marlianus, 310
Márquez, Juan, 361, 469
Marranism, 21-42, 377; and Messianism, 303-6; methodology re, 21-31; persistence of, 31-42
Marrano, definition of, 39-40
Marrano apologetics, 48-50
Marrano martyrology, 395-97
Marrano polemics, 48-49
Marranos: adjustment to Jewish community, 47, 49; attitudes of, 340-41; educational background of emigrants, 44-46; emigration from Spain

and Portugal, 42-50; in 15th century, 21-22; in 16th century, 3; in 17th century, 1-50; in 18th century, 11*n*; in 20th century, 32*n*; Portuguese in Venice, 195-98; religion of, 35-40, 46; sins of, 342; Spanish, 325-26; *see also* New Christians
Martial, 433
Martínez, Ferrand, 395*n*
Martínez Silíceo, Archbishop Juan, 15
Martin V, pope, 464
Mary, Virgin, 190, 192
Masoretic works, permitted by *Index*, 294
Matthew, Gospel of, cited, 185*n*, 187*n*, 430
Maximilian II, emperor, 464, 466
Mazzotta, Benedetto, 236, 237*n*
Medicine: as popular New Christian profession, 70-72; study of, at University of Valladolid, 77-78
Medigo, Elijah del, 300
Medina del Rioseco, Spain, 68-70
Medrano, Sebastián Francisco de, 153
Meir, R., 449
Meir, Don, physician of Henry III of Castile, 445-46, 453
Melancholia, as "Jewish" disease, 130, 437
Meldola, Rafael, 30*n*, 201*n*
Mello, Francisco Manoel de, 37*n*, 92*n*, 193, 277, 310, 368
Melo, David Abenatar, 40
"Men of Affairs," 16-20, 91
"Men of the Nation," 19-21
Mendes Bravo, Hector, 34-35*n*, 196*n*
Méndez, Catalina, 108
Méndez, Pero, 139
Méndez, Victoria, 112-13, 118*n*, 119*n*
Méndez, Violante, 112*n*, 113
Méndez Silva, Rodrigo, 58, 63-64, 178-83, 192, 206, 254*n*, 293; cited, 55, 62, 143*n*

516

Index

Index

Index

Index

Index